The Fighting 10th

(THE TENTH BATTALION,

THIRD INFANTRY BRIGADE,

FIRST AUSTRALIAN DIVISION,

AUSTRALIAN IMPERIAL FORCE)

The Fighting 10th

A SOUTH AUSTRALIAN CENTENARY

Souvenir

OF THE

10th Battalion, A.I.F.

1914 - 19

BY

CECIL BERT LOVELL LOCK
(Late No. 624, Private Original 10th Battalion)

WITH A FOREWORD

BY

BRIGADIER-GENERAL STANLEY PRICE WEIR, D.S.O., V.D.
(First Commanding Officer of the 10th Battalion)

A Collection of Biographical, Historical, and Statistical Records appertaining to the 10th Battalion, Australian Imperial Force, from the Raising of same at Morphettville, South Australia, August 17, 1914, to its Disbandment at Chatelet, Belgium, March 17, 1919.

All Rights Reserved

Issued Without Responsibility

The Naval & Military Press Ltd

Published by
The Naval & Military Press Ltd
5 Riverside, Brambleside, Bellbrook
Industrial Estate, Uckfield, East Sussex,
TN22 1QQ England
Tel: +44 (0) 1825 749494
Fax: +44 (0) 1825 765701
www.naval-military-press.com
www.military-genealogy.com
www.militarymaproom.com

In reprinting in facsimile from the original, any imperfections are inevitably reproduced and the quality may fall short of modern type and cartographic standards.

TO

THE GALLANT OFFICERS AND MEN

OF THE 10TH BATTALION

A.I.F.

WHO LAID DOWN THEIR LIVES

DURING THE GREAT WAR

1914-18

I HUMBLY DEDICATE THESE RECORDS

OF

10TH BATTALION ACHIEVEMENT

ERRATA

Page 2, *line* 38, *for* His Majesty the late King *read* His Majesty the King.

Page 17, *line* 13, *for* Ex-No. 8 Pte. George Dunderdale Gill *read* Ex-No. 8 Pte. Charles Dunderdale Gill.

Page 17, *line* 18, *for* Ex-No. 603 Bugler Ernest Smith *read* Ex-No. 605 Bugler Ernest Clifford Smith.

Page 17, *line* 27, *for* Secretary *read* late Secretary. Also *for* F. H. Reynolds *read* F. E. Reynolds.

Page 39, *line* 3, *for* About this time *read* On January 17, 1915, Also *line* 4, *after* married *add* to Nellie Irene Honeywill, eldest daughter of the late James Honeywill, of Adelaide, South Australia.

Page 45, *line* 26, *for* the Royal Marine Light Infantry *read* companies of the Chatham and Portsmouth Battalions of the Royal Marine Brigade, Royal Naval Division.

Page 55 (BATTALION CHRONOLOGY), *add* April 14, 1916. Battalion Scouting, Intelligence and Sniping Platoon was formed, consisting of 2 officers and 40 other ranks. Capt. W. F. J. McCann was O.C., Lieut. A. W. L. MacNeil 2nd in Command, 634 Sergt. Cecil Stephen Hincks and 2575 Corporal William Samuel Creaser, senior N.C.O's., whilst the other ranks were specially selected. The platoon underwent special training, and visited the front line at frequent intervals for practical experience and patrolling. This platoon, although subsequently reduced in numbers, functioned as an intelligence section throughout the war.

Page 62, *line* 13, *for* Lieut.-Colonel G. F. Redburg *read* Temp. Lieut.-Colonel G. E. Redburg.

Page 128 (MEDICAL OFFICERS), CAPT. DOUGLAS LEWIS BARLOW, M.C., E.D., M.D., *line* 29 *for* Verco Building, 187 North Terrace, *read* Shell House, 170 North Terrace.

Page 131 (REGIMENTAL SERGEANT MAJORS), TEMP. R.S.M. REGINALD TASMAN WHITE, M.M., *line* 2 *for* 32 Avenue Road, Highgate, *read* 22 Avenue Road, Highgate.

Page 134, *line* 20, *for* Shortly after the Battalion returned to Egypt, Lieut. W. F. J. McCann was appointed Signalling Officer at Tel-el-Kebir *read* At Anzac on October 29, 1915, Lieut. W. F. J. McCann was appointed Signalling Officer, and in this capacity accompanied the Battalion to Tel-el-Kebir, Serapeum, and Gebel Habieta.

Page 138 (REGIMENTAL LIST OF OFFCERS—MAJORS), *for* Steele, Alexander, D.S.O., *read* Steele, Alexander, D.S.O., D.C.M.

Page 142 (LIEUTENANTS), *for* Lieut. Denis Courtland Jacob *read* Lieut. Denis Courtauld Jacob. Also *add* 10th Reinforcements. Reg. No. 3041.

Page 145 (BRIEF BIOGRAPHY BRIGADIER-GENERAL S. P. WEIR, D.S.O., V.D.), *line* 5, *delete* and subsequently became a pioneer surveyor in the Northern Territory.

Page 146, *line* 11, *after* the late James Wadham *add* who subsequently became a pioneer surveyor in the Northern Territory.

Page 153, *line* 25, *add* In recognition of his valuable services rendered during the Great War, Price Weir Avenue, near Birdwood, Bridges, Brand, Leane, and MacLagan Avenues, Allenby Gardens, was named in his honour.

Page 154, *line* 13, *after* eighteenth successive year *add* He was the first president of the Returned Soldiers' Association of South Australia, and on Anzac Day, 1917, at the Adelaide Cheer-Up Hut, presided at a reunion of officers and other ranks of the 10th Battalion who had served at Anzac, but through various disabilities had been returned to South Australia.

Page 203, *line* 46, *for* Sgt. L. C. Wickham *read* Sgt. J. C. Wickham.

Page 204, *line* 12, *for* he Battalion *read* the Battalion.

Page 270 (MILITARY MEDALLISTS), *for* 131 Sgt. A. G. P. Neave *read* 131 Sgt. A. G. F. Neave.

Page 275 (ROLL OF HONOUR), *for* BROCK, Leslie Salvador *read* BROOK, Leslie Salvador.

Page 287 (ROLL OF HONOUR), *re* ROBIN, Philip de Quetteville, *for* K.I.A. 25/4/15 *read* K.I.A. 28/4/15.

Page 290 (ROLL OF HONOUR), *for* WATERSTON, Edward Alexander *read* WATHERSTON, Edward Alexander.

Page 298 (NOMINAL ROLL of "F" COMPANY), *for* 809 Pte. Olifent, Douglas Roy Elson, *read* 809 Pte. Olifent, Douglas Roy Elwin.

Page 299 (NOMINAL ROLL OF "G" COMPANY), *for* 605 Bugler Smith, Ernest *read* 605 Bugler Smith, Ernest Clifford.

Page 300 (NOMINAL ROLL OF "H" COMPANY), *for* 309 Pte. Van Driel, W. *read* 309 Pte. Van Driel, William.

Page 301 (NOMINAL ROLL OF "H" COMPANY), *for* 539 Pte. Shaughnessy, Albert G. *read* 539 Pte. Shaughnessy, Albert George.

OBITUARY

Captain Walter Gordon Cornish, *vide* biography herein, *page* 167, died suddenly at Sydney, New South Wales, on May 30, 1936.

CONTENTS

	Page
I FOREWORD: By Brigadier-General S. P. Weir, D.S.O., V.D.	1
II TRIBUTES TO BATTALION: By A.I.F. Commanders, etc.	4
III BATTALION TRADITIONS (Compiler's Note)	6
IV EXPLANATORY	12
V ACKNOWLEDGMENTS	16
VI DEPARTED COMRADES	18
VII BATTLE HONOURS	20
VIII RECORDS ESTABLISHED BY BATTALION	21
IX SONG OF THE BATTALION	23
X BATTALION CHRONOLOGY (Including Bn. War Diary)	24
XI ESTABLISHMENT	103
XII EMBARKATION STATISTICS	107
XIII COMMANDING OFFICERS AND MOVEMENTS OF BATTALION	117
XIV ADJUTANTS	121

CONTENTS (Continued)

	PAGE
XV MEDICAL OFFICERS	124
XVI REGIMENTAL SERGEANT-MAJORS	130
XVII SIGNALLERS	132
XVIII REGIMENTAL LIST OF OFFICERS	138
XIX BRIEF BIOGRAPHY OF BRIGADIER-GENERAL S. P. WEIR, D.S.O., V.D.	145
XX RECORDS OF SERVICE	155
XXI DECORATIONS AND CITATIONS	253
XXII ROLL OF HONOUR	274
XXIII NOMINAL ROLL OF ORIGINAL BATTALION	292
XXIV ORGANIZATION OF FIRST A.I.F. CONVOY	302
XXV MISCELLANEOUS BATTALION ORDERS	304
XXVI MISCELLANEOUS A.I.F. ORDERS, ETC.	310
XXVII DISPOSITION OF WARSHIPS, ETC., AT ANZAC LANDING	318
XXVIII ENVOI	320

I

FOREWORD

BY BRIGADIER-GENERAL STANLEY PRICE WEIR, D.S.O., V.D.
(First Commanding Officer of the 10th Bn., A.I.F.).

Having through the courtesy of the author (Mr. Cecil B. L. Lock) been privileged to peruse the original typescript of this South Australian Centenary Souvenir of the 10th Battalion, A.I.F., which is also widely known as "The Fighting 10th," it affords me extreme pleasure, at his request, to contribute this Foreword regarding same. The idea of compiling such a consummate biographical, historical, and statistical record of the Battalion and releasing it as a Centenary publication originated solely with the compiler, who has devoted considerable time, patience, and labour in the preparation of the following pages, which I feel sure will be more than appreciated and ultimately treasured by all those whose good fortune it will be to procure a copy of "The Fighting 10th."

The immediate object of this original narrative of the Battalion and its achievements in the several theatres of war in which it so worthily upheld the prestige of the A.I.F. and the good name of South Australia, is to add to the written word of the 10th—a unit which I was intensely proud to raise, train, and lead in battle. The history of the Battalion is so varied and comprehensive, and the field of research so vast, that it is impossible to compress into a single volume a complete account of its many aspects. This book, therefore, is not intended as an academic history of the Battalion, but to some extent a guidebook to the movements, activities, achievements, and personnel of the Battalion. It is a book of the Battalion in which the records of Officers, other ranks, Headquarters, Companies, Signallers, Transport, Machine-Gunners, Buglers, specialists and details have been co-ordinated—a volume broad in design, authentic in detail, and pre-eminently a medium of Battalion reference.

The author in determining to commence this work was confronted with a stupendous task, and as he proceeded, problems constantly arose which required considerable research and judgment; but despite the intricacies which presented themselves, he has been able to rise to the occasion and produce a splendid regimental record—a record which we all admit is long overdue, and should have been compiled years ago, when much of the data and many of the details were more verdant within our minds. But as no one else came forward, Mr. Lock has fittingly assembled the records of the old Battalion within this volume, and in so doing has accomplished what no one else had undertaken. As a member of the original Battalion he has attacked the compilation of this record in a very thorough and painstaking manner, and perhaps has been most assisted by an impartial conception of the work in hand. In this way he has produced for us a book which will always be a lasting tribute to the hallowed memories associated with the 10th, and those gallant Officers and men who have emblazoned their name and fame on the A.I.F. escutcheon.

I deemed it a privilege and honour to be associated with "The Fighting 10th" for a period of two years. In looking back I am quite certain of one thing, and it is that the splendid fighting men of the 10th Battalion nobly represented South Australia during the world's greatest war. The Battalion made history, and its great deeds and remarkable achievements can never be forgotten, whilst it is no exaggeration to describe the men of the 10th as "Empire builders every one." From the day I accepted the command of the 10th Battalion I never had one moment's doubt as to whether the Officers I had selected, and other ranks who had enlisted, would render an excellent account of themselves when put to the crucial test. Late in August, 1914, after Colonel E. G. Sinclair-MacLagan, the original Commander of the 3rd Infantry Brigade, had inspected the 10th Battalion at Morphettville for the first time, he expressed surprise that the 10th Battalion was in the main being drilled by its own officers; whereas the other battalions of his command, also then in process of formation, were being drilled primarily by instructors of the permanent forces. This was the first big compliment bestowed upon the 10th, and from that time onward the keenness, reliability, initiative, determination, and indomitable courage of the Battalion as a whole was demonstrated on scores of occasions.

I can plainly visualize the days of arduous training on the sands of the Libyan Desert in Egypt, and though we would all return to Mena camp of a night begrimed with sweat and sand; yet, it was that training—exacting and difficult though it may have been—which fitted the Battalion for "The Great Adventure," and prepared it for the bigger struggles and trials of actual warfare. Out of the blackness that preceded the dawn on Sunday, April 25, 1915, the 10th Battalion, as part of the 3rd Brigade covering force, leapt ashore, scaled the heights of Ari Burnu, and within an incredibly short time was astride the first ridge, and shortly after consolidating, on the second. It was during those days of grim hardship and severe fighting that the Battalion earned for itself the title—"The Fighting 10th." During the gruelling defence of Anzac which followed, the 10th always accepted its share of responsibility, and in no small measure contributed to the glorious "Spirit of Anzac" which was created on the treacherous hillsides and escarpments of rugged Gallipoli. It was this identical spirit which impregnated the A.I.F. and manifested itself in France during the battles of 1916-18. Though the garrisoning of the Anzac area is a story of gallantry and devotion to duty, privations and rigours, successes and misfortunes, barren gains and bitter losses; yet the 10th Battalion can justly claim its share of the honour which has been conferred upon all the British troops who participated in the Dardanelles campaign. The men of the 10th in common with other Anzac troops were named "The White Ghurkas" by the Turks, and were congratulated by His Majesty the late King as "worthy sons of the Empire.'

At Pozieres in July, 1916, the A.I.F.'s first big fight against the Germans was staged, when the dreadful memories of Gallipoli were overshadowed by the horrors of the Western Front. The 10th creditably participated in that onslaught, and though the cost was heavy, the Battalion to a man fought splendidly and repeatedly covered itself with glory. After reluctantly leaving the Battalion I proudly followed the achievements of the 10th with feelings of great admiration and understanding. The penetration of the Hindenburg Line, the stemming of the German tide of invasion, the subsequent wearing-down process, and the thrilling successes of the final phases of the great struggle, and

FOREWORD

all in which the Battalion from time to time participated, only further exemplified the sterling conduct of the Battalion in the field. Gueudecourt, "Hill 60," Flers, Le Barque, and Bullecourt left no doubt as to the fighting qualities and staying powers of the Unit, and after the gallant M. Wilder-Neligan succeeded to the Command, the Polygon Wood, Merris, Crepey Wood, and Jeancourt operations were magnificently carried out and added further laurels to an already long list.

Although two generations have passed since many of us first joined the 10th, yet I am sure this splendid book will bring to our minds many a place, many an incident, and many a good comrade who paid the supreme sacrifice. It is my earnest wish that every survivor of the 10th Battalion, A.I.F., may be enjoying good health and prosperity. To the many who have been less fortunate during the trials of the difficult post-war years, I would take this opportunity of reminding them of the ever-memorable and heroic share they individually took in establishing the wonderful traditions of the 10th, and I further congratulate them upon maintaining through a period of acute adversity that renowned spirit of "The Fighting 10th"—a spirit born on the battle-fields of Anzac and France, a spirit which outlived the Great War and has been carried into the days of peace and everyday life. I also take this opportunity of thanking the Officers, N.C.O.'s and men who served under me in this famous Battalion for the unquestionable loyalty and co-operation which they always rendered to me, and without which the Battalion would never have earned the splendid reputation which it has.

In conclusion, it affords me much pleasure—as the original Commander of the 10th Battalion, A.I.F.—to congratulate Mr. Cecil B. L. Lock on his work, and thank him for preparing such a complete history of the Battalion's activities—a record which I am sure will be read with pleasure and pride by every man who had the honour of serving in the Battalion. I feel that it is a record which from generation to generation will be handed down with pride to the sons and daughters of the men who made the Battalion. Its preparation has involved an enormous amount of research which reflects great credit, not only on the compiler's undoubted ability as an historian and biographer, but on his patience and perseverance which are essential qualifications in a soldier's nature. He has so thoroughly, capably, and exhaustively dealt with the history of the Immortal Battalion—which on one occasion in an Adelaide paper was through a printer's error referred to as "The Immoral Tenth"—that I consider there is little I can add to the wonderful record which he has written.

I heartily commend this book particularly to the survivors of the 10th Battalion, A.I.F., and to the youth of South Australia. As survivors of the Battalion we possess the indefeasible right to claim that the great deeds that made the Battalion famous should not be forgotten, but should be preserved in record form so that the South Australians of to-morrow will have a standard which, should occasion arise, they might well adopt.

1st January, 1936.   Hon. Colonel 10/50th Infantry Battalion, A.M.F.

II
TRIBUTES TO THE 10th BATTALION, A.I.F.

Extracted from messages of greeting forwarded to survivors of the 10th Battalion, A.I.F., to commemorate the Twentieth Anniversary of the embarkation of the Battalion on October 20, 1914.

GENERAL SIR IAN HAMILTON, G.C.B., G.C.M.G., D.S.O., Commander-in-Chief, Mediterranean Expeditionary Force, 1915.

"On the 25th April, 1915, the 10th Battalion from South Australia was about the first, if not the very first of the whole of the Mediterranean Expeditionary Force to spring out of their boats and half swim, half wade on to the unknown and necessarily unreconnoitred wilderness afterwards to be known as Anzac. Of their conduct during the three days and nights of desperate fighting in those desolate mountains which ensued I need not speak. They have become part of the Anzac tradition. Long live the gallant 10th Battalion of the A.I.F. 18/4/34."

FIELD-MARSHAL SIR WILLIAM R. BIRDWOOD, Bt., G.C.B., G.C.S.I., G.C.M.G., C.I.E., D.S.O., Commander A.I.F.

"I think perhaps the fact that the 10th formed part of our advance guard—the very spear point of the whole A.I.F.—at the original landing at Anzac at dawn on April 25, 1915, will probably be the great outstanding event in the history of the regiment. We all of us know well, and can never forget the magnificent bravery, dash, and endurance shown by the 10th on that occasion, and I need only add that that great spirit of determination and loyalty was maintained by the Battalion throughout the whole war. 16/8/34."

LATE LIEUTENANT-GENERAL SIR H. B. WALKER, K.C.B., K.C.M.G., D.S.O., Commander First Australian Division, A.I.F.

"If I recorded all my associations of the 10th Battalion I should be almost writing its minor history. As one of the covering battalions at the landing at Anzac you shared the brunt with the rest of the Third Brigade in that epic attack of the Australian Forces. The deeds of your Battalion in the earlier days in France are inspirited in my memory by your gallantry in the Pozieres first attack. In the deadly and ill-conceived second Pozieres attack on Mouquet Farm the 10th after only ten days' rest again took part with heavy losses. In the second battle of Bullecourt, when the 10th Battalion should have been going into rest billets, it was the Battalion's gallantry that helped to restore a very critical situation in a battle for one objective which exhausted some twenty battalions of the Australian Forces. In the Third Battle of Ypres (Polygon Wood) the 10th played a conspicuous part. Later in front of Hazebrouck the 10th was continually in the line suffering heavily in the hastily planned and ill-supported attack on Meteren, and again in the capture of Mont de Merris, and lastly the brilliant capture of Merris itself on a plan so skilfully conceived. The deeds of your Battalion and its successes filled me with pleasure, and I appreciated the lengthy period I had served with you. 14/8/34."

TRIBUTES TO BATTALION

MAJOR-GENERAL E. G. SINCLAIR-MACLAGAN, C.B., C.M.G., D.S.O., Commander Third Infantry Brigade, A.I.F., August, 1914–December, 1916.

"The 10th Battalion held its own with the other Battalions of the 3rd Brigade, A.I.F., both in training and in the stresses of war. I was intensely proud of the 10th Battalion and the 3rd Brigade, and when the Brigade was selected by General Bridges to be the covering force for the Gallipoli landing, I was most grateful to you for earning that honour—a very high one—though I doubted my own capacity to lead you as you should be led. You did all that was possible there and in the Gallipoli campaign, and in the following campaigns consummated the apparently impossible on more than one occasion. I more especially remember your wonderful work in the Merris Sector in early 1918, when under the command of that splendid officer, Lieut.-Colonel M. Wilder-Neligan, you won great praise for your many feats of arms. September, 1934."

MAJOR-GENERAL H. GORDON BENNETT, C.B., C.M.G., D.S.O., Commander Third Infantry Brigade, A.I.F., December, 1916–November, 1918.

"The Tenth Battalion, like other units of the A.I.F., possessed all the attributes and characteristics associated with the A.I.F. And like all other units it possessed its own individuality. The reputation of the A.I.F. for courage and battle discipline was made by the deeds of the individual units, among which the Tenth played a leading part. From its first action as part of the covering force at the Landing in Gallipoli to its last battle at Jeancourt on September 18, 1918, the Battalion made a history sparkling with brave deeds and wonderful achievements. It produced heroes whose records must bring a thrill of justifiable pride to every Australian. Not only did the Tenth Battalion excel as a fighting unit, but also as one which could "play the game" behind the lines, on the parade ground, and on the field of sport. Every member of this old Battalion has reason to be proud of his association with it, for each individual played his part in giving the A.I.F. that name that the whole world envied. 25/11/35."

COLONEL SIR HENRY GALWAY, K.C.M.G., D.S.O., Governor of South Australia during the Great War, 1914–18.

"I am not likely ever to forget the day when I bid good-bye and God speed to the 10th Battalion at the Outer Harbour on the 20th October, 1914. Twenty years ago, and yet it seems like yesterday. I remember so well, as I stood on the deck of the s.s. *Ascanius* trying to convey to the Battalion in halting phrases how truly my heart went with them on their great adventure. They were as fine a body of soldiers as ever I saw. I knew they would do well, and so they did, magnificently and without any fuss. The building of Empire is a costly business where good lives are concerned. The losses of the 10th Battalion in the several seats of war is a sad reminder of that melancholy fact. May the memory of the Honour and Glory won by the Battalion never fade; and when those who gained that great record have passed away, may the memory of it remain green in the hearts of generations yet unborn. 13/6/34."

III

10TH BATTALION TRADITIONS

COMPILER'S NOTE

Addressed to each survivor of the 10th Battalion, A.I.F.

Comrade,—In offering this South Australian Centenary Souvenir of the 10th Battalion, A.I.F., it is sincerely hoped you will find herein certain biographical, historical, and statistical matter which, because of the sentimental value attached thereto, should prove of more than passing interest to you—a privileged surviving 10th Battalion man. First and foremost, it is necessary for me to state that this little volume of information appertaining to the Battalion in which we served abroad during the Great War, 1914-18, does not principally purport to be a unit history; it is merely a collection of 10th Battalion references and items culled from various official, semi-official, and private sources, assembled in record form, and presumed to concern all ex-10th officers and men as co-producers of those glorious traditions which belong to the 10th. During the last twenty years, it has occasionally been a matter of genuine regret to many of the survivors of the 10th Battalion, A.I.F., that no record has been compiled to show, as it were, "Who was Who" in the old 10th. True, before the Battalion was disbanded in 1919, the late Lieut. Arthur Limb, within the brief period of three weeks, produced a sketchy resumé of the activities of the 10th, from Morphettville to the Armistice. His little book is the only written record of the Battalion that has been issued; but without attempting to disparage his magnificent achievement, it must in all fairness be said that as it was not intended to be a book of reference and detail, it is consequently in many respects obviously deficient. Therefore, in order to supply a long-felt want, I have collected the following facts and figures, details and particulars relevant to the raising, establishment, and history of the old 10th, realising full well, that as a series of records, its chief importance lies in the fact that they have not hitherto been presented in similar form. Firstly, it is an infinitesmal tribute to those illustrious comrades of ours who gave their lives in the great cause; and secondly, as an attempt to preserve a permanent record, it is a small contribution towards the acknowledged traditions of our late unit. I offer no apologies for its many imperfections, for in collating the requisite material I have attempted to please all and offend none, whilst at all times I have been solely actuated by one underlying motive—that of perpetuating 10th Battalion traditions. Seventeen years have passed since the 10th Battalion, A.I.F., was disbanded at Chatelet in Belgium. Before the final 10th Battalion details left France on May 20, 1919, nearly 9,000 men of all ranks had passed through the unit; 61 officers and 949 other ranks had died; 291 officers and 2,252 other ranks had been wounded; the total casualties, not including sickness, had amounted to 3,509; 25 quotas of reinforcements had maintained its fighting strength; its activities had extended over a period of four years and seven months, and its operations had been conducted in three continents and three theatres of war. These comprehensive facts alone have made the task before me all the greater; but if the result of

BATTALION TRADITIONS

my labours only serves as an incentive for another, perhaps more qualified than myself, to take up the historical and biographical cudgels and write the many chapters which even yet could be written, then I shall feel that I could have reaped no greater reward.

Whether originals or reinforcements of the grand old 10th Battalion, we all legitimately pride ourselves on being common creators of the same wartime traditions. The "original" candidly admits that he is more or less proud of the distinctive fact that as an "original" he served in South Australia's first-raised foot-regiment, and as such, was one of the first contingent to leave South Australian shores for active service abroad. Naturally, the original 10th Battalion men unanimously consider that as founders of the original Battalion, they were permitted that rare privilege of seeing and participating in a Battalion in the making. For this reason, if no other, those thrilling days of August, September, and October, 1914, set the traditional pendulum of the old 10th Battalion in motion, and from that time onward the historical nucleus of our unit unmistakably gathered momentum, only to be constantly added to, both in volume and achievement, by our worthy contemporaries—the ever-needed reinforcements, who from time to time were called upon to carry on and fill the breach in the good work first commenced by their original compeers. To-day, out of the fulness of a deep appreciation of the Battalion, some 3,000 or more surviving reinforcements of the 10th also justly pride themselves on the fact that on twenty-five different occasions their numbers swelled the Battalion ranks in Egypt, Gallipoli, France, and Belgium, shared the burdens and brunt of active service, and so permitted the Battalion to function throughout the whole of the Great War. The date of enlistment, time of joining the Battalion, length of service with the Battalion, or date of discharge do not in any way detract from the value of the assistance and co-operation which every man of the 10th, whether original or reinforcement, was called upon to render. Therefore, it is as a member of the original 10th Battalion, animated with exactly the same measure of regimental pride as all other survivors of the unit, that I have compiled this record and submitted it in its present form.

Our 10th Battalion traditions indisputably commenced at the Morphettvile training camp, to be interwoven in a mesh of events which rapidly followed. Route marches over the Brighton Hills or through the City of Adelaide; reviews on the Morphettville Race-course by Governor-General Munro Ferguson, General Bridges, or Colonel MacLagan; the taking of the salute at Parliament House by Governor Galway; the voyage to Egypt on the s.s. *Ascanius*; the sojourn at Mena with those never-to-be-forgotten trudges to Tiger's Tooth and the numerous other events of historical importance which occurred in quick succession, are still mileposts in that long lane of memory. Perhaps, at the time we were not always impressed with their actual or full importance, but now we realize that the intervening years have added lustre to their original setting, and so have brilliantly floodlit the "eternal landscape of the past." To-day we know that all those pre-Gallipoli events had a traditional sentiment attached to them, perhaps relatively less important, but equally as pronounced as any of the later incidents when the achievements of the Battalion were crystallised on the heights of Ari Burnu, through the terrors and chaos of

Pozieres, amidst the mud and slush of Polygon Wood, in the anticipations and realizations of Hell Fire Corner, at the storming of the Passchendaele Ridge, or any of the other trials incidental to front line service whilst on the Western Front. Each and all of these events, whether the former or the latter, besides others too numerous to mention, have their prescribed niche in the traditional shrine of our Battalion. Some may be more outstanding than others, some may have been acquired over the dead bodies of our comrades, others may have been perpetuated whilst winning actual Battalion Honours, others enacted miles behind the firing line; yet, irrespective of place of origin, whether created in the front line, supports, reserves, bivouacs, billets, or camps, they are each and all inseparable links in that grand chain of tradition which from time to time was forged and indissolubly welded by the officers and men of the 10th. Wherever the spotlight of memory may chance to linger—whether at Morphettville or Mitcham before embarkation, at sea on the s.s. *Ascanius* or any other transport, in the land of the Pharaohs, on the s.s. *Ionian* in the Aegean, on rugged Gallipoli, desecrated France or battle-scarred Belgium—they are all dear to memory and occupy an allotted place in that conception of things which death itself alone can obliterate.

In that historic letter to the 3rd Brigade, dated April 21, 1915, Brigadier-General E. G. Sinclair-MacLagan said, "You have a very good reputation you have built up for yourselves, and now you have a chance of making history for Australia and a name for the Brigade that will live in history. I have absolute faith in you, and believe few, if any, finer brigades have been put to the test." He was literally taken at his word, and the immortal traditions of Anzac were the direct answer to his appeal, for within a few days of the Landing, official war commentators and correspondents through the medium of the press apprised the people of South Australia and the world in general of the unique and meritorious history which the 10th Battalion was compiling. Despite the isolation of our unit whilst on Gallipoli, and the suppression of much news by official censorship, all at home interested in the doings of the 10th Battalion abroad confidently realized that the Battalion when put to any test, would ultimately make good and do South Australia credit.

At the Intercessional and Memorial Service for the fallen, held at St. Peter's Cathedral, Adelaide, on August 8, 1915, the Bishop of Adelaide, Right Rev. Dr. Thomas, in his sermon, said, "But I have to tell you something more—something that shows the feeling, the spirit of the famous Tenth—which was as you know essentially South Australian. A letter was read from Sir Ian Hamilton in which he told them 'one unit had to be sacrificed,' the best battalion had to be chosen, and the 10th was that unit, and was to take the central position. 'The Battalion has been given great honour, and I am proud of it.' I quote from the letter written late in the evening before the landing—until it was too late to write any more—written by a 10th Battalion man who laid down his life the next day. He says, 'The pride of place has been given to the Australians, so indeed we should feel proud and honoured. We all feel confident, and please God, we may uphold the judgment of those who chose us, and the honour of good old South Australia'." In this way the traditions of the Battalion were gradually built up, and from time to time recognised and applauded by the general public. As early as February 26, 1916, at Gebel Habieta, Egypt, when 500 of all ranks of the 10th were drawn up for their final 10th Battalion inspection prior to being transferred to the 50th Battalion, the traditional aspect was again most strikingly demonstrated. Lieut.-Colonel M. F. Beevor addressed the parade and impressed upon all those who were about to sever their connection with the 10th, the value of the 10th Battalion traditions which they were taking with them to the sister battalion. He emphasized that whilst in the 10th they had individually established a splendid record pregnant with achievement and tradition, and which in their new unit, as men of the A.I.F., they would be expected to maintain. He pointed out that the incidents of the Battalion during the first eighteen months of its existence had repeatedly proved themselves active service events which had added splendour to the name of the 10th, and which in a survey of the Battalion as a whole could neither be overlooked nor underestimated. This was probably the saddest day the 10th Battalion ever experienced, for staunch friendships formed in Australia, Egypt, and Anzac, caused those who remained in the 10th to genuinely regret the departure of esteemed comrades-in-arms; but the traditions of the 10th Battalion withstood the mighty wrench imposed upon them, and in this manner were infused into the 50th Battalion by those, who at the time were probably more or less indifferent to their transmitting influence.

As the Great War progressed the traditions of the 10th Battalion became better known to rank and file, with the result that many who had not previously considered their existence, quickened to their impulse, and were eventually proud to acclaim them in word and deed. In September, 1917, at Chateau-Segard, in France, where the final preparations for Polygon Wood (Third Battle of Ypres) were in progress, inspiring messages were received from both Divisional and Brigade Commanders urging the men of the 10th Battalion to remember and uphold the traditions which they themselves had made. After the Armistice, when there was more time for historical reflection, the traditions of British regiments from all parts of the British Empire were written up and eulogized. On December 3, 1918, two days following that on which His Majesty the late King inspected the 10th Battalion at Beugnies, in France, Lieut.-Colonel A. M. Ross, C.M.G., D.S.O., who was formerly an officer at the Royal Military Academy and during the Gallipoli campaign was Staff-Captain to Colonel E. G. Sinclair-MacLagan, delivered an interesting lecture to the men of the 10th, entitled "Regimental Traditions." Rank and file of the Battalion listened attentively, but deep down at heart one and all realized that their own beloved war-worn Battalion had emerged from the conflict with traditions of which it could be equally proud—traditions which would be handed down to posterity through the medium of an Anzac Day, traditions which had been built up upon a record of achievement of which any British regiment might feel equally justified in commemorating in an adequate manner.

Only as recently as August 31, 1934, our beloved war-time leader, Field-Marshal Sir William R. Birdwood, in a farewell speech made at Perth, Western Australia, and broadcasted to ex-diggers throughout the Commonwealth, prior to his departure for England, stressed the importance of regimental traditions. In appealing to his war-time associates of the A.I.F., he strongly advised them to lose not the opportunity nor the desire to foster and encourage the recognition and maintenance of those glorious traditions so peculiar to the A.I.F. He pointed out that if we, as returned men, failed in this, our priceless heritage, bought with the blood of our comrades who lie buried in the various theatres of the late war, then the significance of that immortal beginning, Anzac, and the crowning achievements of the years which followed, would neither be wholly understood nor appreciated in their correct historical perspective by the rising generations of the great Commonwealth of Australia. In 1921 an eminent Anglican divine said: "Traditions, which are not valued, which are not guarded, which are not expounded afresh to every generation as in its turn it steps on to the arena of the centuries, that tradition will grow weak and pass." Therefore, there is a real need and a real justification for the survivors of the 10th Battalion to preserve from extinction those traditions steeped in the life-blood of gallant, staunch comrades; traditions to which many of us gave the best years of our lives; traditions which mean so much to us; traditions which are our proudest memories; traditions which require neither definition nor advertisement; traditions which as the years roll by, we will more and more be called upon to guard, interpret, and transmit. As survivors of the old 10th Battalion—an integral unit of the A.I.F.—it is incumbent upon us to stimulate and perpetuate those wonderful traditions associated with our service in the Australian Imperial Force; for if we do not, then the question may be safely asked, who will? We are confronted with the fact that our numbers are slowly but surely diminishing —our post-war establishment is on a very definite sliding scale, and, therefore, growing up in our midst is the present-day generation which knows us only by historical repute and not from personal contact. Approximately one-third of the original Battalion's strength was killed during the Great War, and since demobilization it has been reliably estimated that at least another third has answered "Roll," which means that for every three comrades who stood shoulder to shoulder on the Morphettville parade ground, only one is left—a surviving one-in-three proportion. The same basis of percentage applies to each quota of reinforcements.

At the Dedicatory Service at the Melbourne Shrine of Remembrance on Armistice Day, 1934 (Sunday, November 11), Sir Stanley Argyll, Premier of Victoria, in calling upon H.R.H. the Duke of Gloucester to perform the dedication, said, *inter alia*, "This Shrine of Remembrance is built on foundations of love and honour, and as a lasting symbol of a great tradition that is the saga of the sacrifice, the valour and the sufferings of a generation that placed the national welfare before all." Such eloquent language splendidly portrayed the axiomatic principles underlying the historical origin, development, and world-wide recognition of the established traditions of the A.I.F.—traditions which were as far-flung as the battle-line which it was called upon to defend. We must never lose sight of the fact that it is Tradition—the unwritten record —that rekindles the fires of sacred remembrance; that supplies us with the stark, unvarnished facts of blood-stirring sentiment; that permits us to visualize a kaleidoscopic sequence of incidents and events relevant to our active service abroad; that revivifies the bleached bones of history; that conglomerates the memories of a decade or the recollections of a generation; that reanimates that pulsating urge which thrilled us when we were men of the 10th, and which still is the link divine that bridges years and distances—from Morphettville to Mena, from Alexandria to the Aegean, from Gallipoli to Gebel Habieta, from one battle-field of France to another, and from England to Australia. Therefore, the most cherished traditions of the 10th Battalion are only to be found in that imperishable record of those comrades who never came back; those comrades who as ambassadors of this State worthily represented South Australia abroad, and by their indomitable courage and service helped Australia to attain the status of nationhood. It is those comrades with the traditions enshrining them who will go down to history as builders of Empire, inasmuch as they assisted to erect those A.I.F. and A.N.Z.A.C. copestones of British Imperialism which will endure so long as the story of Anzac and the epic struggles of France and Flanders survive.

Two decades have passed and the children of 1914 are now adults, whilst those born since we enlisted cannot reasonably be expected—on their own initiative—to delve voluntarily into our established traditions. Hence, to keep the home-fires of those same traditions burning throughout the coming years, and as a compliment to our comrades who laid down their lives in the creating of such immortal traditions, and likewise as a just recognition of the individual part, we ourselves took in their making; it devolves upon us who are left to shoulder high the banners of such regimental traditions and all that they imply, if only so that the youth of to-day and the unborn of to-morrow may, when necessary, be properly acquainted with the part South Australia's first infantry regiment played in the Great War. The 10th Battalion traditions, like the sentiment expressed in Francis Barron's rousing barrack-room ballad, are fast becoming a matter of "Ten, twenty, thirty, forty, fifty years ago," and to our dismay the first two of these milestones have already been passed.

Such are the sacrosanct traditions of the 10th Battalion. So much so, that to any 10th Battalion man the name "Morphettville" will always imply more than a place where horse-racing is conducted; the name *"Ascanius"* will always signify more than a vessel of Holt's Blue Funnel Line; Mena, in Egypt, will always be exalted beyond a glorified tourist resort; the name *"Ionian"* will always represent more than a mere Greek archipelago; whilst Pozieres, Louverval, Bullecourt, Polygon Wood, Merris, Crepey Wood, Jeancourt are more than place-names in provincial France. In a similar manner scores of other places connected with the history of the 10th conjure up before us scenes of twenty years ago—visions pregnant with tradition and sentiment. The ranks of the old Battalion may be thinning, the blank files may be increasing annually, but the grand old spirit of 1914–19 still prevails amongst the survivors of the 10th, and will to the last, for it is frequently revived and strengthened by the bonds of comradeship and tradition which will never die. To the last man the unwritten record of our Unit will always form the basis of reminiscences which are still real and strong enough to permeate our very being. There is no end to such traditions, and like "Birdwood's last ridge," the last one is not yet in sight.

"Roll Call," twenty years after, means considerably more to us all than we are perhaps prepared to readily admit. We all deeply deplore that a one hundred per cent. answer cannot be given by every man of the 10th, and that there cannot be a hearty and unanimous response to "All present and correct," as we were wont to reply a score of years ago. Our departed comrades of 1914–18 do not answer roll, and other absentees include many who since demobilization have passed the Great Divide, where battalion, brigade, or division are of no avail. Another twenty years hence, and our numbers will be still further depleted by the incursions of post-war deceases, which to-day are reducing our ranks in no small proportions. The day must eventually dawn when a 10th Battalion man who served in the Great War will be a difficult person to locate. Hence my idea of compiling this record, for I have deemed the South Australian Centenary an appropriate occasion in which to issue this souvenir; for if the year 1936 is a fitting time to commemorate the achievements of the early pioneers who founded the State of South Australia, then the time is also opportune to further perpetuate the memory of their sons and grandsons who became gallant officers and men of the 10th Battalion, A.I.F., and fought and died for their Empire and country in the Great War, and so made the land of their birth "mightier still."

Cecil B. L. Lock.

Ex-No. 624 Pte., "B" and "C" Coys.,
Original 10th Battalion, A.I.F.

28 Trimmer Parade,
  Seaton Park,
    South Australia. 1/1/36.

IV

EXPLANATORY

During the compiling of this volume a lucid picture of the grand old 10th Battalion as a whole has ever been before my mind, and I deeply regret that it has been so difficult to transfer that representation to paper. I can only hope that my readers may not see the difference between the conception and the performance as vividly as I do myself. The subject of each section herein is of sufficient importance to form a book by itself, and it is therefore hoped that the purchaser of this volume will not look for an exhaustive treatment of certain phases. Considerably more could be added in a thousand and one places; each page could be extended indefinitely; an analytical exposition of the Battalion could be presented, until the size of this book would consequently be so unwieldly and the cost so high, that the fundamental object of producing a book of the Battalion would ultimately defeat itself. Therefore, as compiler, I have contended with a difficult problem, inasmuch as from time to time I have been forced to choose discreetly from a mass of materials whatever seemed most suitable for my purpose, and to discard what seemed less appropriate for a complete survey of the Battalion. At no time has it merely been a matter of creating individual chapters or sections, but rather that of curtailing certain portions and eliminating less important data in order to keep within prescribed dimensions. In connection with the selection of material which I have deemed suitable for inclusion herein, it may be advisable for me to append the following remarks which will indicate the general lines upon which I have compressed the facts.

"THE FIGHTING 10TH." The significance of this term is thoroughly understood by all survivors of the 10th Battalion, and in using the words as the title of this book I would at once disclaim any implication regarding the fighting qualities of other units or regiments. When confronted with the task of naming the volume I had compiled, I could decide upon no other than the first unofficial title bestowed upon the Battalion, when during the last week of April, 1915, it was fighting for its very existence upon the slopes and crests of Gallipoli. It was whilst the Battalion was so undergoing its baptismal fire and fighting hard to establish itself upon Turkish soil, that the unique distinction was earned. Throughout the years of the Great War which followed, the 10th Battalion was not infrequently referred to by Divisional, Brigade, and other commanders, as well as the South Australian press, as "The Fighting 10th," a name based upon the realities of Gallipoli, since incorporated in the traditions of the Battalion, and now historically established beyond the need of literary resuscitation.

"10TH" OR "TENTH." Only after mature consideration and much invaluable advice have I intentionally selected the numeral-form "10th" in preference to the word-form "Tenth". It will be remembered that during the Great War all A.I.F. units were officially designated with numerals and not words, and moreover, whenever the unofficial title of the Battalion—"the Fighting 10th"—appeared in print, the same mode of expression was adopted. In retaining the original numeral-appellation of the Battalion I have deemed it advisable not to break away from such strong precedents, whilst it is interesting to note that present-day units of the British Army and the Ausralian Military Forces are also numerically denominated. The numeral-form may be somewhat inelegant in appearance, but the weight of evidence in its favour, is that it more strictly conforms to the traditions of the A.I.F.

HISTORY OF THE BATTALION. I have not attempted to write up the history of the 10th Battalion—battle by battle and chapter by chapter. The unvarnished history of the 10th is portrayed in the chronological section herein, and more especially is detailed by the Commanding Officers themselves in their official despatches more commonly known as "The Battalion War Diary." Those who desire to study the history of the Battalion in relationship to the whole A.I.F., cannot do better than consult Dr. C. E. W. Bean's splendid Official History of the A.I.F. in the Great War. I have deliberately attempted to break away from the conventions defining the usual lay-out and arrangement of Unit records, and in so doing have stressed, wherever possible, the names of Officers and other ranks.

MAPS, DIAGRAMS, AND ILLUSTRATIONS. Whilst admitting that their inclusion would have considerably enhanced this work as a whole, and more or less added to its academic value, their insertion herein would have involved extra cost, which necessarily would have been passed on to the purchaser. Faced with this serious setback it has been imperative for me to decline the generous offers of assistance in this direction received from Major F. G. Giles, D.S.O., V.D., and Messrs. Leonard, Marshall, and George Edmonds.

NOMINAL ROLLS. It will be found that included herein is the nominal roll of the original Battalion only. As over 8,000 men passed through the 10th it will readily be understood that in a book of this size it would be impossible to publish the nominal rolls of all the reinforcement quotas. As much as I desired that this should be so, I have had to content myself by inserting the roll of the original Battalion only, and in so doing, I submit same as the basis upon which the Battalion was raised, embarked, and from time to time was reinforced. I also deeply regret that it has not been possible to submit rolls covering those who participated in the Anzac Landing, served on Gallipoli, participated in each specific operation in France and Belgium, were transferred to the 50th Battalion at Gebel Habieta, or were transferred from the 27th Battalion to the 10th.

CASUALTY LISTS. During the Great War 466 official Casualty Lists were issued by the A.I.F., and the 10th Battalion was represented in all excepting about one dozen. Therefore, it is obvious that these lists could not be included herein.

LETTERS FROM GALLIPOLI. I am in the possession of over 100 copies of letters written by Officers and other ranks of the 10th Battalion whilst at Anzac in 1915. Such letters may rightly be regarded as "The Unofficial History of the 10th Battalion on Gallipoli"; but despite their historical value and interesting contents, I have been most reluctantly compelled to omit same from this publication.

REGIMENTAL LIST OF N.C.O.'s. It has been impossible to obtain an authentic list showing the name of every N.C.O. who passed through the Battalion. Such a list, if compiled, would necessarily have been a long one, but as I could only obtain portions of same, I have had no other alternative than to completely disregard the fragmentary parts to hand.

RANK AND DECORATIONS. In the chronological lists of Commanding Officers, Adjutants, R.S.M.'s, and Medical Officers, rank and decorations only as at time are shown. Subsequent rank attained and decorations won are shown in the Regimental List of Officers and in the individual biographies.

BIOGRAPHIES OF OFFICERS. It is deeply regretted that the magnitude of collating biographical details of every officer who passed through the Battalion and the additional cost same would entail have made it impracticable to include same herein. It may be said that I have unduly given biographical prominence to certain officers, whereas N.C.O's. and privates could also have

EXPLANATORY

been advantageously written up. Despite the merits of this contention, it is generally conceded that the history of any regiment more or less centres upon its officers, and in the first instance no biographical section would be complete without giving just recognition to the officers of that unit.

ACTING-ADJUTANTS, R.S.M.'s, ETC. In the chronological lists of Adjutants and Regimental Sergeant-Majors, those members of the Battalion who were appointed Assistant Adjutants or acted as Adjutant or R.S.M. have not been included. It has not been possible to obtain particulars appertaining thereto.

RECOMMENDATIONS FOR MILITARY MEDALS. These are not included herein. To obtain same a fair amount of research work amongst A.I.F. records at the Australian War Museum would have been necessary, and as the number approximates 160, the compiling of the list would have been a substantial task. The Director of the National War Museum (Major J. L. Treloar, O.B.E.) courteously intimated that M.M. recommendations housed at Canberra were probably incomplete, and contending with these difficulties I have been compelled to exclude them from this book.

PERSONAL OPINIONS AND CRITICISMS. Generally speaking I have purposely refrained from expressing my own personal opinions, and individually I have had no criticisms to offer, comments to make nor judgments to pass, other than those generally accepted and whose historical accuracy is beyond question.

ERRORS AND OMISSIONS. It must be thoroughly understood that whilst I have exerted considerable effort to accurately record matters appertaining to the 10th Battalion, there has existed a decidedly limited sphere of research which has repeatedly proved itself a contributing factor towards finally determining the acceptance or rejection of certain relevant data. If certain errors or omissions have inadvertently been made, then I sincerely trust same are of insufficient importance to mar this volume as a record or wound the dignity of any survivor of the Battalion.

It is generally admitted that no two persons would approach a work of this nature in an identical manner, and therefore, in conforming to my own set plan I have undoubtedly laid myself open to a certain amount of criticism. However justified that may be, I can at least conscientiously claim that I have honestly and without fear or favour done my best to produce a reliable regimental record, and that in so doing I have not intentionally trespassed on the domain of any other author proposing to write up a history of the 10th Battalion. This entire absence of overlapping has indeed given me an extremely wide and unfettered field, and has been a feature which I have been more than pleased to note.

COMPILER.

ACKNOWLEDGMENTS

For some considerable time I have applied myself to the honoured task of collecting reliable and suitable data in order that as a record "The Fighting 10th" should be as authentic and complete as the esteemed assistance of the survivors of the Battalion who have generously aided me in my quest for information, plus my own individual efforts would permit. The obstacles have undoubtedly been many; the old Battalion is scattered far and wide—throughout the Commonwealth of Australia, Britain, Kenya Colony, America, and it is even within the realm of possibility for a 10th Battalion representative to have enlisted with the French Foreign Legion. Notwithstanding the exceedingly wide field over which the members of the 10th Battalion are now geographically distributed and the corresponding difficulties associated with locating same, I have checked up wherever possible with a view to eliminating error. Therefore, the accuracy of the following pages is as perfect as it has been for me under the existing circumstances to obtain. Several minor alterations and corrections may still be necessary, in which case I crave the indulgence of the reader, for it has been my chief ambition, that as a series of records "The Fighting 10th" should above everything else approach being an authoritative and permanent record.

It now remains for me to return my grateful thanks to the various survivors of the 10th Battalion, A.I.F., but for whose aid, even after two years of continuous labour, it would have been impossible for me to complete this work before the South Australian Centenary of 1936. I have received the kind assistance of more comrades than I can mention here, but I must specially thank the following: The subscribers who, by ordering copies of this book in advance, so permitted me to proceed with an unsponsored work and thus accept the individual financial responsibility with a greater degree of confidence and assurance: Brigadier-General S. P. Weir, D.S.O., V.D.; Lieut.-Colonel F. W. Hurcombe, V.D.; Lieut.-Colonel M. F. Beevor, V.D.; Lieut.-Colonel R. B. Jacob, V.D.; Lieut.-Colonel G. D. Shaw, V.D.; Lieut.-Colonel W. F. J. McCann, D.S.O., O.B.E., M.C. and Bar; Major G. E. Redburg, Major F. G. Giles, D.S.O., V.D.; Captain J. Hamilton, and Captain G. C. Campbell, M.C. and Bar, who kindly reviewed the original typescript of this book, and in commending same enabled me to definitely launch the project of publication; Brigadier-General S. P. Weir, who courteously contributed the within foreword, which I consider has more or less added the hall-mark of authenticity to my labours; the 10th Battalion, A.I.F. Club, which granted permission for printed hand-bills to be circulated at the 10th Reunion on September 18, 1935; Captain G. C. Campbell, who made a short appeal at that function on behalf of this book; and Major-General H. Gordon Bennett, who specially forwarded a tribute to the Battalion.

My grateful acknowledgments are also due to Brigadier-General S. P. Weir, Lieutenant-Colonels F. W. Hurcombe, M. F. Beevor, R. B. Jacob, G. D. Shaw, W. F. J. McCann, H. C. Nott, Majors N. M. Loutit, G. E. Redburg, F. G. Giles, J. Newman, C. F. Minagall, C. Rumball, J. Churchill-Smith, H. W. H. Seager, R. K. Hurcombe; Captains J. Hamilton, G. C. Magenis, W G. Cornish, D. L. Todd, H. R. Heming, W. H. Perry, G. C. Campbell,

ACKNOWLEDGMENTS

A. S. Blackburn, J. G. Sinclair, F. J. S. Mead, A. H. Macdonald; Lieutenants A. C. Sommerville, V. H. Robley, J. Davidson, W. S. Bennett, H. W. Scudds, C. R. Allanson, No. 506 Sgt. R. R. Inwood, No. 1327 Corporal P. Davey, who have supplied either biographical or documentary material of historical value and thus permitted me to bridge gaps which otherwise would have flagrantly existed; to Major J. L. Treloar, O.B.E., Director of the Australian War Museum at Canberra, for courteously supplying certain information; to Colonel A. G. Butler, D.S.O., V.D., B.A., M.B., Ch.B. (Camb.), compiler of Part I (The Gallipoli Campaign) of the official history of the Australian Army Medical Service, for supplying a correct list of Medical Officers attached to the Battalion during the war; to Ex-No. 388 Sgt. F. E. Allchin (now S.S.M. Australian Military Forces) for forwarding a resumé of the activities of 10th Battalion signallers and Ex-No. 8 Pte. George Dunderdale Gill, originally of the 10th Battalion Headquarters Signallers, for verifying certain queries in connection with the establishment of the original signallers.

I also have to return my sincere thanks to the following: Ex-No. 809 Corporal Douglas Roy Elwin Olifent, who has continuously supplied me with relevant extracts from his private diary; Ex-No. 603 Bugler Ernest Smith, who made preliminary enquiries at Base Records Office, Melbourne, in connection with the nominal roll of the original Battalion; Ex-No. 190 Pte. George Francis Charles Edmonds, now Secretary of the 10th Battalion, A.I.F. Club, who allowed me the privilege of perusing a nominal roll of "B" Company as at the landing, for instigating certain enquiries through the Department of Defence in connection with nominal rolls, for ascertaining from Dr. C. E. W. Bean, the Australian official war historian, the date of death of Lieut.-Colonel M. Wilder-Neligan, and for his readiness to assist me at every possible turn; the Secretary and Treasurer (Messrs. A. H. Dalziel and F. H. Reynolds), of the R.S.S.I.L., Adelaide, for granting me permission to sight League membership cards in order to verify certain regimental numbers; the Librarian (Mr. H. R. Purnell, F.L.A.) and staff of the Adelaide Public Library for the courteous assistance they have at all times rendered, and for several special favours granted which allowed me to expedite the work in hand; the Archivist (Mr. G. H. Pitt, B.A.) of the State Archives for much invaluable assistance in placing at my disposal certain nominal rolls and casualty lists; and Capt. A. S. W. Arnold, of the 10/50th Battalion, A.M.F., who kindly supplied a copy of the official despatch in connection with the capture of Merris.

To my wife and son, Thomas Berkeley Lovell, I owe thanks for inestimable aid in the work of transcription, and to C.S.M. Raymond Thomas Williams, of the 10/50th Battalion, A.M.F., for much kindly assistance in checking certain typescripts. In conclusion I wish to express my gratitude to my esteemed friend, Ex-No. 308 Sgt. John Tune, to whom I first divulged my intention of compiling this record, and whose instantaneous moral support I have since regarded as collaboration which more or less fired within me the necessary energy and enthusiasm to persevere with this record beyond the embryonic stage; and to the dozens of old 10th men who, from near and far, and from time to time, have courteously supplied essential details and proffered information; and to all, whom I am sincerely indebted, and to whom I offer my very best thanks and appreciation.

COMPILER.

VI

10TH BATTALION DEPARTED COMRADES
"To them the immortality. To us the memory."

LEST WE FORGET!

Proudly and reverently we pronounce the terms "DEPARTED COMRADES" and "SACRIFICE" to be synonymous; but in so doing we momentarily permit ourselves, the surviving members of the 10th Battalion, A.I.F., to pale into insignificance; for all that is to-day, is supremely surpassed by all that was yesterday, when our illustrious 10th Battalion comrades who died were laid to rest under the appalling conditions of modern warfare, which then we all knew only too well, and which now only require a tacit allusion. But the peerless, fadeless memory of those comrades who perished amidst the strife is the one concrete, infallible conclusion that deceives us not. "Nations alter, the years go by," "Change and decay in all around we see;" but the knowledge we possess of those comrades who have gone before, comrades who are gone, but not forgotten, plays no sordid tricks upon our imagination. It requires no amplification; its reality needs not to be intensified; for superlatively eclipsing our comprehension of all that the Great War was, is that paramountly sacred conception of the fallen, and there it remains—immutable, evergreen, and eternal in all its transcendental glory.

Through a maze of conflicting, disturbing, sometimes cross-word- puzzle-like retrospect of our campaigning days, the sacrifice made by our departed comrades is the one thing which at all times pre-eminently stands out; and in its overwhelming importance, in its relationship to everything else, dwarfs every other aspect of the Great War. It is a glorious sacred knowledge acquired only from actual first-hand experience; it is a conception which dies not, nor alters not with the flight of time. True, a lot of water has passed under the bridge since, as men of the 10th Battalion, we partook of our baptismal fire and were each and all initiated into the horrors and realities of the Great War. But nevertheless, there is nothing in this wide, wide world which can ever efface from our minds those indelible impressions, graven upon our very soul cases, as one by one the prime of 10th Battalion manhood passed through the valley of the shadow of death into the Great Beyond—ostensibly to the dirge of Lord Derby's famous war-time recruiting slogan:

> "More men means more might;
> Might is wanted to fight for right.
> And men, might, right, will end the fight."

Twenty years have passed and we still hallow and revere all those human sacrifices which were made by members of the 10th Battalion, and the older we grow, the more fearlessly we gainsay that none can rob us of the precious knowledge we have so acquired. Time may mellow our view-point, our range of focus on those thrilling days may become more strictly limited; but for all that, deep down within us is the moral consciousness of that colossal toll of human sacrifice which was manfully and courageously borne by the 10th Battalion as a fighting unit of the Australian Imperial Force.

And what of this solemn knowledge? Well, it has long since become a fundamental part of our make-up. It is interdependent with our everyday existence; and therefore, we involuntarily do the right thing, and that is unreservedly recognise, acknowledge, and acclaim our departed comrades both in spirit and in word. Call them what we may—"fallen heroes," "departed comrades," "consecrated cannon-fodder," "glorious dead," "those who went west," "those who made the supreme sacrifice"—but the indisputable fact remains that it is our common heritage to honour their memory. In silence we occasionally render unto them the honour that is theirs, but in the bustle of life it is also our bounden duty to epitomize to the very utmost the spirit of their noble sacrifice. The bard may extol them, the orator may eulogize them, the critic may applaud them, the historian may immortalize them; but we who were of them, who knew them, lived with them and fought with them, cannot other than place ourselves with the whole of posterity under a lifelong obligation to them; and in this manner we all, simultaneously as one man, reverently contribute and lay on the altar of our convictions the returned soldier's mite of admiration and remembrance.

Men of the 10th Battalion: survivors of Anzac, Egypt, France, and Belgium. Let us throw our minds back. Back! Back! Back to those stirring days when 10th Battalion blood flowed freely. Why, it was only a glorious yesterday when our Battalion ranks were sadly depleted, and at times practically decimated. From time to time our Unit contributed freely in the form of human sacrifice, when our friends, our comrades, our Digger-pals were numbered with the slain, and fell, never to rise again. True, "their name liveth for evermore;" and true also, we who have survived, go on, participants of a civilization which those very 10th Battalion comrades of ours, as unpretentious idealists, died to save and to better. And thus the indissoluble fact stands for all time, firmly established upon that direct personal contact, when we brushed shoulders with them on the route march, stood with them on the same firebench, occupied the same dug-out, assembled with them at the same jumping-off tape, accompanied them in those helter-skelter rushes across "No Man's Land," shared with them the common joys and sorrows, trials and adventures of a soldier's life, fraternised and associated with them in a thousand and one different ways, or even assisted to lower them into their final resting places. But whilst they have been taken, we have been left, not solely to mourn their loss, but to preserve their undying memory, to venerate their imperishable achievement. "Their glory survives in everlasting remembrance, not graven in stone but enshrined in the hearts of men for all time."

"THEY GAVE THEIR LIVES. FOR THAT PUBLIC GIFT THEY RECEIVED A PRAISE WHICH NEVER AGES AND A TOMB MOST GLORIOUS—NOT SO MUCH THE TOMB IN WHICH THEY LIE, BUT THAT IN WHICH THEIR FAME SURVIVES—TO BE REMEMBERED FOR EVER WHEN OCCASION COMES FOR WORD OR DEED."

VII

10TH BATTALION BATTLE HONOURS

Won during the Great War, 1914-18, by the 10th Battalion, A.I.F., and emblazoned on the 10th Battalion, A.M.F. Regimental Flag, now retained by the 10/50th Battalion Headquarters, A.M.F., at the Drill Hall, Union Street, Kensington, Adelaide.

In 1924 in pursuance of an Army Order the Military Commandant at Keswick requested Brigadier-General S. P. Weir, D.S.O., V.D., to form a 10th Battalion Regimental Committee for the purpose of selecting ten Battalion Battle Honours.

10TH BATTALION REGIMENTAL COMMITTEE

Brigadier-General S. P. Weir, D.S.O., V.D. (President of Committee); Lieut.-Colonel E. K. Baker, V.D. (Commanding Officer 10th Bn., A.M.F.); Major G. D. Shaw, V.D.; Major F. G. Giles, D.S.O., V.D.; Major W. F. J. McCann, D.S.O., M.C. and Bar; Capt. G. C. Campbell, M.C. and Bar; Capt. F. J. S. Mead, M.C., D.C.M.; Lieut. A. S. Blackburn, V.C.; Lieut. J. Davidson, M.C. Lieut.-Colonel R. B. Jacob, V.D., was invited to sit on the committee, but was unable to take part in the deliberations. This committee, after giving the matter exhaustive consideration, finally selected and recommended the following Battle Honours under date of 1st July, 1924:—

THE GREAT WAR—"SOMME, 1916, 18."
"POZIERES", "BULLECOURT", "YPRES 1917"
"MENIN ROAD", "Polygon Wood."
"Broodseinde", "Poelcappelle", "Passchendaele."
"Lys", "HAZEBROUCK."
"Kemmel", "AMIENS."
"Albert 1918."
"HINDENBURG LINE", "Epehy."
"France and Flanders, 1916-18."
"Anzac", "LANDING AT ANZAC."
"DEFENCE OF ANZAC."
"Suvla."
"Sari Bair."
"Gallipoli, 1915."
"Egypt, 1915-16."

The ten Battle Honours shown above in block letters represent the actual Battle Honours allocated by the British War Office upon the recommendation of the 10th Battalion Regimental Committee which was formed in Adelaide for that purpose. These are the honours emblazoned on the 10th Battalion, A.M.F. Regimental Flag, whilst the honours shown above in smaller type have been claimed and verified from the Official Battalion War Diary now in the National War Museum at Canberra, and though officially recognised, cannot be emblazoned on the 10th Battalion, A.M.F. Regimental Flag.

VIII
RECORDS ESTABLISHED BY THE 10TH BATTALION

It has been said that the 10th Battalion's record in victories, decorations, and promotions compares favourably with any other British regiment with a war establishment not exceeding 9,000. The following achievements were placed on record by the Battalion:—

1. The 10th Battalion was the first foot-regiment raised in South Australia for service abroad during the Great War, 1914-18.

2. The first Commanding Officer of the Battalion (Lieut.-Colonel S. P. Weir) was the first South Australian officer to receive a commission in the A.I.F.

3. The 10th Battalion was the first wholly South Australian infantry regiment to march through the city of Adelaide in 1914.

4. The 10th Battalion was the first South Australian infantry regiment to embark for service overseas in 1914. As a unit of the 1st Division, A.I.F., the Battalion accompanied the First Australian and New Zealand Contingent to Egypt; and the convoy consisting of 28 Australian transports, 10 New Zealand transports, and three warships, was the largest fleet of vessels that had ever left the Commonwealth of Australia or crossed the Indian Ocean. This was the greatest number of British troops that had ever been transported at sea at one time. At Port Said the Battalion participated in the greatest demonstration in the history of the A.I.F., and upon arrival at Mena took up an allotted position in the first divisional camp that Australia had ever assembled.

5. The 10th Battalion was the first South Australian regiment in action in the Great War—as part of the 3rd Brigade covering force at the landing at Anzac, April 25, 1915.

6. The 10th Battalion was about the first, if not the very first of the whole of the Mediterranean Expeditionary Force to land on Gallipoli. This feat is acknowledged by General Sir Ian Hamilton, G.C.B., G.C.M.G., D.S.O., in his 1934 tribute to the Battalion.

7. The 10th Battalion penetrated the greatest distance inland on the day of the landing. Dr. C. E. W. Bean, the Australian official war historian, has acknowledged the distances accomplished by Lieut. N. M. Loutit's party and Lance-Corporal A. S. Blackburn and the late Pte. Phil Robin.

8. The first reported South Australian A.I.F. casualty during the Great War was an officer of the 10th Battalion—late Lieut. E. W. Talbot Smith.

9. The first wounded South Australian officer to return to Adelaide from the Dardanelles was a member of the 10th Battalion—Lieut. A. C. Sommerville.

10. The first South Australian recipient of the Victoria Cross was an officer of the 10th Battalion—Temp. Capt. A. S. Blackburn.

11. The capture of Merris on July 29-30, 1918, by two companies of the 10th Battalion was regarded as a master-piece of military art, and is considered by many commentators to be the greatest one-battalion operation executed in France.

12. The 10th Battalion commenced and finished its fighting career by taking the offensive. As the spearhead of the 3rd Brigade covering force at Anzac on April 25, 1915, the Battalion charged the heights and the enemy looming in the breaking light of dawn. Three-and-a-half years later at Jeancourt, France (18/9/18), the final stage of the last operation in which the Battalion participated was accomplished by a spirited charge made by the 10th when the German machine-gunners only retired after severe fighting.

13. More officers and other ranks passed through the 10th Battalion than through any other South Australian A.I.F. unit.

14. The 10th Battalion sustained more casualties than any other South Australian A.I.F. unit.

15. The 10th Battalion was awarded more honours and decorations for service in the field than any other South Australian A.I.F. unit.

IX

SONG OF THE 10TH BATTALION

A MARCHING SONG

Dedicated by special permission to Colonel S. Price Weir, V.D., and the officers and men of the 10th Battalion, 3rd Infantry Brigade, Australian Imperial Force.

Words by C. R. BERESFORD.   Music by H. BREWSTER-JONES.

'Twas not within a barrack yard they put us through our drill,
They licked us into soldier shape in camp at Morphettville;
So khaki-clad and Enfield-armed, we'll fight at Tommy's side,
To hold secure the fields of France against the German tide.

Chorus:
Left, right, left, boys; keep the column swinging;
Every step our destination nears;
Long, long miles we'll shorten by our singing,
Kits are heavy but a chorus cheers—
All our help old Mother England's needing—
Soon we'll have to prove that we are men,
And the 10th Battalion will be leading;
We're Australians in Old Ten.

We hail from busy Rundle Street and north of Goyder's line;
But far from there, beneath strange stars, our glinting bayonets shine.
For half the world is now between us and the crowded quay
Where to the strains of "Auld Lang Syne" our troopship puts to sea.

Chorus.

We long to hear the maxim's purr and smell the cordite strong,
Across the busy firing line the crowded trench along;
The chatter that our rifles make, as down the line it runs
To swell that wartime music grand, the chorus of the guns.

Chorus.

The magic of new lands we see won't banish from our mind
Those bright-eyed, dear Australian maids, the best of all girlkind;
The grand old Jack, wind-blown, above, with all its colours bright,
Means them and home, and all we love; so we march out to fight.

Chorus.

This song was printed and published in September, 1914, by the Mail Newspapers Ltd., who handed over to the Patriotic Fund portion of the proceeds raised by the sale of same.

10TH BATTALION CHRONOLOGY
(Incorporating the *Battalion War Diary*.)

MORPHETTVILLE
August 19 to October 20, 1914

1914.
August 10. Recruiting for Australian Imperial Force commenced.

„ 11. Morphettville camp site decided upon, the State Military Commandant selecting Mr. R. M. Hawker's property at Morphettville. Same had an area of 80 acres, was well watered, accessible by rail to and from city of Adelaide, and in every way was considered suitable for the purpose.

„ 12. Volunteers desirous of serving abroad in the 10th Battalion, A.I.F., applied in great numbers at Keswick Headquarters, the Parade Ground, Adelaide, the military barracks at the rear of the Adelaide Museum, and at various suburban and country area offices. A further batch of written applications for enrolment was received at Keswick, but owing to small staff, could not be acknowledged. It was estimated that at least 1,000 offers had been received from volunteers in all parts of the State of South Australia desirous of enlisting in the Australian Imperial Force.

„ 12. Colonel S. P. Weir received telegram from Military Headquarters at Melbourne offering him the command of a South Australian battalion of infantry (the 10th) with A.I.F. He immediately replied, accepted command of proposed unit, and awaited further instructions.

„ 15. Conditions for enlistment with the A.I.F. were issued at Keswick Headquarters, viz.—Men required, aged 19 to 38; minimum height, 5 ft. 6 in., drivers 5 ft. 4 in.; minimum chest measurement, 34 in., drivers 33 in. Pay for privates, 5/- per day at home, 6/- abroad, 1/- per day to be deferred in the latter case. Period of enlistment—duration of war and for a further term of 4 months, unless discharged, dismissed, or removed. Single men preferred, but married men and widowers with children accepted providing they allotted two-fifths of their pay in favour of dependants.

„ 16. Lieut.-Colonel S. P. Weir instructed by telegram to take command and forthwith raise 10th Battalion. He immediately proceeded with the organization of unit and selection of officers.

„ 17. Lieut.-Colonel S. P. Weir proceeded to Keswick Headquarters and selected Major F. W. Hurcombe as Staff-Major, Capt. F. M. de F. Lorenzo as Adjutant, and Capt. C. F. Minagall as Quartermaster. He also recommended the majority of company commanders and subalterns—all being subsequently confirmed.

BATTALION CHRONOLOGY

1914.
August 19 Morphettville Training Camp opened. First quota of 10th Battalion recruits were sworn in in stables on the property, and the only food issued that day consisted of bread and jam. 200 men enlisted that day, and before the afternoon parade was dismissed for tea, Major F. W. Hurcombe addressed the men and announced that general leave had been granted until eight the next morning.

" 20. Enlistment at Morphettville commenced in earnest. Another 100 men were enrolled, and long queues of men in mufti awaited to take the oath of allegiance.

" 22. Battalion strength increased to 425. Country quotas began to arrive, and Headquarters Staff was extraordinarily busy compiling attestation papers. First quota of Broken Hill recruits arrived with Capt. R. B. Jacob, Lieut. A. J. Byrne and 2nd Lieut. J. Hamilton.

" 24. Original "G" Company under Lieut. F. G. Giles almost up to establishment strength. Blue dungarees were issued pending arrival of uniforms. Second quota of Barrier men arrived with 2nd Lieuts. Perry and Farrier. Colonel Weir sent Lieut. Byrne to the railway station in order to direct them to the camp, and later that day the area officers at Broken Hill were requested by wire to send the remaining men as early as possible.

" 25. Another 245 men added to strength, including 125 trainees from Broken Hill and 110 men without previous military experience. Battalion strength that day increased to 690.

" 26. Imperial Reservists struck off strength of Battalion and placed on supernumerary list pending embarkation for England. This alteration necessitated a further 10 per cent. increase in enrolments. Had this alteration not been made the regimental numbers of the original Battalion would not have exceeded "1,000."

" 26. R. S. M. Whitbourn took in charge 52 men provisionally selected as N.C.O's. for instructional purposes.

" 27. Enlistment proceeded steadily, there being a steady flow of volunteers from all parts of the State. Seven companies almost up to establishment strength, Battalion strength being 745.

" 28. Third quota of troops from Broken Hill arrived, and as they marched into the 10th lines were given an enthusiastic welcome. They were chiefly posted to original "H" Company.

" 28. Lieut.-Colonel S. P. Weir entertained Mr. R. M. Hawker in the Officers' Mess. Colonel Weir mentioned that the Battalion was camped on Mr. Hawker's property, and referred to the patriotic fervour of their guest. Mr. Hawker in reply said that he was merely temporarily giving his property to the defence of his country, whereas the men who were going to the front were giving their lives.

1914.
August 28. Colonel E. G. Sinclair-MacLagan, Commander of the 3rd Infantry Brigade, made his first inspection of the 10th Battalion at Morphettville.

" 29. First list of non-commissioned appointments issued and were confirmed to date from 28/8/14.

" 30. Battalion strength reached 910. Lieut.-Colonel S. P. Weir announced that Mr. C. Tolley had generously undertaken to supply the 10th Battalion with colours. Mrs. Jury and a committee of Glenelg ladies were entrusted with the making of this flag.

" 31. Full Battalion strength reached (1,023).

1914.
September 1. His Excellency the Governor of South Australia (Colonel Sir Henry Galway) visited the Morphettville Training Camp and informally inspected the 10th Battalion at work. During his visit there was no cessation of drilling and instruction. He was accompanied by the District Military Commandant (Lieut.-Colonel Irving), the Camp Commandant (Major de Passey), and Lieut.-Colonel S. P. Weir, C.O. of the 10th.

" 2. 10th Battalion enlistments continued, additional men being required to replace those who had been transferred to the 12th Battalion and other A.I.F. units then being raised.

" 3. Uniforms, rifles and kits were gradually issued. Musketry practice was carried out in the sandhills north-west of the camp. Lieut. Woolley, of Headquarters, had charge of physical training. S. S. M. Bowen instructed the Battalion signallers, and Capt. Hill, of the A.M.C., frequently lectured the troops on camp sanitation and hygienic matters.

" 4. The Governor-General (Right Hon. Sir Ronald Crauford Munro Ferguson) and General Sir William Throsby Bridges reviewed the 10th Battalion on the Morphettville Race-course. The firm of Stott & Hoare, of Adelaide, presented the Battalion with a portable Corona typewriter, which was used in the Orderly Room at Morphettville and Mena, and on the troopships *Ascanius* and *Ionian*.

" 5. Battalion frequently marched to St. Leonards, Glenelg, for bathing purposes. Whilst marching through the streets of Glenelg the Battalion was always lustily cheered, the residents of this sea-side resort always manifesting a particular interest in the 10th.

" 6. Extract from Battalion orders of the day—"The attention of all ranks is directed to the fact that no lights are permitted in tents other than those authorized, after "Lights out" has been sounded. Men on leave who return after 10 p.m. must so arrange their bedding that they will be able to get into bed without using a light and without disturbing their comrades.

BATTALION CHRONOLOGY

1914.
September 6. No talking above a whisper is to take place in tents after "Lights
(continued) out" has been sounded. O.C. Companies will take every advantage of the drums issued to them to train their men to march. The men are to be encouraged to sing on the march. Steps are being taken to introduce regimental marching songs. Men are also to be encouraged to carry and play while on the march a musical instrument that can be carried on active service." A few more non-commissioned appointments were also included in this order.

" 8. All members of Battalion granted three days' "embarkation" leave and free railway passes to destination and return. This was granted in anticipation of the 10th embarking for overseas at an early date.

" 9. Everything in order for Battalion to move off from Morphettville when instruction was conveyed through orders.

" 11. Naval and Military Club entertained Colonel Weir and 10th Battalion Officers. His Excellency the Governor, Sir Henry Galway, also attended.

" 13. A party of nurses from the Adelaide Hospital visited the 10th Battalion lines at Morphettville. The cooks' shelters and butcher's shop claimed special attention. The Adjutant, Capt. Lorenzo, conducted the party and described items of interest.

" 14. Battalion engaged in route march from Morphettville along Tapley's Hill Road to Remount Depot at O'Halloran Hill. Battalion left camp in the morning and returned late in the afternoon. The Battalion scouts extended as the column proceeded, and various tactical exercises were executed.

" 14. Lieut.-Colonel S. P. Weir and Officers of the 10th gave a dinner at Morphettville. Amongst those present were the Premier, Hon. A. H. Peake; the Speaker of the House of Assembly, Hon. L. O'Loghlin; the State Military Commandant, Colonel G. G. Irving, and the Morphettville Camp Commandant, Major de Passey. The Mayors of Adelaide and Glenelg were unable to attend, and forwarded apologies. At this function Lieut.-Col. Weir was presented with a framed photograph of the Officers of the Battalion.

" 16. Camp at Morphettville temporarily struck for sanitary purposes. A considerable amount of influenza had been contracted by the troops, and as an antiseptic the sites of the tents were given a few hours' sunlight. Tents were struck before men went on morning parade and re-erected after afternoon parade.

" 17. Colonel Weir stated that he expected to have the 10th Battalion in readiness to move off before the end of the week.

" 19. Presentation of 10th Battalion colours by His Excellency the Governor on the Morphettville Race-course.

1914.
September 21. First route march through city of Adelaide by all A.I.F. troops in training at Morphettville. The Govt. Offices were closed from 1 to 3 in honour of the occasion. Parade strength of 10th was 1,025, and 1st Reinforcements 100. Battalion left camp at 9.30 a.m., proceeded along the Bay Road to West Terrace, and bivouacked in the West Park lands near the Observatory for lunch. At 1.45 the 10th was marshalled on West Terrace, and moved off about 2 p.m., proceeding along North Terrace, Pulteney Street, Rundle Street, King William Street, Grote Street, West Terrace, and back to camp *via* the Bay Road. The Governor took the salute from the top of Parliament House steps: 2,193 men of the A.I.F. took part in the route march and 725 horses. At the Half-Way House on the Bay Road Mr. Tolley generously supplied free beer to the parched men of the 10th. The ale was brought out in tubs and buckets and ladled into dixies. After such a march through the city under a typically S.A. cloudless sky his kindness was much appreciated by all.

„ 22. Capt. H. W. H. Seager, O.C. of original "C" Coy., was admitted to hospital suffering with pneumonia. Lieut. K. E. Green from "G" Coy. was appointed acting O.C. of "C" Coy., and 2nd Lieut. N. M. Loutit was taken on Battalion strength to fill the vacancy thereby caused in "G" Coy.

„ 23. The issue of equipment to the Battalion was almost completed. A brass band had been established, due to the generosity of several patriotic citizens who supplied various instruments, funds, and music. The Transport Section had received its quota of horses; two Maxim machine guns had been issued to the Machine Gun Section, and the paybooks had been compiled. The S.A. Jockey Club gave permission for the Morphettville Race-course to be used as a manoeuvring ground, where battalion drill was occasionally carried out.

„ 25. Anticipated that this would be the last week of the Battalion at Morphettville prior to embarking. Parents and friends daily visited the Battalion lines in large numbers in order to farewell members of the original Battalion who were prepared to embark at any hour. Twice orders were issued to strike camp, but subsequently these instructions were countermanded.

„ 26. Colonel S. P. Weir stated to the press that his men of the 10th Battalion were second to none, and that his officers were of the first water.

„ 29. First Battalion death occurred. No. 517 Pte. J. W. Poole, of "H" Coy., died of pneumonia, and was buried at the West Terrace Cemetery. 2nd Lieut. J. Hamilton and a firing party from "H" Coy. attended the funeral.

BATTALION CHRONOLOGY

1914.
September 30. Battalion proceeded to Brighton and bivouacked for night, when certain night operations and outpost work was carried out near the Brighton Cement Works.

" 31. Battalion moved off from Brighton, carried out advance and rear-guard work, and late in the afternoon returned to camp at Morphettville.

1914.
October 5. Orders issued to remove camp nearer to Ascot Park, about one mile due south along the Morphettville Road towards Oaklands, in a paddock owned by Mr. Andrew Tennant. A fatigue party from "B" Coy. proceeded with mallets and pegs to define proposed site, but before any pegs were driven the instruction was countermanded, and the party returned to Morphettville, where the Battalion remained until embarkation.

" 6. A water-cart from the Glenelg Corporation was busily engaged in watering the 10th Battalion lines in order to settle the dust which had become a nuisance on account of the 1914 drought.

" 8. Battalion proceeded to Brighton, and en route skirmished in Mr. Fairbairn's paddock and returned along foreshore to Glenelg and back to camp.

" 9. Battalion engaged greater part of day in company and battalion drill on the Morphettville Race-course. The various battalion formations were not easily mastered, and battalion wheeling proved especially difficult.

" 14. Eight Hours' Day found the Adelaide Plains enveloped in a typical brickfielder, when strong north winds and red dust were the order of the day—further omens of the severity of the 1914 drought. General leave was granted that day, and Lieut.-Col. S. P. Weir and several officers proceeded to Glenelg in a vain attempt to free themselves of the climatic rigours of the day.

" 15. Battalion marched from Morphettville to National Park, Belair, and there bivouacked for two nights, whilst certain outposts and advance guard operations were conducted in the park.

" 17. Battalion returned to Morphettville to spend its last week-end in camp prior to embarking.

" 19. No leave whatsoever granted, and camp closed to public. Battalion stood by all day awaiting orders to move off. Greater portion of day spent in finally packing kit-bags for the holds and sea-kit-bags for the troop decks. Lady Galway and an energetic ladies' committee had prepared and donated the sea kit-bags, which were used to contain essential toilet articles for the voyage. Also many woollen articles such as mufflers, gloves, scarves, etc., intended for a cold climate were issued. The

30 THE FIGHTING 10TH

1914.
October 19. remainder of the day was spent in clearing the Battalion lines,
(continued) and the incinerators were burning at their utmost capacity.

„ 19. William Kuhnel & Son presented the Battalion with an Estey organ for use on the transport. Various musical instruments, sheet music and books were also received from several well-wishers.

„ 19. No. 918 Pte. J. Loughran of "C" Coy., fell from a train between McDonalds and Camden, and was removed to a field hospital. He subsequently embarked with the 1st Reinforcements, and was allotted a new regimental number, No. 1156.

„ 20. Battalion struck camp at Morphettville and moved off to the Morphettville Railway Station and entrained for the Outer Harbour, proceeding *via* the Adelaide Gaol loop-line. In many respects there was a genuine feeling of regret that the Battalion was seeing the last of historic Morphettville, as it was there the Battalion was born and came into existence as an integral unit of the A.I.F. The troop-train conveying the Battalion was continuously cheered en route to the Outer Harbour, which was reached about 1 p.m.

AT SEA ON H.M.A.T. A11 *ASCANIUS*
October 20 to December 6, 1914

October 20. H.M.A.T. A11 *Ascanius* was berthed at the Outer Harbour, and after the companies had been allotted their respective quarters, troops were permitted to join friends and relatives who had congregated in large numbers on the wharf. The last Battalion parade in South Australia was then held on the wharf, and Sir Henry Galway, in halting phrases and with a decidedly sad mien addressed the Battalion from the promenade deck of the *Ascanius*. The Battalion then marched up the gangway, and despite the fact that guards had been stationed to prevent the crowd from getting near the boat, it ultimately broke its way through. At 4.30 p.m. the *Ascanius* pulled out, and many of the men of the 10th looked towards the Adelaide Hills for the last time, some with feelings of hope that they would eventually return; but the die in the great game had been cast, and some never returned, and on that occasion viewed their native hills with leave-taking recollections.

„ 20. The Transport Section of the Battalion under 2nd Lieut. T. O. Smyth, with 21 other ranks, embarked on H.M.A.T. A12 *Saldanha* at the Outer Harbour and subsequently joined the convoy proceeding to Egypt.

„ 21. Battalion on *Ascanius* was beginning to settle down for the long voyage ahead. The Orderly-Room Staff and Adjutant were extremely busy in preparing routine orders.

BATTALION CHRONOLOGY

1914.
October 22. Troops on *Ascanius* had commenced routine duties. Several men became ill whilst crossing the Great Australian Bight, and quite a few were prostrated the whole of the voyage.

„ 25. *Ascanius* arrived at Fremantle, where troops were assembled on wharf for church parade during morning. Later in the afternoon a proportion of the 10th was granted leave for the purpose of visiting Perth.

„ 26. Shore-leave continued in accordance with arrangements, whilst each day those companies not on leave proceeded to Osborne for target practice.

„ 27. Shore-leave cancelled. Those companies which had not been on leave requested to be paraded before the Colonel, who refused to grant further leave.

„ 29. 2nd Lieut. H. R. Heming placed in charge of picquet, which proceeded to Perth to escort back those men who had overstayed their leave.

„ 31. Lieut.-Colonel J. L. Johnston, 26 officers, and 759 other ranks of the 11th Battalion embarked on the *Ascanius*, which left Fremantle wharf and anchored overnight in the Gage Roadstead. A huge crowd farewelled the troop-ship, this being the second and final Australian farewell the 10th experienced. Two men of Battalion overstayed leave and missed transport.

1914.
November 1. *Ascanius* lay at anchor all that day and night in Gage Roadstead off Fremantle Harbour. Being a Sunday many residents of Perth and suburbs hired small boats and came alongside the transport to farewell members of the 11th Battalion, there being six companies on board.

„ 1. Important staff alterations were made for the voyage. Lieut.-Colonel S. P. Weir became O.C. of troops; Major F. W. Hurcombe was appointed temporary C.O. of Battalion, and Lieut. E. W. Talbot Smith was appointed Assistant Adjutant. These appointments terminated upon reaching Alexandria.

„ 2. About seven in the morning the *Ascanius* lifted anchor and moved out from the Gage Roadstead for the open sea, when the last glimpse of Australia was partaken of by all on board, and by many who never returned to their native shores.

„ 2. Officers of 10th Battalion were issued with Official A.I.F. textbooks dealing with the French, German, and Austro-Hungarian Armies, notes on the Military Geography of France and Belgium, notes on night operations, physical exercises aboard ship, notes on the laws and customs of war, and a military vocabulary containing English, French, and German military terms.

„ 3. Very early in the morning the *Ascanius* and the *Medic* from Fremantle sighted the Japanese cruiser *Ibuki*, and stood to in

1914.
November 3. (continued) order to take up their allotted positions in the convoy which had assembled at King George's Sound, Albany, and was now commencing the journey across the Indian Ocean. The morning was misty, but as the convoy gradually appeared the whole of the 10th Battalion was thrilled at the prospect of becoming a component of such an assembly of ships, which was the largest convoy to cross the Indian Ocean, the convoy that travelled the greatest distance and transported the greatest number of men. During the afternoon the Japanese cruiser *Ibuki* escorted the *Ascanius* to its allotted position in the 2nd Division of the convoy. The *Ascanius* had come through a storm and had slipped into position behind the *Medic* without any trouble, whilst immediately astern of the *Ascanius* was the *Star of England*.

,, 5. The Orient steamer *Osterley* slowly overhauled the convoy, and at sunset passed close to the starboard column. The *Minotaur* immediately sent a strongly-worded protest to the *Osterley* regretting that her commander had seen fit to come so close to the convoy, and making him responsible for taking all precautions.

,, 5. Captains Brennan and Nott busily engaged in innoculating troops on the *Ascanius*.

,, 7. Precautions were put into operation to prevent the convoy being sighted at night. The suppression of lights was strictly enforced on the *Ascanius*. All lights aboard were screened, and brown paper was pasted over port-holes. Red and green side-lights were discontinued, and the stern-light was covered with a hood so that same should merely cast a glow downwards upon the troubled water in the wake, and only the leading vessels in each division carried a masthead light.

,, 7. The convoy was only 36 hours steam from the Cocos Islands, and during the evening all lights on the *Ascanius* were extinguished for half an hour whilst the troops were ordered to their allotted boat-stations. All cigarettes and pipes were extinguished, whilst barefooted men of the 10th stood motionless until the order was given to "Carry on."

,, 8. The 28 Australian and 10 New Zealand transports travelled through the night, while barely three hours ahead of them the German raider *Emden* was crossing their path.

,, 9. At day-break the whole convoy was due to pass the Cocos Islands. The course had been laid slightly off the track of the mail steamers in order to take the fleet 50 miles east of the Islands. As day broke the siren of the *Orvieto* hooted, and the transports turned in succession a few points to port. They were at that moment swinging round the Cocos Islands at a radius of 50 miles.

BATTALION CHRONOLOGY

1914.
November 9. At 7 a.m. the troops on the *Ascanius* observed H.M.A.S. *Sydney* dash away to the south from the position she had held on the port beam of the convoy, and within ten minutes had disappeared behind a cloud of smoke. She increased speed to 26 knots per hour, with a White Ensign run up to her fore-peak, an Australian ensign at her truck, and the Union Jack floating from her after-mast, and the decks were unmistakably being cleared for action.

„ 9. At 9.30 a.m. the *Sydney* signalled that she had sighted the enemy's ship, and that it was steaming northward. At 9.55 a.m. the *Sydney* wirelessed, "I am engaging enemy," and a little later, "The enemy is escaping north." After an hour of suspense came the message, "Enemy ran ashore to save sinking," and at 11.29, "*Emden* beached herself to save sinking; am pursuing merchant collier." At 11.44 a.m. that morning came the historic message, "*Emden* beached and done for." Cheers rose from the troop-decks of every transport, and spread through the whole convoy as this message definitely stating that it was the *Emden* that had been destroyed was semaphored from ship to ship down the lines. The relief that this destroyer of British merchant-ships had been destroyed and the pride that an Australian ship had done the job were intense. Parades were half-interrupted, and an order from General Bridges on the *Orvieto* caused work for the day to cease. On board the *Ascanius* there was a free issue of beer with dinner to celebrate the event. This was the second occasion when the men of the 10th as a regiment were issued with free beer. This time the cost was borne by the officers of the 10th.

„ 11. *Ascanius* slowed down for a burial at sea, one of the 11th Battalion having succumbed.

„ 13. *Ascanius* crossed equator when no Father Neptune celebrations were staged.

„ 14. The Battalion "stood to" at 5 a.m. on the *Ascanius* in anticipation of H.M.A.S. *Sydney* passing. All troops were warned not to cheer the Australian warship as it passed, for that vessel had requested by signal that there should be no cheering whilst the ship passed through the transports, in view of the fact that the maimed and dying survivors of the *Emden* were temporarily housed on her deck. But the men of the 10th and the whole convoy were denied the inspiring sight, for at 4.30 that morning the *Sydney* and the *Empress of Russia* sped past in the distance. Once in port, however, when any boats from the fleet approached the *Sydney*, hearty ringing cheers came unchecked from all the A.I.F. men.

„ 15. At 12 a.m. the *Ascanius* arrived at Colombo, where the O.C. of troops on the *Ascanius* received a full type-written report of the "*Emden-Sydney* Fight" prepared by Dr. C. E. W. Bean,

1914.
November 15. the Official Press Correspondent accompanying the A.I.F.
(continued) abroad. After leaving Colombo this account was read to each company of the 10th in sequence. No leave was granted to either Officers or men of the 10th Battalion whilst at Colombo. This port proved most interesting. Quaint native junks and mosquito-craft choked the harbour whilst shipping and warships of the Allied Powers predominated. There was the cruiser *Sydney* and several British cruisers, and also the five-funnelled *Askold* belonging to Russia, which earlier in the war had engaged the *Emden* in the China Sea, and according to reports both vessels had fought tooth and nail. The *Askold* was promptly nick-named "The packet of woodbines." There were the huge Empress liners, a Chinese gunboat, the Japanese *Ibuki* staged a washing day, and transports from Bombay, Calcutta, and Singapore were arriving and departing, and others were bringing Territorials from England. So great was the conglomeration of shipping that the harbour at Colombo could not accommodate them all at once, and some of necessity had to lie outside the breakwater and harbour.

„ 17. The *Ascanius* and the 2nd Division of transports left Colombo, and the convoy sailed by Divisions and speeds as were convenient. The 3rd Division, which being the fastest, was the last to leave.

„ 18. Further innoculation parades on *Ascanius*.

„ 20. The 3rd Division of transports caught up to the 1st and 2nd Divisions, but as the *Afric* in the 3rd Division could not maintain the speed required, the *Ascanius* was sent across from the 2nd Division of transports to take her place. Next morning the rest of the fleet came up with the 3rd Division, which was motionless on the high-seas.

„ 21. At 4.25 a.m. the *Ascanius*, in passing over to the 3rd Division of transports, rammed the *Shropshire*. The ships were locked for a moment, and on separating the *Ascanius* came ahead and rammed the *Shropshire* again. Men in the forward holds were violently thrown from their hammocks when the impact occurred, and naturally wondered if the transport had been mined, torpedoed, or had struck a reef. Troops immediately donned life-belts and filed quietly on deck, and there awaited the order to jump overboard. Whilst standing there for over half an hour it was ascertained that during the collision two life-boats of the *Ascanius* had been torn away and a rent 26 feet in length had been made in the side of the forward bow, but fortunately same was well-above the water-line. The siren of the *Ascanius* subsequently hooted, and the impromptu early morning parade was dismissed. Almost immediately after the incident occurred the *Hampshire* came alongside and displayed search-lights on both vessels concerned. The Commander of

BATTALION CHRONOLOGY 35

1914.
November 21. the *Hampshire* seemed disgusted with the affair, and in true
(continued) nautical twang bellowed through his megaphone: "In my whole
career of navigation I have never seen anything so careless. You
are not fit to be in charge of a ferry-boat."

,, 25. *Ascanius* arrived at Aden in morning and took on fresh water
and coal. The other Australian and New Zealand transports
arrived during the day, and found the roadstead at that port
crowded with the traffic of troops to and from India. Transports were either making for India with Territorials or returning with British regulars or native troops. Ships of every size
passed in and out of the harbour all day, and by nightfall 57
vessels were anchored off Aden.

,, 26. At 5 a.m. the *Ascanius* left Aden and passed the tumbled outline
of the Sheikh Said Turkish Fort which appeared on the deserted
foothills. Only a few days previously this enemy fort had been
shelled by the cruiser *Duke of Edinburgh*. At 4 p.m. that day
the *Ascanius* passed through the Straits of Bab-el-Mandeb and
through Hell's Gate into the Red Sea. Even at this time all on
the *Ascanius* confidently anticipated that they were proceeding
to England to train on Salisbury Plain, like the Canadians had
done before proceeding to France. At Aden that morning six
naval engineers had boarded the *Ascanius* to subsequently repair
the damage caused by the *Shropshire-Ascanius* collision.

,, 28. The first official intimation was received on the *Ascanius* as to
where the Battalion was actually to disembark. When Alexandria was named as the port of disembarkation, there was a
certain amount of genuine resentment, which, however, subsided before Egypt was reached, when one and all were agog
to set foot in the land of the Pharaohs, and if necessary to come
to grips with the Turks. The previous night General Bridges
on the *Orvieto* had rceeived the following telegram from Sir
George Reid, the High Commissioner for Australia in London:
"Unforseen circumstances decide that the Force shall train in
Egypt, and go to the front from there. The Australians and
New Zealanders are to form a corps under General Birdwood.
The locality of the camp is near Cairo."

1914.
December 1. About 9 a.m. the *Ascanius* arrived at Port Suez and anchored in
the roadstead, awaiting orders to enter the Suez Canal.

,, 1. *Ascanius* left Suez at 8 that night to traverse the Suez Canal.
The O.C. of troops had been advised that there was a chance of
the transport being fired upon during the night by Bedouins
from the desert to the east. Consequently an armed guard
under 2nd Lieut. H. R. Heming was mounted, and consisted
of 1 officer, 2 sgts., 2 corporals, and 24 men. This guard was
stationed on the boat-deck, where four machine guns had been
mounted. This was the first guard of the Battalion to be issued

December (continued)
1. with ball-ammunition, but the *Ascanius* was neither fired upon nor had to return fire.

" 2. Whilst passing through the Suez Canal the damage sustained by the impact with the *Shropshire* was temporarily repaired by the naval engineers on board. A scaffold was erected over the bows, and an electrical rivetting plant on board created such an all-night din that men of the 10th had little sleep. The strong search-light from the *Ascanius* and the cheering from the Indian camps en route were added attractions which also prevented men from sleeping.

" 2. The *Ascanius* arrived at Port Said about noon and anchored in the harbour. A little later the *Shropshire* passed the *Ascanius*, when troops on both transports vociferously yelled and coo-eed to the other. Above the din of catcalls and cheering an occasional stentorian voice would rend the air with "What ho, she bumps!"—an allusion to the collision of November 21. One by one the Australian transports arrived, each new arrival moving closely between the others already at anchor. On the *Ascanius* and all other transports, too, the decks were thronged and men swarmed in the rigging, and as each vessel passed the gusts and buffets of cheering were deafening. This was undoubtedly the greatest noise within the living memory of Port Said, and could not have been eclipsed even at the opening of the Suez Canal. Dr. C. E. W. Bean said: "This was the first great demonstration in the history of the A.I.F., only perhaps surpassed by the march through London after the Armistice." This was the first time the troops as a whole had had an opportunity of seeing the component parts of the 1st Australian Division, and December 2, 1914, will live for ever in the memories of all surviving original 10th Battalion men who were on the *Ascanius*.

" 2. Whilst anchored at Port Said a naval court of enquiry was conducted on the *Ascanius* in connection with the *Shropshire-Ascanius* incident, and it was generally believed that under the extraordinary conditions which prevailed at the time the collision occurred, both captains were exonerated.

" 3. *Ascanius* left Port Said Harbour and anchored in roadstead about three miles out, and there awaited orders to proceed to Alexandria for disembarkation.

" 4. *Ascanius* left Port Said roadstead for Alexandria at 5 p.m., the transports leaving five at a time.

" 5. *Ascanius* arrived at Alexandria about 7 a.m., and anchored in Alexandria Harbour.

" 6. About 4 p.m. the *Ascanius* moved into the quay at Alexandria, and all troops were prepared and instructed for disembarkation on the morrow. Kit-bags were taken from the holds, and sea kit-bags were finally packed. An advance party from the 10th

BATTALION CHRONOLOGY

1914.
December 6. Battalion and half of the 11th Battalion on board disembarked
(continued) and left for Mena, Cairo, that night by rail.

„ 7. The 10th Battalion disembarked and entrained for Cairo. Companies moved off during the day, "B" Coy. being the last to disembark. Late in the afternoon whilst this company under Capt. G. D. Shaw was assembled on the quay awaiting a troop-train, the *Ascanius* lifted gangways and left for England with Imperial Reservists on board. "B" Coy. of the 10th stood and cheered the *Ascanius* out of sight as she wended her way through the maze of enemy merchantmen which were interned in Alexandria harbour. The 10th had lived on the *Ascanius* for six weeks, and during that time the transport had proved a good friend, even if she had given them a nasty bump. The last 10th Battalion quotas (excluding transport) left Alexandria about 6.30 p.m. for Cairo.

MENA CAMP, EGYPT
December 8, 1914, to February 28, 1915

December 7-8. 10th Battalion entrained in companies for Abu Ela Railway Station, near Cairo. At this station right in the heart of Cairo, near the Egyptian Museum, a committee of women, chiefly wives of British residents in Cairo, met the troop-trains from Alexandria, and provided hot cocoa, cheese, and bread. Strings of electric cars, twenty or more in number, awaited the troops and conveyed them to Mena. The Manchester Regiment then at the Kasr-el-Nil Barracks, gave the Battalion a rousing cheer as it passed, and some of the companies of the 10th were proceeding to their new destination during the early hours of the morning. Alighting from the cars the men of the 10th proceeded along the newly-made road to the site of the Mena Camp. The remaining hours until daybreak were spent on the sands, the tents having not arrived.

„ 8. Before breakfast there was a general rush by all to visit the Giza Pyramids and Sphinx. The expected tents did not arrive from Cairo that day, with the result that a second night was spent in the open, where "As black as Egypt's night" was enjoyed to perfection. The majority of 10th Battalion men spent until midnight in Cairo and returned to Mena during the early hours of the morning. After settling themselves between blankets rain commenced to fall, which somewhat disproved the assertions of the past week that "it never rained in Egypt." Men protected themselves with waterproof sheets, and this was actually the first wet night the Battalion endured without shelter.

„ 9. Tents arrived from ordnance and were erected by the Battalion. Units and details of the 1st Australian Division were arriving daily. Contractors were busy laying water-pipes; tram-lines were being extended to the supply depot; roads were being

1914.
December 9. formed about the camp, and scaffolding around two hastily
(continued) constructed concrete reservoirs for reticulating the camp was
still in existence.

,, 10. The Mena Camp grew bigger each day, and was showing signs of development. Canteens were being erected, and early morning bands and bugles ushered in "Reveille," the "British Grenadiers" being the most popular and best-played tune.

,, 11. Staff divided the desert near the camp into three large training areas, one for each brigade. Lieut.-Col. S. P. Weir was requested by Brigade Headquarters to submit a definite scheme of training, when it was subsequently decided that about a month should be devoted to company training, to be followed by 10 days battalion training, and after that a further ten days training as brigades, and after that, if time permitted, the division would exercise as a whole.

,, 12. Training commenced in earnest. Eight hours per day was the schedule, and a very limited leave was allowed to Cairo after hours. Early each morning the 10th Battalion marched out to the portion of the 3rd Brigade Training Area assigned to it, and all day long groups of men would be drilling, retiring, advancing, or squatting near piled arms listening to an officer. Day after day the Battalion marched through soft sand before the training area was reached, to be marched back to camp again each evening.

,, 13. The 10th Battalion transport arrived, and all units of the 1st Australian Division had disembarked and reached Mena Camp. This was the first time that Australia had assembled a complete division as a body.

,, 14. One of the newly-constructed concrete tanks had been filled with water for reticulating the camp, but unfortunately for the engineers responsible for its construction, the pressure per square inch proved too great, with the result that during the early hours of the morning it burst. The water rolled down the slopes of the Giza Plateau and drenched many who were sleeping in the vicinity.

,, 17. Egypt proclaimed a British Protectorate, thus ending Turkish suzerainty over the country.

,, 20. Great pomp and ceremony at Abdine Palace in connection with the accession of H.H. Sultan Hussein Kamel.

,, 25. Battalion spent its first Christmas abroad. Puddings were made by the Battalion cooks. In the afternoon sports were held, at which some splendid trophies for various events were won. These trophies had been handed to the officers of the 10th prior to leaving Morphettville for competition on the *Ascanius*, but as the deck space on the transport was strictly limited, Col. Weir decided to defer the sports until after dis-

BATTALION CHRONOLOGY

1914.
December 25. embarkation. Lieut. E. W. Talbot Smith was secretary of the
(continued) sports, and many of the trophies had been presented by Mr. C.
Tolley. About this time No. 638 Pte. Phil de Q. Robin was
married in the 10th Battalion Officers' Mess at Mena, and being
a very popular member of "A" Coy. was given a great reception.

„ 28. The 10th Battalion flag formerly presented by Mrs. Jury, of
Glenelg, was taken to Egypt and surmounted a cleverly-worked
Battalion emblem in a conspicuous part near the 10th Battalion
lines. It was constructed in the form of a coat of arms made
of broken bricks, coloured glass, and pebbles. (This flag after
doing heroic service became tattered and torn and unfit for
further service. In consequence thereof, Col. Weir retrieved
the central portion with the magpie upon it, and still has this
exceedingly valuable souvenir in his possession.)

„ 31. Sir George Reid, High Commissioner for Australia, reviewed
and addressed the 1st Australian Division at Mena Camp.

1915.
January 1. Mena Camp had grown in size and importance. It stretched
for nearly a mile up the desert valley. Mena House Hotel was
taken over as a hospital. Headquarters were accommodated in
the manager's house at the rear of the hotel, the ramshackle
grandstand of the old race-course became the ordnance store,
and at the end of the newly-laid tramway were immense stacks
of fodder and supplies. The camp roads were trimly lined
with whitewashed stones, and many of the officers' tents were
bordered with green oats cultivated from the surplus water.
Infantry, artillery, ambulance, transport, and divisional light
horse occupied their allotted areas. Tobacconists, hairdressers,
and improvised shops of all descriptions were erected in a reserve specially set apart for the purpose. Spacious mess-rooms
were in course of construction for the men. The canteens were
well established, and the Battalion pioneers under Pioneer-
Sergt. F. H. G. N. Heritage had the sanitation of the 10th
Battalion lines well in hand.

„ 2. The changeover from the 8-Company system to the 4-Company
system was made. Capt. E. C. Oldham was promoted to the
rank of Major, and Lieut. K. E. Green was promoted to rank
of Captain. Platoon commanders were appointed, and platoon
drill was introduced. In order to perfect the new system of
battalion organization company drill was consequently prolonged until about the end of the month.

„ 5. The name "AUSTRALIAN IMPERIAL FORCE" came to
be generally recognized. White paint was issued to Company
Quartermaster-Sergeants in order that the words "AUSTRALIAN EXPEDITIONARY FORCE," which had been painted
on kit-bags at Morphettville could be obliterated and "A.I.F."
painted in lieu thereof.

THE FIGHTING 10TH

1915.
January
7. Peak caps were issued, but were never as popular with the Battalion as the distinctive Australian felt hats. Nevertheless, large parties of men were to be seen wearing the newly-issued caps.

" 13. No. 23 Lance-Corporal Victor Charles McIntosh, of the 10th Battalion Machine Gun Section, died of meningitis at Mena.

" 26. Towards the end of the month the first part of the training scheme was practically completed, and the 10th Battalion welcomed the second phase—battalion drill. Route marches to Tiger's Tooth, where Napoleon's Army under General Kleber had left cannon-ball souvenirs, were the order of the day. The men generally wore full kit with heavy packs, weighing in all about 70 pounds. The Battalion would march out in the morning and cover six or eight miles across the desert. It was on one of these occasions that the 10th Battalion "Lost Platoon" episode occurred. Capt. R. B. Jacob, O.C. of "C" Coy., reprimanded the platoon of Lieut. J. Hamilton for talking too much whilst on the march. As a result the platoon commander was ordered to take his platoon into the sand-dune. Consequently Lieut. Hamilton marched his platoon into the sandhill near by and there halted and awaited further orders. In the meantime the men were beginning to feel the pinch of hunger, and "Sugar" Cairns approached Lieut. Hamilton and said, "Mr. Hamilton, when do we dine?" The platoon commander replied, "Gentlemen, to-day, you dine with me." After waiting for several hours and receiving no message from Company Headquarters, the defaulting platoon was marched back to Mena Camp. Capt. Jacob insisted that he had intended the platoon to detour around the sandhill as a punishment; whereas with pronounced Scotch accent Lieut. Hamilton maintained that he had carried out orders and marched his men into the sandhill as instructed. The technicalities of the "Lost Platoon" were discussed at some length in the Officers' Mess that night.

" 31. Capt. M. F. de F. Lorenzo, Adjutant of the Battalion, forwarded a letter to Mr. Gordon Green expressing the appreciation of the Battalion for the good work performed by Mr. Green and the Y.M.C.A.

1915.
February
1. 2nd Lieutenants of the Battalion were promoted to the rank of Lieutenant.

" 5. No. 321, Pte. Horace Utting Fordham, of original "A" Coy., died of smallpox at Mena.

" 8. 1st Reinforcements of Battalion under Lieut. A. H. Rowe joined the Battalion at Mena when the training was well advanced.

" 11. No. 601, Pte. Alfred Liersch, of original "G" Coy., died of pneumonia at Mena.

BATTALION CHRONOLOGY

1915.
February 13. Colonel Weir visited the Suez Canal in order to inspect the defences which had withstood the Turkish attack on February 3. Upon his return he reported that in many cases the Turks did not sufficiently bury their dead. He saw several graves with legs of men protruding out of the ground, and the British soldiers had to go round covering them over by rising heaps of sand. He saw two bodies dragged out of the Canal whilst he was there.

„ 14. Brigade training in full swing. 3rd Brigade under Col. E. G. Sinclair-MacLagan would engage in an occasional field-day. The 10th with the 9th, 11th, and 12th Battalions would often camp for a mid-day meal, post outposts, attack a theoretical position in the afternoon, spend the night in entrenching itself, and march back to camp next day. On one occasion the 3rd Brigade marched eight miles to the village of Beni Yusef, and there spent several days and nights in sham-fighting and entrenching, concluding with a night attack and final short rushes.

„ 24. Lieut.-Col. S. P. Weir contradicted certain statements which misrepresented the conditions at Mena Camp. In a letter he said, *inter alia*, "We have a magnificent supply of water laid on right throughout the whole camp. It is the clearest and best water I have ever seen or tasted, and there is an abundant supply which has never been restricted. . . . Our rations consist of an abundant supply of beautiful vegetables, bread, frozen meat from Australia, sugar, salt, tea, and cheese."

„ 28. The 3rd Australian Infantry Brigade having been selected by General Bridges as the landing or covering force for the projected Dardanelles operations, the 10th Battalion marched out of Mena Camp. The 1st and 2nd Brigades lined the camp roads and cheered lustily. Kasr-el-Nil Barracks were reached at eight that night, and the Battalion remained for the night on the barrack square.

„ 28. An unrehearsed incident occurred on the Giza Road whilst the 10th Battalion was marching to Kasr-el-Nil Barracks, Cairo. The Battalion halted outside the residence of Mr. Spathos, the influential Cairene Greek merchant, whereupon Mr. Spathos invited the Officers of the 10th into his villa to partake of refreshment. Mme. de Beneducci and the Misses Meimerachi acted as hostesses. Toasts were drunk and Lieut.-Col. S. P. Weir thanked Mr. Spathos for his friendly greetings towards the British Forces, and pointing to the Greek flag flying side by side with the British ensign expressed the hope that shortly the brave Hellenic troops would be fighting with them in the war for civilization and liberty. Mr. Spathos thanked his guests for the honour they did him in the unexpected visit, and after expressing his wishes for their success in the work before them, said he was convinced of the success of the British cause, which

1915.
February 28. would establish liberty, prosperity, and security for great as
(continued) well as small nations. Before continuing the march the Officers
and men of the 10th burst into cheering.

THE DARDANELLES
March 1 to December 29, 1915

1915.
March 1. Battalion entrained to Alexandria, and with 9th Battalion embarked on *Ionian*. Battalion Transport Section embarked on the *Nizam*.

,, 2. *Ionian* left Alexandria with 2,000 troops on board for a destination "unknown."

,, 4. At 7 p.m. the *Ionian* arrived at Mudros, Lemnos Island, which had been used as a British Base during the Crimean War of 1854-57.

,, 6. The 9th Battalion disembarked, but the 10th remained on board the *Ionian* for another seven weeks.

,, 12. General d'Amade, of the French Expeditionary Force, came aboard the *Ionian*. The 10th guard mounted at the top of the gangway had been on the look-out for him, but unfortunately in the first instance turned out for the wrong officer, who was not entitled to the great honour the guard unwittingly was prepared to confer upon him.

,, 12. Battalion went ashore at Lemnos for first time, and manoeuvres commenced in the rocky, hilly country of the Island, which was presumed to resemble that which the Battalion would subsequently encounter in actual warfare.

,, 16. Battalion again engaged in practising landings at Telikna Point. Heavy rain somewhat marred the day's operations, and one or two small boats went astray.

,, 23. Further training ashore. Men practised in communicating information in battle and carrying a full load, etc.

,, 29. The Battalion left the *Ionian* early in the morning for a three days' bivouac on Lemnos Island. Capt. G. D. Shaw was left on board as O.C. of details, and the men all wore caps. The village of Thermia was reached that night, and the Battalion there camped.

,, 30. Battalion bathed in renowned hot springs of Thermia, and marched to Castro, the capital of the Island, reaching this point at 10.30 a.m., and halted in front of the Hotel de Ville of the town, and drawn up in line presented arms to the Greek flag which was dipped during the ceremony. The Battalion band played the National Anthem and the Song of Australia, after which the 10th marched back to Thermia and encamped for the night.

BATTALION CHRONOLOGY 43

1915.
March
31. Battalion marched off from Thermia at 9.30 a.m. and reached Mudros at 2.30 p.m., having marched about 16 miles whilst on the island. Upon returning to the *Ionian* a large Australian mail was distributed.

1915.
April
2. Good Friday. Lieut.-Colonel S. P. Weir, writing from the *Ionian* said: "I don't know what our next move will be, and if I did, I would not mention it. We hope soon to get to real business, but all things come in good time to those who wait. I am proud of my officers and men. We are a very happy family, indeed, and I hope we will continue to be until the end. One thing we are most delighted about is that General Hamilton is to have charge of all the troops here. I think we have a pretty big and important piece of work to do, and I also think that it will cost us a lot of men. By Jove! my men are a good lot of fellows, and are just longing to get under fire, although they must know that many of them will fall in the first "scrap," but it is the sporting instinct that leads them on, and I am quite sure they will give a good account of themselves."

,, 4. Easter Monday. First official intimation received that the 3rd Australian Infantry Brigade was subsequently to re-embark for the Dardanelles and act as a covering force to a landing to be made somewhere on the Gallipoli Peninsula.

,, 10. The 2nd Reinforcements of the Battalion under Capt. H. W. H. Seager joined the Battalion on the *Ionian*, this being the last reinforcement quota to join the Battalion prior to the landing.

,, 13. Lieut.-Colonel S. P. Weir taken on board *Queen*, which during the afternoon sailed with the staff of the 1st Australian Division, the brigadiers and battalion commanders. They remained on board all that night, and next morning moved at 10 knots past the western coast of the Gallipoli Peninsula, where the landing was to made, at a distance of one-and-a-half miles from land. Gaba Tepe was particularly scrutinized through the field-glasses and various opinions were expressed as to the success or otherwise of the proposed operation.

,, 14. After Lieut.-Col. Weir returned from the *Queen* the landing became more generally anticipated and understood by all ranks of the 10th Battalion which anxiously awaited orders to proceed with the undertaking.

,, 15. Distinguishing colour patches for attaching to upper sleeves of tunics were issued to the Battalion. Saxe-blue and purple was the colour combination, the former representing the 3rd Brigade and the latter the 10th Battalion, corresponding with the unit colours which had beflagged the lines at Mena.

1915.
April

16. The Battalion was taken in boats to H.M.S. *Prince of Wales* for the purpose of acquiring practice in disembarking and landing. This procedure was repeated several times, the men eventually becoming expert in rope-climbing and descent.

18. Operation Order No. 1 in connection with the Gallipoli campaign issued by the Australian and New Zealand Army Corps.

19. 1st Australian Division Orders issued, and a stir was created when orders arrived from G.H.Q. to cease practising the troops at disembarkation.

20. Orders issued that first movement of troops was to commence on the next day, and the landing to take place on April 23. But that day such a wind sprang up, that despite the blue sky none of the smaller craft could work in Mudros Harbour. At 5 p.m. that day it was decided to postpone the move for another 24 hours.

21. The gale blew fiercely throughout the day, and that evening it was again decided to postpone the move.

22. The wind moderated towards nightfall, and the cross-movements of troops between various transports commenced.

24. Shortly after mid-day destroyers came alongside the *Ionian* and transferred "B" and "C" Coys. to the *Prince of Wales*. During the afternoon the *Prince of Wales, London, Queen,* and *Bacchante,* followed by six destroyers and the four 3rd Brigade transports, sailed out of Mudros Harbour and headed for Imbros Island. At 11 p.m. that night "A" and "D" Coys. of the Battalion transferred from the *Ionian* to the destroyers *Scourge* and *Foxhound*.

25. At 1 a.m. the battleships and destroyers stopped on the sea between Imbros and the Peninsula, when the troops were transferred to the small rowing-boats which were brought alongside of each. The small boats were made up into tows of three each. At 2.35 the rowing-boats were full and dropped back in long strings behind the battleships. At 3.30 the battleships stopped and the order was given for the tows to go ahead and land. At 4 a.m. came the first faint signs of dawn, and at 4.30 a.m. the naval steam-boats cast off the tows, when the rowing-boats paddled the last few yards to the shore. The strength of the Battalion on landing was 29 Officers and 921 other ranks. By 6 a.m. the first position was taken by the 3rd Brigade, although the Brigade was considerably mixed. At 7 a.m. the Brigade was reorganized to push on. At 8.10 a.m. a Turkish counter-attack was repulsed, and at 2 p.m. there was heavy fighting, but the Brigade was holding on to its position supported by the Indian Mountain Battery. At 4 p.m. the enemy fire died down under ship's fire and spotting by aeroplane. At 6 p.m. all were ordered to entrench and dig in for night. All night counter-attacks and sniping by enemy followed.

BATTALION CHRONOLOGY

1915.
April

25. *Re* landing at Anzac, Lieut.-Col. S. P. Weir wrote under date of May 15, 1915: "I was in one of the first, if not the first boat to reach the shore on the never-to-be-forgotten morning of April 25. We were about 50 yards from the beach when the Turks fired the first shot. We shot out into the water about four feet deep and made for the shore, and at once fixed bayonets and drove the Turks off the hill from which they were showering us with bullets. How so many of us escaped with our lives I do not know. We had desperate fighting all day long, the shrapnel-shell being very deadly, but our men were game, and dug in for all they were worth with their entrenching tools; of course many were killed during this process, and hundreds were wounded, but we had orders to hold the position gained at all costs, and we did it. We were glad when darkness came at 8 p.m., for we had been fighting hard from 4 a.m. The shrapnel ceased then, but the rifles peppered away all through the night. We dug hard all night; none of us had a greatcoat or waterproof sheet. The night was cold and rain fell, but we never moved from the positions taken up on the Sunday afternoon until Wednesday night, and were under fire night and day during the whole of the time. We kept the firing line supplied with water, rations, and ammunition, etc.; then we had two days' spell on the beach and returned to the trenches."

28. After four days of continuous fighting the 10th Battalion was relieved during the night by the Royal Marine Light Infantry. The men of the 10th were utterly exhausted, and required proper food and rest.

29. In the early hours of the morning the Battalion bivouacked at Shell Green, 13 Officers and 380 other ranks answering roll. Details were still coming in, and the Battalion was rested as much as possible.

30. 10th Battalion casualties included 13 Officers and 453 other ranks.

1915.
May

1. 10th Battalion proceeded from Shell Green and relieved the 9th Battalion on the extreme right flank.

3. A few periscopes were available, but sandbags were urgently required.

4. Capt. C. Rumball led a wire-cutting party of 12 men in an endeavour to co-operate with Capt. R. L. Leane's raid on Gaba Tepe.

5. 10th Battalion relieved the 11th Battalion on the left flank.

7. 3rd Reinforcements arrived under Lieut. W. G. Cornish, and joined the Battalion in the line.

16. Water-fatigues up Shrapnel Gully were commonplace events in the life at Anzac, and water was becoming scarce.

1915.
May

18. For first time since the landing, the Turkish rifle fire subsided, until for minutes together there was hardly a shot. At 5 p.m. that day the Turks opened from all sides the heaviest bombardment yet experienced at Anzac.

,, 19. Severe Turkish attack. Colonel Weir reported: "After several quiet days, on the evening of 18th May, I received a message from the Brigadier to the effect that a Division of the enemy's troops had landed on Square 228M. I at once issued orders for everyone to be particularly watchful during the night and to Stand to Arms at 3 a.m., instead of 3.30 a.m., and it is fortunate that I did, for just at 3 a.m. the enemy attacked in great force and came up in two solid lines, right along our front, only to be mown down by our rifle and machine-gun fire. Three turks actually tried to get over our trenches, but were killed on the parapet. Considering the numbers who attacked us, our losses were very light, our casualties only amounting to 10 killed and 20 wounded. This attack lasted until about 6 AIV."

,, 19. Lieut.-Colonel S. P. Weir, in a letter from Anzac dated May 20, 1915, said: "We had a dreadful battle again yesterday. Had just finished reading my mail Tuesday night when I received word from Headquarters that a Division of Turks were reinforcing the troops against us, so I got busy. Went right along our trenches and firing line and warned every one to be extra vigilant through the night, and ordered all to Stand to Arms at 3 a.m. At half-past three the Turks came along in hordes. They showered our trenches with bullets, and their big guns played havoc with some of the trenches. Then they rushed to within twenty or thirty yards of our position, but our lads mowed them down like grass. Three Turks got to the top, but bayonets and bullets prevented their getting over. It was a gruesome sight to see the dead bodies of the Turks and to see our poor lads being carried to the rear with awful wounds. It was a most anxious time for us all, but against tremendous odds we held our own. Our lads were as cool as if they were shooting ducks, but the game on this occasion were Turks, and they were giants, too—make excellent targets. One poor chap died on his knees not thirty yards from our trenches, and is still in the same position. Capt. Nott would not believe it possible until he went up this morning and saw for himself. Unfortunately we had 11 killed and 23 wounded. The battle lasted from 3.30 a.m. to 10 o'clock, and the noise of the guns and the shrieking and exploding shell was deafening. My dugout was used for our wounded men, as also were those of the M.O. and Q.M. The Turks lost very heavily, but I cannot give an estimate of their casualties. We can see hundreds of dead bodies from our trenches, and in a couple of days we shall

BATTALION CHRONOLOGY

1915.
May (continued)

19. smell them, too. We don't want too many days like yesterday. This morning is all very quiet."

,, 22. Submarine scare at Anzac Cove. The battleships *London* and *Triumph* and the cruiser *Bacchante* were observed by men of the 10th Battalion to suddenly move off in a zig-zag course and escort towards Imbros the remaining four or five transports. After escorting the transports to safety, the battleships returned.

,, 23. German planes occasionally passed over and dropped bombs.

,, 24. After certain negotiations on the suspension of arms had been completed an armistice was observed from 7.30 a.m. to 4.30 p.m., when it was estimated that 3,000 Turkish dead were removed or buried. The burial of the dead was completed by about 3 p.m., and the terms of the temporary cessation of hostilities were correctly observed by both sides.

,, 25. H.M.S. *Triumph* was sunk off Gaba Tepe in broad daylight by an enemy submarine. This unfortunate incident was witnessed from the neighbouring crests and ridges by many men of the 10th Battalion. Under date of June 1, 1915, Lieut.-Col. S. P. Weir wrote: "Just after we sat down to dinner on May 25 we heard a report and saw smoke issuing from the battleship *Triumph*, and at once concluded that something was wrong, for the *Triumph* had a decided list. We noticed destroyers, launches, etc., steaming for all they were worth in the direction of the battleship. Then by the aid of my powerful field-glasses I saw hundreds of men on the deck of the *Triumph*, and soon saw that they were being transferred to our torpedo-destroyers. During the fifteen minutes in which I never took my glasses off the *Triumph* I saw her gradually list and list until at 12.15 she turned right upside down and remained in that position with her keel uppermost until 12.50, when she disappeared altogether. I don't think they lost many men, because there were two destroyers alongside her before she turned over, and a score of smaller craft to pick up any man who might be in the water. When the *Triumph* turned turtle she looked for all the world like a huge red whale. It is an awful calamity, indeed, for so magnificent a boat to be sent to the bottom in less than an hour. It must have been the work of a submarine, and all our destroyers are now going at full speed in all directions trying to locate the culprit."

,, 26. A few cases of dysentery reported, although there appeared to be some doubt as if some of the cases under observation had been correctly diagnosed.

,, 27. The *Majestic* was sunk off Cape Helles by a submarine, and in consequence all large warships were withdrawn from their allotted stations. In consequence of this sudden arrangement, the night of May 27 was the only night during the whole of

THE FIGHTING 10TH

May (continued)

27. the Gallipoli campaign that the flanks at Anzac were not protected by a boat of the British Navy.
" 28. A few periscopic rifles and trench mortars were issued to the 10th Battalion.
" 30. The 4th Reinforcements under Lieut. W. S. de Courcy Ireland arrived and joined the Battalion in the line.
" 31. Battalion still occupied same position. Lieut.-Colonel S. P. Weir reported: "Since the attack on May 19 the enemy has been very quiet—hasn't made any fresh attacks. They continue to shell us every day, but with very little effect. We are still occupying the Third Section of Defence in the trenches, the 9th Bn. holding No. 1 Section, their right resting on beach; then the 12th next ours, with the 11th Bn. on our left."

1915.
June 4. Demonstration at night by 10th Battalion in conjunction with other A.I.F. units in the line at Anzac, designed to prevent the Turks from dispatching any forces next day to Cape Helles.
" 5. The 5th Reinforcements under 2nd Lieut. F. Hancock arrived and joined the Battalion in the line.
" 9. At a conference of battalion commanders it was decided to adopt a scheme whereby a "new" firing line should be constructed in the Right Central Sector.
" 13. Bread issued for the first time at Anzac. It was made by the Field Bakery at Imbros, and lightered across. The bags in which it was placed were often splashed by the choppy seas which prevailed, but despite its dampness it was more than acceptable after the hardness of the "Anzac Wafer."
" 14. The summer heat was becoming oppressive, and flies existed in countless millions.
" 15 & 18. Anzac Beach was violently shelled, and the 23 days' reserve of rations seemed liable to destruction. After this Turkish outburst the 3rd Brigade became more cautious when indulging in a bathe at Anzac Cove.
" 19. The Light Horse were allotted the Right Sector Left, and the 3rd Brigade was allotted the Right Sector North.
" 20. Operations in connection with the new tunnelling scheme as decided upon on June 9 were commenced. Lieut. J. Hamilton, of the 10th Battalion, was placed in charge of a party of experienced miners selected from the 3rd Brigade, and Sergt. W. R. Montgomery was posted to this mining company as senior N.C.O. The average progress by the 3rd Brigade was about 15 or 20 feet per day, depending on the nature of the ground through which the tunnel or sap had to be made. The men worked in four shifts, one man digging, another shovelling, and six carrying the soil to a dump about 50 or 60 yards distant.

BATTALION CHRONOLOGY 49

1915.
June 20. Silt Spur and Tasmania Post were the two schemes concentrated
(continued) upon, and eventually Lieut. Hamilton was able to procure a few wheelbarrows from one of the destroyers. Upon their arrival the men of the mining company were keen to discover the bounder who had been responsible for their appearance.

„ 21. Canteen stores arrived at Anzac, having been purchased on the *Seeang Bee*, and were made available for purchase by the troops. The rush to procure pickles, sauce, tinned fruit, biscuits, tinned milk, chocolate and cigarettes was so great than not many of the 10th Battalion were fortunate enough to procure their requirements before the exhibiting of the "Sold out" notice.

„ 23. The first of a series of orders were issued for extensive additional works to accommodate additional reinforcements and to excavate further terraces sufficient for nearly a division of infantry. These were put in hand to accommodate the 2nd Australian Division. The 10th Battalion supplied digging parties for the "Artillery Road" then in course of construction, and "task-work" was introduced, a fixed amount of work having to be accomplished before each party could be relieved.

„ 28. Another evening demonstration in order to relieve pressure at Cape Helles. This was the second demonstration of this kind.

„ 30. Both sides were busy digging, and evacuations with dysentery were increasing at an alarming rate. The "Peninsula Press" published by G.H.Q. was regularly exhibited on the notice board at "The Cove," and every 10th Battalion man upon returning from the beach was always expected to give a complete *resumé* of the latest issue of the celebrated Anzac publication.

1915.
July 1. At 9 a.m. the 10th Battalion was relieved by the 9th Battalion. The 10th then rested in the rear of the trenches, and were subjected to greater dangers from shell-fire than whilst actually in the trenches. At this stage the water question was very serious, only one pint and a half being issued daily to each man.

„ 8. At 3.30 a.m. 18 Officers and 500 other ranks of the 10th Battion proceeded to Kephalos on Imbros Island for three days' rest. Major G. D. Shaw remained at Anzac with the 5th Reinforcements and various details.

„ 11. At 11 p.m. the Battalion returned to Anzac and went into dugouts at the rear of the line, as vacated by them three days previously. Capt. H. C. Nott stated that the short rest had been a "perfect holiday picnic."

„ 13. Battalion went into line and relieved the 11th Battalion.

„ 19. The 10th completed the works at Silt Spur, and at dawn that day the open bays or "recesses" fringed the whole forward slope of the ridge.

„ 21 & 22. Anzac Beach shelled continuously, this being taken as a sign of an impending Turkish attack.

1915.
July 23. The anticipated attack did not eventuate.
" 24. Dysentery was becoming acute, and cases of extreme collapse were occurring.
" 25. The men of the 10th had by this time become proficient in the use of sandbags, and both sides were still digging day and night.
" 26. Steel loopholes with a movable door had been issued, and were affixed to various vital parts of the front line parapet.
" 27. The cemeteries in the gullies and the main Anzac Cemetery on the beach were assuming large dimensions. Neat wooden crosses and stone edgings had been placed in position by comrades of deceased 10th Battalion Officers and men.
" 30. About this time a few barrels of wine were washed ashore from the sunken *Triumph* off Gaba Tepe. They were eagerly seized by the troops, including a few men of the 10th Battalion who happened to be on the beach at the time, and were amongst those who swam out to expedite the passage of the barrels to shore. The wine was unmistakably saltish and none too palatable, but the men of Anzac drank it with great zest. That night Lieut. Stopp and other 10th Battalion platoon commanders, whilst doing the rounds in the front line, were frequently informed by those who had partaken of the wine dislodged from the holds of the *Triumph* that the Turks were massing in large numbers in the gully.
" 31. Battalion received supplies of jam-tin bombs made at the beach factory, and anti-gas respirators of an early type were issued, and also a number of "helmets" or cloth hoods saturated with anti-gas solution.

1915.
August 4. The 6th Reinforcements under Lieut. C. W. Hooper arrived at Anzac and joined the Battalion in the line.
" 6. Battle of Lone Pine. The 10th Battalion assisted in the defence of this impotant point by placing a machine gun in B7 Tunnel, this gun traversing the area between Sniper's Ridge North and Weir Ridge North, and was allotted "Comb" work in defending the communications between the Pimple and Lone Pine from the south. Those not on duty in the front line stood by with white armbands, full equipment and iron rations ready to reinforce, if necessary, the 1st Brigade which captured the position about 5.30 in the afternoon.
" 7. Suvla Bay landing by British troops and attack on Chunuk Bair in the second and final great attempt to open the Narrows to the Fleet. The attempt failed, though ground was won and lost.
" 8. 10th Battalion from Silt Spur and 11th Battalion from Leane's Trench assisted 1st Infantry Brigade throughout the day in the holding of Lone Pine. Lines were heavily shelled at intervals and also 8·2 shells fell into rear of lines. Saps progressed.

BATTALION CHRONOLOGY

1915.
August 15. The men of the Battalion were sick and run down. At least 45 per cent. had evacuated with diarrhoea.

„ 25. Lieut.-Col. S. P. Weir appointed Acting Brigadier of 3rd Infantry Brigade. Major G. D. Shaw, with rank of temporary Lieut.-Colonel, assumed command of 10th.

1915.
September 2. Great consternation caused in 10th Battalion and all other A.I.F. units when it became known that the *Southland* conveying Australian troops to the Dardanelles had been torpedoed at 9.45 a.m. that day, with a total loss of 32 lives.

„ 3. The health of the men of the 10th was bad, and in consequence the M.O. sent a report to Lieut.-Col. S. P. Weir for transmission to the A.D.M.S. recommending that the men needed rest and change of food.

„ 8. 2nd Australian Division arrived at Anzac, portion taking up positions in line from Wire Gully to Walker's Ridge, and those in reserves and supports occupying the dugouts which the 10th had helped to construct.

„ 11. Lieut.-Colonel S. P. Weir evacuated ill and proceeded to Malta and subsequently to England.

„ 15. 10th Battalion casualties at this date totalled 711, consisting of 150 killed (11 officers and 139 other ranks), 538 wounded (8 officers and 530 other ranks), and 23 missing (all other ranks). Total casualties 711, less rejoined Battalion 210, leaving 501.

„ 16. Ten men per day evacuating with dysentery, and even the M.O. of the Battalion had been forced to evacuate.

„ 17. The 7th Reinforcements under 2nd Lieut. R. G. Wilton joined the Battalion in the line. This was the last quota of reinforcements to join the Battalion on the Peninsula.

„ 18. 3rd Brigade became Divisional troops.

„ 24. Another night demonstration. From 1900 to 2000 the Battalion made every pretence of an intended attack. Dummy figures were shown at Silt Spur, and the Battalion made a show of bayonets. Burnt tins were thrown well out along the whole firing line, and especially from most forward bomb pits. At 2000 a single red rocket was fired from the centre of the 11th Battalion, and from 2000 to 2010 the artillery opened fire, during which period the Battalion maintained complete silence. At 2010 bursts of machine-gun and rifle fire alternated till the enemy fire died away. Watches were set at 1800.

„ 30. Strength of Battalion, 21 officers and 575 other ranks.

1915.
October 1. 3rd Brigade still acting as Divisional troops.

„ 8. First serious storm at Anzac. Interfered with pumping plant at beach, with result that next day the 10th Battalion was

1915.
October 8. placed on short rations of water. In view of the anticipated
(continued) severity of the approaching winter, battalion commanders were
advised to press on with winter preparations.

,, 13. General H. B. Walker, Commanding Officer of the 1st Australian Division, was wounded.

,, 16. General Sir Ian Hamilton was recalled by His Majesty's Government in order that a fresh unbiassed opinion from a responsible commander upon the question of early evacuation could be obtained.

,, 17. General Sir Ian Hamilton left Imbros for England, General Sir William Birdwood becoming temporary Commander-in-Chief of the Mediterranean Expeditionary Force.

,, 17. Sea at Anzac very rough, and the pumping of water from the barge had to cease. Six lighters and a paddle-boat were driven on the beach.

,, 20. Major M. F. Beevor and Capt. R. B. Jacob returned to Anzac from hospital in England.

,, 21. Major M. F. Beevor with temporary rank of lieut.-colonel assumed command of the 10th Battalion. Aeroplane over Anzac.

,, 22. About this time 12th Battalion relieved 10th in the line, and Major G. D. Shaw was temporarily transferred to 9th as C.O.

,, 25. 2nd Lieut. J. C. Smith, who had accompanied the 8th Reinforcements of the 10th to Lemnos, was permitted to join the Battalion in the line at Anzac. He left the quota of reinforcements at Lemnos, and was the last officer to join the Battalion on the Peninsula.

,, 27. General Sir Charles Monro arrived and assumed command of Mediterranean Expeditionary Force.

,, 30. General Sir Charles Monro visited Anzac and Suvla.

,, 31. General Sir Charles Monro telegraphed to Lord Kitchener recommending the evacuation of the Gallipoli Peninsula. His recommendation concluded as follows: "On purely military grounds, therefore, I recommend the evacuation of the Peninsula."

1915.
November 3. 9th Battalion relieved by 1st Brigade.
General Sir Charles Monro transferred to the command of the Salonika Force, and General Sir William Birdwood appointed Commander-in-Chief of Mediterranean Expeditionary Force.

,, 4. Lord Kitchener instructed Birdwood as Commander-in-Chief of the M.E.F. to prepare a plan for evacuating the troops.

,, 12. Turks busily engaged digging at Gaba Tepe.

BATTALION CHRONOLOGY

1915.
November 13. Lord Kitchener inspects positions at Anzac, and in addressing the men, said: "The King asked me to tell you how splendidly you have done—you have done better than ever I thought you would."

" 14. 10th and 12th Battalions in the line with the 9th and 11th in Reserve. 3rd Brigade advance parties left Anzac Cove for Lemnos.

" 15. The effective strength of the 10th Battalion was 25 Officers and 540 other ranks. A half-gale was blowing from the south-east, and water could not be pumped until the next day. Owing to the rough weather the 9th and 11th Battalions could not embark for Lemnos.

" 16. At 2100 the 9th and 11th Battalions embarked for Lemnos.

" 17. 10th and 12th Battalions in Reserve at Anzac.

" 19. "Beachy Bill" had continuously shelled Anzac Beach for 96 hours.

" 21. 10th Battalion left supports at 7.45 p.m. and proceeded to Anzac Cove, and by 3.15 next morning were all taken on lighters and transferred to the *Princess Ena*.

" 22. The *Princess Ena* with the 10th Battalion on board steamed out of Anzac Cove at 6 a.m. and arrived at Mudros, Lemnos Island, at 12.15 p.m. The day was bitterly cold as a result of the blizzard which had raged, causing many deaths amongst troops and putting hundreds on the sick list.

" 23. At 12 noon the Battalion disembarked from the *Princess Ena* and marched to camp, where they were joined by the 8th Reinforcements of the Battalion. These reinforcements had been delayed at Lemnos pending the withdrawal of the 3rd Brigade from Gallipoli.

1915.
December 1. 10th Battalion still in camp at Lemnos.

" 19. The general evacuation of Anzac was completed by 4.10 the next morning. The departing troops were not molested, and only two casualties were incurred.

" 25. The original men of the Battalion experienced their second Christmas dinner away from sunny South Australia.

" 26. At 9 a.m. the 10th Battalion embarked on the transport *Seeang Bee*.

" 27. At 4 a.m. the *Seeang Bee* left Mudros for Alexandria, Egypt.

" 29. At 10.30 a.m. the *Seeang Bee* arrived at Alexandria, and the 10th Battalion disembarked.

EGYPT—TEL-EL-KEBIR, SERAPEUM, GEBEL HABIETA
December 29, 1915, to March 28, 1916

1915.
December 29. At 11.45 a.m. the 10th Battalion at Alexandria entrained for Tel-el-Kebir.
        30. The Battalion arrived at Tel-el-Kebir at 6.30 a.m.

1916.
January 1. The Battalion was encamped at Tel-el-Kebir, where it remained for several weeks chiefly resting, training, and reorganizing.

      " 2. About this time Brigadier-General E. G. Sinclair-MacLagan resumed command of the 3rd Brigade.

      " 15. 10th Battalion reviewed by Sir Archibald Murray, General Officer Commanding British Troops in Egypt.

      " 25. 10th Battalion entrained for Serapeum at 8.30 a.m., arriving at destination at 3.50 p.m.

      " 28. At 11.30 a.m. two companies of the 10th left Serapeum and arrived at Gebel Habieta at 3.45 p.m.

      " 30. Strength of Battalion 27 Officers and 950 other ranks.

1916.
February 1. Headquarters and two remaining companies of 10th proceeded to Gebel Habieta and became engaged in an outpost system in connection with the Suez Canal Defences.

      " 9. 10th Battalion invented sledge box for removing sand.

      " 10. Water scarce, and Quartermaster experiences trying time in attempting to overcome difficulties.

      " 11. General Sir William Birdwood visited the 3rd Brigade.

      " 26. Five hundred of all ranks transferred to 50th Battalion with Lieut.-Col. F. W. Hurcombe in command. Major F. M. de F. Lorenzo was transferred to 49th Battalion as C.O., and Lieut. A. H. Rowe was transferred to 51st Battalion as adjutant. At 10 a.m. that day the left wing of the 10th Battalion was drawn up prior to its transfer to the sister battalion. Colonel MacLagan was present and addressed the parade. He emphasized the importance of the new arrangement which would permit of the newly-formed 4th Division being infused with men who had had fighting experience on Gallipoli. He regretted the breaking-up of his old battalions which for eighteen months had stood shoulder to shoulder. Nevertheless, he realized that the new scheme would work in the best interests of the 4th Australian Division and the A.I.F. in general. Lieut.-Colonel M. F. Beevor then reminded the men that they were taking with them the traditions of the old 10th Battalion.

      " 28. Six officers and 461 other ranks, consisting of reinforcements of the 27th Battalion marched into camp at Gebel Habieta and joined the 10th Battalion.

BATTALION CHRONOLOGY

1916.
March   4. Lieut.-Colonel S. P. Weir returned from hospital in England and assumed command of the 10th, Lieut.-Colonel M. F. Beevor being transferred to the 52nd Battalion as C.O.

,,   5. Battalion, making every preparation for an early departure for France.

,,   9. 10th Battalion left Gebel Habieta and proceeded to Serapeum staging camp.

,,   13. General Birdwood visited the 3rd Brigade lines.

,,   19. 3rd Brigade church parade followed by a march past the G.O.C. 1st Anzac Corps and H.R.H. the Prince of Wales. This was the first occasion that the men of the 10th Battalion had been reviewed by a member of the Royal Family.

,,   25. 10th Battalion Transport Section entrained for Alexandria, and embarked on *Maryland* for France.

,, 26 & 27. Main body of Battalion entrained for Alexandria, and embarked on *Saxonia* with 9th Battalion and 3rd Brigade Headquarters.

,,   28. *Saxonia* left Alexandria for Marseilles.

,,   30. *Saxonia* off Malta.

FRANCE AND BELGIUM
April 2, 1916, to March 17, 1919

1916.
April   2. *Saxonia* arrived at Marseilles, France. Battalion disembarked and entrained for Godewaersvelde. First train conveyed 3rd Brigade Headquarters and 9th Battalion, and second train the 10th Battalion.

,, 3, 4 & 5. Battalion on troop-train travelling through Orange, Montereau, Epluges, Abbeville, and Hazebrouck, arriving and detraining at Godewaersvelde. Proceeded into billets at Moolenacker, near Strazeele.

,,   6. Training commenced, interspersed with gas-helmet practice.

,,   7. 10th Battalion Transport Section arrives.

,,   20. 10th, 11th, and 12th Battalions march to Sailly and occupy billets, becoming Divisional Reserve.

,,   25. Anzac Day. Battalion inspected by Generals Plumer, Walker, and MacLagan.

,,   27. Battalion inspected by Field-Marshal Sir Douglas Haig.

1916.
May   1. Training continues.

,,   12. General Birdwood visits 3rd Brigade.

,,   18. 10th and 12th Battalions relieve the 1st and 2nd Battalions in Reserve billets in the Petillon Sector.

1916.
May 19. Billets occupied by Battalion shelled, two officers and one other rank killed, and seven other ranks wounded.
„ 30. Lieut.-Colonel S. P. Weir reported: "At about 2030 enemy commenced a heavy bombardment, our artillery responding most vigorously, replying by 2100. The noise was terrific, and we were ordered by Brigade Hd. Qrs. to Stand To—at 9.45 (2145). We did—"C" Coy. proceeded to "G" Assembly trenches, "A" and "D" Coys. H.Q. and Lewis M.G. Bombers and Intelligence proceeded to and occupied "J" Assembly trenches, whilst "B" Coy. manned Charged and Windy Post, being in position by 2245. At 2315 I received message from Bde. to resume normal conditions, leaving one Coy. (I detailed "D" Coy.) as Inlying Picquet. Having advised O.C. 9th Battalion that "D" Coy. was occupying "J" trenches, I ordered return of Battalion to billets, and shortly after 0100 we were settled down again. It was a very dark night and cold, and the roads were very sloppy. The enemy's shell fire broke our 'phone line to Bde. Hd. Qrs., and we consequently had to keep in touch by messengers. A raid by Germans was made that night on 11th Battalion."

1916.
June 6. 10th Battalion went into line for first time in France. Lieut.-Colonel Weir reported as follows: "On the night of Tuesday, 6th June, 1916, the 10th Battalion moved from billets—Rouge de Bout—to right sector of firing line Petillon Sector, from Bond St. to near Mine Avenue, in accordance with operation order attached marked A. We suffered only one casualty, viz., Pte. 2958 Searle, of "D" Coy., who was wounded in the neck by indirect M.G. fire whilst coming along Impertinence Avenue. Shortly after midnight our artillery shelled the Germans, otherwise with exception of occasional bursts of M.G. fire the night was quiet." (Fleurbaix.)
„ 16. Gas alarm; no gas.
„ 28-29. Relieved by 51st Battalion, A.I.F., and proceeded to billets situated west of Sailly.

1916.
July 1. 10th Battalion marched from Sailly to Moolenacker, and commenced training raiding party and organizing until about 22nd of month.
„ 9. Marched to Mt. Des Catts and billeted for night.
„ 10-11. Marched to Godewaersvelde and entrained for Doullens.
„ 11. Marched to Halloy.
„ 12. Marched from Halloy to Naours.
„ 16. Marched to Herissart.
„ 18. Marched from Herissart to Forceville.
„ 19. Marched from Forceville to Albert and billeted.
„ 20. Marched from Albert to Sausage Valley, and bivouacked in old British trenches until 2200 on Saturday, 22nd July.

BATTALION CHRONOLOGY

1916.
July 22. Proceeded *via* Black Watch Alley to attack Pozieres.

„ 23. Pozieres. Lieut.-Colonel S. P. Weir reported: "The 9th Battalion having met with strong opposition at X.5.B.21, asked for assistance, and "A" Coy., 10th Battalion, under Capt. McCann, was detailed. This Coy. immediately proceeded to the attack, Capt. McCann working up the centre of the enemy's trench with one platoon, having a platoon on both his flanks as supports. His advance was held up by heavy M.G. fire and bombs, which necessitated the building of a barrier. Capt. McCann, who was wounded, reported the matter to the C.O. 9th Battalion, who thereon asked me for further support. "D" Coy., under Major Giles, was then detailed for this duty. This happened at about 0530 on 23rd July. Lieut. Blackburn with 50 men from "D" Coy. was detailed by Major Giles to report to C.O. 9th Battalion, and on doing so Lieut. Blackburn received order to move up the trench to X.5.d.3½.B. and drive the enemy out. On arrival he found that "A" Coy., 10th Battalion, was suffering heavy casualties from bombs and machine guns. He at once rushed the barricade, breaking it down and bombing the enemy back. The Artillery bombardment had almost obliterated the trench and reduced it to a scene of shell craters which made our advance more difficult, because advancing troops were exposed to the enemy's heavy M.G. fire. The enemy very stubbornly held his position and stopped for a time our advance. Lieut. Blackburn, accompanied by four men, crawled forward to ascertain if possible where the M.G. fire was coming from. The four men who accompanied him were killed, and he had to return to his platoon. He then reported the position to C.O. 9th Battalion, who arranged with the T.M. Battery to bombard the enemy's position at X.5.b.2.½. Under cover of this fire Lt. Blackburn again endeavoured to push forward, but the M.G. fire again prevented him from doing so, another four men being killed in the attempt. He again reported to C.O. 9th Battalion, who then arranged for the Artillery to bombard; under this he managed to push forward some 30 yards when he was again held up by the enemy's bombers. His bomber then engaged the enemy, and under this cover Lieut. Blackburn and Sgt. Inwood crawled forward to reconnoitre the position. They ascertained that the enemy held a trench which cut the one which they were attacking at right angles. Lieut. Blackburn therefore decided to clear this trench, and he succeeded in doing so. The trench was about 120 yards long, and was blind—it ran at right angles to the main trench to the left at X.5.b.1.½. to X.5.b.0.1. The trench was consolidated, and after considerable trouble, communication with the 9th Battalion troops on the left was established. During the work of consolidating, Sgt. Inwood—who had done splendidly—and 3 men were killed. Having taken this trench,

1916.
July 23. another attempt was made to take the strong post at X.5.b.2.1.,
(continued) but the enemy M.G. fire was still strong, and claimed 5 more of his own men; he therefore decided to hold and consolidate the trench gained. Lieut. Blackburn held the trenches gained until 1400, when he was relieved by Lt. Partridge, who held the position until 1800, during which time he had 26 casualties out of the 35 that he took over the positions with."

„ 24. Pozieres. Lieut.-Colonel S. P. Weir reported: "At 0330, "C" Coy. (Commander, Major G. D. Shaw), which Coy. was detailed to support the 9th Battalion, was ordered by the C.O. of that Battalion to reinforce me in O.G.2, and assist in making an effort to take Strong Post X.5.b.4$\frac{1}{2}$.$\frac{1}{2}$. Major Shaw experienced the greatest difficulty getting up trench on account of the number of dead and wounded who were lying about, and being brought down to the Aid Post, but eventually he succeeded in reaching head of the trench held by the 9th Battalion at 0630. It was then being held by 1 officer and 45 other ranks of 9th Battalion and a Lewis gun. As it was then broad daylight it was considered unwise to attack, and as there were sufficient men of the 9th Battalion to hold it, Major Shaw withdrew his men to the support trench near 9th Battalion H.Q. At 1300 on 24th July, No. 11 Platoon, under Lieut. Inglis, was detailed to relieve a Platoon of "D" Coy. in the north of O.G.1, and Platoons 9 and 12 were detailed to assist "A" Coy. of the 10th Battalion in consolidating O.G.1 trench from barricade to 9th Battalion H.Q. At 6.30 (1830) on 24th July, acting under orders from General MacLagan, I ordered Major Shaw with "C" and "B" Coys. and the remnant of "A" Coy. to construct a trench from X.5.d.7.8. to X.5.9.2.9., and to hold same in anticipation of attack to be made by the Second Infantry Brigade at 0200 on the 25th inst. Major Shaw was also instructed to make strong post at X.5.b.2.$\frac{1}{2}$.—this being the post which Lieut. Blackburn had on the previous day made such a gallant attempt to capture. At 2200 on 24th July, "C" and "B" Coys.' men crawled out, each man carrying in addition to his arms and ammunition a pick or shovel, and by midnight they had dug a trench 200 yards long by 3 feet deep, and by 0145 on 25th this trench had been deepened to 6 feet, with sandbag parapets and a fire-step."

„ 25. Pozieres. Lieut.-Colonel S. P. Weir reported: "A party of 36 bombers and 20 bayonet men, under Lieut. Hillier and Lieut. Melville, were detailed for the assault on the strong post. Arrangements were made for the Stokes gun to fire 5 rounds per $\frac{1}{2}$ hour into the post, and as many as possible during the barrage. (0158 to 0200)—140 rounds were fired during these 2 minutes. At 0100 "B" Coy., less 20 men, was by order of the Brigadier withdrawn, and became Brigade Reserve. Immediately the barrage lifted, the raiding party under Lieut. Melville rushed

BATTALION CHRONOLOGY

1916.
July 25. forward and took the strong post in magnificent style. The
(continued) party was strongly counter-attacked, and sent to Major Shaw
for help. He detailed 11 and 12 Platoons to assist, and they
acted as bomb carriers, etc. The fighting then became most
desperate, but eventually the enemy was repulsed, and in addition to the strong post, about 120 yards of trench north of it
taken, held, and consolidated. Subsequently the 120 yards of
trench taken was handed over to the 5th Battalion, "C" and
"A" Coys. holding the Strong Post, in addition to the 200 yards
of trench which they had dug during the night. They continued to hold these positions until at 2200 on the 25th July
they were taken over by the 17th Battalion, who relieved the
10th Battalion. On Tuesday, 25th July, at 0900, I observed
a number of Germans advancing over ridge X.5.a.4.9. These
men were dressed in a dark-coloured uniform, and wore big
packs. I at once got 5 Lewis M.G. and about 50 rifles on to
them at 900 yards, and I saw at least 50 men fall. They retreated over the ridge in a N.E. direction, where they were
met by our shell fire which caused them to again return to ridge,
where our gun fire drove them back, killing a large number.
Those of them that were left retired in great disorder. At
2200 on 25th July the 10th Battalion was relieved by the 5th
Battalion. During these operations, 22-25th July, our artillery
fire was very effective and constant. The enemy's shelling was
very heavy, but on account of lack of observation, rather inaccurate. All ranks in my Battalion worked very hard, and
many gallant actions on the part of individual officers and men
have been brought under the notice of the Brigadier-General.
The bombers had a particularly busy time, and worked splendidly. The messengers or runners did excellent work, and
although the shelling was so constant and deadly, they never
hesitated to deliver a message, and not one message miscarried.
Our own fatigues kept us well supplied with ammunition,
bombs (about 5,000 were used), water, food, and sandbags.
There was a shortage of sandbags, and an inadequate number of
stretchers and stretcher bearers to cope with the large number of
casualties which we suffered." Total casualties for operation,
killed, wounded, and missing, 350.

1916.
August 1. 10th Battalion at Berteaucourt.
,, 9. Battalion marched from Berteaucourt to Bonneville.
,, 14. Marched from Bonneville to Toutencourt.
,, 15. Marched to Vadincourt Wood.
,, 16. Left Vadincourt for Brickfields, near Albert.
,, 18. 10th Battalion marched to Sausage Valley.
,, 19-20. Lieut.-Colonel S. P. Weir reported: "The 10th Battalion relieved the 3rd Battalion of 1st Brigade on the morning of 19th
inst., taking over the line from R.34.A.9½.2½. to R.38.7½.1. to

1916.
August 19-20. R.34.A.9.9.Saps were at once commenced towards the enemy's
(continued) line at points R.28.c.0.3½., C.5.1¼., C.7.½., and C.8.½. These
were run forward a distance from 50 to 70X, and a Lewis Gun
stationed at end of sap N.28.c.7.½. At this time there were
two companies, "B" and "C", occupying the line from
R.34.a.9½. 2½. to R.54.a.9.9., the remaining two companies
being left in Sausage Valley."

„ 22. Mouquet Farm or 2nd Pozieres. Lieut.-Colonel S. P. Weir
reported: "First wave in new line of trench constructed on previous nights, second wave in shell holes between new line and
firing line, third wave and fourth wave in firing line. The
Lewis guns of "D" Coy.—Support Coy.—were handed over
to the attacking Corps. "A" Coy. was detailed to protect right
flank by manning new sap called Annie Sap, and portion of line
until it connected with 1st Battalion. The one gun of H.Q.
M.G. Section was with them, and one gun from 1st Battalion
was stationed in shell hole in No Man's Land to enfilade counter-attack. "A" Coy. instructed to continue sap towards point
R.28.c.9.5. Support Company was moved into firing line as
soon as the attack was launched. At 1700 enemy opened heavy
shell fire on our front and support lines, causing many casualties
and a certain amount of disorganization, and it was decided to
place another platoon (the second) of Support Coy. to strengthen attacking force. This was done. At 1800 the attack was
launched, and owing to heavy casualties went forward in two
waves instead of four, leaving two platoons of Support Coy. in
firing line. At 1830 the objective was reached from R.28.c.3.6.
to C.7.6. The left company had therefore succeeded in occupying their objective, also the left portion of right company,
but the remainder were held up by heavy M.G. fire from point
R.28.c.9.5. The attacking party reported that they met three
lines of enemy's trenches before reaching points 36 and 66, and
the left party reported only two lines of trenches. The first
lines were only lightly held, but the final objective was strongly
held by infantry and machine guns. There was no element of
surprise in the attack, as the moment the first wave left the
trenches it was subjected to heavy fire from machine guns and
rifles, also artillery. The enemy's machine gunners fired
through our barrage. Before launching the attack the Battalion
sustained over 120 casualties from shell fire, and immediately
the attack was launched casualties were heavy and rapid. Only
one officer reached the final objective, and he was wounded
there at once. The remaining seven were killed or wounded
within a few minutes of launching the attack. At 1830 the
position was therefore as shown on attached sketch No. 1 herewith with ink crosses. We were subjected to a heavy fire from
point 95 from mobile machine gunners, and the bombers having failed to make good the sap running south from point 9.5.,

BATTALION CHRONOLOGY

1916.
August 22. our left Coy. could not advance. Another Platoon of Support
(continued) Coy. was sent forward with instructions to join up and make good the line from R.28.c.6.8. to C.9.3. This Platoon advanced, but owing to disappearance in some parts, general thinning of line by casualties, they were compelled to fall back to vicinity of our new line of trench so that by shortly after 2000 the position was as shown in attached sketch No. 2 (ink crosses). It will be seen from this that our left company was "in the air." The enemy was getting behind it, it had no touch on either flanks, and was enfiladed from both flanks. The survivors therefore fell back to new line of trench. The last remaining Platoon was sent to the assistance of left flank, where they dug in. The final position being that we held the new line of trench which we had dug, and is marked on sketch. This line was held from 2100 on night of August 21, until we handed it over to 21st Battalion on night 22-23rd. We joined this line up to connect with 11th Battalion on left of Sunken Road."

,, 23. 10th Battalion entrained at Doullens, and detrained at Proven, in Belgium.

1916.
September 1. Battalion went into Kenora Camp, near Poperinghe, Belgium.
,, 2. Marched to Ottawa Camp.
,, 7. Lieut.-Colonel Weir evacuated sick, and Temp. Lieut.-Colonel G. E. Redburg assumed command of Battalion.
,, 8. Bomb accident; 21 casualties.
,, 13. Battalion moved to reserve position at Chateau Belge.
,, 19. Battalion moved to Railway Dugouts.
,, 24. "Hill 60". Temp. Lieut.-Colonel G. E. Redburg reported: "Sunday. Sent an advance party to front line at 5 a.m. to take over stores, etc. The Battalion moved into the trenches in front of the famous 'Hill 60', the relief taking place at night."
,, 27. Lieut.-Colonel Denton reported: "Lieut.-Colonel Denton, D.S.O., from 11th Battalion, assumed command. Work progressing. A mine was blown by the enemy, but no damage was done to our works, although the trenches are very close together. The gas lip of the crater was under the enemy parapet, and extends towards the centre of our line for 25 feet. We annoyed the Boche during the night with rifle grenades. They retaliated, but did no damage."
,, 30. Temp. Lieut.-Colonel G. E. Redburg returned and took over 10th Battalion from Lieut.-Colonel Denton, D.S.O.

1916.
October 1-2. At 2120 the Battalion was relieved from "Hill 60", and entrained to Brandhoek, and went into Halifax Camp.
,, 9. Battalion moved to Ottawa Camp.
,, 12. At 0900 the Battalion marched to Steenvoorde, and went into billets.
,, 13. Battalion marched to Oosthouck.

1916.
October 14. Battalion marched to Mouille.
„ 15. Marched to Tournehem.
„ 20. At Tournehem, Lieut.-Colonel G. E. Redburg treated the "originals" who embarked on the *Ascanius* to a free drink of beer. Battalion then marched to Ardruicq and entrained for the Somme.
„ 21. Detrained at Pt. Remy, and marched to Buigy-le-Abbaye, reaching destination about 1200.
„ 23. Battalion moved by bus to Buire.
„ 24-30. Battalion marched to Fricourt on fatigues.
„ 30. Battalion marched to Bernafay Wood, taking about six hours.

1916.
November 1-5. Battalion at Bernafay Wood on fatigue duty.
„ 6. Gueudecourt. Lieut.-Colonel G. F. Redburg reported: "Moved forward to front line, and attached to 2nd Infantry Brigade. The relief was carried out satisfactorily."
„ 6-11. Trenches in shocking state, mud everywhere; 150 men evacuated with feet trouble.
„ 12. Battalion marched to Bernafay Wood.
„ 13. Battalion marched to bivouac at Fricourt, and big Australian mail distributed.
„ 14. Marched to Dernancourt, and went into billets.
„ 17. Marched to Buire.
„ 18. Embussed to Cardonette.
„ 30. Battalion marched to Franvillers.

1916.
December 1. Marched to Dernancourt.
„ 3. Marched to Fricourt.
„ 4. Marched to Bernafay.
„ 5. Marched to Flers. Lieut.-Colonel G. E. Redburg reported: "Moved to close supports at Flers Sector with Battalion H.Qrs. in Flers. The Battalion is divided, two companies in camp near Bazentin-le-Grand; "A" and "B" Coys. in trench near Battalion H.Qrs. The move was made at night, and owing to the bad weather it was necessary to leave communication trenches and walk overland. The state of the ground is very bad between shell-holes and the rain. It is very hard work getting over very short distances."
„ 12. Lieut.-Colonel G. E. Redburg reported: "The Battalion moved forward into the line, relieving the 9th Battalion. The ground was in a very bad condition, mud and water. The line is being held by two Coys., with a gap between. There are also gaps on the flanks, all gaps being patrolled at night. In moving up, two men were wounded, otherwise the relief was completely without incident. "A" and "B" Coys. in the line, and "C" and "D" in supports."
„ 15. Whilst in line at Flers men received three hot drinks per day.

BATTALION CHRONOLOGY

1916.

December 22-23. At night the 10th Battalion was relieved in the line by the 9th Battalion. Battalion then moved to Bazentin House.

„ 23. At Bazentin, Lieut.-Colonel G. E. Redburg evacuated sick, and Major Rafferty, from the 12th Battalion, assumed command of the Battalion.

„ 24. Christmas parcels at Bazentin, and fatigues.

„ 25. Christmas Day at Bazentin and fatigues.

1917.

January 1. Battalion moved into Hobart Camp, opposite Bazentin-le-Grand; fatigues.

„ 6. Left by train for Meaulte, and marched to Dernancourt.

„ 14. Marched from Dernancourt to Bresle.

„ 24. Battalion marched from Bresle to Albert.

1917.

February 1. Battalion undergoing training.

„ 4. Marched to Bazentin-le-Petit. Lieut.-Colonel R. B. Jacob assumed command. Fatigues and training.

„ 11. Battalion moved into supports at Hexham Road. Fatigues.

„ 19. Le Barque. Lieut.-Colonel R. B. Jacob reported: "Relief of 12th Battalion completed at 2100. "A" and "D" Coys. in front line, "B" and "C" Coys. in support at Eaucourt L'Abbaye. Battalion H.Qrs. situated at corner of Hexham Road and Pioneer Avenue. Conditions normal, but very muddy."

„ 23. Le Barque. Lieut.-Colonel R. B. Jacob reported: "Our 'heavies' very active on enemy front line in front of us. Enemy's retaliation very heavy, but appeared to pay more attention to his own line than to ours. Pineapple bombing ceased altogether. Our patrols examined enemy wire in front of the Hook, and reported it very little damaged, and no sign of the enemy in his front trench. Very few flares were being used by the Germans. Enemy appears to have evacuated front line opposite us."

„ 24. Le Barque. Lieut.-Colonel R. B. Jacob reported: "During early hours, for about three hours, enemy artillery very active on our front line and his own. During day very quiet, and no sniping or machine gun fire on part of enemy. Our movements and working parties not hindered. At 2230 we moved forward and occupied Grid Trench."

„ 25. Le Barque. Lieut.-Colonel R. B. Jacob reported: "Very foggy. Consolidating and patrolling during morning. 1300, we attacked and occupied Le Barque Switch Trench. Patrols penetrating well into Le Barque. Enemy barraged heavily after positions had been won. Our casualties about 20 per cent (including eight officers, two of which were killed) chiefly due to rifle and machine gun fire. One machine gun captured and one prisoner taken. Relieved by 12th Battalion by midnight, excepting 50 men."

1917.
February 25. Extracts from 3rd Brigade Summary of Operations at Le Barque: "On the night of 23rd-24th there were two battalions in the line: 9th on right from M.18.C.1.6. to M.24.B.6.9., and 10th Battalion on left from M.17.D.0.9. to M.18.C.1.6., with 12th Battalion in support, and 11th Battalion in reserve. On night of 23rd-24th February, 10th Battalion patrols which went out at 2300 reported unusual inactivity in the enemy line, noticing no flares and no rifle or machine gun fire. This was unusual, as the enemy had been very active during the previous day. Both battalions were immediately ordered to send forward more patrols to verify the suspicion that the enemy had cleared out. The patrols could not hear any movement whatever in the enemy lines. They should have endeavoured to enter the enemy trench to ascertain for certain if the enemy were still in the position. The cause for this omission was put down to the effects of trench warfare. Next day, after a conference with the two C.O.'s concerned, preparations were made to occupy the enemy trench after return of patrols, which were ordered to actually enter the enemy trench at dusk should suspicions prove correct. The 9th Battalion sent out their patrol by daylight along a disused sap. This patrol entered the Maze, and found no signs of the enemy. Accordingly at 8.30 p.m. the Maze was occupied and consolidated. The left (10th) battalion patrol was slow in obtaining its information. The right battalion (9th) pushed up a bomb squad to beyond Blue Cut Road, meeting no opposition. At 10 p.m. the left battalion (10th) moved out and occupied the Grid Trench, with posts at Grid Support. About dawn on 25th February, both battalions pushed out and occupied Bank Trench from M.18.D.7.5. to Blue Cut Road. The 10th Battalion was held up on the left by a machine gun firing at short range from somewhere about M.18.A.7.1. A bomb squad with rifle bombers, under Lieut. Whiteford, went forward to drive this opposition back. This officer was killed and his men rushed the gun. The enemy fell back and were lost in the fog. Our line was then extended to M.17.B.4.4. At this stage machine guns and snipers from the left front caused a number of casualties, especially to the 10th Battalion. At 5 p.m. on afternoon of 25th, our line moved forward in attack formation, and occupied the line: Oat Lane-Wheat Trench-Le Barque Switch."

,, 26. Battalion in supports at Le Barque. Fatigues.
,, 27-28. 10th Battalion relieved by 1st Battalion by 10 p.m., and moved to Bazentin-le-Petit. Congratulations were received from Army Corps and Divisional Commanders for the work of the Battalion in the Le Barque operation.

1917.
March 1. Battalion moved from Bernafay Wood to Dernancourt.
,, 8. Battalion moved into Shelter Wood Camp.

BATTALION CHRONOLOGY

1917.
March 23. Battalion moved to Bresle.
" 24-31. Battalion undergoing training.
" 29. Platoon competition.

1917.
April 4. Battalion marched to Montauban.
" 5. Route-marched across country to Fremicourt, and there relieved 29th Battalion in Beugny-Ytres line. (Corps Reserve).
" 7. Moved to front line north of Louverval, relieving two Coys. of 12th Battalion with our "B" 'and "C" Coys. Line held by Platoon posts.
" 8. At 0300 line advanced about 1,000 yards. Strong opposition met by "B" Coy. Lieuts. O'Brien and Fordham killed, and Capt. McCann, M.C., and Lieut. D. J. Walsh wounded. About 40 other casualties.
" 9. Line again advanced in early morning and during the night. Opposition again encountered on our right, where 12th Battalion were attacking Boursies. Casualties about 40. Lieut. Hincks wounded.
" 10. At 0200, with assistance of "C" Coy., 11th Battalion line pushed well forward of Boursies. Practically no opposition, and no casualties. Relieved portion of 12th Battalion lines.
" 11-12. During night relieved by 11th Battalion, and proceeded into Brigade supports.
" 15. Lagnicourt. Heavy attack on our front commenced at about 0420. "A" Coy. ordered to support 11th Battalion, "B" Coy. placed in rear of 12th Battalion near Morchies. Took over portion of 11th Battalion line without incident. "A", "C", and "D" Coys. in line, "B" in reserve.
" 16-17. 10th Battalion relieved by 7th Battalion. Battalion moved to Le Bucquiere.
" 24. Moved into billets at Bancourt.
" 25. "D" Company detailed as Wardens to Villers-au-Flos, Beifvillers line. Remainder of Battalion working on railway construction under Canadian Engineers.
" 27. Lieut.-Colonel R. B. Jacob proceeded on leave, and was relieved by Major Alexander Steele.
" 29. Voting.

1917.
May 1-4. Battalion engaged in fatigues and salvage.
" 5. Battalion moved *via* Fremicourt to trenches. Bullecourt: Major A. Steele reported: "On arriving at Noreuil, some difficulty was experienced in getting guides, after which the move proceeded smoothly. By 0300 the move was complete, and the Battalion was then disposed as under: "A" and "B" Coys. in C.16.A., "D" Coy. at C.10.0. and C.4.D., "C" Coy. at C.B.5. All in sunken roads. H.Q. and Regt. Aid Post in Railway Cut-

1917.
May 5.
(continued)

ting at C.5.D.6.6. Remnants of 17th and 18th Battalions, with their respective H. Qrs., then moved out. At 0200 a party of three officers and 200 other ranks from "A" and "B" Coys. left Brigade Dump carrying S.A.A. and bombs to dump at C.5.D.0.7. This party successfully came through a heavy barrage, their casualties being two other ranks killed and 15 wounded. About 0430, "C" Coy. had Capt. de Courcy-Ireland and Lieut. Hill wounded, also several other ranks. The shelling at this time being very heavy and accurate. At the same time Battalion H.Qrs. was severely shelled, and three other ranks were killed and several wounded in half an hour. During the afternoon a fatigue party of one officer and 65 other ranks carried 400 L.T.M. bombs from Noreuil across the open to 18th Battalion H. Qrs. in C.9.B. with no casualties, although under shell and machine gun barrage. Periodical barrages were placed on C.5.B. and D. throughout the day and night, and "C" Coy.'s casualties had totalled 23 before midnight. During the afternoon Lieut. Partridge had assumed command of "C" Coy., vice Capt. de Courcy-Ireland, wounded."

„ 6. Bullecourt: Action of 10th Battalion supports. Major A. Steele reported: "At 3.30 a.m. orders were received from Brigade to place "C" Coy. at the disposal of the 12th Battalion in the line. This company was established in its position by 4.30 a.m., losing some casualties going in, owing to the shelling of the communication trench. At 3.45 a.m. "C" Coy. Commander reported to 12th Battalion and received instructions to move to O.G.2. and relieve "A" Coy. of the 11th Battalion. The Coy. moved at 4 a.m., and reported to Capt. Vowles of the 12th Battalion in the front line at 4.30 a.m., despite a severe barrage maintained on the communication trench which caused 10 casualties. This Coy. was then allotted by Platoons to both the 11th and 12th Battalions, and materially assisted in repelling the enemy counter-attack. In regaining a portion of trench captured by the enemy, Lieuts. Dougall and Wendt, who were gallantly leading the party, were killed. At 5.15 a.m. "A" Coy. moved up from C.16.A. in four lines across the open, through the enemy barrage, and took up "C" Coy.'s old position in Sunken Road at C.5.B. Enemy's barrage was passed through skilfully and without a single casualty. At 7.20 a.m. orders were received from Brigade by 'phone to push up two more companies into the line. Orders were at once sent to "B" and "D" Coys. at C.16.A. and C.10.C., respectively, to move forward at once, at five paces extension, and in four lines. Coy. Commanders reporting at Battalion Headquarters en route. This was done, and by 9 a.m. "B" Coy. had arrived in O.G.1., and was pushed into O.G.2. "D" Coy., under 10th Battalion was pushed into O.G.2. with orders to at once make good any ground which the enemy still held as a result of his counter-

BATTALION CHRONOLOGY

1917.		attack. The latter Coy. was in O.G.1. by 9.30 a.m., and at once
May	6.	moved to the extreme right and established a bombing stop at
(continued)		U.29.B.8.8., east of the road. Ten enemy other ranks were captured at this period, being members of the 123rd and 124th Wurtemburg Regiment. (A.S.). Consolidation was at once proceeded with in O.G. 1 and 2, and bombs and S.A.A. collected and formed into dumps. The enemy used bombs freely at this stage, but was effectively silenced by rifle grenades, and the work of forming a defensive right flank was continued steadily. At 0945 the remnants of "C" Coy. were withdrawn from O.G.2. to O.G.1., and were placed in support to "D" Coy. (See map "B" attached.) "C" Coy. had suffered 50 casualties, including two officers and nine other ranks killed in less than five hours. During the morning the whole of that portion of the 4th Battalion which had moved into the left of the Brigade Sector during the counter-attack, was relieved by 3 Platoons of "B" Coy. At 2130 "A" Coy. moved from the Sunken Road at O.5.B. to the centre of the Brigade Sector in O.G.2. "B" Coy. then relieved 12th Battalion on the extreme right of the line in O.G.2. Relief completed by 2300. "A" and "B" Coys. at once commenced consolidating. From 2200 to midnight enemy shelling was heavy, and "D" Coy. alone had 8 killed and 20 wounded between these hours. At 0339 "B" and "D" Coys. supplied covering parties in No Man's Land north and east to cover Pioneers and Engineers who, acting under orders from Brigade, were filling in the extreme right of O.G.1. and 2 for a distance of 40 yards. 150 yards of wiring was completed by Engineers on this flank during the night. During the night "C" Coy. went back to O.5.B., and carried up 60 coils of wire to the work above referred to. Posts were established at U.29.B.7.7., where a T-headed work was dug, and U.29.B.8.9., the latter being connected by a sap dug back to C.T. at U.29.B.6.8."
,,	8.	"During the morning our Lewis guns successfully engaged enemy supports moving up against Bullecourt, four guns being in action together. During the afternoon, howitzer and 18-pounder shells reported as coming from the direction of Noreuil, fell into O.G.2. This was reported by high-power buzzer and by runner, but still continued to cause casualties."
,,	8-9.	10th Battalion relieved during night by 53rd Battalion. Proceeded to camp and rested. Casualties for operation: 7 officers and 174 other ranks.
,,	10.	Battalion moved to camp near Bapaume.
,,	19.	Battalion sports held at Bapaume.
,,	22.	At 0900 the Battalion left Bapaume and marched to Bazentin.
,,	23.	At 0900 Battalion left Bazentin and marched to Ribemont.
,,	28.	10th Battalion champion in Brigade with 17 points, and 12th Battalion second with 11 points.

68   THE FIGHTING 10TH

1917. June		10th Battalion engaged in training. Coy. competitions conducted. Results: D.C.A.B. Battalion competition held, with 9th Battalion 1st, and 10th Battalion 2nd.
	1-6.	
,,	12.	Battalion marched from Ribemont to Henencourt and bivouacked.
,,	13.	Divisional sports. ("Ochre" 1st).
,,	14.	Battalion returned to Ribemont.
,,	20.	Final of Divisional Coy. competition, with "D" Coy. of 10th Battalion second in 1st Australian Division.
,,	24.	Marched to Mailly Maillet. Lieut.-Colonel R. B. Jacob transferred to Training Battalion, and Major M. Wilder-Neligan, D.S.O., D.C.M., temporarily in command of 10th Battalion.
,,	24-31.	Battalion engaged in training.
1917. July	1-5.	Battalion still undergoing training.
,,	6.	Battalion marched to Ribemont, and Major F. G. Giles returned and assumed command of Battalion.
,,	8.	Pozieres memorial unveiled.
,,	12.	Inspection by H.M. the late King.
,,	13.	Battalion marched to Bray.
,,	15.	Lieut.-Colonel M. Wilder-Neligan returned to Battalion and assumed permanent command.
,,	26.	Battalion marched to Albert and entrained.
,,	27.	Detrained at Steenbecque, and marched to Staple.
,,	30.	Battalion moved by bus transport by road to Seninghem.
1917. August	1.	Battalion undergoing training.
,,	6.	Battalion returned to Staple.
,,	9.	Battalion marched to Bleu.
,,	10-31.	Battalion engaged in training.
,,	22.	Brigade sports.
,,	24.	Inspection by G.O.C. 2nd Army Corps, General Sir H. Plumer.
1917. September	6.	Brigade Drill Cup, won by 10th Battalion.
,,	13.	Battalion marched to new area near Caestre.
,,	14.	Battalion marched into Connaught Camp.
,,	16.	Battalion marched to Cornwall Camp.
,,	18.	Battalion marched to Chateau Segard.
,,	19-20.	At 2330 Battalion left Chateau Segard and marched to hopping-off line.
,,	20.	Polygon Wood. Lieut.-Colonel M. Wilder-Neligan reported: "On the night of 19-20th, the 10th Battalion left the bivouac area at Chateau Segard at 1130, by route of Shrapnel Corner, Halfway House, Hooge, to assembly point, thence to tape line in front of Jargon Trench. This movement was done more or less in sleeting rain, and up to Halfway House the journey was accomplished without incident. Between Halfway House and

BATTALION CHRONOLOGY 69

1917.
September 20.
(continued)

Hooge, along track marked '3rd Brigade Route', the Battalion was blocked from half to one hour by 2nd Division troops (26th Battalion) passing along in front, and the carrying Company picked up necessary wire, picks, etc., at this point. During the journey between Halfway House and Hooge Crater several gas shells burst near the Battalion, and progress was somewhat reduced by men having to wear gas helmets. After passing Hooge Crater, through Chateau Wood the track became heavy, consequently most trying to carrying parties. The Battalion reached the assembly tapes about 3 a.m., and heavy shelling was indulged in by the enemy, which caused slight disorganization of the Battalion and the loss of a number of men. Capt. W. G. Cornish, M.C., and Capt. G. C. Campbell, M.C., did great work in reorganizing the Battalion into formation for moving forward, and on the barrage coming down at 5.40, the whole of the Battalion moved forward with the remainder of the Brigade. During the advance a strong post was encountered in Glencorse Wood, which was causing considerable trouble. I therefore sent forward one Platoon under Lieut. Leaver, who I regret to say was killed, to asssit the moppers-up of the 11th Battalion. The post was manned by about 50 of the enemy with three machine guns. After capture, about 40 enemy dead were found in and round the post. When barrage halted at 1st objective, the Battalion reorganized into original formation, i.e. "X" and "Y" Companies, Front Line; No. 2 Company Moppers Up; No. 1 Company Carrying Party. At this point Capt. G. C. Campbell, M.C., showed extraordinary ability in handling men and re-organizing them. On reaching the 2nd objective it was found that the 12th Battalion had not occupied the right portion (about 200 yards) of 2nd objective. I therefore decided to put Nos. 1 and 2 Companies (who were carrying and mopping up companies respectively) in to hold right portion of the 2nd objective. I obtained from the C.O. 7th Battalion two Platoons for support at this juncture to make up for the depletion of the two companies so detailed. These Platoons were released later when the 12th Battalion formed a Platoon strong post on the right of their flank. Two machine guns were captured in this line, and one, together with 1 N.C.O. and 5 men were captured by Lieut. Klenner single-handed. This gun was causing great casualties and momentarily held up the advance, but the quick judgment and able action of Lieut. Klenner soon allowed the advance to be continued. On the barrage lifting from the 2nd objective, and moving forward to the 3rd objective, "X" and "Y" Companies moved forward, mopping up their own areas, and established themselves in the 3rd objective. The barrage then rested for two hours in front of the ground gained, which enabled this Battalion to wire their front and consolidate five posts most effectively. Mopping up was found to have been done most thoroughly, and no enemy had been passed over.

1917.
September 20.
(continued)

Large numbers of enemy were found to the east of the strong post in Glencorse Wood. These were in very deep dugouts, and gave considerable resistance. At this point two specially trained Platoons moved up to assist 11th Battalion moppers up. Three machine guns were captured, and about 50 men dead; dugouts were not cleared up, and large numbers of enemy dead were left in them. The final objective was as per attached sketch. The nature of the ground prevented the actual Green Line being adhered to. The enemy endeavoured to counter-attack the position during the afternoon, but was unsuccessful owing to good observation from our lines, and the quick response of the artillery when asked for, on his assembly positions. At dusk (about 7 p.m.) he succeeded in bringing a number of men from behind the Butte situated north-east corner of Polygon Race-course to assembly positions on the right and left of Polygon Wood, but owing to the quick response of the artillery the counter-attack was thoroughly dispersed, and none of the enemy succeeded in getting anywhere near our front line."

" 21. Lieut.-Colonel M. Wilder-Neligan, D.S.O., D.C.M., reported: "During the second day the area between the 2nd and 3rd objectives and the old line were heavily shelled. The new front line remained intact, and came in for very little shelling. During the morning, No. 506 Pte. R. R. Inwood, with a man from the 7th Battalion, located a machine gun, and together went forward and captured it, with one prisoner, killing the remainder of the team. At about 7.30 p.m. S.O.S. signals went up from the 2nd Division on our left, and the 2nd Brigade on our right. This was repeated by the O.P. in front of Brigade centre about a quarter of an hour afterwards. Our barrage came and remained down for one and a half hours, and although none of the enemy were seen, it is probable that a counter-attack was dispersed by the barrage, as the right and left battalions and brigades reported having seen the enemy massing for a counter-attack. The Battalion was relieved about midnight by the 2nd Battalion, 1st Brigade, and the return journey to Dickebusch Area was accomplished without incident. One section of the T.M.B. joined the Battalion at about Halfway House, but owing to the officer in charge of same and three of the crew being wounded, they were reinforced by an officer of another section, who accompanied them to the Assembly Post. The machine gun barrage proved to be most effective, and valuable assistance was rendered throughout by the various Machine Gun Companies. Casualties: As per attached list."

" 23. 10th Battalion embussed for Steenvoorde.
" 29. Battalion embussed to Chateau Segard, the Battalion transport lines being near this point.
" 30. At midnight Battalion moved into line.

1917.
October 1-2. 10th Battalion in line.

BATTALION CHRONOLOGY

1917. October	2-3.	During night, 10th Battalion came out to China Wall. Major C. Rumball, M.C., reported: "The Battalion rested at China Wall all day, having hot meals, etc. At 2345 the head of the Battalion had passed the starting point (Birr Cross Roads) en route back to Anzac Ridge, arriving at Westhoek Ridge without casualties. The Battalion took up a position "C" Coy. on Anzac Ridge, "B" and "C" Coys. in Battalion reserve on Westhoek Ridge, "A" and "C" Coys. relieving companies of the 3rd Battalion."
,,	4.	1st Brigade "stunt": many prisoners. Major C. Rumball, M.C., reported: "The relief was complete, and companies in position at about 0310. The relief so long to allow 3rd Battalion to move right forward to jumping-off line for the "stunt." Zero hour was at 0450, and shortly afterwards prisoners poured in, those who were unwounded being used as stretcher-bearers. The enemy was very quiet, but we continued to shell his back areas. Our total casualties for previous 24 hours being 9 other ranks."
,,	5-6.	10th Battalion relieved 1st Brigade in line during night.
,,	7.	Battalion relieved 12th Battalion.
,,	9.	Celtic Wood. Lieut.-Colonel M. Wilder-Neligan reported: "During the night, 2nd Lieuts. Rae, Laurie, and Fenn, and 42 other ranks, arrived to reinforce Lieut. Scott for the raiding party which went over at zero hour 0520. Results of raid as per attached report: The attacking party consisted of 5 officers and 80 other ranks. The original party was intended to be 109 all told, but the weakness of the Battalion and casualties during the day and night preceding the attack caused the numbers to be reduced; the attack was carried out on the lines as laid down in attached copy of operation order. Our artillery barrage was so weak that all who took part in the operation are agreed that except for the fact that their watches had been synchronized, and the officers and men therefore knew that zero hour had arrived, there was nothing whatever in the very thin artillery fire to indicate that anything in the nature of a barrage was intended. The plus 4 to 10 line seems to have been extraordinarily light. The concentrated fire provided by the 3rd A.L.T.M. Battery was everything that could be desired, and was largely responsible for the successful entry into Celtic Wood. The party entered the wood from the north-western end, and almost immediately met strong opposition by machine guns and rifle fire; machine gun fire coming from the eastern wing of the wood and from both flanks, and rifle fire from strong forces of the enemy, who had entrenched across the spur in the western wing of the wood (D.29.d.9.6.), and another short length of trench running from east to south-west at the southern end of this part of the wood, and from individual snipers who were occupying wooden shelters (much broken by shell fire). The

1917.
October 9.
(continued)

enemy, who at this stage outnumbered us by at least 2 to 1, were strongly attacked by the party, who used rifle fire, bombs, and rifle grenades for this purpose. Lieut. Scott meanwhile led one party round to the right and got behind the last-mentioned trench. At about this stage in the struggle an enemy small artillery barrage—probably entirely 77's—was put down behind our men, cutting them off from our lines. This barrage was strengthened by very heavy hostile machine-gun fire across the greater part of our present front line. In addition, artillery of all calibre opened up on our rear area. A fierce struggle ensued, a temporary mastery was gained; the enemy commencing to retreat as soon as the fire from Lieut. Scott's party was brought to bear from his rear. They were, however, rallied by one officer, and again the struggle was renewed. At this stage a fresh party of the enemy came round the northern end of this part of the wood and commenced to encircle our men. A desperate hand encounter followed, in which heavy casualties were inflicted upon the enemy. The fight gradually concentrated towards Lieut. Scott's party, where the enemy finally gained the mastery. In this operation I regret to say that Lieut. Scott and 2nd Lieut. Rae were killed, Lieut. James and 2nd Lieut. Laurie were wounded, and 2nd Lieut. Wilson missing; also the greater part of the other ranks concerned were either killed or wounded. A few wounded have passed through dressing stations, but up to the present I am only able to account for 14 unwounded members of the party. It is quite possible that a certain number of missing are wounded and prisoners of war, and others may yet come in or be accounted for definitely. Some of the wounded crawled back into shell holes on the western edge of the wood. Every effort was made to get these men. Stretcher bearers with white flags were attempted, but the bearers were shot. After nightfall those that could be found were brought in. Heavy casualties were undoubtedly inflicted on the enemy. The Trench Mortar personnel successfully threw Stokes Mortar bombs into two or three dugouts. Heavy enemy artillery and machine-gun fire was drawn into the Divisional Sector, which could have been employed elsewhere, as there is no doubt from his constant barrage the enemy thought an attack on that sector was intended. The demonstration would have produced extremely good results and probably many prisoners had our artillery preparations been even moderately good, with far less casualties to our men. The episode in no way lowered the morale of our men, but has, if anything brightened it, owing to the fact that it is the first hand to hand struggle against great odds with no great artillery preparation in which they had taken part. The survivors are each now satisfied that he is the equal to any number of Germans. Also the remainder of the Battalion were able to see, as lookers on during the early stage of the fight, what pluck and good leadership can do."

BATTALION CHRONOLOGY 73

1917.
October 9-10. At 0245 the 10th Battalion was relieved in the line by the 32nd Battalion.
„ 11. Battalion at Dominion Lines.
„ 20. 9th and 10th Battalion sports held, the 9th being 1st.
„ 24. Battalion moved to Brigade Reserve line near Ypres at Kruistraat.
„ 30. 10th Battalion moved to Battalion Reserve Area in Railway Dugouts, and relieved 7th Battalion.
„ 31. The Battalion moved to Reserve Area at Westhoek Ridge, arriving without casualties, and took over from the 11th Battalion.

1917.
November 1. Battalion moved forward to support position on Anzac Ridge, and relieved the 9th Battalion. The day was quiet, and no casualties were received.
„ 2-5. Battalion supplied carrying and working parties, the parties being frequently interrupted by enemy shell fire by both gas and high explosive. Casualties, however, were slight. On the afternoon of the 5th, the Battalion moved back to Reserve Battalion position on Westhoek Ridge, relieving the 4th Battalion.
„ 6-8. The 10th Battalion was employed in improving and construcing accommodation.
„ 9. In the morning the Battalion was relieved by the 66th British Division, and moved back to Halifax Camp.
„ 10. 10th Battalion transport left by road for Boulogne area.
„ 11. Battalion embussed to Renescure.
„ 13. Battalion marched 20 miles to Vaudrighem.
„ 18. Battalion marched to Bourthes.
„ 19. At Bezingheim readjustment of Battalion occurred, and "Z" Coy. was formed consisting of 140 men.
„ 27. Readjustment of billets; Battalion H.Q. transferred to Enquin.
„ 27-30. Battalion undergoing training at Enquin.

1917.
December 3-4. Brigade competitions held and 10th Battalion Transport Section successful. Battalion strength at this date: 34 officers and 723 other ranks.
„ 6. Voting in connection with Commonwealth Conscription Referendum.
„ 13. Battalion marched to Vaudrighem and transport proceeded to Elnes.
„ 14. Battalion marched to Remilly, and Transport Section proceeded to Staple.
„ 15. Battalion marched to Wizernes, and entrained to Lindenhoek, and transport proceeded to Bleu.
„ 16. Battalion relieved 31st Battalion in the Messines Sector of the line, and details proceeded to Caestre. Transport arrived at 1200, and remained at Neuve Eglise.
„ 24-25. 10th Battalion relieved early in morning by 12th Battalion, and proceeded to Wulverghem.

74 THE FIGHTING 10TH

1917. Christmas Day spent in reserve trenches at Wulverghem; ex-
December 25. ceedingly cold.

" 26-31. Fatigues to Pollard's Supports and B2, 3 and 4 saps. Weather remained cold; strength of Battalion being 33 officers and 637 other ranks.

1918.
January 1. Relieved 12th Battalion in line, Messines Sector, during evening. Strength with unit, 33 officers and 599 other ranks. Guard placed on rations in ex-German pillbox on Bethlehem Road. Battalion at first in close reserves.

" 5. Battalion proceeded to front line from close reserves.

" 9-10. Battalion relieved during night by 12th Battalion, and proceeded to reserve trenches at Wulverghem.

" 10-16. Battalion engaged in fatigues to Pollard's Supports, and carrying, wiring, and light railway fatigues from Gooseberry Farm and Stinking Farm to front line.

" 16. 10th Battalion marched from Wulverghem to Kemmel, and thence to Rossignol Camp.

" 16-22. Working parties.

" 23-24. Battalion went into line in front of Wytschaete; very quiet.

" 31. During night relieved by 31st Battalion, and marched to Aldershot Camp. Strength: 38 officers and 741 other ranks.

1918.
February 1. Fatigues and training commenced at Aldershot Camp; transport lines at Neuve Eglise.

" 7. Cinemas, concerts, and dinners were frequent, and boxing and football were organized.

" 16. Battalion celebrated its Christmas Day. Prizes were awarded for the best decorated huts, parcels were distributed, and sports were held in the afternoon. The 10th Battalion football team won the 3rd Brigade Cup, and was doing well in the Divisional competition, only being beaten in one match by the 8th Battalion.

" 24. Alarm given; everything completely ready within 20 minutes.

" 28. Battalion moved to Tournai Camp.

1918.
March 1-2. Battalion took over line at Hollebeke. A raid was conducted by the enemy at the time of the relief. Excellent work was performed by Lieut. C. Scott, and the support platoons who succeeded in beating off the attack with heavy casualties. The enemy reached "D" Coy's. Headquarters and carried off Major H. N. Henwood, who refusing to surrender was killed by the enemy on his way across No Man's Land. Seven other ranks were missing, but no information of any importance was obtained.

" 9-10. Battalion was relieved in line during night by the 12th Battalion, and proceeded to supports in Crater Dugouts.

BATTALION CHRONOLOGY 75

1918.
March 24-25. Battalion during night returned to line at Hollebeke and relieved 12th Battalion.
„ 31. Total 10th Battalion casualties for March totalled 141 other ranks.

1918.
April 3-4. During night Battalion relieved by British Division, and moved to Dezon Camp. Strength of Battalion 39 officers and 764 other ranks.
„ 4. Battalion left Dezon Camp by bus for Caestre.
„ 5-6. Battalion entrained at Caestre, and left for the Somme.
„ 6. Battalion detrained at St. Roch (Amiens), and moved to Poulanville. First fire.
„ 7. Resting. Second fire.
„ 8. Resting. Third fire.
„ 9. Battalion marched to Vignacourt.
„ 10. Battalion marched back to Rainneville.
„ 12. Battalion bivouacked outside Amiens.
„ 12-13. At 9 a.m. Battalion marched to St. Roch station, Amiens, and entrained for the north.
„ 13-14. At 11 p.m. Battalion detrained at Hondeghem. Very dark, and Boche near Strazeele. Battalion marched to near Borre in supports, and transport lines established at Morbecque.
„ 19. Battalion relieved Support Battalion of 33rd Division near Besace Farm, south, in the Meteren Sector.
„ 23-24. During night Battalion relieved 11th Battalion in the line.
„ 24-25. Meteren "stunt". Lieut.-Colonel Ross Blyth Jacob reported: "Attack of Meteren (2nd Phase). "A" Coy., left Platoon at X.16.a.2.4., pushed forward to establish post, but encountered strong force of enemy, and finding both flanks in the air, returned to their original position. Coy. H.Qrs., at X.15.b.3.9., was set alight by shell fire, and is now established at Trench location X.15.b.4.7. "B" Coy. advanced post to X.18.c.9.9. and X.16.b.1.C. Heavy opposition was met with, and both flanks became subject to enfilade fire from Meteren and Farm at X.18.d.7.9., which was a nest of machine guns. At the approach of daylight, as the moppers-up had failed to enter the town of Meteren, and as machine guns had not been dislodged from Farm on left, Coy. was compelled to dig in on this line. "C" Coy. advanced and established left flank at X.11.c.4.0., right flank advanced until held up by a nest of machine guns at X.16.d.7.9., which they promptly attacked, getting within 30 yards of Farm. Two Platoon leaders were wounded, and many other casualties occurred. Being unable to capture Farm, and finding right flank in the air, Platoon withdrew to original position, where right flank was subjected to enfilade fire, but is now in trench with "B" Coy. Artillery support was called for to assist advance on left. A barrage was put down at 2.59 a.m., lasting for ten minutes. At 2.30 a.m. "C" Coy. reported

1918.		that with exception of flank opposite X.16.a.7., they were in
April	24-25.	Red Line. "D" Coy. moved out from Coy. H. Qrs. at
(continued)		K.10.c.2.3. at 1.30 a.m., and reached a point opposite jumping-off place, but several hundred yards in rear. As "B" Coy. was held up, head of Coy. pushed up to head of "B" Coy. lines, and Lieut. Du Rieu attempted to push forward, becoming a casualty. Mopping-up party on left appeared to be held up as well. It being considered impossible to move, one platoon dug in, assisting "B" Coy. to consolidate this position. "D" Coy. then withdrew to position in support. Casualties: killed, 2 officers and 19 other ranks; wounded, 3 officers and 55 other ranks."
,,	28-29.	During night 10th Battalion relieved in line by 2nd Battalion.
,,	30.	Battalion moved to Divisional Reserve in Strazeele Sector. Casualties for month of April totalled 169 other ranks.
1918. May	1-3.	Battalion in reserve.
,,	4.	10th Battalion relieved 5th Battalion in reserve, Strazeele Sector.
,,	8-9.	Battalion relieved 12th Battalion in line, Strazeele Sector, right sector.
,,	12.	Lieut.-Colonel R. B. Jacob evacuated sick, and Major G. D. Shaw and subsequently temp. Lt.-Col. J. Newman temporarily commanded the Battalion.
,,	13-14.	Battalion relieved in line by 6th Battalion, and proceeded to Hondeghem Camp.
,,	18.	Battalion relieved by 3rd Battalion, and moved to Divisional Reserve area at Sercus.
,,	21.	Lieut.-Colonel M. Wilder-Neligan returned and assumed command of 10th Battalion.
,,	23.	10th Battalion sports held at Sercus.
,,	26.	10th Battalion relieved 6th Battalion at La Krule, near Hondeghem. Transport lines established near Hazebrouck.
,,	27-28.	During night Battalion relieved 2nd Battalion in line, Merris Sector.
,,	30.	A minor operation was carried out during the night, three counter-attacks being repulsed. Casualties: killed, 2 officers and 10 other ranks; wounded, 4 officers and 52 other ranks. Lieut.-Colonel M. Wilder-Neligan reported: "Object: To advance line and capture enemy posts running from E.6.c.05.70., E.6.c.4.0.-E.6.a.50.15. to E.6.a.35.00. Before operation our line, which advanced on night of 28-29th May, ran E.6.a.10.10-E.6.a.30.30.-E.6.a.75.80.-W.30.c.80.10.-X.25.c.70.30. "B" Coy. held line from E.6.a.10.10. to E.6.a.75.80., and "A" Coy. from E.6.a.75.80. to X.25.c.70.30., with "C" Coy. in support line. "D" Coy. was selected to send out strong fighting patrols with instructions, if possible, to take and consolidate line mentioned in para one (Objects). 11.30 p.m. was selected as zero hour, and artillery support consisting of "hurricane bursts" on objective and Mont De Merris was arranged. Also small

BATTALION CHRONOLOGY 77

1918.
May 30.
(continued)

and medium trench mortars and special rifle grenade protection was arranged. Lieut. A. T. Hill, M.C., in command of "D" Coy. decided to use 3 Platoons to advance in lines of sections, and to keep one Platoon in support to reinforce and help consolidate, if necessary. The jumping-off line was selected on line E.6.a.10.10. to E.6.a.30.30., and was taped out by "B" Coy. early in evening. At 11.15 p.m. "D" Coy. reported on tape line without incident. At 11.30 p.m. our artillery opened "hurricane bombardment," many shells falling short, and I regret to state 2 officers and 20 other ranks casualties are attributed to this. However, the Platoons of "D" Coy. pushed forward, great assistance being obtained from trench mortar and grenade fire. At 11.45 p.m. O.C. "D" Coy. reported having reached objective on left, after heavy fighting. The enemy offered considerable resistance, especially from machine guns, from their main line of defence. Lieut. C. J. Scott, M.C., led the Platoon, and showed great courage and initiative in gaining his objective. One prisoner of 57th I.R. was captured, and some other enemy were killed in hand to hand fighting in the post. The centre and right Platoons pushed forward under heavy machine gun fire from houses at E.6.c.30.40. and E.6.a.75.10. They however reached their objective, overcoming the enemy, who left their trenches with a view of resisting the attack. They however retired in disorder, leaving some dead on the northern side of the trench. The centre Platoon especially met with serious opposition, and O.C. "D" Coy. pushed forward support Platoon to reinforce this section. Lieut. W. H. Blake at this stage did excellent work; wounded in both hands by our own artillery in initial stages, he continued to lead his Platoon forward, and succeeded in capturing his objective. The right Platoon, under Lieut. W. H. Reid, M.C., continued to advance, and at 12.20 a.m. O.C. "D" Coy. reported having gained complete objective. Owing to enemy machine-gun fire, consolidation was exceptionally difficult. At this stage "B" Coy's. carrying parties carried forward wiring material, tools, bombs, and water in a most efficient manner, and consolidation was pushed forward. Owing to casualties it was decided to send forward one Platoon of "B" Coy., under Lieut. R. G. Smith, to assist in withstanding expected counter-attack, and to assist in consolidation. Lieuts. H. W. Reid, M.C., and A. H. Goode of "D" Coy. were wounded badly. Lieut. R. G. Smith was also slightly wounded, but remained on duty. At 1.20 a.m. the enemy made a counter-attack on our new left post which, after being hard pressed, succeeded in repulsing the attack. A German officer was killed (no papers) and several of the enemy. About 1.45 a.m. the enemy made an attempt to retake the right post, without result. A machine gun was captured on the Company first reaching the objective, and at about 1.45 p.m. a second machine gun was taken in front of our new

1918.		lines. Lieut. W. H. Blake (wounded in both hands) was, to a
May	30.	large extent, responsible for this. He succeeded in bombing
(continued)		the gun team, which had been very troublesome, and the belt and lock were brought back to our lines, the gun team having been scuppered. Owing to casualties in officers, Lieut. T. L. Corcoran was sent forward to "D" Coy., but I regret to say that he was badly wounded shortly after joining the Coy., and has since died of wounds. Just before dawn the enemy employed a number of Minenwerfers, and harassed the working party somewhat. They however succeeded in linking up the posts, and when dawn broke the position had been consolidated, and a light belt of wire had been placed along the front. Great assistance was rendered throughout by O.C. "B" Coy., Capt. R. K. Hurcombe, M.C., through whose Company Lieut. A. T. Hill, M.C., led his men. I regret to report that Lieut. A. T. Hill, M.C., O.C. "D" Coy. was badly wounded at dawn, and has since died of wounds. The great leadership of this officer was marked throughout the operation, and his loss is much felt in the Battalion. A Headquarters battery, under command of the R.S.M., and consisting of cooks, batmen, runners, etc., were responsible for excellent work with No. 36 rifle grenades, and greatly assisted the advance, and also the silencing of enemy machine guns. These men had been specially trained during the Battalion's rest in the rear area, with a view of assisting in these operations. Although only one prisoner was sent to the rear during the operation, the enemy suffered severely, and many dead are lying in and around the new line. Our total casualties amount to 2 officers killed, 5 officers wounded, 10 other ranks killed and 47 other ranks wounded. I wish to place on record my high appreciation of the assistance rendered by the 3rd A.L.T.M.B. The guns employed were under the direct supervision of Lieut. T. A. Miles, M.C. The Officer Commanding the Battery, Capt. A. J. Newlands, M.C., remained at my Headquarters throughout the earlier stages of the operation, but later personally guided parties carrying ammunition to guns. Some very fine work was done by the stretcher bearers of this Unit, under very difficult and adverse conditions. Some recommendations for immediate rewards for your favourable consideration will be forwarded by a later despatch. It is proposed to forward the names of 2 N.C.O's. with a view of their obtaining immediate commissions for gallantry in the field. A map showing advances made by the Battalion on night 28-29th, and night 29-30th is attached."
,,	31.	Congratulations received by 10th Battalion from Army Corps, Divisional, and Brigade Commanders.
1918.		
June	1.	10th Battalion in line, Merris Sector.
,,	2-3.	On night of 2nd-3rd, operation was carried out and flanks were pushed forward. Three enemy machine guns and 21 prisoners

1918.	were captured by Platoon on right flank, and 5 machine guns
June 2-3.	and 10 prisoners by Platoon on left flank. Lieut.-Colonel M.
(continued)	Wilder-Neligan reported: "In conjunction with the advance of

the 11th Battalion on Mont de Merris on night of 2nd-3rd June, this Battalion pushed forward with the advance and established posts at E.6.c.70. to E.6.c.95.80. on the right flank, and E.6.b.95.70 on the left flank. The Intelligence Section of this Battalion moved out and laid jumping-off tapes across the front and also forward, marking the advance. At 11.35 p.m. the tapes had been placed on position, and at 12.30 a.m. the 11th Battalion had been guided on to the tapes by our Intelligence personnel. All occupied posts in the line of advance were flagged to avoid the advancing troops meeting our own in mistake. All possible wire was cut before zero hour to allow the attacking companies to pass through. The signals communication were undertaken by this Battalion, and throughout communication was maintained. The Platoons of "A" and "C" Coys. engaged in the advance on the flanks were quick in following the barrage, and at zero plus 21 minutes, the Platoon on the left was reported in position, having taken 5 enemy machine guns and 10 prisoners, and gave help to the flanks. This Platoon then sent out fighting patrols. Shortly after this Platoon on the right flank reported success in gaining their objective. This Platoon took 3 enemy machine guns and 21 prisoners, their work being exceptionally good in view of the fact that they advanced and took a large farm house without casualties. Consolidation and connecting of flanks were pushed forward, and at the ceasing of artillery barrage a strong defensive position had been established. The prisoners were found to be of the 57th and 13th Regiments, and a few taken on the right were of the 50th Regiment; information of identity being forwarded to Brigade 15 minutes after zero hour. A special battery of Headquarters details did exceptionally good work in assisting with barrage. The Battery was under charge of the R.S.M. of this Battalion, and whom, I regret to say, was wounded after performing excellent duty with grenades, and then carrying out a very fine patrol to the front of the 1st objective. Very little resistance was made by the enemy during the advance, and in nearly all cases prisoners came in freely, having been unmistakably surprised during a relief. Forward battle dumps containing the undermentioned stores were established by this Battalion on night of 1st-2nd June, and on zero night were moved immediately after the advance from W.30.c.85.00. to E.6.b.45.85., and from E.6.a.15.35. to E.6.a.75.15. by a Platoon of "D" Coy. of this Battalion. Throughout, the work done by these parties was excellent, and at 3 a.m. all stores had been moved forward. Lieut. F. J. S. Mead, D.C.M., of "D" Coy. played an exceptionally brilliant part in the moving of these dumps. Over 200 prisoners passed through this Battalion

1918. June (continued)	2-3.	Headquarters, and escorts were organized accordingly. I would emphasize the extreme value of a mobile H.Q. Section of from 29 upwards of Rifle Grenadiers. The rapidity and ease with which these grenadiers can move from point to point is of the greatest tactical value. It was found during a previous operation that 24 rifle grenades per man was not an undue load. Our casualties for the operation were exceptionally light, and 2 killed and 1 wounded only were recorded by the attacking Platoons. In other companies and carrying parties the casualties were also very light. Total casualties were: killed 2, and wounded 9. Lieut. F. E. Rice and 2nd Lieut. H. L. Cleworth, and R.S.M. E. A. Holland were wounded during the operation."
,,	3-4.	10th Battalion relieved in line by 11th Battalion, and moved into supports at Pradelles.
,,	4-5.	Battalion relieved in supports by 8th Battalion, and moved to Rouge Croix.
,,	7.	Battalion relieved by 4th Battalion, and moved to Sercus.
,,	10.	Battalion moved to Blaringhem, where sports were held.
,,	11.	Battalion moved back to Sercus.
,,	12.	Brigade sports held, 10th Battalion winning the Challenge Cup. The 10th gained 49 marks; the 12th, 26; the 9th, 22; and the 11th, 11.
,,	15.	Precautionary measures adopted. Battalion moved back to La Krule and bivouacked.
,,	16.	Battalion at La Krule; nothing happened.
,,	17.	Battalion near Borre, with Brigade in line, and 10th Battalion in reserve; transport lines at Hazebrouck.
,,	18-25.	Battalion undergoing training and fatigues.
,,	25-26.	Battalion relieved 11th Battalion in line, Merris Sector. Casualties for month totalled 204 other ranks.
,,	28.	Minor operation carried out near Merris on morning of 28th June, 1918. Lieut.-Colonel M. Wilder-Neligan reported: "Orders in connection with an attack by the Division in the sector on right of 3rd Brigade front were received, and instructions therein ordered an attack on Merris, to be simulated in conjunction with the main attack. The method decided upon of conducting this attack was a demonstration against the enemy positions in front of Merris by rifle grenades, smoke bombs, and Lewis gun fire, in order to divert fire from being directed against the main attacking forces further south. In order to test the possibility of obtaining identification under cover of other operation, it was decided to push forward patrols at or about zero hour to our front. This was done. At 6 a.m. O.C. "C" Coy. (Major C. Rumball, M.C.) sent forward a patrol of Sergt. Leathly and 4 other ranks with a Lewis gun to examine, and if possible capture, an enemy post at E.6.d.10.60. On the trench mortar and rifle grenade barrage lifting at 6.5 a.m., three of this party under covering fire from the Lewis gun rushed the post, capturing 1 prisoner and killed two who tried to escape.

1918.		On the patrol returning and giving the information that an
June	28.	attack on a larger scale would in all probability be successful,
(continued)		it was decided to push out 1 Platoon to mop up enemy positions

along the hedge from E.6.d.10.60. to E.6.d.45.55. This was done at 6.45 a.m. by a Platoon in charge of Lieut. Bennett, and a post was established at E.6.d.45.55., several prisoners being taken. At 6.30 a.m. Lieut. H. W. Scudds, M.C., with one other rank, had captured a German machine gun and 5 prisoners at E.6.d.15.35., and No. 11 Platoon of "C" Coy. was pushed forward and established in this post. At 8.30 a.m. a Platoon of "A" Coy. was sent forward to assist "C" Coy., and if possible move forward. This Platoon was successful in this enterprise, under a light trench mortar and rifle grenade barrage, and local smoke screen worked with "P" bombs and ground flares, pushed forward and established at about E.6.d.35.70. At 8 a.m. the posts of "D" Coy. were moved forward in conjunction with the advance on right, and the line at the end of the first phase was established as per sketch attached. During the advance many enemy were killed, and some prisoners taken, also 6 enemy machine guns. At about mid-day the enemy made an attempt to retake his lost ground; he did this under heavy artillery fire, but failed to regain any portion of the captured position. Our casualties during the morning's operations were slight in comparison with the ground gained and the heavy casualties inflicted on the enemy. They were: 1 officer killed and 2 other ranks killed, 1 officer wounded and 10 other ranks wounded. The first phase of the operations concluded at about 1.30 p.m. Throughout it had been a success, and all objectives had been gained, in spite of heavy fighting, artillery, and machine gun fire. On examination of the position at the conclusion of the 1st phase it was found that, owing to the enemy still occupying positions in very close proximity to our own, it would be beneficial to still further push forward our line. A conference of Company Commanders was held, and 6 p.m. was decided upon as the zero hour for this further advance. The Brigade Major and Senior Artillery Liaison Officer discussed the matter with me in so far as artillery and other support was concerned. Two Platoons of "A" Coy. had been sent forward to assist "C" and "D" Companies in the morning, and the reserve company "B" was moved forward to the support line; "A" Coy. 11th Battalion being placed at my disposal to, if necessary, man the main line of resistance with my "B" Company. Orders were issued for a move forward to the line marked Green (see map attached). The method decided upon was to advance in lines of sections in file under cover of smoke screen and light barrage. This proved most successful, little opposition was encountered, and heavy casualties were inflicted on the enemy. By 7 p.m. the new line had been established and consolidated, and with the exception of patrol engagements the night passed

THE FIGHTING 10TH

1918.
June
(continued)

28. quietly. During the advance 9 enemy machine guns, 2 light Minenwerfers, and a large quantity of rifles, equipment, etc., were collected. Our casualties for the 24 hours were: 1 officer and 6 other ranks killed; 2 officers and 35 other ranks wounded. These include shell casualties in our reserve and support lines. Very severe casualties were inflicted on the enemy, the number killed being estimated at over 100. A number of prisoners, both unwounded and wounded, were taken during the operation. Throughout, the artillery support was excellent, although at one period short shooting was responsible for several of our casualties. A special feature of the operation was the excellent work carried out by the Battalion and Artillery signallers in mending broken wires, under heavy enemy fire. During the day of the 28th inst., very valuable work was carried out by carrying parties from the 11th Battalion, and by other parties drawn from Battalion Headquarters, details and batmen." During this operation 10th Battalion Transport Section first delivered rations to Coy Headquarters.

29. Congratulations received from Army and Corps Commanders.

"
1918.
July
"

1. 10th Battalion still in line, Merris Sector.
4. Battalion in line. Major G. D. Shaw, temporarily commanding 10th Battalion, reported: "Special report of enemy raid on night of July 4, 1918. At 9 p.m. on July 4, 1918, enemy put down a very heavy barrage of gas, 77's, 4·2's and 5·9 shells about 600 yards in depth along the whole of the Battalion front, and that of the 12th Battalion, and under cover of this attempted to raid Nos. 1 and 2 posts. Immediately the barrage came down the Battalion occupied its battalion position, and a request was 'phoned to artillery for counter-battery fire, which was turned on immediately. C.S.M. Storey of "A" Coy. was in the act of firing the S.O.S. when he was wounded by a shell, which destroyed the rifle and rocket. The raiding parties, numbering in all about 100 men, came from copse Sq.E.18.B., one about 20 strong attacked No. 1 post, were met with L.G. and rifle fire, and after suffering several casualties retired. A second party, 60 to 100 strong, which attacked No. 2 post, were met with machine gun (German light and Lewis), and rifle fire, and also enfilade fire from No. 1 post; this party also retired after suffering very heavily. The hedges and shell holes in front of Nos. 1 and 2 posts were searched continuously with No. 36 grenades for an hour, and the ground was swept at intervals with bursts of machine gun and rifle fire; in all 3,000 rounds of German machine gun ammunition, 2,000 rounds of S.A.A., and 30 boxes of No. 36 grenades were used. None of the enemy succeeded in penetrating our wire. Our casualties (4 killed and 6 wounded) were all caused by shell fire. Identification (normal) was obtained from enemy dead, and enemy stretcher bearers could be heard at work during the night."

BATTALION CHRONOLOGY

1918.		During night 10th Battalion was relieved by 4th Battalion,
July	5-6.	and moved to camp near Hondeghem.
,,	8.	Review Parade in honour of G.O.C. 3rd A.I. Brigade. Transport Section was present.
,,	21-22.	Battalion moved into line at Merris Sector, and relieved 11th Battalion.
,,	22.	Lieut.-Colonel M. Wilder-Neligan reported: "At 1 p.m. on 22nd inst. a patrol of 12 men with a Lewis gun, led by Lieut. W. D. Sharland, moved out from post at F.1.A.8.2., moving E. and S.E. This patrol after covering about 500 yards, surrounded and seized an enemy post, captured 8 unwounded prisoners and one machine gun. To exploit this success an Officer patrol of 12 men under Lieut. R. G. Smith, moved out in advance of the area covered by Lieut. Sharland at about 2 p.m., and at the same time a similar patrol under Lieut. C. S. Lightbody moved out from the right flank of the Right Coy. This patrol established a post at E.12.b.7.9. and proceeded to patrol the area E. and N.E. of this point. The left Coy. patrol, under Lieut. R. G. Smith, after proceeding S.E. 100 yards, met with considerable opposition from snipers and machine guns from either the church or monastery in Merris, and it was accordingly decided that further patrolling should be postponed until dusk. The left Coy. patrol returned to the left Coy. line, and Lieut. Lightbody established himself in a post at F.7.A.1.8. at 5.30 p.m. This patrol in moving from E.12.B.7.9. was also sniped at from the direction of Merris. During the afternoon, at 3.15, a small patrol under Lieut. A. P. Chittleborough moved out from E.6.D.4.4. towards E.6.D.9.3., where a small enemy post was located. At 9.30 p.m. patrolling operations were again commenced, with the object of locating enemy posts, improving the line, inflicting casualties, and obtaining identifications. Patrols of Platoon strength accordingly moved out from the right of the Right Coy., and the left of the Left Coy., the former moving E. and the latter S., the intention being to establish new posts along the line of patrol advance, and push forward further patrols from these newly-established posts, eventually linking up at about F.1.D.3.3. on Merris-Outtersteene Road. In the event of this operation being satisfactorily accomplished, the area between the patrol line and the original front line was intended to be mopped up backwards. In order to keep down sniping and machine-gun fire from Merris, which had been reported from several sources during the day, it was arranged that alternative 4·5 in. and 6 in. howitzers should drop into Merris every minute. It was considered that artillery fire on Merris would effectively mislead the enemy as to the possibility of any action of ours on the enemy side of Merris, and the success with which patrols penetrated a long distance into enemy country without attracting attention shows the value of

1918.
July 22.
(continued)

this plan. Reports were received up to 11.10 p.m. from both patrols that they were steadily moving towards the linking up point; at this hour a very heavy field gun barrage opened on the whole of our front. Counter battery work was immediately asked for, and the garrison of posts moved forward to avoid the barrage. As a result of these measures the barrage ceased at 11.26 p.m. without having inflicted more than two casualties. The operation meanwhile was proceeding satisfactorily, when at 11.50 p.m. an order was received from the Divisional Commander, through Brigade Headquarters, that Merris was not be be entered. Orders not to proceed with the operation were then sent to both companies. At this time the Left Coy. had reached its objective on the Merris-Outtersteene Road, while the Right Coy. patrol was moving forward 200 yards from the road, and had reported having taken prisoners and machine guns while mopping it up. In order that the benefits of the advance already made should not be entirely lost, both Companies were ordered to fall back to a "Pincer" line round Merris. The Right Coy. had no difficulty in carrying this order out, establishing its line of posts finally at E.12.B.7.9.-F.7.A.1.6.-F.1.C.1.1.-F.1.C.2.5.-F.1.C.1.8., but the Left Coy. as soon as it commenced its withdrawal, was heavily attacked. This withdrawal in face of an expectedly determined enemy, was a most delicate operation, and great credit devolves on Captain R. K. Hurcombe, M.C., and Coy. Commander, for the skilful way in which he handled the situation, personally leading and controlling the rear-guard action. When he reached the line laid down to form the left "pincer" he was still being harassed by the enemy, and the hour was too late to permit of the construction of good new posts, so he withdrew his Coy. back into the original line of posts. The operation was carried out throughout strictly in conformity with plan, and the ultimate withdrawal in obedience to the order of the Divisional Commander in no way mitigated its success. Between 60 and 70 of the enemy were killed, 4 prisoners (2 unwounded) taken, and one heavy trench mortar, two heavy machine guns, and four light machine guns captured; while our right flank was advanced 400 yards, and a corresponding advance made in alignment towards the left. Our total casualties for the entire operation were: 1 officer and 1 other rank killed, 1 officer and 6 other ranks wounded."

„ 29-30. During night Merris was captured by "A" and "B" Coys. of the 10th Battalion. 187 prisoners were taken, and only three casualties sustained.

„ 29-30. 3rd Brigade reported re capture of Merris. "At 12.14 a.m. artillery opened fire, 12.30, 10th Battalion asked for C.B. work, and at 12.31, 10th Battalion reported prisoners having been captured. At 12.35, 10th Battalion asked for standing

BATTALION CHRONOLOGY

1918.
July 29-30.
(continued)

barrage to be kept at the same rate for a while. At 12.41, artillery carried on normal programme; and at 12.42, 10th Battalion reported prisoners having "14" on shoulder straps. At 12.51, 10th Battalion reported gas barrage on the Battalion front; and at 12.45, 10th reported prisoners of 8th Coy., 14th I.R. At 1.9, 10th reported casualties very light. At 1.26, 10th asked that both barrages be lifted 50 yards after 2 plus 90; and at 1.29, 10th asked that lanes "A" and "B" be lifted 150 yards. At 1.30, lanes "C" and "D" were lifted another 50 yards. At 1.40, 10th Battalion reported Right Coy. again established contact in centre, from which they were driven by our shell fire. At 1.41 a.m., 10th Battalion reported 140 I.R. prisoners captured; and at 1.47, reported touch gained in centre and now digging in, all prisoners from left are 140th I.R. At 2.2, 10th Battalion reported small local counter-attack towards Gerbedoen Farm, and think they have dealt with it successfully. At 2.6, 10th Battalion asked for standing barrage to drop, and 1 Platoon of 11th Battalion to go to left line Coy. H.Q. At 2.17, 10th advised barrage can die down again; and at 2.28, 10th Battalion in touch with Coys. and report situation O.K. At 2.40, Battalion think that there are some Boche about Merris inside our lines—they are to clean these up by patrols after the shoot at 4.15 a.m. At 3.46, artillery fire opened, and at 3.47, 10th only want burst, so artillery told to slow down and stop. At 3.56, barrage ceased; and at 4.10, 10th Battalion O.K., and also O.K. at 4.13. At 7.30, 10th reported 2 officers and 143 other ranks passed through 10th lines and Battalion H.Q. as prisoners; also 1 officer and 6 other ranks wounded. At 9.10, 10th reported 2 machine guns still firing from centre of Merris, and is sending 2 Platoons to endeavour to bring them in. Estimated casualties: 2 officers wounded, 1 other rank killed and 31 other ranks wounded. Cannot get touch with enemy in front of Merris. Our men wiring still on our front. At 9.30, 10th Battalion reported machine gunners in Merris captured 1 officer and 27 other ranks in Merris; 5 machine guns captured in centre of Merris. At 10.10, 10th Battalion reported prisoners still being captured in Merris."

„ 29-30. Lieut.-Colonel M. Wilder-Neligan reported on capture of Merris: "Reference Map No. 9341 of 15/7/18. Object: The object proposed was to envelop the village of Merris by a simultaneous movement from the N.E. and S.W., and to establish a new line of posts east of Merris, at approximately F.7.A.30.95.; F.7.A.60.95.; F.7.V.10.99.; F.I.D.30.10; F.I.D.30.40; F.I.D.55.50; F.I.D.60.80; F.I.B.65.05. Method of Attack: For the attack two Companies of this Battalion ("A" and "B") were used, "A" Coy. moving out from right flank of the Battalion in an easterly direction, and "B" Coy. from the left flank in a southerly direction; Platoons being dropped at selected points to form a continuous line of posts

1918.
July 29-30.
(continued)

east of Merris. The remaining two Companies ("C" and "D") which were holding the line, continued to do so, and their line of posts, the original front line, after the objective had been gained became the support line. There was one novel feature in the scheme of attack. Merris itself was known to be occupied by two Coys.' H.Qs., with numerous machine guns located in cellars, so the following plan was adopted to deal with this dangerous area. A continuous howitzer and trench mortar fire was kept on the village during the time the Coys. were encircling it. At the end of an hour this ceased, to enable Merris to be mopped up, and at the end of a further hour commenced again. It was considered that a doubly valuable purpose would be served by this, to deal with any enemy who had evaded mopping up, and to mislead the enemy as to our actual position. That this ruse was fully successful is shown by several different incidents. A captured message from one of the Coy. Commanders time 5.30 a.m., stated that he held Merris, but that the situation was very obscure. One of our runners on leaving a post in the front line at 5 a.m., walked into a party of the enemy which was occupying a hedge, and was captured. This party knew nothing about our position, and when captured soon after, were much surprised. The bombardment of Merris was again stopped at 4.25 a.m. to enable the village to be mopped up a second time. On both occasions the "moppers up" were able to surprise the enemy, who throughout were quite in the dark as to our position. The novelty of the plan adopted undoubtedly appealed to the men and served to increase their confidence. The Attack: Zero was fixed for 12.15 a.m. on night 29-30th July, and the Left Company in moving up to its jumping-off position, which had been previously dug, sustained casualties by artillery fire to 1 officer and 11 other ranks—all the Platoon which was to gain touch with the Right Coy. and occupy the post furthest from the old line. This necessitated a reorganization of the Company, but as Companies moved to their jumping-off positions in ample time, the reorganization was satisfactorily accomplished before zero hour. At zero the attacking Coys. moved forward under a barrage, and keeping well up to the barrage, with excellent direction, the objective was reached and contact gained at 12.36 a.m. At 1.28 a.m. Right Coy. reported that our artillery was falling short, and that it has been necessary to evacuate the right posts at F.7.B.10.99. and F.I.D.30.10. The artillery lifted, the Right Coy. regained touch with the Left Coy., and the work of consolidation proceeded under cover of Lewis guns. The Barrage: At least one battery in the artillery barrage commenced firing between 3 and $3\frac{1}{2}$ minutes before zero, which made the opening of the barrage ragged and irregular. By zero hour the barrage had become regular and intense, and was well maintained from thence onwards. It is thought, however, that the opening of barrage of this kind, i.e., in lanes, should be

1918.
July 29-30.
(continued)

absolutely synchronized, otherwise it is quite possible for it to be from 100 to 200 yards ahead in parts of lanes, or that part of lane for which barrage opened too soon, and has therefore passed on in sufficient time for the enemy to recover from the surprise, and thus liable to cause a hold-up in the attack. Craters: The cratering of road by "heavies" does not appear to have been successful. Until aerial photos are available it is not possible to locate the actual craters formed. It is known, however, that no craters were formed sufficiently near to the objective line on the main Merris-Outtersteene Road to have been of any value to the troops. A valuable crater was discovered on the right leading from Merris to Albert Crossing, but it is thought this was formed at an earlier date, owing to so much water being in it. Vickers Machine Guns: A carefully prepared programme of covering fire with two four-gun and two two-gun batteries was, in the main, most accurately carried out. A little short shooting was noticed from the right during preparation shoot, which was reported to the O.C. Machine Gun Battalion, and corrected. Trench Mortars: The 3rd A.L.T.M.B. rendered most valuable assistance in the bombardment of Merris, and in dealing with special strong points in preliminary work. An unusually large quantity of ammunition was got up to the guns prior to the attack, and this enabled the mortars to fire continously for a long period. The principle of having two silent guns on the extreme flank of the attack was found valuable, as these guns were not interfered with owing to no flash giving away their positions, consequently were later able to deal with enemy machine guns on the flanks which were clear of the actual barrage line. This was most effectively done, especially on the right. Dumps: A dump was made on each flank of the Battalion front prior to the attack, and as the flank posts in the scheme of attack did not have to advance, this meant that each of the attacking Coys. had a dump in its own lines. The system, however, was not entirely satisfactory owing to the fact that in moving stores forward congestion occurred at the dumps. Men when endeavouring to pick out No. 36 grenades often picked up boxes of 23's, and finding out that they had the wrong boxes threw them down indiscriminately on top of wire, S.A.A., and other stores. This caused unnecessary work to other parties coming along in sorting out the stuff to obtain what they required. I am of the opinion that it is essential before an attack to have a specially trained N.C.O. in charge of a dump, to supervise issue of stores, and take no other part in the attack whatever. Each of these dumps contained the following: 20 coils French wire, 40 coils barbed concertina, 20 boxes S.A.A. (ordinary), 5 boxes Bundles packed S.A.A., 50 boxes No. 36 grenades, 20 boxes No. 23 grenades, 100 short corkscrews, 20 tins water, 2 boxes Very lights, 5 S.O.S. signals, 50 shovels, 15 picks, 32 L.G. magazines (filled). In addition 200 boxes of grenades, 80 coils

1918.
July 29-30.
(continued)

of wire, 20 boxes S.A.A. were placed in a dump at a point central to both forward dumps. Resistance: In most instances this was more robust than usual, and as the attack developed, the enemy apparently became confident that it had failed owing to the reopening of shelling of Merris. Considerable trouble was given by parties of the enemy, numbering from 25 to 50 men, who were obviously moving up to reinforce. Both officers and men of these parties seemed to have no idea that the village had been captured. This I entirely attribute to the shelling of Merris after the cessation of artillery barrage. Identification: The prisoners taken belonged to the 4th Division, and represented the following regiments: 14th J.R.; 57th R.I.R.; 140th J.R.; and 19th Machine Gun Coy. Particulars of identification were reported to Brigade Headquarters within half an hour of the opening of the attack. Prisoners and Killed: The number of prisoners taken totalled 5 officers and over 200 other ranks, and the number of enemy killed is estimated at between 200 and 300. As an example, in front of No. 7 post (see attached map), no less than 47 dead Germans were counted, and in front and on flanks of No. 3 post 61 dead were counted. These are merely examples of similar instances that occurred along the whole line. Signals: 5-legged ladder lines, metallic lines, a buried cable, a direct line, and two loop sets were used. The loop sets did good work, but communication was hard to maintain with the left flank owing to splinters hitting one of these sets. On the whole communication was well kept. Light Signals: The Light Signals were not altogether satisfactory. They did not rise to a sufficient altitude, and the various colours are not easily read during battle, being too liable to be mistaken for enemy signals. It is suggested that the Mortared Light—a long tail with many colours—which was in use about 12 months ago, be revived, as a group of colours can be altered by Battalions to suit their own arrangements. Incendiary Shells: The incendiary shells were most effective, two or three appeared to have been overtimed and ricocheted before exploding. It is a valuable and easily seen signal. Casualties: As referred to previously, there were 1 officer and 11 other ranks wounded moving up to the jumping-off position. In the actual operation the total casualties were 4 other ranks killed, 30 other ranks wounded, and 1 officer wounded. Most of these were accounted for by after shelling. Material Captured: Over 20 machine guns were actually brought in, and many more, also trench mortars, were left on the ground. In addition a large quantity of rifles, bombs, etc., are in and between old enemy posts. Mopping Up: The system of mopping up by small parties within limited areas from old front line proved most effective. A special Platoon detailed to mop up the actual village of Merris did valuable work. I would like to point out this Platoon was composed almost entirely of Headquarter's details,

BATTALION CHRONOLOGY 89

1918.
July 29-30.
(continued)

viz., batmen, pioneers, cooks, etc. Suggested Movement of Enemy Artillery: From several different posts on the night following the attack sounds of heavy traffic, resembling the movement of guns, were reported at about 10 p.m. Taken in conjunction with the excessive and wild expenditure of ammunition during the whole of the day succeeding the attack, suggesting that the enemy was disposing of all he had in the gunpits, the conclusion is that he moved his guns back on night 30th-31st July. Formations: Platoons moved forward between lanes of artillery along the objective line in file, with approximately 150 yards between Platoons. Two scouts took the lead, and flank guards carrying Lewis guns were posted on each flank. The leap-frog method of passing Platoons through was adopted. It was thought and proved to be correct, that this would lend additional confidence to Platoons moving to the attack, as they would know that a complete chain of communication held between them and our general line. General: The combined strength of the two attacking Companies was less than the actual number of prisoners taken. Towards dawn enemy reinforcements began to arrive from the direction of the Becque. In the main, few of these were permitted to reach our own new line of posts. From the fact that they came forward by hedges and along tracks in close formation with rifles slung, it would appear they were still under the impression that Merris was in their hands. This is again substantiated by the fact that an officer and his runner (the officer carrying a walking stick) were allowed to actually walk into one of our new posts. The Intelligence Officer of this unit, when returning from the front line, came across a party of between 30 and 40 Germans moving between our old and new front lines. From the quiet way in which they were moving, the I.O. imagined them to be prisoners, but when getting a nearer view, discovered they had no escort. A few men were immediately obtained from the new posts, who attacked the party in rear and captured most of them. Two or three distinct counter-attacks were attempted, one against No. 3 post, and one against No. 7 post, also old No. 8 post. In each case the attacks failed, and heavy casualties were inflicted on enemy. A strong post was still holding out after daylight, at about F.I.C. Central; but this was captured by an N.C.O. and 5 men, and yielded 1 officer and 27 other ranks prisoners, 15 killed, and 5 machine guns. They were attacked from their rear, and were obviously under the impression that our line had not advanced. It was discovered in the course of mopping up the village of Merris that there were three shafts leading to dugouts under the Asylum, and as the occupants seemed disinclined to come out, an ample supply of "P" bombs were flung down same, with the result all three shafts were left in flames. At various times during the operation, and on the day succeeding it, enemy machine guns firing on to our old and new posts from the flanks were

1918.
July 29-30.
(continued)

engaged, silenced, and captured. Some of these guns were stubbornly contested by the enemy, and were by no means easy to deal with. A heavy fog during the morning allowed wiring and digging to be pushed on with until nearly 8 o'clock, by which time all posts were at least 5 feet deep, and sufficiently wired to prevent surprise attacks. At least one enemy M.G. was mounted in each of these posts, and were freely used against the enemy. The enemy shelling during the actual attack was weak and scattered, and caused no serious inconvenience; machine guns, however, from the flanks were fairly active. An endeavour was made to silence enemy batteries shelling our posts during the day following the attack, but the counter battery work seemed weak and did not have any appreciable effect in reducing his shelling. The early morning hot meal was delivered to the men in the new posts before daylight. This was done by placing hot food containers, filled with stew, on the battle dumps a few minutes before the operation commenced. In most cases these containers were actually moved forward with the attack. The food was much appreciated by the men, and undoubtedly assisted in reducing their attitude to normal after the excitement of the attack. The whole operation appealed very much to the imaginations of the men, and unquestionably increased their interest and greatly added to their dash in the execution of the operation. I wish to put on record the daring and masterly leadership of both Captain R. K. Hurcombe, M.C., and Captain W. F. J. McCann, M.C., also the brilliant work accomplished by Lieut. A. MacNeil, D.S.O., in fighting his Stokes Mortars. Many other names have come before me in connection with the operation, and a list of recommendations will be forwarded as soon as these can be compiled. Lessons Learnt: Large dumps are not a complete success; small dumps containing different kinds of ammunition and stores are better. In the dark it is impossible to distinguish boxes of No. 23 grenades from 36's. It is suggested that either the boxes of 23's or 36's be painted a different colour. Our steel hats are very easily picked out even at a considerable distance, unless absolutely stationary. Reports go to show that the German helmet is less easily seen, probably owing to the fact that the brim of our helmet has such a very clear-cut line. Camouflaging of helmets by covering them with sacking is not very effective, except in wet weather; even helmets that are "sanded" usually reflect light. More aerial photographs down to section Commanders should be available before a minor operation of this nature. All ranks can now read aerial photos moderately well, and such photos are particularly valuable in distinguishing hedges from ditches, picking up German posts and traps, and verifying locations of objectives. The loop set of Trench Wireless would, if more known and greater number be available, be far more valuable than any number of lines.

BATTALION CHRONOLOGY

1918. July 29-30. (continued)		They should, however, if possible be protected from splinters, which could easily be done after dark on the night of an operation, if the ground did not allow of adequate emplacements being built. Appendices Attached: Battalion Operation Order No. 109, Diary kept during the operation, Map No. 9341 and Intelligence Officer's Report."
„	30-31.	10th Battalion relieved in line at Merris by 8th Battalion, and moved to Hondeghem.
1918. August	1.	10th Battalion strength: 45 officers and 715 other ranks.
„	1.	Battalion left Hazebrouck at 8.30 p.m. and embussed to Heurighem, arriving at 11 p.m.
„	6.	Battalion marched to Wizernes, and entrained for the Somme at 1815.
„	7.	At 0530 Battalion detrained at Pont Remy and marched to Cocquerel. Battalion left Cocquerel by bus, and transport proceeded by road. Battalion arrived at Poulanville at 0100.
„	8.	Battalion left Poulanville at 1430 and arrived at trenches near Hamel about 2200.
„	9.	Battalion left Hamel-Bayonvillers-Gillducourt, and bivouacked near Harbonnieres. Lieut.-Colonel M. Wilder-Neligan reported: "On the night 9-10th August the 10th Battalion arrived in bivouac position near Harbonnieres, and orders were received that the advance was to be continued at 8.0 a.m. on the morning of 10/8/18 with a view to capturing the Blue Line (see attached map). The order of battle was 9th Battalion on Right, 11th Battalion on Left, 10th Battalion Right Support, and 12th Battalion Left Support. At 6.30 a.m. the 10th Battalion commenced the advance in artillery formation, and were disposed in support of 9th Battalion at zero hour, and the orders received were to move 1,000 yards in rear of the attacking battalions. Early in the attack it was seen that the attacking battalions had to a certain extent lost direction. It was therefore decided to push on the 10th Battalion to a very close support in order that, if necessary, flanks could be protected. The Battalion was therefore disposed in trenches X.29.b. and d. From this point a complete view of the battle was obtained. It was observed that the objective had not been reached, and that a stiff fight was taking place in the area of Crepey Wood, which seemed to be held strongly by the enemy; further the left battalion appeared to be in considerable difficulty, and had made a small advance only. The Brigade on our right also appeared to be held up in the neighbourhood of the Railway Line. At about 9.30 a.m. touch was gained with the Headquarters of the 9th Battalion, and I was informed that they would require assistance to clear up the situation in Crepey Wood. I therefore sent "A" Coy. 10th Battalion to carry out this operation. Capt. W. F. J. McCann, M.C., O.C., "A" Coy., was sent back to 9th Battalion Headquarters to receive instructions from Lieut.-

1918. August (continued)	9.	Col. Mullin, D.S.O., under whose command this Coy. had now passed. Capt. McCann accordingly went forward and worked through the wood from south to north; heavy opposition was encountered, and all four platoons of the Coy. had to be used in the attack. A platoon of the 5th Battalion reported at this stage to Capt. McCann, who used them as support for his attack. As "A" Coy. moved forward and cleared each portion of the wood, posts were established along the northern and eastern edges of the wood, four of which were occupied by "A" Coy. and the remainder by the 9th Battalion. At about 4.0 p.m. on the same day, after a heavy bombardment, the enemy launched a counter-attack against Crepey Wood, during which two out of the four of "A" Coy's. posts were completely blown out, and the posts occupied by the 9th Battalion evacuated. The remaining two posts of "A" Coy. garrisoned by Capt. McCann, one other Officer, and 7 men, put up a strong resistance to the enemy, and after one hour's strong fighting the attack was driven off, leaving 90 of the enemy dead in this area. During this period "A" Coy. suffered casualties to the extent of 3 Officers killed, 12 other ranks killed, and 16 other ranks wounded."
„	10-11.	Lieut.-Colonel M. Wilder-Neligan reported: "During the night 10-11th August an order was received that an attack would be carried out by the 10th and 12th Battalions under the command of C.O. 10th Battalion with the object of reaching the Blue Line. Zero hour was fixed for 4.0 a.m., which allowed very little time for preparation. The order of battle was: 2 Coys. 10th Battalion on right, 1 Coy. 12th Battalion on left, 2 Coys. 12th Battalion in support, 1 Coy. 12th Battalion in reserve, 2 sections Vickers guns on right, 1 section Vickers guns on left, 3 tanks supporting right of the attack, and 1 tank supporting left of the attack. A slow artillery barrage commenced at Zero, lifting 100 yards every three minutes. (For barrage line see attached map.) The morning was very misty and dark, and great difficulty was experienced in maintaining direction. Touch had not been gained with the battalion of brigade operating on our right, it therefore became necessary to extend our flank to cover the whole of village of Lihons, which it was recognised would be dangerous to leave open. Up to this hour one tank only had reported; the remainder did not turn up until 5.0 a.m., their officers complaining that they had no maps, consequently guides had to be provided them. The barrage was effective, and at 5.15 a.m. the final objective had been reached, the main opposition being experienced in Auger Wood. Throughout the whole attack strong concentrations of enemy machine-gun fire hampered the movement of our troops. In the main, however, his fire was high and did not cause many casualties. As the attack progressed machine gun fire became less concentrated, chiefly owing to the fact that a considerable

BATTALION CHRONOLOGY

1918.
August 10-11.
(continued)

number of guns were captured and the crews killed. My right Company, after passing through the village of Lihons, put out of action the crews of some light field guns, which were on the eastern side of the village. At 5.15 a.m. it was found that both flanks were in the air; patrols were sent out to endeavour to gain touch with the 8th Battalion on the right and the 11th Battalion on the left, These patrols were working for over an hour before touch was gained. At about 6.0 a.m. an Officer of the 8th Battalion came into touch with my Right Company Commander and asked him if he could still hold the area in front of Lihons as he was unable to gain touch with his own men to the right. My Right Company agreed to do this until the 8th Battalion could get up into position. By 7 a.m. this flank was secure, and the 8th Battalion took over a portion of my Right, thus freeing troops in order to create a spare line. A quarter of an hour later my line was re-adjusted and a spare line was established, but it was then discovered that a gap of over 1,000 yards existed between my left and the remainder of the Brigade. Touch was gained with the C.O's. 11th and 12th Battalions, and they were asked to assist in filling up this gap by swinging forward their flanks. About this time a series of counter-attacks developed against my left, and a number of the enemy succeeded in breaking through the gap on my left flank. To deal with this situation I sent forward the remaining Company of the 10th Battalion ("D" Coy.) to assist my "A" Coy. (attached to 9th Battalion) to hold their ground, and the reserve Company of the 12th Battalion was also ordered to move up and endeavour to fill the gap. Some fierce fighting took place between Crepey Wood and the new line in the course of which heavy casualties were inflicted on the enemy and a good number of prisoners taken. In order to strengthen the support line the Brigade Mining Coy. was sent forward and took up a position behind Crepey Wood, and placed under the command of Major MacPherson, of the 12th Battalion, to be used as a last resort. At this stage Colonel Stevens, of the 2nd Battalion, visited my Headquarters, and he was asked to move a Company of his battalion into the Red Line. He stated he was unable to do this without authority from his own Brigade. Close touch was at all times maintained with the C.O's. 9th and 11th Battalions, and they were kept posted as to the situation as it developed. The main brunt of the attack was against Crepey Wood and Hospital in S.19. At about this time a further counter-attack in considerable force was seen to be in preparation in the woods in Square S.20. It is estimated that at least 1 battalion of the enemy was employed for this counter-attack. An artillery was placed down in this square, and a very heavy machine-gun fire was brought to bear on the advancing troops, with the result that the enemy was unable to reach our lines in any force. Very heavy casualties must have been inflicted on the enemy. Our

1918.
August 10-11.
(continued)

field of fire was so good that any of the enemy moving in the open could not fail to be caught in the M.G. barrage employed. Against this, however, the enemy had ample opportunity of getting close to our lines by utilising the very complicated system of trenches in this area. From thence on a constant succession of counter-attacks developed, mainly against our left, and at times small parties got through our lines, but invariably these were either killed or ejected. The greatest credit is due to Capt. McCann and his Coy., who were attached to the 9th Battalion, and that part of the 9th Battalion under Lieut. Miers, in repulsing these attacks. These troops were so heavily engaged throughout the day that they were unable to be utilised to fill the gap. The C.O. 11th Battalion was asked if he could assist by sending forward a Company, but it appears his troops were equally as much involved, consequently the remainder of the 12th Battalion under Capt. Jorgensen were sent forward to report to Capt. McCann, and the latter was instructed to dispose this Company on the left to the best possible advantage, with a view to creating a defensive flank. This was eventually done, with the result by 4.0 p.m. a general line was established which left no gap of sufficient dimensions to cause further anxiety. Late in the afternoon Col. Stevens, C.O. 2nd Battalion, informed me he had received orders to move his battalion into the Red Line as support to the Brigade. I am not aware of the time that this move was completed as no liaison was maintained between my Headquarters and the 2nd Battalion. During the first two hours of the operation my Right Flank appeared to be in grave danger owing to the fact that the 8th Battalion on my right did not gain touch until late in the afternoon. The Brigade front between squares S.19 and W.24 was a constant source of danger, and it is thought this could have been rectified had necessary touch been maintained with the left of my attack by troops occupying this area. A series of remarks is appended for various arms attached to me for the operation. Artillery: For the advance on morning 11th inst. artillery barrage was very well arranged and carried out. It was thick and regular, and no difficulty was experienced in keeping close to it. Later in the day, however, when artillery assistance was called for by the battalion on Right of 10th Battalion, great trouble was caused to both 10th Battalion Line Coys. by our own fire, several posts having to be evacuated in consequence. This was soon cleared up and the range re-adjusted. Vickers M.G's.: One section of Vickers M.G's. was attached to each of the attacking battalions and advanced with the attacking companies. Taking up positions in the front line they were able to render valuable assistance during consolidation by their protective fire. Trench Mortars: One section of the 3rd Trench Mortar Battery was attached to attacking battalions and proved of value in dealing with wooded country on the left during the period enemy was

BATTALION CHRONOLOGY 95

1918.
August 10-11.
(continued)

preparing to launch a counter-attack. Tanks: The Tanks attached to me for the operation would have been of vast assistance if liaison could have been maintained. They, however, were over an hour late and very uncertain of the role they had to play in the operation. The first two Tanks to report to me were sent to the village of Lihons, as it was doubtful whether this village had been properly mopped up, and orders were given to continually promenade the streets until the mist lifted, or until they were certain that no considerable number of enemy were left behind. Small mopping-up parties of such troops as could be spared were also sent into the village to assist these tanks. The two other tanks did good work round about Auger Wood and in front of Crepey Wood, and one tank was ordered to move in front of the 11th Battalion and assist them. The Commander of this Tank, however, reported that if this work was carried out his tank was practically certain to become a casualty as it was then too light. The order was therefore cancelled and the tank released. Communication: Owing to the fact that very little information was available from the left, communication was established between the Coy. of 10th Battalion attached to the 9th Battalion and my Headquarters direct, and this information was passed to the C.O. 9th Battalion as it became available. Carrying Parties: The 3rd Brigade Mining Coy. under Capt. Richardson acted as carrying party for the attacking battalions, and great praise is due to them for their untiring efforts throughout the morning of the attack. This Company also assisted later in the day in repelling an enemy counter-attack. Prisoners: Owing to the continual alteration in dispositions of the various units engaged in the advance, it is impossible to give a definite number of prisoners captured. Casualties: The casualties of the 10th Battalion during the whole operation totalled 3 Officers and 29 other ranks killed, 60 other ranks wounded, and 11 other ranks missing. The enemy casualties were heavy, particularly in the vicinity of Crepey Wood; here the ground was specially thick with their dead bodies. Material Captured: This has not been co-ordinated, but a considerable number of machine guns, some field guns, a large canteen in Lihons, transport wagons, and a quantity of equipment, rifles, etc., were captured. At no time during the operation were there any men to spare to collect captured material, with the result the bulk of the material was left on the ground, and was no doubt collected by the 2nd Battalion after they relieved the troops engaged in the area in question. Identification: Prisoners captured belonged to the 21st Bavarian I.R., 5th Division; 19th Bavarian I.R., 5th Division; 26th R.I.R., 109th Division, and 94th I.R., 38th Division. General: It is apparent that the enemy made no preparation for a retirement, as everywhere in the course of the advance it was noticed he had cleared out hurriedly, leaving equipment, meals on

1918. August 10-11. (continued)		tables, and other gear, all of which pointed to the surprise of the attack. Attached is a copy of the relief order issued to the elements of Brigade when relieved by the 2nd Battalion, which will make clear the disposal of the troops at the conclusion of the day's operations. I would like to place on record the exceptional good work done by the C.O., Officers and men of the 12th Battalion. Major McPherson throughout the operation gave his whole-hearted support. His Headquarters were established in Evacuation Valley, where a general Report centre was formed. Some recommendations for immediate awards will be forwarded as soon as possible. I have asked the C.O. 12th Battalion to forward his own recommendations direct to Brigade."
,,	11-12.	10th Battalion relieved in line at Lihons by 2nd Battalion.
,,	12-13.	10th Battalion proceeded during night into line again.
,,	13.	Battalion moved to Harbonnieres, "D" Coy. being temporarily disbanded, half joining "A" Coy. and the other half "B" Coy.
,,	14-15.	During night 10th Battalion moved into supports. Bombs in Transport lines: 5 men and 8 horses being wounded.
,,	15-16.	During night Battalion left Harbonnieres for Vaire.
,,	21.	Battalion left Vaire and proceeded to Brigade Reserve near Morcourt.
,,	22-23.	Battalion went forward to jumping-off line. Lieut.-Colonel M. Wilder-Neligan reported: "At 1 a.m. Battalion moved to R.10, companies being situated approximately as follows: "A" Coy., R.19.d.3.7.; "C" Coy., 4.Q0.b.3.3.; "B" Coy. in rear; H.Q. Coy. in Battalion H.Q. at R.19.a.3.4. During the morning "A" and "B" Coys. assisted 1st Brigade in clearing Luc Wood. They established a line on left flank of 1st Brigade, 500 yards in advance of Luc Wood. Having on afternoon of 21st August moved from Vaire to trenches near Morcourt, orders were received on following day that an attack would be made by the 1st Australian Division on morning of 23rd August. A copy of the 3rd Aus. Inf. Brigade Operation Order (No. 139) is attached. As the 3rd Brigade was to carry out the second phase of the attack Units moved forward on night 22-23rd August; the 10th Infantry Battalion occupying position at and near R.8.C.8.2. Zero hour was 4.45 a.m. on 23/8/18, and at 6.10 a.m. an order was received that the 10th Battalion would protect the Left flank of the Left Brigade. Accordingly "A" and "B" Coys. were sent forward at 6.15 a.m. to form a defensive Flank under command of Capt. McCann, M.C., and took up a position in quarries and trenches in R.2.D. On the left of the first phase of the advance and in front of position taken up by "A" and "B" Coys. was Luc Wood, with Long Wood to the right of this, and as the line moved forward these woods checked the advance on the Left. The Left attacking battalion were early in difficulties, especially opposite Luc and Long Wood. Therefore, at about 7 a.m. Capt. McCann was

BATTALION CHRONOLOGY

1918.
August 22-23.
(continued)

ordered to move his Companies forward to clear Long Wood and gain touch with left of 1st Battalion and right of Third Division. On the West side of the Wood a platoon of the 59th Battalion was not incorporated into the attacking party. Enemy Artillery was very heavy, and on the least sign of movement enemy machine guns opened fire from the Woods and the Ridge between Marly and Caronne Woods. "A" and "B" Coys. worked their way steadily through Luc Wood, the Left of the advance being taken by "B" Coy., enemy machine guns being engaged by the section of Vickers Guns attached to "A" Coy., which also covered the marshy flat ground on the left of Luc Wood in R.S.A. and R.s. B. & D. At 8.30 a.m. the Wood had been cleared and touch gained with the Left Platoon of 1st Battalion; a series of posts then being established at Northern edges of Luc Wood in R.3.B., the whole position being firmly established by 9.15 a.m., patrols being sent forward. During this part of the operation 15 prisoners were captured, together with one heavy machine and 3 light machine guns. At 10.45 a.m. after conference with C.O. 1st Battalion, it was arranged that this Battalion should take over responsibility for ground between Road through R.3.B.R.4.A., L.34.C., and the River. It was then decided to push forward as far as the Red Line (see attached map), in order to make a continuous line extending to the Left as far as the River before the commencement of the second phase of the attack. Accordingly four platoons were pushed forward under cover of 4 Vickers and 12 Lewis Guns, and at 1.45 p.m. the final line of posts was established at L.33.-D.6.8., L.33.D.8.8., L.34.C.2.1., L.34.C.4.2. with Supports at R.3.b.3.4. and R.3.b.2.3. Meantime at 11.45 a.m. the remaining Coy., "C" Coy., was moved forward to support this movement to mop up the flats along the Southern banks of the River. During this portion of the operation 9 prisoners were captured, together with 1 heavy and 1 light machine gun. One other heavy machine gun was captured and handed over to the Platoon of the 59th Battalion involved, in order to assist them. Large quantities of material, such as shells, huts, horse-shoes, etc., were also captured."

„ 24. Battalion advanced line in front of Proyart and Olympia Wood.

„ 25. Lieut.-Colonel M. Wilder-Neligan reported: "The advance continued in fine clear weather, the 10th with its usual determination pushing forward in bounds soon had reached Chateau Orchard. The 11th pushed on gradually over the open ground on right, getting a good deal of trouble from field guns at Dompiere. The line as follows was handed over to the 6th Brigade on relief at midnight. From the high ground on the S. Bank of the River to Salmon Wood, which was held by patrols, thence S.W. to G.27.B., thence South through

August	25.	G.33.B.N.3., Central to M.9.A.8.7. On completion of relief
(continued)		Units moved back to bivouac at St. Germains Wood."
August	26.	10th Battalion moved forward to beyond Chateau Orchard.

At 2 p.m. Coys. again moved to G.32.c.4.9. At 4 p.m. Coys. again moved forward and established a line running from G.21.d.4.8.-G.33.b.3.3. Battalion was relieved by the 21st Battalion the same night, and moved back to R.8.b.7.0. Lieut.-Colonel M. Wilder-Neligan reported on operations about Cappy: "On the evening of 25th August the line held by the 9th Battalion which had been operating during the day with the 12th Battalion on the right, lay at approximately from G.25.d.4.8.-G.25.d.5.0.-South along road to G.31.d.9.8. (See map attached —Reference Combined Sheet 62D S.E. & N.E. and 62D N.W. and S.W.). Red Line: It was decided to continue the advance on the following day with the object of keeping touch with the enemy, gaining ground, and inflicting casualties. Accordingly Battalion moved from the area it was occupying in L.34.D. and relieved 9th Battalion in the line at 2 a.m. On morning of 25th August with "C" Coy. on the right, "B" Coy. in the centre, and "A" Coy. on the left, zero hour for the advance was fixed at 6 a.m. An artillery barrage, to commence at zero, creeping forward with 100 yard lifts every three minutes for 1,000 yards was to cover the advance. Three sections of Machine Guns and two sections of Trench Mortars were placed at disposal of the Battalion Commander, together with two Brigades of Horse Artillery. At zero Companies advanced steadily towards their objective, meeting with little opposition on the way. The objective, a line running approximately South from Quarry in G.26.C. was reached at 6.30 a.m., where Companies settled down to prepare for the second stage of the advance. To assist in dealing with any centre of opposition not touched by artillery a special platoon under Lieut. F. J. S. Mead, M.C., D.C.M., made up of Battalion Headquarters details, moved forward with the attacking Companies, and although their services were not required for any particular work they did excellent work in the advance. During this portion of the operations the left platoon of "A" Coy. advanced through the village of Cappy, clearing it of the remnants left behind by the enemy, finally securing firm possession of the village. Having successfully overcome the enemy first line of resistance, it was at once decided to push on and exploit the initial success. Accordingly Companies were at once ordered to move forward by means of patrols well supported, with a view of reaching a line approximately through G.21 Central-27 Central and 35 Central. It was not considered to employ artillery to cover this advance, but in order to cover the large area between the left Company and the River Somme, one section of Machine Guns was emplaced behind left flank of advance. Of the remaining two sections, one moved forward

BATTALION CHRONOLOGY 99

1918.
August 26.
(continued)

with the left Company and one with the right. During this portion of the advance the chief opposition encountered was from machine guns, lightly manned and evidently left with the idea of impeding rather than holding up the advance, for as the Companies swung forward the enemy hastily fled, giving no opportunity to get to close quarters, nor capture any material. This was especially the case in Chateau Orchard, which was finally in our possession by 7 a.m. At this stage the position in front of Chateau Orchard was the most advanced portion of our line, which bent back on the right towards Yakko Wood, and on the left to the East of Justice Wood. The latter wood had not been taken without a sharp struggle in which the enemy was not forced to retire until the left Company had worked its way round the flank of the Wood and attacked the garrison in the rear. At this stage the line was as shown by Blue Line on attached map. Having fed and rested the troops, the advance was continued at 8.30 a.m., with the object first of straightening the line, and then of pushing the whole line forward. By this time the enemy artillery, which hitherto had taken little part in the defence, had become very active, especially harassing the right flank Company from Nameless Wood. As the operation was not one in which casualties were to be disregarded it was necessary to move forward in very small groups, taking advantage of all ground cover. In this manner "C" Company moved forward slowly to the position it finally occupied at 7 a.m. (see map). Meanwhile "A" Coy. on the left being further protected on its left flank by artillery fire from two batteries which had been brought up into a position near Olympia Wood, was pushing forward in a most spirited manner, small patrols boldly investigating likely enemy positions and clearing the way for the advancing Company. 20th of October Wood provided strong opposition, and had to be attacked in a most determined manner before the enemy was forced to fly in disorder. In this fight casualties were inflicted on the enemy, and two prisoners taken. Having defended 20th of October Wood with great vigour the enemy retired to the next defensive position in Salmon Wood, which was defended with equal tenacity, but before the end of the afternoon at 6 p.m. Salmon Wood had been entirely cleared of the enemy. On account of the ground contours, a line of posts was dug behind Salmon Wood, and the Wood kept clear of enemy by patrols, and the final line was taken up at 7 p.m., as shown in Green in attached map. During the whole of the day's operations there were of necessity many gaps between Companies and also between the flanking Companies and neighbouring Battalion, but at all times these gaps were adequately protected by Vickers and Lewis Guns, and during the whole advance, which realized from a minimum of 1,600 yards to a maximum of 2,500 yards in one day, there was not at any time an unprotected flank or gap in the line. As

1918.
August 26.
(continued)
explained above, captures in prisoners or material were necessarily small on account of the elusive nature of the enemy defences, but the operation was carried out with only one man killed and five men wounded, while of the enemy a much larger number were killed and wounded and two prisoners taken. Herewith is attached map of the area of operation and copy of diary."

" 26-27. 10th Battalion relieved by 21st Battalion at Cappy.
" 27. Battalion moved to Cerisy area.
" 27-31. Battalion engaged in training, bathing, etc., strength consisting of 39 officers and 597 other ranks.

1918.
September 6. Brigade competition conducted; rifle and Lewis gun events won by 10th.
" 7. Battalion moved up to Peronne area.
" 10. Battalion moved up to Tincourt area.
" 13. Four enemy 'planes brought down during raid.
" 17-18. About 8 p.m. Battalion moved into Jeancourt area.
" 18. Battalion provided hot meal by limber.
" 18. About 0700 Battalion left Jeancourt and by 1 p.m. had advanced 5,000 yards and consolidated line. Lieut.-Colonel M. Wilder-Neligan reported: "The Attack from Brown Line to Red Line. Right Battalion, 10th. Order of Battle: "C" Coy. on right, "B" Coy. on left, and "A" Coy. in support. The Battalion to avoid casualties did not follow too closely on the heels of the 12th Battalion, but were closed on to the Brown Line during the barrage halt, and on it lifting at zero plus 190 minutes, moved forward to the attack with vigour. Companies moved in lines of sections at approximately 50 paces interval and distance. The troops along the high ground in L.17.D.-L.18.C. keeping touch throughout with the 9th Battalion. The low ground in L.23.B. and L.24.A. was left to the Mopping-up Platoon of the Support Companies. Opposition developed mainly in (a) the strong trench system between the Brown and Red Lines, and (b) in the equally strong system situated just short of the Exploitation Line. In the first of these systems, "C" Coy. after hard fighting captured nearly 100 prisoners, 12 M. Guns, and 77 mm. Guns. 2nd Lieut. W. S. Bennett, of "C" Coy., accomplished an exceptionally brilliant individual achievement. Entirely by himself he captured three enemy guns and crew which were retarding the progress of the platoon. On reaching the Red Line the formation of the Coy. had not been broken, and on the lifting of the barrage after it had rested for 15 minutes on the protection line in front of the Red Line, the Coys. again went forward and the enemy offered a stubborn resistance, hotly contesting the high ground, which it was essential to the success of the operation to capture. The final stage was accomplished by a spirited charge, the enemy machine-gunners only retiring after severe fighting. Posts were

BATTALION CHRONOLOGY

1918.
September 18. (continued)
established in the proximity of the Blue Line (shown on attached map). Touch had been maintained with the Left Battalion during the whole of the advance, but the 14th Battalion on the right did not go forward to the line of Exploitation with the 10th Battalion. This resulted in a gap between two battalions. On the 10th Battalion reaching the Blue Line this was, however, rectified by the sending out of Liaison patrols on the Right Flank of the Battalion. Frontal patrols operated throughout the remainder of the day, and on several occasions dealt with enemy machine guns and strong posts."

„ 21-22. 10th Battalion relieved by 12th Battalion and moved into supports.

„ 23-24. 3rd Brigade moved to Tincourt Wood and 10th relieved by 4 Coys. of 59th American Brigade.

„ 25. Transport left Tincourt for a three-days' "trek" to Longpre.

„ 26. At 7 p.m. Battalion left Tincourt by train and arrived at Brucamps at 11 p.m.

„ 26-30. Battalion engaged in training and resting, strength being 35 officers and 482 other ranks. Casualties for month, 140.

1918.
October 1-31. Battalion at Brucamps, engaged in training and sports.

„ 11. At 1200 Brigade Transport Competition conducted; 10th Battalion winning Cup.

„ 16. About this time the Allied Advance commenced, and Ostend, Lille, Douai, Roubaix, and Turcoing were taken.

„ 30. Divisional Musketry Competitions conducted; 12th Battalion 1st and 10th Battalion did some very good shooting.

1918.
November 5. Battalion preparing to leave Brucamps. Move postponed for another 24 hours.

„ 8. About 2 p.m. Battalion left Brucamps for Hangest, to entrain about 6 a.m. on 9th.

„ 9. Train late; left at 5 p.m. in evening. Rumours were being circulated *re* Armistice.

„ 10. Troop-train conveying Battalion stopped at Ham, St. Quentin, Roisel and Epehy.

„ 11. Battalion detrained at Epehy. Armistice signed. Left Epehy at 11.30 a.m.; Battalion by bus and Transport by road. Battalion proceeded to Mazinghem and Transport to Premont.

„ 12. At 1300 Transport rejoined Battalion.

„ 14. At 0930 Battalion left Mazinghem for Bohain; arrived at 1630.

„ 22. Battalion left Bohain for Mazinghem.

„ 23. Battalion left Mazinghem for Cartignies.

„ 24. Battalion left Cartignies for Beugnies.

1918.
December 1. 10th Battalion inspected by H.M. the late King.

„ 2. Bishop Long delivered lecture entiled "The British Empire."

THE FIGHTING 10TH

1918. December		Colonel Ross delivered lecture entitled "Regimental Traditions."
"	3. 5.	Football match, 10th Battalion *versus* 11th Battalion. Won by 10th Battalion.
"	6.	Lecture by Major Flood entitled, "My Experience while a Prisoner in the Raider *Wolf*."
"	17.	Battalion moved from Beugnies area to Barbencon.
"	18.	Battalion moved from Barbencon to Gourdonnes.
"	19.	Battalion moved from Gourdonnes area to Chatelet, near Charleroi.
"	25.	Battalion appreciated Christmas dinner.
"	30.	Investiture of medals by H.R.H. the Prince of Wales.
1919. January	1.	Lieut.-Colonel M. Wilder-Neligan, C.M.G., D.S.O., and Bar, D.C.M., C. de G. (Fr.), finally left Battalion, and Major W. F. J. McCann, D.S.O., M.C. and Bar, assumed command, retaining same until Battalion was finally disbanded.
"	20.	About this time several officers and men of the 10th Battalion availed themselves of facilities offered by the A.I.F. Educational Scheme.
February	1.	Battalion still at Chatelet, Belgium, demobilization proceeding steadily. Drafts frequently left the Battalion for England, and the strength of the 10th was consequently diminishing, both in officers and other ranks.
March	1.	Battalion still at Chatelet, Belgium, and was further reduced in strength by departure of several drafts.
"	10.	Major W. F. J. McCann selected to conduct a party of American delegates through the war-devastated areas of France and Belgium.
"	16.	Field-Marshal Sir Douglas Haig completed his final despatch in which four 10th Battalion Officers and three other ranks were mentioned.
"	17.	Demobilization drafts had reduced the 10th Battalion to a skeleton unit, and the various remaining details merged with similar details of the 9th Battalion as Brigade Details, this being the last day that the 10th Battalion existed as a separate unit of the A.I.F.
May	20.	Final 10th Battalion details, including band, left Chatelet and entrained at Charleroi for Le Havre, where one week was spent before embarking for England and subsequently proceeding to Sandhill Camp, near Warminster, Wiltshire.
July	18.	Final 10th Battalion detachment left Sandhill Camp and entrained at Warminster for Devonport, and at 3 p.m. that day embarked on the *Takada*, and next day sailed for Australia.
"	20.	Capt. F. J. S. Mead, M.C., D.C.M., as O.C. of the A.I.F. Divisional Colour Party of five carried the 10th Battalion Regimental Flag in the triumphal Victory March through Paris At the time same was not emblazoned with Battle Honours as these had yet to be selected, recommended and awarded.

1919.
September 5.
Final 10th Battalion detachment on *Takada* arrived at Outer Harbour, South Australia, at 8 a.m. with Lieut.-Colonel M. Wilder-Neligan, C.M.G., D.S.O. and Bar, D.C.M., C. de G. (Fr.), on board. Members of the Battalion arriving back after this date returned independently or with details from other units.

XI

ESTABLISHMENT

PERSONNEL OF THE ORIGINAL BATTALION
(As at Embarkation 20/10/14)

(For Regimental Numbers, etc., see Nominal Roll, *vide* Section XXIII)

HEADQUARTERS
(Establishment strength—55 all ranks)

Administrative: Commanding Officer: Lieut.-Colonel Stanley Price Weir.
2nd in Command: Major Frederick William Hurcombe.
Adjutant: Captain Francis Maxwell de Frayer Lorenzo.
Quartermaster: Captain Charles Francis Minagall.
R.S.M.: Wesley Armstrong Whitbourn.   R.Q.M.S.: George Charles Magenis.
Orderly-Room Sgt.: Benjamin Bennett Leane.   Pioneer Sgt.: Felix Hereward Gordon Norfolk Heritage.
Sgt.-Cook: John Goldsack Parker.   Armourer-Sgt.: Claude Oswald Provis.
Bugler-Sgt.: Gordon Clyde Taylor.
Signalling Section: Captain Sydney Raymond Hall, Sgt. Leonard Reid Walker, and nine signallers.
Transport Section: 2nd Lieut. Trevor Owen Smyth, Sgt. Edward Charles Gill, Lance-corporal Roy Kintore Hurcombe, and fifteen drivers.
Medical Section: Captain Harry Carew Nott, A.A.M.C.; Corporal Charles Beauchamp Davinett, A.A.M.C.; four orderlies, A.A.M.C., and Lance-corporal Jean Pierre Becker.
Miscellaneous Details: Eight privates as grooms, batmen, orderlies, etc.

MACHINE GUN SECTION
(Establishment strength—18 all ranks)

Officer-in-charge: 2nd Lieut. Vernon Hermann Robley.
Sregeant: Edgar Geoffrey Sawer.
Corporal: William Edgar.
Lance-corporals: Victor Charles McIntosh, James Stanley Harden.
Drivers: Francis Davison Forsyth, Harold Lennox Williams.
Complement of privates—eleven.

THE FIGHTING 10TH

"A" COMPANY
(Establishment strength—119 all ranks)

Officer Commanding: Major Miles Fitzroy Beevor.
Subalterns: Lieut. Herbert Champion Hosking, 2nd Lieut. Clarence Rumball.
Colour-Sergeant: Thomas Brown Oliver.
Sergeants: John Rutherford Gordon, Horace Norman Henwood, Sydney Earl Rigney, Tom Stuart Tidy.
Corporals: Charles James Barclay, Victor Cromwell, Melville Basil Dunk, John Albert McAulay, Frederick John King.
Lance-corporals: Cecil Edgar Annis, Clarence Eugene Bradley, Hubert Clarke, Eric Murray Inglis, Arthur James Vallis.
Buglers: Frederick John Broughton, Oscar George Witcomb.
Transport drivers: George Reginald Brokenshire, Percy Edward Leonard Raffen.
Complement of privates—ninety-seven.

"B" COMPANY
(Establishment strength—119 all ranks)

Officer Commanding: Capt. George Dorricutt Shaw.
Subalterns: 2nd Lieut. Eric John Carl Stopp, 2nd Lieut. Charles Percy Farrier.
Colour-Sergeant: Oscar Donald Hassam.
Sergeants: George Hall, Sydney John Howe, Adolphus Wilmot Jarrett, Charles Lister.
Corporals: Edward Cheney, John Paul, Albert Edward Phillips, George Debney Lloyd Prince, Albert Alfred Osmond Whitbread.
Lance-corporals: Donald McDonald Carroll, Cyril Jolley, Royce Spinkston, Cecil Roy Westwood.
Buglers: Thomas Stanley Gordon, Edward Richard Hill.
Transport drivers: John James Allen, Henry Law Spencer.
Complement of privates—ninety-eight.

"C" COMPANY
(Establishment strength—121 all ranks)

Officer Commanding: Lieut. Keith Eddowes Green.
Subalterns: Lieut. Eric James Sexton, 2nd Lieut. Robert James Mansfield Hooper.
Colour-Sergeant: Charles Alfred Aspinall.
Sergeants: Charles James Backman, James Courtenay, Leslie Kenneth Temple Fry, Anthony Basil Hall.
Corporals: Oswald Kolb, Clarence Harcroft Mollett, Roy Pickering, Walter Batley Seaman, Robert William Wilson-Todd.
Lance-corporals: Charles Colin Cussion, Michael Foggarty, Michael Coughlan, William John Nagle, Walter Gordon Read, Stephen Ruddock, Clarence Gordon Youds.
Buglers: Walter Stanley Manchip, Thomas Lindsay Noble.
Transport drivers: Walter Bergin, Hurtle John Watson Lynch.
Complement of privates—ninety-seven.

ESTABLISHMENT

"D" COMPANY

(Establishment strength—118 all ranks)

Officer Commanding: Capt. Mervyn James Herbert.
Subalterns: 2nd Lieut. William Stanley Frayne, 2nd Lieut. David Leslie Todd.
Colour-Sergeant: Harry Coward.
Sergeants: William Francis James McCann, Ivor Eric MacGillivray, Albert George Ferdinand Neave, Alan John Newlands.
Corporals: Edward Keith Blunt, John Boyle, Edward Bruce Oliver, Stanley Alexander Outerbridge.
Lance-corporals: Herbert Addison, Harold Kent, Alexander William Lauchlan MacNeil, George Tippett.
Buglers: James Battye, William Taylor Edis.
Transport drivers: Victor Malcolm Barnes, Harold Gabriel.
Complement of privates—ninety-eight.

"E" COMPANY

(Establishment strength—120 all ranks)

Officer Commanding: Captain Edward Castle Oldham.
Subalterns: 2nd Lieut. Hector Roy Heming, 2nd Lieut. Alfred Cyril Sommerville.
Colour-Sergeant: Charles Henry Jones.
Sergeants: Charles Joseph Bates, John Ellis Pearce, George Colin Steer, Alfred Martin James Tucker.
Corporals: William Russell de la Poer Beresford, Henry Arthur Kinnish, Michael John McMahon, Frederick Rixon, John Mitchell Sinclair.
Lance-corporals: Walter Harold Davidson, Andrew John Moore, John Forrest Reading, Arnold Cooper Sandland, Karl Frederick Timcke.
Buglers: Herbert Alexander Bartholomaeus, Fred Freeman.
Transport drivers: Archie Gordon Hooper, Percy George Marriott.
Complement of privates—ninety-eight.

"F" COMPANY

(Establishment strength—119 all ranks)

Officer Commanding: Captain George Ernest Redburg.
Subalterns: Lieut. Louis Gordon Holmes, Lieut. Eric Wilkes Talbot Smith.
Colour-Sergeant: Samuel Walter Coombe.
Sergeants: Tennyson George Clarke, Charles Frederick English, Charles Albert Tomlinson, Claude Arnold Percival Virgo.
Corporals: Stanley Clarke Coffey, Geoffrey Cowan, Leon Maxwell Gellert, Thomas Ernest Martin, Thomas Victor Storey.
Lance-corporals: Thomas Henry Adams, James Davidson, Arthur Manning, Rupert Livingstone Mayman.
Buglers: John Michael Flood, Thomas Stewart.
Transport drivers: Edward Henderson Boag, Joseph Thomas Marshall.
Complement of privates—ninety-eight.

"G" COMPANY
(Establishment strength—119 all ranks)
Officer Commanding: Capt. Felix Gordon Giles.
Subalterns: 2nd Lieut. Noel Medway Loutit, 2nd Lieut. William Howard Perry.
Colour-Sergeant: George Francis Henderson.
Sergeants: Andrew Stewart Duncan, William Horace Lionel Evans, Francis Charles Ford, Wilfred Francis Huggert Lodge.
Corporals: Walter Henry Blake, Thomas Esson James Rule, John William Searcy, Herbert Hurtle White.
Lance-corporals: William Reginald Batty, Rodney Vernon Franklin, George William Edward Hazelwood, Arthur Harold Robinson, Thomas Norris Catlow, Edgar Kent.
Buglers: John Evans, Ernest Smith.
Transport drivers: Roderick McKinnon, James Ogilvy.
Complement of privates—ninety-seven.

"H" COMPANY
(Establishment strength—119 all ranks)
Officer Commanding: Capt. Ross Blyth Jacob.
Subalterns: Lieut. Albert John Byrne, 2nd Lieut. John Hamilton.
Colour-Sergeant: Harold Baker Shaw.
Sergeants: Roy George Baynes, Anthony Simpson Gilpin, Charles Laurence Hunt, William Henry Munro.
Corporals: Ambrose Henry Baynes, Albert John Edwards, George Deane Mitchell, Peter Molloy.
Lance-corporals: Donald Chisholm, Frederick Foster, Robert Finlay McNeil, William Rockliff Montgomery, Cyril Charles Smith.
Buglers: John McNeil, James Gilbert Slee.
Transport drivers: Alfred George Bottom, Thomas Edward Kelly.
Complement of privates—ninety-eight.

COMPANY REORGANIZATION AT MENA, JANUARY, 1915.

In accordance with the 1914 Manual of Infantry Training issued by the War Office on August 10, 1914, certain company reorganization was effected. As the amended manuals were not available prior to embarkation, the change-over was deferred until Egypt was reached and text-books were procured. The 8-Company System under which the Battalion was originally raised was then superseded by the 4-Company System in which platoons of 60 men each were introduced and trained as fighting units. Each re-formed company consisted of four platoons, and former company subalterns were appointed platoon commanders. Other important changes consisted of the abolition of Colour-Sergeants, and the appointment of Company Sergeant-Majors, and Company Quartermaster-Sergeants. Under this reorganization the following company mergers occurred:

Original "A" and "F" Companies became the new "A" Company.
Original "C" and "E" Companies became the new "B" Company.
Original "B" and "H" Companies became the new "C" Company.
Original "D" and "G" Companies became the new "D" Company.

XII

EMBARKATION STATISTICS

A complete list showing the establishment of the original Battalion as at embarkation and figures appertaining to the subsequent quotas of reinforcements specially raised in South Australia to maintain Battalion strength, or reinforcements transferred from the 27th Battalion at Gebel Habieta, or others drafted from the South Australian General Service Reinforcements in France.

ANALYSIS OF RANKS

The following 10th Battalion ranks embarked on H.M.A.T. A11 *Ascanius* and H.M.A.T. A12 *Saldanha* on October 20, 1914:—

Officers: 1 lieut.-colonel, 2 majors, 9 captains, 6 lieutenants, 13 second lieutenants	31
N.C.O's.: 1 R.S.M., 1 R.Q.M.S., 7 H.Q.Sgts., 8 colour-sergeants, 33 sergeants, 38 corporals, 44 lance-corporals	132
Buglers:	16
Drivers:	33
Privates (including signallers, drummers, bandsmen, batmen, cooks, stretcher-bearers, scouts, machine-gunners, etc.):	809
A.A. Medical Corps details attached: 1 capt., 1 corporal, 4 privates	6
Grand Total	1,027

THE ORIGINAL BATTALION

(Excluding 1 officer and 15 drivers of Transport Section, and 6 Coy. drivers) Embarked at Outer Harbour, South Australia, per H.M.A.T. A11 *Ascanius*, October 20, 1914.

Gross tonnage of transport 10,048, accommodating 70 officers, 1,750 other ranks and 12 horses.

Strength of Companies, etc., on embarkation:

Headquarters	5	officers,	28	other ranks	=	33
A.A.M. Corps attached	1	,,	5	,,	=	6
Machine Gun Section	1	,,	17	,,	=	18
"A" Company	3	,,	115	,,	=	118
"B" Company	3	,,	115	,,	=	118
"C" Company	3	,,	117	,,	=	120
"D" Company	3	,,	114	,,	=	117
"E" Company	3	,,	116	,,	=	119
"F" Company	3	,,	115	,,	=	118
"G" Company	3	,,	116	,,	=	119
"H" Company	3	,,	116	,,	=	119

Grand Total .. 31 officers, 974 other ranks = 1,005

Approximate range of regimental numbers, 1–1100.

Disembarked at Alexandria, Egypt, December 7, 1914, entrained to Abu Ela, Cairo, and proceeded to Mena Camp, near Giza Pyramids.

THE FIGHTING 10TH

THE ORIGINAL TRANSPORT SECTION

(Excluding thirteen drivers who embarked with the main body of the Battalion, 1 being included in H.Qrs., 2 in M.G. Section, and 10 in Company totals as above.)

Embarked at Outer Harbour, South Australia, per H.M.A.T. A12 *Saldanha*, October 20, 1914.

Gross tonnage of transport 4,594, accommodating 5 officers, 50 other ranks, and 300 horses.

Strength on embarkation:

Headquarters	..	1 officer,		14 drivers,		1 N.C.O.	=	16
"A" Company	..	—	,,	1	,,	—	,, =	1
"B" Company	..	—	,,	1	,,	—	,, =	1
"C" Company	..	—	,,	1	,,	—	,, =	1
"D" Company	..	—	,,	1	,,	—	,, =	1
"E" Company	..	—	,,	1	,,	—	,, =	1
"F" Company	..	—	,,	1	,,	—	,, =	1
Grand Total	..	1 officer,		20 drivers,		1 N.C.O.	=	22

(and 108 horses).

Accompanied First Australian Contingent to Egypt; disembarked at Alexandria early in December, 1914, and proceeded to Mena Camp.

1st REINFORCEMENTS.

Embarked at Melbourne, Victoria, per H.M.A.T. A32 *Themistocles*, 27th December, 1914.

Gross tonnage of transport, 11,231, accommodating 100 officers, 1,220 other ranks, and no horses.

Strength on embarkation: 1 Officer and 100 other ranks.

Approximate range of regimental numbers, 1101–1199.

Officer: 2nd Lieut. Albert Henry Rowe.

Accompanied 2nd Australian Contingent to Egypt, arrived at Alexandria February 1, 1915, and proceeded to camp at Zeitoun, near Heliopolis, Cairo.

Joined Battalion at Mena on February 8, 1915.

2nd REINFORCEMENTS.

Embarked at Melbourne, Victoria, per H.M.A.T. A46 *Clan MacGillivray*, 2nd February, 1915.

Gross tonnage of transport, 5,023, accommodating 17 Officers, 1,079 other ranks, and no horses.

Strength on embarkation: 2 Officers and 153 other ranks.

Approximate range of regimental numbers, 1301–1449.

Officers: Captain Harold William Hastings Seager, 2nd Lieut. Alexander Henry Macdonald.

Joined 10th Battalion on *Ionian*, Mudros Harbour, Lemnos Island, Aegean Sea, April 10, 1915.

EMBARKATION STATISTICS

3RD REINFORCEMENTS.
Embarked at Melbourne, Victoria, per H.M.A.T. A54 *Runic*, 19th February, 1915.
Gross tonnage of transport, 12,490, accommodating 90 officers, 1,534 other ranks, and no horses.
Strength on embarkation: 2 Officers and 151 other ranks.
Approximate range of regimental numbers, 1451–1613.
Officers: Lieut. Walter Gordon Cornish, 2nd Lieut. Hedley Elbert Cullen.
Joined Battalion in line at Anzac, May 7, 1915.

4TH REINFORCEMENTS.
Embarked at Outer Harbour, South Australia, per H.M.A.T. A17 *Port Lincoln*, 1st April, 1915.
Gross tonnage of transport, 7,243, accommodating 25 Officers, 370 other ranks, and 376 horses.
Strength on embarkation: 2 Officers and 150 other ranks.
Approximate range of regimental numbers, 1702–1857.
Officers: Lieut. William Stanley de Courcy Ireland, Lieut. Charles Launcelot Moule.
Joined Battalion in line at Anzac, Gallipoli, May 30, 1915.

5TH REINFORCEMENTS.
Embarked at Outer Harbour, South Australia, per H.M.A.T. A20 *Hororata*, 20th April, 1915.
Gross tonnage of transport, 9,400, accommodating 67 Officers 2,000 other ranks, and 124 horses.
Strength on embarkation: 2 Officers and 150 other ranks.
Approximate range of regimental numbers 1901–2063.
Officers: 2nd Lieut. Frank Herbert Hancock, 2nd Lieut. Harold Edwin Salisbury Armitage.
Joined Battalion in line at Anzac, Gallipoli, June 5, 1915.

6TH REINFORCEMENTS.
Embarked at Outer Harbour, South Australia, per H.M.A.T. A30 *Borda*, 23rd June, 1915.
Gross tonnage of transport, 11,136, accommodating 26 Officers, 550 other ranks, and 260 horses.
Strength on embarkation: 2 Officers and 151 other ranks.
Approximate range of regimental numbers, 2102–2265.
Officers: Lieut. Charles William Hooper, 2nd Lieut. William Murray Fowler.
Joined Battalion in line at Anzac, Gallipoli, August 4, 1915.

7TH REINFORCEMENTS.
Embarked at Outer Harbour, South Australia, per H.M.A.T. A61 *Kanowna*, 23rd June, 1915.
Gross tonnage of transport, 6,942, accommodating 82 officers, 980 other ranks, and no horses.
Strength on embarkation: 2 Officers and 150 other ranks.
Approximate range of regimental numbers, 2326–2600.

Officers: 2nd Lieut. Richard Gladstone Wilton, Captain George Edwin Cresswell* (*Did not join Battalion. Appointed captain in A.I.F. 7/5/15. Previously served in Senior Cadets. Upon arrival in Egypt was appointed C.O. of 3rd T.Bn. at Zeitoun. Subsequently returned to South Australia, services with A.I.F. terminating on 13/1/16).

2nd Lieut. R. G. Wilton and other ranks of this quota joined the Battalion in the line at Anzac, Gallipoli, September 17, 1915. This was the last quota of reinforcements to join the Battalion prior to being withdrawn from the Peninsula.

8TH REINFORCEMENTS.

Embarked at Outer Harbour, South Australia, per R.M.S. *Morea*, 26th August, 1915.

Strength on embarkation: 2 Officers and 152 other ranks.

Approximate range of regimental numbers, 2601–2750.

Officers: 2nd Lieut. James Churchill Smith (landed on Gallipoli), 2nd Lieut. Colin MacPherson Smith.

Joined Battalion at Mudros, Lemnos Island, November 22, 1915.

9TH REINFORCEMENTS.

Embarked at Outer Harbour, South Australia, per H.M.A.T. A15 *Star of England* (later *Port Sydney*), 21st September, 1915.

Gross tonnage of transport, 9,136, accommodating 29 Officers, 499 other ranks, and 476 horses.

Strength on embarkation: 2 Officers and 150 other ranks.

Approximate range of regimental numbers, 2750–3000.

Officers: 2nd Lieut. Joseph Ronald Harniman, 2nd Lieut. Morris James Coffey.

Joined Battalion at Mudros, Lemnos Island, November 22, 1915.

10TH REINFORCEMENTS.

Embarked at Outer Harbour, South Australia, per H.M.A.T. A70 *Ballarat*, 14th September, 1915.

Gross tonnage of transport, 11,120, accommodating 48 Officers, 1,577 other ranks, and no horses.

Strength on embarkation: 2 Officers and 155 other ranks.

Approximate range of regimental numbers, 3001–3225.

Officers: Lieut. Gordon Cathcart Campbell, 2nd Lieut. Ernest Joseph Battye.

Joined Battalion at Mudros, Lemnos Island, November, 1915.

11TH REINFORCEMENTS.

Embarked at Outer Harbour, South Australia, per H.M.A.T. A24 *Benalla*, 27th October, 1915.

Gross tonnage of transport, 11,118, accommodating 50 Officers, 1,200 other ranks, and 12 horses.

Strength on embarkation: 3 Officers and 302 other ranks.

Approximate range of regimental numbers, 3226–3568.

Officers: 2nd Lieut. Jesse Gilmour Jamieson, 2nd Lieut. Victor Gillard Dridan, 2nd Lieut. Maxwell Gore.

Majority of this quota was transferred to the 50th Battalion at Gebel Habieta, Egypt, February 26, 1916.

EMBARKATION STATISTICS 111

12TH REINFORCEMENTS.

Embarked at Outer Harbour, South Australia, per R.M.S. *Malwa*, 2nd December, 1915.

Strength on embarkation: 3 Officers and 304 other ranks.

Approximate range of regimental numbers, 3676–3982.

Officers: 2nd Lieut. Walter Charles Chinnery, 2nd Lieut. Alexander Ralph Walker, 2nd Lieut. John Albert Smith* (*Did not join Battalion. Appointed 2nd lieut. in A.I.F. 16/9/15. Promoted to lieut. 1/4/16. Transferred to 50th Battalion, and subsequently to Permanent Supernumerary List.) Disembarked at Egypt, and subsequently proceeded to France. Joined the Battalion at Fleurbaix early in June, 1916, being the first quota of reinforcements to join the Battalion in France.

13TH REINFORCEMENTS.

Embarked at Outer Harbour, South Australia, per H.M.A.T. A30 *Borda*, 11th January, 1916.

Gross tonnage of transport, 11,136, accommodating 26 Officers, 550 other ranks, and 260 horses.

Strength on embarkation: 2 Officers and 199 other ranks.

Approximate range of regimental numbers, 4126–4328.

Officers: 2nd Lieut. Albert Edward Willmer, 2nd Lieut. Harry Thomson* (*Did not join Battalion. Appointed 2nd lieut. in A.I.F. 16/9/15. Promoted to rank of lieutenant on 1/5/16. Attained captaincy 20/4/17, and majority 1/1/19. Won M.C. Served with 50th Battalion. Subsequently transferred to 4th Infantry Brigade and A.I.F. Education Service).

Joined 10th Battalion in France, 1916.

14TH REINFORCEMENTS.

Embarked at Outer Harbour, South Australia, per H.M.A.T. A28 *Miltiades*, 7th February, 1916.

Gross tonnage of transport, 7,814, accommodating 42 Officers, 977 other ranks, and no horses.

Strength on embarkation: 4 Officers and 200 other ranks.

Approximate range of regimental numbers, 4426–4644.

Officers: 2nd Lieut. Herbert Youngman Collison, 2nd Lieut. Alexander Lorimer Miller, 2nd Lieut. Thomas Arthur Table Heward, 2nd Lieut. Arnold William Collins.

Joined 10th Battalion in France, 1916.

15TH REINFORCEMENTS.

Embarked at Outer Harbour, South Australia, per R.M.S. *Mongolia*, 9th March, 1916.

Strength on embarkation: 4 Officers and 201 other ranks.

Approximate range of regimental numbers, 4726–4937.

Officers: 2nd Lieut. Sydney Sylvanus Mills, 2nd Lieut. Wallace Westerfield Baker, 2nd Lieut. George Roy McGregor Dey, 2nd. Lieut. Kenneth Robert Wyllie* (*Did not join Battalion. Appointed 2nd lieut. in A.I.F. 16/12/15. Promoted to rank of lieutenant 6/9/16, and attained captaincy on 8/8/17. Served with 38th, 53rd, and 55th Battalions).

Joined 10th Battalion in France, 1916.

16TH REINFORCEMENTS.

Embarked at Outer Harbour, South Australia, per H.M.A.T. A9 *Shropshire*, 25th March, 1916.

Gross tonnage of transport, 11,911, accommodating 57 Officers, 878 other ranks, and 461 horses.

Strength on embarkation: 4 Officers and 201 other ranks.

Approximate range of regimental numbers, 5028–5257.

Officers: 2nd Lieut. Rufus Phillip Ford, 2nd Lieut. Eric Charles Harvey, 2nd Lieut. John Gladstone Sinclair, 2nd Lieut. James Bichan McLean* (*Did not join Battalion. Appointed 2nd lieut. in A.I.F. 20/1/16. Promoted to rank of lieutenant 1/9/16. Served with 27th Battalion).

Proceeded to Tel-el-Kebir, Egypt, 25/4/17, and subsequently re-embarked for England. Joined 10th Battalion in France, arriving in several drafts between August and October, 1916.

17TH REINFORCEMENTS.

Embarked at Outer Harbour, South Australia, per H.M.A.T. A60 *Aeneas*, 11th April, 1916.

Gross tonnage of transport, 10,049, accommodating 60 Officers, 1,742 other ranks, and 10 horses.

Strength on embarkation: 2 Officers and 129 other ranks.

Approximate range of regimental numbers, 5326–5460.

Officers: Captain Eric James Sexton, Lieut. Felix Hereward Gordon Norfolk Heritage.

Joined 10th Battalion in France, 1916.

18TH REINFORCEMENTS.

Embarked at Melbourne, Victoria, per H.M.A.T. A37 *Barambah* (ex-enemy *Hobart*), 27th June, 1916.

Gross tonnage of transport, 5,923, accommodating 5 Officers, 120 other ranks, and 498 horses.

Strength on embarkation: 2 Officers and 156 other ranks.

Approximate range of regimental numbers, 5646–5870.

Officers: Lieut. William Stanley de Courcy Ireland, 2nd Lieut. Colin MacPherson Smith.

Joined 10th Battalion in France, 1916.

19TH REINFORCEMENTS.

Embarked at Outer Harbour, South Australia, per H.M.A.T. A70 *Ballarat*, 12th August, 1916.

Gross tonnage of transport, 11,120, accommodating 48 Officers, 1,577 other ranks, and no horses.

Strength on embarkation: 2 Officers and 153 other ranks.

Approximate range of regimental numbers, 5966–6150.

Officers: Lieut. Herbert Champion Hosking, 2nd Lieut. Magnus Graham Saunders.

Joined 10th Battalion in France, arriving in several drafts between December, 1916, and January, 1917.

EMBARKATION STATISTICS 113

20TH REINFORCEMENTS.
Embarked at Outer Harbour, South Australia, per H.M.A.T. A68 *Anchises*, 28th August, 1916.
Gross tonnage of transport, 10,046, accommodating 45 Officers, 1,736 other ranks, and no horses.
Strength on embarkation: 2 Officers and 148 other ranks.
Approximate range of regimental numbers, 6211–6442.
Officers: Lieut. Eric John Carl Stopp, Lieut. Patrick Gerald Browne.
Joined 10th Battalion in France, 1917.

21ST REINFORCEMENTS.
Embarked at Outer Harbour, South Australia, per H.M.A.T. A16 *Port Melbourne* (originally *Star of Victoria*), 23rd October, 1916.
Gross tonnage of transport, 9,152, accommodating 30 Officers, 511 other ranks, and 537 horses.
Strength on embarkation: 2 Officers and 151 other ranks.
Approximate range of regimental numbers, 6456–6621.
Officers: Lieut. Alexander Henry Macdonald, 2nd Lieut. William Roy Jenkins,
Joined 10th Battalion in France, 1917.

22ND REINFORCEMENTS.
Embarked at Outer Harbour, South Australia, per H.M.A.T. A19 *Afric*, 7th November, 1916.
Gross tonnage of transport, 11,999, accommodating 49 Officers, 1,300 other ranks, and 12 horses.
Strength on embarkation: 2 Officers and 151 other ranks.
Approximate range of regimental numbers, 6701–6873.
Officers: 2nd Lieut. John Hubert Kennare, 2nd Lieut. Richard Graham Smith.
Joined 10th Battalion in France, 1917.

23RD REINFORCEMENTS.
Embarked at Outer Harbour, South Australia, per H.M.A.T. A35 *Berrima*, 16th December, 1916.
Gross tonnage of transport, 11,137, accommodating 60 Officers, 1,500 other ranks, and no horses.
Strength on embarkation: 2 Officers and 150 other ranks.
Approximate range of regimental numbers, 6946–7122.
Officers: 2nd Lieut. William Arthur Ditchburn, 2nd Lieut. Edward Laurence Angove.
Joined 10th Battalion in France, April 19, 1918.

24TH REINFORCEMENTS.
Embarked at Outer Harbour, South Australia, per H.M.A.T. A30 *Borda*, 23rd June, 1917.
Gross tonnage of transport, 11,136, accommodating 26 Officers, 550 other ranks, and 260 horses.
Strength on embarkation: 2 Officers and 150 other ranks.
Approximate range of regimental numbers, 7191–7389.
Officers: 2nd Lieut. Claude Arnold Percival Virgo, 2nd Lieut. Cecil Claude Marcelin Chabrel.
Joined 10th Battalion in France, 1918.

25TH REINFORCEMENTS.

Embarked at Melbourne, Victoria, per H.M.A.T. A60 *Aeneas*, 30th October, 1917.

Gross tonnage of transport, 10,049, accommodating 60 Officers, 1,742 other ranks, and 10 horses.

Strength on embarkation: 4 Officers and 146 other ranks.

Approximate range of regimental numbers, 7436–7590.

Officers: Lieut. Harold Leslie Boyce, 2nd Lieut. Herbert Leighton Cleworth, 2nd Lieut. Ernest Percy Orman, 2nd Lieut. John James Affleck Younger.

Arrived at Plymouth, England, 25/12/17, and joined 10th Battalion at Meteren, France, about April 19, 1918. Lieut. H. L. Boyce remained in England, having been appointed R.T.O. This quota of reinforcements was partly recruited by Lieut. H. L. Boyce, and was the last quota of reinforcements specifically raised in South Australia for the 10th Battalion.

27TH BATTALION REINFORCEMENTS TRANSFERRED TO 10TH BATTALION.

On February 26, 1916, after 500 of the Battalion had been transferred to the 50th Battalion, 6 officers and 461 other ranks of the 27th Battalion were taken on strength of 10th. The undermentioned were the 27th Battalion reinforcement quotas affected:—

4TH REINFORCEMENTS OF 27TH.

Embarked at Outer Harbour, South Australia, per H.M.A.T. A15 *Star of England* (later *Port Sydney*), 21st September, 1915.

Gross tonnage of transport, 9,152, accommodating 20 Officers, 499 other ranks, and 476 horses.

Officers transferred to 10th: 2nd Lieut. Robert James Bradley Hillier, 2nd Lieut. Phillip George Melville.

No other ranks of this quota were transferred to 10th Battalion.

6TH REINFORCEMENTS OF 27TH.

Embarked at Outer Harbour, South Australia, per H.M.A.T. A24 *Benalla*, 27th October, 1915.

Gross tonnage of transport, 11,118, accommodating 50 Officers, 1,200 other ranks, and 12 horses.

Strength on embarkation: 3 Officers and 310 other ranks.

Approximate range of regimental numbers, 2525–2875.

Officers transferred to 10th: 2nd Lieut. Harold Ewart Partridge, 2nd Lieut. Hugh William Thomas, 2nd Lieut. William Hill Dunn Stewart.

A large number of this quota was transferred to 10th Battalion.

7TH REINFORCEMENTS OF 27TH.

Embarked at Outer Harbour, South Australia, per H.M.A.T. A7 *Medic*, 12th January, 1916.

Gross tonnage of transport, 12,032, accommodating 31 Officers, 1,076 other ranks, and 283 horses.

Strength on embarkation: 3 Officers and 302 other ranks.

EMBARKATION STATISTICS

Approximate range of regimental numbers, 3000-3351.
No Officers transferred to 10th.
Almost the whole of this quota was transferred to the 10th Battalion.

8TH REINFORCEMENTS OF 27TH.

Embarked at Outer Harbour, South Australia, per H.M.A.T. A30 *Borda*, 12th January, 1916.
Gross tonnage of transport, 11,136, accommodating 26 Officers, 550 other ranks, and 260 horses.
Strength on embarkation: 2 Officers and 202 other ranks.
Approximate range of regimental numbers, 3451-3653.
Officer transferred to 10th: 2nd Lieut. Douglas James Walsh.
A large number of this quota was transferred to the 10th Battalion.

MISCELLANEOUS TRANSFERS TO AND FROM 10TH BATTALION.

Whilst in France, various temporary and permanent transfers were made. On one occasion the Battalion was reinforced from the 43rd Battalion, which in turn was reinforced by the 10th; but invariably on occasions of this nature the troops were eventually redrafted to their original units. Occasionally officers and men were permanently transferred to Machine Gun Battalions, Trench Mortar Batteries, and other A.I.F. units.

GENERAL SERVICE REINFORCEMENTS.

After the 25th Reinforcements joined the Battalion, six quotas of reinforcements, known as General Service Reinforcements, embarked for overseas. These reinforcements were recruited in South Australia, but were not allotted to any particular unit until arrival overseas, when they were drafted to various battalions according to the exigencies of the situation. The following are the details:

1ST SOUTH AUSTRALIAN GENERAL SERVICE REINFORCEMENTS.

Embarked at Sydney, New South Wales, per H.M.A.T. A14 *Euripides*, 1st May, 1918.
Gross tonnage of transport, 15,050, accommodating 136 Officers, 2,204 other ranks, and 20 horses.
Strength on embarkation: 2 Officers and 117 other ranks.
Approximate range of regimental numbers, 51761-51909.
No Officers, and probably only a few other ranks of this quota joined the 10th Battalion in France.

2ND SOUTH AUSTRALIAN GENERAL SERVICE REINFORCEMENTS.

Embarked at Sydney, New South Wales, per R.M.S. *Orontes*, 5th June, 1918.
Strength on embarkation: 2 Officers and 120 other ranks.
Approximate range of regimental numbers, 51883-51906 and 55791-55915.
Officers: 2nd Lieut. Clarence George Perry, 2nd Lieut. Henry Weall.
Both Officers and a good number of other ranks of this quota joined the 10th Battalion in France.

3RD SOUTH AUSTRALIAN GENERAL SERVICE REINFORCEMENTS.

Embarked at Melbourne, Victoria, per H.M.A.T. A74 *Marathon*, 23rd July, 1918.

Gross tonnage of transport, 7,827, accommodating 44 Officers and 1,202 other ranks.

Strength on embarkation: 2 Officers and 150 other ranks.

Approximate range of regimental numbers, 55800–55906 and 56026–56179.

Officers: 2nd Lieut. Joseph Daniel Willshire, etc.

One Officer and a number of this quota were drafted to the 10th Battalion in France. Subsequently two privates evacuated with illness and were included in the final Australian Casualty List—No. 466—issued in June, 1919, these being the only two General Service Reinforcements appearing amongst 10th Battalion casualties. The name of one private of this quota appears on the Roll of Honour. He died of illness in England.

4TH SOUTH AUSTRALIAN GENERAL SERVICE REINFORCEMENTS.

Embarked at Outer Harbour, South Australia, per transport *Gaika*, 6th August, 1918.

Strength on embarkation: 2 Officers and 151 other ranks.

Approximate range of regimental numbers, 56176–56184 and 62046–62188.

No Officers and probably only a few other ranks of this quota joined the 10th Battalion in France.

5TH SOUTH AUSTRALIAN GENERAL SERVICE REINFORCEMENTS.

Embarked at Melbourne, Victoria, per H.M.A.T. A37 *Barambah*, 31st August, 1918.

Gross tonnage of transport, 5,923, accommodating 5 Officers, 120 other ranks, and 498 horses.

Strength on embarkation: 2 Officers and 100 other ranks (fifty other ranks accompanied the 6th General Service Reinforcements).

Approximate range of regimental numbers, 62281–62383.

Officers: 2nd Lieut. William Percival Allan Lapthorne, etc.

One Officer and several other ranks joined the 10th Battalion in France after the Battalion had fought in its last engagement.

6TH SOUTH AUSTRALIAN GENERAL SERVICE REINFORCEMENTS.

Embarked at Outer Harbour, South Australia, per H.M.A.T. A36 *Boonah*, 22nd October, 1918.

Gross tonnage of transport, 5,926, accommodating 5 Officers, 120 other ranks, and 498 horses.

Strength on embarkation: 2 Officers and 150 other ranks (also 50 other ranks of 5th General Service Reinforcements, 62466–62515).

Approximate range of regimental numbers, 62516–62678.

This quota was at sea when the Armistice was signed on November 11, 1918, and consequently no Officers or other ranks joined the 10th Battalion in France.

XIII
COMMANDING OFFICERS AND MOVEMENTS OF BATTALION

A chronological list including all A.I.F. officers who at any time from the raising of the Battalion at Morphettville on August 17, 1914, to the disbandment of same at Chatelet, Belgium, on March 17, 1919, either permanently or temporarily commanded same for any period in excess of one day.

LIEUT.-COLONEL STANLEY PRICE WEIR. August 16 to October 31, 1914. Battalion raised and encamped at Morphettville, South Australia; bivouacked at Brighton and Belair, and embarked per H.M.A.T. A11 *Ascanius* and proceeded to Fremantle, Western Australia.

MAJOR FREDERICK WILLIAM HURCOMBE. November 1 to December 6, 1914. *Ascanius* left Fremantle and took up allotted position in convoy conveying 1st Australian Contingent to Alexandria, Egypt, *via* Colombo, Aden, and Suez Canal. During the voyage, Lieut.-Colonel Weir acted as O.C. Troops on transport.

LIEUT.-COLONEL STANLEY PRICE WEIR. December 7, 1914, to August 25, 1915. Battalion disembarked at Alexandria, proceeded to Cairo, and encamped at Mena. Later returned to Alexandria, embarked on *Ionian* for Dardanelles, and proceeded to Mudros Bay, Lemnos Island. Subsequently transferred to *Prince of Wales*, *Foxhound*, and *Scourge*, and landed at Anzac, Gallipoli, and remained on Peninsula during defence of Anzac. Proceeded to Imbros Island for short rest, and returned to Anzac.

TEMP. MAJOR (ACTING LIEUT.-COLONEL) GEORGE DORRICUTT SHAW. August 25 to October 21, 1915. Upon Lieut.-Colonel Weir going to Brigade, and subsequently evacuating ill, Major Shaw assumed command of Battalion, and retained same for two months until the return of a senior officer.

LIEUT.-COLONEL MILES FITZROY BEEVOR. October 21, 1915, to March 4, 1916. Returned to Anzac from hospital in England, and at first was appointed temp. lieut.-colonel, but subsequently was promoted to rank of lieut.-colonel. Battalion was withdrawn from Anzac under his command, proceeded to Lemnos, and later re-embarked on the *Seeang Bee* for Alexandria, and upon disembarkation proceeded to Tel-el-Kebir, Serapeum, and subsequently occupied a position in the Suez Canal Defences at Gebel Habieta.

LIEUT.-COLONEL STANLEY PRICE WEIR. March 5 to May 8, 1916. Battalion moved from Gebel Habieta to Serapeum, then to Alexandria, and subsequently embarked on *Saxonia* for France. Disembarked at Marseilles, and entrained to Godewaersvelde *via* Orange, Montereau, Epluges, Abbeville, and Hazebrouck. Billeted at Strazeele, Moolenacker, and then moved to Sailly.

MAJOR GEORGE DORRICUTT SHAW. May 8, to 16, 1916. Temporarily commanded Battalion whilst Lieut.-Colonel Weir acted as Brigadier of 3rd Infantry Brigade. Battalion remained at Sailly.

LIEUT.-COLONEL STANLEY PRICE WEIR. May 16 to August 23, 1916. Battalion moved into billets in Petillon Sector, and then into line at Fleurbaix. Returned to Sailly, proceeding to Moolenacker, Mt. Des

Catts, Godewaersvelde, Doullens, Halloy, Naours, Herissart, Forceville, and Albert. Subsequently moved to Sausage Valley, Black Watch Alley, and into line at Pozieres, afterwards proceeding to Berteaucourt, Bonneville, Toutencourt, Vadincourt Wood, Albert Brickfields, Sausage Valley, and into line at Mouquet Farm. Here Lieut.-Colonel Weir relinquished the command of the Battalion.

TEMP. LIEUTENANT-COLONEL GEORGE ERNEST REDBURG. August 23 to September 27, 1916. Battalion moved to Proven, Kenora Camp, and Ottawa Camp, where Lieut.-Colonel Weir made his final appearance with the Battalion, and subsequently evacuated through illness. Battalion then moved to reserve positions at Chateau Belge, occupied the Railway Dug-outs, and then moved into line at "Hill 60", at Ypres.

LIEUTENANT-COLONEL JAMES SAMUEL DENTON, D.S.O. September 27 to 30, 1916. Battalion remained in line at "Hill 60", Ypres.

TEMP. LIEUTENANT-COLONEL GEORGE ERNEST REDBURG. September 30 to November 19, 1916. Battalion returned from "Hill 60" to Ottawa Camp, and then proceeded to Steenvoorde, Oosthouck, Mouille, Tournehem, and Ardruicq. Subsequently entrained for Somme, detraining at Pt. Remy, moving to Buigny-le-Abbaye, Buire, Fricourt, Bernafay Wood, and into line at Gueudecourt. Later returned to Bernafay Wood, and moved to Fricourt, Dernancourt, Buire, and Cardonette.

MAJOR FELIX GORDON GILES. November 19 to December 6, 1916. Assumed command of Battalion whilst Major Redburg proceeded to Britain on furlough, the Battalion moving from Cardonette to Franvillers, Dernancourt, Fricourt, Bernafay, and Flers.

TEMP. LIEUTENANT-COLONEL GEORGE ERNEST REDBURG. December 6 to 23, 1916. Battalion moved into line at Flers, and then proceeded to Bazentin House, where through illness he was forced to evacuate. This was his final appearance with the Battalion.

MAJOR RUPERT ANSTICE RAFFERTY, D.S.O. December 23, 1916, to February 4, 1917. Battalion moved from Bazentin to Hobart Camp, opposite Bazentin-le-Grand, and then proceeded to Meaulte, Dernancourt, Bresle, Albert, and Bazentin-le-Petit.

LIEUTENANT-COLONEL ROSS BLYTH JACOB. February 4 to April 27, 1917. Battalion moved from Bazentin-le-Petit into supports at Hexham Road, and into line at Le Barque. Then returned to Bazentin-le-Petit, and subsequently moved to Bernafay Wood, Dernancourt, Shelter Wood, Bresle, Montauban, Fremicourt, and into line at Louverval and Lagnicourt. Later moved to Le Bucquiere, from where Lieut.-Colonel Jacob proceeded on furlough.

MAJOR ALEXANDER STEELE, D.S.O., D.C.M. April 27 to May 11, 1917. Relieved Lieut.-Colonel Jacob whilst on leave, the Battalion moving from Le Bucquiere into billets at Bancourt, and then to Fremicourt, and into the line at Bullecourt, and afterwards into camp near Bapaume.

LIEUTENANT-COLONEL ROSS BLYTH JACOB. May 11 to June 23, 1917. Battalion moved from Bapaume to Bazentin, then to Ribemont. After bivouacking at Henencourt, returned to Ribemont, where he was transferred to the command of a Training Battalion in England.

COMMANDING OFFICERS AND MOVEMENTS OF BN. 119

MAJOR MAURICE WILDER-NELIGAN, D.S.O., D.C.M. June 23 to July 5, 1917. Transferred from 9th Battalion. Battalion moved from Ribemont to Mailly Maillett.

MAJOR FELIX GORDON GILES, D.S.O. July 5 to 15, 1917. Battalion proceeded from Mailly Maillett to Ribemont, and then to Bray.

LIEUTENANT-COLONEL MAURICE WILDER-NELIGAN, D.S.O., D.C.M. July 15 to September 25, 1917. Returned to Battalion with rank of Lieutenant-Colonel. Battalion moved from Bray to Albert, Steenbecque, Staple, and Seninghem. Subsequently returned to Staple and proceeded to Bleu. Later moved to Caestre, Connaught Camp, Cornwall Camp, Chateau Segard, and marched to hopping-off line, the Polygon Wood operation following. Then proceeded to Steenvoorde.

CAPTAIN GORDON CATHCART CAMPBELL, M.C. AND BAR. September 25 to 28, 1917. Lieut.-Colonel Wilder-Neligan proceeding on leave it devolved upon Capt. Campbell to temporarily command the Battalion until the return of a senior officer, the Battalion remaining at Steenvoorde.

MAJOR CLARENCE RUMBALL, M.C. September 28 to October 9, 1917. Returning to the Battalion at Steenvoorde, Major Rumball took over the command from Capt. Campbell. Battalion embussed to Chateau Segard, and moving into the line in the Zonnebeke area, subsequently rested at China Wall. From Birr Cross Roads the Battalion afterwards took up positions at Anzac Ridge and Westhoek Ridge. He relinquished command of the Battalion on the eve of the Celtic Wood raid.

LIEUTENANT-COLONEL MAURICE WILDER-NELIGAN, D.S.O., D.C.M. October 9, 1917, to January 11, 1918. From Celtic Wood the Battalion moved into Dominion Lines, and subsequently into the Brigade Reserve Line at Kruitstraat, near Ypres. Later the Railway Dug-outs in Reserve were occupied, and then into supports at Anzac Ridge. After proceeding into reserves at Westhoek, the Battalion moved to Halifax Camp, proceeding to Renescure, Vaudrighem, Bourthes, Bezinghem, and Enquin. Then proceeded to Vaudrighem, Remilly, Wizernes, and into line in the Messines Sector, afterwards proceeding into supports at Wulverghem, where Lieut.-Colonel Wilder-Neligan sprained an ankle and was forced to leave the Battalion for a few days.

MAJOR GEORGE DORRICUTT SHAW. January 11 to 18, 1918. Temporarily commanded Battalion during absence of Lieut.-Colonel M. Wilder-Neligan. Battalion moved from Wulverghem to Rossignol Camp, near Kemmel.

LIEUTENANT-COLONEL MAURICE WILDER-NELIGAN, D.S.O., D.C.M. January 18 to 23, 1918. Battalion moved from Rossignol Camp into line in front of Wytschaete.

MAJOR GEORGE DORRICUTT SHAW. January 23 to 31, 1918. Battalion moved from line near Wytschaete to Aldershot Camp.

LIEUTENANT-COLONEL MAURICE WILDER-NELIGAN, D.S.O., D.C.M. January 31 to February 11, 1918. Battalion remained in Aldershot Camp.

MAJOR GEORGE DORRICUTT SHAW. February 11 to March 30, 1918. Battalion moved from Aldershot to Tournai Camp, then into line at Hollebeke, and into supports at Crater Dug-outs, and subsequently back into line at Hollebeke.

LIEUTENANT-COLONEL ROSS BLYTH JACOB. March 30 to May 11, 1918. Battalion moved from line at Hollebeke to Dezon Camp, proceeding to Caestre, Poulanville, Vignacourt, Rainneville, bivouacking outside Amiens. Then moved to St. Roch, Hondeghem, near Borre, and into Meteren Sector near Besace Farm. Subsequently moved into line at Meteren, and then into reserves in the Strazeele Sector, where Lieut.-Colonel Jacob evacuated ill, and was transferred to the General List. During this period Lieut.-Colonel Wilder-Neligan was temporarily commanding the 9th Battalion.

CAPTAIN ROY KINTORE HURCOMBE, M.C. AND BAR. (Commanded the Battalion for a few days between May and September, 1918, but the exact period has not been ascertained.)

MAJOR GEORGE DORRICUTT SHAW. May 11 to 16, 1918. Battalion moved from Strazeele Sector into Hondeghem Camp.

TEMP. LIEUTENANT-COLONEL JOHN NEWMAN, D.S.O.. May 16 to 20, 1918. Battalion moved from Hondeghem Camp to Sercus.

LIEUTENANT-COLONEL MAURICE WILDER-NELIGAN, C.M.G., D.S.O., D.C.M. May 20 to June 28, 1918. Battalion moved from Sercus to La Krule, and into the line in the Merris Sector, and then into supports at Pradelles, proceeding to Rouge Croix, Sercus, and Blaringhem. Subsequently returned to Sercus, bivouacking at La Krule, and then moved near Borre, and into line again at Merris.

MAJOR GEORGE DORRICUTT SHAW. June 28 to July 7, 1918. Battalion in line at Merris, subsequently moving into camp near Hondeghem.

LIEUTENANT-COLONEL MAURICE WILDER-NELIGAN, C.M.G., D.S.O. AND BAR, D.C.M. July 7 to August 12, 1918. Battalion moved into line at Merris again, and then returned to Hondeghem, proceeding to Hazebrouck, Heurighem, Wizernes, Pt. Remy, Coquerel, Poulanville, and into line at Hamel. Subsequently moved to Bayonvillers, Gillducourt, and bivouacking near Harbonnieres, moved into line at Crepey Wood, Lihons.

MAJOR GEORGE DORRICUTT SHAW. August 12 to 16, 1918. Battalion in line at Lihons, subsequently moving to Harbonnieres.

LIEUTENANT-COLONEL MAURICE WILDER-NELIGAN, C.M.G., D.S.O. AND BAR, D.C.M. August 16 to 27, 1918. Battalion moved from Harbonnieres to Vaire, Morcourt, Proyart, Cappy, and Cerisy area.

MAJOR WILLIAM FRANCIS JAMES McCANN, D.S.O., M.C. AND BAR. August 27 to September 6, 1918. Battalion remained at Cerisy.

LIEUTENANT-COLONEL MAURICE WILDER-NELIGAN, C.M.G., D.S.O. AND BAR, D.C.M. September 6 to 30, 1918. Battalion moved from Cerisy to Peronne, Tincourt, and then into line at Jeancourt, subsequently proceeding to Tincourt Wood, Longpre, and Brucamps.

MAJOR WILLIAM FRANCIS JAMES McCANN, D.S.O., M.C. AND BAR. September 30 to October 4, 1918. Battalion remained at Brucamps whilst Lieut.-Colonel Wilder-Neligan proceeded on a four days' lecture tour of the battle-fields.

ADJUTANTS

LIEUTENANT-COLONEL MAURICE WILDER-NELIGAN, C.M.G., D.S.O. AND BAR, D.C.M., C. de G. (Fr.), October 4, 1918, to January 1, 1919. Battalion moved from Brucamps to Hangest, and entrained for Epehy, via Ham, St. Quentin, Roisel, subsequently moving to Mazinghem, Bohain, Cartignies, Beugnies, Barbencon, Gourdonnes, and thence to Chatelet, near Charleroi, in Belgium.

MAJOR WILLIAM FRANCIS JAMES McCANN, D.S.O., M.C. AND BAR. January 1 to March 17, 1919. Battalion remained at Chatelet until finally disbanded on St. Patrick's Day, 1919.

XIV

ADJUTANTS

A complete list, arranged chronologically, from the raising of the Battalion at Morphettville, South Australia, on August 19, 1914, to disbandment of same at Chatelet, Belgium, on March 17, 1919.

1. CAPTAIN FRANCIS MAXWELL DE FRAYER LORENZO.
   August 20, 1914, to May 9, 1915.
   Subsequently promoted to rank of major and attained lieutenant-colonelcy, vide separate biography herein, No. 29.

2. CAPTAIN CLARENCE RUMBALL.
   May 9 to June 27, 1915.
   Subsequently promoted to rank of major, vide separate biography herein, No. 46.

3. TEMPORARY CAPTAIN WESLEY ARMSTRONG WHITBOURN.
   June 27 to October 29, 1915.
   Born 19/9/84, and at the outbreak of the Great War was a Staff Sergeant-Major on the A. & I. Staff at Keswick Headquarters. Enlisted in the 10th Battalion at Morphettville on 19/8/14, and was the first R.S.M. of the Battalion. He was promoted to rank of 2nd lieutenant at Anzac on May 25, 1915; attained his lieutenancy on July 1, 1915, and was appointed a temporary captain on August 18, 1915. In addition to his duties as Adjutant of the Battalion, he also officiated as Signalling Officer. On October 29, 1915, he evacuated ill, and reverting to his substantive rank of lieutenant proceeded to the General Hospital at Gibraltar, subsequently re-embarking for England. He rejoined the Battalion at Gebel Habieta on March 11, 1916, and was promoted to rank of captain on March 12, 1916. He accompanied the Battalion to France on the *Saxonia*, and was wounded at Pozieres in July, 1916. He then proceeded to England, and subsequently rejoined the Battalion in France on July

17, 1917. Remaining with the Battalion until October 22, 1917, he was seconded for duty with the 3rd Training Battalion in England, where he remained until the end of the war. In October, 1919, he was granted six months' leave by the Australian Military Forces for the purpose of attending to urgent private business, such leave to commence upon the termination of his special A.I.F. duty. He subsequently returned to Australia and resumed duties with the permanent forces. He was appointed Quartermaster and honorary captain in the Australian Instructional Corps on July 1, 1920, and on April 15, 1921, was posted as temporary Adjutant and Quartermaster of the 19th Battalion, 2nd Military District. On July 1, 1930, he was promoted to the rank of honorary major and temporarily attached to Headquarters of the 9th Infantry Brigade. He resigned from the military forces on December 21, 1931, and in 1935 was residing at "The Warren", Liverpool Road, Cabramatta, New South Wales. Whilst in the 10th Battalion he was affectionately known to rank and file as "Klinko".

4. LIEUTENANT BENJAMIN BENNETT LEANE.
October 29, 1915, to January 28, 1916.
Born 5/5/89, and was one of five brothers who served abroad in the A.I.F. He was a brother of Brigadier-General R. L. Leane, C.B., C.M.G., D.S.O., M.C., and also had six nephews serving abroad in the A.I.F., his family being known in South Australia during the Great War as "The Fighting Leanes". He was the first Orderly-Room Sergeant of the Battalion, his regimental number being "3". He landed at Anzac with Battalion Headquarters from the *Prince of Wales* at the historic landing on April 25, 1915, and shortly after was wounded. He subsequently proceeded to England, where he was admitted to the Whitworth Street Hospital at Manchester. During his absence from the Peninsula he was promoted to the rank of 2nd lieutenant on May 28, 1915, and to lieutenant on August 21, 1915. Returning to the Dardanelles from England he assumed the adjutancy of the Battalion, and after the Battalion was withdrawn from Anzac subsequently accompanied the Battalion to Serapeum, Egypt, where he was transferred to the Camel Corps and later to the 48th Battalion; his brother, Raymond L., being Commanding Officer of same. He was promoted to the rank of captain on March 23, 1916, and received his majority on November 6, 1916. For his splendid work in the field during September and October, 1916, he was awarded the Serbian Order of the White Eagle, 5th Class with swords. This decoration was promulgated in the London Gazette on 13/2/17. He was killed in action at the first Battle of Bullecourt on April 10, 1917, and was mentioned in despatches, *vide London Gazette*, 5/11/15 and 1/6/17.

5. CAPTAIN GEORGE CHARLES MAGENIS, D.S.O.
January 28, 1916, to January 14, 1917.
Relinquished adjutancy of Battalion upon being invalided from France, *vide* separate biography herein, No. 33.

ADJUTANTS

6. **LIEUTENANT FRANK JOHN SCOTT.**
    January 14 to July 15, 1917.
    Enlisted in original Battalion at Morphettville on August 22, 1914, his regimental number being "278". Born August, 1894, and promoted from rank of sergeant to 2nd lieutenant on August 5, 1916, and attained his lieutenancy on November 27, 1916. He was killed in action during the Celtic Wood Raid of October 8, 1917. He led his party behind a German trench where a fierce struggle ensued, the enemy being strongly reinforced. A desperate hand-to-hand encounter followed, the fight gradually concentrating towards his party, where the enemy gained the mastery, and he was mortally wounded. He was mentioned in despatches *vide London Gazette*, 1/6/17. He enlisted from Gawler, and was a brother of Lieutenant Cleve James Scott, M.C., who was killed in action at Merris on July 22, 1918.

7. **CAPTAIN WALTER GORDON CORNISH, M.C.**
    July 15, 1917, to July 13, 1918.
    Relinquished adjutancy of Battalion upon being transferred to 3rd Brigade Headquarters, *vide* separate biography herein, No. 7.

8. **CAPTAIN GORDON CATHCART CAMPBELL, M.C., and Bar.**
    July 13 to October 12, 1918.
    Subsequently promoted to rank of temporary major, *vide* separate biography herein, No. 6.

9. **CAPTAIN WILLIAM HOWARD PERRY, M.C.**
    October 12 to December 4, 1918.
    Relinquished adjutancy of Battalion upon finally leaving France, *vide* separate biography herein, No. 41.

10. **LIEUTENANT ALAN PERCIVAL CHITTLEBOROUGH.**
    December 4, 1918, to March 17, 1919.
    Born 15/7/95 and educated at St. Peter's College, Adelaide, where he distinguished himself by winning a five-year voice scholarship. He was also a chorister at St. John's Anglican Church, Adelaide. He embarked with the First Australian Contingent in October, 1914, as a corporal in No. 4 Company, Divisional Train, Australian Army Service Corps. Appointed 2nd lieutenant on February 2, 1918, and transferred to 10th Battalion. Promoted to rank of lieutenant on June 20, 1918. On July 23, 1918, at Merris, he carried out an important daylight patrol. At 3.15 in the afternoon he moved out with a small patrol and advanced towards where a small enemy post was located. He remained Adjutant of the Battalion until same was finally disbanded at Chatelet, Belgium, and after the 9th and 10th details merged and became known as the 3rd Brigade Battalion, he officiated as Adjutant of same until the final draft left France for England on May 20, 1919. He subsequently returned to South Australia, his services with the A.I.F. terminating on March 7, 1920. He has married, and in 1935 was residing at Maryborough, Queensland, where he was managing a branch of the Dunlop Perdriau Rubber Co. Ltd. Whilst in France he was wounded on two occasions.

XV

MEDICAL OFFICERS

From Australian Army Medical Corps
A complete Regimental List arranged chronologically:

1. CAPTAIN HARRY CAREW NOTT, M.B., B.S., D.M.R.E.
   August 20, 1914, to July 18, 1915.
   Born 1/8/88, and served with Battalion at Morphettville, Mena, and Dardanelles. Evacuated sick and proceeded to Egypt, but subsequently returned to the Battalion.

2. CAPTAIN BERTRAM INGRAM, F.R.C.S., L.R.C.P.
   July 19 to August 15, 1915.
   Born 18/12/77, and was admitted as a licentiate of the Royal College of Physicians of London in 1904, and became a fellow of the Royal College of Surgeons at Edinburgh in 1907. Appointed captain in A.I.F. on 20/8/14. Originally served with 3rd Field Ambulance, and relieved Capt. H. C. Nott during his absence in Egypt. Returned as M.O. in December, 1915.

3. CAPTAIN HARRY CAREW NOTT, M.B., B.S., D.M.R.E.
   August 16 to September 29, 1915.
   Returned from Egypt and remained with 10th until forced to evacuate sick a second time. Never returned to Battalion. Subsequently transferred to No. 1 Aus. C.C. Station, and finally became O.C. of No. 1 Aus. G. H. Promoted to rank of major on 14/11/16, and to lieut.-colonel on 5/11/18, vide separate biography herein, No. 37.

4. CAPTAIN CLAUDE MORLET, D.S.O., M.B., B.S., F.R.A.C.S.
   September 30 to December 16, 1915.
   Born 11/8/88, and is a son of the late Jean Stanislaus Morlet. He was educated at the University of Melbourne, where he graduated M.B., B.S., in 1913. Appointed captain in A.I.F. on 14/11/14. Originally Quartermaster of 2nd Field Ambulance, and afterward transferred to 1st A.G.H. Served with Battalion at Anzac, and accompanied 10th to Lemnos when withdrawn from Gallipoli, and three weeks later evacuated sick. Subsequently proceeded to France and served with 13th and 2nd Field Ambulances. Promoted to rank of major on 14/11/16, and to temporary lieut.-colonel on 5/11/18. M.I.D. vide London Gazette 31/12/18, and awarded D.S.O. promulgated amongst NewYear's Honours in London Gazette on 1/1/19, the official citation being: "For distinguished service in connection with military operations in France and Flanders." Returned to Australia and appointed major, 5th Military District, Reserve of Officers, 1/10/20, and transferred to A.A.M.C. with same rank 1/9/21. Listed on Reserve of Officers 1/1/22, and placed on Unattached List 1/10/22. Retransferred to A.A.M.C. 1/9/26, and placed on A.A.M.C. Reserve 1/9/30. He is a member of the British Medical Association, and in 1931 was admitted as a

MEDICAL OFFICERS

fellow of the Royal Australian College of Surgeons. He is a member of the Weld Club, Perth, and in 1935 was residing at Glyde Street, Mosman's Bay, Perth, and practising as an eye specialist at 252 St. George's Terrace, Perth, Western Australia.

5. CAPTAIN BERTRAM INGRAM, F.R.C.S., L.R.C.P.
December 17, 1915, to January 14, 1916.
Second occasion served with Battalion accompanying same on *Seeang Bee* to Egypt. Left 10th at Tel-el-Kebir, and later served in France with No. 3 Australian Auxiliary Hospital, and later appointed R.M.O. 13th Field Ambulance. Promoted to rank of major on 14/11/16, and appointed honorary major in Australian Military Forces on even date. Subsequent to his return was appointed major, Reserve of Officers, 1/1/21, and placed on Senior Executive Hospital Staff, 6th Military District. On 1/7/25 he was listed on A.A.M.C. Rseerve. He is a member of the British Medical Association, and in 1935 was residing and practising at Sorell, Tasmania.

6. CAPTAIN DEAN DAWSON, M.B., B.S.
January 15 to August 1, 1916.
Born 13/3/81, and appointed captain in A.I.F. on 26/8/15. Graduated in Faculty of Medicine, University of Adelaide, in 1905, and appointed a captain in A.A.M.C. on 3/8/14. Proceeded to Egypt in 1915, and subsequently transferred from 2nd A.G.H. to 10th Battalion then stationed at Tel-el-Kebir. He moved to Gebel Habieta with 10th, and later accompanied Battalion to France on *Saxonia*. Served through Fleurbaix and Pozieres, and at Berteaucourt was transferred to 1st Field Ambulance, with which he remained until August 30, 1916. He subsequently returned to Australia, his services with the A.I.F. terminating on November 20, 1916. He was appointed captain, Reserve of Officers, 22/8/19, and transferred to A.A.M.C. Reserve, 1/7/25. He is a member of the British Medical Association, and in 1935 was residing and practising at 58 King William Road, Hyde Park, and also at Verco Building, 178 North Terrace, Adelaide.

7. CAPTAIN FRANCIS TEULON BEAMISH, O.B.E., M.B., B.S.
August 1 to 10, 1916
Born 22/9/90, and was educated at the University of Melbourne, where he graduatd M.B., B.S. in 1913, and that year was appointed Resident Medical Officer at St. Vincent's Hospital, Melbourne. Appointed captain in A.I.F. on 14/1/15. Embarked from Australia with 3rd Reinforcements of A.M. Corps, and subsequently joined 10th Battalion at Berteaucourt, remaining with Battalion for 10 days only. Evacuated sick, and afterwards appointed R.M.O., 3rd Battalion, and later appointed D.A.D.M.S., A.I.F. Depots in United Kingdom, and eventually served with 1st Field Ambulance. Awarded O.B.E., Military Division on 1/1/19, order of precedence No. 3231. He was promoted to rank of major on 29/1/17, and appointed honorary major in Australian Military Forces, 5th Military District, on even date. Listed on Reserve of

Officers, 3rd Military District,, with rank of major on 1/10/20, and transferred to 5th Military District with same rank on 1/11/21, and placed on A.A.M.C. Reserve on 1/7/25. He is a member of the British Medical Association, and in 1935 was residing and practising at 65 Wellington Street, Northam, Western Australia.

8. CAPTAIN OSWALD RYLE HORWOOD, M.R.C.S., L.R.C.P.
August 10 to November 20, 1916.
Born 23/8/83, and graduated in London in 1913. Registered as member of British Medical Association on 31/10/13, and before proceeding to Australia resided at Tunstall Rectory, Suffolk. Appointed captain in A.I.F. on 20/8/15, and originally served with Australian Auxiliary Hospital. Awarded Medaille Du Roi Albert (Belgian), his services with A.I.F. terminating on the last day he officiated as M.O. to the Battalion. Proceeded to England, and subsequently to Australia, where he was appointed captain, Reserve of Officers, 4th Military District 1/1/20, and transferred to A.A.-M.C. Reserve 1/7/25. In 1935 he was not listed on Reserve of Officers, and was not practising within the Commonwealth of Australia; but according to an unauthenticated report is believed to be serving with a Christian mission in China.

9. CAPTAIN JOHN LESLIE HARRISON, M.B.
November 20, 1916, to February 12, 1917.
Born 15/4/93, and graduated M.B. at University of Sydney in 1916. Appointed captain in A.I.F. on 1/3/16. Served with No. 3 Australian Auxiliary Hospital before being attached to 10th. Later served with 10th Field Ambulance. Appointed honorary captain, Australian Military Forces, on 1/3/16, and promoted to rank of captain, Reserve of Officers on 1/1/21, and placed on A.A.M.C. Reserve, 1/7/25. He was appointed Resident Medical Officer at the Sydney Hospital in 1919, and for some time resided at Manly, but in 1935 was residing and practising at Wade Avenue South, Lecton, New South Wales.

10. CAPTAIN HERBERT ODILLO MAHER, M.B., Ch.M.
February 12 to September 3, 1917.
Born 28/1/93, and graduated M.B. Ch.M. at University of Sydney in 1915. Appointed captain in A.I.F. on 1/3/16, and originally served with 3rd Field Ambulance. Left Battalion at Bleu Tours shortly after arrival of Lieut.-Col. M. Wilder-Neligan, D.S.O., D.C.M. Subsequently transferred to No. 3 Aus. C.C. Station, and served in France until July, 1918. Appointed honorary captain, Reserve of Officers, 1/3/16, and on 1/1/21 was appointed captain, Reserve of Officers, and transferred to A.A.M.C. Reserve on 1/7/25. Appointed Hon. Assistant Ophthalmic Surgeon at St. Vincent's Hospital, Sydney, 1923-24, and officiated as Hon. Ophthalmologist since 1934. He is also Hon. Ophthalmic Surgeon at the Mater Misericordiæ Hospital, North Sydney. He registered as a member of the British Medical Association on 12/5/20, and in 1935 was residing at 8 Pine Hill Avenue, Double Bay, Sydney, and practising at 195 Macquarie Street, Sydney.

11. MAJOR SYDNEY VERE APPLEYARD, D.S.O., M.C.R.S., L.R.C.P.
    September 3, 1917, to March 1, 1918.
    Born 6/6/83, and appointed captain in A.I.F. on 1/3/16, and promoted to rank of major on 20/6/17. Commenced service in France with 3rd Field Ambulance on October 29, 1916, and finally left France on September 28, 1918. Awarded D.S.O. whilst serving with 10th Battalion, *vide* separate biography herein, No. 1.

12. CAPTAIN JAMES MANN HENDERSON, M.C., M.B., B.S.
    March 1 to August 17, 1918.
    Born 17/7/82, and graduated M.B., B.S. at University of Melbourne in 1916. Appointed captain in A.I.F. on 11/9/16. Shortly after Lihons in August, 1918, he was transferred to 12th Battalion as Medical Officer. Whilst serving with this unit he won the Military Cross, which was promulgated in the *London Gazette* on February 15, 1919, and the details on July 30, 1919, the official citation being: "During the attack near Jeancourt on 18th September, 1918, he established his regimental aid post immediately in rear of the jumping-off place, and attended to the wounded of his and of a supporting battalion under heavy shell fire in an exposed position. As the attack progressed he moved forward and treated large numbers of casualties in the open. By his energy, disregard of danger, and clever organization he relieved a great deal of suffering, and throughout set a splendid example to those under him." He subsequently returned to Australia, and was appointed a captain in the A.M. Corps on 1/1/20, and transferred to Reserve of Officers with same rank on even date, and was listed on Junior Hospital Staff, 3rd Military District, as captain, A.A.M.C. Reserve, 1/7/25. He is a member of the British Medical Association, and for some years has served as a Surgeon Commander in the Royal Australian Navy. He was appointed in this capacity to H.M.A.S. *Canberra* with seniority from 15/2/32. He was subsequently transferred to H.M.A.S. *Cerberus*, and in 1935 his address was "Flinders Naval Depot, Westernport, Victoria".

13. CAPTAIN ROBERT PERCY YOUNG, M.B., B.S.
    August 17 to September 18, 1918.
    Born 29/12/89, and educated at Caulfield Grammar School and Ormond College, University of Melbourne, where he commenced his medical course in 1909 and graduated M.B., B.S. in 1914, his degrees being conferred on 14/8/14. He attended the University of Melbourne at the same time as Capt. Claude Morlet, who also became an A.I.F. Medical Officer, and was attached to the 10th Battalion. Appointed captain in A.I.F. on 14/3/16, and served in Egypt and France. He was formerly attached to the 3rd D.A.C., and subsequently served with the 1st, 2nd and 3rd Field Ambulances. Transferred to 10th Battalion from No. 1 Field Ambulance, and remained with Battalion exactly one month, until killed in action at Jeancourt on September 18, 1918. On this day the 12th Battalion "hopped over" at 5 a.m., followed by the 10th at 6 a.m.—the 10th

leap-frogging over the 12th at a specified time. As the 10th Battalion moved forward the enemy artillery opened up, and casualties were heavy before the Battalion reached the tape line. During this initial advance Capt. Young came to the door of his aid post to witness the 10th men move off, when a shell landed at his feet and he was instantly killed. This was the last occasion the Battalion was in action during the Great War, and he was extremely unfortunate not to have survived the operation. Immediately following his death, Capt. Horace Crotty, M.A. (A.I.F. Chaplain), who was formerly Bishop of Bathurst, New South Wales, and in November, 1935, accepted the living of St. Pancras, London, came forward and assisted with the wounded.

14. CAPTAIN DOUGLAS LEWIS BARLOW, M.C., E.D., M.D.
September 18 to October 4, 1918.
Born 18/6/94. Appointed captain in A.I.F. on 20/5/16. Graduated M.B., B.S. in Faculty of Medicine at University of Adelaide in 1915. First served with A.I.F. on No. 1 Hospital Ship, and subsequently appointed Medical Officer of the 7th Battalion. Whilst serving with this unit he won the M.C. at Broodseinde early in October, 1917. His award was promulgated in the *London Gazette* on 26/11/17 and the details on 6/4/18, the official citation being: "For conspicuous gallantry and devotion to duty during an attack. He advanced with the battalion, established his aid post, and dressed the wounded, and assisted in their removal under constant shelling. Owing to casualties among bearers he was cut off from the ambulance clearing post for several hours, and it was mainly owing to his exertions that the wounded received attention and shelter during this period." He was appointed an honorary captain in the Australian Military Forces on 20/5/16, and upon his return to South Australia was promoted to rank of captain, A.A.M.C. on 1/9/21, and listed as major, Reserve of Officers, 1/7/20. He was appointed Medical Officer, Area 27, 4th Divisional Area at Keswick, from 1/7/32, and Commander of 8th Field Hygienic Section from 19/10/32. He attained his majority in the A.A.M.C. on 18/11/32, and on September 1, 1935, was appointed to the command of the 6th Cavalry Brigade Field Ambulance, and was promoted to the rank of lieutenant-colonel. He has been awarded the Efficiency Decoration. He registered as a member of the British Medical Association on 19/4/20, and in 1922 obtained the degree of M.D. at the University of Adelaide. He has subsequently been appointed Hon. Assistant Physician to the Asthma Clinic at the Adelaide Children's Hospital. In 1935 he was residing and practising at 36 Portrush Road, Tusmore, and also practising at Verco Building, 178 North Terrace, Adelaide.

15. CAPTAIN CLARENCE ARCHIBALD MITCHELL, M.B.
October 4, 1918, to February 15, 1919.
Born 28/1/85, and graduated M.B. at University of Sydney in 1916. Appointed captain in A.I.F. on 31/1/17. Transferred to

10th from 3rd Field Ambulance in which he had officiated as R.M.O. Listed on Reserve of Officers as captain, 1/1/20, and transferred to A.A.M.C. Reserve 1/7/25, 2nd Military District. He is a member of the British Medical Association, and for some years resided at Teralba, New South Wales, but in 1935 was residing at Toronto and practising at Boolaroo, Newcastle, New South Wales.

16. CAPTAIN JOHN SYDNEY GREEN, M.D., Dip. G.O., M.C.O.G., F.R.A.C.S.
March 25, etc., 1919.
An interim of six weeks occurred between the departure of Capt. Mitchell and the arrival of Capt. J. S. Green. During this period the 9th and 10th Battalion details merged into Brigade Details when the medical services were supplied by Brigade Medical Officers. Born 3/5/95, and graduated M.B., B.S. in Faculty of Medicine at University of Melbourne in 1917, and officiated as Resident Medical Officer at Melbourne Hospital, 1917-18. Appointed captain in A.I.F. on 6/5/18, and originally served with A.I.F. Depots. Subsequent to returning to Australia was appointed captain A.A.M.C. on 1/1/20, 3rd Military District, and was placed on Reserve of Officers 1/7/20, and on 1/7/25 was placed on A.A.M.C. Reserve. He was Hon. Clinical Assistant to the Gynæcologist at the Melbourne Hospital, 1924-33, and has been Hon. Assistant to the Gynæcologist since 1933. He is now Hon. Surgeon (midwifery) Women's Hospital, Melbourne. In 1920 he obtained the Diploma of Gynæcology and Obstetrics of the Dublin University, and in 1922 obtained the degree of M.D. at the University of Melbourne. He is a member of the College of Obstetricians and Gynæcologists of England, and is a fellow of the Royal Australian College of Surgeons. He is a member of the British Medical Association, and a member of the Branch Council of Victoria. In 1935 he was residing and practising at 84 Maribyrnong Road, Moonee Ponds, and was also practising at No. 12 Collins Street, Melbourne.

XVI

REGIMENTAL SERGEANT-MAJORS

A complete list arranged chronologically, from the raising of the Battalion at Morphettville, August 19, 1914, to disbandment of same at Chatelet, Belgium, March 17, 1919, but excluding any who only acted in that capacity.

1. No. 1, R.S.M. WESLEY ARMSTRONG WHITBOURN.
   August 19, 1914, to June 27, 1915.
   Subsequently promoted to rank of 2nd lieutenant, and attained captaincy, *vide* particulars on page 121.

2. No. 2, R.S.M. GEORGE CHARLES MAGENIS.
   June 27 to August 17, 1915.
   Subsequently promoted to rank of 2nd lieutenant, and attained captaincy, *vide* separate biography herein, No. 33.

3. No. 748, R.S.M. DONALD CHISHOLM.
   August 17, 1915, to August 17, 1916.
   Born 15/8/84 at Ross-shire, Scotland, and one of five brothers who served in the Great War, four being killed in action. Enlisted at Morphettville 29/8/14, and posted to original "H" Company, in which he was promoted to rank of lance-corporal prior to embarkation. Served for seven years in 1st Bn. (79th Foot), Queen's Own Cameron Highlanders, and participated in the Sudan War of 1898 and the South African War, receiving the Khedive's Medal for the former and the Queen's with five clasps and the King's Medal for the latter. Promoted to rank of 2nd lieutenant on August 5, 1916, and attained lieutenancy on November 27, 1916, services with A.I.F. terminating on June 15, 1918. Employed for several years as commissionaire at Commonwealth Bank, Adelaide, and now employed at Mental Hospital, Parkside, and residing at No. 34 Duthy Street, Malvern.

4. No. 365, R.S.M. SAMUEL EDMUND DOLEY.
   August 17 to September 23, 1916.
   Born August, 1879, and enlisted at Morphettville 19/8/14, and posted to original "C" Company. Promoted to lance-corporal on transport *Ascanius*, 1/12/14, and received first commission as 2nd lieutenant on September 23, 1916. Seconded for duty with 3rd Training Battalion on January 20, 1917, and attained his lieutenancy on February 6, 1917. Subsequently returned to Australia, services with A.I.F. terminating on June 15, 1918. Died at Adelaide Hospital on February 26, 1929, as result of scaffolding accident at Cresco Fertilizer Building, Birkenhead. Survived by a widow and daughter now residing at No. 19 Clifford Street, Torrensville.

5. No. 324, R.S.M. FREDERICK JAMES STANLEY MEAD, D.C.M.
   September 23, 1916, to January 24, 1917.
   Subsequently promoted to rank of 2nd lieutenant, and attained captaincy, *vide* separate biography herein, No. 35.

REGIMENTAL SERGEANT-MAJORS 131

6. No. 470, R.S.M. GEORGE GUTHRIE, M.C.
   January 24 to May 6, 1917.
   Born 3/8/87, and enlisted at Morphettville on 24/8/14, and posted to original "D" Company. Appointed Warrant Officer, Class I, 11/2/17, and awarded M.C., which was promulgated in *London Gazette* amongst King's Birthday Honours on June 3, 1917. Wounded in Bullecourt action, 6/5/17, and did not return to Battalion. On July 5, 1921, appointed clerk in Soldier Settlement Department, Adelaide, and on December 1, 1927, transferred to Children's Welfare and Public Relief Department. Subsequently left South Australian Public Service, and now residing in Sydney, New South Wales. Affectionately known to men of 10th as "Snowy".

7. No. 621, TEMPORARY R.S.M. ERNEST STANLEY LEWIS, D.C.M.
   May 6 to July 28, 1917.
   Born 1892, and enlisted at Morphettville on August 26, 1914, and posted to original "B" Company. Prior to joining A.I.F. was a butcher by occupation, and was residing at Torrensville. Won D.C.M. at Bullecourt on May 7, 1917. Appointment as R.S.M. not confirmed, but promoted to rank of 2nd lieutenant on July 28, 1917, and killed in action at Broodseinde Ridge on October 2, 1917.

8. No. 503, R.S.M. ERNEST ALFRED HOLLAND, D.C.M., M.M. (Fr.)
   July 28, 1917, to June 2, 1918.
   Born 8/8/89, and enlisted at Morphettville on August 24, 1914, and posted to original "H" Company. Appointed Warrant Officer, Class I, 7/8/17. French Decoration (Medaille Militaire) won at Pozieres in July, 1916, and D.C.M. at Merris, May 29, 1918. Mentioned in despatches, *vide London Gazette* 7/4/18, and also mentioned in 1st Anzac Routine Orders of 28/2/17. Wounded at Merris on June 2, 1918, and did not return to Battalion. Affectionately known to men of 10th as "Raggy", and now residing at Wall Flat, River Murray, where he has settled on a small block.

9. No. 116, R.S.M. EDWARD GEORGE WILSON, D.C.M., M.M.
   June 2 to September 20, 1918.
   Born 14/3/93, and enlisted at Morphettville on 19/8/14, and posted to original "C" Company. Won M.M. as sergeant at Bullecourt in May, 1917, and D.C.M. at Polygon Wood, September, 1917. Wounded at Mouquet Farm, and finally left Battalion on September 20, 1918. Affectionately known to men of 10th as "Ned". Now in business as cabinetmaker at Morgan Street, Hindmarsh, and residing at No. 40 Cedar Avenue, Croydon Park.

10. No. 3, TEMPORARY R.S.M. REGINALD TASMAN WHITE, M.M.
    September 20, 1918, to March 17, 1919.
    Born at Quorn, South Australia, 21/5/95, and son of Rev. Thomas Geddes White, Methodist clergyman, now of 32 Avenue Road, Highgate. Prior to his birth his parents had resided in Tasmania,

which fact was perpetuated when he was christened "Tasman". Enlisted at Morphettville on 3/9/14 with 3rd Brigade Headquarters, by whom his low regimental number was allotted. Embarked as private in this unit with 1st Australian Contingent in October, 1914, and proceeded to Egypt and subsequently to the Dardanelles. Returned to South Australia from the Peninsula, and in August, 1916, re-embarked with the 19th Reinforcements of the 10th Battalion with rank of staff-sergeant. Subsequently joined Battalion in France, and won M.M. at Lihons on August 11, 1918. His appointment as R.S.M. was not confirmed, owing to the impending disbandment of the Battalion. Now residing at No. 27 Roberts Street, Strathfield, New South Wales.

11. No. 1587, TEMPORARY R.S.M. JOHN CLIFFORD WICKHAM, M.M.
March 17 to April, 1919.
Born 24/1/90, and enlisted in A.I.F. on 23/11/14. Embarked with 3rd Reinforcements of 10th Battalion, and joined Battalion in the line at Anzac on May 7, 1915. Won M.M. at Jeancourt, September 18, 1918, and appointed Warrant Officer, Class II, 30/10/18. His appointment as R.S.M. was not confirmed owing to disbandment of Battalion. Painter by occupation, now residing at No. 116 Kenilworth Road, Parkside.

XVII

SIGNALLERS

The Signallers of the 10th Battalion, although only small numerically, played an important part in assisting the men of "The Fighting 10th" in their many battles. Termed "the nerves of the Unit", they maintained requisite communication between Battalion Headquarters and the Companies, and between Battalion Headquarters and Brigade under circumstances invariably dangerous, difficult, and diverse. Throughout the history of the 10th the Signalling Section always magnificently co-operated, and was justly recognized as an efficient component, whilst the men who constituted it were regarded as a happy family.

Synchronizing with the raising of the main body of the Battalion, the nucleus of the 10th Signalling Section first came into existence at Morphettville in the middle of August, 1914. It may be said that the men selected from the original Battalion and drafted into the Signalling Section were men of considerable experience, either acquired in the British Navy, the British Army, or as enthusiastic trainees under the Commonwealth compulsory training systetm. Captain S. R. Hall—the first Signalling Officer—was an expert in his work, and immensely popular with his men, and from the very beginning set an example that lived long with the Battalion and the Signalling Section. During those early days at Morphettville it devolved upon S.S.M. Bowen, of the A. & I. Staff, to mould the Headquarters and Company Signallers into a technical adjunct, whilst S.S.M. L. R. Walker, who embarked as Signalling Sergeant, was proficient both in organizing and sketching.

Throughout the whole of the voyage to Egypt the Signallers were functioning with full effect. Communication was maintained day and night with the *Orvieto*, the flagship of the convoy, and between the other transports by means of the international code—semaphore and Morse, both flag and lamp. It was on the transport *Ascanius* that the Signallers came into the lime-light by winning the tug-of-war match against all teams from the Battalion.

At Mena the Signallers tramped over the dunes of the desert with the Battalion, and the glaring sun proved ideal for the use of the heliograph, and with this instrument they became adept. It was well known that they preferred sacrificing the Sunday morning Church Parade in order to take up a vantage point on the Great Pyramid in order to establish communication between that eminence and the Citadel situated on the Mokattam Hills on the opposite side of the River Nile. Subsequently embarking with the Battalion on the *Ionian* for the Dardanelles, they settled down to the new training and new scenery of Lemnos with a zest which undoubtedly contributed in no small measure to their physical and technical fitness. Then came Saturday, April 24, 1915, when they boarded the *Prince of Wales* with "B" and "C" Companies of the Battalion, each signaller taking with him a bicycle, which was ultimately discarded.

In the historic landing at Anzac on April 25, 1915, the Signallers were amongst the first men of the Battalion ashore, and most of them, upon setting foot on Turkish soil immediately rejoined their companies as fighting men. Battalion Headquarters Signallers remained in proximity to Lieut.-Colonel S. P. Weir, and from the very outset were used in carrying messages, whilst later, if not in the firing line, were employed in carrying messages or lugging ammunition to the front. That day their leader, Captain S. R. Hall, was seen on a small plateau calmly wagging a pair of red and yellow flags, whilst bullets sprayed the dirt about his feet; but before dusk he had fallen, and the news of his death came as a severe blow to his men, who had always said he would either win a V.C. or meet his death whilst in action. It was during the tension of the first day and night on Gallipoli, whilst the men of the 10th were engaged in that desperate and grim struggle of fighting off attacks against the positions that had been won, that the Signallers developed that great admiration which ever after they maintained of the wonderful fighting qualities of the men of the Companies of the 10th. When the 10th was first relieved and proceeded to the Anzac Beach, it moved along in full view of the formidable Gaba Tepe. As the troops wearily trudged along the beach, their safety was the paramount question of the moment within the mind of Lieut.-Colonel S. P. Weir. He accordingly instructed the Signallers to get in touch with one of the warboats. A heliograph was quickly set up, and a message flashed to a stationary warship which quickly replied: "Keep under the cliff, and go no farther south. Advise move into gullies." The required check-up on direction being obtained, the Battalion detoured to Shell Green, where a bivouac was struck, and the memorable first roll call occurred.

After the Battalion moved into the line from Shell Green D.3 'phones were used for the first time as a means of communication between Brigade, Battalion, and the Companies. These instruments saved the runners a great deal of work, and for several weeks after the landing touch was maintained with the troopship *Ionian* by means of large flag and heliograph signalling. In August, 1915, Lieutenant W. A. Whitbourn was appointed Signalling Officer, and carried out the duties appertaining thereto, in addition to his other duties as Adjutant of the Battalion; and during the difficult months associated with the Defence of Anzac the 10th Signallers performed their duties in a thoroughly satisfactory manner.

In November, 1915, after the Battalion had been withdrawn from the Peninsula and went into camp on the island of Lemnos, the sadly-depleted ranks of the Signalling Section were strengthened by additions from several reinforcement quotas which had been held up at Mudros, and thus precluded from serving on Gallipoli. These new men were of a splendid type—young, intelligent, and fit. They had received excellent training, and with the survivors of Anzac brought the Section up to a high standard. Shortly after the Battalion returned to Egypt, Lieut. W. F. J. McCann was appointed Signalling Officer at Tel-el-Kebir, but before the Battalion embarked on the *Saxonia* for France he had been transferred back to his company. At Gebel Habieta several signallers were transferred to the 50th Battalion and the Pioneer Battalion, and a few were promoted to the rank of 2nd Lieutenant.

Before entering the line at Fleurbaix, France, the 10th Battalion Signallers were billeted at Madame George's Farm, and at what was subsequently known as the nursery sector, experienced several weeks under ideal conditions. At Rouge-de-Bout on June 6, 1916, they underwent their first experience of repairing lines under shell and machine-gun fire. Lieut. R. K. Hurcombe became Signalling Officer at Pozieres, in July, 1916, and with Signallers Kay and Wilson moved up as an advance party to the front, leaving the main body of the Battalion resting in Sausage Valley. Before dusk the move came, and then the struggle into the line. The Company Signallers returned to the Companies to again become fighting men of their Unit, whilst Headquarters Signallers were used as runners. It was impossible to maintain line communication, and in many instances the difficulties were insuperable. Incredible as it may appear, the Signallers had been issued with reels of wire insulated with black enamel. About one-sixteenth of an inch in gauge, springy but unpliable in the extreme, this wire would not lie flat; yet, when bent, it was easily broken. Orders were issued for a line to be laid to Brigade at Contalmaison, but the enamelled wire was broken almost as fast as it was put down. It was a complete failure. Earlier in the day Signallers Kay and Wilson had carried in a large French electric lamp, which proved most invaluable as a means of maintaining communication. With this big lamp twenty to thirty messages daily were forwarded to Brigade, but its flash at night had to be dimmed, and still was dangerous, as it drew enemy fire; but fortunately no direct hit resulted. When the Germans made their heavy counter-attack a message was sent to Brigade by this lamp for artillery support. The exact map reference was given, and the artillery quickly responded. Apart from this big boon lamp the Signallers possessed one other small lamp in one Company line; but it was impossible to use it, and the only other means of communication was by runner. At Pozieres the Signallers also assisted to carry bombs to the front line, where they saw their comrades fighting under the terrific conditions of that inferno.

At the Second Pozieres (Mouquet Farm) Lieut. L. R. Stephens became Signalling Officer, and was regarded as a perfect gentleman and an efficient Signaller. All communications in this operation were by runner, except a few short messages on the panel to observation planes, and several messages sent by carrier-pigeon. The birds were invaluable in emergency, but could only be used in daylight. They were sent off in pairs with the message attached to their legs by means of a small cylinder. Their loft would be situated at Division, which they could reach quickly. Owing to the limited number of birds available only extremely urgent messages were sent by them. Mouquet Farm was another furnace of shell-fire, and the Signallers were caught in a barrage when going over some exposed ground. In the resulting scramble for cover some were lost, and did not report to the Battalion until late the following day.

The Railway Dugouts which were occupied by the Battalion in September, 1916, before moving into the trenches at "Hill 60" at Ypres, established a precedent for the number of night patrols operating in "No-Man's-Land". Minenwerfers were prevalent, and the chief task of the Signallers was to take a line out each night. Here the Fullerphones were used in the line for the first time. These instruments were an ingenious arrangement that prevented the enemy from picking up the messages through faulty earthing of the wires. These instruments required expert men on the code, and even though the Signalling Section provided men specially skilled in the work, the 'phones on the whole were found to be unsatisfactory, as they were so easily put out of adjustment.

The dreary months of the 1916-17 winter were spent in and out of the trenches at Bernafay Wood, Gueudecourt, Flers, Bazentin, Le Barque, etc., where the Signallers, in common with the rest of the Battalion, existed and suffered in a morass of mud and slush. Repairing broken wires in the snow and sleet was a new experience, and day and night, often under fire, the repairs were executed. Often the wire would be buried deep down under the slush and ice, and hours would sometimes be spent in locating and fixing one break. The 10th Signallers still vividly recollect the treacherous spot in front of Gueudecourt, where one of the enemy 'planes had great sport in "potting" them.

At Bullecourt, in May, 1917, men were pounded to death by heavily-massed artillery, and shells of all sizes fell continuously about Battalion Headquarters in the sunken road. Lines were impossible to maintain, except to the 12th Battalion Headquarters and Brigade. Despite the frightful conditions prevailing the Signallers did wonderful work under such merciless fire. When repairing the line between Battalion Headquarters and the 12th Battalion it seemed that during the day the enemy would deliberately snipe those moving about in the open with 4·9 shells, as these shells persistently followed the men and accompanied and harassed their every effort to maintain communication. A line was attempted to the front line by way of Pioneer Trench, which though considerably battered offered some little cover in reaching the front line. It was crowded with men going in and coming out, fatigue parties both ways, and wounded going out. In addition to the congestion necessarily caused by such troop movements in the heat of battle, it was littered with the debris of war, including smashed woodwork, twisted iron, gear dropped by fatigue parties, and worst of all obstacles, a maze of twisted and tangled telephone wires. It was in this conglomeration of men and materials and munitions that the Signallers heroically attempted to lay the new wire; and despite the heavy shelling, the wire was eventually taken to a dug-out in the front line, and was actually spoken through to Battalion Headquarters. Proud of this accomplishment, the Signallers returned only to be informed that the line had barely lasted five minutes. The question of putting the line over the top was next considered, but not carried out, as the open ground between the line and the sunken road was continuously swept with shells of all sizes, and to show above the ground near the front line was to be exposed to the deadly rattle and swish of enemy machine guns. This ground was a veritable shambles, consisting of shell hole on shell hole, heaps of rusted wire, piles of dead Germans, and the same was being churned over and over by each successive salvo of shells. Immediately the line was reported broken two signallers volunteered to try and repair same, but after successfully negotiating such difficult terrain, and after three hours' indefatigable effort, were reluctantly compelled to give it up. Communication in this area was then maintained by High-Power Buzzer and by runner.

It was at Bullecourt that the Germans made that early morning thrust and actually penetrated our first line of trenches, whilst No. 3132 Private E. Williams, a Company Signaller, complacently remained in a dug-out operating the High-Power Buzzer. Whilst the Germans were bombing down the trench he sent out urgent messages for help. His messages got through, and reinforcements eventually arrived, with the result that the Germans were driven out. For his splendid work and bravery he was awarded the D.C.M. A few days later at Bullecourt, No. 388 Sergeant F. E. Allchin presented a neat incident of cool bravado. This episode of splendid conduct whilst under fire is one of the many examples of devotion to duty for which the Signallers as a body were noted. At dawn the enemy attacked, and Battalion Headquarters desired that a message should be sent through to Brigade for support. The Brigade line was found to be broken, and Sergeant Allchin and two other Signallers went out to locate the fault. From a rise they saw the line pass over a sunken road which had recently been occupied by one of the batteries. The enemy had placed on this position a box barrage that was almost perfect in design. The outer square was of light shells whilst the centre about the road was pummelled with "heavies". The N.C.O. told the other two men to wait whilst he attempted the job on his own. With the 'phone on his shoulder and trailing the wire, he trotted to the edge of the barrage, and there calmly waited until four shells had burst in front of him, and then dashed through the outer line. Then down into the smoke of the sunken road he passed and found the break, whilst shells fell only twenty yards on his right. He completed the repair, and subsequently scrambled up the opposite bank when a shell seemed to burst in front of him. He was flung back rolling down the bank, but picked himself up unhurt, and serenely climbed up again with the wire still intact and running through his hand. He then moved clear of the outer shells, and sitting down tapped in to both Battalion and Brigade, the line still being sound. For this act of bravery on the field he was awarded the Military Medal.

Shortly after Bullecourt, Lieutenant L. R. Stephens temporarily left the Battalion, and in July, 1917, Lieut. A. B. Baker was appointed Signalling Officer, but almost immediately afterwards was transferred to a company. In September, 1917, Lieutenant E. L. Angove was appointed Signalling Officer, and then followed the fighting at Polygon Wood on 20/9/17, where the Signallers under the eagle-eye of Lieut.-Colonel M. Wilder-Neligan had their work cut out; but there was always a reason for everything, and everyone worked willingly.

In 1918 the Signallers carried out an important part in the successes achieved by the Battalion in the Merris Sector. During the operation of June 3, 1918, signals communications were undertaken by the 10th Signallers, and throughout intercourse was maintained. On June 28, 1918, a special feature of the operation was the excellent work carried out by the 10th Battalion and Artillery Signallers in mending broken wire under heavy enemy fire; and in the culminating capture of Merris on July 30, 1918, the Signallers in order to maintain the communications employed 5-legged ladder lines, metallic lines, a buried cable, a direct line and two loop sets. The two loop sets did good work, but communication was hard to maintain with the left flank, owing to splinters hitting one of these sets; but on the whole communication was well kept.

During all the fighting in which the 10th Battalion was from time to time engaged, the Signallers determinedly, successfully, and skilfully carried out the work entrusted to them. With new men filling up the vacancies created by those who had passed on, the old spirit survived, and on no occasion, when put to the test, were the Signallers of the 10th ever found wanting. The rank and file of the Battalion always appreciated the assistance and co-operation rendered by this technical arm of the Unit, and the high esteem in which they were so held was always fully reciprocated by the Signallers themselves. Ex-No. 388 Sergeant F. E. Allchin, of the 10th Signalling Section, has paid the men of "The Fighting 10th" the following valuable tribute: "And now as the years pass by the Signallers look back on those days of war and remember the wonderful comrades with whom they served, and cannot find words to express feelings of pride in having been associated with the splendid men of the 10th Battalion, A.I.F. The Signallers saw them in action, and will never forget how they stood up to those grim struggles, bringing glory to the Unit—the Tenth, the name of which ranks with the best in the A.I.F. But their fondest memory is of those who fell—comrades who paid the supreme sacrifice for our Great Empire and for us. And remembering this, although the years of the Great War are long past, the memory of fallen comrades will never die, nor will the efforts of those who remain ever cease to prevent the lives of those who died having been given in vain. 28/10/35."

XVIII

REGIMENTAL LIST OF OFFICERS

Including all Officers who passed through the Battalion during the Great War, and showing the following details:
1. Decorations won before, during, or after serving with 10th Battalion.
2. Highest substantive rank attained whilst serving in 10th Battalion, but promotions subsequent to transfer to other units are not all shown.
3. Officers transferred to and from the 10th Battalion.
4. Pre-commissioned rank upon receiving first commission.
5. Temporary rank and reversions of 10th Officers.
6. If original or reinforcement quota Officer.

HONORARY COLONEL

Weir, Stanley Price, D.S.O., V.D. Appointed Lieutenant-Colonel with rank of Honorary Colonel, 17/8/14.
(Russian Order of St. Anne),
M.I.D.

LIEUTENANT-COLONELS

	2nd Lieut.	Lieut.	Capt.	Major.	Lt.-Col.
Beevor, Miles Fitzroy, V.D. To 52nd Bn. as C.O., 4/3/16.	—	—	—	19/8/14	1/2/16
Denton, James Samuel, D.S.O., V.D., M.I.D. From 11th Bn. temp., Sept., 1916.	—	—	25/8/14	1/1/15	27/9/16
Jacob, Ross Blyth, V.D. To 50th Bn., subsequently commanded 10th twice.	—	—	—	19/8/14	20/2/16	4/2/17
Wilder-Neligan, Maurice, C.M.G., D.S.O., and Bar, D.C.M., Croix de Guerre (Fr.), M.I.D. 4 From 9th Bn. (O.R. Sgt.)	28/4/15	11/8/15	12/3/16	21/10/16	30/6/17

MAJORS

	2nd Lieut.	Lieut.	Capt.	Major.	
Hurcombe, Frederick William, V.D.	—	—	—	19/8/14	To 50th Bn. as C.O. 1/3/16, M.I.D.
Oldham, Edward Castle	—	—	19/8/14	1/2/15	K.I.A., 25/4/15.
Lorenzo, Francis Maxwell de Frayer, D.S.O. (Montenegrin Order of Danilo)	—	—	19/8/14	26/4/15	To 49th Bn. as C.O. 12/3/16, M.I.D. 2.
Redburg, George Ernest	—	—	19/8/14	20/2/16	Temp. Lt.-Col. 23/8/16, Res. Com., 28/2/17, M.I.D.
Rafferty, Rupert Anstice, D.S.O.	28/8/14	1/2/15	22/5/15	1/3/16	From 12th Bn. as Lt.-Col., 26/3/17, M.I.D. 2.
Shaw, George Dorricutt, V.D.	—	—	19/8/14	12/3/16	Temp. Lt.-Col. when Commanding Bn., M.I.D.
Giles, Felix Gordon, D.S.O., V.D.	—	19/8/14	19/9/14	12/3/16	Commanded Bn. twice, M.I.D.
Steele, Alexander, D.S.O. (M.G. Sgt.)	28/4/15	4/8/15	20/2/16	5/8/16	From 9th Bn. as C.O., K.I.A., 7/9/17.
Newman, John, D.S.O.	19/8/14	1/2/15	20/2/16	23/9/16	From 11th Bn. as C.O., Temp. Lt.-Col. M.I.D.

REGIMENTAL LIST OF OFFICERS

MAJORS—continued.

Name	2nd Lieut.	Lieut.	Capt.	Major.	
Rumball, Clarence, M.C.	19/8/14	1/2/15	26/4/15	30/3/17	Commanded Bn. once. M.I.D.
Henwood, Horace Norman (Sgt.)	28/5/15	9/11/15	16/4/16	19/9/17	K.I.A., 1/3/18, M.I.D.
McCann, William Francis James, D.S.O., O.B.E., M.C. and Bar. (C.S.M.)	4/8/15	14/11/15	16/4/16	21/10/18	Commanded Bn. early 1919, M.I.D.

HONORARY MAJOR

Name	2nd Lieut.	Lieut.	Capt.	Hon. Major.
Minagall, Charles Francis, D.S.O. Quartermaster, M.I.D.	—	—	19/8/14	22/11/15

CAPTAINS

Name	2nd Lieut.	Lieut.	Capt.	
Seager, Harold William Hastings, M.C.	—	—	19/8/14	Original and 2/10th, to 50th; Major, 23/7/17.
Herbert, Mervyn James	—	—	19/8/14	Original to 50th; Major 12/3/16.
Hall, Sydney Raymond	—	—	19/8/15	Original; K.I.A. 25/4/15.
Green, Keith Eddowes	—	19/8/14	1/1/15	Original; K.I.A. 25/4/15.
Sexton, Eric James, O.B.E.	—	19/8/14	26/4/15	Original and 17/10th, to M.G. Coy.; Major, 14/2/17.
Hamilton, John	19/8/14	1/2/15	20/2/16	Original.
Loutit, Noel Medway, D.S.O. and Bar	19/9/14	1/2/15	20/2/16	Original to 50th; Temp. Lt.-Col., 1/12/18. M.I.D. 3.
Hooper, Charles William	—	22/4/15	12/3/16	6/10th, K.I.A., 25/7/16.
Whitbourn, Wesley Armstrong (R.S.M.)	28/4/15	1/7/15	12/3/16	To 3rd T. Bn.
Sawer, Edgar Geoffery, M.C. (M.G. Sgt.)	28/4/15	1/7/15	12/3/16	To 12th M.G. Coy.; Major, 1/3/17. M.I.D.
Magenis, George Charles, D.S.O. (R.Q.M.S.)	4/8/15	8/10/15	12/3/16	Adjutant, 1916-17. M.I.D.
Bates, Charles Joseph (C.S.M.)	4/8/15	14/11/15	16/4/16	K.I.A., 19/5/16.
Hurcombe, Roy Kintore, M.C. and Bar (Cpl.)	12/5/15	14/11/15	25/5/16	Temp. Major, 23/9/18; did not revert to Capt. M.I.D.
Heming, Hector Roy	19/8/14	1/2/15	26/7/16	Original.
Campbell, Gordon Cathcart, M.C. and Bar	16/7/15	24/3/16	24/10/16	10/10th, Temp. Major, 7/10/18; Rev. Capt., 8/11/18.
De Courcy-Ireland, William Stanley	—	10/2/15	25/10/16	4/10th and 18/10th.
Cornish, Walter Gordon, M.C., C. de G. (Fr.)	—	16/12/14	30/10/16	To Brigade and Div. Hdqrs.; 3/10th. M.I.D. 2.
Coyle, James Edward Fitzgerald	—	—	20/3/17	To Div. Train A.A.S.C.
Perry, William Howard, M.C.	19/8/14	1/2/15	30/3/17	Original.
Macdonald, Alexander Henry	1/1/15	4/8/15	1/11/17	2/10th and 21/10th.
Partridge, Harold Ewart	16/7/15	10/5/16	1/11/17	6/27th
Thomas, Hugh William	16/7/15	10/5/16	1/11/17	6/27th
Inglis, Eric Murray, M.C. (L.Sgt.)	4/8/15	20/2/16	1/11/17	M.I.D.
Newlands, Alan John, M.C. (Sergt.)	12/3/16	21/6/16	22/12/18	Temp. to 3rd A.L.T.M. Bty., 15/4/16.
Sinclair, John Gladstone	20/1/16	6/2/17	23/12/18	16/10th. M.I.D.
Saunders, Magnus Graham, M.C.	3/3/16	1/6/17	14/1/19	Temp. transferred to 32nd Bn.; 19/10th.
Mead, Frederick James Stanley, M.C., D.C.M. (R.S.M.)	24/1/17	24/5/17	14/1/19	—

THE FIGHTING 10TH

LIEUTENANTS

Name	2nd Lieut.	Lieut.	Notes
Smith, Eric Wilkes Talbot	—	14/8/14	K.I.A., 30/4/15; M.I.D., Posthumous; Original.
Byrne, Albert John	—	19/8/14	Original; K.I.A., 25/4/15.
Holmes, Louis Gordon	—	19/8/14	Original. To Bde. Hqrs. Capt., 26/4/15; D. of Wounds, 23/6/15.
Hosking, Herbert Champion	—	19/8/14	Original and 19/10th.
Kayser, Julius August William	—	27/8/14	Original. To 12th Bn. Sept. 1914. To Temp. Major, K.I.A., 16/2/17.
Harrison, John de Courcy	—	21/9/14	Imp. Reservist; Temp. Capt. 11/2/17; subsequently to 27th Bn.
Todd, David Leslie	19/8/14	1/2/15	To 50th Bn.; Capt. 9/5/16; P.O. War 2/4/17; Original.
Sommerville, Alfred Cyril	19/8/14	1/2/15	Original.
Stopp, Eric John Carl	19/8/14	1/2/15	Original and 20/10th.
Farrier, Charles Percy	19/8/14	1/2/15	Original. K.I.A. 9/5/15.
Hooper, Robert James Mansfield	19/8/14	1/2/15	Original. K.I.A. 27/4/15.
Frayne, William Stanley	28/8/14	1/2/15	Original. Temp. Capt. 6/8/15. K.I.A. 6/8/15.
Haig, James Leslie	1/11/14	1/2/15	Imp. Reservist. To 50th Bn. and Cyclist Corps.
Moule, Charles Launcelot, M.C.	—	18/3/15	4/10th. To 50th Bn. Capt. 1/3/16.
Rowe, Albert Henry (Serbian Order of White Eagle)	15/9/14	25/4/15	1/10th. To 51st. Major 1/10/16.
Robley, Vernon Hermann	19/8/14	28/4/15	Original. Left Bn. ill before landing at Anzac.
Smyth, Trevor Owen	11/9/14	28/5/15	K.I.A. 16/5/15. Posthumous lieutenancy. Original Transport Officer.
Hancock, Frank Herbert	24/3/15	4/8/15	5/10th. To 50th Bn. Capt. 1/4/16. M.I.D.
Armitage, Harold Edwin Salisbury	24/3/15	4/8/15	5/10th. To 50th Bn. Capt. 1/3/16. K.I.A. 2/4/17.
Leane, Benjamin Bennett (O.R. Sgt.), (Serbian Order of White Eagle)	28/4/15	21/8/15	To Camel Corps and 48th Bn. Major 16/11/16. K.I.A. 10/4/17. M.I.D. 2.
Heritage, Felix Hereward Gordon Norfolk (Pioneer Sgt.)	28/4/15	21/8/15	17/10th. M.I.D. K.I.A. 20/9/17.
Dodson, William Francis Lyon	29/3/15	22/10/15	From Engrs. Signalling Officer. K.I.A. 20/9/17.
Fowler, William Murray, M.C.	22/4/15	9/11/15	6/10th. To 50th Bn. Major 1/12/17.
Henderson, George Francis, D.C.M. (C.S.M.)	28/4/15	14/11/15	D.C.M. won in Boer War whilst serving with Wales (S.) Borderers. M.I.D.
Wilton, Richard Gladstone	20/5/15	20/2/16	7-10th. To 50th Bn. Capt. 16/5/16.
Smith, James Churchill, M.C. and Bar	16/6/15	20/2/16	8/10th. To 50th Bn. Major 21/10/18.
Clarke, Tennyson George, M.C. (Sgt.)	4/8/15	20/2/16	To 50th Bn. Capt. 1/4/16.
Blackburn, Arthur Seaforth, V.C. (Lance-Corporal)	4/8/15	20/2/16	Temp. Capt. 1/8/16; Reverted to Lieut. 7/9/16.
James, Charles Albert (Sgt.)	8/10/15	20/2/16	3rd Reinforcements. Reg. No. 1496.
Harniman, Joseph Ronald	16/6/15	24/3/16	To Machine Gun Company; 9/10th.

REGIMENTAL LIST OF OFFICERS 141

LIEUTENANTS—continued.	2nd Lieut.	Lieut.	
Hillier, Robert James Bradley ..	16/6/15	10/5/16	4/27th. K.I.A. 25/7/16.
Melville, Phillip George ..	16/6/15	10/5/16	4/27th.
Coffey, Morris James ..	16/7/15	10/5/16	9/10th. To 70th Bn. Temp. Appt. Transport Officer, Jan., 1916.
Stewart, William Hill Dunn ..	16/7/15	10/5/16	6/27th.
Walsh, Douglas James, M.C. ..	16/9/15	10/5/16	8/27th. Died of sickness 12/8/18.
Browne, Patrick Gerald ..	—	9/6/16	Rank and precedence pre-dated to 9/12/16.
Coombe, Samuel Walter (R.Q.M.S.)	16/3/16	21/6/16	Services terminated 16/3/18. Seniority predated to 7/7/16.
Sandland, Arnold Cooper (Sgt.)	16/3/16	21/6/16	Died of wounds 4/8/16.
Kinnish, Arthur Henry (Sgt.)	16/3/16	21/6/16	K.I.A. 21/8/18.
MacNeil, Alexander William Lauchlan, D.S.O. (Sgt.)	16/3/16	21/6/16	To 3rd L.T.M.B. Bty. 12/1/17. Temp. Capt. 23/9/18. Resigned Commission in England 3/2/19.
Boyce, Harold Leslie ..	15/5/15	8/7/16	From 27th Bn. 25/10th. Resigned Commission in England 12/3/20.
Walker, Alexander Ralph ..	16/9/15	8/7/16	Died of wounds 23/8/16.
Walker, Albert Reginald ..	24/3/16	8/7/16	From 47th Battalion.
Mills, Sydney Sylvanus, M.C. ..	16/9/15	27/11/16	15/10th. K.I.A. 20/9/17.
Ford, Rufus Phillip ..	16/12/15	27/11/16	16/10th. K.I.A. 7/10/17.
Stephens, Leonard Ralph, M.C.	29/7/16	27/11/16	Signalling Officer 1917.
Chisholm, Donald (R.S.M.) ..	5/8/16	27/11/16	
Davidson, James, M.C. (R.Q.M.S.)	5/8/16	27/11/16	To 3rd T. Bn. 12/7/17. Temp. Capt. 23/9/18. M.I.D.
Watson, Frederick Robert (Sgt.)	5/8/16	27/11/16	To Machine Gun Company.
Lynch, Horace Warner (Sgt.)	5/8/16	27/11/16	
Hill, Alfred Thomas, M.C. (Sgt.)	5/8/16	27/11/16	M.I.D. Died of wounds, 30/5/18.
Corcoran, Thomas Leo, M.C. (Sgt.)	5/8/16	27/11/16	Died of wounds, 30/5/18. M.I.D.
Scott, Frank John (Sgt.)	5/8/16	27/11/16	M.I.D. K.I.A. 8/10/17.
Carson, Reginald ..	10/7/15	13/12/16	From 9th Bn.
Collison, Herbert Youngman ..	16/9/15	1/1/17	K.I.A. 25/2/17; 14/10th.
Harvey, Eric Charles ..	16/12/15	6/2/17	Lewis Gun Officer 1918; 16/10th.
Colbey, Frank Hammond (C.Q.M.S.)	6/9/16	6/2/17	To 70th Bn. Temp.
Doley, Samuel Edmund (R.S.M.)	23/9/16	6/2/17	To 3rd T. Bn. 20/1/17.
Whiteford, Clarence George (C.S.M.)	23/9/16	6/2/17	K.I.A. 25/2/17.
Miller, Alexander Lorimer ..	16/9/14	17/3/17	D. of Wounds 8/5/17; 14/10th.
Dougall, Norman, M.C. (Posthumous) (Sgt.)	23/10/16	17/3/17	From 11th Bn.; ex Cadet School. K.I.A. 6/5/17.
Sutton, Charles Ronald (L.-Cpl.)	23/10/16	17/3/17	Ex Cadet School.
Searcy, John William, M.C. (Sgt.)	10/6/16	21/5/17	Ex Cadet School.
Jenkins, William Roy, C. de G. (Fr.)	1/5/16	1/6/17	21/10th.
Smith, Colin MacPherson ..	12/6/15	1/6/17	8/10th and 18/10th. D. of Wounds 6/10/17.
Hincks, Cecil Stephen (Sgt.) ..	24/1/17	1/6/17	
Leaver, Graham Holland (Pte.)	25/1/17	1/6/17	Ex Cadet School. K.I.A. 20/9/17.

142 THE FIGHTING 10TH

Name	2nd Lieut.	Lieut.	Notes
LIEUTENANTS—continued.			
Allanson, Charles Reddie, M.C., M.S.M. (Staff Sgt.)	25/1/17	1/6/17	From 5th Bn. Reg. No. 426. M.S.M., vide London Gazette, 17/10/16.
Jorgenson, Carl Fritz Stanton ..	1/3/17	5/6/17	3rd Reinforcements 4th F. Ambulance. Ex Cadet School.
Gatliff, Michael Penrose (C.Q.M.S.)	3/3/17	5/6/17	From 8th Bn.
Paisley, Cyril John (Cpl.) ..	3/3/17	21/7/17	From 11th Bn.
Cruickshank, Errol (L.Cpl.) ..	3/3/17	21/7/17	From 3rd Field Ambulance. M.I.D. K.I.A. 25/12/17.
Singleton, Phillip Arthur ..	28/3/17	21/7/17	
Bowers, Thomas William (C.S.M.)	28/3/17	21/7/17	Ex Cadet School.
Angove, Edward Laurence ..	16/9/16	22/8/17	23/10th. K.I.A. 23/8/17.
Klenner, Arthur George, M.C. (C.Q.M.S.)	26/4/17	22/8/17	M.I.D.
Coffey, Stanley Clarke, M.M. (Sgt.)	1/5/17	22/8/17	
Rice, Frank Edwin (C.Q.M.S.)	19/5/17	4/9/17	
James, Roy Pickard (Sgt.) ..	19/5/17	4/9/17	
Baker, Alan Boyton (Pte.) ..	19/5/17	4/9/17	Signalling Officer 1917.
Martin, Frederick William Scott, M.M. (Cpl.)	28/5/17	4/9/17	From 9th Bn. K.I.A. 20/9/17.
Gaston, Malcolm Bruce (Sgt.)	28/5/17	4/9/17	From 11th Bn.
Reid, Harold Willis, M.C. (Sgt.)	28/5/17	4/9/17	From 2nd F. Coy. Engineers.
Pennington, Francis Ernest, M.C., D.C.M. (Sgt.)	28/5/17	4/9/17	From 2nd F. Coy. Engineers.
Limb, Arthur (Cpl.) ..	28/5/17	4/9/17	Ex Cadet School. M.I.D. 2. 16/10th. D. of sickness 7/5/20.
Brown, Wilfred Douglas ..	31/5/17	4/9/17	From 11th Bn.
Scudds, Howard Wilson, M.C. and Bar (Sgt.)	28/6/17	17/11/17	Ex Cadet School.
Jacob, Denis Courtland, M.M. (Sgt.)	23/7/17	17/11/17	
Smith, Richard Graham, M.C. ..	25/7/16	17/11/17	22/10th.
Fuller, Basil ..	1/9/17	1/12/17	To 3rd Machine Gun Coy.
Virgo, Claude Arnold Percival (Sgt.)	25/7/16	1/1/18	24/10th.
Chabrel, Cecil Claude Marcelin	1/10/16	1/1/18	24/10th.
Du Rieu, Desmond Theodore ..	3/8/17	1/1/18	
Holloway, Percy Edgecumbe (L.-Cpl.)	3/8/17	1/1/18	Ex Cadet School.
Schneider, Ferdinand James William	3/8/17	1/1/18	From Field Ambulance.
Grant, Keith ..	13/8/17	1/1/18	
Blake, William Harvey, M.C.	27/9/17	22/1/18	From Army Service Corps.
Paxton, Robert Armytage (Pte.)	27/9/17	22/1/18	Ex Cadet School.
Scott, Cleve James, M.C. (L.Cpl.)	27/9/17	22/1/18	From 43rd Bn. Ex Cadet School. K.I.A. 22/7/18.
Davidson, Walter Harold (Sgt.)	1/10/17	22/1/18	
Fenn, Charles Bradshaw (Cpl.)	1/10/17	22/1/18	
Laurie, Leonard Buxton ..	1/10/17	22/1/18	Died of Wounds 27/4/18.
McInerney, John Morris, M.M. (Cpl.)	1/10/17	22/1/18	K.I.A. 28/6/18.
Sprott, John, M.M. (Sgt.) ..	18/10/17	22/1/18	K.I.A. 24/4/18.
Jackson, Albert Heyward, M.M. (Sgt.)	18/10/17	22/1/18	K.I.A. 24/4/18.
Robinson, Arthur Harold (Cpl.)	18/10/17	22/1/18	
White, Alexander Deucher ..	—	18/2/18	D. of wounds 18/9/18

	2nd Lieut.	Lieut.	
LIEUTENANTS—continued.			
Sharland, Wilfred Drew, M.C. (Sgt.)	29/11/17	29/2/18	10th Reinforcements. Reg. No. 3102.
Mining, Arthur Eugene, M.C. (Pte.)	1/12/17	1/3/18	From 21st M.G. Coy.
Goode, Arthur Hedley (Pte.)	19/12/17	19/3/18	
Lightbody, George Sidney, M.C. (Sgt.)	19/12/17	19/3/18	6th Reinforcements, Reg. No. 2188.
Younger, John James Affleck ..	25/7/16	1/6/18	25/10th. K.I.A. 10/8/18.
Cleworth, Herbert Leighton ..	1/10/16	1/6/18	25/10th.
Orman, Ernest Percy, M.C. ..	1/10/16	1/6/18	25/10th.
Chittleborough, Alan Percival (Cpl.)	2/2/18	20/6/18	From 4th A.A. Service Corps.
Bain, Thomas Tangye ..	1/10/16	15/9/18	
Cox, Albert Charles ..	10/2/18	15/9/18	
Cooper, William Osborne, M.C.	16/2/18	15/9/18	
Shepherd, Charles Raymond ..	16/2/18	15/9/18	
Allen, Reginald Stanley (Sgt.)	1/5/18	15/9/18	Ex Cadet School.
Bennett, William Stanley, D.S.O. M.C. (Sgt.)	1/6/18	15/9/18	Ex Cadet School. From 24th Bn. Reg. No. 6924. M.I.D.
Collett, Leonard Walter, M.C. (Sgt.)	1/6/18	15/9/18	Ex Cadet School.
Mitchell, Ronald Eric, M.M. (Sgt.)	1/6/18	15/9/18	Ex Cadet School.
Edwards, Charles, M.M. (Sgt.)	15/6/18	15/9/18.	
Edwards, Hartley James, M.M. and Bar (Cpl.)	15/6/18	15/9/18.	
Wishart, James Leslie ..	16/2/18	26/12/18	
Mussared, Joseph Llewellyn (Sgt.)	23/9/18	26/12/18	No. 5157 16th Reinforcements.
Allen, Uveydale (Cpl.) ..	9/11/18	26/12/18	
Weall, Henry ..	25/4/18	27/12/18	2nd South Australian General Service Reinforcements.
King, Robert, M.M. (Sgt.) ..	26/8/18	27/12/18	
Sykes, John Wilfred (Sgt.)	13/9/18	27/12/18	
Slocombe, William George, C. de G. (Fr.), (C.S.M.)	13/9/18	27/12/18	M.I.D.
Perry, Clarence George ..	15/4/18	20/1/19	
Vaughan, John Howard, C.B.E. (Pte.)	23/11/18	1/3/19	2nd South Australian General Service Reinforcements.
Harris, Alexander Ross (L.Sgt.)	1/1/19	1/3/19	To General List, A.I.F. Education Service.
Glasson, George Roy (Pte.) ..	14/12/18	14/3/19	
Willshire, Joseph Daniel ..	6/6/18	1/4/19	3rd South Australian General Service Reinforcements.
Lapthorne, William Percival Allen (Hon. Lt.)	8/8/18	1/4/19	5th South Australian General Service Reinforcements.
Segnit, Ralph Walter (Sgt.) ..	1/1/19	1/4/19	From A.A. Medical Corps. Ex Cadet School.
Bowen, Thomas Stuart (Cpl.) ..	3/1/19	3/4/19	
Jury, Alfred Ellis (L.Cpl.) ..	5/1/19	5/4/19	
Hocking, Keith Bower, M.M.	3/1/19	3/4/19	From 3rd Field Ambulance.
Baker, Arthur James Kendall ..	6/1/19	6/4/19	
Phillips, John Harold Keast ..	3/1/19	6/4/19	

HONORARY LIEUTENANT

	2nd Lieut.	Hon. Lieut.
Perry, William McDonald (Sgt.) Quartermaster	18/10/17	6/11/17

2ND LIEUTENANTS

Name	Appointed.	Notes
Cullen, Hedley Elbert	12/12/14	3/10th; to Zion Mule Corps; K.I.A. 10/8/15.
Jamieson, Jesse Gilmour	16/6/15	11/10th.
Dridan, Victor Gillard	16/6/15	To 50th Bn.; 11/10th.
Gore, Maxwell, M.C.	16/7/15	11/10th; to 50th Bn.; M.I.D. Capt. 29/3/17.
Battye, Ernest Joseph	16/7/15	10/10th; to 4th Aus. Div. Artillery. Lieut., 25/3/17.
Mayman, Rupert Livingstone, O.B.E. (L.Cpl.)	4/8/15	To No. 4 "D" Group, A.I.F. Depots in U.K. as Staff Capt.; M.I.D.; Temp. Capt. 21/7/18; Lieut. 1/1/17.
Gordon, John Rutherford, M.C. (Sgt.)	4/8/15	To Aus. Flying Corps, 1/5/17.
Baker, Wallace Westerfield	30/8/15	15/10th; K.I.A. 22/8/16.
Chinnery, Walter Charles	16/9/15	12/10th.
Heward, Thomas Arthur Table	16/9/15	14/10th.
Willmer, Albert Edward	16/12/15	13/10th; rank and precedence predated to 1/1/17.
Collins, Arnold William	16/12/15	14/10th.
Dey, George Roy McGregor	16/12/15	15/10th; K.I.A. 23/8/16.
Smith, R. W.	19/1/16	
Burt, Gilbert Rosewell	3/3/16	To 32nd Bn.; Lieut. 21/3/17.
Rogers, James Keith (Sgt.)	16/3/16	To 48th Bn. and T. Mortar Battery. Commission cancelled 4/1/17.
Shaw, Harold Baker (C.Q.M.S.)	28/4/16	K.I.A. 19/5/16.
Ditchburn, William Arthur	1/5/16	23/10th.
Kennare, John Hubert	25/7/16	23/10th. To 4th M.G. Coy., 22/10th.
Crowle, Herbert Walter (Sgt.)	5/8/16	Died of Wounds 25/8/16.
Kent, Edgar (Sgt.)	5/8/16	K.I.A. 22/8/16.
Wickham, Lindsay Claude, M.M. (Sgt.)	24/7/16	Posthumous Commission; K.I.A. 25/7/16
Montgomery, William Rockliff, M.C., M.M. (Sgt.)	9/8/16	To 3rd L. Trench M. Battery.
O'Brien, William (Sgt.)	6/9/16	K.I.A. 9/4/17.
Coombe, Harry Heyward	1/10/16	K.I.A. 23/8/18.
Caust, Leslie George William (Cpl.)	23/10/16	Ex Cadet School. To Permanent Supernumerary List. Lieut. 1/12/17.
Wendt, Kenneth	1/3/17	Ex Cadet School; K.I.A. 6/5/17.
Fordham, Roy Ogilvie	8/2/17	K.I.A. 8/4/17.
Kelly, L. B.	23/7/17	
Lewis, Ernest Stanley, D.C.M. (Temp. R.S.M.)	28/7/17	Died of wounds 2/10/17.
Hardy, Clifford Bettsworth	1/8/17	
Wilsdon, Walter Harry, D.C.M.	3/8/17	From A.A. Medical Corps; K.I.A. 8/10/17.
Rae, Albert Norman	1/10/17	K.I.A. 8/10/17.
Virgoe, Randall Gordon (L.-Cpl.)	18/10/17	K.I.A. 21/12/17.
Ronald, Stuart Douglas (Sgt.)	30/11/17	
Houghton, William Henry (L.Sgt.)	31/1/18	From 6/27th. Reg. No. 2688.
Sharpe, Frederick	16/2/18	K.I.A. 23/8/18.
Pearce, Alfred Alexander	16/2/18	K.I.A. 10/8/18.
Hastwell, Hugh Norman (Pay Sgt.)	1/6/18	Ex Cadet School. K.I.A. 30/6/18. From 3rd L.T.M. Battery.
Daunt, Achilles John Laurence	7/10/18	

MEDICAL OFFICERS ATTACHED TO THE 10TH BATTALION
(From Australian Army Medical Corps)
Arranged Chronologically but not according to Seniority

	Capt.	Major.	
Nott, Harry Carew	20/8/14	—	To Major 14/11/16 and Lieut.-Colonel 11/11/18
Ingram, Bertram	20/8/14	—	To Major 14/11/16
Morlet, Claude, D.S.O.	14/11/14	—	To Major 14/11/16 and Temp. Lt.-Col. 5/11/18. M.I.D.
Dawson, Dean	26/8/15	—	
Beamish, Francis Teulon, O.B.E.	14/1/15	—	To Major 29/1/17.
Horwood, Oswald Ryle	20/8/15	—	Awarded Medaille Du Roi Albert (Belgian).
Harrison, John Leslie	1/3/16	—	
Maher, Herbert Odillo	1/3/16	—	
Appleyard, Sydney Vere, D.S.O.	1/3/16	20/6/17	D.S.O. won whilst serving with 10th Bn. M.I.D.
Henderson, James Mann, M.C.	11/9/16	—	M.C. won whilst M.O. of 12th Bn., 18/9/18.
Young, Robert Percy	14/3/16	—	K.I.A. whilst serving with 10th Bn., 18/9/18.
Barlow, Douglas Lewis, M.C.	20/5/16	—	M.C. won whilst M.O. of 7th Bn., 7/10/17.
Mitchell, Clarence Archibald	31/1/17	—	
Green, John Sydney	6/5/18	—	

XIX

BRIEF BIOGRAPHY OF BRIGADIER-GENERAL S. P. WEIR, D.S.O., V.D.

First Commanding Officer of the 10th Bn., A.I.F.

Brigadier-General Stanley Price Weir, D.S.O., V.D., is the son of the late Alfred Weir, who, as an early South Australian pioneer, arrived at Port Adelaide from Aberdeen, Scotland, in the ship *Prince Regent*, in the year 1839, only two years after the founding of the colony at Glenelg by Governor Hindmarsh, and subsequently became a pioneer surveyor in the Northern Territory. He is distantly related through his father to Justice Weir, of the Superior Court of Quebec, Canada, and on his maternal side the family tree is well rooted in the green fields of old England. He was born at Norwood, South Australia, on April 23, 1866, his parents never for a moment anticipating that St. George's Day was destined to play such an all-important part in the life of their son; for exactly forty-nine years later it was decreed that he should command a battalion of South Australian infantry in the world's greatest war, when to the day, he was finalizing arrangements according to an operation order, for his men to land on a foreign shore in one of the greatest combined naval and military feats in the history of the world.

He was educated at Moore's School, the Norwood Public School, and the Pulteney Street Grammar School. On April 13, 1879, at the age of thirteen, he entered the Surveyor General's Department, Adelaide, as office assistant to the Survey Storekeeper. Whilst in this office it devolved upon him to accompany the late Charles Hope Harris as a sort of chainman to cut off the piece of land for the Parade Ground at the back of Government House, on which, until then, survey department horses grazed. By strict attention to duty he merited and received promotion. On July 1, 1889, he was appointed clerk in the Storekeeper's Branch, and on July 1, 1890, was reappointed clerk and storekeeper. On May 14, 1890, he married Rosa, daughter of the late James Wadham, there being one son, Lionel Wadham, and one daughter, Beryl Price (now Mrs. Ian Tapley), of the union. At the outbreak of hostilities in 1914 he had attained the office of Survey Storekeeper, Custodian of Plans, and Custodian of Government Motor Cars, receiving the latter appointment on July 1, 1911.

As regards his military career he accurately may be termed a "ranker", having worked his way up in the Australian Military Forces from a private, through the various non-commissioned and commissioned ranks to that of brigadier-general. In March, 1885, during the Russian War scare he enlisted as a private in the 1st Battalion of the old Adelaide Rifles. His first Commanding Officer was Colonel L. C. Madley, and by examinations he rose step by step through the non-commissioned ranks to colour-sergeant. He received his first commission in the 3rd Battalion of the Adelaide Rifles under Colonel J. C. Lovely, V.D., being appointed to rank of lieutenant on March 19, 1890, when he was posted to "C" Company under the command of Captain M. G. Hipwell. He was advanced to the rank of captain on May 25, 1893. Whilst holding this rank the South African War occurred, and though he offered his services to the South Australian Bushmen's Corps, he was not accepted, as the contingent raised was small, and mounted Officers were invariably given the first preference. On July 1, 1903, the old Adelaide Rifles was converted into the 10th Australian Infantry Regiment, to which he transferred and secured some distinction by being appointed Adjutant from September 1, 1902, to January 1, 1904, when he received his majority, and consequently was appointed 2nd in Command of his regiment. On June 22, 1908, he was promoted to the rank of lieutenant-colonel, and became Commanding Officer of the 10th A.I.R. He retained this command until January 1, 1912, when he was placed on the Unattached List, where he remained for the brief period of six months. On July 1, 1912, when the universal training scheme was brought into operation, he was given the command of the S.A. 19th Infantry Brigade, and on September 9, 1913, he was made a full colonel. He held this commission at the outbreak of the Great War, such appointment to terminate on June 30, 1917. The clash of arms in Europe in 1914 brought this important chapter in his life to a sudden conclusion, when others opened, which neither he nor anyone else had been able to prophesy.

On August 5, 1914, the day when confirmation of the historic declaration of war made by England was received in Adelaide, he was appointed a colonel in the British forces, and on August 12, 1914, he received a telegram from Colonel E. G. Sinclair-MacLagan, Commander of the 3rd Australian Infantry

Brigade, A.I.F., offering him the command of the 10th Battalion. He immediately accepted same, and on August 17, 1914, was appointed a lieutenant-colonel in the A.I.F., and subsequently was made an honorary colonel. He was thus the first South Australian officer to obtain a commission in the A.I.F. On August 16, 1914, he assumed command of the first infantry unit raised in South Australia for service abroad in the Great War. His first task was to proceed to Military Headquarters at Keswick and make certain recommendations as to suitable officers selected by him for the positions of 2nd in Command, Adjutant, Quartermaster, Company Commanders, subalterns, and such other officers required as would bring the personnel of his unit up to establishment strength. In September, 1914, he was granted leave by the S.A. Government to command the 10th Battalion abroad, his position being kept open, and he being entitled upon his return to apply for reinstatement as Survey Storekeeper. On September 16, 1914, the Commissioner of Crown Lands, Hon. F. W. Young, and staff of the Surveyor-General's Department, assembled in the Land Office, where he was presented with a valuable pair of field-glasses and a compact shaving set. The Commissioner in officially bidding him farewell said his department was proud of the fact that Colonel Weir had been chosen to command the 10th Infantry Battalion. Every man in the service was inspired by a feeling of loyalty, and many would be pleased to have the opportunity to follow Colonel Weir to the front. They looked forward to the time when they would be able to welcome him back victorious, some time next year (1915). Colonel Weir, in reply, said he hoped he would do as well as the Commissioner of Lands seemed to expect. He had a very fine Battalion under his command, and if he could only make proper use of it, he thought the result would be as good as they hoped.

He embarked with his Battalion per H.M.A.T. A11 *Ascanius* on October 20, 1914, and when that transport arrived at Fremantle six infantry companies of the 11th Battalion came on board. He was then made O.C. Troops for the voyage, receiving his orders from the flagship *Orvieto*, in which Major-General Sir W. T. Bridges and his staff were travelling. He served abroad with the A.I.F. in Egypt, Gallipoli, Sinai, France, and Belgium, and holds the unique distinction of having commanded the 10th Battalion from its formation, through the vigorous days at Morphettville, through the exacting training at Mena, Egypt; through the difficult practice operations in landing at Mudros Harbour, Lemnos Island; through the famous Anzac Landing on April 25, 1915; through the ordeals and privations associated with the Defence of Anzac; through the rigours of the Battalion's first summer in France, and its first conflicts with the Hun.

Early in 1915, if not before, he had definite cause to be more than regimentally proud of the Battalion under his command. At Mena in Egypt, long before the syllabus of company, battalion, brigade, and divisional training had been completed, the signal distinction befell the 3rd Australian Infantry Brigade, of which the 10th Battalion was an integral unit, of being selected to act as the covering force in a projected landing of British troops somewhere in the Dardanelles theatre, at a place and time which had yet to be decided. The 10th Battalion, like the sister battalions of the 3rd Brigade, consisted largely of men who at first were somewhat tough against discipline, but the most hardened in rough places, inasmuch as quite a number were miners from Mount Morgan (Queensland), Broken Hill (New South Wales), Kalgoorlie (Western Australia), and Moonta (South Australia). Therefore, geographically, the 3rd was the most Australian Brigade of the 1st Australian Division, and the handling and training of this composite brigade, which represented four States of the Australian Commonwealth, greatly pleased General Bridges. Lieut.-Colonel Weir had carried the training of the 10th to a degree of precision, and the keenness of his men had impressed all Australian Staff Officers who had watched them during their desert training. The C.O., his Officers N.C.O's. and men had a way of relying on themselves which won the confidence and esteem of those who knew them, and it may be said that these characteristics were in common possessed by the 9th, 11th, and 12th Battalions. The initiative of the 3rd Brigade had become an established fact, and thus, when it was necessary to decide as to which brigade should first be thrown into action, General Bridges readily chose the 3rd. This was indeed a compliment to Lieut.-Colonel Weir, who proudly accepted the distinction at its full value, for the Battalion to a man realized that it was indeed no ordinary honour for the 10th to be included in a brigade specially selected to act as a covering force, especially when General Bridges had the choice of four brigades and sixteen battalions at his disposal—units which represented the prime of Australian manhood, and units equally as eager to become storm troops as those of the 3rd Brigade. Thus Lieut.-Colonel Weir and the 10th Battalion, justly proud of the great honour conferred upon it, left Egypt some six weeks before the balance of the 1st Australian Division struck camp at Mena. The Battalion embarked on the *Ionian* and proceeded to Mudros Harbour, Lemnos Island, where Lieut.-Colonel Weir specially trained his men in landing and re-embarking on a sloping beach, communicating information in battle, and carrying a maximum load. Constant landings and rushes up the foothills at Telikna Point became the order of the day, and twice he took the Battalion on board H.M.S. *Prince of Wales* to practise disembarking and landing. In this manner he saw his men pass from the stage of the raw recruit and develop into highly-trained and efficient soldiers. He insisted that they should all pass a very severe grade-test preparatory to the "great adventure", which loomed ahead. Morning, noon, and night he instilled it into the men under his command that as advance troops they were expected to push inland on as wide a front as possible, so that if part of the 3rd Brigade was held up, other parts could still penetrate. He specially instructed all ranks of the 10th to push on as rapidly as they could to the covering position on the ridge as outlined to them on the maps. It is safe to assume that if Lieut.-Colonel Weir had not handled the 10th Battalion in such a capable manner, from Morphettville to Mena, and if he had not forced his men to distinguish themselves in their arduous training, then the honour would probably not have befallen the 10th of being the first ashore on the Gallipoli Peninsula. His leadership at the landing was determined and reliable. He landed from the 10th Battalion scouts' boat, and No. 899 Pte. J. W. A. Bradford, writing from Anzac, said: "I was in the scouts' boat pulling No. 2 oar, and Colonel Weir, Capt. Lorenzo, and Lieut. Talbot Smith (the latter in charge of the scouts), were in the next seat. Our chaps bent down as far as possible in order to present a smaller target for the bullets, but for some time the Officers continued to sit erect. A bullet passed between the Colonel and me, and many others nearly found their mark, so somebody leant against the Colonel, thereby compelling him to bend over. This action probably saved him from getting shot. All our Officers were recklessly brave."

Shortly after his men had jumped or waded from the tows he observed a proportion of the 9th Battalion (Queensland) together with a number of the 10th Battalion discarding their packs under the bend on the southern end of Ari Burnu. He shouted to them to immediately continue the advance, and invigorated upon hearing his orders, they clambered up the precipitous slopes of the hill. Others soon followed, and seeing the forms of Colonel Weir's party advancing in the dark set off after them. The result of his orders delivered at this critical stage in the operation was that in a few minutes after the actual landing had been made by the covering force of the 3rd Australian Infantry Brigade, about six companies of infantry began the difficult ascent, and were gradually moving inland, although any idea of keeping touch or maintaining formation was entirely out of the question. This front line was known throughout the day of the landing as "Weir's Line", and from time to time, soldiers who had become detached from their officers joined up with it, irrespective of unit or brigade. Stragglers from the beach and gullies reinforced it until certain strategical positions were consolidated, until what was originally "Weir's Line" in reality became the first firing-line. Despite the repeated attempts of the Turks that day to drive the Australians into the sea, the "Weir Line" held on, and with the assistance of the New Zealanders and the 1st, 2nd, and 4th Brigades which followed the 3rd, the A.I.F. succeeded in the seemingly impossible task of establishing itself on Turkish soil. The "Weir Line" advanced and made its way across Shrapnel Gully, or the Valley of Death, until it reached the 400 Plateau. Between six and seven o'clock that morning many of the 10th men climbed the steep slopes which led to this high ground, and there Colonel Weir again forcibly demonstrated his leadership, for during a lull in the firing he inspired his men to advance upon the 3rd Ridge, which was about a mile ahead, and which the Turks were occupying. In this manner he put his name on the map at Anzac, and Weir Ridge on the Lone Pine (Southern) end of the 400 Plateau was named after him to commemorate the gallant stand made at that point by him and his men. As such it was known throughout the whole of the Gallipoli campaign, and is still remembered by all 10th men who served on Gallipoli. He landed with a rifle, and throughout the day moved amongst the rank and file. In fact he was the only Colonel of the 3rd Brigade to pass the 1st Ridge. Colonel Lee, of the 9th Battalion, sprained his ankle and could not advance; Colonel Johnson, of the 11th Battalion, was nearly drowned whilst getting ashore; whilst Colonel Clarke, of the 12th Battalion, was killed on the 1st Ridge. Dr. C. E. W. Bean at the time wrote: "The 3rd Brigade went over the hills with such dash that within three-quarters of an hour of landing some had charged over three successive ridges; each ridge was higher than the last, and each party that reached the top went over it with a wild cheer."

He landed at Anzac with the 10th, which consisted of 29 officers and 921 other ranks, and his saddest Anzac recollection appertains to the consequent dwindling of those numbers, as revealed at the first roll call at Shell Green, three days after the landing had been accomplished. After incessant fighting his men became utterly exhausted, and a bivouac was struck for reorganization purposes. It was then discovered that the strength of the 10th Battalion had decreased to 13 Officers and 385 other ranks, over one-half being either killed or temporarily put out of action. He remained with the Battalion until a few weeks after the Battle of Lone Pine, and on August 25, 1915, was appointed Acting-Brigadier; but on September 11, 1915, being completely run down in health, he was forced to evacuate. He proceeded to Malta, where he was admitted to the Blue Sisters' Hospital, and later re-embarked for England, where he was admitted to the 3rd London General Hospital at Wandsworth. In reference to his service on Gallipoli, Dr. C. E. W. Bean, in his "Official History of Australia in the War", Vol. 1, p. 135, paid him a well-deserved compliment when he said: "Colonel Price Weir, though somewhat above the average in years, took his Battalion into the front line, commanded it there through its first battle, and remained longer in the field than almost any of the senior military Officers who had left with the original force."

After gaining convalescence he spent the greater portion of his furlough as the guest of Mr. and Mrs. Ernest Toms, of Surbiton, London. His host was an old friend, and at that time was London representative of the Adelaide firm of Good, Toms & Co. During his stay in England the Agent-General for South Australia (Hon. F. W. Young) answered numerous enquiries as to his whereabouts, and many were the letters and cablegrams he received from sunny South Australia conveying congratulatory messages for the part Colonel Weir and his Battalion had achieved in the Dardanelles. Eager to return to the 10th, he proceeded to the Australian Details Camp at Weymouth, where in January, 1916, he was appointed Camp Commandant. Before his health was properly regained he embarked on the *Olympic* for Egypt, where on March 4, 1916, he resumed command of the 10th Battalion which, during his absence, had been withdrawn from Gallipoli and was stationed at Gebel Habieta, about 15 miles east of Serapeum on the Suez Canal. Nine days later General Birdwood visited the Battalion lines, and a week later returned with H.R.H. the Prince of Wales, when the 10th defiled before him in a grand march past. This was the first occasion that the 10th Battalion had been reviewed by a member of the Royal Family.

From Gebel Habieta he accompanied the Battalion on the *Saxonia* to France, where soon after its arrival it was inspected by Generals Plumer, Walker, and MacLagan, followed shortly after by General Birdwood and Sir Douglas Haig. During his command of the 10th in France, the Battalion fought three important engagements:
1. Fleurbaix, June 6-29, 1916, in the Armentieres Area.
2. Pozieres (1st attack), July 22-25, 1916, in the Somme Area.
3. Pozieres (Mouquet Farm), August 19-23, 1916, in the Somme Area.

His most poignant reminiscence of France takes him back to Pozieres, when the casualties of the Battalion for the 1st attack totalled 350, including killed, wounded, and missing. So great was the onslaught that many of the dead had been piled up in barricade formation and used for defensive purposes.

On August 23, 1916, immediately following the Mouquet Farm attack, he was appointed Acting-Brigadier of the 3rd Brigade, and consequently handed over the command of the Battalion to Major G. E. Redburg. On September 7, 1916, he was reluctantly compelled to leave France, when continued ill-health precluded his return to the 10th Battalion. He was invalided to England, and with a somewhat heavy and sorrowful heart severed his connection with the unit which he had been instrumental in raising, training, and leading, and whose traditions had become a by-word. Dr. C. E. W. Bean, in his Official History, Vol. 3, p. 798, says: "Colonel Price Weir, the senior Australian Regimental Commander, though he had actively led his men through most of the Anzac fighting, found the lack of sleep at Pozieres too trying for him, and was forced to ask for relief." Before relinquishing command of the 10th he had seen his officers and men initiated into the conditions and hardships of modern warfare, and had seen them opposed to a scientific enemy armed with every weapon twentieth century warfare could invent. For distinguished service in the Pozieres and Mouquet Farm attacks he was mentioned in despatches by Field-Marshal Sir Douglas Haig, *vide London Gazette*, 2/1/17. He was subsequently awarded the D.S.O., which was promulgated in the *London Gazette*, amongst the New Year Honours on January 1, 1917. It is interesting to note that he was awarded the D.S.O. the same day as he commenced duties as Public Service Commissioner of South Australia. In October, 1916, he embarked in England on the *Barambah*, and arrived back in Adelaide on November 16, 1916, his services with the A.I.F. terminating on December 14, 1916.

Whilst in the A.I.F. he was senior infantry lieutenant-colonel, and on the gradation list was only preceded by Lieut.-Colonel G. H. Dean, V.D., who commanded the 13th Light Horse Regiment. On three occasions during the Great War he officiated as acting-brigadier, the first time at Anzac from August 25 to September 11, 1915, the second in France from May 8 to 16, 1916, and the third in France from August 23 to September 7, 1916. It will go down to his credit as well as the history of the 10th Battalion that he was Commanding Officer for a longer period than any other C.O. who succeeded him. He actually commanded the 10th from August 17, 1914, to August 25, 1915, and from March 4 to August 23, 1916—an aggregate of nineteen months. It is also a matter of history that he led his Battalion in its first battle at Anzac, and in its first battle in France, and that he was C.O. of the 10th during its two biggest engagements, namely Anzac and Pozieres, as revealed by casualties. He also had the honour of leading the Battalion in action when Lieut. A. S. Blackburn won the first V.C. on behalf of the 10th and South Australia. It redounds to his credit and also bears excellent testimony to his sound and thorough leadership that whilst he commanded the 10th Battalion, that unit earned for itself the inimitable distinction, "The Fighting 10th".

As Commanding Officer of the 10th Battalion he was always held in high esteem by his Officers and men, and was looked up to, both as an Officer and a gentleman. Rank and file alike regarded him as being distinctly non-vindictive, scrupulously fair, and humane above the average. His conduct in the Battalion's baptismal fire won for him the reputation of being a good soldier. Whether on the parade ground or in the firing-line he was invariably esteemed by those under him for his commonsense decisions and a peremptory mode of execution. Without exception he made a punctilious habit of addressing both Officers and men in a thoroughly gentlemanly manner, whilst his verbal orders and commands, without exception, were delivered in a way which courted respect and obedience. He was never a bully, and his commands were couched in language which bore not the slightest suggestion of brusqueness or pomposity. Many are the men of the old 10th Battalion who have sought his advice and assistance on a variety of subjects, and have so placed themselves under an obligation to him in some way or another. He was also admired for the tactful manner in which he handled the men under his command, and though firm and resolute, he seldom adopted an extreme expedient unless other means had failed and a last resource was necessary. Quite a number of men who served under him in Egypt, Gallipoli, and France can look back and fairly admit that the inadequate punishments they sometimes received did not always "fit the crime", whilst others know full well that occasionally they escaped penalties for offences worthy of severe military punishment. To many a defaulter he extended a sporting chance, and the fact that only forty of his men were returned from Egypt for either medical or disciplinary reasons speaks volumes in his favour. At a public meeting held in the Adelaide Town Hall on August 27, 1915, by the Mayor of Adelaide in honour of the third lot of wounded men to return to South Australia from the Dardanelles, No. 231, Sergeant J. E. Pearce, in responding on behalf of the returned men, said: "I am proud of the fact that I belong to the 10th Battalion under Colonel Weir. No praise of Colonel Weir could be exaggerated. That officer has acted magnificently throughout. He is a very fine leader, and one whom the men love to follow."

On December 19, 1916, he resumed duties as Survey Storekeeper, and two days later (December 21, 1916) was appointed Public Service Commissioner of South Australia, being the first occupant of the newly-created office. In 1923 he was reappointed for a further term of seven years. On February 1, 1926, he was also appointed Chairman of the Public Service Classification and Efficiency Board, he formerly being chairman of the old Classification Board which was abolished when the new board came into existence. On December 24, 1929, he was also appointed Chairman of the Children's Welfare and Public Relief Department, and Chairman of the Central Board of Health. To the satisfaction of several governments, the general public, and the Public Service he discharged the duties appertaining to these important offices in a highly commendable manner. As Public Service Commissioner he proved himself a genuine soldier's friend to those whose efficiency and qualifications warranted appointment or promotion in the Public Service, and on more than one occasion, all things being equal, there was never any doubt as to whether he would extend a preference to the returned man. Many returned soldiers were at first appointed in a temporary capacity by him, and after a short probationary period were permanently appointed. On April 16, 1929, he completed 50 years in the Public Service, and that day was the recipient of many expressions of goodwill from members of his office staff, who presented him with an address of appreciation and congratulation, and also a handsome silver-mounted cigar case. He retired from the Public Service on June 15, 1931, and during 52 years' service naturally had witnessed many important changes within the Public Service, probably the most important being the higher standard of education possessed by Officers. In reference to this change he said: "Many Officers are studying accountancy and taking other courses at the University, knowing that they will receive promotion in accordance with their efficiency. In years gone by an Officer might stay in one department practically all his life. The State is getting the benefit of the Public Service in better Officers and improved service." The day following his retirement from the Service he was the recipient of several handsome presents given as tokens of appreciation from Officers of the late departments under his control.

In 1916, on the recommendation of Field-Marshal Sir William Birdwood, he was appointed A.D.C. to his Excellency the Governor-General of Australia (Sir Ronald Crauford Munro Ferguson, P.C., G.C.M.G.) and officiated in that capacity during 1917-18. He retired as Commander of the 20th Infantry Brigade on March 17, 1921, when his name was transferred to the Retired List of the A.M.F. That same day he was promoted to the rank of brigadier-general, and in obtaining same holds the distinction of being the second South Australian Officer by birth to attain same. He was appointed Honorary Colonel of the 10th Battalion, A.M.F., on March 31, 1921, and has held this appointment continuously, being reappointed again in 1935. He was appointed a Justice of the Peace on September 10, 1914, and is also a Commissioner for taking Affidavits in the Supreme Court of South Australia. His decorations and medals include the Long Service Medal awarded in 1905; the Colonial Auxiliary Volunteer Decoration, awarded April 11, 1908; Commander of St. Anne of Russia (2nd Class with swords), awarded for services in France, by Field-Marshal His Imperial Majesty, the late Emperor of Russia, on September 12, 1916, and promulgated in the *London Gazette* on February 13, 1917; Companion of the Distinguished Service Order awarded for services in France, and conferred upon him on January 1, 1917; the All Service Medal; the Peace Medal, and the late King's Silver Jubilee Medal, which was awarded on May 6, 1935.

After years of indifferent health his first wife died on June 8, 1923, and on April 27, 1926, at Kensington Park, he married Lydia Maria, daughter of the late Alfred Schrapel. Hearty and hale after half a century in the Public Service, he was still fit for community service, and on July 1, 1931, was appointed secretary of the Adelaide Benevolent and Strangers' Friend Society, which position he still holds. On February 22, 1933, he was appointed secretary of the Royal Society of St. George. He was a member of the Norwood Church of Christ for over forty years, and during this period served as Sunday-school teacher, secretary, and superintendent. He also officiated as deacon, secretary, and treasurer of the same church, and for many years was church organist. He is a past president of the Church of Christ Conference, which office he held in 1924. He is now a member of the Maylands Church of Christ. For many years he has been prominently connected with Freemasonry in South Australia. He was initiated in Lodge of Friendship No. 1, S.A.C., in 1900, and became master in 1908. In April, 1925, he was installed as master of the United Service Lodge No. 37, which after being in recess for 30 years was resuscitated. He is a past First Principal of the St. Peters Royal Arch Chapter No. 13, and is also the First Principal of the United Service Royal Arch Chapter, and in this capacity installed as his successor the late Governor of South Australia, Sir Alexander Hore-Ruthven. He is a past master of the Payneham Mark Lodge No. 23. He is also a past Grand Sword Bearer in the Grand Lodge of South Australia, and past Grand Sword Bearer in the Supreme Grand Royal

Arch Chapter. In connection with the centenary celebrations of the Lodge of Friendship No. 1, S.A.C., held in October, 1934, he was made an honorary life member, and presented with a gold centenary jewel.

His numerous activities in connection with charitable and educational interests have carried him into many ramifications of life. He is president of the League of the Empire, and senior vice-president and a life honorary member of the South Australian Ambulance Transport Inc. He was president of the Adelaide Y.M.C.A., 1919-24, also a member of the board of directors, and is still chairman of the finance committee and on the executive of three. He is a past president of the Commonwealth Club, which during his presidency increased its membership to one thousand. He is president of Our Boys' Institute, and on July 1, 1935, was re-elected president of that institution for the eighteenth successive year. In 1919 he represented the Returned Soldiers' Association on the South Australian State Repatriation Committee, and at the same time was on the executive of the Trench Comforts Fund. He was the first President of the St. Peters Returned Soldiers' Association, and held this office for four years. He is past president of the Norwood Public School Old Scholars' Association, and has been a president of the East Adelaide Cricket Club. He is treasurer of the Partially Blinded Soldiers' Association, and president of the South Australian Deaf and Dumb Mission and Angas Home for aged and infirm deaf mutes. He is senior vice-president of the Soldiers' Home League, and officiated as treasurer of the Armenian Relief Fund and Save the Children Fund. He was for five years a member of the Board of Commercial Studies at the University of Adelaide, and is a past chairman of the Institute of Public Administration, and is still a member of the council. Since its inception in 1923 he has been chairman of the Father Adelaide Christmas Fund, and is honorary treasurer of the Truby King Mother Craft League, president of the Volunteer Infantry Old Comrades' Association, and in August, 1935, was made a life member of the 10th Battalion A.I.F. Club. He is patron of the Forestville Boy Scouts, and holds the distinction of being a silver wolf in that movement. His recreations consist of bowls, and he is a member of the St. Peters Bowling Club, and the Commercial Travellers' Club (Adelaide). He is interested in gardening, and in 1935 was residing at No. 64 2nd Avenue, St. Peters, Adelaide.

For over half a century he has been well to the forefront in South Australia in connection with military, masonic, religious, educational, and charitable works, and has a splendid record of achievement, in many respects unique and unexcelled. In 1936, when the State of South Australia celebrates its centenary, Brigadier-General Stanley Price Weir, D.S.O., V.D., will become a septuagenarian, when he will be in the esteemed position of being able to proudly survey an honoured retrospect in which he has played a manly and reputable part, always giving his best for his country, and living an unselfish life usefully spent in the betterment of his fellow men.

XX

RECORDS OF SERVICE OF V.C. WINNERS AND SELECTED OFFICERS

"History is only innumerable biography."—*Carlyle*.

INDEX

To Biographical particulars relating to various Officers, etc., of the 10th Battalion, A.I.F., arranged alphabetically and numerically, and according to the undermentioned groups:

GROUP No. 1

Every A.I.F. Officer who at any time during the Great War commanded the Battalion either permanently or temporarily:

No. 2 Beevor, M. F.	No. 42 Rafferty, R. A.
No. 6 Campbell, G. C.	No. 43 Redburg, G. E.
No. 10 Denton, J. S.	No. 46 Rumball, C.
No. 13 Giles, F. G.	No. 50 Shaw, G. D.
No. 24 Hurcombe, F. W.	No. 54 Steele, A.
No. 25 Hurcombe, R. K.	No. — Weir, S. P. (*vide* separate biography)
No. 27 Jacob, R. B.	
No. 34 McCann, W. F. J.	No. 57 Wilder-Neligan, M.
No. 38 Newman, J.	

GROUP No. 2

Officers of the original Battalion and the 1st, 2nd, and 3rd Reinforcements:

No. 2 Beevor, M. F.	No. 31 Macdonald, A. H.
No. 5 Byrne, A. J.	No. 36 Minagall, C. F.
No. 7 Cornish, W. G.	**No. 39 Nott, H. C. (*A.A.M.C.*)**
No. 8 Cullen, H. E.	No. 40 Oldham, E. C.
No. 11 Farrier, C. P.	No. 41 Perry, W. H.
No. 12 Frayne, W. S.	No. 43 Redburg, G. E.
No. 13 Giles, F. G.	No. 44 Robley, V. H.
No. 14 Green, K. E.	No. 45 Rowe, A. H.
No. 16 Hall, R. S.	No. 46 Rumball, C.
No. 17 Hamilton, J.	No. 48 Seager, H. W. H.
No. 19 Heming, H. R.	No. 49 Sexton, E. J.
No. 20 Herbert, M. J.	No. 50 Shaw, G. D.
No. 21 Holmes, L. G.	No. 51 Smith, E. W. T.
No. 22 Hooper, R. J. M.	No. 52 Smyth, T. O.
No. 23 Hosking, H. C.	No. 53 Sommerville, A. C.
No. 24 Hurcombe, F. W.	No. 55 Stopp, E. J. C.
No. 27 Jacob, R. B.	No. 56 Todd, D. L.
No. 28 Kayser, J. A. W.	No. — Weir, S. P. (*vide* separate biography)
No. 29 Lorenzo, M. F. de F.	
No. 30 Loutit, N. M.	No. 58 Willshire, W. S.

GROUP No. 3

Certain Officers who accompanied Imperial Reservists and upon disembarkation were attached to the Battalion:

No. 15 Haig, J. L.	No. 18 Harrison, J. de C.

INDEX—continued.

GROUP No. 4

Every 10th Battalion Officer who was killed on Gallipoli:

No. 5 Byrne, A. J.
No. 8 Cullen, H. E.
No. 11 Farrier, C. P.
No. 12 Frayne, W. S.
No. 14 Green, K. E.
No. 16 Hall, S. R.

No. 21 Holmes, L. G.
No. 22 Hooper, R. J. M.
No. 40 Oldham, E. C.
No. 51 Smith, E. W. T.
No. 52 Smyth, T. O.

GROUP No. 5

Every member of the 10th Battalion who won the Victoria Cross:

No. 4 Blackburn, A. S.
No. 9 Davey, P.

No. 26 Inwood, R. R.

GROUP No. 6

Every Officer who was awarded the Distinguished Service Order, or any two Decorations whilst serving with the Battalion.

No. 1 Appleyard, S. V., *D.S.O.*, (*A.A.M.C.*)
No. 3 Bennett, W. S., *D.S.O.* and *M.C.*
No. 6 Campbell, G. C., *M.C.* and *Bar*
No. 13 Giles, F. G., *D.S.O.*
No. 25 Hurcombe, R. K., *M.C.* and *Bar*
No. 29 Lorenzo, M. F. de F., *D.S.O.*
No. 32 MacNeil, A. W. L., *D.S.O.*
No. 33 Magenis, G. C., *D.S.O.*
No. 34 McCann, W. F. J., *D.S.O.*, *M.C. and Bar*

No. 35 Mead, F. J. S., *M.C.*, *D.C.M.*
No. 36 Minagall, C. F., *D.S.O.*
No. 37 Montgomery, W. R., *M.C.*, *M.M.*
No. 47 Scudds, H. W., *M.C. and Bar*
No. — Weir, S. P., *D.S.O.* (*vide* separate biography)
No. 57 Wilder-Neligan, M., *C.M.G.*, *D.S.O. and Bar*, *D.C.M.*, *C. de G. (Fr.)*

1. APPLEYARD, SYDNEY VERE, was born at London, England, on June 6, 1882, and was the son of Walter Appleyard, at present living in that city. He was educated at Buxton College, and soon gave evidence of his mental ability. He played football for his school, and was fond of outdoor sports. His parents intended him to enter the Navy, and with that end in view sent him to the Training Ship *Conway* to study for his entrance to that service. He discovered when he was sitting for his entrance examination that by an unfortunate mistake he had left it too long, and that he was just one month too old. He determined, however, not to give up the sea, and entered the service of the Peninsular and Oriental Steam Navigation Company. In the service of this company he advanced to the rank of third officer. At the time of the South African War he was anxious to serve, and when at length he was free and was on his way to the Cape, the Boer War ended. After this he gave up the sea and determined to study medicine. He entered the Medical School at Saint Thomas's Hospital, London, and in 1910 was admitted as a member of the Royal College of Surgeons of England, and licentiate of the Royal College of Physicians of London. He registered as a member of the British Medical Association on 11/11/10, and for some time resided at Eversfield, New Balderton, Nottinghamshire. He then proceeded to Dublin, and acted as

external Maternity Assistant at the Coombe Hospital. Returning to London he became Casualty Assistant at Saint Thomas's Hospital in 1911 and 1912. From this post he went as House Physician to Bethlem Royal Hospital, and later in 1912 became Medical Officer in charge of a British Red Cross Society unit in Turkey in the Balkan War. In 1913 he was Senior Medical Officer in Turkey for the British Red Cross Society. Here he did a great deal of hard work and shouldered much responsibility. Major C. H. M. Doughty-Whyte, the Director of the British Red Cross Society in Turkey, wrote in the terms of highest praise of his work and of his devotion to duty in the hardest times that were experienced in that campaign. On relinquishing the post he received a medal in recognition of his services from Queen Alexandra. At this time he became co-author with C. M. Page of two articles published in *The Lancet*, in which were reviewed the medical and surgical experiences of that campaign. Perusal of these articles will show that their findings coincided in many instances with conclusions which were later reached in the Great War. It was then that he turned to Australia, and *en route* broke the journey at Singapore, where he was appointed Medical Officer to the Eastern Extension Cable Company. In 1914 he arrived in Australia and took up practice at Elderslee, Crow's Nest, North Sydney. He had only been in practice a short time when war broke out. He offered his services immediately, and on August 18, 1914, received his first commission in the Australian Army Medical Corps, being appointed captain He remained in Australia for over a year on home service, and on March 1, 1916, joined the A.I.F. with rank of captain A.A.M.C. He subsequently proceeded overseas, and arrived in France on October 29, 1916, and was attached to the 4th Field Ambulance. He was promoted to the rank of major on June 20, 1917, and was transferred to the 10th Battalion as Medical Officer on September 3, 1917. He was not content until he was right in the thick of fighting with the Battalion, and it was in the second "stunt" at Polygon Wood, September 19-22, 1917, that his work attracted most attention. It was here that he won his D.S.O., which was promulgated in the *London Gazette* on November 19, 1917, and the details on March 23, 1918. He was mentioned in despatches, *vide London Gazette* 25/12/17. He remained with the 10th Battalion until March 1, 1918, when he was transferred to a Field Ambulance unit. On September 28, 1918, he was forced to leave France owing to a severe attack of trench fever which laid the foundation of the illness from which he subsequently died. His condition caused his medical advisers some concern, and he was seen by the late Clifford Allbutt. Allbutt wrote to him under date October 15, 1918, and told him that he regarded trench fever as being in all probability the cause of his illness. He was also advised that he should not in future engage in practice of too active a nature. He subsequently returned to Australia and took up practice in Glebe, and tried to go gently. He was not to do so, for influenza began to rage; doctors were smitten with the complaint, and the populace had to be treated. He could not sit still while work was waiting to be done. This did his health no good, and finally he was compelled to relinquish practice. In 1920 he was appointed an honorary major, 2nd Military District, and on January 1, 1922, was appointed to the Senior Executive Staff, A.A.M.C. Reserve with rank of major. He did some work at the Repatriation Department until his failing health made him give up altogether. In 1923 he changed his residence to "The Straths", Killara,

Sydney, and in 1924 removed to Devonside, Owen Street, Lindfield, New South Wales. Broken in health as a direct result of his war service, and after a long and trying illness, he died at Lindfield on August 28, 1926, of uraemia. He bore his long illness with wonderful patience, and *The Medical Journal of Australia* on October 2, 1926, paid him the following tribute: "Sydney Vere Appleyard was a man of boundless enthusiasm. He was quiet and unobtrusive, but knew how to strive for and attain an objective. What he did he did with all his heart. His sense of humour was keen, and must have been a great asset to him. To his wife the sympathy of the medical profession and of his former comrades in the A.I.F. is wholeheartedly given."

2. BEEVOR, MILES FITZROY, was born at North Adelaide on February 27, 1883, and is the son of the late Miles Horatio Beevor, who was formerly a farmer and later a mercantile broker, and had been a captain in the Georgetown Company of Volunteers, and subsequently joined the S.A. Garrison Artillery at the same time as Lieut.-Colonel F. W. Hurcombe was serving therein. His grandfather, Horatio Beevor, had served with the 13th Madras Light Infantry, took part in the Burmese and South African Wars, was wounded and subsequently settled in Australia. He was educated at various schools, and at the age of fourteen entered the service of the English and Australian Copper Company at Port Adelaide, where he subsequently rose to the position of chief accountant, and later that of manager for South Australia. He associated himself with the activities of the Australian Natives' Association in 1900, and in 1906 was made president of the Adelaide branch. For several years he served with the board of directors, and as chairman of the metropolitan committee. Later he was appointed auditor to the board, and held this position for a number of years. In 1908 he became an associate of the South Australian Society of Accountants, which was later absorbed by the Commonwealth Institute of Accountants. He also obtained the diploma of the society, and later became a fellow (F.S.A.S.A.). From his youth he was keenly interested in military matters, and with an athletic appearance was always considered a fine type of Australian manhood. He joined the South Australian Military Forces in 1900, enlisting as a private in the old Adelaide Rifles, in which he served one year as a private, one as a corporal, and one as a sergeant. On May 9, 1903, he received his first commission as a lieutenant in the same regiment. He was transferred with same rank to the 10th Australian Infantry Regiment on July 1, 1903, and promoted to rank of captain, and appointed to the command of a company on February 4, 1908. He received his majority on September 11, 1911, and with the introduction of universal military training was transferred to the 74th (Boothby) Infantry on July 1, 1912. He was appointed Area Officer (Unley Training Area, 74A District of Senior Cadets) on June 21, 1911, this appointment terminating on April 30, 1918. His certificates from various military schools of instruction include: Infantry School, issued January 15, 1904; Infantry School, issued December 23, 1907; Duties in Field, issued May 29, 1911; Technical Fitness to Command, *vide* Section 21A, Defence Acts 1903-12, issued January 29, 1913; and Light Horse School, issued December 11, 1912. He was a well-known figure on the rifle ranges, his best achievement being the winning of the Simpson trophy in 1909 with a score largely in excess of any before or since. He captained the rifle team which secured the Tennyson Cup, which is now in the South Australian Art Gallery, by winning it three times.

At the outbreak of the Great War he was one of the first Officers selected by Colonel Weir for the 10th Battalion, and on August 19, 1914, was appointed major and Officer Commanding "A" Company, and was thus senior Company Commander at Morphettville. From the earliest days at Morphettville the men of his company were invariably referred to as "Beevor's Little Lambs", whilst it is almost a tradition of the Battalion that he was one of the principals in the reputed "Ha! ha! no shave!" incident. He accompanied the original Battalion to Egypt on H.M.A.T. A11 *Ascanius*, and at Mena, in January, 1915, his company merged with original "F" Company and became the new "A" Company, when he retained command of same, with Capt. G. E. Redburg, formerly of original "F" Company as 2nd in Command. He landed with his Company from the destroyer *Foxhound* at the historic landing on April 25, 1915, but during the afternoon of that day was wounded in the foot and forced to evacuate. Referring to his wound, No. 125 Corporal S. A. Outerbridge wrote: "All our Officers turned out trumps and nearly all got hit. Major Beevor got wounded in the foot. He was crawling backwards and forwards to the firing-line with ammunition after he was wounded, and left the firing-line only when reinforcements came up. He'll do me." He proceeded to England and was admitted to the Whitworth Street Hospital at Manchester. In a small book entitled "My Landing on Gallipoli", with considerable literary skill he has recorded the various experiences which befell him on that occasion. He returned to Gallipoli on October 20, 1915, and next day took over the command of the 10th Battalion from Temporary Major and Acting Lieut.-Colonel G. D. Shaw. On November 21, 1915, he accompanied the Battalion when withdrawn from Anzac, and proceeded with it to Lemnos, where it was reorganized with the 8th, 9th, and 10th Reinforcements. At the end of 1915 he embarked with the Battalion for Egypt on the transport *Seeang Bee*. The Battalion was first encamped at Tel-el-Kebir and then moved into the Suez Canal Defences, first at Serapeum and later at Gebel Habieta. On November 19, 1915, just prior to leaving Anzac, he was promoted to the rank of temp. lieutenant-colonel, and on February 1, 1916, was promoted to the full rank of lieutenant-colonel. At Gebel Habieta he received instructions from Brig.-adier-General F. G. Sinclair-MacLagan authorizing the transfer of about half of the 10th Battalion of all ranks to the 50th Battalion, which was then in the process of formation, and was to become a unit of the newly-formed 4th Division. It was impressed upon him to be scrupulously fair in the changeover, and to include fifty per cent. of the troops both in efficiency and numbers. On February 26, 1916, he saw the old 10th Battalion marshalled for the last time, and before those who were detailed to join the 50th moved off he impressed upon all the necessity of maintaining the traditions of the 10th Battalion, traditions which they themselves had created in Australia, Egypt, and Anzac. It was with a sad heart that he witnessed 13 Officers and 490 other ranks march off from the 10th lines to join their new unit. Two days later 6 Officers and 461 other ranks marched in, to bring the 10th up to establishment strength again. He rode out to meet them, and addressed them on the heights overlooking the camp and the defensive lines which they were to occupy. He explained to them in the simplest of terms that as reinforcements they were to become part of a Battalion which had made itself famous at Anzac, and that nothing but the best would do. His Adjutant, Capt. G. C. Magenis, then directed them to the various companies to which they had been allocated. On March 4, 1916, his service with the 10th Battalion terminated, when he wsa transferred to the 52nd Battalion as Commanding Officer. This unit at the time was being raised, and much organization and ground work was necessary, the backbone of the battalion consisting of about 500 of all ranks from the 12th Battalion. On June 6, 1916, he accompanied the 52nd Battalion on the *Ivernia* to France, and arrived at Marseilles on June 12, 1916, and within a fortnight his battalion was in the front line of trenches. Whilst in France, for a short time, he was in command of the 13th Infantry Brigade. He was wounded during the Mouquet Farm attack on September 2, 1916, and left his battalion on a stretcher, his headquarters then being situated at Pozieres. He thus relinquished command of the 52nd Battalion and proceeded to England, where he was admitted to the 4th London General Hospital at Denmark Hill. He desired to rejoin his unit, and fully anticipated doing so until General Sir William Birdwood wrote to him as follows: "You have been two years on active service and have been twice wounded, so we will send you back to Australia for a while." He returned to Australia on the *Orsova*, and arrived back in Adelaide about November 16, 1916, his services with the A.I.F. terminating on December 7, 1916. On February 1, 1916, whilst absent from South Australia, he was appointed an honorary lieut.-colonel in the Australian Military Forces. On October 1, 1918, he was appointed a major in the 2/27 Infantry, and on March 31, 1921, was transferred to the 27th Battalion with same rank. On July 1, 1922, he was placed on the Unattached List and promoted to rank of lieutenant-colonel. He was transferred to Reserve of Officers with same rank on July 1, 1927. He was appointed Brigade Major of the 19th Brigade Area on January 1, 1918, such appointment terminating on June 30, 1920, and was also Brigade Major of the 19th Infantry Brigade from May 7, 1917, to June 30, 1920. On May 9, 1919, he was appointed secretary of the S.A. Society of Accountants, and on May 3, 1922, was appointed president of the Commonwealth Institute of Accountants, S.A. Division. Since the war he has practised as a public accountant, and in 1935 his office was located at 13 Grenfell Street, Adelaide. From 1927-31 he officiated as secretary of the Mount Osmond Country Golf Club Ltd.; has been on the board of directors of same, and is now chariman of the finance committee. He is also treasurer of the House of Mercy and Retreat for Women, Walkerville, Inc. In 1925 he was invited to join the board of directors as chairman of the Army and Navy Stores, and retained that position until same was ultimately liquidated. He was awarded the Volunteer Decoration and also the Long Service Medal. He is a member of Masonic Lodge of Friendship No. 1, and with Lieut.-Colonel S. P. Weir in December, 1916, was accorded an enthusiastic reception upon returning to South Australia. On May 23, 1925, he married Ethel, daughter of Peter McD. Morrison, of Balcanoona Station, there being no children of the union, and is now residing at 28 Halsbury Street, Kingswood.

3. BENNETT, WILLIAM STANLEY, was born in Victoria on April 30, 1879, and is a son of the late George Jesse and late Charlotte Braie Bennett. For many years his father was schoolmaster of the Balwyn State School, whilst his brother, Brigadier-General H. Gordon Bennett, C.B., C.M.G., D.S.O., succeeded Major-General E. G. Sinclair-MacLagan, C.B., C.M.G., D.S.O., as Commander of the 3rd Aus-

tralian Infantry Brigade on December 3, 1916. He was educated at the Balwyn State School and New College, Box Hill, Victoria, and prior to joining the A.I.F. had not served with any Australian Military Force unit. On February 1, 1916, he enlisted at Melbourne as a private in the A.I.F., his regimental number being "6924". He entered camp on March 1, 1916, but was not posted to any particular unit, and on March 6, 1916, was promoted to the rank of lance-corporal. In April, 1916, he was further promoted to the rank of acting-corporal, and in July, 1916, proceeded to Duntroon, where he remained for two months and qualified for a commission. He subsequently returned to camp as a private, and was retained for instructional purposes, holding the acting ranks of sergeant and company sergeant-major. In May, 1917, at Port Melbourne, he embarked with a quota of reinforcements of the 24th Battalion on H.M.A.T. A11 *Ascanius*, and held the rank of acting-sergeant. He proceeded to England, and disembarking at Plymouth proceeded to Salisbury Plain, where he was encamped by July, 1917. Shortly after he was transferred to the 10th Battalion as a private, and proceeding to France joined the Battalion on September 6, 1917. He remained with the 10th until December, 1917, when he proceeded to England and entered an Officers' Training School at Oxford. He was promoted to the rank of 2nd lieutenant on June 1, 1918, and returning to France rejoined the Battalion about June 15, 1918, at Borre. He was then posted to "C" Company as a Platoon Commander under Capt. W. H. Perry. He first distinguished himself in the fighting at Justice Wood on August 23, 1918, and was awarded the M.C., which was promulgated in the *London Gazette* on February 1, 1919, he being the 33rd officer of the Battalion to receive this decoration. For his conspicuous gallantry at Villeret, France, on September 18, 1918, he was awarded the D.S.O., which was promulgated in the *London Gazette* on March 15, 1919. He was the 9th officer of the Battalion to win the D.S.O., and probably created a record for the whole of the A.I.F., inasmuch as his two decorations were won within less than a month. In reference to his D.S.O., Lieut.-Colonel M. Wilder-Neligan, C.M.G., D.S.O., D.C.M., in a confidential report submitted to 3rd Brigade Headquarters, stated: "2nd Lieut. W. S. Bennett of "C" Company accomplished an exceptionally brilliant achievement. Entirely by himself he captured three enemy guns and crew which were retarding the progress of his platoon." He was promoted to the rank of lieutenant on September 15, 1918, and was mentioned in Sir Douglas Haig's final despatch, *vide London Gazette*, 11/7/19. After the Armistice he was appointed Education and Repatriation Officer to the 10th Battalion, and when the 9th and 10th Battalion details merged he became Education Officer to the 3rd Brigade. He finally left the Battalion in April, 1919, and proceeding to England was granted final leave five times pending embarkation. He subsequently embarked for Australia on the *Katoomba*, and arrived back in Melbourne in September, 1919, his services with the A.I.F. terminating on October 30, 1919. On January 1, 1920, he was listed as a lieutenant in the Reserve of Officers, but on March 31, 1921, was transferred to the 24th Battalion, and on April 5, 1924, was transferred back to the Reserve of Officers. On May 24, 1932, he married Maud May, daughter of the late Thomas and late Ellen Cromb, of Moe, Victoria, there being one son of the union (Roger Phillip). In 1935 he was residing at Winterbourn, Burwood Road, Burwood, Victoria, and was employed as head of the securities department of the Australian Mutual Provident Society, Collins Street, Melbourne.

4. BLACKBURN, ARTHUR SEAFORTH, was born at Woodville, South Australia, on November 25, 1892, and is a son of the late Canon T. Blackburn, who was rector of St. Margaret's, Woodville, for 27 years. He resided at Woodville for 20 years, and was baptised and confirmed in St. Margaret's, and also sang as a chorister in the same church. He is a step-brother of the well-known Sydney physician, Lieut.-Colonel C. Bickerton Blackburn, O.B.E., B.A., who served with distinction in Egypt, and now resides at Pott's Point. He was educated at St. Peter's College and the University of Adelaide, where he graduated LL.B. in 1913, and was called to the Bar on December 13, 1913. Prior to the Great War he had not served with any Australian Military Force unit, and was practising as a solicitor with an Adelaide legal firm, and was residing at Hyde Park. He was one of the first South Australians to offer his services for abroad, and enlisted as a private in the 10th Battalion at Morphettville on August 19, 1914. His regimental number was "31", and he was drafted into original "A" Company, and embarked with the original Battalion per H.M.A.T. A11 *Ascanius* on October 20, 1914. He landed with the Battalion scouts from the *Prince of Wales* at the historic landing on April 25, 1915, and distinguished himself that day by penetrating the greatest distance inland. With the late Pte. Phil Robin he reached his farthest point after circling the east side of Scrubby Knoll to the north of it, a direct distance of about 2,000 yards from the beach at Anzac Cove. Until 1934 it was generally conceded that Lieut. N. M. Loutit and Pte. Fordham, of the 10th, reached the farthest inland point; but in 1934 Dr. C. E. W. Bean intimated that Blackburn and Robin could probably claim that distinction. In reference to this incident he said: "All that I have done is to supply Dr. Bean, at his request, with charts and descriptions of the course that Phil Robin and I took after leaping from the boats at dawn on April 25, 1915. I do not know precisely how far we or anyone else went, and a statement as to who went farthest into Gallipoli is Dr. Bean's responsibility based on information which he has gathered from myself, other men, and official documents. On the morning of that April 25 Robin, who was my old tent mate, and I were in the prow of one of the early boats to land. Our instructions were in effect, 'Go like hell for Third Ridge'. We leapt ashore and scrambled through the scrub by a winding route. We believed that we passed Third Ridge. Phil Robin was killed later that day." Shortly after the landing he was promoted to the rank of lance-corporal, and whilst holding this rank was detailed to take charge of the 10th Battalion post office for one month. On August 4, 1915, he was promoted on the field at Anzac to rank of 2nd lieutenant, and posted to "A" Company as a Platoon Commander. He remained with the Battalion during the whole of the Defence of Anzac, and on November 21, 1915, accompanied same when it was withdrawn. He accompanied 10th to Lemnos and Gebel Habieta, Egypt, where on February 20, 1916, he was promoted to the rank of lieutenant. He subsequently accompanied the Battalion to France, where as a Platoon Commander in "D" Company he distinguished himself in the attack on Pozieres on July 23, 1916. For his conspicuous bravery he was awarded the Victoria Cross, which was promulgated in the *London Gazette* on September 9, 1916. It was actually in the heat and burden of the bomb fight in O.G.2 that he won

the V.C., and Lieut.-Colonel S. P. Weir, in recommending him for the highest decoration, said: "Matters looked anything but cheerful for Lieut. Blackburn and his men, but Blackburn lost neither his heart nor his head." He was promoted to the rank of temporary captain on August 1, 1916, but through sickness was compelled to evacuate on September 7, 1916. He proceeded to England, where he was admitted to the 3rd London General Hospital at Wandsworth, and thus reverted to his substantive rank of lieutenant. Late in 1916, with Capt. W. F. J. McCann, he attended an investiture at Buckingham Palace, where His Majesty the late King decorated him with the V.C. He was the 10th member of the A.I.F. to win this coveted distinction, and also the first member of the 10th Battalion and the first South Australian to obtain this decoration during the Great War. Ill-health prevented him returning to the 10th in France, and he subsequently embarked on the hospital ship *Karoola*, arriving back in Adelaide in December, 1916, his services with the A.I.F. terminating on April 10, 1917. On March 16, 1917, he married Rose Ada, second daughter of J. H. Kelly, of Walkerville, there being four children of the union (two sons and two daughters). He returned to the legal profession and became a principal in the firm of Fenn & Hardy. He was appointed a Justice of the Peace on August 29, 1918, and represented the District of Sturt in the South Australian House of Assembly from 1918-21. He was president of the Returned Soldiers' Association of S.A. 1919-20, and was also a member of the Citizens' and Business Men's Committee. In 1925 he entered into partnership with Lieut.-Colonel W. F. J. McCann, who was associated with him in the Pozieres attack, and for his splendid work was awarded the M.C. They have since practised as barristers and solicitors at Trustee Building, 22 Grenfell Street, Adelaide, and in this manner have carried their war-time partnership into the days of peace. He was appointed City Coroner on September 9, 1933, which position he still holds. He was appointed an honorary lieutenant in the Reserve of Officers, Australian Military Forces, on February 20, 1916, and a full lieutenant, Reserve of Officers, on October 1, 1920. He was transferred to the 43rd Battalion with same rank on October 30, 1925, and promoted to rank of captain on February 21, 1927. He was transferred to the 23rd Light Horse Regiment on July 1, 1928, and the 18/23 Barossa Light Horse on July 1, 1930, and in 1935 was still serving with this unit. He is a member of the Royal Adelaide Golf Club and the Adelaide Branch of the Royal Society of St. George, and on August 31, 1935, was chairman of the A.I.F. Cup competition conducted at the Kooyonga Golf Links. On May 6, 1935, he was a recipient of the late Kings' Silver Jubilee Medal, and in 1935 was residing at No. 5 Salisbury Terrace, Collinswood.

5. BYRNE, ALBERT JOHN, was born on September 21, 1890, and was the son of the late S. T. Byrne, of Gaffney Street, Railway Town, Broken Hill, N.S.W. From the introduction of universal military training he took an enthusiastic interest in military matters, and received his first commission as a 2nd lieutenant in the 81st (Wakefield) Infantry on November 18, 1912. On July 1, 1914, he was transferred to the 82nd (Barrier) Infantry, and promoted to rank of lieutenant. He held this commission at the outbreak of the Great War, and was considered a most capable instructor in Area 82B. At the time of enlisting in the A.I.F. he was 24 years of age, and both his parents were dead. He was one of the first six men medically examined at Broken Hill by

Surgeon-Captain Hains for service abroad, and anxious to get into camp at Morphettville, he left as a N.C.O., but upon arriving at Morphettville was appointed a lieutenant in the 10th Battalion, his commission being dated August 19, 1914. He was posted to original "H" Company, which at Mena, Egypt, in January, 1915, merged with original "B" Company and became the new "C" Company, in which he was appointed a Platoon Commander. He landed with his company from the *Prince of Wales* at the historic landing on April 25, 1915, and was killed in action during the fighting which occurred in the afternoon of that day. No. 1005 Signaller W. Pavey, of "C" Company, referring to his death, wrote under date of May 4, 1915: "About 4 p.m. there was a slight lull in the firing. Then I heard a pitiful cry of 'Water! water!' I asked the Captain who was next to me at the time, 'Who is it?' He said, 'Lieut. Byrne' (my platoon commander); 'will you go and give him a drink?' He was lying out in the open, so I had to crawl to him. I reached him in safety, and quenched his thirst. There was a clump of thick bushes on the left of us, about 20 yards away, and if we could reach it he might be there in comparative safety. As he was shot in both legs and in the left side, I had no alternative but to carry him. I raised him as gently as I could and got under him; then staggered to my feet, and had gone half-way when 'thud', and down I went on top of my unfortunate Officer. I felt a stinging in my thigh, and it was not until I endeavoured to get up and have another try that I realized I had got a bullet and could not use my leg. After lying still for a few minutes (during which the Lieutenant gave another cry, indicating that he had received another bullet) I decided that to stay there was certain death, and started to crawl to the bushes, as I could do no more for Byrne." In his contribution to the "Anzac Book" entitled "The Landing", No. 525 Pte. A. R. Perry wrote: "All the time shrapnel was hailing down on us. 'Oh-h!' comes from directly behind me, and looking around I see poor little Lieutenant Byrne of "C" Company has been badly wounded. From both hips to his ankles blood is oozing through pants and puttees, and he painfully drags himself to the rear. With every pull he moans cruelly. I raise him to his feet, and at a very slow pace start to help him to shelter. But, alas! I have only got him about fifty yards from the firing-line when again, bang-swish! and we were both peppered by shrapnel and shell. My rifle-butt was broken off to the trigger-guard, and I received a smashing blow that laid my cheek on my shoulder. The last I remembered was poor Lieutenant Byrne groaning again as we both sank to the ground." He was the first Broken Hill member of the A.I.F. reported killed in the Great War, and at the first meeting of the Broken Hill Council following the announcement of his death it was unanimously resolved upon the motion of Alderman Booth that the council express its deep sympathy to his relatives. At the outbreak of the Great War he was undergoing a map-reading course at a military school of instruction held at Gawler, but upon same being suddenly disbanded he returned to Broken Hill.

6. CAMPBELL, GORDON CATHCART, was born at Adelaide on June 4, 1885, and is the son of the late Dr. Allan Campbell, who for many years was a member of the South Australian Legislative Council, and founded the Adelaide Children's Hospital, the "Allan Campbell' wing at that institution perpetuating his memory. He is a nephew of the late Lieutenant-Governor and Chief Justice of South Australia, Sir Samuel J. Way. His brother,

Captain Allan J. Campbell, served in the South African War, and died during that campaign, whilst another brother, Lieutenant Neil Campbell, served in the South African War, and was killed in action in the Great War at Strazeele in 1918. He was educated at St. Peter's College and the University of Adelaide, where in 1906 he graduated in arts and obtained his B.A., and completing a law course graduated LL.B. in 1909. He was called to the Bar on April 22, 1911, and at the outbreak of the Great War was practising as a solicitor on his own account. In 1915 he married Iris, daughter of the late I. A. Fisher, there being one son and one daughter of the union. He had a brilliant athletic career, excelling in cricket, football, lacrosse, running, and gymnastics, and during the prime of his achievement was regarded as one of the best athletic all-rounders in the State, his collection of medals totalling fifty. Whilst at St. Peter's College in 1901 and 1902 he won the 100, 150, 220, and 440 yards events both in school and inter-collegiate sports. In 1901 his time for the 220 yards flat race was 23 seconds, which still remains a record. He won the cup and championship twice, and at this time captained the St. Peter's running team. It is a remarkable coincidence that his son, Allan J., on the same day in January, 1934, became the holder of both the Junior and Senior State Sprint Championships, and later won the Inter-University 100 Yards Championship, which thirty years previously his father had also annexed. He played inter-collegiate football for five years, and captained St. Peter's in 1903. He also played inter-collegiate cricket for three years and captained St. Peter's in 1901 and 1902. In inter-collegiate gymnastics he accomplished seven feet six inches in tiger-leaping. In inter-collegiate contests in Adelaide he, in 1904, held a record in six out of thirteen events. In Melbourne in 1909 he captained the Adelaide team at inter-varsity sports, at which five universities were represented. He played lacrosse in South Australia from 1908-14, and was interstate goalkeeper and State captain. He played cricket for South Australia from 1909-14 as wicket-keeper, and captained the State team, and in 1913 accompanied Mayne's Eleven to America. In June, 1914, he was selected in the Australian Eleven for South Africa, but the declaration of war in August of that year caused this tour to be abandoned. He has been a South Australian Cricket selector, and for six years was on the Australian Board of Cricket Control. For several years he was chairman of the S.A. Cricket Association, chairman of the S.A. Lacrosse Association, and president of the S.A. Amateur Sports Association. Prior to joining the A.I.F. he had not served with any Australian Military Force unit. In May, 1915, he attended an Officers' School for one month at Mitcham. Upon completing this course his appointment as a 2nd lieutenant in the A.I.F. was predated to May 1, 1915, and on May 11, 1915, he was posted to the 10th Reinforcements of the 10th Battalion. With Lieutenant Ernest Joseph Battye he embarked with this quota of reinforcements at the Outer Harbour, per H.M.A.T. A70 *Ballarat* on September 14, 1915, and proceeded to Egypt, being encamped at Zeitoun for a short period. Towards the end of October, 1915, he and the 10th Reinforcements of the 10th (leaving Lieut. Battye in Egypt) proceeded to the Dardanelles where at Lemnos on November 2, 1915, they disembarked and subsequently joined the Battalion after it had been withdrawn from the Peninsula on November 21, 1915. Early in 1916 he accompanied the Battalion to Tel-el-Kebir and Gebel Habieta, Egypt, where at the latter place he attended a Lewis gun school, subsequently being appointed O.C. of the first Lewis Gun Section of the Battalion. On March 24, 1916, he was promoted to the rank of lieutenant, and accompanied the Battalion to France, where he retained command of the Lewis Gun Section, which with great skill and daring he led in the attack on Pozieres in July, 1916. For his excellent work in this attack he was awarded the Military Cross, which was promulgated in the *London Gazette* amongst the New Year Honours on January 1, 1917. He was promoted to the rank of temporary captain on August 1, 1916, when he relinquished command of the Lewis Machine Gun Section, which then merged into a battalion machine gun company. At this juncture he was posted to the command of "C" Company which he commanded, with a few short intermissions, until he was appointed Adjutant of the Battalion. In September, 1916, he proceeded to the 2nd Army School at Wisques, near St. Omer, and rejoined the 10th again on October 12, 1916. He was promoted to the rank of captain on October 24, 1916. On February 25, 1917, in the Le Barque attack, he was wounded in the foot, and proceeded to England where he was admitted to the 3rd London General Hospital at Wandsworth. He returned to France and rejoined the Battalion at Ribemont in June, 1917. In August, 1917, two special 10th Battalion companies were formed, trained as raiding parties, and designated "X" and "Y" Companies. He was posted to the command of "Y" Company, 200 strong, and in addition to the training of these companies being extraordinarily hard and exacting, they were under the constant supervision of Battalion, Brigade, and Divisional Officers. At no time during the whole of the Great War did the 10th possess two companies of men who were physically fitter than either his "Y" Company or "X" Company, which was under the command of Captain R. K. Hurcombe. The Third Battle of Ypres found the 10th Battalion at Polygon Wood. On September 20, 1917, after his company had reached the 2nd objective in this operation, he co-operated with Captain Hurcombe in reorganizing the companies which had become hopelessly mixed. When the barrage lifted his company moved forward and established itself in the 3rd objective. For his distinguished service in this engagement he was awarded a Bar to his M.C., being the first 10th Battalion Officer to win a second decoration. His award was promulgated in the *London Gazette* on November 16, 1917. During the Celtic Wood raid he was in hospital at an Australian Field Hospital behind the line; but his "Y" Company which was employed in this operation was brought out of Celtic Wood by Corporal C. C. Cooke, M.M.; on October 2, 1917, with its strength reduced to 34 men, whereas only three weeks previously it had consisted of nine Officers and 200 other ranks. After one week's absence from the 10th he rejoined the Battalion at Steenvoorde, and being the senior Officer temporarily commanded the Battalion until Major C. Rumball subsequently took over. He also commanded the Battalion on two other occasions. Early in 1918 he was one of three Officers specially selected from the 1st Australian Division by Brigadier-General Walker, for service with a special corps which was then being formed for duty at picked places in Europe and Mesopotamia. However, as single Officers only were eligible for inclusion, he was precluded from accepting this signal distinction. He remained with the Battalion until February, 1918, when at the Aldershot Camp he was invalided to England and admitted to the 3rd London General Hospital at Wandsworth. He subsequently returned to France and rejoined the

10th at Sercus on June 7, 1918. On July 13, 1918, he was appointed Adjutant of the Battalion, taking over the adjutancy from Capt. W. G. Cornish, who had been transferred to 3rd Brigade Headquarters. In this capacity it devolved upon him to prepare the plans for the capture of Merris, which occurred on July 29-30, 1918. He retained the adjutancy of the Battalion until October 12, 1918, when Captain W. H. Perry relieved him of the position. He was promoted to the rank of temporary major on October 7, 1918, and whilst the Battalion was training at Brucamps he injured a leg, which necessitated his lying-up. In anticipation of an order being issued whereby temporary rank could be retained after leaving the field, though indisposed he remained with the 10th as long as possible in order to preserve his temporary rank. On November 8, 1918, the Battalion moved forward again, and he was then compelled to proceed to Abbeville Hospital, thereby reverting to his substantive rank of captain. Three days after he evacuated the Armistice was signed, and on November 15, 1918, the long-expected instruction *re* retention of temporary rank was issued. By this narrow margin he missed his majority. After being discharged from hospital he was seconded for duty as Divisional Courts-Martial Officer, 1st Australian Division, on December 6, 1918. He relinquished this appointment on December 27, 1918, and in January, 1919, his knee occasioning him further trouble, he proceeded to England for medical attention. He was admitted to the 3rd London General Hospital at Wandsworth, and for the third time during the war was admitted to the same ward, with same nurses and doctors, and occupied almost the identical bed. He subsequently negotiated with A.I.F. Headquarters at Horseferry Road in connection with the formation of the A.I.F. Cricket Team, which subsequently successfully toured Britain. He embarked for Australia in March, 1919, on the *Czarina*, an arctic exploration ship, which conveyed him to Alexandria, and there he remained a month prior to re-embarking on the *Dunraven Castle*. He arrived back in Adelaide in May, 1919, and his services with the A.I.F. terminated on August 8 of that year. He subsequently returned to the legal profession and became a principal in the firm of Bennett, Campbell & Ligertwood, but in 1928 commenced practising on his own account. In 1920 he was appointed an honorary captain in the Reserve of Officers, 4th Military District, but for some years has not associated himself with the Australian Military Forces, and at present is not listed on the Reserve of Officers. In 1920 he became State vice-president of the South Australian branch of the R.S.S.I.L., and in 1920-21 officiated as chairman of the War Gratuity Board. He has been prominently connected with the 10th Battalion A.I.F. Club, and in 1934-35 was president, and in September, 1935, was re-elected to that position for a further term. He was one of the originators of the Army and Navy Stores, the inaugural meeting being held at his private residence. His partner (Mr. Bennett) rendered invaluable assistance in securing the passage of a special Commonwealth Bill which permitted war gratuities to be negotiated for bonds in the stores. In 1935 he was practising as a solicitor and company director at Albion House, Waymouth Street, Adelaide, and was residing at No. 108 Finniss Street, North Adelaide.

7. CORNISH, WALTER GORDON, was born at Maylands, South Australia, on February 9, 1893, and is a son of the late Alfred J. Cornish, who was a jeweller by profession. He was educated at the East Adelaide Public School and the South Australian School of Mines and Industries, and at the outbreak of

the Great War was employed as a warehouseman by G. & R. Wills & Co. Ltd., of Gawler Place, Adelaide. He commenced his military career in the old Adelaide Rifles, which he joined as a private in 1911, and subsequently held the non-commissioned ranks of corporal and sergeant. On July 1, 1912, with the introduction of compulsory military training he received his first commission as a 2nd lieutenant in the 79th (Torrens) Infantry, and was promoted to rank of lieutenant in same regiment on July 16, 1914, holding this commission at the time of joining the Australian Imperial Force. He also officiated as Adjutant of the 79th Infantry from August 16, 1914, to December 15, 1914, and next day was appointed a lieutenant in the A.I.F., and posted to the 3rd Reinforcements of the 10th Battalion, with which he embarked as O.C. per H.M.A.T. A54 *Runic* on February 19, 1915. He proceeded to Egypt and the Dardanelles, where he joined the 10th Battalion in the line at Anzac on May 7, 1915. He was posted to "C" Company as a Platoon Commander, and on May 25, 1915, was promoted to the rank of temporary captain. On August 19, 1915, he evacuated ill, and was taken on board the hospital ship *Gascon*, proceeding to Malta where he was admitted to the Blue Sisters' Hospital, and thus reverted to his substantive rank of lieutenant on September 10, 1915. He subsequently re-embarked on the *Oxfordshire* for England, where he was admitted to the 3rd London General Hospital at Wandsworth. He rejoined the 10th Battalion in France at Delville Wood in September, 1916, when he was posted to "D" Company as 2nd in Command. On October 30, 1916, he was promoted to the rank of captain, and appointed O.C. of "D" Company. On May 30, 1917, at Ribemont, his company won the Brigade Cup for the Battalion, and in June, 1917, was placed 2nd in the Division in the Company competition. He retained command of "D" Company until July 15, 1917, when he was appointed Adjutant of the Battalion by Lieut.-Colonel M. Wilder-Neligan, D.S.O., D.C.M. He retained the adjutancy of the 10th until July 13, 1918, when he was transferred to 3rd Brigade Headquarters as a Staff Trainee. He first was appointed Asst. Staff Captain, then Asst. Brigade Major, and subsequently his former appointment of Staff Captain was confirmed. He was later transferred to 1st Australian Division Headquarters as D.A.A.G., which appointment he held until November, 1918, when he was transferred to England, where on March 13, 1919, he was appointed Staff Officer, No. 1, A.I.F. Demobilization Group at Longbridge Deverill, Wiltshire. In November, 1919, he embarked on the *Morea* as Ship's Adjutant, and arrived back in Adelaide in December, 1919, his services with the A.I.F. terminating on February 10, 1920. For his splendid work at Bullecourt in May, 1917, he was awarded the Military Cross, which was promulgated in the *London Gazette* on August 14, 1917. He was also mentioned in despatches on two occasions, *vide London Gazette* 25/5/18 and 11/7/19. In 1919 he was awarded the Croix de Guerre *avec palme*, he and Field-Marshal Sir William Birdwood, Major-General Sir T. William Glasgow, K.C.B., C.M.G., D.S.O., V.D., and Major-General E. G. Sinclair-MacLagan, C.B., C.M.G., D.S.O., being the only four A.I.F. recipients of this particular form of that French decoration. During his absence from Australia he was appointed a lieutenant in the 2/32 Infantry on October 1, 1918. On October 30, 1921, he was listed as a captain in the Reserve of Officers, 4th Military District, and on November 11, 1923, transferred with same rank to the 1st Battalion, 2nd

Military District. On March 1, 1924, he was appointed Staff Officer "G" Branch, 2nd Division Headquarters, and retained this position until October 2, 1924. He officiated as Adjutant and temporary Quartermaster of the 1st Battalion from October 4, 1924, until October 31, 1924. He subsequently officiated as Staff Officer "G" Branch, 2nd Division Headquarters, from March 1, 1925, until April 19, 1925. He was placed on the Unattached List, 3rd Military District, on April 21, 1925, and transferred to the Retired List on July 1, 1927. Early in 1920 he proceeded to Fiji, where he was appointed Resident Commissioner of Rotumah Island, holding this position for three years. He then returned to Australia and entered into business with Major-General H. Gordon Bennett, C.B., C.M.G., D.S.O., trading under the name of "H. G. Bennett & Co." Two years later he entered the Economic Manufacturing Co. at Bendigo, Victoria, and in 1933 returned to Sydney and commenced with the firm of Snowball Bros., mantle and costume manufacturers of Hall House, 367 George Street. Representing this firm he last visited Adelaide in July, 1935. In 1915 he married Vera, daughter of Albert Kirston, of Kew, Victoria, there being two sons of the union. He is an enthusiastic member of the 3rd and 13th Brigades, A.I.F. Association, Sydney, and in 1935, was residing at No. 13 Awaba Street, Balmoral Beach, Sydney.

8. CULLEN, HEDLEY ELBERT, was born at Terowie, South Australia, on August 8, 1894, and was a son of the late William and Caroline Edith Cullen, who at the outbreak of the Great War were residing at Victoria Terrace, Hawthorn, his father carrying on business as a wood and chaff merchant on the Unley Road. He was educated at the Terowie Public School, and whilst in that town commenced a most promising military career. He quickly rose to the rank of sergeant in the cadets, and in 1910 accompanied his parents to Hawthorn, eventually entering his father's business, which he left to proceed overseas. He was a member of the Rechabite Order, and had filled all the offices in the juvenile and adult tents. He was also a prominent worker in the Malvern Methodist Church and Sunday-school. He was a member of the Hawthorn Tennis Club, and a member of the Adelaide Choral Society. He was of a bright and genial disposition, and was an exceedingly popular young man. He was a compulsory trainee and became an ardent student and worker in the 74th (Boothby) Infantry, and in this capacity attended many camps and schools of military instruction. He received his first commission in that regiment on August 1, 1913, when he was provisionally appointed to the rank of 2nd lieutenant. He held this commission at the time of joining the A.I.F. On December 1, 1914, he joined the Officers' Camp at Brighton, from which he was chosen as one of the instructors for duty at the Oaklands and Morphettville training camps, where he was admired and respected by all with whom he came in contact. At the Oaklands Camp on December 12, 1914, he was appointed a 2nd lieutenant in the A.I.F., and appointed 2nd in charge of the 3rd Reinforcements of the 10th Battalion. With Lieutenant W. G. Cornish and this quota of reinforcements he embarked per H.M.A.T. A54 *Runic* at Melbourne on February 19, 1915, and proceeded to Egypt, subsequently re-embarking for the Dardanelles, where he joined the 10th Battalion in the line at Anzac on May 7, 1915. He had three months' service at Anzac, and became attached to No. 1 Mule Cart Convoy, Indian Mule Train, 1st Australian Division, of which he was eventually appointed 2nd in Command. On August 9, 1915,

he was wounded by a sniper at Lone Pine, and was subsequently conveyed to the hospital ship *Dongala*, but next day died from his wounds and was buried at sea. Only a few days before his death he had dispatched a cable to his father notifying him of his promotion, and following his death his parents received many letters of appreciation from Officers and men, including Lieut.-Colonel S. P. Weir and Major G. D. Shaw. Major H. M. Alexander, D.S.O., who commanded the Indian Mule Corps, writes appreciatively of him in his book, "On Two Fronts". The following is an extract from a letter received by his parents from Major Alexander: "I was very sorry to lose your son, who was an efficient and excellent Officer, very hard-working, and faithful in whatever I gave him to do. I could always be sure that he wouldn't come back until he had done it. He was very popular, and respected by the men and all connected with him." Whilst at Anzac he compiled a very accurate map of "C" Company trenches, and same is now in the possession of Lieut.-Colonel G. D. Shaw, V.D. He left a large circle of friends, both in the 10th Battalion and in South Australia.

9. DAVEY, PHILLIP, was born at Unley, South Australia, on October 10, 1896, and is a son of William George Davey, and a brother of No. 1456 Corporal Claude Davey (3rd Reinforcements), who distinguished himself in the Le Barque attack of 24/2/17, and was awarded the M.M., and was subsequently killed in action at Bullecourt, 6/5/17. He was educated at the Flinders Street and Goodwood Public Schools, and prior to joining the A.I.F. was a driver by occupation. On December 22, 1914, he enlisted in the A.I.F. at Morphettville as a private, his regimental number being "1327", and was posted to the 2nd Reinforcements of the 10th Battalion, with which he embarked at Melbourne on February 2, 1915, per H.M.A.T. A46 *Clan MacGillivray*. He proceeded to Egypt, and later joined the 10th Battalion on the *Ionian* in Mudros Harbour, on April 10, 1915. He participated in the historic landing at Anzac on April 25, 1915, and remained on the Peninsula until subsequently forced to evacuate with enteric fever, and proceeding to No. 1 Australian General Hospital at Heliopolis, Egypt, was subsequently invalided to South Australia. On June 27, 1916, at Melbourne he re-embarked per H.M.A.T. A37 *Barambah* with the 18th Reinforcements of the 10th, and proceeding to England joined the 10th Battalion in France during September, 1916, before the 10th moved into the line at "Hill 60" in the Ypres Sector. He remained with the 10th, and at Warneton, Belgium, in the Messines Sector, on January 3, 1918, for an act of bravery was awarded the Military Medal, which was promulgated in the *London Gazette* on April 2, 1918. For his gallantry in the Merris Sector on June 28, 1918, he was awarded the Victoria Cross, which was promulgated in the *London Gazette* on August 17, 1918. He was the third and final member of the Battalion to win this coveted distinction. Whilst winning this decoration he was severely wounded, and finally leaving the Battalion proceeded to hospital at Weymouth, England. Before leaving France he had attained the rank of corporal, and subsequently returning to South Australia was discharged from the A.I.F. on February 24, 1919. On August 25, 1928, at Toorak, he married Eugene Agnes, daughter of Alfred James Tomlinson, and in 1935 was residing at No. 144 Barton Terrace, North Adelaide, and was employed in the signal and telegraph section of the South Australian Railways. General Sir W. R. Birdwood congratulated him

upon winning the V.C. as follows: "Headquarters, 23/8/18. Dear Corporal Davey.—I am very glad to have this opportunity of sending you my heartiest congratulations on the very high distinction you have gained in the award of the Victoria Cross in recognition of your exceptionally gallant and good work. While your platoon was consolidating a portion of the enemy line which had just been captured, the enemy pushed a machine gun forward under cover of a hedge, and at close range brought effective fire to bear upon your platoon. Alone, and in broad daylight, you moved forward in the face of direct fire, and attacked the gun with hand grenades, by means of which you put half the gun crew out of action. Having exhausted your supply of bombs you returned to the original jumping-off trench, secured a further supply, and again attacked the enemy gun. Although during this time the enemy had been reinforced, you succeeded in your task, killing the crew of eight Germans and capturing the gun. You then very promptly mounted the gun in the new post, and used it in repelling a determined counter-attack, in which I am so sorry that you were, I fear, severely wounded. As a result of your extremely gallant and determined action, the consolidation of a position of great importance was successfully completed, and heavy casualties in your platoon were averted. I sincerely trust that you are making satisfactory progress in hospital, and that you are not undergoing too much suffering. With good wishes, and again my warm congratulations on your fine record in having gained the V.C. and M.M. (Signed) W. R. Birdwood." Lieut.-Colonel M. Wilder-Neligan also forwarded him the following letter: "I wish to offer my sincere congratulations to you upon receiving the highest military honour which can be bestowed upon a soldier of Britain. Your career in the 10th Battalion has been marked throughout by keenness and efficiency to an unusually high degree. The especially fine work which secured the V.C. to you was only the culmination of a series of acts of coolness and bravery for which you have been noted in the past. News of your decoration is particularly pleasing to your comrades in the 10th, whose best wishes are with you during your days of convalescence. The Corps, Divisional and Brigade Commanders also desire me to pass on their congratulations to you. (Signed) M. Wilder-Neligan. 19/8/18."

10. DENTON, JAMES SAMUEL, is the son of Cinncinattius Denton, of Fremantle, Western Australia, and is a native of South Australia, being born at Port Adelaide on December 11, 1875. He was educated in Melbourne, and subsequently proceeded to Western Australia, where he was residing at the outbreak of the Great War. In 1896 he entered the Western Australian Government Railways, and for some time held the position of 2nd in command of the Ways and Works Workshop at West Midland. He subsequently left the Western Australian Government Railways to go farming. In 1899 he married Eleanor Anne, daughter of the late John Hembry. He was always keenly interested in military training, and on November 11, 1890, received his first commission as a 2nd lieutenant in the 11th Australian Infantry Regiment. He was promoted to the rank of lieutenant in the same regiment on August 1, 1902, and attained his captaincy on November 1, 1907. He officiated as militia Adjutant from July 1, 1910, to June 30, 1911. Upon the introduction of universal military training on July 1, 1912, he was transferred to the 88th Infantry with rank of captain, and attained his majority in that unit on August 3, 1914. He held this commission at the time of joining

the A.I.F., and was one of the first Officers in Western Australia to offer his services for abroad. He was one of the first Company Commanders selected by Lieut.-Colonel Johnston, of the 11th Battalion, and was appointed a captain in the A.I.F. on August 25, 1914. He first came in contact with the 10th Battalion at Fremantle, Western Australia, when on November 1, 1914, he embarked with his company on the transport *Ascanius*, and in this manner accompanied the 10th to Egypt. At Mena during the company reorganization he was appointed commander of "D" Company of the 11th Battalion and promoted to rank of major on January 1, 1915. He accompanied the 11th Battalion to the Dardanelles, and landed with his company from the destroyer *Chelmer* at the historic landing on April 25, 1915. Shortly after the actual landing had been made he distinguished himself in the fighting, and was mentioned in despatches, *vide London Gazette*, 3/8/15, the official citation being: During the operations in the neighbourhood of Gaba Tepe on April 25, 1915, for valuable services in obtaining and transmitting information to ship's guns, field and mountain batteries, and subsequently for holding a trench, with about 20 men, for over six days during which he repulsed several determined attacks." He was the first Officer of the 3rd Brigade, and also of the 11th Battalion, to receive the D.S.O., which was promulgated in the *London Gazette* on June 3, 1915, amongst the King's Birthday Honours, the official citation being: "For gallantry and devotion to duty in connection with the operations in the Dardanelles (Mediterranean Expeditionary Force)." After the landing at Anzac he received a severe wound in the leg through slipping down a slope on to one of the bayonets of his men. He was compelled to evacuate, and after receiving hospital attention returned to Gallipoli on May 12, 1915. He remained on the Peninsula until July 18, 1915, when he evacuated the second time, and was invalided to Malta, where he was admitted to St. Andrew's Hospital, being an inmate there at the same time as Captain C. F. Minagall, of the 10th Battalion. On January 3, 1916, he rejoined his unit in Egypt, and subsequently accompanied the 11th Battalion to France, where he arrived on April 5, 1916. He commanded the 11th Battalion in France from September 22 to October 11, 1916, with the exception of September 27 to 30, 1916, when he temporarily commanded the 10th Battalion during temp. Lieut.-Colonel G. E. Redburg's three days' absence. He was promoted to the rank of lieutenant-colonel on September 27, 1916, and that day assumed command of the 10th Battalion, which at the time was in the line at the famous "Hill 60" at Ypres. This was the first occasion that the 10th had been commanded by any other than an original 10th Officer. He returned to the 11th Battalion as C.O. until October 11, when he proceeded to England, where at Windmill Hill he was appointed Commanding Officer of the 70th Battalion. He was subsequently appointed C.O. of the 49th Battalion on March 20, 1917, and returned to France on September 10, 1917, remaining on the field until May 22, 1918, when he was wounded and forced to evacuate. During his absence from Australia he was made an honorary lieut.-colonel in the Australian Military Forces on September 27, 1916. On October 1, 1918, he was appointed major in the 2/11th Infantry, and on January 1, 1920, was listed on Reserve of Officers with same rank. He was promoted to lieut.-colonel, Reserve of Officers on October 1, 1920. He represented the District of Moore in the Western Australian Legislative Assembly from April 13, 1921, to 1927. In

1935 he was general secretary of the New Settlers' League Branch, 89 St. George's Terrace, Perth. He was awarded the Volunteer Decoration, and in 1935 was residing at 21 Clarke Street, Nedlands Park, Perth.

11. FARRIER, CHARLES PERCY, was the son of William Charles Valentine Farrier, who at the outbreak of the Great War was residing at Thomas Street, Broken Hill, being a N.S.W. Government mining inspector on the Barrier Mines. He was apprenticed as a surveyor at the British Mine. He was interested in military matters, and on April 30, 1913, received his first commission (provisionally) as a 2nd lieutenant in the 81st (Wakefield) Infantry, and on July 1, 1914, his appointment was confirmed. He held this commission at the time of joining the A.I.F. At the outbreak of the Great War he was undergoing a map-reading course at a military school of instruction being conducted at Gawler; but upon same being suddenly abandoned he returned to Broken Hill and offered his services for overseas. He was appointed a 2nd lieutenant in the 10th Battalion on August 19, 1914, and arrived in camp at Morphettville on August 28, 1914, when he was posted to original "B" Company. At Mena, Egypt, when this company merged with original "H" Company and became the new "C" Company, he was appointed a Platoon Commander in same, and promoted to rank of lieutenant on February 1, 1915. He landed with his company from the *Prince of Wales* at the historic landing on April 25, 1915. On May 9, 1915, whilst standing and observing through a pair of field-glasses, he was shot through the head, and never regained consciousness. He was killed by a Turkish sniper whom he was trying to locate. At the time of his death he was standing only a few yards from Capt. G. D. Shaw, O.C. of "C" Company, and Lieut. W. G. Cornish, also of that company. Colonel Weir had just completed his morning round of the trenches, and had barely passed him when the tragic happening occurred. On May 14, 1915, his parents were advised that he had been wounded, and advice that he had been killed in action did not arrive until June 3, 1915. On the day that his father received notification of his death, his mother underwent a serious operation and died the next day. She passed away in complete ignorance of the death of her son. It was a sad coincidence that mother and son, although so many miles apart, should die within such a short time of each other. He was twenty-one years of age when he was mortally wounded, and was a very popular young officer.

12. FRAYNE, WILLIAM STANLEY, was born on December 14, 1892, and was the eldest son of William and Nellie Frayne. He was educated at the Hindmarsh Public School and Muirden College, and at the outbreak of the Great War was residing with his parents at 41 Henley Beach Road, Mile End. He was a clerk by profession, and at the time of joining the A.I.F. was employed in the insurance department of Dalgety & Co. Ltd. He was a member of the Caledonian Society and the Glenelg Amateur Swimming Club. He was well-known in Adelaide military circles, formerly being a member of the old Scottish Rifles. On the introduction of universal training he transferred to the 76th (Hindmarsh) Infantry on July 1, 1912, and received his first commission in that regiment on October 28, 1912, as a 2nd lieutenant. He held this commission at the time of joining the A.I.F. He was one of the first South Australian Officers to offer his services for overseas, and within six hours after the news arrived in Adelaide of the declaration of war he obtained leave from his

office and immediately set about getting his company together, the 76th Infantry being the first South Australian regiment mobilized. He was appointed a 2nd lieutenant in the 10th Battalion at Morphettville on August 28, 1914, and was posted to "D" Company, a vacancy having existed in that company for a subaltern consequent upon the transfer of Lieutenant J. A. W. Kayser to the 12th Battalion. When the new "D" Company was formed in Egypt in 1915, he was appointed a Platoon Commander in same, and promoted to rank of lieutenant on February 1, 1915. He landed with his company from the *Scourge* at the historic landing on April 25, 1915, and served continuously at Anzac from that day to the time of his death. On August 6, 1915, he was on duty in the front line with "D" Company at the section known as the Lone Hand, and was shot through the head whilst attempting to locate a Turkish sniper through his field-glasses. Only a few minutes prior to being mortally wounded Capt. D. L. Todd, of the same company, drew his attention to the fact that perhaps he was unnecessarily exposing himself too much, as the 10th Battalion could ill afford to lose further Officers through misadventure. He was killed in circumstances almost identical with those when Lieut. C. P. Farrier was killed earlier in the Gallipoli campaign. Capt. M. J. Herbert, the original Officer Commanding "D" Company, upon hearing of his death, wrote: "An excellent Officer, well liked by his men, for whom he always had the greatest consideration, and I had learnt to have the utmost confidence in him." He had been promoted to the rank of temporary captain shortly before his death, such promotion being retrospective to May 25, 1915. He was highly respected by rank and file of the 10th Battalion for his genial disposition.

13. GILES, FELIX GORDON, was born at Darwin in the Northern Territory on November 23, 1885, and is the son of the late Alfred Giles, pastoralist and explorer of fifty years' residence in the Northern Territory, and author of "Exploring in the 'Seventies", his note-books compiled whilst on his several exploratory trips now being deposited in the State Archives Department. He was educated at St. Peter's College, and showing a distinct aptitude for engineering, took up an electrical engineering course at the S.A. School of Mines and Industries, subsequently completing same at the University of Adelaide. In 1902 he commenced as a cadet in the electrical branch of the General Post Office, but in 1904, desirous of entering into a wider field of experience, commenced duties with the Adelaide Electric Lighting and Traction Co. On July 24, 1909, he married Elsie Kilpack, daughter of Arthur Kilpack Marshall, who for many years was G.S.M. at Keswick Headquarters; there being five children of the union, two sons and one daughter surviving; and at the outbreak of the Great War was residing at Dulwich. In May, 1908, he joined the S.A. Scottish Infantry as a private, and on March 8, 1910, was promoted to rank of corporal, and on September 3 of same year was promoted to rank of sergeant. He received his first commission as a 2nd lieutenant in the same regiment on August 21, 1911, and on July 1, 1912, upon the introduction of universal training, transferred to the 79th (Torrens) Infantry, and was posted to the command of "A" Company. He was promoted to the rank of lieutenant on January 31, 1913, and held this commission at the time of joining the Australian Imperial Force. At the outbreak of the Great War he offered his services for overseas,

and was appointed a lieutenant in the 10th Battalion at Morphettville on August 19, 1914, and posted to the command of original "G" Company. He was promoted to the rank of captain on September 19, 1914, and embarked with the original Battalion on H.M.A.T. A11 *Ascanius*, on October 20, 1914. At Mena, in Egypt, his company merged with original "D" Company and became the new "D" Company, of which he was appointed 2nd in Command. He participated in the historic landing at Anzac on April 25, 1915, and landed with his company from the destroyer *Scourge*. That day he distinguished himself by leading 150 men along Wire Gully and through Monash Valley in a determined but futile attempt to bridge the gap existing between the latter and Baby 700, which was the key position. He and his men who had been fighting since the dawn of the landing, were one of the last parties to be relieved when the Royal Marine Light Infantry arrived, and the 10th bivouacked at Shell Green. After Captain M. J. Herbert evacuated wounded on the day of the landing, he was appointed O.C. of "D" Company. For his splendid work at the landing he was mentioned in A.C. Routine Orders. During the Turkish attack on May 19, 1915, he was slightly wounded, but not forced to evacuate. He was promoted to rank of temporary major on August 18, 1915, and was 2nd in Command of the Battalion from August 25 to October 21, 1915, when he resumed the command of "D" Company. On November 8, 1915, the return of a senior Officer necessitated his reversion to his substantive rank of captain. He was one of two original Officers of the Battalion who remained continuously on the Peninsula from the landing to the withdrawal of the Battalion on November 21, 1915. He was also one of the four original 3rd Brigade Officers who could claim the same distinction. Whilst at Anzac he was recommended for honours, including a foreign decoration. He accompanied the Battalion to Lemnos and then to Egypt, and at Gebel Habieta Lieut.-Colonel M. F. Beevor allocated to him a key position in the Suez Canal Defences, "D" Company taking up a defensive line in the wadi. He was promoted to the rank of major on March 16, 1916, and accompanied the Battalion to France, retaining command of "D" Company. In June, 1916, he led his company into the trenches at Fleurbaix, this being the Battalion's first appearance on the Western Front. In July, 1916, he led his company in the attack on Pozieres, and performed valuable work in linking up the two objectives, "D" Company eventually being detailed to assist "A" Company under Captain W. F. J. Mc-Cann. It was during this engagement that his Platoon Commander, Lieutenant A. S. Blackburn, won the first 10th Battalion V.C. On July 23, 1916, he was wounded and gassed, and proceeding to England, was admitted to the 3rd London General Hospital at Wandsworth. He subsequently returned to France and rejoined the 10th in the line at Gueudecourt on November 3, 1916, and was then appointed 2nd in Command of the 10th Battalion, and from November 19 to December 6, 1916, he temporarily assumed command during the absence of temp. Lieut.-Colonel George Ernest Redburg. During the rigours of Flers he contracted trench fever and was forced to evacuate on December 22, 1916, being admitted to the Becordel Rest Station in immediate rear of the line. There he spent two weeks, and then temporarily commanded the 12th Battalion, returning to the 10th as 2nd in Command, just prior to the attack on Le Barque on February 25, 1917. His good work in the capture of Le Barque, including his harassing of the enemy rear-guards during the German withdrawal, earned for him further recommendations for honours. During April, 1917, in the operations in the vicinity of Boursies and Beugny, he was further recommended. On April 8, 1917, he was seconded to the Senior Officers' School at Aldershot, and on April 13, 1917, proceeded to England. He received an excellent report from this school, and completed his course on June 16, and returning to France rejoined the 10th at Ribemont on July 6, 1917, taking over the command of the Battalion from Major M. Wilder-Neligan, D.S.O., D.C.M. He retained the command of the 10th until July 15, 1917, when it was confidently anticipated by Officers and men of the Battalion that he would be permanently appointed to the command. It was decreed otherwise, for Major M. Wilder-Neligan, D.S.O., D.C.M., was promoted to the rank of lieutenant-colonel and appointed C.O. of the 10th. Major Giles was then seconded for duty with the 1st Anzac Corps School, and on July 19, 1917, was transferred to same as Assistant Commandant. That was his last appearance with the 10th, much to the regret of Officers and men. The school to which he proceeded was established on the heights of Thiepval, overlooking the Ancre, at D'Eveloy, near Albert, and later was removed to Merkinhem near Volcringhem, and finally to Rue, near the French aerial base of Le Crotmer on the coast. He was later appointed Acting-Commandant of this school, and gained a reputation for efficiency and executive ability. Before relinquishing command of same he was requested to consign available official documents, orders, and reports appertaining to the working of the school to the Royal Military College at Duntroon, where they are now housed. He was mentioned in despatches, *vide London Gazette*, 1/6/17, and for his services in the prosecution of the war was awarded the D.S.O., which was included in the King's Birthday Honours and promulgated in the *London Gazette* on June 4, 1917, and was the fourth 10th Battalion Officer to receive this coveted distinction. He had previously been recommended for honours five times, and his final mention for good work at Boursies and Beugny in April, 1917, probably secured for him the award. On October 5, 1918, he became due for Anzac 1914 leave, and relinquishing command of the Australian Corps School proceeded to England, where he embarked at Tilbury for Plymouth, and there re-embarked for Montreal in Canada, proceeding to Vancouver via the Canadian Pacific Railway. At the Pacific port he embarked on the *Makura* via Auckland for Sydney, and with Major G. D. Shaw, of the 10th Battalion, arrived back in Adelaide on Christmas Eve, 1918, his services with the A.I.F. terminating on February 21, 1919. During his absence from Australia he was promoted to the rank of captain in his pre-war unit on October 18, 1914 (79th Infantry), gazetted an honorary major on Marsh 12, 1916, and was appointed captain in the 2/32nd Infantry on October 1, 1918. Upon his return he was promoted to the rank of major in the 2/32nd Infantry on August 1, 1920, and was promoted to rank of temporary lieutenant-colonel from October 1, 1920, to March 29, 1921. He was placed on the Unattached List on March 30, 1921, and listed on Reserve of Officers as major on March 31, 1926. He has been awarded the Volunteer Decoration. During his sojourn on the Peninsula he secured a remarkable set of photographs of various positions, etc., and these he has kindly placed at the disposal of the National War Museum at Canberra. One very fine view shows the raid on Gaba Tepe on May 4, 1915, by Capt. R. L. Leane, of the 11th Battalion, when Captain C. Rumball and a party of

12 men from the 10th were detailed to cut the wire defences and assist them to get through. This unique view shows the destroyers covering the embarkation with gun-fire, and the same picture, with his permission, has been used by Dr. C. E. W. Bean in his "Story of Anzac," Vol. 1, p. 570. He also secured a remarkable view of Walker's Ridge, and both negative and print show a well-defined cross projecting above the skyline. This inexplicable cross, which did not exist, is both distinct and geometrical in outline. It would be interesting to know if the Imperial War Graves Commission has erected a memorial anywhere in the vicinity of the spot where this phenomenon occurred. Upon his return to Australia he recommenced duties with the Adelaide Electric Supply Co. Ltd., and in 1935 was meter superintendent at the Hilton depot of that company, and was residing at No. 35 Winchester Street, East Adelaide. Always slow in speech and gait, he was the acme of solidity and reliability, and was affectionately known to all men of the 10th as "Farmer". He also possesses a very fine collection of battle-field souvenirs, including shell cases, helmets, etc. His recreations consist of shooting and motoring.

14. GREEN, KEITH EDDOWES, was born at Glenelg on January 29, 1893, and was the only son of the late Thomas Walker and Mary Phillis Green. His father, who predeceased him, had for many years been chief clerk in the Chief Secretary's Office, Adelaide, and at the outbreak of the Great War he resided with his mother at Marian Place, Prospect. He was educated at Kyre College and St. Peter's College, and at the time of leaving for overseas he was employed in the accountant's branch of the Adelaide Steamship Co., Ltd. He lived formerly in the Mitcham district, and for some time attended Archdeacon Clampett's Sunday-school in connection with St. Colombia's Church, Hawthorn, and as a lad filled an enthusiastic part in the Boy Scout movement. He was a keen oarsman, and as a member of the Adelaide Rowing Club competed in a number of events, for which he received various club trophies. His widowed mother resided with his married sister (Mrs. T. Horton) at Joyce Park, Lower Mitcham, and this address was quoted in connection with his next of kin. He received his first commission in the 10th Australian Infantry Regiment on June 24, 1912, and was transferred with same rank to the 79th (Torrens) Infantry on July 1, 1912. He was promoted to rank of lieutenant on February 1, 1914, and held this commission at the time of joining the A.I.F. He was one of the first South Australian Officers to offer his services for overseas, and was appointed a lieutenant in the 10th Battalion at Morphettville on August 19, 1914, and posted to original "G" Company. About September 20, 1914, when Captain H. W. H. Seager, the original commander of "C" Company, became ill with pneumonia, he was transferred to "C" Company as Acting-Company Commander. Captain Seager being precluded from embarking on the *Ascnaius*, he was appointed Commanding Officer of the company, and when at Mena his company merged with original "E" Company and became the new "B" Company, he was appointed 2nd in Command of same, and promoted to the rank of captain on January 1, 1915. He landed with his company from the *Prince of Wales* at the historic landing on April 25, 1915, and during the heavy fighting of the first two days was killed in action. Colonel Weir, in writing to his mother under date of May 7, 1915, said: "Your dear son was killed in action on April 25 or 26 while bravely fighting for the Empire. I am sure that you will be glad to know that he was leading his men

and bravely urging them to stick to their position, which we had to hold at all costs. The cost was, indeed, dreadful! Your dear son was a brave soldier, and no soldier desires a more glorious death than to be killed in action."

15. HAIG, JAMES LESLIE, was born in Great Britain on December 3, 1886, and is the son of a retired army officer who had attained his majority in the 18th Hussars, and during the Great War was engaged in war work, and was residing at Rumbling Bridge, Kinross-shire, Scotland. He is a nephew of the late Field-Marshal Sir Douglas Haig, and is connected with the proprietors of the famous Haig distilleries. He served with the Royal Highlanders (Black Watch); had been stationed with that regiment in India, and at the outbreak of the Great War was an Imperial Reservist residing in Western Australia. He was well-educated, much travelled, and possessed the happy knack of imparting military knowledge in an attractive and masterly manner. He was one of a select band of five Imperial Reservist Officers who, by special arrangement, were permitted to accompany Imperial Reservists to England or Egypt, and upon disembarkation become available for duty with the Australian Imperial Force. He was appointed a 2nd lieutenant in the A.I.F. on November 11, 1914, but pending embarkation with reservists was not posted to any A.I.F. unit. He subsequently embarked at Fremantle with reservists and proceeded to Egypt with the 2nd Australian Contingent. At Alexandria on February 1, 1915, he left the transport on which the reservists were travelling and proceeded to the 1st Austalian Divisional Headquarters at Mena House, where he reported for attachment to an A.I.F. unit. Late in January, 1915, when Lieutenant L. G. Holmes was transferred from the 10th Battalion to 3rd Brigade Headquarters as permanent Orderly Officer to Colonel E. G. Sinclair-MacLagan, a vacancy was created in "A" Company for a Platoon Commander. It was this appointment which he received, and on February 1, 1915, he was attached to the 10th Battalion and promoted to the rank of lieutenant. He first appeared at Mena in a uniform which was neither Imperial nor A.I.F., and after same had caused some little comment, he selected No. 997 Pte. R. S. Brown for his batman. Pte. Brown considered that he was a fine type of man and a good soldier. He accompanied the 10th Battalion to the Dardanelles on the *Ionian*, and landed with his company from the destroyer *Foxhound* at the historic landing on April 25, 1915. After the landing he joined up with Lieutenant N. M. Loutit's party and reached the Third Ridge, but was ultimately forced to retire to Johnston's Jolly on the 400 Plateau. He was subsequently invalided ill from the Peninsula and admitted to the Ras-el-Tin Military Hospital at Alexandria. At first it was reported that he had been killed, when his O.C. (Major M. F. Beevor) forwarded a letter of condolence to his parents; but his mother subsequently replied that the announcement of his death had been officially contradicted. Major Beevor, after leaving hospital at Manchester and before returning to Gallipoli, visited his parents in Scotland, and speaks highly of the hospitality he received. He subsequently received the appointment of Assistant Provost-Marshal at Lemnos, but rejoined the Battalion again at Gebel Habieta, and in February, 1916, was transferred to the 50th Battalion, where he remained a very short time before subsequently being transferred to the Cyclist Training Battalion, which he commanded from 1916-17. He was appointed an honorary lieutenant in the Australian Military Forces on 25/6/18.

16. HALL, SYDNEY RAYMOND, was born on December 17, 1884, and was the eldest son of the late Thomas William Hall, who was carrying on business as a land agent at Unley. His elder brother had been accidentally drowned at Henley Beach a few years before the Great War. On May 14, 1908, he married May, daughter of the late John Drummond, of Sandford & Co., Adelaide, there being two young children of the union, and with his family he resided at No. 48 Wattle Street, Frewville. In June, 1900, he entered the Education Department, but in 1901 transferred to the Lands Titles Office, and at the time of his departure for the front was senior counter-clerk in the Register-General of Deeds Office, Victoria Square. He always took a keen interest in military matters, and received his first commission as a 2nd lieutenant in the Corps of Signallers on March 6, 1911. Upon the introduction of compulsory military training he was transferred on July 1, 1912, to the Engineers, and for some time he was a lieutenant of signalling in the 74th (Boothby) Infantry. On August 3, 1914, he was transferred to the 22nd Signal Troop and promoted to rank of captain. He held this commission at the time of joining the A.I.F. He was anxious to join the 1st Australian Contingent, and on August 19, 1914, was attached to the 10th Battalion Headquarters at Morphettville as Signalling Officer with rank of captain. He landed with his signallers from the *Prince of Wales* in the historic landing on April 25, 1915, and during that morning with great skill and determination established communicaion with Brigade and Divisional headquarters, which at the time had not landed. It was one of his signallers who first transmitted the message that the landing had been successfully accomplished, and the actual flag used on this occasion by No. 966 Pte. G. B. Carter is now in the National War Museum at Canberra. Later that day he was killed in action, having the misfortune to be shot down, and never regained consciousness. News of his death was first received in Adelaide on May 5, 1915, and the late Registrar General of Deeds (G. Wilfred Anthony), when hearing of his death, said: "The sad announcement has cast a gloom over the department. He was a splendid fellow. I had the highest opinion of him as an officer and a man." At a meeting of the Unley City Council on May 11, 1915, the Mayor of Unley (Mr. T. E. Yelland) said: "The war has been brought very close to Australia by the first engagement of the Australian soldiers in Turkey. Of the many residents of Unley who offered their services to the Empire at the commencement of the war, Capt. Hall, son of Mr. T. W. Hall, had unfortunately been killed in action."

17. HAMILTON, JOHN, was born at Auchinleck, Ayrshire, Scotland, on August 20, 1870, and is a son of the late Samuel Hamilton, who was a mine surveyor by profession. He was educated at the Auchinleck Public School and the Edinburgh Academy. In 1892 he proceeded to South Africa and held various positions on the mines at Johannesburg, including clerk, storekeeper, surface-manager, and assistant underground manager. In 1894 he joined the Chartered Company Mounted Police, and working his way through the non-commissioned ranks subsequently obtained a lieutenancy. He participated in the 1st Jameson Raid of December 31, 1895; was captured by the Boers, but managed to escape en route to prison at Pretoria. He participated in the Matabele War of 1896 and received a medal for same. In 1897 he resigned his commission and returned to the Transvaal, and became employed on cyanidation

works at Johannesburg. In October, 1899, he joined Thorneycroft's Mounted Infantry, and served until the termination of the Boer War in 1902. He took part in practically every important engagement from Colenzo to the Relief of Ladysmith. In 1899 he married at Johannesburg, Miss Mary Elizabeth Martin, of Moonta, South Australia, there being two children of the union, one son and a married daughter. For his services in the South African War he received the Queen's Medal with seven clasps. In 1902 he returned to Scotland for a nine months' holiday, and the next year arrived in Australia, proceeding to Broken Hill, where he became engaged sampling on the mines. In 1903 he went to Kalgoorlie, Western Australia, as a gold sampler on the Golden Mile, and later that year proceeded to Pine Creek in the Northern Territory, and took charge of a cyanide plant. He remained in the Northern Territory until 1905, and then returned to Broken Hill, where he remained employed on the mines in various capacities until 1909. In 1910 he qualified as an assayer at the Broken Hill Technical College, becoming an assayer at the Zinc Corporation, where he was employed at the outbreak of the Great War. He interested himself in military training, and on December 16, 1913, was appointed a 2nd lieutenant in the 81st (Wakefield) Infantry, and on July 1, 1914, was transferred to the 82nd (Barrier) Infantry, holding this commission at the time of joining the A.I.F. In May, 1914, he completed an Officers' Training Course at a school of instruction held at Keswick. He was one of the first Broken Hill Officers to offer his services for overseas, and with Capt. R. B. Jacob and Lieut. A. J. Byrne proceeded to Adelaide, and was present at the opening of the Morphettville training camp. He was appointed a 2nd lieutenant in the 10th Battalion on August 19, 1914, and was posted to original "H" Company. He was promoted to rank of lieutenant at Mena on February 1, 1915, although he had been recommended for this rank before embarking on the *Ascanius* on October 20, 1914. He landed with his platoon from the *Prince of Wales* at the historic landing on April 25, 1915, and remained on the Peninsula for the whole of the occupation by the 10th Battalion, with the exception of one week when he was invalided to Lemnos. He was promoted to the rank of temporary captain on August 6, 1915, and his captaincy was confirmed on February 20, 1916. Whilst at Anzac he was appointed Officer-in-Charge of a tunnelling company, which consisted of experienced miners from the 11th Battalion (Western Australia) and 10th Battalion (Broken Hill). This company executed important excavations at Quinn's Post, Courtney's Ridge, and Pope's Hill, and was engaged in this class of work for about three months. After the Battalion was withdrawn from Anzac he accompanied same to Egypt, and at Gebel Habieta received orders to transfer to the 50th Battalion, but at the last moment same were rescinded, and he remained on the strength of the 10th. He proceeded with the Battalion to France, and served first in the Armentieres area and then in the Somme, where he took part in the Pozieres and Mouquet Farm attacks. At Doullens in September, 1916, he left the Battalion and proceeded to the Bull Ring at Etaples, and was subsequently invalided to England with bronchitis. He was admitted to the 3rd London General Hospital at Wandsworth; subsequently entered Lark Hill Camp on Salisbury Plain; was boarded and returned to France, where he rejoined the Battalion at Bancourt early in May, 1917. He participated in the Bullecourt operation, which was his last time in the line. He was seconded for duty with the 3rd

Training Battalion on August 28, 1917, and after another severe attack of bronchitis finally left the Battalion early in September, 1917, when the 10th was moving forward for the Passchendaele Ridge (Polygon Wood) operation. This was his farewell appearance with the Battalion, and much to his regret, he was invalided to England, where he was admitted to the 3rd London General Hospital at Wandsworth. Upon regaining convalescence he proceeded to the Lark Hill Camp, where he was appointed 2nd in Command of the 3rd Training Battalion under Lieut.-Colonel R. B. Jacob. Upon the disbandment of this training battalion he was transferred to the 2nd Training Battalion at Sutton Veney under Temporary Lieut.-Colonel John Newman, with Lieut. E. J. C. Stopp as Adjutant. In May, 1918, he was transferred to Westham Camp at Weymouth, where he was appointed Officer-in-Charge of the Boat Company, his most important duty at Weymouth being to make arrangements for the embarkation of eight Australian Victoria Cross winners who were returning to the Commonwealth. He retained this position until January, 1919, when he embarked on the *Margha*, and arrived back in Adelaide in March, 1919, his services with the A.I.F. terminating in April, 1919. During his absence from Australia he was promoted to the rank of captain in his pre-war unit, but in 1920 he resigned his commission in the 82nd (Barrier) Infantry, and has not since associated himself with the Australian Military Forces. In 1920 he returned to the Zinc Corporation at Broken Hill as an assayer, but in June, 1922, resigning this position, he proceeded to Adelaide, where he has since retired from business. His health at this time was none too robust, and on January 16, 1924, he was admitted to the Bedford Park Sanatorium, from which he was discharged on August 9 of the same year. His wife died in 1933, and in 1935 he was residing at No. 5 Fernleigh Street, Underdale. He was the only original Officer of the Battalion who could claim the rare distinction of having served in three wars. He was affectionately known to his men as "Jock", and noted for his ready wit—he was a particularly popular Officer.

18. HARRISON, JOHN DE COURCY, was born on June 2, 1886, and subsequently served with the Royal Irish Regiment, in which he obtained a commission as lieutenant on September 5, 1908. After retiring from this regiment he proceeded to Australia, where at the outbreak of the Great War he was residing in New South Wales, somewhere in the outback pastoral country near Wilcannia on the River Darling. In August, 1914, he proceeded to Morphettville, and went into camp with the Imperial Reservists, and by special arrangement was permitted to accompany a quota of Imperial Reservists abroad, and upon disembarkation become available for duty with the Australian Imperial Force. He was appointed a lieutenant in the A.I.F. on September 21, 1914, but pending embarkation with Reservists was not attached to any A.I.F. unit. He subsequently proceeded overseas, and arrived at Anzac about May 15, 1915, when he was attached to the 10th Battalion, and promoted to the temporary rank of captain on May 25, 1915. He remained with the Battalion until August 23rd, 1915, when he evacuated ill. He proceeded to Malta, and subsequently re-embarked for England, where he was admitted to hospital, and thus reverted to his substantive rank of lieutenant. He subsequently proceeded to France, and at the end of 1916 when Temp. Lieut.-Colonel G. F. Redburg commanded the Battalion, he was attached to 1st Divisional Headquarters. Shortly after this he returned to the 10th Battalion, was placed in

charge of a company, and promoted to temporary rank of captain as and from February 11, 1917. He was wounded during the Le Barque attack on February 25, 1917, and forced to evacuate, thereby again reverting to his substantive rank of lieutenant. He was subsequently transferred to the 27th Battalion. He was the second Imperial Reservist Officer attached to the 10th, and was affectionately known to rank and file as "Shrapnel Jack" or "Telescope Jack", owing to his ability to compress himself within an absolute minimum of space, should the occasion warrant. In 1935 he was managing the late Sir Sidney Kidman's Ivanhoe Station, via Broken Hill.

19. HEMING, HECTOR ROY, was born at Adelaide on October 28, 1888, and is a son of the late Thomas and Grace Heming. His father, prior to leaving England for Australia, had served as a life-guardsman in H.M. Household Cavalry, and in 1908 acquired the licence of the Selborne Hotel, Pirie Street, Adelaide, but following his decease, the licence on 14/12/09 was transferred to his mother, who relinquished same on March 1, 1911. He had two brothers in the A.I.F.—Capt. L. D. Heming, of the 16th Battalion, who was killed in action on Gallipoli, and Major T. G. Heming, of the 43rd Battalion. He received his education in Adelaide, and at the outbreak of the Great War was undergoing a course of training for the Commonwealth Military Forces, and was residing with his mother at No. 15 McKinnon Parade, North Adelaide. As a young man he was keenly interested in military matters, and received his first commission as 2nd lieutenant in the 78th (Adelaide Rifles) Infantry on March 17, 1913, and was promoted to rank of lieutenant in same unit on August 24, 1914. He also officiated as Adjutant of his regiment for some considerable time, and was holding this commission at the time of joining the A.I.F. He was one of the first South Australian Officers to offer his services for overseas, and was appointed a 2nd lieutenant in the 10th Battalion at Morphettville on August 19, 1914, and posted to original "E" Company. He embarked with the original Battalion per H.M.A.T. A11 *Ascanius* on October 20, 1914, and at Mena, in Egypt, January, 1915, when his company merged with original "C" Company and became the new "B" Company, he was appointed a Platoon Commander in same and promoted to rank of lieutenant on February 1, 1915. He was noted for being the tallest Officer in the original Battalion. He accompanied the Battalion on the *Ionian* to the Dardanelles, and landed with his company from the *Prince of Wales* at the historic landing on April 25, 1915. Later that day he had the unique experience of being the only surviving Officer of his company—the first and second Officers in Command being killed, one Platoon Commander killed, and two other Platoon Commanders wounded and forced to evacuate. When the 10th Battalion was relieved by the Royal Marines on April 29, 1915, he and his party of 20 men were one of the last posts to be relieved. They had occupied a position difficult to reach, and were short of food and water. He was invalided from the Peninsula on August 5, 1915, suffering with enteric fever, and proceeded to the 3rd London General Hospital at Wandsworth. He arrived in France on April 16, 1916, and joined the 10th Battalion at Sailly in May, 1916. He was then posted to the command of "B" Company. He was promoted to the rank of captain on June 27, 1916, and in July, 1916, was appointed Brigade Bombing Officer. He remained in France until March 2, 1917, when he was seconded for duty with the 3rd Training Battalion. In this capacity he proceeded to

England, where he was appointed O.C. of the 10th Training Battalion. He returned to France on December 19, 1917, and was O.C. of "C" Company whilst the Battalion was in the line in the Messines Sector. He served through various operations with the Battalion until he finally left the 10th at Pradelles on July 18, 1918. He then proceeded to England where, in August, 1918, he embarked on the *Malta*, arriving back in Adelaide the next month, his services with the A.I.F. terminating on October 8, 1918. During his absence from Australia he was appointed an honorary captain in the Australian Military Forces on June 27, 1916, and was appointed a lieutenant in the 2/10th Infantry on October 1, 1918. On December 12, 1919, he was promoted to the rank of captain, and listed on the Reserve of Officers. Returning to civil life he decided to settle on the land, and obtained an irrigation perpetual lease of $16\frac{1}{2}$ acres in the Waikerie irrigation area, taking possession of same on May 24, 1919. On September 1, 1924, he increased his holding by securing an additional lease of $35\frac{1}{2}$ acres situated in the same area. On June 16, 1920, at St. Peter's Church, Glenelg, he married Ruby Margaret, daughter of James Allen, there being two sons of the union. He is a member of Masonic Lodge of Truth, No. 8. He was affectionately known to men of the 10th as "Long Tom" or "Boof", and in 1935 his private address was "Box 34, Waikerie".

20. HERBERT, MERVYN JAMES, was born at Melbourne on September 15, 1887, and at the outbreak of the Great War was residing at Marlborough Street, New Glenelg. He received his first commission as a 2nd lieutenant in the S.A. Scottish on August 28, 1911, and was transferred to the 78th (Adelaide Rifles) Infantry on July 1, 1912. He was promoted to the rank of lieutenant on January 31, 1913, and obtained his captaincy on July 16, 1914, and held this commission at the time of joining the A.I.F. On April 16, 1914, he was appointed Area Officer at Prospect. He was one of the first Company Commanders selected by Colonel Weir for the 10th Battalion, and was appointed a captain in the 10th at Morphettville on August 19, 1914. He was posted to the command of original "D" Company, and embarked on H.M.-A.T. A11 *Ascanius* on October 20, 1914. He landed with his company from the destroyer *Scourge* at the historic landing on April 25, 1915, and later that day was wounded in the hand, which necessitated the amputation of a finger. He evacuated and proceeded to Egypt, and subsequently returned to Adelaide with the second lot of wounded to return to Australia on the *Ballarat*. He arrived in Adelaide on August 3, 1915, and was the third original Battalion Officer to be invalided home. After leaving Anzac he had been transferred to the 9th Battalion. On August 4, 1915, he attended a monster recruiting meeting at the Adelaide Exhibition Building, and with other wounded Officers and men was requested by the Governor, Sir Henry Galway, to go up on the platform. After recovering from his wounds he returned to Egypt, and was retransferred to the 10th, rejoining the Battalion at Lemnos on December 5, 1915. He proceeded with the Battalion to Egypt, and on March 1, 1916, was transferred to the 50th Battalion, and on March 12, 1916, was promoted to the rank of major. He arrived in France with the 50th Battalion on June 6, 1916, and remained with this unit until November 8, 1916. On October 28, 1916, he was seconded for duty as O.C. of the 13th Infantry Training Battalion, and subsequently proceeded to England. On May 4, 1917, he was seconded for duty as Permanent President Courts-Martial, A.I.F. Depots in

United Kingdom. He subsequently returned to Australia, his services with the A.I.F. terminating on April 26, 1919. During his absence from Australia he was appointed an honorary major in the Australian Military Forces on March 3, 1916. Returning to civil life he commenced duties with the Department of Defence, but subsequently decided to settle on the land, and on June 1, 1921, secured an irrigation perpetual lease over $20\frac{1}{2}$ acres situated in the Moorook irrigation area. In 1923 he acquired a further 45 acres, in 1927, $29\frac{1}{2}$, and also $4\frac{3}{4}$ acres, and in 1930, 14 acres, making a total holding of approximately 114 acres. On August 26, 1911, at New Glenelg, he married Dorothy Matilda, daughter of James John Royals, there being two sons and one daughter of the union, and in 1935 was residing on his block, and was also manager of the Moorook Distillery Ltd. Upon relinquishing command of "D" Company at Anzac in 1915, the following letter under date of July 23, 1915, was dispatched to him: "As we have heard definitely that you are not returning to us, we wish to express our regret, and hope that you will soon make a speedy recovery. You, no doubt, sir, have heard of the gallantry of the old 'Don' Company, and in your disappointment at not being able to return to us we hope it has been of some consolation to you. There have been two D.C.M's. gained by the 10th Battalion, and it will please you to know they are both men of your old company, namely Privates C. P. Green and Lance-corporal J. C. Weatherill. It will be needless for us to tell you news of our Battalion, as it will be given you by others. In conclusion we thank you for your sound instruction in the past, and our sincere wish is that when we return we shall see you well. (Signed) Sgts. A. R. Baker, G. Tippett; Lance-corporals F. J. S. Mead, J. C. Weatherill; Ptes. S. G. Pack, S. C. Toovey; Dvr. C. King." He received this letter of commendation whilst in Adelaide in August, 1915, before returning temporarily to the 10th Battalion. After leaving Anzac, and whilst in hospital in Egypt, he succeeded in preparing a splendid article dealing with the landing of the 10th Battalion at Anzac, and same was subsequently published in *The Advertiser*.

21. HOLMES, LOUIS GORDON, was born at Launceston, Tasmania, on July 7, 1892, and was the only son of Dr. Louis and Lucy Holmes, of Norwood and Ballarat. He was educated at Scotch College, Launceston, and Wesley College, Melbourne, where he gained his blue for football and rowing. He also attended the University of Melbourne, where he had a successful athletic career, being a prominent member of the rowing and football teams. He was well known in athletic circles in South Australia, and on several occasions rowed with the University of Adelaide eights. Shortly before the outbreak of the Great War he commenced studying for a military career. He received his first commission as a 2nd lieutenant (provisionally) in the 79th (Torrens) Infantry on February 16, 1913, and was promoted to rank of lieutenant in the same regiment on July 16, 1914, and held this commission at the time of joining the A.I.F. He was appointed a 2nd lieutenant in the 10th Battalion at Morphettville on August 19, 1914, and was posted to original "F" Company, with which he embarked per H.M.A.T. A11 *Ascanius* on October 20, 1914. On February 1, 1915, at Mena, Egypt, he was promoted to the rank of lieutenant, and attached to 3rd Brigade Headquarters as permanent Orderly Officer to Colonel E. G. Sinclair-MacLagan. Whilst holding this position he had much to do with Major Brand, Brigade Major of the 3rd Brigade, and other

Staff Officers. Before leaving the Battalion his many admirers presented him with a riding whip and a pair of spurs in recognition of the splendid services he had rendered in connection with fostering sport. He accompanied the 3rd Brigade Headquarters to Anzac, landed with the 3rd Brigade, and often came in contact with his late associates of the 10th. On June 13, 1915, he was returning to his dug-out after bathing in the cove, when the Olive Grove guns opened fire, and he was mortally wounded by the notorious "Beachy Bill". He was widely popular, and when it was first announced that he was wounded it was hoped by his many scholastic and other friends that his injury would not prove fatal. He had attained his captaincy on April 26, 1915.

22. HOOPER, ROBERT JAMES MANSFIELD, was born at Kapunda on July 11, 1895, and was the only son of James and the late Liby Louisa Hooper, of Prince's Street, Alberton. He was educated at the Alberton Public School, and as a compulsory trainee took a zealous interest in military training, even whilst at school. He received his first commission as a 2nd lieutenant (provisionally) in the 76th (Hindmarsh) Infantry on August 1, 1913, and held this commission at the time of joining the A.I.F. The death of his mother shortly before the outbreak of the Great War influenced him to some extent in deciding to proceed overseas. He was appointed a 2nd lieutenant in the 10th Battalion at Morphettville on August 19, 1914, and was posted to original "C" Company, and embarked with same per H.M.A.T. A11 *Ascanius* on October 20, 1914. At Mena, in Egypt, in January, 1915, when his company merged with original "E" Company and became the new "B" Company he was appointed a Platoon Commnader in same, and promoted to rank of lieutenant on February 1, 1915. He accompanied the Battalion on the *Ionian* to the Dardanelles, and landed with his company from the *Prince of Wales* at the historic landing on April 25, 1915, and shortly after was killed in action. After leading a ration party from the beach to "C" Company line of trenches he proceeded to return, but whilst attempting to penetrate a perfect hail of shells and bullets was killed in the act of crossing between two trenches. Lieut.-Colonel S. P. Weir assisted to bury him, most of the Officers at the time being in the front line. He had been a chorister at St. Paul's Church, Port Adelaide, and had been prepared for confirmation in the same church by the rector, Rev. M. Williams, who was asked to break the sad news of his death to his father. He was one of the youngest lieutenants in the 10th, and was of a cheerful disposition. In his last letter to his father he said: "I have by now learnt to take care of myself; and, whatever happens, never regret you let me go, as nothing would have kept my heart away from it. I simply had to go, and simply do or die; and remember, I am only doing my duty as a soldier is bound to. You and I always used to love the verse of Longfellow's which read: 'Lives of great men all remind us, we can make our lives sublime; and, departing, leave behind us footprints on the sands of time.' If I do not manage to leave any footprints, you can remember you brought up a son of British blood, and who was not frightened, but took it as an honour to give his life for his King and Country. Whatever comes, I trust I will not die in any way that would disgrace my country or my friends. Many a noble family will have to suffer loss, and why not take it in the best light possible. Take it as an honour that you help to pay for the nation's misfortune. Even if I knew I was to meet the most violent death I would not flinch, but would go

ahead. So whatever happens, do not worry and think I have not my whole heart in the game."

23. HOSKING, HERBERT CHAMPION, was born on March 8, 1895, and is the son of the late Edward Champion and Edith Hosking. His father was a grocer, and at the outbreak of the Great War he resided with his parents at Magill Road, St. Peters. He passed the State Civil Service Examination in 1910, and was subsequently appointed a junior clerk in the accountant's branch, Surveyor General's Department, commencing duties on April 19, 1910, but resigned from the Public Service on May 12, 1912. He was a compulsory trainee, and received his first commission as a 2nd lieutenant in the 79th (Torrens) Infantry on May 31, 1913, and on July 16, 1914, was promoted to the rank of lieutenant in the same regiment. He held this commission at the time of joining the A.I.F. He was appointed a lieutenant in the 10th Battalion at Morphettville on August 19, 1914, and was posted to original "A" Company, with which he embarked per H.M.A.T. A11 *Ascanius* on October 20, 1914. At Mena, Egypt, when his company merged with original "F" Company and became the new "A" Company, he was appointed a Platoon Commander in same. He accompanied the Battalion to the Dardanelles on the *Ionian*, and landed with his company from the destroyer *Foxhound* at the historic landing on April 25, 1915. He remained on the Peninsula until August 20, 1915, when through illness he was compelled to evacuate, and proceeding to England was admitted into hospital. He subsequently returned to South Australia in 1916, but proceeded overseas again as O.C. of the 19th Reinforcements of the 10th Battalion, which embarked per H.M.A.T. A70 *Ballarat*, at the Outer Harbour on August 12, 1916. He joined the Battalion in France on November 11, 1916, and on January 4, 1917, evacuated sick, leaving France for England on January 14, 1917. He subsequently returned to Australia, his services with the A.I.F. terminating on August 6, 1917. He was one of the youngest Officers of the original Battalion, and with Lieutenants R. J. M. Hooper and W. H. Perry shared this distinction. In 1918 he commenced a first-year course in the Faculty of Medicine at the University of Adelaide, and under the Commonwealth Vocational Training Scheme completed his second to fourth years, both inclusive. His academic career was outstanding. In 1920 he topped the 2nd year students, and won the Elder Prize; later tied with another student for the Everard Prize, and finally won the Dr. Charles Gosse Medal for opthalmology. In 1923 he graduated M.B., B.S., his degrees being conferred on December 12, 1923. He was appointed Junior Medical Officer at the Parkside Mental Hospital on March 1, 1924, and by December 31 of that year had become Senior Medical Officer. On January 1, 1925, he was appointed Deputy Superintendent, which position he resigned on February 3, 1925. On the same day he was appointed a medical officer in the Commonwealth Public Service, Department of Health, and subsequently proceeded to New Britain to take up his new appointment. On August 22, 1927, at the Kent Town Methodist Church, he married Lorna Ellen, daughter of William Reynolds Bayly, and in 1935 he was stationed at Ravalion, Rabaul. He is a member of the British Medical Association, and is local secretary of the Royal Society of Tropical Medicine and Hygiene. It will be remembered that whilst on the *Ascanius* in November, 1914, he and Major M. F. Beevor staged the first boxing bout in order to popularize the ring with the troops. His name was removed from the Retired

RECORDS OF SERVICE

List of the Australian Miliary Forces on November 11, 1916, but was replaced on same with rank of 2nd lieutenant on July 23, 1925.

24. HURCOMBE, FREDERICK WILLIAM, was born at Hindmarsh on August 16, 1867, and is a son of the late William Hurcombe, who was a brewer. He was practically a self-educated man, attending no school in particular for any period worthy of mention, with the exception of a small quaker school at North Adelaide. Keen on a military career he enlisted with the South Australian Garrison Artillery as a gunner, and after holding the non-commissioned ranks of bombadier, lance-corporal, sergeant, and quartermaster-sergeant, received his first commission as a lieutenant in that regiment on July 18, 1894, and was promoted to the rank of captain on August 8, 1898. In 1899 he joined the Imperial Bushmen's Corps, which was the first regiment raised by the British Government in Australia for service in the South African War. He embarked as a senior lieutenant; was promoted to rank of captain shortly after leaving, and received his majority before completing a year's service. It was in South Africa that he first met Sir William Birdwood, being attached to Birdwood's Staff as Officer Commanding Australian Details, which appointment necessitated his carrying despatches from Lord Kitchener's headquarters at Pretoria to Government House at Cape Town. He served in South Africa for two years and nine months, and participated in several operations in the Transvaal and Orange River Colony, including the action at Wittenbergen. He received the Queen's Medal with three clasps, and the King's with two. During his absence in South Africa he was appointed a captain on the Supernumerary List in the Commonwealth Forces as and from July 5, 1901, and was appointed an honorary major on July 7, 1901. He was listed on the Reserve of Officers on December 12, 1904, and transferred to the Unattached List on July 8, 1905, and at the time of joining the A.I.F. he was still listed on same. He was appointed a temporary Area Officer at Port Adelaide on September 16, 1912, and held this position at the outbreak of the Great War. On December 26, 1885, he married Eva Victoria Alice Birkenshaw, daughter of an English sea captain who navigated his own vessel and sailed to various British and foreign ports with his wife and two daughters aboard. It was during one of these trips made by Capt. Birkenshaw that Lt.-Col. Hurcombe met his future wife, there being five children of the union, three sons and two daughters. In private life he was a shipping agent employed by George Ferguson & Co., of Port Adelaide, and was well-known throughout the Port Adelaide district. Due to his extensive South African War experience he was one of the first Officers selected by Lieut.-Colonel S. P. Weir, and on August 19, 1914, was appointed a major on the 10th Battalion staff at Morphettville, whilst on October 2, 1914, he was appointed 2nd in Command of the Battalion, although he had virtually held this appointment from the opening of the Morphettville training camp. He embarked on H.M.A.T. A11 *Ascanius* on October 20, 1914, and one week later (November 1, 1914), when Colonel Weir was appointed O.C. Troops on transport, he assumed temporary command of the 10th Battalion until same disembarked at Alexandria on December 6, 1914. He accompanied the 10th to Lemnos as 2nd in Command, and on the Saturday night preceding the historic landing had the Battalion Officers assembled on the *Ionian*, when he outlined to them the field-conditions they were likely to encounter on the morrow. He instructed

them to expose themselves as little as possible, and push on for the objectives, seeking cover as frequently as possible. He landed with the Battalion from the *Prince of Wales*, and as senior field-officer performed every task necessary to help the troops to advance. At one time he would be carrying machine-gun belts to Lieut. E. W. Talbot Smith, who had run short of ammunition, or at another he would be moving along the line advising, instructing, commending, as the circumstances warranted. He was always a popular Officer with the men, and his outspoken candid demeanour constantly gained for him the esteem of the original Battalion as well as the respect of the reinforcements. A few hours after landing at Anzac he had a very narrow escape from death caused by a shrapnel pellet. Referring to this incident in a letter to his wife, dated May 15, 1915, he said: "I had a very narrow escape. A bullet tore away the ribbon on the bar, went through my pocket-book, broke up my fountain pen, and remained in my pocket. It was the hottest thing I ever saw." He still possesses this pocket-book and the actual pellet, which are his most treasured Gallipoli souvenirs. Shortly after this miraculous escape he left Signalling Officer Capt. S. R. Hall to proceed to the right flank, and returning within ten minutes was advised of the death of Capt. Hall. who during his absence had been instantaneously killed by a shell. On July 2, 1915, he was invalided from the Peninsula, and proceeded to hospital at Heliopolis, Egypt, later to Helouan near Cairo, and subsequently to the 3rd London General Hospital at Wandsworth. For his splendid work on the Gallipoli Peninsula he was mentioned in Army Corps Routine Orders, and for his conspicuous work was further mentioned in despatches, *vide London Gazette*, November 5, 1915. He returned to Egypt on December 15, 1915, and was posted to a training battalion at Heliopolis, Cairo, being specially selected to reorganize and train a brigade of reinforcements. On March 1, 1916, he was appointed Commanding Officer of the 50th Battalion, and in this capacity on March 12, 1916, proceeded to Tel-el-Kebir, where he raised his new battalion, partly from a quota of 10th Battalion Officers and men who had been specially transferred for the purpose, and partly from A.I.F. reinforcements then in training in Egypt. Early in June, 1916, he proceeded with the 50th Battalion to France on the *Arcadian*, and led his unit in the attacks on Pozieres and Mouquet Farm. He sustained shell-shock at Pozieres and was invalided to England about August 15, 1916, and was admitted to the 3rd London General Hospital at Wandsworth, and subsequently to "The Boltons", a convalescent depot near Hyde Park, London. Shortly before leaving England for Australia he received the following letter from General Sir William Birdwood: "My dear Hurcombe—I am so sorry not to have seen you before you left here, as I should have so much wished to have done so, to say good-bye, and to thank you for all the work which you have put in for us with the A.I.F. for close on the last two years. I so well realize what a very great strain this has necessarily been on you, more especially in the responsible and very difficult position of a Commanding Officer, which I always think myself is perhaps one of the most difficult and trying in the whole of our service. That you have stood this as you have done for all these months is, I think, highly creditable, and I feel I cannot let you leave us without expressing to you my gratitude and thanks. I am convinced that you must yourself realize how very advisable it is that you should go home for a thorough rest, and let others who have not been so long in the field come forward and take their turn. With my heartiest wishes to you on your return to Australia, and again, my most grateful thanks. Yours sincerely, (Signed) W. R. Birdwood." He spent two months in England before embarking for South Australia, arriving back in Adelaide about November 20, 1916, his services with the A.I.F. terminating on January 23, 1917. After a short period of convalescence he considered himself again fit to assist the Empire, and before the Armistice occurred in 1918 he made three separate trips to England as O.C. of A.I.F. troops on transports conveying details and reinforcements. His first trip on transport duty was completed on July 3, 1917, and his third and final on May 24, 1918. Two of these trips were made via the Suez Canal and one via the Cape. He was subsequently placed on the Reserve of Officers with rank of lieutenant-colonel, and on August 16, 1927, was transferred to the Retired List. In 1920 his wife died, and since then he has retired from business pursuits, and in 1935 was residing at "Fricourt", No. 75 Third Avenue, East Adelaide. He is a recipient of the Volunteer Decoration. From the first day of the Morphettville Camp he was admired for his straight talks to the men. He was never guilty of "beating around a corner", and was always admired by rank and file for calling "an ace an ace", or "a spade a spade". By many of the younger volunteer recruits he was looked upon as a counsellor, and was invariably sought after for his fatherly advice, and for this reason was affectionately known as "Dad Hurcombe". On April 8, 1935, in referring to the 10th Battalion, he stated to the compiler of this record as follows: "Never a corps existed that equalled them for enthusiasm, and in spite of a little gaiety of spirit they were very attentive to their duties, which were always well carried out." His son, Roy Kintore, was also an original member of the Battalion; enlisting as a private and attaining the rank of temporary major.

25. HURCOMBE, ROY KINTORE, was born at South Terrace, Adelaide, on February 8, 1889, and is a son of Lieut.-Colonel F. W. Hurcombe, V.D., who was originally 2nd in Command of the 10th Battalion, and subsequently first C.O. of the 50th Battalion. From early youth he possessed an adventurous spirit, his chief ambition being to see as much of the world as possible. He successfully accomplished his desire by residing one and a half years in England, one year in South Africa, and four and a half years in the United States of America, besides visiting many other foreign parts. He was educated at various public schools which he attended during the course of his travels; but chiefly graduated in the bigger school of cosmopolis. In 1914 he returned to South Australia from America, and at the outbreak of the Great War was employed as a storeman at Port Adelaide. He resided with his parents at Mile End, and prior to joining the A.I.F. had not served with any Australian Military Force unit. On August 19, 1914, he enlisted as a private in the 10th Battalion at Morphettville, his regimental number being "52", and was subsequently drafted as a driver to the Transport Section of the Battalion. Before embarking on H.M.A.T. A12 *Saldanha* with portion of the Battalion Transport Section he had attained the rank of lance-corporal, and before reaching Alexandria had been promoted to the rank of corporal. He accompanied the 10th Battalion Transport Section to the Dardanelles on the *Nizem*, and when various troop transfers were being made in Mudros Harbour, Lemnos, with 2nd Lieut. T. O. Smyth was transferred to the *Ionian*, whilst the balance of the Transport Section was transferred to the *Malwa*. Whilst the main body of the Battalion

participated in the historic landing on April 25, 1915, the Battalion Transport Section unwillingly and discontentedly stood by daily awaiting instructions to land. Whilst waiting for orders which never came the troopship on which he was stationed made one voyage to Alexandria with wounded, and trips to Gaba Tepe and Cape Helles. On May 12, 1915, shortly after Lieut. T. O. Smyth was killed, he was promoted to the rank of 2nd lieutenant, and was appointed Transport Officer of the Battalion. He subsequently received unwelcome orders that his section was not to land on the Peninsula, but return to Egypt. On May 30, 1915, he left Lemnos with the Battalion transport, arriving at Alexandria on June 6, 1915, and then proceeded to Mex, where the Transport Section encamped for several months; but subsequently removed to Maadi near Cairo. On November 14, 1915, he was promoted to the rank of lieutenant, and early in 1916 at Tel-el-Kebir, the transport rejoined the main body of the Battalion. On January 25, 1916, at Serapeum, he was transferred to the Battalion as a Platoon Commander, and posted to "B" Company, whilst Lieut. M. J. Coffey was appointed Transport Officer. He accompanied the Battalion to France on the *Saxonia*, and in April, 1916, proceeded to Wisques, near St. Omer, where he attended the Corps School for six weeks. He returned to the Battalion, and on May 25, 1916, was promoted to the rank of captain, shortly before the Battalion went into the line at Fleurbaix. At the attack on Pozieres he was 2nd in Command of "B" Company, and upon the death of Capt. C. W. Hooper on July 25, 1916, assumed command of that company. On September 14, 1916, whilst the Battalion was at Chateau Belge, he proceeded on his first furlough, and rejoined the 10th whilst it was in the line at the famous "Hill 60", at Ypres. He remained with his company until November 12, 1916, when at Bernafay Wood, following the Gueudecourt action, he evacuated sick, and proceeded to England, where he was admitted to the 3rd London General Hospital at Wandsworth. He was mentioned in despatches, *vide London Gazette*, 2/1/17. He subsequently returned to France and rejoined the Battalion a few days before it proceeded into the line at Louverval on April 7, 1917. He then retained command of "B" Company until the two special raiding companies were formed. He was then appointed Officer Commanding "X" Company, which he led in the Polygon Wood operation on September 19-22, 1917, and distinguished himself by reorganizing and leading it to the final objective, for which he was awarded the M.C., which was promulgated in the *London Gazette* on November 16, 1917, and the details on March 19, 1918. He was seconded for duty with the 3rd Training Battalion on September 29, 1917, and shortly after the Polygon Wood action proceeded to England, where he was attached to the 3rd Training Battalion under the command of Lieut.-Colonel R. B. Jacob, and when same was disbanded and the 2nd Training Battalion formed at Durrington, he was transferred to same, and appointed Training Adjutant, which position he retained until relieved by Capt. W. F. J. McCann. He subsequently returned to France and rejoined the Battalion in the line in front of Merris at the end of May, 1918, and resumed command of "B" Company, which he led in the Mont de Merris operation on May 30, 1918. During the preparations proceeding the capture of Merris on July 29-30, 1918, he acted as Assistant Adjutant of the Battalion, and the night that Merris was taken his company co-operated with "A" Company, when less than a dozen casualties were sustained. For his splendid work in this operation he was awarded a Bar to his M.C., which was promulgated in the *London Gazette* on November 7, 1918. He subsequently received the following letter from Headquarters, A.I.F., B.E.F., France: "Dear Hurcombe—This is just a line to send you my heartiest congratulations on the award to you of a Bar to the Military Cross, which you have fully deserved for your excellent work in command of one of the attacking companies in our operations at Merris on July 29. Although you came under heavy fire immediately prior to the attack, you succeeded in reorganizing your company, which you led with great dash and courage. After gaining your objective, you personally led an attack on an enemy machine-gun nest, and in the hand-to-hand fighting which ensued accounted for several Germans. Later you surprised and captured a German Officer and two men. Thank you very much for your soldierly conduct, and with good wishes. Yours sincerely, W. R. Birdwood, 24/9/18. P.S.: I hope you have good news of your father, to whom please give my very kindest regards." He was promoted to the rank of temporary major on September 23, 1918, and before finally leaving the Battalion at Brucamps on September 30, 1918, he temporarily commanded the 10th for over a week during the absence of Lieut.-Colonel M. Wilder-Neligan, C.M.G., D.S.O., D.C.M., and Major W. F. J. McCann, D.S.O., M.C., and Bar. Due for 1914 Anzac leave he proceeded to England, where at Southampton he embarked on the *Olympic* and travelled to New York, thence overland to San Francisco, and at that port embarked on the *Sonoma* for Sydney, arriving back in Adelaide in November, 1918, his services with the A.I.F. terminating on January 18, 1919. After five months in Adelaide he proceeded to the United States of America and recommenced his pre-war life of general adventure, in which he travelled extensively between the Canadian and Mexican borders. After an absence from Australia of six and a half years he returned to Adelaide in 1927, and accepted a position in the production department office of General Motors Ltd. He retained this occupation for two years, but in 1929 was appointed Labour Superintendent at Port Adelaide of the Employers of Maritime Labour of S.A. Inc., and still holds this position. In 1933 he married Jean Mary, daughter of Charles John Conley, there being no children of the union. During his absence from Australia he was appointed an honorary captain in the Australian Military Forces on May 25, 1916, and is now listed on the Reserve of Officers with rank of captain as and from October 1, 1920. Since the war he has annexed 18 Australian weight-lifting records, and also two world's championships. In 1935 he was residing at Sewell Avenue, Rugby, Payneham.

26. INWOOD, REGINALD ROY, was born at North Adelaide on July 14, 1890, and is a son of Edward Inwood and a brother of No. 1533 Sergeant Robert Minney Inwood (3rd Reinforcements) who first distinguished himself in the fighting at Rouge-de-Bout in the Armentieres Sector on 6/6/16, and later at Pozieres on 24/7/16 made a reconnaissance with Lieut. A. S. Blackburn and was killed in action during the same operation. He was educated at the North Adelaide Public School and the Broken Hill Model School, and at the outbreak of the Great War was employed on the Broken Hill mines. He enlisted in the A.I.F. at Railway Town, Broken Hill, on August 24, 1914, and shortly after proceeded to Morphettville training camp with the 10th Battalion quota from that city. His regimental number was "506", and he was drafted to original "H" Company. He embarked as a private with the original Battalion

per H.M.A.T. A11 *Ascanius* at the Outer Harbour, South Australia, on October 20, 1914, and proceeded to Egypt. At Mena in January, 1915, when his company merged with original "B" Company and became the new "C" Company, he was transferred to same. He subsequently re-embarked with the Battalion on the *Ionian* for the Dardanelles, and landed with his company from the *Prince of Wales* at the historic landing at Anzac on April 25, 1915, and whilst on the Peninsula was promoted to the rank of lance-corporal. He subsequently served with the Battalion in France, and for his exceptionally gallant and good work in the Polygon Wood operation on September 20-21, 1917, was awarded the Victoria Cross, which was promulgated in the *London Gazette* on November 26, 1917. He was the second member of the Battalion to win this coveted distinction, and after winning his decoration was congratulated by letter from General Sir W. R. Birdwood. Shortly after the Polygon Wood action he was promoted to the rank of corporal, and subsequently attained the rank of sergeant. He remained with the Battalion until May 30, 1918, when in a minor operation carried out in the Merris Sector he finally left the Battalion and subsequently returned to South Australia, being discharged from the A.I.F. on December 21, 1918. In 1927 he married Evelyn, daughter of John Owens, there being no children of the union. In 1935 he was employed by the Adelaide City Council, and was residing at No. 6 Argyle Street, Prospect. Dr. C. E. W. Bean, in the "Official History of Australia in the War, 1914-18, Vol. IV, A.I.F. in France 1917," pp. 786 and 787, says in reference to him in the Battle of Menin Road: "Patrols went deep into Polygon Wood. Lance-Corporal R. R. Inwood of the 10th went 600 yards and found that there were Germans in the shelters near the Butte. . . . During the morning of the 21st some movement 200-300 yards ahead of the line in Polygon Wood suggested that the enemy was trying to establish his front there. In this wood in the morning a German machine gun was detected by Lance-Corporal Inwood and some soldier of the 7th. Creeping behind the gun they bombed it and made a surviving German gunner carry it in to the Australian lines for them. For this and for his scouting operations Inwood received the Victoria Cross. The name of the 7th Battalion man was not recorded."

27. JACOB, ROSS BLYTH, was born at Snowtown, South Australia, on July 5, 1885, and is a son of the late William Edwards Jacob, who was formerly a mounted trooper in the S.A. Police, but upon retirement from that force acquired near Kadina, 5,000 acres of land on which he built a homestead, and subsequently became the proprietor of the Royal Exchange Hotel at Kadina. He was one of seven brothers, six of whom enlisted in the A.I.F., five proceeding overseas and one remaining in Australia on home service. He was educated at the Snowtown Public School, the Norwood Public School, and Professor Bill's Grammar School at Moonta. On July 1, 1901, at Kadina, he entered the Postmaster-General's Department as a postal assistant, and later was trnsferred to the Adelaide office as a telegraphist, which position he resigned on November 11, 1912. As a young man he was an enthusiast in military matters, and commenced his military career by joining the South Australian Infantry Regiment as a 2nd lieutenant, receiving his commission in that regiment on July 27, 1908. He was transferred to the 10th A.I.R. with same rank on August 9, 1909, and was promoted to rank of lieutenant on March 25, 1912. Upon the introduction of compulsory military training on July 1, 1912, he was transferred to

the 81st (Wakefield) Infantry and promoted to rank of captain in that unit on March 31, 1913. He was Area Officer at Kadina from November 1, 1910 to April 30, 1914. On July 1, 1914, he was transferred to the 82nd (Barrier) Infantry as Commanding Officer, such appointment to terminate on September 30, 1918, and held this commission at the time of joining the A.I.F. He was one of the first Broken Hill officers to offer his services for overseas, and with Lieutenants Byrne and Hamilton arrived in Adelaide for the opening of Morphettville training camp. He was appointed a captain in the 10th Battalion at Morphettville on August 19, 1914, and posted to the command of original "H" Company, which was composed almost entirely of Broken Hill men. He embarked with the original Battalion per H.M.A.T. A11 *Ascanius* on October 20, 1914, and at Mena, Egypt, in January, 1914, when his company merged with the original "B" Company and became the new "C" Company he was appointed Officer Commanding same. He accompanied the Battalion on the *Ionian* to the Dardanelles, and landed with his company from the *Prince of Wales* at the historic landing on April 25, 1915. On April 28, 1915, he was wounded and forced to evacuate, and proceeding to England was admitted to the Whitworth Street Hospital at Manchester. For his splendid work at the landing he was mentioned in Army Corps Routine Orders. He subsequently returned to the Dardanelles, and rejoined the 10th in the line at Anzac on October 20, 1915, and was promoted to the rank of temporary major, reverting to his substantive rank of captain on December 10, 1915. He accompanied the Battalion when withdrawn to Lemnos on November 21, 1915, and subsequently embarked on the *Seeang Bee* for Egypt, where he proceeded with the 10th to Tel-el-Kebir, Serapeum, and Gebel Habieta. He was promoted to the rank of major on February 20, 1916, and on March 16, 1916, was transferred to the newly-formed 50th Battalion as 2nd in Command. He left Egypt with this unit on June 5, 1916, and arrived in France on June 12, 1916, and served with the 50th through the Pozieres and other operations, until at Windmill, near Flers, in December, 1916, he was appointed Chief Instructor of the 1st Divisional School at La Chausee, where he remained for one month, and was promoted to the temporary rank of lieutenant-colonel. He was transferred to the 10th Battalion as Commanding Officer, and promoted to the rank of lieutenant-colonel on February 4, 1917. He took over the command of the Battalion from Major R. A. Rafferty, D.S.O., and retained same until June 23, 1917, with the exception of one fortnight he spent on furlough, when he was relieved by Major Alexander Steele, who led the Battalion in the Bullecourt operation of May, 1917. At Ribemont, on June 21, 1917, he was seconded for duty as Commanding Officer of the 3rd Training Battalion at Lark Hill, England. Subsequently, when all training battalions were transferred to Warminster and reorganized, he was appointed O.C. of the 1st Training Battalion, with Capt. J. Hamilton as 2nd in Command. He subsequently returned to France, and commanded the 10th Battalion for the second time—from March 30 to May 11, 1918. He left France on June 10, 1918, when he was invalided to England and transferred to the General List as from May 16, 1918. Owing to the fact that there happened to be a surplus of A.I.F. colonels in England, and also for family reasons, he was desirous of returning to Australia. He embarked on the *Malta*, and returned to South Australia *via* the Cape, arriving back in Adelaide early in October, 1918, his services with the A.I.F. terminating on October 8, 1918. Whilst returning on this boat he became acquainted with Staff-Nurse Maude Beatrice Beetham of the A.I.F., who was also returning from active service abroad, and in March, 1919, they married, there being one son of the union. During his absence from Australia he was appointed an honorary lieutenant-colonel in the Australian Military Forces on February 4, 1917. He was appointed a captain in the 2/5 Pioneers on October 1, 1918, and placed on the Unattached List on February 1, 1919. He was listed on the Reserve of Officers with rank of lieutenant-colonel on August 1, 1920, and transferred to the Unattached List on April 19, 1926. He was again transferred to the Reserve of Officers on February 1, 1930. Since 1930 he has taken a keen interest in the affairs of the R.S.S.I.L. of Australia. He was first elected to the State Board in 1930, and the following year was re-elected. He succeeded the late Harry Thomson (late 13th Reinforcements, 10th Battalion) as president, after officiating as vice-president for three consecutive years and acting-president for six months. In 1935 he was occupying the presidential chair for the third year, and in this important position displayed a great aptitude for the high office, and a particularly keen interest in the work of the League, especially in the matter of soldier settlement. In this capacity it has frequently devolved upon him to represent the returned soldiers of South Australia at many important conferences, functions, and services. In December, 1935, he declined to re-offer his services as president of the League, and is now retained on the board as immediate past president. For many years he has been associated with his brothers in pastoral pursuits, and is a large shareholder in the firm of Mt. Eba Ltd., and is also a member of the Mt. Eba Vermin Board, to which position he was appointed on November 27, 1934. He has business interests at Kadina, and in 1935 was residing at the Royal Exchange Hotel, of which his brother, G. H. Jacob, is the licensee, the freehold being part of the estate of his late father. He was appointed a Justice of the Peace on February 4, 1920, and in 1932 was awarded the Volunteer Decoration, whilst on May 6, 1935, he became the recipient of the late King's Silver Jubilee Medal.

28. KAYSER, JULIUS AUGUST WILLIAM, was born at Lyndoch, South Australia, on October 4, 1877. He was educated at Prince Alfred College, and was a schoolmaster by profession. On December 24, 1904, at Maitland, he married Helen Elizabeth, daughter of Edward Prosser Henry Hopewell, and at the outbreak of the Great War was residing at James Street, Franklin, Alberton, and was teaching at the Alberton Public School. He was appointed a 2nd lieutenant in the 76th (Hindmarsh) Infantry on March 16, 1913, and was promoted to the rank of lieutenant in the same regiment on March 1, 1914, and held this commission at the time of joining the A.I.F. He was one of the first South Australian officers desirous of proceeding overseas, and on August 27, 1914, was appointed a lieutenant in the 10th Battalion at Morphettville, where he was posted to original "D" Company, but when it was decided to raise two companies of the 12th Battalion in South Australia he was immediately transferred to original "F" Company of that unit. He was actually with the 10th for such a short period that many of the original men did not know he had served amongst them for a few weeks. On September 21, 1914, after the first A.I.F. march through the city of Adelaide, he entrained for Melbourne with "E" and "F" Companies of the 12th Battalion, and proceeded to Tasmania, where he subsequently joined the main body of the 12th Battalion.

He embarked with his battalion on September 20, 1914, and accompanied the First Australian Contingent to Egypt. On October 18, 1914, he was promoted to the rank of captain, and during the company reorganization at Mena, Egypt, in January, 1915, was transferred to "C" Company of the 12th Battalion, and appointed 2nd in Command of that company. He accompanied the 12th Battalion to the Dardanelles, and landed with half of his company from one of the destroyers at the historic landing on April 25, 1915. He remained on the Peninsula until October 20, 1915, when he was wounded, and subsequently returned to Australia. On March 3, 1916, he re-embarked for overseas and proceeded to France, where he was wounded at Pozieres in August, 1916. He proceeded to England, and was admitted to the Palace Green Hospital at Kensington West, London, and later was transferred to Moray Lodge, Camden Hill. He subsequently returned to France, where he was promoted to the rank of temporary major, and killed in action at Le Barque on February 16, 1917.

29. LORENZO, FRANCIS MAXWELL DE FRAYER, was born at Roselle, Sydney, New South Wales, on March 7, 1880. He served in the South African War in 1902, and took part in the operations in the Western Transvaal and British Bechuanaland, and received the Queen's Medal with three clasps. Upon returning to Australia from South Africa he decided to take up soldiering as a profession, and after qualifying in certain military examinations became an officer in the Australian permanent forces. He received his first commission as a lieutenant in the Administrative and Instructional Staff on June 14, 1907, and was promoted to the rank of captain (A. and I.) on October 1, 1911, and held this commission at the outbreak of the Great War, being attached to the 4th Military District Headquarters at Keswick under Major Brand, Chief of Staff. He was also appointed Brigade Major of the 19th Infantry Brigade and 19th Brigade Area on July 1, 1913, retaining this position until August 19, 1914. In this capacity he was well known to numerous compulsory trainees. He married prior to arriving in South Australia, and his wife (Amy Ella) is not a South Australian by birth. At the outbreak of Great War he was residing at Falcon Avenue, West Adelaide. He was one of the first officers selected by Colonel S. P. Weir for the personnel of the 10th Battalion, in which he was appointed a captain on August 19, 1914, and on August 20, 1914, was appointed Adjutant of the Battalion. He experienced a busy time in the early days of the Morphettville training camp, when recruits were arriving in large numbers and attestation papers could not be filled in quickly enough. He accompanied the Battalion to Egypt on H.M.A.T. A11*Ascanius*, and retained the adjutancy of the 10th until after the landing. He landed from the *Prince of Wales* in the historic landing on April 25, 1915, and the next day was promoted to the rank of major and posted to the command of "A" Company, although he did not actually assume command of his company until a few weeks later, when he relinquished the adjutancy of the Battalion. He was subsequently invalided ill from the Peninsula, and proceeded to hospital at Malta. He eventually returned, and joined the Battalion in the line at Anzac about October 30, 1915, and was appointed 2nd in Command of the Battalion. He accompanied the Battalion to Lemnos when withdrawn on November 21, 1915, and proceeded with the 10th to Egypt, where at Gebel Habieta, on March 1, 1916, he was transferred to the 49th Battalion as Com-

manding Officer, and on March 12, 1916, was promoted to the rank of lieut.-colonel, and commanded the 49th Battalion until January 23, 1917. On June 5, 1916, he embarked on the *Arcadian* with the 49th Battalion and disembarked at Marseilles on June 12, 1916. This transport also conveyed 13th Infantry Brigade Headquarters and Lieut.-Colonel F. W. Hurcombe, and the 50th Battalion. He remained on the field until January 23, 1917, and subsequently returned to Australia, his services with the A.I.F. terminating on October 2, 1917. For his services on Gallipoli he was mentioned in despatches *vide London Gazette*, 5/11/15, and for his services in France, *vide London Gazette*, 2/1/17. For his distinguished service on the field during the operations at the Dardanelles he was awarded the D.S.O., which was promulgated in the *London Gazette* on November 8, 1915. He was the first 10th Battalion officer to become a companion of this order. After returning to Australia he was awarded the Order of Danilo (4th class with swords), which was conferred by H.M. the late King of Montenegro and promulgated in *London Gazette* of 21/8/17. Whilst he was C.O. of the 49th Battalion that unit received a consignment of sandbags made by children attending the Heathfield School, South Australia. These sandbags were used in connection with the Suez Canal Defences, and after same had been filled and placed in position by the troops under his command he had a photograph taken, which with a letter of thanks was forwarded to the Director of Education for transmission to the Heathfield School. Upon returning to Australia he was transferred to the 2nd Military District Headquarters at Sydney. During his absence from Australia he was appointed a major in the A. and I. on December 1, 1915, and promoted to rank of honorary colonel on March 12, 1916. On November 26, 1919, he became seriously ill, which necessitated him absenting himself from military duty for six weeks, resuming again on January 7, 1920. On October 1, 1920, he was transferred from the A. and I. to the Staff Corps, with rank of major, and on October 1, 1923, was promoted to rank of lieutenant-colonel, and attained the rank of colonel on June 1, 1935. Since the Great War he has held the following important Australian Military Force appointments: Assistant Quartermaster-General, 2nd Military District, from October 22, 1917, to April 12, 1919; Brigade Major (Light Horse), from April 13, 1919, to April 30, 1921; Inspector-General of Cavalry, 4th Division (Victoria), May 1, 1921, to July 31, 1922; Staff Officer "A-Q" Branches, 3rd Division (Victoria), August 1, 1922, to December 31, 1924; Inspector-General of Cavalry, 3rd Division (Victoria), September 1, 1923, to December 31, 1924; Assistant Adjutant and Quartermaster-General and Inspector-General of Cavalry, 3rd Division (Victoria), January 1, 1925, to April 30, 1926; Assistant Adjutant and Quartermaster-General and Inspector-General of Cavalry, 1st Cavalry Division (New South Wales and Queensland), May 1, 1926, to October 14, 1928; Assistant Adjutant and Quartermaster-General, 11th Mixed Brigade, 5th Division (Queensland), 1st District Base, 1st Military District, October 15, 1928, to June 14, 1935, when, having attained the rank of colonel, he was transferred from Brisbane to Sydney, and appointed Assistant Adjutant and Quartermaster-General, 2nd District Base, as from June 15, 1935, which appointment he still holds. With a soldierly carriage, and whether with or without a military helmet, he was always a conspicuous parade ground figure, and possessed an unmistakable barrack-square voice, which for volume and penetrability could not be excelled. Early in 1935 his name was mentioned in military circles in connection with higher command vacancies created by the retirement and transfer of certain A.M.F. officers, he being preceded by only four other colonels on the Gradation List of the Australian Staff Corps.

30. LOUTIT, NOEL MEDWAY, waas born at St. Peters, Adelaide, on March 8, 1894, and is a son of Thomas Inkster Loutit, who for a number of years was secretary of Geo. P. Harris, Scarfe & Co. He was educated at the Norwood Public School, and in 1919 commenced an engineering course at the South Australian School of Mines and Industries. He started as a cadet in the fitting department of that institution, but in 1911 discontinued the course. At the outbreak of the Great War he was still a student of engineering, and was residing with his parents at Salop Street, Kensington. He was a compulsory trainee, and received his first commission as a 2nd lieutenant in the 78th (Adelaide Rifles) Infantry on October 16, 1913, and held this commission at the time of joining the A.I.F. He was the last officer to be taken on the strength of the original 10th Battalion prior to embarkation. He was appointed a 2nd lieutenant in the 10th Battalion at Morphettville on September 19, 1914, and was posted to original "G" Company in lieu of Lieutenant K. E. Green, who through the illness of Captain H. W. H. Seager was Acting-Commanding Officer of original "C" Company. He accompanied the Battalion to Egypt on H.M.A.T. A11 *Ascanius*, and at Mena, Egypt, in January, 1915, when his company merged with original "D" Company, he was appointed a Platoon Commander in same and promoted to the rank of lieutenant on February 1, 1915. He landed with his company from the destroyer *Scourge* at the historic landing on April 25, 1915. During the actual landing he succoured No. 722 Bugler F. T. Broughton, who was mortally wounded, and whom he lifted out of the boat. Later that day he distinguished himself by penetrating a great distance inland, which for many years was considered to be a record established that day by any member of the A.I.F. He led his party of thirty-two men. He and Pte. Fordham then left the party at a knoll and went forward to another (Scrubby Knoll), about a quarter of a mile away, to see what was there. They saw no one but Turks, and then returned to the rest of the party. In 1934, from fresh evidence supplied, Dr. C. E. W Bean considered that Pte. A. S. Blackburn and Pte. Phil Robin probably exceeded the distance travelled inland by Loutit and Fordham. On the additional evidence submitted he said: "With Pte. Fordham I passed Third Ridge and saw the waters of the Narrows. I saw no one in front of me nor on either side but Turks. I wish I had seen some of our men. I would have been glad of their help. I don't know how far it was inland in direct distance. When we got back to the Battalion four days later there were only about eleven men." He subsequently was invalided sick from the Peninsula, and after being admitted to hospital rejoined the Battalion again in the line at Anzac about October 31, 1915. He accompanied the 10th when withdrawn to Lemnos on November 21, 1915, and proceeded to Egypt with the Battalion, and at Gebel Habieta, on March 1, 1916, was transferred to the 50th Battalion as Adjutant, having been promoted to the temporary rank of captain whilst on the Peninsula. On February 20, 1916, he was promoted to the rank of full captain, and for his valuable services rendered in connection with the landing at Anzac was mentioned in Army Corps Routine Orders. He proceeded with the 50th Battalion to France, and on October 28, 1916, attained his majority. For his gallantry at Noreuil on April 2-4, 1917, he was awarded

the D.S.O., which was promulgated in the *London Gazette*, amongst the King's Birthday Honours, on June 4, 1917, the official citation being: "In recognition of his services in the prosecution of the war." Only fourteen days later he was awarded a Bar to his D.S.O., which was promulgated in the *London Gazette* on June 18, 1917, the official citation being: "For conspicuous gallantry and devotion to duty in laying out the jumping-off tape under heavy shell and rifle fire. Later he took forward a machine gun and platoon and opened a surprise burst of fire into the enemy, thus relieving the pressure at a critical time. He did not leave the front until the whole front was secure." Probably within the whole British Army during the Great War no D.S.O. and Bar were won by the same officer within such a remarkably short time. He was mentioned in despatches on three occasions, *vide London Gazette*, 1/6/17, 25/12/17, and 11/7/19. On October 22, 1917, he was seconded for duty with the 13th Training Battalion, and on the 29th of the same month was appointed to command same. After several months in England he subsequently returned to France, and on March 22, 1918, was first appointed to the command of the 45th Battalion, and did not relinquish same until subsequently wounded and forced to evacuate. On September 2, 1918, he was promoted to the rank of temporary lieutenant-colonel, and appointed to temporarily command the 45th. On December 1, 1919, he was promoted to the rank of lieutenant-colonel, and permanently appointed C.O. of the 45th Battalion. He subsequently proceeded to England, where he embarked on the *Raranga*, arriving back in Adelaide on November 25, 1919, his services in the A.I.F. terminating on January 7, 1920. During his absence from Australia he was appointed a lieutenant in the 78th (Adelaide Rifles) Infantry on July 1, 1915, and with the same rank was transferred to 2/10 Infantry on October 1, 1918. He was promoted to the rank of captain in 2/10 Infantry on August 1, 1920, and placed on Reserve of Officers with rank of major on October 1, 1920. He was transferred to the 27th Battalion on May 19, 1927, and commanded that unit from June 15, 1927, to June 14, 1930, when he assumed the provisional rank of lieutenant-colonel. With rank of major he was placed on the Unattached List on June 13, 1930. On November 13, 1920, he married Stella, daughter of W. J. Ponder, there being one son and one daughter of the union. During the South Australian waterfront dispute in October, 1928, he was appointed Commanding Officer of the Essential Services Maintenance Corps by the South Australian Government. For several years he officiated as manager of Yellow Cabs Ltd.; but on July 31, 1935, resigned that position, and next day commenced duties with the Shell Co. of Australia Ltd. as general administrative officer, transport of Australia. It is anticipated that in this capacity he will subsequently be transferred to Melbourne. In 1935 he was residing at Rossington Avenue, Fullarton Estate.

31. MACDONALD, ALEXANDER HENRY, was born at Perth, Western Australia, on February 12, 1894, and is a son of the late Donald Macdonald, who by occupation was a warehouse manager. During the Great War his mother (Mrs. N. Macdonald) resided at No. 14, Craven Terrace, Lancaster Gate, London, W.2. He was educated at North Adelaide, and at the time of joining the A.I.F. was employed as a warehouseman by D. & W. Murray Ltd., of Adelaide, and was residing at Hyde Park. He was a compulsory trainee, and had joined the 78th (Adelaide Rifles) Infantry, in which he was appointed a 2nd lieutenant, provisionally, on July 1, 1915, i.e., six

months after receiving his first commission in the A.I.F. He was appointed a 2nd lieutenant in the A.I.F. on January 1, 1915, and on January 16, 1915, was posted to the 2nd Reinforcements of the 10th Battalion, of which Capt. H. W. H. Seager was O.C. With this quota of reinforcements he subsequently entrained for Melbourne, where he embarked per H.M.A.T. A46 *Clan MacGillivray* on February 2, 1915, and proceeding to Egypt subsequently joined the 10th Battalion on the *Ionian* in Mudros Harbour on April 8, 1915. He was then posted to "D" Company, and landed with his platoon from the destroyer *Scourge* at the historic landing on April 25, 1915. Whilst on the Peninsula (4/8/15) he was promoted to the rank of lieutenant, but through illness was forced to evacuate on September 23, 1915, and passing through the Field Hospital at Lemnos was subsequently admitted to the 2nd Australian General Hospital (Gezireh Palace) at Cairo. Later he embarked on the *Wandilla*, and arriving back in Adelaide in December, 1915, his services with the A.I.F. terminated on 28/1/16, amended to 24/3/16, and re-amended to 5/5/16. Desirous of returning overseas, he rejoined the A.I.F. at Mitcham about September, 1916, and was posted to the 21st Reinforcements of the 10th Battalion, which embarked at the Outer Harbour, South Australia, per H.M.A.T. A16 *Port Melbourne*, on October 23, 1916. He proceeded to England, and joined the 10th Battalion in France on February 25, 1917, but in March, 1917, evacuated ill, and returning to England was admitted to the 3rd London General Hospital at Wandsworth. He returned to France and rejoined the Battalion about August, 1917, and was promoted to the rank of captain on 1/11/17. On March 1, 1918 (prior to the Hollebeke operation) he was appointed O.C. of a special raiding party, but that night, when he first led his party in action, he was badly wounded in an ear and forced to evacuate, Lieut. F. J. S. Mead assuming command of the party. Proceeding to England, he was admitted to the 3rd London General Hospital at Wandsworth, and subsequently embarked on the *Arawa*, arriving back in Adelaide in November, 1918, his services in the A.I.F. terminating on 3/12/18. Returning to civil life, he subsequently entered into business partnership with Lieut. A. B. Baker, of the 10th Battalion, A.I.F., and in 1923 proceeded to Sydney, where as a manufacturers' agent he controls the Sydney branch at Strand Arcade, George Street, there being branches also in Adelaide, Brisbane, and Melbourne. On May 5, 1920, at St. Theodore's Church, Rose Park, he married Zillah Elsie, daughter of John Hunter, of Rose Park, and in 1935 was residing at Valley Road, Springwood, New South Wales. Whilst in the 10th Battalion he was affectionately known to rank and file as "Fighting Mac."

32. MacNEIL, ALEXANDER WILLIAM LAUCHLAN, was born at Inverness, Scotland, on August 24,. 1892, and is the son of the late Alexander and Grace MacNeil. He was educated at Inverness, and subsequently arrived in Australia, where at the outbreak of the Great War he was residing at Largs Bay, South Australia, and was a boilermaker by trade. He enlisted in the 10th Battalion at Morphettville on August 29, 1914, and was posted to original "D" Company, his regimental number being "746." He was promoted to the rank of lance-corporal prior to embarking on H.M.A.T. A11 *Ascanius* on October 20, 1914, when he accompanied the original Battalion to Egypt. He subsequently proceeded to the Dardanelles with the 10th on the *Ionian*, and landed with his

company from the destroyer *Scourge* at the historic landing on April 25, 1915. Whilst on the Peninsula he was promoted to the rank of sergeant, and on March 16, 1916, at Gebel Habieta, Egypt, he received his first commission as a 2nd lieutenant in the 10th Battalion, and subsequently accompanied the 10th to France on the *Saxonia*. He was wounded in the Fleurbaix operation on June 6, 1916, and forced to evacuate. Proceeding to England, he was subsequently seconded for duty with the 3rd Training Battalion, and on June 21, 1916, was promoted to the rank of lieutenant. He subsequently rejoined the 10th Battalion in France, and became temporarily attached to the 3rd Trench Mortar Battery. At East of Bullecourt, on May 6, 1917, for most conspicuous gallantry, he was awarded the D.S.O., which was promulgated in the *London Gazette* on August 16, 1917. He was the fifth officer of the 10th Battalion to become a companion of this order. His conduct in the field, for which he was awarded the D.S.O., is regarded by many as one of the most brilliant and outstanding episodes of its kind in the whole history of the A.I.F. Brigadier-General H. Gordon Bennett, C.B., C.M.G., D.S.O., in a *Smith's Weekly* article headed "Great Deeds in the A.I.F.," and published on May 24, 1930, wrote: "MacNeil realised that something must be done, and done quickly, for our men were being slaughtered, and were unable to help themselves. He had noted that the enemy kept the flammenwerfer playing in the trenches, relying upon the supporting troops to shoot down any who tried to escape over the top. Seizing a Lewis gun, he wormed his way over the parapet, and then from shell-hole to shell-hole towards the approaching enemy. After going some little distance he waited until the man with the flammenwerfer—his attention concentrated on the trench before him—had advanced a few yards past him. MacNeil then stood up, and firing from the hip emptied the Lewis gun into the flammenwerfer merchant and those accompanying him. As the leading Prussian fell, the nozzle of the infernal machine turned back upon his own comrades, inflicting upon some the fate so recently suffered by many of our men, and causing the rest to retire. MacNeil, who had dropped to the ground immediately the Lewis gun was empty, perceived the confusion and ran back to his trench mortar. Seizing half-a-dozen of the ten-pound bombs, he again clambered on to the parapet, and ran along, dropping one into each traverse occupied by the Germans, thus effectively clearing fifty or sixty yards of the trench we had so recently lost. Badly shaken as they were, our men were slow to realize that the flammenwerfer attack was ended; but before the Germans could reorganize MacNeil rallied his men and counter-attacked. Not only did he regain lost ground, but he pushed fifty yards farther along the trench, where he erected another bomb-stop and held it against all attacks. In the darkness and confusion no definite news had gone back to Headquarters as to how the fight went. There was no opportunity for MacNeil to telephone, and all runners sent had been killed before reaching their destination. At dawn, however, it was realized that the situation was desperate, and a fresh company of the 10th Battalion was ordered to reinforce the trench and continue our attack. When the fresh troops jumped into the trench, MacNeil, white as a sheet, blood streaming down his face from a head wound, and hardly able to stand, threw his arms around the Commanding Officer's neck, saying, 'Thank Christ you've come, old man. We're all in.' But for MacNeil's cool courage and devotion to duty the flammenwerfer attack would have succeeded, and all those in our front line cut off and taken prisoner." Shortly after the Bullecourt operation in which he distinguished himself, he proceeded to England, and on June 23, 1917, was seconded for duty with the 2nd Training Battalion. For his splendid work with the 3rd Light Trench Mortar Battery he was mentioned in despatches, *vide London Gazette*, 28/12/17. He subsequently returned to France, and on June 13, 1918, was seconded for duty with the 3rd Australian Light Trench Mortar Battery. During the capture of Merris by the 10th Battalion on July 29-30, 1918, he did exceptionally brilliant work in fighting his Stokes mortars, and on August 23, 1918, he was promoted to the rank of temporary captain, but such appointment was subsequently cancelled. After the cessation of hostilities he eventually resigned his commission in Britain, his services with the A.I.F. terminating on February 3, 1919. In 1918 he married Mary, eldest daughter of C. Morrison Rose, of Welwyn, Hertfordshire, England, and in 1935 was residing at No. 230, Upper Spit Road, Mosman, Sydney, New South Wales, where for several years he has unfortunately been enjoying indifferent health.

33 MAGENIS, GEORGE CHARLES, was born at Warrington, Lancashire, England, on October 4, 1883, and is a son of the late Richard John Magenis, who served in the South Lancashire Regiment (Prince of Wales' Volunteers), accompanied his regiment to New Zealand and Australia, and in 1854, at the Eureka Stockade Riot at Ballarat, Victoria, was ordered to attack the miners. His elder brother, Richard John, No. 3535, also served in the A.I.F., enlisting with the 8th Reinforcements of the 27th Battalion, and at Gebel Habieta, Egypt, on February 26, 1916, was transferred to the 10th Battalion. He was educated at Warrington, and at an early age joined his father's regiment (South Lancs), and at the age of fifteen was a drummer-boy serving in the South African War, subsequently attaining the non-commissioned rank of lance-sergeant. After his discharge from the South Lancashire Regiment he proceeded to America, where he spent five years, and later arrived in Australia in 1910. He joined the Instructional Staff, 4th Military District, on December 9, 1912, his appointment being confirmed on June 2, 1913. For some time he was attached to the 20th Infantry Brigade, but upon the completion of Keswick Barracks was transferred to District Headquarters, where he was stationed at the time of joining the A.I.F. On December 5, 1913, he married Margaret, daughter of John Green, of Warrington, England, at the Church of St. Mary Magdalene, Adelaide, there being two children of the union, one son and one daughter. His son, as the third successive Magenis generation, is now serving with the South Lancashire Regiment, and in 1935, had attained the non-commissioned rank of corporal. At the outbreak of the Great War he was an Imperial Reservist, and was residing at Glandore. He was one of the first South Australian officers of the Administrative and Instructional Staff at Keswick to offer his services for abroad, and enlisted in the 10th Battalion at Morphettville on August 19, 1914. He was appointed Regimental Quartermaster-Sergeant of the Battalion, and was the senior non-commissioned officer of the original 10th. His regimental number was "2," and with Capt. C. F. Minagall he experienced a busy time at Morphettville in 1914 in equipping the 10th for overseas. He embarked with the Battalion on H.M.A.T. A11 *Ascanius* on October 20, 1914, and proceeded to Egypt. He re-embarked with the Battalion on the *Ionian*, and proceeded to the Dardanelles, landing from the *Prince of Wales* at the his-

toric landing on April 25, 1915, and from June 27 to August 17, 1915, officiated as R.S.M. of the Battalion. On July 16, 1915, he was appointed Acting-Quartermaster in lieu of Captain C. F. Minagall, and carried out the duties appertaining to this position until the return of Capt. Minagall in October, 1915. On August 4, 1915, he was promoted on the field at Anzac to the rank of 2nd lieutenant, and on October 8, 1915, was promoted to the rank of lieutenant, and posted to "C" Company as a Platoon Commander, but was subsequently transferred to "B" Company and then to Headquarters as Q.M. He accompanied the Battalion when withdrawn on November 21, 1915, and subsequently proceeded to Egypt, where at Serapeum, on January 28, 1916, he was appointed Adjutant of the Battalion. He took over the adjutancy from Lieut. B. B. Leane, and retained same until he finally left the Battalion a year later. He accompanied the Battalion to Gebel Habieta, and in February, 1916, as Adjutant it devolved upon him to complete arrangements for 500 of all ranks of the 10th to be transferred to the 50th Battalion, and the admission of six officers and 461 other ranks to the 10th. He was promoted to the rank of captain on March 12, 1916, and accompanied the Battalion to France, and there remained with the 10th for nine months until January 14, 1917, when he was forced to evacuate with a severe attack of neurasthenia. He had served continuously with the Battalion from August, 1914, and with the exception of ordinary furlough had not left the unit once. This was a remarkable achievement, not approached by any other member of the original 10th. He proceeded to England, where he was admitted to the 4th London General Hospital at Denmark Hill, where he remained for several months, until transferred to an auxiliary hospital of the 4th London General, where neurasthenic cases were specially treated. In October, 1917, he embarked on the *Benalla* for Australia, and arrived back in Adelaide at the end of November, 1917, his services with the A.I.F. terminating on December 3, 1917. After eighteen months' sick leave he returned to the A.I.C. staff at Keswick, and on November 1, 1921, was appointed to the War Disability Supernumerary List. On March 1, 1923, he was appointed warrant officer, 1st class, and S.S.M., 2nd class, Field Troops, 4th Military District. He is also eligible for honorary rank of captain should he receive a commission or cease to belong to the Australian Military Forces as and from March 12, 1916. For his splendid work at the attack on Pozieres in July, 1916, he was mentioned in despatches *vide* the *London Gazette*, 2/1/17, and for his distinguished service in the field was awarded the D.S.O., which was promulgated in the *London Gazette* amongst the New Year's Honours on January 1, 1917. This decoration was awarded simultaneously with that of Colonel S. P. Weir. He has practically been a professional soldier all his life, and in 1935 was residing at No. 10, Byron Road, Black Forest Estate.

34. McCANN, WILLIAM FRANCIS JAMES, was born at Glanville, South Australia, on April 19, 1892, and is a son of Jack Francis McCann, who for a number of years was employed as an engine-driver in the South Australian Railways. He was one of three brothers who served in the A.I.F.—Lance-Corporal J. S. S. McCann, of the 43rd Battalion, being killed at Hamel on July 4, 1918, and Lieutenant C. J. J. McCann, M.C., of the 27th Battalion, who was twice wounded. He was educated at various public schools, the Adelaide High School, and the University of Adelaide. In December, 1913,

he completed his training as a teacher in the Education Department, and on January 1, 1914, was appointed to the Ethelton Public School, and held this position at the outbreak of the Great War. Prior to joining the A.I.F. he had not served with any Australian Military Force unit, except the old volunteer cadets. He was one of the first South Australians to offer his services for abroad, and reported for duty at the Parade Ground, Adelaide, on August 17, 1914, but subsequently proceeded to Morphettville, where he enlisted as a private in the 10th Battalion on August 22, 1914. His regimental number was "405," and he was allotted to original "D" Company. A few weeks later his name appeared in the first list of non-commissioned appointments, when he was promoted to the rank of sergeant. He embarked with the original Battalion on H.M.A.T. A11 *Ascanius* on October 20, 1914, and proceeded to Egypt. At Mena, in January, 1915, when his company merged with original "G" Company, he was appointed a platoon sergeant in the new "D" Company. He landed with his company from the destroyer *Scourge* at the historic landing on April 25, 1915, and four days later (April 29, 1915) was promoted to the rank of company sergeant-major, and although at the time he did not know, he was gazetted in Australia as a warrant officer, 2nd class. For his good work at the landing he was mentioned in Army Corps Routine Orders, and was further recommended on three other occasions. He received his first commission in the A.I.F. on August 4, 1915, when he was promoted on the field at Anzac to the rank of 2nd lieutenant, at the time when the 10th Battalion was standing by ready to reinforce, if necessary, the 1st Brigade attack on Lone Pine. He served without a break through the Gallipoli campaign, and was promoted to the rank of lieutenant on November 14, 1915, one week before the Battalion was withdrawn from the Peninsula. Whilst at Anzac he was appointed Intelligence and Signalling Officer, and in this capacity from various sources compiled for Lieut.-Colonel Beevor a contoured map of the Anzac area. In reference to this map Lieut.-Colonel Beevor said, "A map I still have, and which is a monument of his capacity and thoroughness." He accompanied the Battalion to Gebel Habieta, where he was given charge of patrols performed by the Bikanir Camel Corps, which performed various reconnaissances in the Sinai Desert. He was later posted to the 2nd in Command of "D" Company. As Scouting, Intelligence, and Sniping Officer he accompanied the Battalion to France, and on arrival at Marseilles commanded a composite guard of honour drawn from the 9th and 10th Battalions. He was promoted to the rank of captain on April 16, 1916, and appointed 2nd in Command of "A" Company. He distinguished himself in the attack on Pozieres on July 23, 1916, when his company was the first of the 10th to enter the bomb fight in O.G.1, in support of the 9th Battalion. Dr. C. E. W. Bean describes this incident as follows: "McCann, recognising that the enemy post must be seized, lined out in front of it in shell-holes, the ten or twelve men who were with him. With bombs they thoroughly subdued the German bombers, and smashed one machine gun—McCann's success in this bold movement being partly due to his having with him two old Gallipoli sergeants—G. D. Beames and L. C. Wickham. When bombs began to run out, McCann passed the word on to charge with the bayonet, and he was on the point of giving the word when he was hit in the head by a machine-gun bullet." For his good work in this engagement he was awarded the

Military Cross, being the first 10th Battalion recipient of same, as well as the first 10th Battalion officer to win an award in the field in any specific action. At daybreak, following the attack on Pozieres, though his skull was severely fractured, he managed to report to Colonel Robertson, of the 9th Battalion, that the fighting of the last hour and a half had not altered the position. He then proceeded to England, and was admitted to the 2nd London General Hospital (St. Mark's). His M.C. was promulgated in the *London Gazette* on September 1, 1916, and later, with Lieutenant A. S. Blackburn, who had also distinguished himself in the same action, he had the unique distinction of attending an investiture at Buckingham Palace, where His Majesty the late King conferred on these two 10th Battalion officers respectively, the first Victoria Cross and the first Military Cross awarded to he Battalion. He was subsequently boarded for Australia and marked "Hospital Ship," but determined to rejoin his unit he managed to evade the hospital ship. Recovering from his head injuries, he returned to France, and rejoined the 10th at Dernancourt on November 13, 1916, when he was posted to the command of "B" Company. He remained with the Battalion until shortly before the Le Barque attack in February, 1917, when he evacuated ill, and afterwards entered the 4th Army School at Flixecourt, where he remained for one month. He rejoined the Battalion in March, 1917, and in a night attack on Louverval on Easter Sunday, April 8, 1917, although wounded in the neck, refused for several hours to leave the line. With a bandage round his neck, and scarcely able to speak, he was a great inspiration to his men. After the situation had clarified he reported for medical attention, and proceeded to England, where he was admitted to the 3rd London General Hospital at Wandsworth. After an absence of about six weeks he returned to France, and rejoined the 10th Battalion at Ribemont about the end of May, 1917. He then assumed command of "A" Company, and remained with the Battalion through all the Flanders fighting of 1917. At Polygon Wood, in September, 1917, he was appointed Liaison Officer to the 7th Brigade Headquarters. On December 30, 1917, he was seconded for duty with the 2nd Training Battalion, and next day, after the Battalion moved out of the line in the Messines Sector, proceeded to Warminster, England, where he was posted to the command of "C" Company, and later officiated as Assistant Adjutant. Whilst in England he was ordered to return to France in order to inspect the working of the various army schools. This inspection in France lasted about a week, and he arrived back in England on March 31, 1918. He subsequently returned to France and rejoined the 10th Battalion at Sercus on June 7, 1918. The first event of importance after his return was the silent raid by the Germans at Merris on the night of June 28-29, when seventeen of the enemy were killed. On July 4, 1918, two American officers and five other ranks were temporarily attached to the Battalion, when the Germans made two determined raids within a week, sustaining heavy casualties, about eighty killed and several machine guns captured. On the night of July 29-30, with Captain R. K. Hurcombe, he led his company in the envelopment of Merris, when that village and its entire garrison were captured. He succeeded in severing the enemy lines of communication, and for this achievement was awarded a Bar to his M.C., which was promulgated in the *London Gazette* of November 7, 1918. The Germans twice raided Mont de Merris, held by his company once silently, and the second occasion, supported by artillery fire; but each time were driven back with loss of prisoners. He then proceeded south with the Battalion, and on August 10, 1918, two days after the great offensive opened, the Battalion started for the line again, but encountered trouble at Crepey Wood. With one officer and seven other ranks he held back a heavy counter-attack and prevented the recapture of Crepey Wood by the Germans. At all costs he was determined to hold Crepey, which was literally "boiling" under an inferno of enemy fire, shells, machine guns, bullets, and bombs, in the midst of which he directed his men with the greatest coolness and resource, eventually driving back the attacking forces, who left ninety of their dead behind. The next day Lihons was taken, and dumps containing thousands of bottles of wine were discovered, but unfortunately for the men of the 10th the same was not palatable. For his brilliant and conspicuous defence of Crepey Wood he was recommended by Lieut.-Colonel M. Wilder-Neligan, D.S.O., D.C.M., for the highest decoration, and was subsequently awarded the D.S.O., which was promulgated in the *London Gazette*, of February 1, 1919. On September 23, 1918, he was promoted to the rank of temporary major, and from August 28 to September 6, 1918, whilst at Cerisy, temporarily commanded the Battalion during the absence of Lieut.-Colonel M. Wilder-Neligan, D.S.O., D.C.M., and on October 21, 1918, he received his majority. He also commanded the Battalion from September 30 to October 3, 1918, whilst Lieut.-Colonel Neligan proceeded on a lecture tour of the recent battle-fields. About this time daylight raids were carried out by the Battalion, this being the commencement of what my be termed semi-open warfare, or the beginning of the last phase of operations on the Western Front. During these operations several important posts of the enemy were captured without any opposition after they had been evacuated by the enemy. About the end of October, 1918, he proceeded to England, and commenced a course in tactics and strategy at the Staff College, Camberly. He returned to France in November, 1918, and was appointed 2nd in Command of the Battalion, and early in January, 1919, was appointed Commanding Officer of the 10th. Having been raised from the rank of private to Commanding Officer of the unit in which he enlisted, he commanded same until it was finally disbanded at Chatelet, Belgium, on March 17, 1919, after it had existed as a fighting unit of the A.I.F. for four years and seven months. At this date the details of the 9th and 10th Battalions merged into Brigade Details whilst awaiting transfer to England. On March 10, 1919, he was selected to conduct a party of American delegates around the war zone, and in this capacity travelled over 2,000 miles through the war-devastated areas of France and Belgium. He was mentioned in Sir Douglas Haig's final despatch of March 16, 1919, *vide London Gazette* of July 11, 1919. Early in April he left the Brigade Details, and on Anzac Day, 1919, led the 3rd Brigade group in the march of Australian troops through the city of London. On May 3, 1919, he made his second appearance at Buckingham Palace, where he was decorated with his D.S.O. and Bar to M.C. He embarked on the *Nestor* in May, 1919, and arriving back in Adelaide in June, 1919, was admitted to the Keswick Hospital for three months, his services with the A.I.F. terminating on September 8, 1919. In November, 1919, he resigned as a teacher in the Education Department, and in October of that year entered on rural pursuits at Truro and Manoora, with a view to obtaining a qualification certificate from the State Repatriation Department. In August, 1920, he was forced to abandon this idea, owing to the great handicap imposed upon him by his war injuries. He then commenced studies as an articled law clerk in December, 1920, and in March, 1922, took up a course at the University of Adelaide, and subsequently obtained his final certificate in law, being called to the Bar on July 25, 1925. He then entered into partnership with Capt. A. S. Blackburn, and they have since practised as the firm of Blackburn and McCann, barristers and solicitors, of 22 Grenfell Street, Adelaide—a peacetime partnership perpetuating their first associateship in the O.G. trenches at Pozieres in July, 1916. On August 22, 1921, he married Mildred, daughter of the late J. H. Southcott, there being three children of the union, two sons and one daughter. On January 17, 1935, he was appointed a Justice of the Peace. During his absence from Australia he was appointed an honorary major in the Australian Military Forces on October 21, 1918, this being his first commission in the A.M.F. After his return he was promoted to rank of major on October 1, 1920, and transferred from Reserve of Officers to the 10th Battalion on May 19, 1927. He was transferred to the 43rd Battalion with same rank on July 1, 1927, and made a lieutenant-colonel in that unit on December 1, 1927, and transferred to the Unattached List on July 1, 1930. He actually commanded the 43rd Battalion from July 1, 1927, to June 30, 1930. He has been actively associated with the South Australian branch of the R.S.S.I.L. of Australia from 1921 to 1931, excepting 1930. He was a vice-president from 1921 to 1924, acting president in 1925, and president continuously from 1926 to 1931, with the exception of a break in 1930, when he resigned to contest a Commonwealth election as a Liberal candidate for the Boothby seat in the House of Representatives. He has represented the South Australian branch at federal congress on four occasions —1925 to 1928, both inclusive. On September 18, 1935, His Excellency the Governor of South Australia (Major-General Sir Winston Dugan), in opening the R.S.S.I.L. Annual Conference, presented him, on behalf of the R.S.A., with an illuminated address in recognition of his ten years' service to the League. In June, 1929, he proceeded to London as the senior Australian delegate at the biennial conference of the British Empire Service League. He has filled many important positions in connection with returned soldiers' associations, being chairman of trustees of the S.A. Returned Soldiers' Association Building Trust, chairman of the Poppy Day Fund, trustee of the A.I.F. Cemetery Trust, trustee of the Partially Blinded Soldiers' Provident Fund, committeeman of the Soldiers' Children Education Board and the Red Cross Society, a foundation member of the Legacy Club, State War Council, and South Australian Soldiers' Fund. He is also an administrator and a member of the executive and finance committee of the Soldiers' Fund, and is a member of the committee and executive of the Soldiers' Home League (Myrtle Bank Home for Soldiers). He was chairman of the War Gratuity Board from 1921-22, and has been prominently connected with the 10th Battalion A.I.F. Club, having served as committeeman and president. He has officiated as honorary solicitor to various bodies connected with the welfare of returned soldiers, and has been especially popular amongst 10th Battalion men. He frequently fills the position of Acting City Coroner, and on May 6, 1935, he became a recipient of the late King's Silver Jubilee Medal, and on the recommendation of the Commonwealth Government was awarded the O.B.E., Civil Division, which was announced in the late King's Silver Jubilee and Birthday Honours of June 3, 1935. In December, 1935, he unsuccessfully contested the presidency of the R.S.S.I.L. of South Australia, and was residing at 52 Tusmore Avenue, Tusmore.

35. MEAD, FREDERICK JAMES STANLEY, was born at Parkside, Adelaide, on June 30, 1890, and is a son of the late John Mead, who was a French polisher by occupation. He was educated at the Parkside Public School, and at the outbreak of the Great War was residing with his parents at the Semaphore, and was a wharf-builder by occupation. Prior to joining the A.I.F. he had not served with any Australian Military Force unit. Early in August, 1914, he proceeded to the Naval Depot at Largs Bay for the purpose of enlisting with the Australian Naval and Military Expeditionary Force which sailed for New Guinea on August 19, 1914. With several other applicants he was rejected, and then presented himself at the Parade Ground, Adelaide, for enlistment with the A.I.F. He subsequently joined the 10th Battalion at Morphettville on August 19, 1914, and as a private was allotted to original 'D" Company, his regimental number being "324." He embarked with the original Battalion on H.M.A.T. A11 *Ascanius* on October 20, 1914, and proceeded to Egypt, where he eventually embarked on the *Ionian* for the Dardanelles. He landed with his company from the destroyer *Scourge* at the historic landing on April 25, 1915. A few weeks later he was promoted to the rank of lance-corporal, and on May 30, 1915, was wounded, and proceedeed to Egypt, where he was admitted to No. 1 General Hospital at Heliopolis. He returned to Gallipoli, and arrived at Anzac on July 8, 1915, as the main body of the Battalion was about to proceed to the island of Imbros for three days' rest. Shortly after he was promoted to the rank of corporal, and when the Battalion was withdrawn from Anzac on November 21, 1915, he had attained the rank of temporary sergeant, and whilst in Lemnos, December, 1915, he was made a full sergeant. He accompanied the Battalion to Egypt on the *Seeang Bee*, and subsequently to France on the *Saxonia*. In the Pozieres attack in July, 1916, he was acting-company sergeant-major, and then reverted to the rank of sergeant, and in the Mouquet Farm attack of August 19-23, 1916, he distinguished himself by directing a lost platoon, for which he was awarded the D.C.M. Early in September, 1916, whilst in the Ottawa Camp, he was promoted to the rank of company sergeant-major, and on September 27, 1916, whilst in the line at the famous "Hill 60," Ypres, was promoted to the rank of R.S.M., which rank he retained until January 24, 1917, when he was promoted to the rank of 2nd lieutenant, and appointed a Platoon Commander in "B" Company, under the command of Capt. W. F. J. McCann, Prior to the Le Barque attack in February, 1917, he was transferred to "A" Company under the command of Captain C. Rumball. Early in May, 1917, he attended the Divisional School at Piquigny, where he remained a month, and was thus precluded from taking part in the Bullecourt operations. On May 24, 1917, he was promoted to the rank of lieutenant, and seconded for duty with the 3rd Training Battalion. He subsequently returned to the Battalion, with which he remained until July 14, 1917, when at Bray he was attached to the permanent cadre and transferred to the 3rd Training Battalion

at Lark Hill, England, under the command of Lieut.-Colonel R. B. Jacob. Seven months later he returned to France, and rejoined the 10th Battalion at the Aldershot Camp in February, 1918. On April 1, 1918, at Hollebeke, he was appointed 2nd in Command of a special raiding party, of which Capt. A. H. Macdonald was O.C. The first night this raiding party was put in action the O.C. was wounded and forced to evacuate, when it devolved upon him to assume command of the party. At Meteren he was 2nd in Command of "B" Company, under Major C. Rumball, and when the Battalion moved into supports he was appointed Liaison Officer and sent for duty to the 11th Battalion until the 10th was relieved. In the attack on Mont de Merris, on June 2-3, 1918, he commanded No. 13 Platoon of "D" Company, and played an exceptionally brilliant part in the moving forward of stores. For this splendid work he was awarded the M.C., which was promulgated in the *London Gazette* on September 16, 1918. He was thus the only member of the 10th Battalion who could claim the distinction of winning both the M.C. and D.C.M. When the Battalion moved south after the capture of Merris he was appointed Battalion Intelligence Officer, and retained this position until August 26, 1918, when he was appointed Orderly Officer to Lieut.-Colonel M. Wilder-Neligan, D.S.O., D.C.M., and became permanently attached to Battalion Headquarters. At Cappy, on August 26, 1918, he had to hurriedly gather every spare man and rush him to the part of the line which was being most hard-pressed. In a confidential report to Brigade Headquarters, Lieut.-Colonel Neligan said: "To assist in dealing with any centre of opposition not touched by artillery, a special platoon was organised by Lieut. F. J. S. Mead. It was made up of Battalion Headquarters, and moved forward with the attacking companies, and although its services were not required for any particular work, it did excellent work in the advance." He shortly after proceeded on furlough, and in this manner missed the final operation of the Battalion at Jeancourt. He subsequently rejoined the 10th in France, and on October 28, 1918, whilst the Battalion was at Brucamps, he was appointed O.C. Headquarters Company and promoted to the rank of temporary captain. On January 14, 1919, he received his captaincy, and remained with the Battalion until it was finally disbanded at Chatelet on March 17, 1919, after which he stayed on with the Brigade details until early in April, 1919. He then proceeded to England, where at the Sandhill Camp, near Warminster, he was appointed O.C. of Staff Company during demobilization. Early in July 1919, he was selected as O.C. of a party of five to form a 1st Divisional Colour Party. In this capacity he proceeded with his party to Paris, where he carried the 10th Battalion Regimental Colours in the Victory March through that city on July 20, 1919. He then returned to London for a similar march through that city. Returning to Sandhill Camp, he proceeded on extended leave, and in August, 1919, at Tilbury, embarked on the *Wahehe* with his wife, whom he had married at Bristol, on September 5, 1918, there being two daughters of the union. He arrived back in Adelaide late in December, 1919, his services with the A.I.F. terminating on December 30, 1919. Returning to civil life, he recommenced his pre-war occupation of wharf-building, but on September 8, 1927, he joined the staff of the Adelaide City Council, and subsequently was appointed ward foreman, which position he still holds. He was appointed a lieutenant on the Reserve of Officers as and from January 1,

1920. He has been an executive member of the Semaphore sub-branch of the R.S.S.I.L. of Australia for several years, and also has been prominently connected with the 10th Battalion A.I.F. Club. In 1935 he was residing at 42 South Terrace, Semaphore. He was affectionately known to his comrades of the 10th Battalion as "Butcher."

36. MINAGALL, CHARLES FRANCIS, was born at Flinders Street, Adelaide, at the site now occupied by the Dunlop Perdriau Rubber Co., Ltd., on March 28, 1873, and is a son of the late Peter Minagall, who was a native of Ireland, and for many years resided in Edinburgh, Scotland, and by occupation was a foreman in the leather industry. He was educated at the Goodwood Public School. For eight years he was employed first in the office and later in the factory of the Hooker Engineering Works, which were established on the land now occupied by John Shearer & Sons, Ltd., of Kilkenny. He was later associated with Forwood, Down & Co. and Simpson & Son, but in 1912 opened a foundry of his own at Goodwood. On April 11, 1911, he married Ada Esperanza, daughter of the late Captain C. F. Bray, there being three sons and one daughter of the union. The eldest son, who was born before the Great War, was accidentally killed whilst riding a motor cycle near Kapunda in February, 1935. The three surviving children were born since the war. At the outbreak of the Great War he resided at Goodwood, and worked his garden with considerable success, being a recognised rose enthusiast. He also owned a five-acre block at Oaklands. In 1891, at the age of eighteen years, he joined the 1st Adelaide Rifles as a private, and for the first three months of his military career was allotted to "D" Company at Port Adelaide. He was then transferred to "B" Company, in the same regiment, and subsequently transferred to the Army Medical Corps, in which he attained the rank of staff-sergeant. Before the introduction of universal training he was a captain in the old senior cadets, and commanded the 1st Battalion. He later commanded the Hindmarsh Company of Cadets, which for two years in succession won the Regimental Colours and King's Colours presented by Lady Dudley, wife of the Governor-General of Australia. He led this company to Melbourne in January, 1910, and personally received the colours from Lord Kitchener, who at that time was visiting Australia. On August 16, 1912, he was temporarily appointed Area Officer at Goodwood, the Headquarters of the 75th Infantry, and was placed on the Unattached List. He held this position at the time of joining the A.I.F., and with Major F. W. Hurcombe and Lieut. E. W. Talbot Smith was one of the three original 10th Battalion officers who were not on the Active List. At the outbreak of the Great War he was carrying on business at his foundry in addition to the duties appertaining to Area Officer. He was one of the first South Australian officers selected by Colonel Weir for the personnel of the 10th Battalion, and on August 19, 1914, was appointed Quartermaster, with rank of captain. He was the first officer to report for duty with the 10th Battalion at Keswick on August 18, 1914. For the first week at Morphettville his stores were merely dumped in open spaces, uncovered and unprotected, and chaos and confusion reigned supreme. Without proper provision for storage it was no easy matter to check supplies and supervise issues, but due to his untiring energy and efficiency the Battalion within a few days of the opening of that camp was fed and equipped. He embarked with the Battalion on H.M.A.T. A11 *Ascanius* on October 20, 1914, and from that day

to the day of the landing at Anzac acted as official 10th Battalion Correspondent to *The Advertiser*. Whilst on the transport the companies continually drew stores and supplies, as some of the men had not been properly equipped. At Mena, Egypt, his duties worked smoother, but upon embarking on the *Ionian* for the Dardanelles he found the position of Quartermaster almost impossible. "A quartermaster's lot is not a happy one" could be most appropriately applied to his *Ionian* experiences. In the first place the *Ionian* had transported Indian troops, and had not been overhauled and prepared to receive a battalion of infantry which was to remain on it for a month, and in the second place it was not provisioned with sufficient stores for that purpose. Consequently the impossible position which presented itself from day to day when the troops had to be fed. He speaks in glowing terms of Captain Henry, of that boat, and his officers, who from day to day eked out the rapidly diminishing supplies, wondering how long this unsatisfactory state of affairs would continue without a replenishment of supplies. He did not land with the main body of the Battalion at the historic landing on April 25, 1915, but remained aboard the *Ionian* with Captain H. W. H. Seager. He had only been instructed a few hours prior to landing that he would not be permitted to accompany the covering force provided by the 3rd Brigade. The *Ionian* stood off the Peninsula, whilst day and night the process of cramming every available portion of the vessel with wounded continued, until with gangways, decks, and holds literally filled with maimed and dying men it sailed for Alexandria. During that never-to-be-forgotten voyage to Egypt he voluntarily collaborated with the medical staff on board, and with Captain Carlyle, of the A.A.M.C., attended to the wounded and dying, and acted as a trained dresser, which duties for three whole days and nights precluded him from having a minute of sleep. After a few hours in Alexandria and a quick return to Gallipoli, the *Ionian* arrived back on April 29 ,1915. The vessel then stood by awaiting instructions, and a message was transmitted to 10th Battalion Headquarters at Anzac, when to his joy a reply was heliographed back that he was to land and join the Battalion, then in bivouac at Shell Green. Then followed the daily task of arranging water fatigues and beach parties—asking for forty men and being allotted twenty, arranging for rations and stores to be transported up the gullies and over the ridges, which necessitated running the daily gauntlet of "Beachy Bill." He was invalided ill from Gallipoli on July 16, 1915, and proceeded to Alexandria, but all hospitals at that port being full, he was taken on to Malta, where he was admitted to St. Andrew's Hospital. He remained at St. Andrew's for about three weeks, until early in August, 1915, when he re-embarked for Syracuse, in Sicily, disembarked, and proceeded to Florence, where he became an officer-guest of Lady Cutting, who is a cousin of Lord Lascelles. He was one of a few A.I.F. officers who had the unique privilege of proceeding to Italy, where the officers of the American Consulate and many others entertained them in a most cordial manner. After a delightful convalescence in Italy he returned to Malta, and reported back to St. Andrew's Hospital, and subsequently proceeded to Alexandria, where he embarked on the *Minneapolis*, arriving back at Anzac and joining the Battalion in the line about the end of October, 1915. He accompanied the 10th when withdrawn from the Peninsula on November 21, 1915, and upon arrival at Lemnos, November 22, 1915, was promoted as Quartermaster of the Battalion to the rank of honorary major. He served with the Battalion in Egypt, first at Tel-el-Kebir, and then at Gebel Habieta. He considered the latter place a quartermaster's nightmare, where water supplies were his eternal concern—eight miles to get the precious liquid, and a fight to get it upon arriving there. He accompained the Battalion to France on the *Saxonia*, and remained with it until December, 1916, when he proceeded to England and Ireland on furlough. He returned to France, and rejoined the 10th in January, 1917. In June, 1917, he left the Battalion at Ribemont, when Lieut.-Colonel Jacob was in command, and proceeded on three weeks' special leave to Italy, where he had an opportunity of renewing associations with the many friends he had made in Florence in 1915. He was mentioned in despatches on two occasions, *vide London Gazette*, 1/6/17 and 25/12/17. Returning to the Battalion, he remained on the field until November 6, 1917, when he was seconded for duty with the 1st Australian Divisional Base Depot at Le Havre. He left the Battalion at Westhoek Ridge to take up his new appointment as Quartermaster of the 1st Australian Division. He retained this appointment for one month, until certain reorganization had been effected, and then proceeded to England, where he remained on furlough for one month, prior to embarking for Australia on the *Balmoral Castle*. He was appointed Quartermaster on this boat, and arrived back in Adelaide on March 24, 1918, his services with the A.I.F. terminating on April 6, 1918. For his distinguished service in France he was awarded the D.S.O., which was promulgated in the *London Gazette* on January 1, 1918, amongst the New Year Honours, he being the seventh 10th Battalion recipient of same. Early in 1918, before leaving England, he attended an investiture at Buckingham Palace, and received his decoration from the hands of His Majesty the late King. During his absence from Australia he was appointed an honorary major in the Australian Military Forces on November 22, 1915. On October 1, 1920, he was placed on the Reserve of Officers, with rank of major, and in 1935 was transferred to the Retired List. In October, 1918, he worked for several months on different horticultural properties, in order to gain experience before acquiring a holding of his own. On November 4, 1919, he was allotted a fruit-growing block in the Berri irrigation area, and later increased his holding by thirteen acres. Ill-health prevented him from continuing on the land, and on May 29, 1931, he was forced to relinquish same. He then proceeded to North Kapunda, where for several years he has been retired. Whilst at Berri he was appointed a member of the board of the Berri Distillery, and held this position for a period of two years. On several occasions he represented the Berri sub-branch of the R.S.S.I.L. of Australia and other River Murray sub-branches at various conferences in Adelaide. During the war he was associated with the Montenegrin Red Cross and Relief Fund, and for his services was recommended for a Montenegrin decoration, but the ultimate collapse of Montenegro nullified same. He has always been a lover of the antique, and possesses a fine collection of war souvenirs, including various calibred shell-cases, an actual "Beachy Bill" shell, pebbles from Anzac Cove, carved wooden panels from the cathedral doors of Bapaume, and the drum stick of the original bass drum of the original 10th Battalion. On the *Balmoral Castle* he was the recipient of an illuminated address from twenty-four hospital patients travelling thereon, given to him as a slight token of the esteem in which he was held by one and

all, and bearing the following verses:—
"He comes amongst us with a smile,
And makes our living on worth while
By treating us in friendly style:
   Our Major.
Who sees that we get proper care,
With best of tucker and fresh air,
And does good as if unaware:
   The Major.
There's no one else we wish so well,
When go we must to heaven or hell,
We'll raise our glasses and we'll yell,
   The toast of Major."

7/3/18.

37. MONTGOMERY, WILLIAM ROCKLIFF, was born in 1883, and at the outbreak of the Great War resided at Broken Hill, where he was a miner by occupation, and had not previously served with any Australian Military Force unit prior to joining the A.I.F. He was one of the first men at Broken Hill to offer his services for overseas, and proceeding to Morphettville enlisted in the 10th Battalion as a private on August 24, 1914. He was allotted to original "H" Company, his regimental number being "514." Prior to embarking on H.M.A.T. A11 *Ascanius* on October 20, 1914, he had attained the rank of lance-corporal, and during the voyage to Egypt, on October 23, 1914, he was promoted to the rank of corporal, and on November 16, 1914, was raised to the rank of acting-sergeant. At Mena, Egypt, in January, 1915, when original "H" Company merged with original "B" Company and became the new "C" Company, he was promoted to the rank of sergeant in same. He landed with his platoon from the *Prince of Wales* at the historic landing on April 25, 1915, and in the early stages of the Gallipoli campaign was wounded, but not seriously enough to cause him to be away from the Battalion for very long. Returning to Anzac, he was subsequently appointed senior non-commissioned officer in a special tunnelling company under the command of Captain J. Hamilton. This company of experienced miners moved to various sectors of the Anzac area, and performed important excavations at Quinn's Post, Pope's Hill, Courtney's Ridge, and was engaged in this class of work for several months. For an individual act of bravery performed by him at Anzac he was awarded the Military Medal, which was gazetted in November, 1915, he being the second 10th Battalion recipient of this decoration. He served with the Battalion in France, and on August 9, 1916, was promoted from the rank of sergeant to 2nd lieutenant. He was subsequently transferred to the 3rd L.T.M. Battery, and for his conspicuous gallantry at "Hill 60," Ypres, on September 24-25, 1916, was awarded the M.C., which was promulgated in the *London Gazette* on December 12, 1916, he being the third officer of the 10th Battalion to receive this decoration, whilst he was the only member of the 10th who could claim the distinction of having won both the M.C. and M.M. He was eventually wounded, and left the Battalion on October 18, 1916, and subsequently returned to Australia, his services with the A.I.F. terminating on August 8, 1917. Shortly after he was appointed a recruiting officer, and in this capacity visited many

South Australian country centres, where he distinguished himself in making eloquent appeals and obtaining large quotas of reinforcements for the A.I.F. After the Armistice (11/11/18) he was appointed an organizing officer of the A.I.F. Volunteer Reserve Scheme, which was introduced to perpetuate the A.I.F., consisting chiefly of four day's mobilization and reunion each year with senior cadet rates of pay. In connection with the activities of this system he was at first stationed at Keswick Headquarters, and subsequently at Dalgety's Building, Currie Street, Adelaide. The scheme was ultimately abandoned, when he returned to Broken Hill, and unsuccessfully contested the District of Willyama seat in the New South Wales State elections. After making a trip to Rabaul he returned to Adelaide, where on April 4, 1927, he was appointed manager of the Returned Soldiers' Club, Angas Street, Adelaide, and retained this position until May 1, 1928. He has since managed several hotels, and in 1935 was manager of the South African War Veterans' Club in Melbourne. He last visited Adelaide in 1934, during the visit of H.R.H. the Duke of Gloucester, and unfortunately has since not been enjoying the best of health. He was always affectionately known to all men of the 10th as "Big Bill" or "Monty," and was especially popular amongst the Broken Hill members of the Battalion.

38. NEWMAN, JOHN, was born at Port Pirie, South Australia, on March 1, 1880, and is a son of the late John Newman, who for many years was a mining and company promoter. At the age of six he went to Victoria, but returned to South Australia at the age of thirteen, receiving his education at various public schools in both States. He served in the South Australian Garrison Artillery for one year, and after attaining his sixteenth birthday left South Australia for Esperance Bay, Western Australia, and from that port tramped to Coolgardie, where for several years he was engaged in sundry occupations. He proceeded to Perth in 1907, and entered the employ of Faulding & Co., Ltd., but subsequently returned to Kalgoorlie as branch manager of the company. In 1910 he married Irene May, daughter of Lieut. Tandy, R.N., there being one daughter of the union. He received his first commission as a 2nd lieutenant in the Goldfields' Infantry Regiment on December 10th, 1910, and on July 1, 1912, upon the introduction of compulsory military training was transferred with same rank to the 84th Infantry. He held this commission at the time of joining the A.I.F., and was one of the original subalterns of the 11th Battalion at Blackboy Hill. He received his 2nd lieutenancy in that unit on August 19, 1914, and was posted to original "D" Company of same. He embarked with his company on H.M.A.T. A11 *Ascanius* at Fremantle on November 1, 1914, and in this manner first came in contact with the 10th Battalion, which also proceeded on the same transport to Egypt. During the company reorganization at Mena in January, 1915, he was appointed a Platoon Commander in the new "B" Company of the 11th Battalion, and promoted to the rank of lieutenant on February 1, 1915. He subsequently proceeded to the Dardanelles on the *Nizam*, on which he officiated as Ship's Quartermaster, subsequently rejoining the 11th Battalion on the *Suffolk* during the troop-movements which occurred in Mudros Harbour. He landed with his company from the destroyer *Chelmer* at the historic landing on April 25, 1915, and that day distinguished himself by penetrating a great distance inland. With a composite platoon, including

two of his own men, and others from A.I.F. and New Zealand units, he advanced beyond the 400 Plateau towards Third Ridge, from which the Narrows opposite could be seen. At this time he was in close proximity to Lieut. N. M. Loutit's party, of the 10th Battalion. He subsequently retired along Wire Gully, and with his platoon took up a defensive position near Lieut. E. J. C. Stopp, of the 10th, and for the next three days was under the command of the 10th Battalion. On June 14, 1915, he was appointed Adjutant of the 11th Battalion, and held this position until August 8, 1915, when he contracted enteric fever and was compelled to evacuate. He proceeded to Alexandria on the *Gloucester Castle*, and after several weeks returned to Lemnos on the *Huntsgreen*. Upon arrival at Mudros he was appointed O.C. of Stores Transit Department, with quarters on the *Aragon*, being delegated the duty of collecting stores and parcels from the numerous transports assembled in Mudros Harbour and distributing same to their correct destinations. He eventually returned to the Peninsula, and rejoined the 11th Battalion in the line at Anzac in October, 1915. He was posted to the command of "D" Company, and remained with his unit until same was withdrawn on November 16, 1915. He then accompanied his Battalion to Lemnos, and subsequently proceeded to Egypt on the *Empress of Britain*. At Gebel Habieta, on February 20, 1916, he was promoted to the rank of captain, and in April, 1916, accompanied the 11th Battalion to France on the *Corsican*. He remained with this unit until July 19, 1916, when during the Pozieres attack he was wounded and forced to evacuate. He proceeded to England, and was admitted to the 2nd London General Hospital (St. Mark's), Capt. W. F. J. McCann, of the 10th, being an inmate at the same time. He attained his majority on September 23, 1916, and in October, 1916, was posted to the Command Depot at Lark Hill, and appointed O.C. of Depot Company. Keen on organization, and noted for his thoroughness of system, he was subsequently transferred to Wareham, where he was appointed C.O. of the new camp which provided accommodation for 6,000 men. He quickly organized a new system, and as a nucleus body took with him 1,400 men from Lark Hill, and in a very short time had over 4,600 men under his command. Early in December, 1916, he was appointed C.O. of the 3rd Training Battalion, Capt. John Hamilton, of the 10th, being one of his training officers, and Lieut. E. J. C. Stopp, of the 10th, his training Adjutant. He returned to France in July, 1917, and during the operations at Broodseinde Ridge on October 7, 1917, upon the death of Major Alexander Steele, D.S.O., D.C.M., it devolved upon him temporarily to command the 11th Battalion. He subsequently became 2nd in Command of that battalion retaining such appointment until December 25, 1917, when he was seconded for duty with the Senior Officers' School at Aldershot, England. After completing a three months' course he returned to France in March, 1918, and on April 3, 1918, was posted to temporarily command the 9th Battalion, which appointment he relinquished on May 11, 1918. He then returned to the 11th Battalion for a few days, and on May 16, 1918, was transferred to the command of the 10th Battalion, relinquishing same on May 21, 1918. He was then holding the rank of temporary lieutenant-colonel, the 10th Battalion at the time moving from Hondeghem to Sercus during the absence of Lieut.-Colonel M. Wilder-Neligan, D.S.O., D.C.M. Temp. Lieut.-Colonel J. Newman took over the command of the 10th from Major G. D. Shaw, and subsequently handed same over to Lieut.-Colonel Wilder-Neligan. On May 28, 1918, he returned to the 11th Battalion as C.O., when his battalion on June 3, 1918, attacked Mont de Merris, taking over 300 prisoners and several anti-tank guns, trench mortars, machine guns, ammunition, and equipment. He later drew up the operation order for the 11th Battalion to capture the village of Merris, but the taking of this strategical point was subsequently deferred, when the task was allocated to the 10th Battalion. He remained with the 11th Battalion as C.O. until September 15, 1918, when due for Anzac leave he proceeded overland to Toronto, Italy, and there embarked for Alexandria, Egypt. After a fortnight at Suez he embarked for Western Australia on the *Dorset*, his services with the A.I.F. terminating on January 13, 1919. He was mentioned in despatches on May 28, 1918, and for his distinguished service in connection with military operations in France and Flanders was awarded the D.S.O., which was promulgated in the *London Gazette* on June 3, 1918, amongst the King's Birthday Honours. He was affectionately known amongst rank and file as "Sir John." During his absence from Australia he was appointed a lieutenant in the 84th Infantry on July 1, 1915, and promoted to rank of honorary major on September 23, 1916. On October 1, 1918, he was appointed a lieutenant in the 2/2 Pioneers, and on October 1, 1919, was transferred to the 2/51 Infantry with the same rank. He received no appointment as a captain, and on March 31, 1921, was listed as a major on the Reserve of Officers, 5th Military District. He was transferred to the 3rd Military District, Victoria, with the same rank, Reserve of Officers, on May 10, 1926, and transferred to the 22nd Battalion on March 26, 1917. He was transferred back to the Reserve of Officers on December 31, 1929. Returning to civil life, he rejoined the staff of Fauldings Ltd. at Perth, Western Australia, and managed a department until 1926, when he proceeded to Melbourne, and became interstate representative of Ponsford, Newman & Benson Pty. Ltd., of 234 Flinders Street, Melbourne, and in this capacity occasionally visits Adelaide. His first wife died in 1925, and in 1927 he married Marie Theresa, daughter of C. R. Barry, there being one daughter of the union. In 1935 he was residing at No. 24, Gray Street, Brighton Beach, Melbourne.

39. NOTT, HARRY CAREW, was born at Walkerville, Adelaide, on August 1, 1888, and is a son of Albert Edward Nott, who for many years was manager of the South Australian Brewing Co. He was educated at St. Peter's College, and the University of Adelaide, where, after a successful scholastic career, he graduated in the Faculty of Medicine, the degrees of M.B., B.S., being conferred on him in 1913. He was appointed a captain (provisionally) in the Australian Army Medical Corps on August 3, 1914, and held this commission at the time of joining the A.I.F. On August 20, 1914, he was appointed a captain in the A.I.F. and posted to the A.A.M.C., and attached to the original 10th Battalion at Morphettville as Medical Officer. During August and September, 1914, his time was fully occupied in medically examining recruits for the 10th Battalion. He embarked with the original Battalion on H.M.A.T. A11 *Ascanius* on October 20, 1914, and accompanied the 10th to Egypt. With Capt. E. T. Brennan, Senior Medical Officer on the *Ascanius*, he experienced a busy time in innoculating and vaccinating the men of the 10th and 11th Battalions. He subsequently proceeded to the Dardanelles, and landed at Anzac on April 25, 1915, and that day established an aid-post in

Monash Valley, immediately behind the firing-line. On July 18, 1915, he evacuated sick, and proceeded to Egypt, where he was admitted to the 19th General Hospital at Alexandria, and subsequently transferred to No. 1 Australian General Hospital at Heliopolis, where he remained a week before re-embarking for the Dardanelles. He arrived back at Anzac on August 16, 1915, and resumed duties as Medical Officer of the Battalion. On September 2, 1915, when the health of the 10th Battalion troops became very bad, and an average of ten men per day were evacuating with dysentery, he forwarded a report to Lieut.-Colonel S. P. Weir for transmission to the Assistant Director of Medical Services, pointing out the poor health of the men, and suggesting that change of food and rest were urgently needed. On September 29, 1915, he was invalided a second time from the Peninsula, and proceeded to Egypt, arriving at Alexandria on October 2, 1915. He remained in Egypt until January 3, 1916, when he embarked for South Australia. On February 22, 1916, at Adelaide, he married Marjory, daughter of William Lowe, there being two children of the union. After three months' rest in Adelaide he returned to Egypt, and later that year proceeded to England, where he became attached to the 3rd Training Battalion on Salisbury Plain, where on November 14, 1916, he was promoted to the rank of major. On January 4, 1917, he arrived in France, where he was attached to the 2nd Field Ambulance at Bapaume, where he remained until July 25, 1918. He was then promoted to the temporary rank of lieutenant-colonel, and transferred to Rouen as C.O. of the 1st Australian General Hospital. On November 11, 1918, he was promoted to the rank of lieutenant-colonel, and transferred to Le Havre as C.O. of the 1st Australian Convalescent Depot. He retained this appointment until the depot was ultimately disbanded, but for several months afterwards he was retained as Senior Medical Officer at the Australian Base at Le Havre, and in that capacity controlled the medical side of the evacuation of the A.I.F. troops until the last Australian soldier had crossed the English Channel in June, 1919. He then proceeded to London, and obtained extended leave, which enabled him to commence studies at the University of Cambridge under the Commonwealth Vocational Training Scheme. In 1920 he obtained the diploma of Medical Radiology and Electrology, and subsequently embarked on the *Wahehe* (late *Marella*), arriving back in Adelaide on October 19, 1920, his services with the A.I.F. terminating shortly after. On September 1, 1921, he was appointed a Senior Specialist with the rank of major in the A.A.M.C., and on April 1, 1922, was placed on the Reserve of Officers with rank of lieutenant-colonel. On July 1, 1925, he was attached to the A.A.M.C. Reserve, 4th Military District. In 1921 he was appointed Honorary Radiologist at the Adelaide Hospital, and is also radiologist at the Repatriation General Hospital at Keswick and a tutor in radiology at the University of Adelaide. On February 23, 1922, at a meeting of the S.A. Branch of the British Medical Association, of which he is a member, he presented a paper entitled "The treatment of malignant disease by radiation." After he had delivered same, Dr. Bronte Smeaton, the president, thanked him for his contribution, and expressed the opinion that his paper and the discussion which followed would tend to the more extensive use of radio-therapy by members of the branch. In 1934 he proceeded to England, in order to keep abreast with medical and surgical science. He is a member of the Royal Adelaide Golf Club, and for a number of years was keenly interested in amateur aviation. He is an acknowledged X-ray specialist, and in 1935 was practising at his surgery attached to his residence at 111 Hutt Street, Adelaide.

40. OLDHAM, EDWARD CASTLE, was born at Gawler on August 8, 1876, and was educated at Prince Alfred College. He subsequently became a clerk by profession, and at the outbreak of the Great War resided at Edward Street, Evandale. On April 19, 1912, at the Registry Office, Adelaide, he married Elsie Sophia, daughter of Frank Johnson. He received his first commission as a lieutenant in the 10th Australian Infantry Regiment on February 6, 1904, and was promoted to the rank of captain in the same unit on July 1, 1908. On July 1, 1912, upon the introduction of universal military training, he was transferred to the 78th (Adelaide Rifles) Infantry with rank of Captain, and held this commission at the time of joining the A.I.F. On November 1, 1910, he was temporarily appointed Area Officer at St. Peters, where at the outbreak of the Great War he was well known by many compulsory trainees. He underwent a military course of training in India during 1909-10, and was regarded as one of the finest infantry officers in the Commonwealth. He was one of the first Company Commanders selected by Lieut.-Colonel S. P. Weir for the 10th Battalion, and was appointed a captain at Morphettville on August 19, 1914, when he was posted to the command of original "E" Company. He embarked with the original Battalion on H.M.A.T. A11 *Ascanius* on October 20, 1914, and at Mena, Egypt, in January, 1915, when his company merged with original "C" Company and became the new "B" Company, he was appointed to the command of same and promoted to the rank of major on February 1, 1915. He embarked with the Battalion on the *Ionian* for the Dardanelles, and landed with his company from the *Prince of Wales* at the historic landing on April 25, 1915. During the severe fighting of that day he unnecessarily exposed himself, and whilst in the act of so doing was shot dead. His attention had been drawn by one of his men, and standing up in order to make a fuller observation, he was mortally wounded. He was a strict disciplinarian, but after associating with his men for some months softened considerably. One of his own men, No. 172 Bugler H. A. Bartholomaeus, in writing from Gallipoli after the landing, referred to his death as follows: "You remember how hard we used to think the major was at Morphettville. Well, he turned out differently at Mena, and I don't think any company had a better officer than the one under his command." He was affectionately known to rank and file of the Battalion as "Froggy". He was particularly popular in military circles in South Australia, where his mother resided at Hackney and his wife and son at Bakewell Road, Evandale.

41. PERRY, WILLIAM HOWARD, was born at Broken Hill, New South Wales, on March 22, 1895, and is a son of William Francis Perry, of 168 Chappel Street, Broken Hill. His brother, Frank, enlisted with the 5th Reinforcements of the 10th Battalion, his regimental number being "2006," and died of wounds October 2, 1917. He was educated at the Broken Hill State School, and was a foundation scholar of the Broken Hill High School. At the outbreak of the Great War he resided with his parents, and was apprenticed as an ironmoulder at the Central Mine. He was a compulsory trainee, and received his first commission as a 2nd lieutenant in the 81st (Wakefield)

Infantry on December 16, 1913, and was transferred with the same rank to the 82nd (Barrier) Infantry on July 1, 1914, and held this commission at the time of joining the A.I.F. At the outbreak of the Great War he was undergoing a map-reading course at a military school of instruction being conducted at Gawler, but within a few hours of the declaration of war being made known in South Australia the same was abandoned, when he returned to Broken Hill, and was one of the first Barrier officers to offer his services for overseas. He was appointed a 2nd lieutenant in the 10th Battalion at Morphettville on August 19, 1914, and arrived at Morphettville with 2nd Lieut. C. P. Farrier and a large quota of Broken Hill recruits for the 10th on August 28, 1914. At all stations *en route* from Broken Hill he and his party received a great ovation, and the 10th men in camp at Morphettville turned out to a man and gave them a rousing reception as they marched into the lines. He was posted to original "G" Company, and embarked with the original Battalion on H.M.A.T. A11 *Ascanius* on October 20, 1914. At Mena, Egypt, in January, 1915, when his company merged with original "D" Company and became the new "D" Company, he was appointed a Platoon Commander in same, and promoted to the rank of lieutenant on February 1, 1915. He accompanied the Battalion to the Dardanelles on the *Ionian*, and landed with his company from the destroyer *Scourge* at the historic landing on April 25, 1915. At Lemnos before the landing he was officer-in-charge of a 10th Battalion guard mounted on shore for forty-eight hours for Sir Ian Hamilton. It was then that he first met this great soldier, and in a letter to his mother described the leader of the Mediterranean Expeditionary Force as follows: "A tall, thin man, bushy eyebrows, piercing eyes, and very alert, and on the whole looks a soldier." At the Battalion bivouac at Shell Green, with Lieut. H. R. Heming, his was one of the last posts to be relieved. He was then transferred to "B" Company. On the night of May 18 he was on duty in the line, and upon discovering that the Turks were massing in large numbers preparatory to an attack, roused his Company Headquarters as well as the Machine Gun Officer. The Turkish attack was precipitated before dawn, and in all aspects completely failed. On June 4, 1915, he evacuated with dysentery, and proceeded to Egypt, where he was admitted to hospital at Heliopolis. Within a month he was on his way back to Gallipoli, and rejoined the Battalion on July 5, 1915. He was appointed Battalion Intelligence Officer on August 20, 1915, but on August 31, 1915, he was forced to evacuate a second time with dysentery and enteric fever. He proceeded to Malta, where he was admitted to the Blue Sisters' Hospital, and later transferred to the Imtarfa Barracks. He subsequently re-embarked for England, where he was admitted to the 3rd London General Hospital at Wandsworth. On May 6, 1916, he proceeded to France with the first A.I.F. draft from England, and was appointed Adjutant at the 3rd Brigade Details Camp at the Etaples Base. He rejoined the Battalion on August 18, 1916, the day preceding the Mouquet Farm operation. He served on with the Battalion, and on March 30, 1917, was promoted to the rank of captain. During his service in France he was wounded twice, but only forced to evacuate once, when at Merris, on May 8, 1918, he was forced to leave, passing through the 15th Casualty Clearing Station at Ebblinghem, where he proceeded to No. 8 British Red Cross Hospital at Boulogne, and finally to the 3rd London General Hospital at Wandsworth. He rejoined the

Battalion in France on July 5, 1918, and for his distinguished work at Jeancourt on September 18, 1918, was awarded the M.C., which was promulgated in the *London Gazette* on February 11, 1919, and the details on July 30, 1919. He was appointed Adjutant of the Battalion on October 12, 1918, and in this capacity succeeded Temp. Major G. C. Campbell. He retained this appointment until December 4, 1918, when at Chatelet, in Belgium, he finally left the Battalion and proceeded on 75 days' 1914 Anzac leave, Lieut. A. P. Chittleborough succeeding him as Adjutant. On August 29, 1918, whilst on furlough, at St. Matthew's Church, Chelston, Torquay, he married Louisa Ivy Vera, daughter of W. H. Sampson, there being two sons and two daughters of the union. He subsequently embarked for Australia on the *Konigen Louise*, arriving back in Adelaide on August 11, 1919, his services with the A.I.F. terminating on August 25, 1919. During his absence from Australia he was appointed an honorary captain in the Australian Military Forces on March 30, 1917, and was promoted to rank of lieutenant in the 82nd (Barrier) Infantry on July 1, 1918. On October 1, 1918, he was transferred to the 2/5 Pioneers, and on August 1, 1920, was promoted to rank of captain, in the same unit, and on December 1, 1920, was placed on the Reserve of Officers with rank of captain, and is still listed thereon. He has been employed for several years by Metters Ltd., and in 1935 was residing at No. 47, Broadway, Glenelg. He was one of the three youngest subalterns of the original Battalion, and was affectionately known to his men as "Bill."

42. RAFFERTY, RUPERT ANSTICE, was born at Bedford, England, on March 2, 1875, and at the outbreak of the Great War was residing in Tasmania, being a schoolmaster by profession. He served in the South African War, 1899-1902, and was appointed a 2nd lieutenant in the 91st (Tasmanian Rangers) on January 16, 1914, and held this commission at the time of joining the A.I.F. He was appointed a 2nd lieutenant in the 12th Battalion on August 28, 1914, and at Mena, Egypt, in January, 1915, during the company reorganization was appointed a Platoon Commander and promoted to the rank of lieutenant on February 1, 1915. He landed with his company from the destroyer *Ribble* at the historic landing on April 25, 1915, and on May 22, 1915, was promoted to the rank of captain, attaining his majority on March 1, 1916. He accompanied the 12th Battalion to France, and on December 23, 1916, when Temp. Lieut.-Colonel George Ernest Redburg evacuated sick he was transferred from the 12th Battalion to temporarily command the 10th. He remained C.O. of the Battalion until February 4, 1917, when Lieut.-Colonel R. B. Jacob assumed command. He was the first officer to command the 10th Battalion who was not a South Australian by birth. In recognition of his services in the prosecution of the war he was awarded the D.S.O., which was promulgated in the *London Gazette* on June 4, 1917, amongst the King's Birthday Honours. He attained the rank of lieutenant-colonel, and temporarily commanded the 11th Battalion, and subsequently commanded the 12th Battalion, 1918-19. He was seconded to command the 1st Training Battalion in England on May 28, 1918. During his absence from Tasmania he was promoted to the rank of lieutenant in the 91st Infantry on July 1, 1915, and was transferred to the 2/12 Infantry on October 1, 1918. He received no appointment as captain or major in the Australian Military Forces, but on July 1, 1920, was promoted to the rank of

lieutenant-colonel and commanded the 5/12 Infantry. He was subsequently transferred to the 52nd Battalion on March 31, 1921, and listed on Reserve of Officers on July 1, 1922. He commanded the 5/12 Infantry from July 1, 1920, to March 30, 1921, and commanded the 52nd Battalion from March 31, 1921, to June 30, 1922. He was short and wiry, very alert and active, and was pleasant and well liked. He commanded the 10th Battalion in France shortly after Flers, and accompanied the 10th to Bazentin, where Christmas, 1916, was spent. The Battalion under his command subsequently moved to Hobart Camp, Dernancourt, Bresle, Albert, and Bazentin-le-Petit, where he handed over the command to Lieut.-Colonel R. B. Jacob. He was mentioned in despatches on two occasions, *vide London Gazette*, 1/6/17 and 25/12/17. In 1935 he was residing at Currie, King Island, Tasmania.

43. REDBURG, GEORGE ERNEST, was born at Adelaide on October 8, 1881, and is a son of the late George Augustus Redburg, who for many years was employed as a well-boring artisan by the South Australian Water Conservation Department. He was educated at the Norwood Public School, and in 1909 commenced his military career as a private in the South Australian Scottish Corps, in which he subsequently held the non-commissioned ranks of corporal and sergeant. He received his first commission as a 2nd lieutenant in the same regiment on July 3, 1911, and on the disbandment of the Scottish Rifles, consequent upon the introduction of universal military training, he was transferred with same rank on July 1, 1912, to the 79th (Torrens) Infantry. He was promoted to the rank of lieutenant on January 31, 1913, and to captain on February 1, 1914. He held this commission at the outbreak of the Great War, and was also officiating as Adjutant of his regiment. At the time of joining the A.I.F. he was employed as manager of the manufacturing department of Foy & Gibson Proprietary Ltd. He was one of the first Company Commanders selected by Lieut.-Colonel S. P. Weir for the 10th Battalion, and was appointed a captain in the 10th at Morphettville on August 19, 1914. He was posted to the command of original "F" Company, and embarked with the original Battalion on H.M.A.T. A11 *Ascanius* on October 20, 1914. At Mena, Egypt, in January, 1915, when his company merged with the original "A" Company and became the new "A" Company, he was appointed 2nd in Command of same. He accompanied the 10th on the *Ionian* to the Dardanelles, and landed with his company from the destroyer *Foxhound* at the historic landing at Anzac on April 25, 1915, and that day, about 5 p.m., was shot through both legs and forced to evacuate. He proceeded to England, where he was admitted to the Whitworth Street Hospital at Manchester. He subsequently returned to the Dardanelles, and rejoined the 10th Battalion on the island of Lemnos on December 8, 1915. He subsequently accompanied the Battalion on the *Seeang Bee* to Egypt, and at Gebel Habieta, on February 20, 1916, was promoted to the rank of major. On March 1, 1916, he was appointed 2nd in Command of the Battalion, and in this capacity accompanied the 10th to France on the *Saxonia*. He participated in the Fleurbaix, Pozieres, Mouquet Farm, Gueudecourt, and Flers operations, and prepared the operation order for the attack on Mouquet Farm. On August 23, 1916, upon Lieut.-Colonel S. P. Weir being appointed Acting-Brigadier, he temporarily commanded the 10th Battalion, with the rank of temporary lieutenant-colonel. He retained the command of the Battalion until December 23,

1916, when through illness he was forced to evacuate. During the period he was C.O. of the Battalion he was twice relieved of the command, in the first instance by Temp. Lieut.-Colonel J.S. Denton, and in the second by Major F. G. Giles. Finally leaving the Battalion, he proceeded to England, where he was admitted to the 3rd London General Hospital at Wandsworth, and upon gaining convalescence resigned his commission in the A.I.F. on February 28, 1917. He subsequently accepted employment with the British Ministry of Munitions, and was engaged at various works in the north and east of Scotland. Whilst on furlough he married into a Scottish family, and returned to South Australia with his wife on the *Cluny Castle* in October, 1918. Returning to civil life, he was gazetted a captain in the 2/32 Infantry on October 1, 1918, and placed on Reserve of Officers with same rank on January 1, 1920, and promoted to rank of major, Reserve of Officers, as and from October 1, 1920. On February 21, 1919, he entered the Public Service of South Australia, and was appointed clerk at the Pompoota Training Farm, and subsequently was promoted to clerk-in-charge, and in this capacity supervised the clerical work and accounts of training farm, and also prepared pay-sheets, received revenue, and supervised work of storekeeper. He was subsequently transferred to the Jervois area, but resigned this position on August 8, 1923. He then came to Adelaide, and on August 20, 1923, became an employee of John Martin & Co., Ltd., and in 1935 had attained the position of floor superintendent. For services in France he was mentioned in despatches, *vide London Gazette*, 2/1/17. He has two children, and in 1935 was residing at Henley Beach Road, Brooklyn Park.

44. ROBLEY, VERNON HERMANN, was born at Walkerville on April 26, 1894, and is a son of James Hindhaugh Robley. He was educated at a small Church of England school, the Walkerville Public School, and St. Peter's College. At the outbreak of the Great War he was employed as a clerk by Elder, Smith & Co., Ltd., and was residing with his parents at Gilbert Street, Gilberton. He was a compulsory trainee, and becoming interested in the universal training scheme quickly sought promotion. He was appointed a 2nd lieutenant in the 78th (Adelaide Rifles) Infantry on March 1, 1914, and held this commission at the time of joining the A.I.F. He was appointed a 2nd lieutenant in the 10th Battalion at Morphettville on August 19, 1914, and posted to the command of the Machine Gun Section, which comprised sixteen men, consisting of two machine-gun teams. Both the guns allotted to his section were practice guns with barrels and mechanism considerably worn, one being obtained from Unley and the other from Adelaide. He embarked with the original Battalion on H.M.A.T. A11 *Ascanius* on October 20, 1914, and proceeded to Egypt, subsequently re-embarking on the *Ionian* for the Dardanelles. On April 5, 1915 (Easter Monday), the actual day when the first intimation of the Gallipoli landing was received on the *Ionian*, there was much excitement on board; but late that night he was stricken with rheumatic fever, and on April 7, 1915, was transferred to No. 1 Stationary Hospital Ship, and subsequently to another vessel, which sailed for Alexandria on April 14, 1915. He disembarked at Alexandria on April 17, 1915, and proceeded to Heliopolis, where he was admitted to the 1st Australian General Hospital. Shortly after he boarded the *Ceramic* at Suez, this vessel taking 29 days 11 hours to accomplish the direct run to Melbourne. After leaving the

Battalion on the *Ionian*, Lieut, E. W. T. Smith was hurriedly appointed Machine Gun Officer, and Lieut. Robley was promoted to the rank of lieutenant on April 28, 1915. Under these unfortunate conditions he was the first original 10th officer to return to South Australia, his services with the A.I.F. terminating on September 21, 1915. Commenting upon several original officers of the Battalion who were killed in action on Gallipoli shortly after the landing, he said: "Lieut. Talbot Smith, who has since been killed, took charge of my section when I went to hospital; Capt. Hall and Lieut. Owen Smyth, both fine fellows, were tent mates of mine." He subsequently made three trips to Europe, including one to Italy, on A.I.F. transport duty. Whilst engaged in this work he was appointed an honorary captain, and accompanied several quotas of South Australian reinforcements and details abroad. He was promoted to the rank of lieutenant in the 78th (Adelaide Rifles) Infantry on July 1, 1915, and on October 1, 1918, was transferred to the 2/10 Infantry with same rank. On December 16, 1919, he was placed on the Reserve of Officers as lieutenant. He has had a varied business career, being employed at different times as manager and clerk. He commenced duties as a clerk in the Public Service of South Australia on February 2, 1932, and in 1935 was employed by the Unemployment Relief Council at Kintore Avenue, Adelaide. On September 11, 1920, at St. Paul's, Adelaide, he married Irene Pretoria Emily, daughter of Frederick Henry Newcombe, and in 1935 was residing at No. 27, Coombe Road, Allenby Gardens.

45. ROWE, ALBERT HENRY, was born on July 26, 1894, and at the outbreak of the Great War was residing at Gawler, where he was employed as a draughtsman by the engineering firm of James Martin & Co. He was a compulsory trainee, and received his first commission as a 2nd lieutenant in the 79th (Torrens) Infantry on July 1, 1913, and with same rank was subsequently transferred to the 80th (Gawler) Infantry, holding this commission at the time of joining the A.I.F. He was appointed a 2nd lieutenant in the A.I.F. on September 14, 1914, and posted to the 1st Reinforcements of the 10th Battalion. This quota of reinforcements was raised and encamped at Morphettville before the original Battalion embarked, and on September 21, 1914, marched with the original Battalion in the first A.I.F. route-march through the city of Adelaide. As O.C. of this quota of reinforcements he entrained for Melbourne, and embarked on H.M.A.T. A32 *Themistocles* on December 27, 1914, and with the 2nd Australian Contingent proceeded to Egypt, arriving at Alexandria on February 1, 1915. Upon disembarkation he accompanied his reinforcements to Zeitoun, near Cairo, where he remained for about a week, prior to joining the 10th in camp at Mena on February 8, 1915. He was posted to "A" Company, and subsequently embarked with the Battalion on the *Ionian* for the Dardanelles, and landed with his platoon from the destroyer *Foxhound* at the historic landing on April 25, 1915. That day he was promoted to the rank of lieutenant, and on August 28, 1915, was wounded and forced to evacuate. He proceeded to hospital in London, and rejoined the Battalion at Tel-el-Kebir on January 2, 1916. At Gebel Habieta, on March 5, 1916, he was transferred to the 51st Battalion as Adjutant, which appointment he retained until October 1, 1916. On March 12, 1916, he was promoted to the rank of temporary captain, and on March 16, 1916, his substantive rank of captain was confirmed. On June 5, 1916, he embarked on

the *Ivernia* with the 51st Battalion under Lieut.-Colonel A. M. Ross, and disembarked at Marseilles on June 12, 1916, and on October 2, 1916, attained his majority. He was subsequently wounded in France and awarded the Serbian Order of the White Eagle, 5th Class, *vide London Gazette*, 13/2/17. For some considerable time he was 2nd in Command of the 51st Battalion and also temporarily commanded same. From November 18 to December 28, 1918, with rank of temporary lieutenant-colonel, he temporarily commanded the 50th Battalion during the absence on furlough of Lieut.-Colonel A. G. Salisbury, D.S.O. He subsequently returned to South Australia, his services with the A.I.F. terminating on July 10, 1919. During his absence from Australia he was promoted to the rank of lieutenant in the 80th (Gawler) Infantry on July 1, 1915. Returning to civil life, he resided at North Adelaide for several years, and accepted employment with Horwood Bagshaw Ltd. at Mile End. He married in England during the war, and subsequently proceeded to Ireland to take up an appointment in the brewing firm of Arthur Guinness & Sons, of Dublin. On November 11, 1925, he was transferred to the Retired List of the Australian Miliary Forces.

46. RUMBALL, CLARENCE, was born at Fowler's Bay, Eyre's Peninsula, on August 13, 1892, and is the third son of H. S. Rumball, who for many years was a Commonwealth Public Servant, and at the outbreak of the Great War was postmaster at Thebarton. His brother Arnold enlisted with the 9th Reinforcements of the 10th Light Horse, and his younger brother, Francis, joined the 1st Signalling Company. He resided for several years at Kingscote, Kangaroo Island, and was educated at various public Schools, G. A. Newman's Academy, and the S.A. School of Mines and Industries. In 1910 he took up a position with the Vivian Lewis Company of Adelaide, and on March 1, 1912, commenced duties as a clerk in the paymaster's office of the South Australian Railways, and held this position at the outbreak of the Great War. From boyhood he had been an ardent military enthusiast, and devoted most of his spare time in studying for military examinations. When England declared war on Germany he was attending a map-reading course at an instructional school at Gawler; but upon same being hurriedly abandoned he returned to Adelaide to await mobilization with the 78th (Adelaide Rifles) Infantry, in which he held a commission. He was appointed a 2nd lieutenant in this regiment on January 1, 1914, and shortly after leaving Australia (July 1, 1915) was promoted to the rank of lieutenant. He was appointed a 2nd lieutenant in the 10th Battalion at Morphettville on August 19, 1914, and was posted to original "A" Company. He embarked with the original Battalion on H.M.A.T. A11 *Ascanius* on October 20, 1914, and accompanied the 10th to Egypt. At Mena, in January, 1915, during the company reorganization, he was appointed a Platoon Commander in the new "D" Company, and promoted to rank of lieutenant on February 1, 1915. He re-embarked with the Battalion on the *Ionian*, and proceeded to the Dardanelles, and landed with his company from the destroyer *Scourge* at the historic landing on April 25, 1915. Three days later, when the Battalion reorganized at Shell Green, he was posted to the command of "A" Company. On May 9, 1915, he was appointed Adjutant of the Battalion in lieu of Major F. M. de F. Lorenzo, who then relieved him of the command of "A" Company. He was later promoted to the rank of captain, which was made retrospective to April 26, 1915. He figured conspicuously in connection with the raid on Gaba Tepe, con-

ducted at dawn on May 4, 1915, when he was delegated the duty of leading a party of twelve 10th Battalion men southward along the beach, from Anzac to cut the northward belt of Turkish wire along the beach, in order to facilitate the withdrawal of Capt. R. L. Leane's raiding party of 100 strong, who landed in tows from the destroyer *Chelmer*. His party succeeded in achieving the task allotted it, but the raid failed, owing to the impregnability of the objective. Dr. C. E. W. Bean, in his "Story of Anzac," Vol 1, p. 562, says: "The place was by far the most formidable stronghold which the Australian troops attempted to raid during the war." He retained the adjutancy of the Battalion until June 27, 1915, when he returned to his company. On September 25, 1915, he evacuated the Peninsula with enteric, and proceeded to Malta, where he was admitted to the Blue Sisters' Hospital. For his good work at Anzac he was mentioned in despatches, *vide London Gazette*, 5/11/15. He subsequently returned to Egypt, and at Tel-el-Kebir, in January, 1916, was attached to the staff of Brigadier-General E. G. Sinclair Mac-Lagan, and in this capacity assisted in organizing the camp for A.I.F. units, which were then returning from the Dardanelles. He was subsequently appointed R.T.O. at Tel-el-Kebir, and retained this position during the troop-movements. He subsequently rejoined the 10th Battalion at Gebel Habieta, and was posted to "A" Company. When the Battalion finally moved off from Serapeum to embark for France, he remained in charge of details, with which he was subsequently transferred to the 13th Brigade. Later he proceeded to England, and was appointed Adjutant of the 3rd Training Battalion on Salisbury Plain. He arrived in France on December 12, 1916, and for his splendid work whilst commanding "A" Company in the Le Barque attack on February 25, 1917, was awarded the M.C., which was promulgated in the *London Gazette* on April 26, 1917. This was the fourth M.C. won by an officer of the Battalion. He attained his majority on March 30, 1917, and immediately after the Polygon Wood operation of September 20, 1917, it devolved upon him, as senior officer, to temporarily command the Battalion, during the absence of Lieut.-Colonel M. Wilder-Neligan, D.S.O., D.C.M. He was C.O. of the 10th at Broodseinde and Westhoek Ridge, and took over the command from Capt. G. C. Campbell, M.C., and retained same for about one week. He subsequently handed over to Lieut.-Colonel Wilder-Neligan on the eve of the Celtic Wood raid. He served on with the Battalion, and at Meteren, May 19-29, 1918, he commanded "A" Company, and at Merris, June 28, 1918, he was O.C. of "C" Company. On July 10, 1918, he finally left the Battalion, and proceeded to England, where he attended a Senior Officers' Instructional Course at Aldershot. On September 5, 1918, he was seconded for duty with the Machine Gun Training Depot at Grantham, where he officiated as Senior Instructor in machine-gun tactics. He subsequently embarked on the *Somerset* as O.C. of Troops, and arrived back in Adelaide on January 19, 1919, his services with the A.I.F. terminating on March 19, 1919. He then returned to the South Australian Railways as a clerk. On June 1, 1920, he was transferred to the South Australian Public Service, and appointed receiver of revenue in the Motor Vehicles Department. In February, 1919, he married Dorothy, daughter of H. W. Schroeder, there being two sons and one daughter of the union. Keen to settle on the land, he set himself out to acquire gardening and horticultural experience, with the result that on February 17, 1921, he obtained his qualification certificate from the Superintendent of Soldier Settlements. On March 1, 1921, he was allotted a block, consisting of 26 acres, in the Berri irrigation area. Prior to going on the land he was Area Officer at Alberton and Kilkenny. During his absence from Australia he was appointed an honorary major in the Australian Military Forces on March 30, 1917. In 1920 he was listed as a lieutenant in the 5/10 Infantry. He was subsequently transferred to the Unattached List, but was later transferred back to the Reserve of Officers. At present he is not listed on same. In 1935 he was residing on his block at Winkie, in addition to carrying out the duties of a fruit inspector at various River Murray centres.

47. SCUDDS, HOWARD WILSON, was born at Stirling, South Australia, on August 12, 1895, and is a son of Benjamin Scudds, who for a number of years was employed as overseer by the Crafers District Council. He was educated at the Stirling Public School, and for three years was employed as a footman at Government House, Adelaide, by Admiral Sir Day Hort Bosanquet, and subsequently held the position of usher at the King's Theatre. He was a compulsory trainee, and was serving as a private in the 78th (Adelaide Rifles) Infantry at the time of joining the A.I.F. He enlisted as a private in the 10th Battalion at Morphettville on August 20, 1914, his regimental number being "176." He was allotted to original "E" Company, and embarked with the original Battalion on H.M.A.T. A11 *Ascanius* on October 20, 1914, and proceeded to Egypt. At Mena, in January, 1915, when original "E" Company merged with original "C" Company and became the new "B" Company, he was retained on strength of same. He embarked with the Battalion on the *Ionian* for the Dardanelles, and landed with his company from the *Prince of Wales* at the historic landing on April 25, 1915. He remained on the Peninsula until August 30, 1915, when he evacuated ill and proceeded to Lemnos, where he embarked on the *Ascanius* and proceeded to Malta, where he was admitted to the Floriana Hospital. He subsequently returned to Egypt, and rejoined the Battalion at Habieta in February, 1916. He accompanied the 10th to France on the *Saxonia*, and served continuously with the Battalion until early February, 1917. He was raised to the rank of lance-corporal at Fleurbaix in June, 1916, to corporal at Pozieres in July, 1916, and to sergeant at Mouquet Farm in August, 1916. In February, 1917, shortly before the Le Barque attack, he was sent to an N.C.O.'s and Officers' School at Piquigny, where he remained for two weeks as a trainee and one month as an instructor, subsequently being transferred to an Officers' Training Corps at Keble College, Oxford, England, where he received his first commission as a 2nd lieutenant on June 18, 1917. He returned to France, and rejoined the Battalion at Bray on June 30, 1917, and served continuously with the 10th for another three months. In September, 1917, he distinguished himself in the Polygon Wood operation, for which he was awarded the Military Cross, which was promulgated in the *London Gazette* on November 10, 1917, and the details on March 19, 1918. General Sir W. R. Birdwood, under date of October 24, 1917, forwarded him the following congratulatory message: "1st Anzac Corps, B.E.F., France.—Dear Scudds, I write to congratulate you very heartily upon the award to you of the Military Cross in recognition of your good work in the operations near Ypres from 19th to 22nd September. I know what great courage and initiative you displayed in lead-

ing your platoon against an enemy strong point, which was holding up the company on your flank, and your capture of which enabled the advance to continue. Your work, too, in the capture and consolidation of the final objective was of a very high order, and I thank you so much for it. With good wishes for your future, Yours sincerely, W. R. Birdwood." Immediately after the Polygon Wood operation he proceeded on special furlough to England, and thus missed the Celtic Wood raid. He subsequently returned to France, and rejoined the Battalion at the horse-lines near the Chateau behind the front line the day before the Battalion moved forward into the trenches, and there awaited the return of the 10th from the raid. He served on with the 10th, and was promoted to rank of lieutenant on November 17, 1917, and at Merris on June 28, 1918, again distinguished himself, for which he was awarded a Bar to his M.C., which was promulgated in the *London Gazette* on October 15, 1918. General Sir W. R. Birdwood again congratulated him as follows: "Headquarters, A.I.F., Attached Headquarters Fifth Army, B.E.F.—Dear Scudds, I am very pleased to have this opportunity of congratulating you most heartily on the award of a Bar to the Military Cross, which you have fully deserved for your good and gallant work during our operations near Merris on the morning of 28th June last. You led your platoon in the attack with great skill and determination, and, as a result of your good leadership, quickly reached your objective, where you inflicted heavy casualties upon the enemy. Having done this, you displayed commendable resource and initiative in moving forward with three members only of your platoon, and capturing three enemy machine guns and 21 Germans. Thank you very much for your fine example of bravery and devotion to duty, and with good wishes, Yours sincerely, W. R. Birdwood. 30/8/18." At the capture of Merris in July, 1918, he was posted to the command of "C" Company, which he took over from Major C. Rumball, M.C., and retained command of this company until the Crepey Wood operation of August 12, 1918. Early in September, 1918, at a bomb smash near Peronne, he was wounded in the head and both legs and forced to evacuate, proceeding to the 8th General Hospital at Rouen. He subsequently returned to the Australian Base at Le Havre, where he was detailed to proceed on three days' escort duty to the Citadel at Peronne. He rejoined the Battalion at Brucamps shortly before the Armistice, but during the Armistice was attending a six days' gas course at a military school near Amiens. He subsequently rejoined the 10th *en route* to Charleroi, where he was appointed officer-in-charge of the 3rd Brigade section of a special guard mounted in honour of H.R.H. the Duke of Connaught. The section under his command consisted of picked men from the 9th, 10th, 11th, and 12th Battalions. In December, 1918, he was detailed to proceed to England with a draft of men from the 10th, but upon the cancellation of this instruction he finally left the Battalion by himself on December 25, 1918. He proceeded to Paris, and then to England, where he obtained extended leave and accepted non-military employment in connection with cinematography work, and in this capacity continued until August, 1919. He subsequently embarked on the *Ascanius* for Australia, arriving back in Adelaide early in November, 1919, his services with the A.I.F. terminating on November 21, 1919. This was his third and final trip on the *Ascanius* during the war. On June 28, 1922, at North Adelaide, he married Linda Jessie Octavia, daughter of Percy Walsingham Wood, there being one son of the union. On July 1, 1920, he was placed on the Reserve of Officers as a lieutenant, and on August 3, 1926, was transferred to the 10th Battalion with same rank. On November 24, 1926, he was again listed on the Reserve of Officers, and in 1935 was still on same. He is also listed as a lieutenant in the Regimental Reserve List of the 10th Battalion as and from June 1, 1930. In 1935 he was employed as a mechanic at the Hackney depot of the Municipal Tramways Trust, and was residing at No. 29, Asquith Street, Prospect Gardens.

48. SEAGER, HAROLD WILLIAM HASTINGS, was born at Powlett, Victoria, on July 6, 1893, and is a son of the late Clarendon James Seager, who was an ex-captain of the 8th Hussars, and for many years was engaged in the pastoral industry in Queensland. He comes of a fighting stock, his grandfather, Lieut.-General Seager, C.B., as a young lieutenant of the 8th Hussars taking part in the historic charge of the Light Brigade at Balaklava, in the Crimean War of 1854, whilst Hugh Seager fought against the Spanish Armada on H.M.S. *Nonperilla*, whilst another ancestor, Sir Halsall Seager, served in the land forces at the same time, and was buried in York Minster. He is one of three brothers who served in the A.I.F., and his mother, Alexandrina Seager, during the Great War supervised the Adelaide Cheer-Up Hut for over four years. He was educated at Christchurch Grammar School, Victoria, and the Pulteney Street Grammar School, Adelaide, and for a short time was employed as a clerk by the Alliance Assurance Co., Ltd. On March 21, 1910, he commenced duties at the Bank of Australasia, and at the time of joining the A.I.F. had attained the position of teller, having served in both the Adelaide and Port Adelaide branches. As a youth he was interested in military training, and commenced his military career in 1908 by joining the old senior cadets as a private. He subsequently joined the 10th Australian Infantry Regiment, in which he was promoted to the rank of sergeant, and on July 21, 1911, received his first commission as a 2nd lieutenant. On July 1, 1912, consequent upon the introduction of universal military training, he was transferred to the 74th (Boothby) Infantry with same rank. On November 18, 1912, he was transferred to the 78th (Adelaide Rifles) Infantry, in which he was promoted to rank of lieutenant on January 31, 1913. He received his captaincy on February 16, 1914, and held this commission at the outbreak of the Great War. He was one of the first South Australian officers to offer his services for overseas, and was also one of the first Company Commanders selected by Lieut.-Colonel S. P. Weir for the 10th Battalion. He was appointed a captain in the 10th at Morphettville on August 19, 1914, and was posted to the command of original "C" Company. Early in September, 1914, he became seriously ill with pneumonia, and was thus precluded from leading his company in the memorable first A.I.F. routemarch through the city of Adelaide on September 21, 1914. He was admitted to hospital, and thus prevented from accompanying the original Battalion on the *Ascanius* to Egypt, Lieutenant K. E. Green, of original "G" Company, being posted to the command of "C" Company. After regaining health he embarked as O.C. of the 2nd Reinforcements of the 10th Battalion at Melbourne on H.M.A.T. A46 *Clan MacGillivray* on February 2, 1915, and disembarked at Alexandria, Egypt, on March 7, 1915. He then proceeded to Mena Camp, and in the absence of the 3rd Brigade, which had been dis-

patched to the Dardanelles ahead of the other units of the 1st Australian Division, he became attached to the 1st Brigade. He subsequently re-embarked at Alexandria on the *Piraeus* for the Dardanelles, being entrusted with confidential papers for the Commanding Officer of the 3rd Brigade and £18,500 in cash to pay A.I.F. troops. This transport also carried the first two flying officers dispatched to the Dardanelles. He joined the Battalion on the *Ionian* at Mudros Harbour, Lemnos, on April 10, 1915, and a few days later was appointed Ship's Transport Officer, which appointment prevented him from landing with the main body of the Battalion in the covering force at the historic landing at Anzac on April 25, 1915. In the capacity of Ship's Transport Officer it devolved upon him to act as the medium of communication between the British Navy and the captain of the *Ionian*. With Capt. C. F. Minagall he stood off the Peninsula on the *Ionian*, and at first obtained a wonderful panoramic view of the naval and military operations then being staged in the vicinity, but as the land-battle progressed was kept more than busy with the hundreds of wounded and dying, who day and night were packed into the transport. The vessel was converted into a temporary hospital ship, and when no more could be admitted, proceeded to Alexandria, and then immediately returned to Cape Helles with troops, and afterwards came on to Anzac, where he landed and rejoined the Battalion in the line about May 4, 1915. His experience as a Ship's Transport Officer on board the *Ionian*, to say the least of it, was most gruesome, and in a letter to a friend from Anzac he said: "Never again do I want to be on a temporary hospital ship. The poor mangled, quivering pieces of humanity were placed on the decks, in the saloons, cabins, boat decks, and even down the holds." At Anzac he was posted to the command of "B" Company, which included his old "C" Company of Morphettville, and by his fearless conduct both in and out of the line earned for himself the name of "Daredevil Harry." On September 17, 1915, he was invalided ill from Gallipoli, and proceeded to hospital at Malta, and later re-embarked for England, where he was admitted to the 3rd London General Hospital at Wandsworth. He subsequently returned to the Dardanelles on the *Olympic*, and rejoined the Battalion at Lemnos on November 21, 1915, this being the day that the 10th arrived from the Peninsula when the blizzard was blowing at its hardest. He eventually accompanied the Battalion to Egypt on the *Seeang Bee*, and at Gebel Habieta, on February 26, 1916, was transferred to the 50th Battalion. He subsequently embarked on the *Arcadian* and accompanied the 50th to France, where he had many marvellous escapes. In June, 1916, he was seconded for duty with the 13th Training Battalion at Codford, England. Returning to France, he rejoined the 50th Battalion in December, 1916. At Noreuil, on April 2-4, 1917, he distinguished himself in the fighting, and was awarded the Military Cross, which was promulgated in the *London Gazette* on June 15, 1917, the official citation being: "For conspicuous gallantry and devotion to duty. He rendered valuable service while in command of a rescue company. He attacked with the utmost skill and determination, thereby relieving the pressure at a very critical time. He set a fine example of courage and coolness throughout." He attained the rank of major on July 23, 1917, but on September 26, 1917, was wounded, and subsequently invalided from France with severe head-wounds. He proceeded to hospital at Boulogne, and later was transferred to the 3rd London General Hospital at Wandsworth. In November, 1917, he embarked on the *Karoola*, and returned to Adelaide, his services with the A.I.F. terminating on January 25, 1918. In August, 1918, he embarked at Sydney as O.C. Troops on the *Bakara*, which proceeded to England *via* the Cape. This transport was escorted by H.M.S. *Africa*, which was the last British naval ship to be torpedoed during the Great War. He subsequently embarked for Australia as O.C. Troops on the *City of York*, which proceeded to Brisbane *via* the Suez Canal, his services with the A.I.F. finally terminating on July 10, 1919. Returning to civil life, he resigned his position with the Bank of Australasia on July 29, 1918, having no desire to resume a sedentary occupation, but was keen on applying himself to an outdoor occupation. In October, 1922, he was residing at Ashbourne Avenue, Mitcham, and on November 14, 1924, with his brother, Edward Clarendon, late of the 4th Light Horse, A.I.F., obtained a pastoral lease of sixty-six square miles at Hawke's Nest South and White Lagoon South, Kangaroo Island, situated south-south-west of Queenscliffe. This tract of country is a long distance from the coast, over chiefly bush road, which is bad in parts. On December 12, 1924, he individually secured a pastoral lease over 1,780 acres, also at Hawke's Nest, and on December 1, 1933, he and his brother were allotted 3,284 acres under an acquired soldier's agreement, and situated in the Hundred of MacGillivray, County of Carnarvon. On January 31, 1935, they were allotted another 1,228 acres, also in the Hundred of MacGillivray. On October 28, 1930, he was granted permission by the Hon. Minister of Repatriation to allow officers of the Commonwealth Council of Scientific and Industrial Research (Division of Animal Nutrition) to investigate diseases amongst his sheep known as "coast." On July 28, 1925, he married Joy Debenham, daughter of Professor Tearne, of Sydney, there being one son of the union. His wife is a qualified medical practitioner, and assists in the research investigations, acting as a liaison officer by extracting thyroid glands from sheep killed for food on the station, and forwarding same to the Adelaide laboratories of the council, and also conducts blood tests and mixes sheep licks. Various soil and pot culture tests have also been conducted on his holdings by the Waite Research Institute. He was awarded the Volunteer Decoration, and was appointed a captain in the 2/10 Infantry on October 1, 1918, and promoted to rank of major in the same unit on April 2, 1919. On March 31, 1921, he was transferred to the 10th Battalion, and on January 1, 1922, was placed on the Unattached List. On January 1, 1927, he was listed on the Reserve of Officers with rank of major. In 1935 he was enggaed in sheep-farming with his brother on the above-mentioned holdings, his postal address being, "Hawke's Nest, Kangaroo Island."

49. SEXTON, ERIC JAMES, was born at Mount Gambier on March 20, 1893, and is the fourth son of the late R. J. Sexton, who at the outbreak of the Great War was postmaster at Port Adelaide, and had formerly held a similar appointment at Mount Gambier. He was one of a family of seven, consisting of six sons and one daughter. Three of his brothers also served with the A.I.F., and at one time during the Great War were all attached to the 43rd Battalion—the Rev. H. E. Sexton, who in 1914 was a curate at All Saint's Anglican Church at Hindmarsh, and in 1935 was appointed Coadjutor Bishop of British Columbia, was attached to the 43rd as chaplain with rank of captain; R. C. Sexton attained the rank of major in the same battalion; and L. B.

Sexton, formerly of Duntroon College, was a sergeant in the same unit; whilst another brother, F. C. Sexton, was rejected for service abroad. He was educated at the Mount Gambier Grammar School, and in 1910 commenced as a clerk with Dalgety & Co., Ltd., and at the time of joining the A.I.F. was stationed at Angaston, having served with that company for three years and nine months. As a youth he interested himself in military training, and in military circles was looked upon as a promising subaltern. He received his first commission as a 2nd lieutenant in the 76th (Hindmarsh) Infantry on March 16, 1913, and was promoted to the rank of lieutenant in the same unit on March 1, 1914, and held this commission at the time of joining the A.I.F. He also acted as Adjutant of his regiment from March 1, 1914, such appointment terminating on July 1, 1915. He was one of the first lieutenants selected by Lieut.-Colonel S. P. Weir for the 10th Battalion, in which, at Morphettville on August 19, 1914, he was appointed a lieutenant. He was posted to original "C" Company, and embarked with the original Battalion on H.M.A.T. A11 *Ascanius* on October 20, 1914, and proceeded to Egypt. At Mena, in January, 1916, when his company merged with original "E" Company and became the new "B" Company, he was appointed a Platoon Commander in same. He re-embarked on the *Ionian*, and accompanied the Battalion to the Dardanelles, and landed with his platoon from the *Prince of Wales* at the historic landing at Anzac on April 25, 1915. About 4.30 during the afternoon of that day, whilst his company was engaged in holding on to the 2nd Ridge, and before it had dug itself in, shrapnel shattered his left forearm, a bullet tore away a portion of his left ear, and another missile penetrated his right shoulder. These injuries were all sustained within ten minutes, with the result that he was forced to evacuate, but in so doing managed to crawl back behind the line for about fifty yards. He then proceeded along one of the Anzac gullies, and ultimately reached the beach in a very weak state. At 6.30 p.m. that day he was removed to a transport, and arrived at Alexandria on Friday, April 30, 1915, whereupon he was admitted to the Bombay Presidency Hospital at San Stefano, near Alexandria. This hospital prior to the war had been a casino, but subsequently staffed with English nurses. He eventually returned to Australia on the *Ballarat* with the second quota of wounded from the Dardanelles, arriving at the Outer Harbour on August 3, 1915. Capt. M. J. Herbert and 23 other ranks of the 10th Battalion also returned on the same boat. After regaining convalescence he returned to Egypt as O.C. of the 17th Reinforcements of the 10th Battalion, embarking at the Outer Harbour on H.M.A.T. A60 *Aeneas* on April 11, 1916. He attained his captaincy the day after he was wounded (April 26, 1915), and disembarked at Alexandria on May 11, 1916. Proceeding to Tel-el-Kebir, he was appointed Camp Adjutant, and retained this appointment until August 2, 1916, when he embarked for England. On February 14, 1917 he was promoted to the rank of major, and transferred to a Machine Gun Company, being subsequently appointed O.C. of the Australian Machine Gun Corps Training Depot at Grantham. On January 1, 1918, in recognition of his services during the war, he was awarded the O.B.E., Military division, *vide London Gazette*, 7/1/18, being No. 725 on the precedence list. He was mentioned in despatches, *vide London Gazette*, 4/1/18. He eventually returned to South Australia, his services with the

A.I.F. terminating on June 8, 1918. Shortly after returning to civil life he was appointed Quarantine Officer on Torrens Island, but later proceeded to Melbourne, where for some time he was employed at the Commonwealth Bank in connection with the raising of a Commonwealth war loan. He has since followed various business pursuits, and besides entering into business on his own behalf has been employed by the Victorian Wheat Commission. On January 19, 1928, at Melbourne, he married Queenie, only daughter of the late Claude R. Johnson, who was an architect of that city, there being one daughter of the union. During his absence from Australia he was transferred to the 77th Infantry with rank of lieutenant as and from July 1, 1915, and on December 1, 1916, was promoted to rank of captain in same unit. He was promoted to rank of honorary major on February 14, 1917, and gazetted a full major in the A.M.F. on September 1, 1918. He was transferred to 2/10 Infantry on October 1, 1918, and commanded that unit until May 4, 1920. He was transferred to the 3rd Military District (Victoria) on May 5, 1920, and placed on Unattached List, and listed on Reserve of Officers with rank of major on May 5, 1925. In 1935 he was residing at No. 305, "Alberta," Dandenong Road, Armidale, Victoria, whilst his mother (Mrs. Lucy Sexton) and his sister (Rita Muriel Sexton) are now residing at No. 25, Belmore Terrace, Woodville Park, Adelaide.

50. SHAW, GEORGE DORRICUTT, was born at Hindmarsh on July 5, 1883, and is a son of the late John Shaw, who for many years was principal of the firm of John Shaw & Co. He was educated at Whinham College, North Adelaide, where he acquired the rudiments of chemistry, and subsequently at the South Australian School of Mines and Industries, where he specialized in metallurgy. After becoming an associate of the School of Mines he entered the employ of the Wallaroo Mining and Smelting Company as a chemist and assistant metallurgist. In 1908 he married Beatrix, daughter of the late William Ogle Bennett, there being three daughters of the union. At the outbreak of the Great War he was a manufacturer on his own account, and for several years prior to the clash of arms in Europe in 1914 had evinced a keen interest in military matters. He obtained his first commission as a 2nd lieutenant in the South Australian Infantry Regiment on August 14, 1911, and consequent upon the introduction of universal military training and the disbandment of his regiment he was transferred to the 81st (Wakefield) Infantry on July 1, 1912. He was promoted to the rank of lieutenant in that unit on October 14, 1912, and transferred to the 78th (Adelaide Rifles) Infantry on December 2, 1912, and promoted to rank of Captain on February 16, 1914, and held this commission at the time of joining the A.I.F. He was one of the first South Australian officers to volunteer for service abroad, and also was one of the original Company Commanders selected by Lieut.-Colonel S. P. Weir for the 10th, in which he was appointed a captain at Morphettville on August 19, 1914. He was posted to the command of original "B" Company, and embarked with the original Battalion on H.M.A.T. A11 *Ascanius* on October 20, 1914, and proceeded to Egypt. At Mena, in January, 1915, when his company merged with original "H" Company, and became the new "C" Company, he was appointed 2nd in Command of same. He subsequently re-embarked with the Battalion on the *Ionian* for the Dardanelles, and landed with his company from the *Prince of Wales* at

the historic landing on April 25, 1915. He actually remained on the Peninsula from the day of the landing until the 10th Battalion was subsequently withdrawn on November 21, 1915. He was the only original 10th officer to establish this record, the only officer to approach his achievement being Capt. F. G. Giles, who served at Anzac three days less than he, on account of proceeding to Imbros in July, 1915, when the main body of the Battalion had a temporary respite for three days. He was appointed a temporary major at Anzac in May, 1915, and on August 25, 1915, being the senior officer remaining with the Battalion, it devolved upon him to assume command of the 10th upon Lieut.-Colonel S. P. Weir being temporarily appointed Brigadier. He was then appointed acting liuetenant-colonel, and retained command of the Battalion until October 21, 1915, when Major M. F. Beevor, returning from England, became C.O. He was then temporarily transferred to the 9th Battalion as C.O., and remained with that unit for one month, and finally accompanied the 9th to Lemnos, when same was withdrawn from Gallipoli. At Lemnos he rejoined the 10th Battalion, and reverted to his substantive rank of captain on December 8, 1915 (due to the return of a senior officer). He subsequently accompanied the Battalion to Egypt on the *Seeang Bee*, and at Gebel Habieta, on March 12, 1916, attained his majority. He was later appointed Divisional Entraining Officer, which appointment necessitated his proceeding to France early in March, 1916. He left the 10th about a fortnight before the Battalion embarked on the *Saxonia*, and remained at Marseilles for two weeks, until the whole of the 1st Australian Division had disembarked. He then rejoined the Battalion, and in May, 1916, again assumed command of the Battalion during the temporary absence of Lieut.-Colonel S. P. Weir, who at the time was Acting-Brigadier. He commanded "C" Company at Fleurbaix and Pozieres, and during the attack on the latter place his company dug a new defensive line during the night, and thus secured the flank of the position. Early in August, 1916, a little before the Mouquet Farm attack, he was invalided to England sick, and admitted to the 4th London General Hospital at Denmark Hill. For his splendid work at Pozieres he was mentioned in despatches, *vide London Gazette*, 2/1/17. He was subsequently recommended for home service, and appointed 2nd in Command of the Wareham Command Depot on Salisbury Plain, and retained this position until April, 1917. He was then boarded and transferred to the 6th Australian Division, then in process of formation at Windmill Hill, where he was appointed 2nd in Command of the 67th Battalion. Upon the 6th Division being subsequently disbanded he returned to France, and rejoined the 10th Battalion as 2nd in Command during November, 1917. Between January 11 and August 16, 1918, he commanded the Battalion on six different occasions, approximating a period of two months. It was whilst he was in command of the 10th on March 2, 1918, that the Germans at Hollebeke raided the position occupied by "D" Company and carried off Company Commander Major H. N. Henwood, who, refusing to surrender, was killed. On August 18, 1918, he was appointed to the command of the 12th Battalion, *vice* Lieutenant-Colonel H. C. Elliott, who had been wounded. He retained the command of the 12th for ten days, and in September, at Chuignes, on the Somme, he was wounded. (It was at Chuignes where the monster German gun was discovered by the A.I.F.) Proceeding to England, he was admitted to the 3rd London

General Hospital at Wandsworth. Shortly after, his 1914 Anzac furlough became due, and at Tilbury, in October, 1918, he embarked on the *Themistocles*, and disembarked at Quebec, Canada. Proceeding by the Canadian Pacific Railway to Vancouver, he re-embarked on the *Makura*, and arrived back in Adelaide on Christmas Eve, 1918. It was a coincidence that Major F. G. Giles should return with him on the same boat, they being the two senior majors of the 10th Battalion and the two officers with the longest service at Anzac to their credit. His services in the A.I.F. terminated on February 22, 1919, and on March 1 of that year he was appointed a chemist in the Chemistry Department of the Public Service of South Australia (at Kintore Avenue, Adelaide). He has since been appointed an analyst under the Fertilisers Act, and is a fellow of the Australian Chemical Institute, and is president of the South Australian branch. During his absence from Australia he was appointed an honorary major in the Commonwealth Military Forces on March 12, 1916, and attained his captaincy in the 2/10 Infantry on October 1, 1918. Upon his return to Adelaide he continued his connection with the military forces, and on April 2, 1919, was appointed a major in the 2/10 Infantry, and with this rank was transferred to the 10th Battalion on March 31, 1921, and again to the 43rd Battalion on July 1, 1922. He was further promoted to the rank of lieutenant-colonel in that unit on February 7, 1925, and transferred to the Unattached List on July 1, 1927, and to the Reserve of Officers on July 1, 1932. He was Commanding Officer of the 10th Battalion Senior Cadets from March 31, 1921, to June 30, 1922, and commanded the 43rd Battalion from July 1, 1922, to June 30, 1927. In 1927 he was awarded the Volunteer Officers' Decoration, and in all has had fifteen years' commissioned service in the forces. By his outstanding personality during five years he built up the 43rd Battalion from a skeleton formation to a fully organized unit. Starting with four officers he finished with seventeen, including nine voluntary enlisted returned officers. He is a past master of Princess Royal Masonic Lodge, Wallaroo, No. 23, and a past master of the United Service Lodge, No. 37, Adelaide. He has consistently taken a keen interest in the activities of the Returned Sailors' and Soldiers' Imperial League of Australia, and in addition to being the first president of the Walkerville R.S.A., has been connected with the same sub-branch for five years. In 1933 he was elected a member of the Walkerville District Council, and on July 6, 1935, was re-elected as a member of the Walkerville Ward. In 1935 he was also elected to the Metropolitan County Board. He is well known in Adelaide literary circles, and has contributed largely both in prose and verse to the Sydney *Bulletin* and other Australian papers. He is a past president of the Adelaide Dual Club, and is a member of the Adelaide Repertory Theatre, at which, in September, 1933, his play, entitled "Personal Effects," was staged. The proceeds of this production were devoted to the Legacy Club. It was considered remarkable for the number of finely contrasted character studies it contained, all typical of men who served in the A.I.F., and with whom he came in contact during his service abroad. At one time he contemplated writing a history of the 10th Battalion, but for various reasons decided not to proceed with the arduous labours which a work of such magnitude would necessarily entail. Short in stature, thorough, energetic, and well-balanced, he always commanded the esteem of his fellow-officers and men. On the day of the landing at Anzac, 2nd Lieut. Meager, of the 3rd Battalion was detailed to reinforce the 10th Battalion, and was posted to Capt. Shaw's "C" Company. Subsequently Lieut. Meager wrote from Gallipoli: "Any man would be proud to work under such a man as Capt. Shaw of the 10th has proved himself to be." One of Capt. Shaw's own men (No. 519 Pte. H. W. H. McCarthy, of "C" Company) also wrote: "Capt. Shaw is our commander. He is one of the gamest officers we have struck. We will follow wherever he likes to lead us." Peculiarly, he had an A.I.F. namesake, George D. Shaw, of the 28th Battalion. (He was originally a machine-gun officer, and subsequently attained the rank of major and won the M.C.) Chemistry, soldiering, freemasonry, and literature have been his main interests, and though diversified he has retained his love for home life. In 1935 he was residing at Warwick Street, Walkerville.

51. SMITH, ERIC WILKES TALBOT, was born on April 28, 1892, and was the second son of Sydney Talbot Smith, M.A., solicitor, of 62 Halton Terrace, Kensington Park, and the late Florence Oliver Smith, who on her 70th birthday (21/9/35) died as the result of a motor accident. He was a grandson of the late Sir Edwin Smith, K.C.M.G., whilst his brother, Donald Lang Talbot, embarked on the *Ascanius* with the original Battalion as a private (No. 114) in the A.A.M.C., and subsequently re-embarked as a private (No. 5157) with the 16th Reinforcements of the Battalion. He was educated at the Canterbury House School, conducted by the Rev. F. Slaney Poole, M.A., and at St. Peter's College, where he captained the school rifle club. In 1911 he entered the Royal Military College of Australia at Duntroon, being one of the first South Australians to enter same, having proceeded from Adelaide with the son of Colonel F. M. Rowell, and at the time of joining the A.I.F. was within a year of completing a four-year course. His regimental number at Duntroon was "15," and at the outbreak of the Great War he had attained the rank of corporal. On August 14, 1914, with all the Duntroon cadets, he was gazetted a lieutenant in the A.I.F., and therefore held the distinction of being the first officer of the 10th Battalion to obtain a commission in the A.I.F. He was appointed a lieutenant in the 10th Battalion at Morphettville on August 19, 1914, and was posted to original "F" Company. At Morphettville he was placed in charge of the Battalion scouts, and subsequently embarked with the original Battalion on H.M.A.T. *All Ascanius* on October 20, 1914, and proceeded to Egypt. At Mena, in January, 1915, when his company merged with original "A" Company and became the new "A" Company, he was appointed a Platoon Commander in same. Whilst on the *Ascanius* he acted as Assistant Adjutant from November 1, 1914, to December 6, 1914, and at Mena was appointed secretary of the 10th Battalion sports, which were held on Christmas Day, 1914. He skilfully trained the scouts at Mena, and re-embarked on the *Ionian* with the Battalion for the Dardanelles. When practically at the eleventh hour before the landing 2nd Lieut. Robley was invalided from the *Ionian*, and thus prevented from taking part in the landing, he was appointed Machine Gun Officer in his stead. On the Saturday night preceding the landing he had efficiently prepared certain plans for Colonel S. P. Weir. At 10 o'clock that night, on board H.M.S. *Prince of Wales*, he lectured his men in one of the gun casements, and illustrated his remarks with sketches on one of the 6-inch guns.

His task after landing was to hurry on and reach the Turkish battery near the objective ridge, and with this end in view he had requested one of the ship's gunners to show his party how to damage a gun by burring the screw in the breach. He was amongst the first to land on the Peninsula, and on the tip of Ari Burnu south, which his party of 32 scouts of the 10th Battalion, reached the shore just after the first shot was fired. From the very onset he went about his duty in a fearless manner, which earned for him the admiration of both rank and file. Inspiriting his men, he cried, "Come on, boys; they can't hit you!" Instructing his men to leave their packs in the boats, he ran across the beach and cried, "10th Battalion scouts, are you ready?" With grim and fearless determination he led them up the height, the Turks firing over their heads. From the left-hand edge of the plateau above they could see the flash of a machine gun, and with great deliberation and dash he directed his scouts towards it. As the first men were reaching the 400 Plateau he and his men were silently advancing on the Turks, who seeing them approach in the dim light began to shoot. Rifle-fire came from the enemy somewhere on the heights across the valley, and with his men he stood for a few moments on the edge of a gravel precipice and studied his map. Then they all plunged down the path by the three enemy tents to their task of finding the enemy guns. Later that day he was in the act of firing one of the Battalion machine guns when he was mortally wounded in the head. His death was the first reported casualty in South Australia, and at a meeting of the Adelaide City Council in the afternoon of May 3, 1915, the same day as his casualty was released for publication, the Mayor of Adelaide (Mr. A. A. Simpson) made sympathetic reference to his death, when it was unanimously resolved that a letter of sympathy be sent to his parents. At the Norwood Council the same evening Alderman Essery referred to his death, when it was resolved that a letter of condolence be sent to his relatives. In one of his final letters to his father he wrote: "We have been given a very responsible piece of work, which will probably mean a large percentage of casualties, but will give us an opportunity to make a name for Australians." No. 172 Bugler H. A. Bartholomaeus, writing from Gallipoli after his death, referred to him as follows: "He was as brave a man as one could meet. If you had only been here to see him lead a charge you would have thought the same. He was simply wonderful, and it did our hearts good to be with a man like that." In another letter Bugler Bartholomaeus again referred to him: "Poor old Lieut. Eric Talbot Smith was killed, as you know. I was right alongside of him. He shouted, 'Come on, Australians; give them the bayonet. That's all they want,' and we charged up a big hill, but when we reached the top the Turks hadn't waited for us." He was posthumously mentioned in despatches by Sir Ian Hamilton in his first Dardanelles despatch, *vide London Gazette*, 5/8/15. At a monthly meeting of the council of the S.A. Institutes Association, of which his father was chairman, it was unanimously resolved that a letter of condolence be forward to his father. Colonel S. P. Weir, in a letter from Anzac to his mother, dated May 7, 1915, said: "Your son Eric died at his post bravely fighting for the Empire. He was among the first to land on Sunday, April 25, at about 4.15 a.m. He had charge of the scouts, and went about his duty in a fearless manner. After he had done all that was possible with his scouts, he took charge of our machine guns, and was in the act of firing one when he was wounded in the head. From the first we considered his wound would prove fatal, but he was taken aboard the hospital ship, and it was not until yesterday afternoon, when one of our wounded officers returned to duty, that I learned that Eric had passed away. I sincerely sympathize with you in your sad bereavement. Eric was a soldier who most certainly would have distinguished himself had he been spared. He proved himself of the greatest assistance during the training of the regiment at Mena. At Morphettville he had charge of the training of the Battalion scouts, whom he handled most skilfully. I was in close touch with him on the evening before we landed. He prepared some plans for me, little dreaming that we were to lose nearly half of our Battalion during the first twenty-four hours after landing."

52. SMYTH, TREVOR OWEN, was born in 1887, and was the elder of two sons of the late C. E. Owen Smyth, C.M.G., I.S.O., who for many years was Superintendent of Public Buildings, and on August 5, 1914, convened a patriotic demonstration in Victoria Square, Adelaide, founded the Adelaide branch of the Royal Society of St. George, and resided at "Egryn," Kensington Park. He was educated at St. Peter's College, and for some time had been associated with the Bank of New South Wales in Adelaide, first proceeding as a cadet to the bank's Cuthroo sheep station on the River Murray, and subsequently proceeding to Frome Downs Station. He was appointed a lieutenant in the 2nd Australian Infantry Regiment on May 19, 1908, at the time Colonel S. P. Weir was officiating as Adjutant of the regiment. During the last few years preceding the Great War he had lived principally in the back country of Northern Queensland, where he was looking for sheep land. He had decided to take up a small holding west of Rockhampton, and had paid a deposit on it. The outbreak of the Great War, however, altered his plans, and he returned immediately to Adelaide to enrol for overseas. He straightway enlisted as a private in the 10th Battalion at Morphettville, his regimental number being "625." On September 11, 1914, he was promoted to the rank of 2nd lieutenant, and appointed Transport Officer of the Battalion. He embarked with his Transport Section on H.M.A.T. A12 *Sadhana* on October 20, 1914, and proceeded to Egypt. He subsequently embarked with the Transport Section on the *Nizam* for the Dardanelles, and was sorely disappointed upon receiving instructions that the men of his section would not be permitted to land with the main body of the Battalion. He subsequently returned to Alexandria, where his horses were exchanged for mules, and returned to Lemnos Island. Still anxious to get his men on the Peninsula, he managed to get ashore himself, with the express object of making enquiries as to the possibility of his section eventually landing at Anzac. On the morning of May 16, 1915, when returning to the beach at Anzac, with the intention of re-embarking for Lemnos, he was killed by shrapnel. He was a man of a lovable disposition, of powerful physique, and a splendid horseman. He was noted for his skill with the rifle and revolver. No. 721 Driver P. Young, of the Battalion Transport Section, and one of his men, in writing from Lemnos after his death, said: "While there (Alexandria) our officer exchanged our horses for mules, as the horses were getting ship-weary, and he also reckoned we had a better chance of getting ashore (on Gallipoli) with mules. Poor fellow! He went ashore to get us off, and was right up in the firing-line

taking photos. He was killed on the beach when returning to the boat. He was one of the gamest and best." He had been recommended for a lieutenancy prior to his death, and same was confirmed on May 28, 1915.

53. SOMMERVILLE, ALFRED CYRIL, was born at Hindmarsh on January 21, 1887, and is a son of the late William S. Sommerville, who by occupation was a warehouseman. His brother, Lieutenant J. R. Sommerville, of the 27th Battalion, A.I.F., was killed in action in France during the Great War. At the outbreak of the war he was residing with his mother at Croydon, and was employed as a salesman by Colton, Palmer & Preston Ltd. He was educated at the Hindmarsh Public School, and in 1910 commenced his military career as a private in the old 10th Australian Infantry Regiment, and subsequently held the rank of corporal, and later sergeant. He was eventually transferred to the 7th Company of the Australian Signalling Corps. On December 9, 1912, he received his first commission as a 2nd lieutenant in the 78th (Adelaide Rifles) Infantry, and later commanded the Regimental Signallers of that unit. holding this commission at the time of joining the A.I.F. He was appointed a 2nd lieutenant in the 10th Battalion at Morphettville on August 19, 1914, and posted to original "E" Company. He embarked with the original Battalion on H.M.A.T. A11 *Ascanius* on October 20, 1914, and proceeded to Egypt. At Mena, in January, 1915, when his company merged with original "C" Company and became the new "B" Company, he was appointed a Platoon Commander in same and promoted to rank of lieutenant on February 1, 1915. He subsequently re-embarked with the Battalion on the *Ionian* for the Dardanelles, and landed with his company from the *Prince of Wales* at the historic landing on April 25, 1915. About 12.30 p.m. that day, upon reaching the 2nd Ridge, where the fighting was severe, he sustained a shrapnel injury to his left side, and was forced to evacuate. He remained in the firing-line until about 8 p.m. that night, when he was carried out and transferred to a destroyer. Under these distressing circumstances he remained for seven and a half hours in the thick of the fighting, until the conditions of nightfall permitted of his removal. He subsequently proceeded to Alexandria, where he was admitted to the Deaconess Hospital. Later he embarked on the hospital ship *Kyarra* for Australia, being the first South Australian officer who had been in action at the Dardanelles to return to Adelaide. The *Kyarra* made a direct run from Suez to Melbourne, there being fourteen N.C.O.'s and men of the 10th on board, this quota arriving in Adelaide on July 18, 1915. At first he confidently anticipated that his wound would not prevent him from rejoining the Battalion, but his best hopes were not realized, for he was eventually fitted with a surgical appliance, which he still wears. His services with the A.I.F. terminated on March 31, 1916, and on September 29, 1918, he married Constance Jean, daughter of the late T. I. Loutit, and sister of N. M. Loutit, who embarked with the original Battalion as a 2nd lieutenant. There is one daughter of the union. Returning to civil life, he commenced duties as Staff Officer in connection with the embarkation of A.I.F. troops, and in this capacity was stationed at Keswick Headquarters. He subsequently became a clerk in the Repatriation Commission as and from April 8, 1918, and retained this position until June 30, 1923. On July 9, 1923, he returned to Colton, Palmer & Preston Ltd. as a suburban traveller, but relinquished same on July 13, 1929. Since then he has followed various

business pursuits. During his absence from Australia he was promoted to the rank of lieutenant in the 78th (Adelaide Rifles) Infantry on July 1, 1915. On October 1, 1918, he was appointed a lieutenant in the 2/10 Infantry, and on October 1, 1920, was transferred to the Reserve of Officers with same rank. Upon his return to Adelaide from Egypt he refused to be interviewed by a representative of *The Register*, declining publicity, and also at the time did not feel equal to the task of relating his experiences. In August, 1914, an amusing inaccuracy occurred when an Adelaide daily paper published his photograph above the name of "Lieut. D. L. Todd," and after the Battalion embarked on the *Ascanius* a pictorial publication was issued by *The Advertiser*, giving the names of rank and file of the 10th Battalion, and his was the only officer's name omitted. At a meeting of the Hindmarsh Council on July 19, 1915, the Mayor of Hindmarsh (Mr. W. Wood) said it was a remarkable thing that the first wounded officer to arrive home resided in the Hindmarsh municipality. To Lieut. Sommerville he extended a hearty welcome home, and on behalf of the council expressed the hope that he soon would be sufficiently restored to normal health to return to the firing-line. The Town Clerk of Hindmarsh was instructed to convey these sentiments to him by letter. He is a member of the Payneham Masonic Lodge, No. 87, S.A.C., and in 1935 was residing at No. 9, Coolibah Avenue, Kensington Gardens.

54. STEELE, ALEXANDER, was born at Mount Gambier on August 20, 1888, and was educated at the Mount Gambier Grammar School. As a youth he worked for a bootmaker by the name of "Beevor," who was a member of the local volunteer corps, and whilst at this occupation undoubtedly became determined to embark upon a military career. On August 16, 1910, he joined the Instructional Staff of the Australian Military Forces, and for some considerable time was stationed at Gawler. He was subsequently transferred to the Royal Military College of Australia at Duntroon, where he was instructing at the time of joining the A.I.F. He was one of the first permanent officers to offer his services for overseas, and enlisted in the 9th Battalion at Brisbane, his regimental number being "41." He was subsequently appointed a staff sergeant-major, and placed in charge of the Machine Gun Section of the 9th Battalion. In 1914 he accompanied the original 9th Battalion on the *Omrah* to Egypt, and later proceeded on the *Ionian* to the Dardanelles, where he participated in the historic landing on April 25, 1915. He distinguished himself in the early fighting at Anzac, and was awarded the D.C.M., *vide London Gazette*, 3/6/15, the official citation being: "From 25th to 29th April, 1915, during operations near Gaba Tepe, for distinguished conduct in manning and maintaining his machine gun, which he continued to work after the remainder of his section had been killed or wounded." His rise to commissioned rank in the A.I.F. was rapid. On April 28, 1915, at Anzac, he was promoted to the rank of 2nd lieutenant, and on August 4, 1915, also at Anzac, he was made a lieutenant. He was promoted to the rank of temporary captain whilst at Gebel Habieta, Egypt, on January 28, 1916, and attained his full captaincy on February 20, 1916. He accompanied the 9th Battalion to France, where he received his majority on August 5, 1916, having previously been appointed to the command of the 3rd Machine Gun Company. He temporarily commanded the 10th Battalion during the absence on furlough of Lieut.-Colonel R. B. Jacob

from April 27 to May 11, 1917. During this period the Battalion moved into billets at Bancourt, and then into trenches via Fremicourt, the Bullecourt operation ensuing. This was the third occasion that an officer from another unit temporarily commanded the 10th. He was mentioned in despatches, and received the D.S.O., which was promulgated in the *London Gazette* amongst the New Year Honours on January 1, 1917. He commanded the 3rd Machine Gun Company from 1916-17, and was killed in action at Broodseinde on October 7, 1917, whilst temporarily commanding the 11th Battalion. He was engaged to be married, and went over the top singing "Drink to me only with thine eyes," but never completed the first line. He was regarded as a capable officer, keen on details, and a good soldier. It is interesting to note that "Steele's Post" on Gallipoli was not named after him, but after Major T. H. Steel, of the 14th Battalion, A.I.F.

55. STOPP, ERIC JOHN CARL, was born at Gawler on March 28, 1894, and is a son of Richard Charles Stopp, who for several years was a resident engineer in the South Australian Railways at Port Wakefield. He was educated at the Pulteney Street Grammar School and St. Peter's College, and at the outbreak of the Great War was residing at Kent Town, being employed as a clerk in the shipping department of D. & W. Murray, Ltd., of Gawler Place, Adelaide. He was a compulsory trainee, and received his first commission as a 2nd lieutenant in the 78th (Adelaide Rifles) Infantry on February 28, 1913, and held this commission at the time of joining the A.I.F. He was promoted to the rank of lieutenant in this regiment on August 24, 1914. He was one of the first South Australian officers to offer his services for overseas, and was appointed a 2nd lieutenant in the 10th Battalion at Morphettville on August 19, 1914, and posted to original "A" Company, but shortly after was transferred to original "B" Company. He embarked with the original Battalion on H.M.A.T. A11 *Ascanius* on October 20, 1914, and proceeded to Egypt. At Mena, in January, 1915, when his company merged with original "H" Company and became the new "C" Company, he was appointed a Platoon Commander in same, and promoted to rank of lieutenant on February 1, 1915. He subsequently embarked with the Battalion on the *Ionian* for the Dardanelles, and landed with his company from the *Prince of Wales* at the historic landing on April 25, 1915. On August 17, 1915, he was invalided seriously ill from the Peninsula, proceeding to the New Zealand Stationary Hospital at Port Said, and later re-embarked for Malta. He subsequently returned to South Australia, and on August 28, 1916, re-embarked at the Outer Harbour on H.M.A.T. A68 *Anchises* as O.C. of the 20th Reinforcements of the 10th Battalion. He proceeded to England, and on January 1, 1917, was seconded for duty with the 3rd Training Battalion at Durrington, where he was appointed Messing Officer under Lieut.-Colonel R. B. Jacob, the 2nd in Command being Capt. J. Hamilton. He was later transferred to the 2nd Training Battalion under Temp. Lieut.-Colonel John Newman, by whom he was appointed Training Adjutant. He eventually returned to South Australia, his services with the A.I.F. terminating on June 28, 1918. He was appointed a lieutenant in the 2/10 Infantry on October 1, 1918, and placed on the Unattached List on January 1, 1920. On April 11, 1923, he was transferred to the Retired List, but on May 3, 1923, was listed on Reserve of Officers with rank of lieutenant. On July 1, 1918, he was appointed private secre-

tary to his Excellency the Governor of Tasmania (Sir Francis Alexander Newdigate Newdegate). He retained this appointment until November 15, 1919, when he secured the position of secretary of the Hobart Stock Exchange, and also became owner of a racehorse. In 1925 he was appointed private secretary and A.D.C., with rank of honorary captain, to the Governor of Tasmania (Sir James O'Grady, K.C.M.G.), and held this position until February 1, 1927, when he was appointed private secretary to Major-General V. C. M. Sellheim, C.B., C.M.G., Administrator and Chief Magistrate of Norfolk Island. The Commonwealth Govt. subsequently appointed him postmaster, clerk, and assistant to the registrar of the magistrate's court as and from July 1, 1929. On July 1, 1930, he was further appointed Deputy Registrar of Lands, and on December 18 of the same year was appointed a Justice of the Peace and authorized to administer oaths and take affirmations for the purpose of any court within the territory of the island. On October 18, 1930, and during the absence on leave of the Collector of Customs, he was appointed Collector of Customs, Registrar of Magistrate's Court, Registrar of Births, Marriages and Deaths, Registrar of Wills, Probate, and Administration, and Curator of Intestate Estates. He was appointed Registrar of Motor Cars on October 18, 1930, and on January 19, 1931, his appointment as postmaster terminated, and he was reappointed Collector of Customs. He was appointed Inspector of Plants and Fruits on July 27, 1933. He is a member of St. Peter's Collegiate Masonic Lodge, No. 53, and at Sydney in May, 1927, married Miss Eileen Chancellor, there being two sons of the union. His married sister (Mrs. C. J. Fulton) resides at 111 North Terrace, Kensington Gardens. He was affectionately known to men of the 10th as "Stoppy", and in 1935 was residing at Kingston, Norfolk Island.

56. TODD, DAVID LESLIE, was born at Adelaide on June 29, 1891, and is a son of the late John Todd, who founded the engineering and blacksmithing firm of J. Todd & Son. He was educated at the Grote Street School, and from 1902-8 resided in Scotland, where he completed his education. For several years he was employed in a clerical capacity by the firm of Todd and Samuel, and three months before the outbreak of the Great War took up a position in the import department of D. & W. Murray Ltd. In 1909 he commenced his military career by joining the South Australian Scottish Corps, and whilst in this regiment became intimate with Lieut. W. S. Frayne, who also secured a commission in the original 10th Battalion, A.I.F. On July 1, 1912, when the universal training scheme was brought into operation he had attained the rank of corporal, and then voluntarily enlisted with the 76th (Hindmarsh) Infantry, in which he received his first commission as a 2nd lieutenant on October 28, 1912. He held this commission at the time of joining the A.I.F., and on August 24, 1914, was promoted to the rank of lieutenant in the same regiment. On August 5, 1914, when news of the declaration of war was officially received in Adelaide, he mobilized his company of the 76th (Hindmarsh) Infantry, and proceeded with it to Fort Largs, where he remained about a fortnight. On August 19, 1914, he was appointed a 2nd lieutenant in the 10th Battalion at Morphettville and posted to original "D" Company. He embarked with the original Battalion on H.M.A.T. A11 *Ascanius* on October 20, 1914, and proceeded to Egypt. At Mena, in January, 1915, when his company merged with original "G" Company and

became the new "D" Company, he was appointed a Platoon Commander in same and promoted to rank of lieutenant on February 1, 1915. He reembarked with the Battalion on the *Ionian* for the Dardanelles, and landed with his company from the destroyer *Scourge*. On May 25, 1915, he was promoted to the rank of temporary captain, and on August 4, 1915, he was only a few yards from his old associate of the Scottish Corps, Temp. Capt. W. S. Frayne, when he was mortally wounded by a Turkish sniper. On October 3, 1915, he evacuated the Peninsula with typhoid fever, and proceeded to England, where he was admitted to the 3rd London General Hospital at Wandsworth. Early in 1916 he entered the Details Camp at Weymouth, when Colonel Weir unsuccessfully attempted to have him placed on the same draft for Egypt as that in which he was proceeding. In March, 1916, he succeeded in getting away with the first draft after Colonel Weir's departure. He proceeded to Egypt and entered a camp near Giza, and then proceeded to Tel-el-Kebir, and had an interview with Lieut.-Colonel F. W. Hurcombe, with the result that he was immediately transferred to the 50th Battalion, then stationed on the Suez Canal Defences at Serapeum. On June 5, 1916, he embarked on the *Arcadian* and accompanied this battalion as part of the 13th Infantry Brigade, 4th Australian Division to France. He disembarked at Marseilles on June 12, 1916, and remained with the 50th Battalion until April 2, 1917, when at the fighting at Noreuil, with several others of his regiment, he was taken a prisoner of war by the Germans. His unit suffered severely in this action, losing more than half its strength. He remained a prisoner of war until after the Armistice, and in December, 1918, returned to England. He then remained in London on non-military employment until November, 1919. On April 12, 1919, at All Saints' Church, Langham Place, London, he married Violet Lilian, daughter of Mrs. V. L. Lawes, of Weymouth, there being two children of the union—John Trevor David, born in 1920, and Rosemary Lesley Trevor, born in May, 1923. He returned to Australia on the *Aeneas*, his services with the A.I.F. terminating on January 20, 1920. He entered the Public Service of South Australia on February 9, 1920, when he was appointed a clerk in the Soldier Settlement Department. On April 20, 1920, he was transferred to the accountant's branch, Department of Lands and Survey, but subsequently resigned from the Public Service on June 30, 1921. In July, 1921, he entered into partnership with his brother in the firm of J. Todd & Son, but in 1930 became sole proprietor of the firm. which is now carrying on business at 192 Pirie Street, Adelaide. On October 1, 1918, he was appointed a lieutenant in the 2/43 Infantry, and on August 1, 1920, was promoted to rank of captain. He was transferred to the 10th Battalion on March 31, 1921, and placed on Reserve of Officers on March 1, 1923. On October 28, 1925, he was transferred to the Active List of the 43rd Battalion, and on September 27, 1926, was again listed on Reserve of Officers. Capt. H. W. H. Seager, under date of May 3, 1915, writing to a friend from Anzac said *inter alia*: "Poor little Todd had a leg blown off." Capt. Seager whilst on the *Ionian* during the time of the landing, had been misinformed, but the receipt of his letter in Adelaide caused no little concern to Lieut. Todd's parents, who immediately dispatched cables in order to obtain verification or otherwise, and no one was better pleased than their son to be able to refute the misrepresentation of facts which had unfortunately occurred. He attained the rank of captain on May 9, 1916, and was affectionately known to the men of the 10th as "Toddy." In 1935 he was residing at 84 Burnside Road, Kensington Gardens. Prior to the war he was interested in swimming, and was a member of the Glenelg Amateur Swimming Club, and was one of the first South Australians to receive the bronze medallion of the Royal Life Saving Society.

57. WILDER-NELIGAN, MAURICE, was born at Tavistock, Devon, England, on October 2, 1882, and was a son of the late Rev. Canon John West Neligan, D.D., at one time Incumbent of Christ Church, Leeson Park, Dublin, and who for some time resided at Bray Head, Bray, County Wicklow, Ireland. He was an elder brother of the Right Rev. Moore Richard Neligan, B.A., M.A., D.D., who officiated as Bishop of Auckland, New Zealand, from 1903-10, and who died on April 24, 1922, whilst another brother, George Ernest Neligan, M.C., M.A., M.B., L.R.C.P., F.R.C.S., is a well-known Harley Street specialist, practising at 33 Wimpole Street, London West. He was educated at Queen Elizabeth's Grammar School, Ipswich, England, and the Bedford Grammar School, and it was generally believed that he had been at school with the late Lieut-General Sir H. B. Walker, K.C.B., K.C.M.G., D.S.O., Commander of the 1st Australian Division, with the result that both were intimate and lifelong friends. He had served as a captain in the exclusive Royal Horse Artillery—"The right of the line, pride of the regiment, and terror of the whole damned army," but being a romantic military figure, with a vivid and unique personality, he always more or less defied classification. It may be said that at times he was a mass of human contradiction, and concerning him numerous legends were in circulation. He was believed to be the scion of an influential English family and was highly connected, his blood relations including several eminent Anglican ecclesiastical dignitaries. He had been brought up in King Edward's household, had been a page boy to Queen Victoria, and boasted that the old Queen had boxed his ears. He was once on the staff of the Egyptian Government, had been connected with the Fijian Constabulary, and had a son in the British Navy who had attained the rank of submarine commander. Undoubtedly some of these things were true, but despite the many performances attributed to him which lacked authoritative verification he was always considered an educated and much-travelled man, possessed with a charming personality. During the war he possessed a London house at No. 10, Mount Street, near Park Lane, where his wife and daughter lavishly entertained, several officers of the 10th Battalion having partaken of their unstinted hospitality. He served in the Boer War, but for some considerable time after joining the A.I.F. did not wear his South African ribbons. He arrived in Australia a few years before the outbreak of the Great War, and straightway proceeded from Sydney to Queensland, where he subsequently officiated as clerk, Court of Petty Sessions, at Roma, and later his restless energy and initiative abilities found scope in a large sugar mill at Prosperine, where he was brought into considerable favour with his employers. At the outbreak of the war he was serving as a mounted trooper in the Queensland police, and shortly after the declaration of war in August, 1914, enlisted as a private in the 9th Battalion at Brisbane, under the name of "Maurice Wilder," his regimental number being "974." He often told the story of his enlistment. The recruiting clerk asked his name and age, and demanded to know what family ties he possessed. He declared his name, gave his correct

age, and owned to a wife and family. Whereupon he was informed that young and single men were offering in great numbers and he would not be required. Nothing daunted the wily Wilder, so he rejoined the queue and supplied amended particulars to another clerk. This time his age had dropped to 31 and he became a bachelor with no encumbrance. He emerged from that recruiting office under his second Christian name, which had been accepted as his surname, and as an approved volunteer for the A.I.F. he proceeded into camp at Enoggera with the 9th Battalion, commanded by Lieut.-Colonel H. W. Lee, V.D. He embarked as a corporal with the 9th Battalion at Brisbane on September 23, 1914, per H.M.A.T. A5 *Omrah*, which the next day sailed for Melbourne, being actually the first Australian transport to leave port with A.I.F. troops. At Melbourne his battalion was detained nearly a month awaiting the sailing of the First Australian Contingent. He subsequently accompanied the 9th Battalion to Egypt, where his knowledge of routine soon gained for him the rank of orderly-room sergeant. He proceeded on the *Ionian* to the Dardanelles, where as a member of the 3rd Brigade covering force he participated in the historic landing at Anzac on April 25, 1915. A few hours after the landing he was performing the work of an adjutant, and for some time, with Major A. G. Salisbury, of "A" Company of the 9th Battalion, was practically working the 9th Battalion. For his splendid work the day following the landing he was awarded the D.C.M., which was promulgated in the *London Gazette* amongst the King's Birthday Honours on June 3, 1915, the official citation being: "For conspicuous gallantry on 26th April, 1915, near Gaba Tepe (Dardanelles). Assisted by another non-commissioned officer, who was subsequently killed, he carried a wounded man into a place of safety under very heavy fire. Later on he was instrumental in collecting stragglers, who he led back into the firing-line." At Anzac, on April 28, 1915, he was promoted to the rank of 2nd lieutenant, and from the very beginning proved himself an outstandingly dashing leader. On May 19, 1915, during the Turkish onslaught, he unmistakably showed his capacity to command at a difficult moment. On May 27, 1915, he led a party of 63 men of the 9th Battalion on the right flank near Gaba Tepe, and in conjunction with the *Rattlesnake* completely hoodwinked the Turks who were holding a certain trench. As a preliminary the destroyer shelled the position by firing twenty rounds, after which he led his party to the trench, where twenty dazed Turks were in occupation. He ordered his men to use the bayonet, with the result that without firing a single shot six Turks were killed and captured, his party being enabled to return without sustaining a casualty. He was promoted to the rank of lieutenant on August 11, 1915, and on November 9, 1915, was promoted to the rank of temporary captain. About this time, for family reasons, he changed his name, the official gazettal being: "Lieut. (Temp. Capt.) Maurice Wilder having changed his name will in future be known as Maurice Wilder-Neligan, dated 9/11/15." As a temporary captain on the Peninsula it shortly after devolved upon him to temporarily command his battalion, owing to senior battalion officers being absent either through wounds or sickness. After the withdrawal from Gallipoli he proceeded to Egypt with the 9th Battalion, which was subsequently stationed on the Suez Canal Defences. In February, 1916, with the first appearance of Turkish patrols, he asked to be allowed to take out a patrol of camels and cut them off.

He was granted permission, but despite his daring and initiative no enemy were sighted. In March, 1916, he volunteered again to go out, and in conjunction with the Bikanir Camel Corps he made an extensive reconnaissance, and upon returning reported as follows: "It is quite certain that there have been no enemy patrols or other movements of recent date over any of the area." He was promoted to the rank of captain on March 12, 1916, and subsequently accompanied his battalion to France on the *Saxonia*. About this time he was appointed Adjutant of the 9th Battalion, and proudly recounted that he had enlisted as a private, had officiated as cook, batman, orderly-room corporal, orderly-room sergeant, intelligence officer, adjutant, and had held practically every job which the A.I.F. could offer. Flanders was undoubtedly a more congenial sphere for him than either Gallipoli or Egypt, for in the main it provided greater dangers and a broader setting for his dash and daring. It was in France and Belgium that he was destined to become a notable commander, a tactician and a diplomat. On the night of July 1-2, 1916, South of Fleurbaix, he conducted a raid, since described by Dr. C. E. W. Bean as "perhaps the most brilliant raid that Australians undertook." His party consisted of four officers, 144 other ranks, including two telephonists and two messengers. It was personally organized and led by him, being known as a "silent raid," there being no preliminary bombardment. At this time rumours had been circulated that the Germans expected the men of the A.I.F. to be black, so in order to create a most grotesque appearance, as well as strike terror into the heart of the Hun, he and several others of his raiding party had their faces blackened and streaked with phosphorus. During this raid he was severely wounded in the shoulder by a bomb, and a piece of shell ricochetted off the parapet and grooved his scalp, which mark he bore until his death; but nevertheless by sheer determination and perseverance he carried on and commanded throughout. After this raid he recommended that knuckleberries (short, stout sticks headed with bolts of iron) should in future be dispensed with. For this brilliant and dashing enterprise he was awarded the D.S.O., which was promulgated in the *London Gazette* on August 25, 1916, the official citation being: "For conspicuous gallantry when commanding a raid in force. His careful training and fine leading were responsible for the successes attained. Fifty-three of the enemy were killed and prisoners taken, besides a machine gun, many rifles, and much equipment. Though wounded in the head he stuck to his command." He was promoted to the rank of major on October 21, 1916, and in the Bullecourt action of May 6 and 7, 1917, he was in charge of a stubborn attack made by three companies of the 9th Battalion. On this occasion he was once again in his element, disregarding dangers at every turn. He made his first appearance with the 10th Battalion at Bray on June 23, 1917, when he temporarily took over the command of the Battalion from Lieut.-Colonel R. B. Jacob, who had been transferred to England. At this time he was junior to forty majors in the A.I.F., including Major F. G. Giles, D.S.O., who relieved him of the command of the 10th Battalion on June 30, 1917. It was confidently anticipated that as he was well down in the gradation list, Major Giles stood an excellent chance of being the officer selected to permanently command the 10th Battalion. To the astonishment of many Brigade and Battalion officers he returned to the 10th Battalion on July 15, 1917, with the rank of lieutenant-colonel, and retained the command of the

10th from that day until December 31, 1918, with the exception of several breaks, when he was temporarily relieved by Capt. G. C. Campbell, Major C. Rumball, Major G. D. Shaw, Lieut.-Colonel R. B. Jacob, Major J. Newman, Major W. F. J. McCann, and Capt. R. K. Hurcombe. He first appeared amongst the officers of the 10th in a somewhat dramatic and sensational manner. The officers were assembled in the Officers' Mess, and with frankness and deliberation were discussing the merits and demerits of having to serve under a junior major from the 9th Battalion. At this critical moment there was a knock on the door, and the newly-created Lieut.-Colonel M. Wilder-Neligan, D.S.O., D.C.M., stood before them. They all appeared nonplussed, and the atmosphere immediately became electrical. No one ventured to speak until he broke the silence. "Gentlemen," he said, "is no one going to offer your Colonel a seat?" Still silence reigned supreme. He continued, "Has no one anything to say?" Then with great presence of mind, and master of an exceedingly awkward situation, he said, "Then if *you* have nothing to say, *I* have a hell of a lot to say. This Battalion has never been a battalion, but I am now going to make it one. Cornish! you will be my Adjutant. We will start all over again, and the first Battalion Order issued will be No. 1. Take this down: 'The Battalion will move off in the morning for a destination unknown,' etc. Get the runners busy immediately and have this order distributed." In this extraordinary manner he installed himself amongst the officers of the 10th, and "became the commander of the most famous of all the South Australian battalions," *vide* Adelaide *Mail*, 21/4/27. He spoke French fluently, and at Chateau Segard, where the Countess gave a dinner to A.I.F. officers, he surprised all present by responding in French for at least fifteen minutes. His organizing powers as a Commanding Officer were first put to the test in the Polygon Wood action of September 19-22, 1917. For this engagement he had specially trained the 10th Battalion, organizing it into two special "storm companies." Before the operation commenced he promised leave to all those who distinguished themselves in the fighting, and, true to his word, a quota of officers and other ranks proceeded on special leave immediately after the Battalion moved out of the line. His operation order for Polygon Wood consisted of 28 folios, and is considered a master-piece of military art. It is now deposited at Base Records, Melbourne, and is an epitome, *par excellence*, of his military brilliance and sagacity. During the fighting at Polygon Wood he was positively brilliant, for whilst the actual fighting was in progress he inspirited all under his command, and whilst certain of his officers were reorganizing and waiting for the barrage to lift before proceeding with the advance he had specially detailed certain men of the 10th as "newspaper boys" to distribute copies of the *Daily Mail* and *Daily Mirror*, which he had specially procured. Next day he was billed in London by a certain newspaper as "The Eccentric Colonel." At one stage, when he ascertained that Lieut. Graham Leaver had been shot through the head he described his men as "going mad." There was never a greater organizer in the A.I.F., and his conduct of operations on the field of battle was never surpassed. He never went into battle unless he possessed definite plans to cover the average emergency, and on these lines he always prepared the 10th Battalion as thoroughly as human mind and human energy could contrive. He undeniably possessed a temperament of many contrasts; but his self-command, mental efficiency and agility were remarkable, and whether directing operations on the telephone, planning an operation, or writing a despatch, his remarkable latent capacity always permitted him to rise to the occasion, when his great powers as a leader were rarely extended. The 10th Battalion's long list of successes in 1918 was largely due to the brain and personality of this eclectic soldier of fortune. During his regime no failure ever marred the record of the Battalion. Many successful operations were achieved which were largely due to his aggressiveness, his initiative, his unconventionality, and his military brilliance. His scheme for the capture of Merris in June, 1918, for which he was awarded a Bar to his D.S.O., and which was promulgated in the *London Gazettee* on November 7, 1918, provided the 1st Australian Division with what was probably its neatest, and on a small scale, its most brilliant achievement. The whole operation was daring in the extreme, and typical and symbolical of the officer who propounded it. It was meticulously carried out according to plan, with the result that the village was isolated from the Germans behind it. The enemy garrison at Merris were unaware of the envelopment which was occurring, and even the German commander was tricked, for he confidently sent a message to his headquarters, describing how he had beaten off an attack on his front. But the "Wilder-Neligan" strategy triumphed and was eulogized by Army, Corps, Divisional, Brigade, and Battalion officers, who came in person to inspect the work that had been achieved and to offer their congratulations. Many British officers considered his attack on Merris to be the greatest one-battalion operation carried out in France. He was a keen believer in the Napoleonic maxim that "an army moves on its stomach," and no battalion was better fed than the 10th. He was always admired by rank and file alike for the indefatigable efforts he repeatedly made to have the front line rations delivered in suitable quantity and quality. Sentiment found no place in his complex nature, but he deemed it a crime to see his men go into action without ample supplies. Capt. J. G. Sinclair, of the 10th Battalion, wrote: "As a 'wangler' he was never eclipsed. He always made a point of owning a staff friend who would loan him a motor car or lorry. He gave regimental dinners—and his guests all paid their way. If he was short of wire for a 'stunt,' the C.R.E., who controlled wire supplies would be a certain guest. If he contemplated a special 'shoot' by the artillery when next he was to occupy the line, the commanding officer of that arm of the service would be sure of a dinner invitation. If his men were getting shabby the requisite officer would receive a pressing request to put aside an evening when he could be entertained by the Battalion. To make sure that he would obtain good supplies of clothing he adopted a simple yet effectual plan. He called a parade, and any man whose tunic showed the slightest signs of wear would find his C.O.'s finger inserted in the slightest hole, and the next instant a tear would be made which would quite disqualify the garment for further wear. Thus the 10th Battalion was noted for its smart appearance." He soon made his personality felt as Commander of the 10th, and though he played several exceptionally brilliant parts he never assumed the role of harbinger of peace and quiet. To be closely associated with him without paying the price was impossible. Eventually he quarrelled with practically all his closest associates within his Battalion—which was his kingdom. He was a great disciplinarian, but a law unto himself in respect to his methods of gaining results. He was the most regimental Commander the

Battalion had served under, and quite irrespective of the climatic rigours and the mud and slush of Flanders during the 1917-18 winter, it was a routine matter for him to have the Battalion drawn up for a C.O.'s inspection, when the slightest defect in equipment, rifle, or uniform would never escape his penetrating eye. He also had an exceedingly strong penchant for battalion drill, and apparently revelled in seeing his Battalion quick-marching, double-marching, wheeling, forming, inclining on a large open field. On the parade ground he was complete master, and delighted in issuing orders which would bewilder his officers, the while he roared out personal remarks through his megaphone to any hapless subaltern whom he detected in error. In fact, he never supervised battalion drill unless the officers of the 10th were more or less made to suffer with an inferiority complex. He evidently gained much satisfaction in seeing them puzzled and at a loss to carry out his instructions, when his parade ground remarks would only make things infinitely worse. At Bleu, early in September, 1917, he excelled himself on one of these occasions by completely staggering the Platoon Commanders. Mounted on his black pony, and with megaphone in hand, he so tangled his officers that in exasperation he finally chased them off the parade ground. Galloping after them a certain distance, he then returned to the parade ground and handed over the platoons to the platoon sergeants. Despite such eccentricities these interludes were invariably enjoyed by one and all, and within a few days all concerned would be the best of friends again. His renowned brigade parade, when he was acting-brigadier, "took the wind out of everybody's sails," and astonished officers and bewildered men have retained the memory of this occasion through the years that have followed. He was a splendid specimen of virile manhood, but never aspired to pose as a paragon of perfection. Even if he showed unmistakable traits of intense selfishness in his aims and ruthlessness in his methods, he possessed the magic touch with his men, and could invariably get the last ounce out of them. He was never a staunch believer of military etiquette, and if occasion warranted would not hesitate to reprove or admonish an officer before his men. On February 7, 1918, at the Aldershot Camp in Belgium, the Battalion Quarter Guard was paraded before him for inspection, but disgusted and dissatisfied with its appearance, he censured one and all responsible. To the astonishment of many men of the 10th gathered in the vicinity, as well as the guard itself, he ordered that the guard before him be dismounted and a new guard be immediately mounted, consisting of sergeant-majors and sergeants. This novel guard when mounted was duly paraded before him, much to the interest and amusement of officers and other ranks of the Battalion, who were finally relieved when they discovered he had proceeded on leave at midnight that day. Through the annals of British regimental traditions it would be difficult to find a precedent for such a unique battalion quarter guard. He possessed a quick wit, which held a rapier thrust for the unwary. In this respect he rarely let an occasion pass where a caustic reply would leave few in doubt as to its inference. A 10th corporal and his party were occupying a billet near Neuve Eglise early in 1918, when quite a number of empty bottles were deposited through a window. When inspecting that billet he seemed to be instinctively drawn towards that window, when his eyes immediately alighted on the "empties," whereupon he enquired of the corporal why they were there. The corporal suavely replied that they were there when his party moved into the billet. He sardonically replied, "Well, I have heard some lies in my time, but that is the best damn lie I have yet heard," and then passed on his round of inspection without further comment. He rarely indulged in conversation with his men, who invariably stood somewhat aloof, fearing he would maintain his reputation by finding fault with their appearance. In fact, very few men of the Battalion, whether in camps, billets, or the line had spoken to him, other than to receive orders or censure. He had a unique and inspiring manner of getting the best out of his officers in the field, and the following is a copy of a letter addressed by him to one of his officers during the Merris operation in June, 1918: "Dear Hurcombe—Best of good luck in your patrols. Don't place too much reliance on artillery to start with, as I won't be able to fix a new line until you have yours. The low-flying bird can be got, but read my memo. first, perhaps it may alter your idea about that for a bit. As you may not know yet, the 11th have boned Gerbedon Farm, which should help you a lot as a jump off. Allah be with you. You're too good to lose. Yours, M. Wilder-Neligan." (The low-flying bird mentioned was an aeroplane which he had instructed to fly low and drop results of observations to the officer of his patrol.) He was noted for his periodical outbursts of anger, and on occasions of this nature his language knew no bounds. At Messines, early in January, 1918, when the A.I.F. Artillery was inadvertently killing some of the 10th in the forward trenches, he telephoned the Officer Commanding the offending battery as follows: "You murderer! You hound of hell fire let loose! Man alive, your shells are dropping in my trenches and killing my men. If you don't increase your range, by the powers of Hades I'll come over and fix the damn lot of you." At Merris, on July 23, 1918, when he received instructions that Merris was not to be entered, he gave vent to his feelings, but with rage and disappointment tactfully worded his despatch to Brigade Headquarters: "and the ultimate withdrawal in obedience to the order of the Divisional Commander in no way mitigated its success (the operation)." At Lihons, on August 12, 1918, he was frantic at the non-arrival of certain tanks delegated to assist him in the advance; but when they arrived, and contrary to expectations, his anger melted, and he accepted the explanation offered by the Officer-in-Charge. Woe betide the officers or men who overstayed their leave, when he would not hesitate to heap coals of fire on the heads of the delinquents. As a technician he would concentrate on preparing the 10th Battalion for anticipated action. A model or map of the particular sector in which the fighting was likely to occur would be exhibited and demonstrations staged for the guidance of both officers and men. Officers would be posted to relative positions in accordance with his plans and expectation, and then excluding officers he would lecture to each platoon in sequence, constantly referring to positions and details as outlined on the model or map before them. He was an effective speaker and a brilliant conversationalist, and was never at a loss to instil confidence into his men, who would leave one of his lectures feeling that the impending attack in which they were to participate would be quite an ordinary manoeuvre, in which chances of failure had been considerably eliminated by the master mind of their C.O. behind the scenes. He always maintained a high opinion of the Australian soldier, and though he professed more confidence in the men than in their leaders, yet he was always the first to recognise

RECORDS OF SERVICE 249

and praise the initiative of the troops under his command. A Devonian by birth, he undoubtedly inherited in no small measure much of the traditional dash, fire, and brilliance common amongst such Elizabethan prototypes as Hawkins, Raleigh, Drake, and other men of Devon famous in history. With these rare gifts he stood out as "the most picturesque figure of South Australia's most picturesque battalion," *vide* Adelaide *Mail*, 21/4/27. He was wounded on three separate occasions and mentioned in despatches on four occasions, the first whilst serving with the 9th Battalion and the latter three whilst serving with the 10th Battalion, *vide London Gazette*, 2/1/17, 25/12/17, 28/5/18, and 31/12/18. He was affectionately known to men of the 10th at "Mad Wilder," and amongst divisional and brigade officers was referred to as "Neligan of the 10th." In 1934 the late Sir H. B. Walker, K.C.B., K.C.M.G., D.S.O., in a message of greeting to survivors of the 10th Battalion, referred to him as the "Gallant Wilder-Neligan." Dr. C. E. W. Bean in his "Official History of the A.I.F.," has referred to him as a "dashing leader," "a restless, daredevil officer, but free from the carelessness with which these qualities are often associated," "a gay, wild young Englishman, clever soldier, and inevitably a leader wherever he was," and "a mercurial commander." He led the 10th in several major actions during 1917-18, and subsequently through the final phase of the epic struggle. His career in the A.I.F. was phenomenal, inasmuch as he was one of a very select band who could claim the distinction of having enlisted as a private and attained the rank of lieutenant-colonel, commanding a battalion on active service for the best part of eighteen months. On March 30, 1918, he temporarily commanded the 9th Battalion, in which he first commenced his meritorious A.I.F. career. On June 3, 1918, he was awarded the C.M.G., and on October 10, 1918, was the recipient of the French Croix de Guerre. He was awarded more decorations than any other officer who commanded the 10th Battalion, and his C.M.G. was the highest decoration bestowed on a 10th C.O. His name, with its long string of decorations, is a self-explanatory way of illustrating the romantic nature of his career, and more remarkable still is the fact that no courtesy honours were included in his awards. After handing over the command of the Battalion to Major W. F. J. McCann, D.S.O., M.C. and Bar, he remained in France on Brigade and other duties until May 20, 1919. On this day, with the final 10th Battalion details, including the band, he left Chatelet and proceeded to Le Havre, and subsequently to Sandhill Camp, near Warminster, England. On July 18, 1919, with the final 10th Battalion detachment, he embarked at Devonport on the *Takada*, which arrived at the Outer Harbour, South Australia, on September 5, 1919. Continuing its journey to the Eastern States, the *Takada* arrived at Brisbane on September 9, 1919, but he had previously disembarked at Sydney, and consequently did not reach the Queensland capital until September 15, 1919. Upon his arrival in that city about fifty officers of the 9th and 49th Battalions assembled in his honour, and gave him an enthusiastic welcome. Major A. R. Knightley, M.C. (now Secretary of the Randwick Prince of Wales Hospital, Sydney), stressed the fact that Lieut.-Colonel Wilder-Neligan had started his A.I.F. career as a private, and had risen to his present rank in his own unit. During his five years' service with the A.I.F. he had made a success of every job he had undertaken, and had made a name, not only for himself, but for his old battalion. His wonderful progress was largely due to his personality, tact, and a unique manner of handling men. From the "brass hat" to the private he was not only admired but loved. Leaving Australia in 1914, a corporal with nothing on the breast of his tunic, he had returned to them a lieutenant-colonel with a double row of magnificent decorations, which were not only well earned, but thoroughly deserved. It was to be sincerely hoped that he would bring those sterling soldierly qualities to bear in respect of the civil life of the soldiers. Major Walsh said his career in the A.I.F. was a splendid example to all soldiers. He had won his rank and honours by sheer skill and bravery, the two characteristics which stood for most in the soldier. Capt. McIntyre, M.C., said his record wanted no "boosting." Australia wanted many more men of his calibre—men who knew what they wanted and then went and got it. In Queensland the "diggers" sadly lacked a forceful, virile leader, and no one was more admirably suited for that leadership than the man whose wonderful force had been a power in the A.I.F. The hope of the Queensland returned soldiers lay in their becoming a united force, and if Lieut.-Colonel Wilder-Neligan would make his influence felt in civil life, as he had done in the army, that force would ultimately become an established fact. In reply, Lieut.-Colonel M. Wilder-Neligan said that the returned officers should really try to do something for the returned "digger." Many of the returned soldiers did not appear to realize that they had their officers to fall back upon. It was the officers' duty to look after the men as they came back, especially those men who did not just know where to turn to find employment. "Let us try to make it a bit easier for the chap who comes back and doesn't quite know his way about." His services with the A.I.F. terminated on October 12, 1919, when his address was quoted, "Athenaeum Club, Melbourne." He subsequently interested himself in the formation in Queensland of a soldiers' parliamentary party, and toured the country delivering brilliant speeches from the back of a lorry. He was appointed a lieutenant-colonel in the Australian Military Forces on January 1, 1920, and on March 26, 1920, was transferred to the Australian Naval and Military Expeditionary Force to New Guinea with rank of lieutenant. For some time afterwards he lived a quiet life on the north coast of Queensland, and then returned to Brisbane on May 1, 1920, in order to take part with the returned men in the welcome accorded to Field-Marshal Sir William Birdwood on his first visit to Australia. On May 2, 1920, at an investiture conducted by Sir William Birdwood, he received his French Croix de Guerre. Later in 1920 he proceeded to Rabaul, New Guinea, where he was subsequently appointed District Officer at Talasea, with honorary rank of lieutenant-colonel. He was vested with police and magisterial powers, and travelled extensively through the wilds of his district. He died under tragic circumstances on January 10, 1923. With his faithful native servants, Yami and Kubik, to whom he was known as the "Kiap," he was proceeding to headquarters at Rabaul, and passing through the villages of Eurango and Pera Pera whilst on patrol duty, arrived at Ekerapi on January 6, 1923. He there directed his Chinese cook to convey his surplus belongings to Rabaul, and then divulged his intention of remaining at the Government Rest House for a few days. On the night of January 9, 1923, before finally retiring, he told both his native servants that he did not wish to rise early next morning. At 9 a.m. next day Yami made tea and went to rouse him, but upon calling him twice and grasping his hand discovered that he was dead. The natives of Ekerapi were then instructed to prepare a canoe, on which the body of the deceased was conveyed to the Government Rest Station at Garua. Threatening weather compelled the natives in the canoe to follow the coast instead of taking a more direct route, the journey taking twenty-six hours. The Medical Assistant (Francis John Giles) subsequently examined the body, and reported, *inter alia*, that the body was in a natural position of rest, the left hand quietly clasping the right wrist, and there were no external causes of death visible. At an inquisition held in the District Court at Talasea on January 11, 1923, Edward Taylor, the Acting District Officer, who officiated as coroner, certified that the cause of his death was unknown, and that there were no suspicious circumstances to suppose that death was due to other than natural causes. Lieut. C. R. Allanson, M.C., M.S.M., of the 10th Battalion, and now of Sydney, possesses certain copies of the depositions taken at the inquest in connection with his death. He is buried close to the sea on the hillside of a lonely island in New Guinea, and his isolated grave is marked by an elaborate monument impressive to his memory. The 10th Battalion A.I.F. Club was anxious that his remains, if possible, should be reinterred in the A.I.F. Cemetery, West Terrace, Adelaide, and with this object in view an expression of opinion was sought from his widow, who courteously replied that, whilst appreciating the great interest manifested by her late husband's comrades, she thought that if he had a say in the matter he would undoubtedly prefer that his grave should remain in the lonely outpost of Empire where his death had occurred. The 9th and 10th Battalion A.I.F. Clubs were willing to contribute to his monument, but Mrs. Neligan reluctantly declined such offers, and defrayed the cost herself. He will never be forgotten while any man of the 10th Battalion who served under him survives. For bravery, initiative, and military brilliance he was unrivalled. Despite his many eccentricities, he was every inch a born soldier, and no one could be associated with him for any length of time without perceiving that there was that indefinable "something" about him which invariably removed him so far from his contemporaries. Capt. J. G. Sinclair, of the 10th Battalion, A.I.F., in his article "The Colonel," published in the *Express and Journal* on February 28, 1923, wrote: "The Colonel is dead. Some very glowing drawbacks existed in his character, but as a soldier he was wonderfully endowed by Nature and training. It is safe to say that for years to come, whenever any of the old Battalion foregather, and throwing back their minds to the days of the war, let their tongues tell of the march, of camp, of trench, or of the battle-field, so long will his men bring to mind the words, and the ways, and the wisdom in war, of their old leader, the Colonel."

"He sleeps his last sleep, he has fought his last battle;
No sound can awake him to glory again."

Leonard Heath.

58. WILLSHIRE, WILLIAM STANLEY, was born on May 11, 1895, being the only son of his parents. He was a compulsory trainee under the universal training scheme which became operative on July 1, 1912, and received his first commission as a 2nd lieutenant in the 81st (Wakefield) Infantry on December 16, 1913, but was transferred with same rank to the 82nd (Barrier) Infantry on July 1, 1914, and held this commission at the

time of joining the A.I.F. At the outbreak of the Great War he was a commercial traveller by occupation, and was residing with his mother at Hebbard Street, South Broken Hill. He was popularly known in Broken Hill, and on account of his slender build was affectionately known as "Splinter." He was amongst the first quota of Broken Hill officers to offer his services for overseas, and was appointed a 2nd lieutenant in the 10th Battalion on August 19, 1914, but on September 19, 1914, his A.I.F. commission was cancelled, owing to his parents declining to give their necessary consent. He was on the strength of the 10th Battalion for exactly one month, but did not enter the Morphettville camp, subsequently proceeding to Fort Largs with citizen force trainees from Broken Hill. On May 28, 1915, he was reappointed a 2nd lieutenant in the A.I.F., and was posted to the 3rd Reinforcements of the 27th Battalion, with which he embarked at the Outer Harbour, South Australia, per R.M.S. *Morea*, on August 26, 1915, and subsequently served with his unit in Gallipoli, Egypt, and France. He was promoted to the rank of lieutenant on January 7, 1916, and attained his captaincy on March 19, 1917. Later in 1917 he was temporarily transferred to the newly-formed 70th Battalion, but upon subsequent disbandment of same returned to the 27th. In the Villers-Brettoneux fighting early in August, 1918, he distinguished himself, and was awarded the Military Cross, which was promulgated in the *London Gazette* on September 24, 1918, the official citation being: "For conspicuous gallantry and devotion to duty in action with his company. He led his men to the attack with great dash. During the consolidation, when other company commanders became casualties, he took charge of the front line, and moved about at great risk, supervising the consolidation. His energy and spirit were great factors in the success of the operations." He was subsequently killed in action in France on August 28, 1918, at Biaches, in the fighting near Peronne. After joining the 27th Battalion, A.I.F., he was promoted to the rank of lieutenant in the 82nd (Barrier) Infantry, on July 1, 1915.

XXI
DECORATIONS AND CITATIONS

10TH BATTALION RECIPIENTS OF THE VICTORIA CROSS.
"FOR VALOUR."

Official citations extracted from the *London Gazette* and arranged chronologically.

During the Great War 577 Victoria Crosses were bestowed on British soldiers, and of this number the Australian Imperial Force received 63. 18 were awarded to privates, 1 to a driver, 11 to corporals, 9 to sergeants, 18 to lieutenants, 5 to captains, and 1 to a major who at time was acting lieutenant-colonel.

1.   LIEUTENANT ARTHUR SEAFORTH BLACKBURN.
Original 10th Battalion.
Won at Pozieres, France, July 23, 1916.
Awarded September 9, 1916.

The 10th V.C. awarded to a member of the A.I.F., and the first won during the Great War by a South Australian or a member of the 10th Battalion.

"For most conspicuous bravery. He was directed with 50 men to drive the enemy from a strong point. By dogged determination he eventually captured their trench after personally leading four separate parties of bombers against it, many of whom became casualties. In face of fierce opposition he captured 250 yards of trench. Then after crawling forward with a sergeant to reconnoitre he returned, attacked and seized another 120 yards of trench, establishing communication with the battalion on his left."

2.   No. 506 PRIVATE REGINALD ROY INWOOD.
Original 10th Battalion.
Won at Polygon Wood, East of Ypres, September 19-22, 1917.
Awarded November 26, 1917.

The 33rd V.C. awarded to a member of the A.I.F. and the second won by a member of the 10th Battalion.

"For most conspicuous bravery and devotion to duty during the advance to the second objective. He moved forward through our barrage alone to an enemy strong post and captured it, together with 9 prisoners, killing several of the enemy. During the evening he volunteered for a special all-night patrol, which went out 600 yards in front of our line, and there —by his coolness and sound judgment—obtained and sent back very valuable information as to the enemy's movements. In the early morning of September 21, Pte. Inwood located a machine gun which was causing several casualties. He went out alone and bombed the gun and team, killing all but one, whom he brought back as a prisoner with the gun."

3.   No. 1327 CORPORAL PHILLIP DAVEY, M.M.
2nd Reinforcements, 10th Battalion.
Won at Merris, France, June 28, 1918.
Awarded August 17, 1918.

The 39th V.C. awarded to a member of the A.I.F. and the third and final won by a member of the 10th Battalion.

"For most conspicuous bravery and initiative in attack. In a daylight operation against the enemy position, his platoon advanced 200 yards, capturing part of the enemy line, and whilst the platoon was consolidating, the enemy pushed a machine gun forward under cover of a hedge and opened fire from close range, inflicting heavy casualties and hampering work. Alone, Corporal Davey moved forward in the face of a fierce point-blank fire, and attacked the gun with hand grenades, putting half the crew out of action. Having used all available grenades, he returned to the original 'jumping-off' trench, secured a further supply, and again attacked the gun, the crew of which had in the meantime been reinforced. He killed the crew, eight in all, and captured the gun. This very gallant N.C.O. then mounted the gun in the new post and used it in repelling a determined counter-attack, during which he was severely wounded. By this determination Corporal Davey saved the platoon from annihilation and made it possible to consolidate and hold a position of vital importance to the success of the whole operation."

MOST DISTINGUISHED ORDER OF SAINT MICHAEL AND SAINT GEORGE.

Appointment for services rendered in connection with Military Operations in France and Flanders: Additional Member of the Third Class or Companion of the said Most Distinguished Order—

LIEUT.-COLONEL MAURICE WILDER-NELIGAN, D.S.O., D.C.M., *vide London Gazette*, 3/6/18. (King's Birthday Honours).

COMPANIONS OF THE DISTINGUISHED SERVICE ORDER.

Official citations extracted from the *London Gazette* and arranged chronologically.

Distinguished Service Orders were awarded either for distinguished service in the field or specific acts of gallantry. Five 10th Battalion Officers were decorated for the former and four for the latter, and one was awarded a Bar to the D.S.O., which he won whilst serving in another A.I.F. unit. In two cases the details of services were gazetted some time after the award had first been promulgated in the *London Gazette*.

1. MAJOR FRANCIS MAXWELL DE FRAYER LORENZO.
Original 10th Battalion Officer.
Won during Defence of Anzac, April 25-November 21, 1915.
Gazetted November 8, 1915.
"For distinguished service in the field during the operations at the Dardanelles."

2. CAPTAIN GEORGE CHARLES MAGENIS.
Original 10th Battalion R.Q.M.S.
Won during service in France, chiefly at Mouquet Farm, August 19-23, 1916.
Gazetted January 1, 1917 (New Year's Honours).
"For distinguished service in the field."

DECORATIONS AND CITATIONS 255

3. **LIEUT.-COLONEL STANLEY PRICE WEIR.**
(Honorary Colonel) 1st C.O. of 10th Battalion.
Won during service in France, chiefly at Pozieres, July 22-25, 1916.
Gazetted January 1, 1917 (New Year's Honours).
"For distinguished service in the field."

4. **MAJOR FELIX GORDON GILES.**
Original 10th Battalion Officer.
Won during service in France.
Gazetted June 4, 1917 (King's Birthday Honours).
"In recognition of services in the prosecution of the war."

5. **LIEUTENANT ALEXANDER WILLIAM LAUCHLAN MacNEIL.**
(L.T.M. Battery.)
Formerly Private in original Battalion.
Won East of Bullecourt, France, May 6, 1917.
Gazetted August 16, 1917.
"For conspicuous gallantry and devotion to duty. He handled his mortar with great courage and determination against an overwhelming attack. He held off the enemy with his revolver until his men had got the mortar away to safety. He then took part in the counter-attack, and did great execution with a machine gun."

6. **MAJOR STANLEY VERE APPLEYARD.**
(Australian Army Medical Corps, M.O. attached to 10th Battalion.)
Won at Polygon Wood, France, September 19-22, 1917.
Gazetted November 19, 1917.
Details gazetted March 23, 1918.
"For conspicuous gallantry and devotion to duty. He established a forward dressing station immediately in rear of the front line during an attack and attended continuously to the wounded, frequently going out and dressing cases in the open under heavy shell fire. His dressing station was hit by a shell, and, though he was badly shaken, he continued his work with great determination and devotion to duty. His fearlessness was an inspiration to all, and was the means of saving many lives."

7. **MAJOR CHARLES FRANCIS MINAGALL**
Original 10th Battalion Officer.
(Quartermaster and Honorary Major.)
Won during service in France.
Gazetted January 1, 1918 (New Year's Honours).
"For distinguished service in the field."

8. **BAR TO D.S.O.—LIEUT.-COLONEL MAURICE WILDER-NELIGAN, C.M.G., D.S.O., D.C.M.**
Commanding Officer of 10th Battalion, 1917-18.
Won at Merris, France, July 29-30, 1918.
Gazetted November 7, 1918.
"For conspicuous gallantry in a night attack on a village. Owing to his skill and courage, the plan of enveloping the village was successfully carried out, resulting in the capture of 200 prisoners and 30 machine guns. The attacking force suffered less than 20 casualties."

9. CAPTAIN (Temp. Major) WILLIAM FRANCIS JAMES McCANN, M.C.
Formerly Sergeant in original 10th Battalion.
Won near Lihons, France, August 10, 1918.
Gazetted February 1, 1919.

"For conspicuous gallantry and devotion to duty near Lihons on August 10, 1918. After the attack had failed at Crepey Wood, he successfully captured the position with his company in face of very heavy fire; and, when the enemy in greatly superior numbers counter-attacked, he held them off, personally killing many of the enemy, and exposing himself freely until reinforcements enabled him to drive off the enemy and re-establish his original line. His courage and fine leadership prevented an important position falling into the hands of the enemy."

10. LIEUTENANT WILLIAM STANLEY BENNETT, M.C.
Transferred to Battalion in France in September, 1917.
Won near Villeret, France, September 18, 1918.
Gazetted March 15, 1919.
Details gazetted July 30, 1919.

"For most conspicuous gallantry near Villeret on September 18, 1918. Whilst leading his platoon with the first wave he observed a nest of machine guns firing through our barrage and holding up our advance. He ran out ahead of his men into the barrage, worked his way round to the rear of the nest, and shot five of the enemy with his revolver, made 30 men surrender, and captured their five guns. Thanks to this fine action, which was accomplished single-handed under a hail of bullets, the advance was enabled to continue."

RECIPIENTS OF THE MILITARY CROSS.

Awarded in recognition of gallantry and devotion to duty in the field.
Official citations extracted from the *London Gazette* and arranged chronologically.

Thirty-four officers of the 10th Battalion were awarded the Military Cross and four were awarded a Bar to the M.C. In four instances the award was not made for any specific act of gallantry, but was conferred for general services in France.

1. CAPTAIN WILLIAM FRANCIS JAMES McCANN. Won at Pozieres, July 23, 1916.

"For conspicuous gallantry in action. He led his company in the attack, bombing the enemy back, and, in spite of heavy casualties, pressed forward until severely wounded by a bomb."

Vide London Gazette, 1/9/16.

2. CAPTAIN GORDON CATHCART CAMPBELL. Won at Pozieres, July 23, 1916.

"During a bomb attack on the German trenches he exhibited great courage and marked ability as a leader. In addition to directing and serving his Lewis machine guns which he commanded, he showed great energy and organizing powers by arranging bomb teams to replace the heavy casualties which we were suffering. He exhibited great gallantry, skill, and leadership. Three men in succession who were assisting him on the gun which he was working were killed, and when he could no longer work his guns with effect, he stood on the parapet of the Germans' trench and threw bombs thereon. He also had his Lewis gun fired at the enemy whilst resting on his shoulder."

Award *vide London Gazette*, 1/1/17. (New Year's Honours.)
Details *vide* Colonel Weir's Recommendation.

3. 2ND LIEUTENANT WILLIAM ROCKLIFF MONTGOMERY, M.M. Won at "Hill 60," Ypres, September 24-25, 1916.

"For conspicuous gallantry in action. On one occasion when he and two men were buried, he extricated himself, and at once set to work to dig out the men. He fought his trench mortars with great courage and determination throughout the operation."

Vide London Gazette, 12/12/16.

4. CAPTAIN CLARENCE RUMBALL. Won at Le Barque, February 25, 1917.

"For conspicuous gallantry and devotion to duty. He made several reconnaissances of unknown ground under heavy fire, and by his quick appreciation of the situation and prompt action greatly assisted in the success of the operations."

Vide London Gazette, 26/4/17.

5. No. 470 REGIMENTAL SERGEANT-MAJOR GEORGE GUTHRIE.
"For services in France."

Vide London Gazette, 4/6/17. (King's Birthday Honours.)

6. 2ND LIEUTENANT NORMAN DOUGALL. (Posthumous.) Won at Louverval, April 7-11, 1917.

"For conspicuous gallantry and devotion to duty. He organized and gallantly led forward a counter-attack which drove the enemy back, and undoubtedly saved a critical situation."

Vide London Gazette, 12/6/17.

7. LIEUTENANT ALFRED THOMAS HILL. Won at Boursies, April 15-17, 1917.

"For conspicuous gallantry and devotion to duty. He led his platoon forward in the face of a very hostile fire, and was largely responsible for checking the enemy's advance at a critical time."

Vide London Gazette, 12/6/17.

8. LIEUTENANT DOUGLAS JOHN WALSH. Won at Louverval, April 7-11, 1917.

"For conspicuous gallantry and devotion to duty. Although wounded, he led his men forward in the most gallant manner, and succeeded in driving the enemy out of the trench."

Vide London Gazette, 12/6/17.

9. CAPTAIN WALTER GORDON CORNISH. Won at Bullecourt, May 4-9, 1917.
"For conspicuous gallantry and devotion to duty. He led his company from the reserve line to the firing-line through heavy artillery barrage, where he rendered the greatest assistance in clearing up the situation. Two hours after entering the trench he had captured fifty yards of the new enemy trench and ten prisoners. Throughout he showed a fine example of leadership and courage under heavy fire."
Vide London Gazette, 14/8/17.

10. LIEUTENANT ERIC MURRAY INGLIS. Won at Bullecourt, May 6, 1917.
"For conspicuous gallantry and devotion to duty. When under heavy hostile shell fire a bomb dump was set on fire. He at once dashed forward and assisted to remove the boxes and extinguish the fire, thus preventing a serious explosion. His prompt action undoubtedly saved many lives."
Vide London Gazette, 14/8/17.

11. LIEUTENANT SYDNEY SYLVANUS MILLS. Won at Bullecourt, May 7, 1917.
"For conspicuous gallantry and devotion to duty. Under heavy bombardment by the enemy he carried out the work of consolidation. His section of the trench was repeatedly blown in, but with great tenacity and courage he hung on and prevented the enemy from regaining his position."
Vide London Gazette, 14/8/17.

12. BAR TO M.C.—CAPTAIN GORDON CATHCART CAMPBELL, M.C. Won at Polygon Wood, September 19-22, 1917.
"For conspicuous gallantry and devotion to duty. While his battalion was assembling for an attack it came under a very heavy enemy barrage. With great coolness and determination, and utter disregard of personal safety, he reorganized his own company, and then assisted in reorganizing the rest of the battalion. Throughout the operations his work was admirable, and he was largely responsible for the success achieved."
Vide London Gazette, 16/11/17.
Details, 19/3/18.

13. CAPTAIN ROY KINTORE HURCOMBE. Won at Polygon Wood, September 19-22, 1917.
"For conspicuous gallantry and devotion to duty. His company came under a heavy barrage when assembled for the attack. By his determination, cheerfulness, and disregard of danger he reorganized the company and led it successfully to the final objective, and consolidated the captured position. His ability and untiring energy contributed largely to the success of the operation."
Vide London Gazette, 16/11/17.
Details, 19/3/18.

14. LIEUTENANT ARTHUR GEORGE KLENNER. Won at Polygon Wood, September 19-22, 1917.

"For conspicuous gallantry and devotion to duty. Single-handed he captured an enemy machine gun which was holding up the advance and captured or killed the whole of the team. When the final objective was captured he showed great judgment in placing his men so that heavy casualties were inflicted on the enemy."

Vide London Gazette, 16/11/17.
Details, 19/3/18.

15. 2ND LIEUTENANT MAGNUS GRAHAM SAUNDERS. Won at Polygon Wood, September 19-22, 1917.

"For conspicuous gallantry and devotion to duty. His platoon came under a heavy barrage, and, though badly shaken by the explosion of a shell, he collected his men and led them successfully to the final objective. He consolidated the position, and by his splendid example and cheerful manner he kept his men steady under difficult circumstances."

Vide London Gazette, 16/11/17.
Details, 19/3/18.

16. 2ND LIEUTENANT HOWARD WILSON SCUDDS. Won at Polygon Wood, September 19-22, 1917.

"For conspicuous gallantry and devotion to duty in leading his platoon against a strong point which was holding up the advance. His prompt and skilful action enabled the advance to continue, and he then led his platoon to the capture of the final objective. He showed great ability and fearlessness during the consolidation."

Vide London Gazette, 16/11/17.
Details, 19/3/18.

17. LIEUTENANT HAROLD WILLIS REID. Won at Zonnebeke, September 30, 1917.

"For conspicuous gallantry and devotion to duty when in command of his platoon during nine days' operations. When the company guides became casualties he led his platoon forward to the correct position under a heavy enemy barrage. After his trench was heavily bombarded he cleared it and reorganized the defence."

Vide London Gazette, 14/12/17.
Details, 23/4/18.

18. LIEUTENANT CLEVE JAMES SCOTT. Won at Hollebeke, March 1-2, 1918.

"For conspicuous gallantry and devotion to duty during an enemy raid on his position. From a post on the right of the one raided he at once opened Lewis gun and rifle fire, causing the enemy many casualties. He drove off the attack upon his own post, and fired on the enemy while they were returning to their own lines. He then reconnoitred the position under heavy artillery and machine-gun fire, re-established the raided post and assisted in bringing in the wounded. He acted throughout with a total disregard of danger, and set a splendid example to his men."

Vide London Gazette, 13/5/18.

19. LIEUTENANT THOMAS LEO CORCORAN.
"For services in France."

Vide London Gazette, 3/6/18.
(King's Birthday Honours.)

20. LIEUTENANT WILLIAM HARVEY BLAKE. Won at Merris, May 29-30, 1918.
"For conspicuous gallantry and devotion in charge of a platoon of his battalion in an attack on enemy posts. Although wounded in both hands, early in the action, he continued to lead his platoon, rushed objective, capturing and consolidating it under heavy machine-gun fire. Later with three men he rushed an enemy machine-gun post, killing the garrison and bringing back portion of the gun. Although badly wounded, he remained on duty until his post had been consolidated. His splendid courage and example throughout were admirable."

Vide London Gazette, 16/9/18.

21. LIEUTENANT FREDERICK JAMES STANLEY MEAD, D.C.M. Won at Merris, June 2-3, 1918.
"For conspicuous gallantry and devotion to duty in operations when he was responsible for the moving of bombs to a captured objective. His skilful handling of the carrying parties, and his courage and untiring energy in leading them forward through the hostile artillery and machine-gun fire, enabled new dumps to be established, and thus greatly helped with the consolidation of the new position. Throughout the operations his coolness and splendid example enabled the supply of material to the troops in the forward positions to be kept up."

Vide London Gazette, 16/9/18.

22. LIEUTENANT LEONARD RALPH STEPHENS. Won at Merris, June 2-3, 1918.
"For conspicuous gallantry and fine leadership in charge of a platoon in action. He led his men with great courage and skill, and on gaining the objective immediately began the work of consolidation. Throughout the operations his splendid example greatly encouraged all ranks with him."

Vide London Gazette, 16/9/18.

23. 2ND LIEUTENANT ERNEST PERCY ORMAN. Won at Merris, June 1-2, 1918.
"For conspicuous gallantry and devotion to duty in command of a fighting patrol sent out to obtain identification from an enemy position at a farm. Finding the farm strongly held, and large enemy working parties in the vicinity, he sent back his patrol, and with his platoon sergeant made a careful reconnaissance of the position under machine-gun and rifle fire. Next night, when his company attacked over the same ground, he led his platoon with great dash, and captured three machine guns and eighteen men."

Vide London Gazette, 24/9/18.

24. BAR TO M.C.—LIEUTENANT HOWARD WILSON SCUDDS, M.C. Won at Merris, June 28, 1918.
"For conspicuous gallantry and determination in leading his platoon forward to the attack. By good leadership and skilful handling he

quickly reached his objective and inflicted heavy casualties on the enemy. Later, with one of his platoon, he moved forward again and captured a machine gun and five prisoners."
Vide London Gazette, 15/10/18.

25. LIEUTENANT GEORGE SIDNEY LIGHTBODY. Won at Merris, July 22-23, 1918.

"For conspicuous gallantry during an attack. He led his platoon brilliantly, shooting three of the enemy himself and accounting for three more while making a reconnaissance in front of his post. After gaining his objective he established touch with the flanks. He set a fine example of cool determination and courage."
Vide London Gazette, 7/11/18.

26. LIEUTENANT FRANCIS ERNEST PENNINGTON, D.C.M. Won at Merris, July 22-23, 1918.

"For conspicuous gallantry while commanding a platoon during an attack. Discovering a party of the enemy in a house in front of his post, he went forward with one man, under cover of Lewis gun fire, and after throwing a bomb into the house rushed it and captured nine prisoners. He showed splendid dash and resourcefulness."
Vide London Gazette, 7/11/18.

27. LIEUTENANT WILFRED DREW SHARLAND. Won at Merris, July 22-23, 1918.

"For conspicuous gallantry and devotion to duty. He led his platoon with great dash during an attack. With one N.C.O. he crept forward and rushed an enemy post, capturing a machine gun and seven prisoners. He set a fine example of courage and determination."
Vide London Gazette, 7/11/18.

28. LIEUTENANT RICHARD GRAHAM SMITH. Won at Merris, July 22-23, 1918.

"For conspicuous gallantry and devotion to duty. When in charge of a fighting patrol he attacked an enemy post, capturing the two machine guns and killing the garrison. After reaching his objective he withdrew his men most ably under heavy fire, making full use of the captured guns. He set a fine example of courage and good leadership."
Vide London Gazette, 7/11/18.

29. BAR TO M.C.—CAPTAIN ROY KINTORE HURCOMBE, M.C. Won at Merris, July 29-30, 1918.

"For conspicuous gallantry and devotion to duty during an attack. He led his company splendidly, and with great dash gained his objective, after which he personally led an attack on a machine-gun nest and accounted for many of the enemy. Later he captured an officer and two men. He set a very fine example to all under his command."
Vide London Gazette, 7/11/18.

30. BAR TO M.C.—CAPTAIN WILLIAM FRANCIS JAMES McCANN, M.C. Won at Merris, July 29-30, 1918.

"For conspicuous gallantry and fine leadership during an attack. He led one of the attacking companies with great dash, and helped very materially in the success of the operation. Wherever the situation was most critical he was to be found directing and encouraging his men, and his fine example inspired all under his command."

Vide London Gazette, 7/11/18.

31. 2ND LIEUTENANT LEONARD WALTER COLLETT. Won at Lihons, August 11, 1918.

"For conspicuous gallantry during operations near Lihons. He led his platoon with great dash through very heavy shell and machine-gun fire, and, by skilful use of ground, penetrated the enemy's positions, capturing three machine guns, seven prisoners, and inflicting severe casualties."

Vide London Gazette, 1/2/19.

32. LIEUTENANT ARTHUR EUGENE MINING. Won at Lihons, August 11, 1918.

"He displayed great gallantry in the fighting before Lihons, on 10th-12th August, 1918, and in the defence of Crepey Wood. When the company on his flank withdrew and most of his men had become casualties, he very skilfully extricated the remainder and reinforced a neighbouring post, which was in serious difficulties. It was largely due to his action that the position was saved."

Vide London Gazette, 1/2/19.

33. LIEUTENANT WILLIAM STANLEY BENNETT. Won at Justice Wood, August 23, 1918.

"For conspicuous gallantry and devotion to duty on 23rd August, 1918, near Cappy, when he found his platoon strongly opposed from Justice Wood. He crept forward with a small party regardless of his personal safety, and outflanking the enemy, forced them to retire. This effort greatly facilitated the day's advance."

Vide London Gazette, 1/2/19.

34. LIEUTENANT WILLIAM OSBORNE COOPER. Won at Luc Wood, August 23, 1918.

"For conspicuous gallantry and devotion to duty. In clearing Luc Wood on 23rd August, 1918, he led his platoon against three enemy machine-gun nests in succession, and by his dash succeeded in overwhelming the enemy resistance before the remainder of his company got up. His fine example assisted the main advance considerably."

Vide London Gazette, 1/2/19.

35. CAPTAIN WILLIAM HOWARD PERRY. Won at Jeancourt, September 18, 1918.

"In the operations near Jeancourt, on 18th September, 1918, he was in charge of the attacking line. Under the most difficult conditions caused by darkness, smoke, and the barrage, he led his men with complete accuracy to the jumping-off line and the second objective, and then quickly organized and sent out patrols to exploit forward. Throughout the attack he showed marked gallantry and splendid control of his men. He was wounded early in the attack, but carried on."

Vide London Gazette, 11/2/19.
Details, 30/7/19.

36. LIEUTENANT JOHN WILLIAM SEARCY. Won at Jeancourt, September 18, 1918.

"In the operations near Jeancourt on 18th September, 1918, he was responsible for the direction of the Battalion. In order to successfully fulfil his task under very difficult circumstances he fearlessly exposed himself, advancing up to and across our barrage frequently in order to correct direction. His gallantry was an inspiration to all who saw him, and contributed largely to the morale which carried so few men so long a distance."

Vide London Gazette, 11/2/19.
Details, 30/7/19.

37. LIEUTENANT (Temp. Captain) JAMES DAVIDSON. "For services in France."

Vide London Gazette, 1/1/19.

38. LIEUTENANT CHARLES REDDIE ALLANSON, M.S.M. "For services in France."

Vide London Gazette, 3/6/19.

RECIPIENTS OF THE DISTINGUISHED CONDUCT MEDAL.

Awarded for acts of gallantry and devotion to duty in field.
Official citations extracted from the *London Gazette* and arranged chronologically.

1. No. 122 PRIVATE C. P. GREEN. Won at Anzac Landing, April 25, 1915.

"For conspicuous gallantry on the 25th April, 1915, during the landing at Gaba Tepe (Dardanelles). He had reached shelter on the beach, when he saw a wounded man struggling in the surf, which was under heavy fire. Without hesitation, he turned back, reached the man in the water, and brought him successfully to shore, and subsequently to a place of shelter."

Vide London Gazette, 6/9/15.

2. No. 456 PRIVATE J. C. WEATHERILL. Won at Anzac, April 25, 1915.

"On April 25, 1915, during operations near Gaba Tepe, for exceptionally good work in scouting and in an attack resulting in the capture of two of the enemy's guns."

Vide London Gazette, 3/6/15.

3. No. 1157 CORPORAL V. G. R. McDONALD. Won during Defence of Anzac, 1915.

"For conspicuous gallantry. He threw his greatcoat over a bomb, and held it down till the bomb exploded, thereby probably saving several casualties."

Vide London Gazette, 3/6/16.
Details, 20/6/16.

4. No. 882 PRIVATE G. E. A. BAKER. Won at Anzac, November 7, 1915.

"For conspicuous gallantry at Anzac, Gallipoli Peninsula, on 7th November, 1915. One of the enemy's shells fell in a gun-pit, exploded seven rounds of 18-pr. ammunition, and set fire to the brushwood, threatening a magazine containing 300 rounds of 18-pr. ammunition. Private Baker was one of a small party which beat out the fire, regardless of the danger of being blown up by the explosion of the magazine."

Vide London Gazette, 15/3/16.

5. No. 2593 PRIVATE R. L. BONYTHON. Won at Pozieres, July 22-25, 1916.
"For conspicuous gallantry in action. Though wounded in the head, he refused to withdraw, and, working his way round the enemy's flank, used his machine gun with great effect."

Vide London Gazette, 20/10/16.

6. No. 2948 PRIVATE D. H. McKENZIE. Won at Pozieres, July 22-25, 1916.
"For conspicuous gallantry in action. When the N.C.O.'s had become casualties, he took charge of the bayonet team, and, though three times knocked over by shells, continued to lead them with great dash."

Vide London Gazette, 20/10/16.

7. No. 324 SERGEANT F. J. S. MEAD. Won at Mouquet Farm, August 19-23, 1916.
"For conspicuous gallantry during operations. He went out and directed a platoon which had lost its way, under heavy shell fire. On other occasions he has done fine and gallant work."

Vide London Gazette, 20/10/16.

8. No. 248 CORPORAL A. WHITE. Won at "Hill 60," Ypres, September 24-25, 1916.
"For conspicuous gallantry in action. Although wounded he remained at his post and fought his trench mortar with great gallantry." (Attached to 3rd Light Trench Mortar Battery.)

Vide London Gazette, 13/2/17.

9. No. 3132 PRIVATE ELISHA WILLIAMS. Won at Bullecourt, May 5-9, 1917.
"For conspicuous gallantry and devotion to duty. Although wounded and a section of the trench had been captured, he calmly continued to send through the S.O.S. signal, thereby enabling the brigade to call down the S.O.S. barrage without delay."

Vide London Gazette, 2/8/17.

10. No. 5712 PRIVATE H. T. PALMER. Won at Bullecourt, May 5-9, 1917.
"For conspicuous gallantry and devotion to duty. During a hostile attack a Lewis gun was knocked out of action, the crew becoming casualties, by the enemy. He, though wounded at the time, managed to secure the gun and get it into action again, inflicting many losses on the enemy, who by this time were retreating. He continued to serve his gun single-handed until wounded a second time."

Vide London Gazette, 31/7/17.

DECORATIONS AND CITATIONS 265

11. No. 621 SERGEANT (Temp. Sergeant-Major) E. S. LEWIS. Won at Bullecourt, May 5-9, 1917.

    "For conspicuous gallantry and devotion to duty. When all his officers had been killed he took charge of his company during a heavy hostile attack, and displayed qualities of leadership and courage that were beyond praise. He personally and at great risk, under heavy fire, dug out two men who had been buried by a shell in their trench, thereby saving their lives. His splendid example had a wonderful effect upon the men."

    Vide London Gazette, 17/7/17.

12. No. 116 COMPANY SERGEANT-MAJOR E. G. WILSON, M.M. Won at Polygon Wood, September 19-20, 1917.

    "For conspicuous gallantry and devotion to duty in reorganizing and steadying the men after they were caught in the enemy barrage. When the company ran short of bombs and ammunition he organized a party and by skilful handling had very few casualties, bringing up ammunition when required."

    Vide London Gazette, 1/3/18.

13. No. 503 REGIMENTAL SERGEANT-MAJOR E. A. HOLLAND. Won at Merris, May 29-30, 1918.

    "For conspicuous gallantry and devotion to duty in night operations against hostile posts, when he showed the greatest courage and efficiency in arranging and leading forward carrying parties to the front lines. Later he took charge of a mobile section of rifle grenadiers, and moved the party with great courage from place to place, silencing a hostile machine gun and allowing a consolidation to be pushed on. His leadership and devotion to duty under heavy machine-gun fire and bombing was beyond praise."

    Vide London Gazette, 3/10/18.

14. No. 5734 CORPORAL A. J. DUNCAN, M.M. Won at Merris, June 28, 1918.

    "For conspicuous skill and courage during a daylight operation, when he advanced with his platoon and captured an enemy post. To cover consolidation he pushed his Lewis gun forward under heavy fire. In spite of losing the whole crew, he kept his gun in action, silencing one enemy machine gun and keeping down the fire of two others, thus enabling his platoon to consolidate in time to resist a heavy counter-attack."

    Vide London Gazette, 30/10/18.

15. No. 7103 LANCE-CORPORAL R. S. BEATTY, M.M. Won at Jeancourt, September 18, 1918.

    "For most conspicuous gallantry and dash. In the operations near Jeancourt, on 18th September, 1918, he, followed by his section, rushed a machine-gun nest in a small quarry, and in face of heavy fire advanced, firing his Lewis gun from the hip. He succeeded in putting one of the enemy gun crews out of action, and swept the parapet of the trench. Having ordered six prisoners to the rear, he handed his Lewis gun over to his section, and with bombs and a revolver mopped up the remaining

enemy in the quarry. His total captures from this quarry were 3 officers, 43 other ranks, and three machine guns. He did splendid work."
Vide London Gazette, 8/3/19.
Details, 2/12/19.

16. No 2263 LANCE-CORPORAL S. CURYER. Won at Jeancourt, September 18, 1918.

"In the operations near Jeancourt, on 18th September, 1918, whilst carrying his Lewis gun, he got somewhat in advance, but under heavy machine-gun fire he immediately brought his gun into action, and by his determined use of same drove one of the crew of five men to surrender, whilst two others fled. Later, he engaged a low-flying enemy 'plane, and caused it to make a forced landing on fire. He showed great gallantry and initiative throughout."
Vide London Gazette, 8/3/19.
Details, 2/12/19.

10TH BATTALION RECIPIENTS OF THE MILITARY MEDAL.

Awarded for bravery in the field.
Extracted from *London Gazette* and arranged chronologically.

MILITARY MEDAL AND TWO BARS.

2700 Corporal (afterwards Sergeant) C. A. Williams.
    M.M. won at Bullecourt, May 5-9, 1917, *vide London Gazette*, 4/6/17.
    1st Bar won at Polygon Wood, September 19-22, 1917, *vide London Gazette*, 12/12/17.
    2nd Bar won at Merris, July 29-30, 1918, *vide London Gazette*, 29/3/19.

MILITARY MEDAL AND ONE BAR.

890 Cpl. H. J. Edwards. M.M. won at Pozieres, July 22-25, 1917, *vide London Gazette*, 10/11/16.
    Bar won at Mouquet Farm, August 19-23, 1916, *vide London Gazette*, 16/11/16.

2696 L.-Cpl. R. Turpin. M.M. won at Mouquet Farm, August 19-23, 1916, *vide London Gazette*, 16/11/16.
    Bar won at Bullecourt, May 7, 1917, *vide London Gazette*, 17/7/17.

4390B Pte. A. M. M. Buik. M.M. won at Bullecourt, May 6-9, 1917, *vide London Gazette*, 17/7/17.
    Bar won at Polygon Wood, September 19-22, 1917, *vide London Gazette*, 17/12/17.

2860 Cpl. G. T. Easther. M.M. won at Zonnebeke, October, 9, 1917, *vide London Gazette*, 19/3/18.
    Bar won at Warneton, January 3, 1918, *vide London Gazette*, 2/4/18.

DECORATIONS AND CITATIONS

3734 Cpl. A. J. Duncan. M.M. won at Louverval, April 15, 1917, *vide London Gazette*, 14/6/17.
    Bar won at Hollebeke, March 1-2, 1918, *vide London Gazette*, 25/4/18.

9 Sgt. C. B. McIvor. M.M. won at Polygon Wood, September 19-22, 1917, *vide London Gazette*, 12/12/17.
    Bar won at Merris, July 29-30, 1918, *vide London Gazette*, 24/1/19.

355 Sgt. W. Faint. M.M. won at Merris, July 22-24, 1918, *vide London Gazette*, 24/1/19.
    Bar won at Merris, July 29-30, 1918, *vide London Gazette*, 29/3/19.

1959 Pte. C. Holt. M.M. won at Merris, May 20-30, 1918, *vide London Gazette*, 7/10/18.
    Bar won at Lihons, August 11, 1918, *vide London Gazette*, 13/3/19.

2761B Cpl. G. L. Pike. M.M. won at Pozieres, July 22-25, 1916, *vide London Gazette*, 16/11/16.
    Bar won at Lihons, August 11, 1918, *vide London Gazette*, 13/3/19.

3864 L.-Cpl. H. E. Beaton. M.M. won at Merris, July 29-30, 1918, *vide London Gazette*, 24/1/19.
    Bar won at Jeancourt, September 18, 1918, *vide London Gazette*, 17/6/19.

MILITARY MEDAL.

GALLIPOLI.

455 Cpl. C. Rule. Won at Anzac, April 25, 1915, *vide London Gazette*, 27/10/16.

617 C.S.M. W. H. Ebborn. Won at Anzac, November, 1915, *vide London Gazette*, 27/10/16.

514 Sgt. W. R. Montgomery. Won at Anzac, November, 1915, *vide London Gazette*, 27/10/16.

FRANCE.

Pozieres, July 22-25, 1916.

3041 L.-Cpl. D. C. Jacob	*Vide London Gazette,*	21/9/16
3210 Pte. W. E. J. Boama	*Vide London Gazette,*	21/9/16
1342 Pte. G. F. Foote	*Vide London Gazette,*	21/9/16
162 Sgt. W. Dommett	*Vide London Gazette,*	20/10/16
447 Sgt. L. C. Wickham	*Vide London Gazette,*	20/10/16
1356 Pte. A. J. Holt	*Vide London Gazette,*	20/10/16
2566 L.-Cpl. D. Barr	*Vide London Gazette,*	16/11/16
2745 Pte. J. Macmillan	*Vide London Gazette,*	16/11/16

Mouquet Farm, August 19-23, 1916.

333 Cpl. S. C. Coffey	*Vide London Gazette,*	16/11/16
4449 Pte. T. Campbell	*Vide London Gazette,*	16/11/16
1474 Pte. J. Russell	*Vide London Gazette,*	16/11/16
771 Pte. P. Straney	*Vide London Gazette,*	16/11/16

Le Barque, February 24-25, 1917.

1456 L.-Cpl. C. Davey	Vide London Gazette,	11/5/17
2587 L.-Cpl. R. Davey	Vide London Gazette,	11/5/17
815 Pte. W. C. Attwood	Vide London Gazette,	11/5/17
4472 Pte. J. V. Glanville	Vide London Gazette,	11/5/17
3970 Pte. R. F. Witte	Vide London Gazette,	11/5/17

Louverval, April 15, 1917.

3634B Sgt. J. Young	Vide London Gazette,	14/6/17
4640 Cpl. J. M. Marion	Vide London Gazette,	14/6/17
2622B Pte. W. B. Crispe	Vide London Gazette,	14/6/17
6081 Pte. J. R. Marks	Vide London Gazette,	14/6/17
5713 Pte. R. K. Humphries	Vide London Gazette,	14/6/17
3813 Pte. C. Mitchell	Vide London Gazette,	14/6/17
3948 Pte. A. F. Von Duve	Vide London Gazette,	14/6/17
2454A Sgt. H. C. Milton	Vide London Gazette,	19/3/18

Bullecourt, May 7, 1917.

2714 Sgt. R. E. Mitchell	Vide London Gazette,	14/6/17
5184 Pte. H. J. Purvis	Vide London Gazette,	14/6/17
388 Sgt. F. E. Allchin	Vide London Gazette,	17/7/17
1800 Sgt. H. G. Radbone	Vide London Gazette,	17/7/17
116 Sgt. E. G. Wilson	Vide London Gazette,	17/7/17
1418 T. Cpl. J. Sprott	Vide London Gazette,	17/7/17
5765 L.-Cpl. R. N. Varcoe	Vide London Gazette,	17/7/17
1086 Pte. R. Fisher	Vide London Gazette,	17/7/17
2611 Pte. T. R. Giles	Vide London Gazette,	17/7/17
6068 Pte. B. J. Halliday	Vide London Gazette,	17/7/17
3366 Pte. R. R. Montgomery	Vide London Gazette,	17/7/17
2964 Pte. A. C. Sailing	Vide London Gazette,	17/7/17
4594 Pte. C. R. Wallace	Vide London Gazette,.	17/7/17

Polygon Wood, September 19-22, 1917.

2829 Sgt. L. M. Cowley	Vide London Gazette,	12/12/17
5338 Cpl. R. E. Adcock	Vide London Gazette,	12/12/17
772 Cpl. F. M. Bradley	Vide London Gazette,	12/12/17
2846 L.-Cpl. P. J. R. Harrison	Vide London Gazette,	12/12/17
3469 Cpl. W. P. Chinner	Vide London Gazette,	12/12/17
6218A Cpl. S. E. Rigney	Vide London Gazette,	12/12/17
532 L.-Cpl. W. J. Rawlins	Vide London Gazette,	12/12/17
5026 Pte. W. D. Allbrecht	Vide London Gazette,	12/12/17
551 Pte. G. R. Bates	Vide London Gazette,	12/12/17
5351 Pte. G. W. Davis	Vide London Gazette,	12/12/17
2641A Pte. E. O. Fidge	Vide London Gazette,	12/12/17
5242 Pte. E. L. Wilkins	Vide London Gazette,	12/12/17
144 L.-Sgt. J. P. Becker	Vide London Gazette,	17/12/17
2128 Cpl. C. C. Cooke	Vide London Gazette,	17/12/17
6301 Pte. J. P. Morris	Vide London Gazette,	17/12/17

Zonnebeke, September 30 to October 9, 1917.

1010 Sgt. A. H. Jackson	Vide London Gazette,	28/1/18
3242 Sgt. F. T. A. Wood	Vide London Gazette,	19/3/18

DECORATIONS AND CITATIONS

3638	Pte. R. M. Bell	*Vide London Gazette,*	19/3/18
4638	Pte. J. W. R. L. C. Scobie	*Vide London Gazette,*	19/3/18
4578	Pte. A. T. Smith	*Vide London Gazette,*	19/3/18
6584	Pte. H. E. Spencer	*Vide London Gazette,*	19/3/18
2817B	Pte. A. Vale	*Vide London Gazette,*	19/3/18

Celtic Wood, October 9, 1917.

1194	Cpl. E. Williams	*Vide London Gazette,*	19/3/18
493	Pte. L. A. Green	*Vide London Gazette,*	19/3/18
3882	Pte. D. A. Rhodes	*Vide London Gazette,*	19/3/18
5228	Pte. C. C. Toll	*Vide London Gazette,*	19/3/18
1841	Pte. T. Wilson	*Vide London Gazette,*	19/3/18

Warneton, January 3, 1918.

1327	L.-Cpl. P. Davey	*Vide London Gazette,*	2/4/18

Hollebeke, March 1-2, 1918.

2246	Sgt. S. Ball	*Vide London Gazette,*	25/4/18
2849	L.-Cpl. F. J. J. Baker	*Vide London Gazette,*	25/4/18
5410	Pte. G. F. J. Kotz	*Vide London Gazette,*	25/4/18
7288	Pte. F. J. Roach	*Vide London Gazette,*	25/4/18

Merris, May 20-29, 1918.

2647B	Pte. H. T. Fyfe	*Vide London Gazette,*	15/10/18
3181	Pte. M. Musgrave	*Vide London Gazette,*	7/10/18

Merris, May 29-30, 1918.

362	Sgt. R. King	*Vide London Gazette,*	7/10/18
7437	Sgt. W. J. Mitchell	*Vide London Gazette,*	7/10/18
113	Pte. L. K. T. Fry	*Vide London Gazette,*	7/10/18

Merris, June 2-3, 1918.

963	Sgt. J. L. Partridge	*Vide London Gazette,*	7/10/18
2765B	Sgt. E. A. Pullen	*Vide London Gazette,*	7/10/18
2381	Cpl. W. E. Hanson	*Vide London Gazette,*	7/10/18
2242	L.-Cpl. W. V. Wright	*Vide London Gazette,*	7/10/18
2813	Pte. T. H. Morris	*Vide London Gazette,*	7/10/18
6089	Pte. T. Perkins	*Vide London Gazette,*	7/10/18
2760B	Pte. J. H. Phillips	*Vide London Gazette,*	7/10/18

Merris, June 28, 1918.

2187	Sgt. P. C. Leathley	*Vide London Gazette,*	15/10/18
6244	L.-Cpl. E. M. Edwards	*Vide London Gazette,*	15/10/18
5126	L.-Cpl. A. K. Harris	*Vide London Gazette,*	15/10/18
6463	Pte. G. Groves	*Vide London Gazette,*	15/10/18

Merris, June 30, 1918.

217	Sgt. T. Mooney	*Vide London Gazette,*	15/10/18
5187	L.-Cpl. J. H. Quinn	*Vide London Gazette,*	15/10/18
7334	Pte. V. A. Hall	*Vide London Gazette,*	15/10/18
5404	Pte. J. R. Mitchell	*Vide London Gazette,*	15/10/18
700	Pte. T. Ryan	*Vide London Gazette,*	15/10/18
952	Dvr. H. E. Jacobs	*Vide London Gazette,*	15/10/18

Merris, July 22-24, 1918.

7103	L.-Cpl. R. S. Beatty	*Vide London Gazette,*	24/1/19
63A	Pte. F. W. Fry	*Vide London Gazette,*	24/1/19
1769	Pte. H. Lorymer	*Vide London Gazette,*	24/1/19

Merris, July 26, 1918.

1469 Sgt. E. Mann	*Vide London Gazette,*	24/1/19
6606 Sgt. A. Warner	*Vide London Gazette,*	24/1/19
6607 Cpl. H. B. Bassham	*Vide London Gazette,*	24/1/19
7219 Pte. W. A. Cilento	*Vide London Gazette,*	24/1/19
964B Pte. D. Winter	*Vide London Gazette,*	24/1/19

Merris, July 29-30, 1918.

131 Sgt. A. G. P. Neave	*Vide London Gazette,*	24/1/19
2057 L.-Cpl. F. T. Elvidge	*Vide London Gazette,*	24/1/19
2739 L.-Cpl. D. J. Melville	*Vide London Gazette,*	24/1/19
5340 Pte. A. Bache	*Vide London Gazette,*	24/1/19

Lihons, August 11, 1918.

3504B Sgt. H. A. Green	*Vide London Gazette,*	14/5/19
3 Sgt. R. T. White	*Vide London Gazette,*	14/5/19
2609B Cpl. G. F. Clarke	*Vide London Gazette,*	14/5/19
1935 L.-Cpl. C. T. Howe	*Vide London Gazette,*	14/5/19
6574 L.-Cpl. S. H. Quicke	*Vide London Gazette,*	14/5/19
3460B Pte. C. J. S. Bott	*Vide London Gazette,*	14/5/19
4446 Pte. L. H. Broadbent	*Vide London Gazette,*	14/5/19
6969 Pte. R. P. S. Brooks	*Vide London Gazette,*	14/5/19
1316 Pte. C. W. Busbridge	*Vide London Gazette,*	14/5/19
6988 Pte. F. Cain	*Vide London Gazette,*	14/5/19
3477 Pte. J. P. Davies	*Vide London Gazette,*	14/5/19
6508 Pte. A. R. Fisher	*Vide London Gazette,*	14/5/19
6783 Pte. W. C. Manser	*Vide London Gazette,*	14/5/19
3267 Pte. G. G. Nutt	*Vide London Gazette,*	14/5/19
5170 Pte. P. Olds	*Vide London Gazette,*	14/5/19
5174 Pte. R. H. Pearman	*Vide London Gazette,*	14/5/19
1795 Pte. J. W. Pitick	*Vide London Gazette,*	14/5/19
7313 Pte. F. S. Williams	*Vide London Gazette,*	14/5/19

Jeancourt, September 18, 1918.

2568B Sgt. C. F. B. Schenscher	*Vide London Gazette,*	17/6/19
1587 Sgt. J. C. Wickham	*Vide London Gazette,*	17/6/19
244 Cpl. A. Glover	*Vide London Gazette,*	17/6/19
3585B Cpl. J. H. Priest	*Vide London Gazette,*	17/6/19
3451 Cpl. J. F. Zwolsman	*Vide London Gazette,*	17/6/19
6464 L.-Cpl. J. J. Heffernan	*Vide London Gazette,*	17/6/19
3553B L.-Cpl. B. F. Murphy	*Vide London Gazette,*	17/6/19
2630B Pte. P. J. Dowd	*Vide London Gazette,*	17/6/19
2865B Pte. R. J. Simpson	*Vide London Gazette,*	17/6/19
1801 Dvr. W. Rayner	*Vide London Gazette,*	20/8/19
2825 L.-Cpl. N. C. Collings	*Vide London Gazette,*	30/1/20
2365 Pte. E. Gardiner	*Vide London Gazette,*	30/1/20

MERITORIOUS SERVICE MEDAL.

In recognition of valuable service rendered with the Armies in France and Flanders, and for gallantry in the performance of military duty.

371 T.R.Q.M.S. J. Boyle	*Vide London Gazette,*	17/6/18

DECORATIONS AND CITATIONS

531 S. Sgt. E. L. Randell (Arm. Sgt., A.O.C.)	*Vide London Gazette*, 17/6/18
3682 Sgt. C. Barker	*Vide London Gazette*, 18/1/19
2584A S. Sgt. J. V. Bartlett (Aus. Section, 3rd Echelon)	*Vide London Gazette*, 18/1/19
967 Sgt. H. H. Coffin	*Vide London Gazette*, 18/1/19
5186 Sgt. W. D. Pyle	*Vide London Gazette*, 18/1/19
1571 Sgt. D. Morton	*Vide London Gazette*, 3/6/19
2755 Cpl. C. F. Pavey	*Vide London Gazette*, 3/6/19
6848 Pte. (T. Cpl.) J. N. Winkworth	*Vide London Gazette*, 3/6/19

FOREIGN DECORATIONS.

Decorations and Medals awarded by the Allied Powers at various dates to members of the 10th Battalion, A.I.F., for distinguished services rendered during the course of the Campaign. His Majesty the late King has given unrestricted permission in all cases to wear the Decorations and Medals in question.

RUSSIAN.

Conferred by Field-Marshal His Imperial Majesty the late Emperor of Russia.

Order of St. Anne (2nd Class with Swords).
Hon. Colonel Stanley Price Weir, D.S.O., V.D.
Vide London Gazette, 13/2/17.

FRENCH.

Conferred by the President of the French Republic.

Croix de Guerre.

Lieut.-Col. M. Wilder Neligan C.M.G., D.S.O. and Bar, D.C.M.	*Vide London Gazette*, 10/10/18
Lieutenant W. R. Jenkins	*Vide London Gazette*, 17/3/20
2791 C.S.M. W. G. Slocombe	*Vide London Gazette*, 7/1/19

Croix de Guerre avec Palme.

Captain W. G. Cornish	*Vide London Gazette*, 20/9/19

Medaille Militaire.

503 R.S.M. E. A. Holland	*Vide London Gazette*, 1/5/17

BELGIAN.

Conferred by His Majesty the late King of the Belgians.

Croix de Guerre.

847 L.-Cpl. J. Henry	*Vide London Gazette*, 12/7/18
3739 Sgt. M. A. Earl	*Vide London Gazette*, 12/7/18
5218 L.-Cpl. A. W. Swanson	*Vide London Gazette*, 5/4/19

Decoration Militaire.

2128 L.-Cpl. C. C. Cooke	*Vide London Gazette*, 14/9/17

ITALIAN.

Conferred by His Majesty the King of Italy.

The Bronze Medal for Military Valour.
1946 Cpl. T. F. Whiting (formerly Griffith), attached to L.T.M. Battery.
Vide London Gazette, 26/5/17.

MENTIONED IN DESPATCHES.

Extracted from *London Gazette* and arranged chronologically.

1. BY GENERAL SIR IAN HAMILTON, Commander-in-Chief of the Mediterranean Expeditionary Force:—

    1st Dardanelles Despatch, dated 12/6/15,
    Vide London Gazette, 5/8/15.

Lieut. E. W. T. Smith (posthumous)	413 Pte. J. C. Weatherill
122 Pte. C. P. Green	

2nd Dardanelles Despatch, dated 22/9/15 (Supplementary to 26/8/15),
Vide London Gazette, 5/11/15.

Major F. W. Hurcombe	7 M.G. Sgt. E. G. Sawer
Major F. M. de F. Lorenzo	3 O.R. Sgt. B. B. Leane
Captain C. Rumball	234 C.S.M. G. F. Henderson

3rd Dardanelles Despatch, dated 11/12/15,
Vide London Gazette, 28/1/16.

Lieut. F. H. Hancock	500 Corporal T. Hill
Lieut. F. G. H. N. Heritage	1157 Pte. V. G. R. McDonald

2. BY GENERAL SIR CHARLES MONRO, Commander-in-Chief of the Mediterranean Expeditionary Force:—

    Dardanelles Despatch, dated 10/4/16, *vide London Gazette*, 11/7/16.
    1157 Pte. V. G. R. McDonald

3. BY FIELD-MARSHAL SIR DOUGLAS HAIG, G.C.B., Commander-in-Chief of British Armies in France:—

    Despatch dated 13/11/16, *vide London Gazette*, 2/1/17.

Colonel S. P. Weir	Capt. H. N. Henwood
Major G. E. Redburg	Capt. R. K. Hurcombe
Major G. D. Shaw	Lieut. E. M. Inglis
Capt. G. C. Magenis	

Despatch dated 9/4/17, *vide London Gazette*, 1/6/17.

Major F. G. Giles	531 S. Sgt. E. L. Randall
Hon. Major C. F. Minagall	84 C.Q.M.S. A. G. Klenner
Lieut. F. J. Scott	

Despatch dated 7/11/17, *vide London Gazette*, 28/12/17.

Lieut.-Colonel M. Wilder-Neligan	1336 C.S.M. S. A. Dyer
Major S. V. Appleyard (A.A.M.C.)	2791A Pte. W. G. Slocombe
Hon. Major C. F. Minagall	5218 Pte. A. W. Swanson
Lieut. T. L. Corcoran	

Despatch dated 7/4/18, *vide London Gazette*, 28/5/18.

Lieut.-Colonel M. Wilder-Neligan	Lieut. A. Limb
Capt. W. G. Cornish	503 R.S.M. E. A. Holland

Despatch dated 8/11/18, *vide London Gazette*, 31/12/18.

Lieut.-Colonel M. Wilder-Neligan	Lieut. A. Limb
Lieut. J. Davidson	3457 Sgt. A. Bartlett

DECORATIONS AND CITATIONS

Despatch dated 16/3/19, *vide London Gazette*, 11/7/19.

Major W. F. J. McCann	71 C.Q.M.S. C. W. Amber
Capt. W. G. Cornish	2861 Sgt. L. W. Featherstone
Capt. J. G. Sinclair	(Aus. A. Pay Corps)
Lieut. W. S. Bennett	5270 T.C.Q.M.S. S. W. Howie

MENTIONED IN ARMY CORPS ROUTINE ORDERS, GALLIPOLI, 1915.
(Incomplete.)

Major F. W. Hurcombe	Capt. F. G. Giles
Capt. M. F. de F. Lorenzo	Lieut. N. M. Loutit
Capt. M. J. Herbert	405 Sgt. W. F. J. McCann
Capt. R. B. Jacob	931 L.-Cpl. R. H. Pritton
Capt. G. D. Shaw	(also 2 others)

MENTIONED IN 1st ANZAC ROUTINE ORDERS.
503. R.S.M. Holland.
Vide Para. 58, Part I 12/1943 E of 28/2/17.

MENTIONED IN A.I.F. ORDERS, APRIL, 1917.
1585 C.S.M. S. H. Towner

SUMMARY OF THE 10TH BATTALION HONOURS AND REWARDS FOR SERVICE IN THE FIELD.

BRITISH AWARDS:
- Victoria Crosses 3
- Companion Order of St. Michael and St. George 1
- Companions Distinguished Service Order 9
- Bar to Distinguished Service Order 1
- Military Crosses 34
- Bars to Military Crosses 4
- Distinguished Conduct Medals 16
- Military Medals 149
- Two Bars to Military Medal 1
- Bars to Military Medals 11
- Meritorious Service Medals 9
- Mentioned in Despatches 48
- Mentioned in Army Corps Routine Orders 11
- Mentioned in A.I.F. Orders 2

FOREIGN DECORATIONS:
- Russian Order of St. Anne (2nd Class with Swords) .. 1
- French Croix de Guerre 3
- French Croix de Guerre avec Palme 1
- French Medaille Militaire 1
- Belgian Croix de Guerre 3
- Belgian Decoration Militaire 1
- Italian Bronze Medal for Military Valour 1

Grand Total .. 310

XXII

ROLL OF HONOUR

The *South Australian National War Memorial*, North Terrace, Adelaide, records 1,005 names of officers and other ranks of the 10th Battalion who during the Great War, 1914-18, were killed in action, died of wounds, sickness, or injuries. The following Battalion Roll of Honour includes five other names which have been omitted from the National War Memorial.

Regt. No.	Rank.	NAME. (Showing Decorations)	Nature of Casualty.	Date of Casualty.	Place of Casualty.
6475	Pte.	ACASON, Leonard Laxton	K.I.A.	24/4/18	France
2780	Pte.	ADAMS, Charles	K.I.A.	8/10/17	Belgium
1857	Sgt.	ADAMS, Douglas Bernard Matthew	D.O.W.	7/7/15	Gallipoli
731	Pte.	ADAMS, John Albert	K.I.A.	27/4/15	Gallipoli
6473	Pte.	ADAMS, Thomas Clifford	K.I.A.	21/9/17	Belgium
2576	Pte.	AHERN, James Phillip	K.I.A.	11/8/18	France
1073	Pte.	ALFORD, Gordon James	D.O.W.	7/5/15	Gallipoli
73	Pte.	ALLARD, Alfred Donald M.	K.I.A.	18/5/15	Gallipoli
6713	Pte.	ALLCHURCH, Clifford	K.I.A.	21/9/17	Belgium
6957	Pte.	ALLEN, Charles Alexander	D.O.I.	27/2/17	England
984	Pte.	ALLEN, Charles Henry	K.I.A.	19/5/15	Gallipoli
2104	Pte.	ALLEN, David William	D.O.W.	20/8/16	France
6707	Pte.	ALLEN, Eustace Reveley	K.I.A.	6/10/17	Belgium
591	Pte.	ALSTON, Harry	K.I.A.	27/4/15	Gallipoli
1301	Pte.	ALTHORP, Algar Hampton (P.O.W.)	D.O.W.	15/12/16	France
1452	Pte.	ALTREE, William	K.I.A.	29/5/15	Gallipoli
	Lieut.	ANGOVE, Edward Laurence	K.I.A.	23/8/18	France
810	Pte.	ANTRAM, Harry	K.I.A.	25-29/4/15	Gallipoli
2783	Pte.	ARCHIBALD, Clifford Harrold	K.I.A.	24/4/18	France
1719	L/Cpl.	ARGALL, John Hosking (P.O.W.)	D.O.W.	9/9/16	France
3678	Cpl.	ARNOLD, Frederick William	K.I.A.	15/4/17	France
5030	Pte.	ARRING, Carl Hjalmar	K.I.A.	7/10/17	Belgium
387	Sgt.	ASH, Arthur Addison	K.I.A.	25/2/17	France
5031	Pte.	ATKINS, Alfred	D.O.C.	19/11/17	England
1878	Pte.	ATKINSON, Ernest Albert	K.I.A.	18/4/18	France
6955	L/Cpl.	ATKINSON, Frederick James Edward Richard	K.I.A.	26/8/18	France
299	Pte.	ATWELL, Thomas Arthur	K.I.A.	19/5/15	Gallipoli
77	Sgt.	BACKMAN, Charles James	K.I.A.	25-29/4/15	Gallipoli
1880	Sgt.	BADGER, David Gibson Jude	K.I.A.	21/8/16	France
6480	Pte.	BAGLEY, Charles James	K.I.A.	10/8/18	France
5052	Pte.	BAILEY, Richard Edwin	K.I.A.	17/2/17	France
882	L/Cpl.	BAKER, George Ernest Anthony (D.C.M.)	K.I.A.	8/4/17	France
1903	Pte.	BAKER, Henry Squire	K.I.A.	10/8/18	France
2330	L/Cpl.	BAKER, Horace Frank Charles	K.I.A.	22/8/16	France
3679	L/Cpl.	BAKER, Howard Emery	D.O.W.	6/5/17	France
	2/Lt.	BAKER, Wallace Westerfield	K.I.A.	22/8/16	France
3681	Pte.	BARBER, Alfred Douglas	K.I.A.	22/8/16	France
6728	L/Cpl.	BARCLAY, Percy James	K.I.A.	24/4/18	France
187	Pte.	BARKER, Oliver Albert Mortimer	K.I.A.	25/7/16	France
3978	L/Cpl.	BARLOW, George Alwynne Garfitt	D.O.W.	21/8/16	France
7213	Pte.	BARNES, Edwin William	K.I.A.	18/9/18	France
5037	L/Cpl.	BARNES, William Henry	K.I.A.	7/5/17	France
2506	Cpl.	BARR, Daniel (M.M.)	K.I.A.	9/5/17	France
2108	Pte.	BARROW, Harold William	K.I.A.	8/10/17	Belgium
2583	Pte.	BARRY, John Joseph	D.O.W.	24/5/16	France
6040	Pte.	BARTSCH, Theodor Bernhard	K.I.A.	6/5/17	France

ROLL OF HONOUR 275

Regt. No.	Rank. NAME. (Showing Decorations)	Nature of Casualty.	Date of Casualty.	Place of Casualty.
1558	Pte. BASWICK, Albert (stated to be Routledge, John)	K.I.A.	19/5/15	Gallipoli
1595	Pte. BATCHELOR, William Henry Edwin Cyril	K.I.A.	6/5/17	France
	Capt. BATES, Charles Joseph	K.I.A.	19/5/16	France
551	Pte. BATES, Glen Roy (M.M.)	K.I.A.	8/10/17	Belgium
477	Pte. BATT, Frank	K.I.A.	25/4/15	Gallipoli
5969	Cpl. BAWDEN, Hugh	K.I.A.	10/8/18	France
3004	Pte. BAYLIS, Charles Henry	D.O.I.	24/11/15	Lemnos
2585	Pte. BEALE, Lionel Cosmore	K.I.A.	19-23/8/16	France
3458	Pte. BEATTIE, George	D.O.I.	10/7/17	France
2729	Pte. BEATTY, William James	K.I.A.	24/4/18	France
6345	Pte. BEECKEN, Herman Ernest (P.O.W.)	D.O.W.	8/4/17	France
2588	Pte. BELL, William Solomon	K.I.A.	21/8/16	France
4436	Pte. BELLIS, Thomas Henry	D.O.W.	4/3/17	France
1914	Pte. BELTON, Robert William	K.I.A.	21/8/15	Gallipoli
6110	Pte. BENNETT, Francis	K.I.A.	10/8/18	France
1559	Pte. BENNETTS, Edward James	D.O.W.	15/5/15	Gallipoli
75	Dvr. BERGIN, Walter	K.I.A.	6/8/15	Gallipoli
2104	Pte. BEST, George Harold	K.I.A.	24/7/18	France
3689	Pte. BIRKIN, Ebenezer	K.I.A.	23/8/16	France
5045	Pte. BISHOP, Roy Amos Raymond	K.I.A.	8/4/17	France
1028	Pte. BLACK, Harold Frederick	K.I.A.	25-29/4/15	Gallipoli
6217	Pte. BLEECHMORE, Eric Frank	D.O.W.	14/10/17	Belgium
3459	Pte. BLYTHMAN, Albert George	D.O.I.	27/4/17	France
1913	Pte. BOCK, Charles Heinrich	D.O.I.	8/12/16	France
6457	Pte. BOLTON, Frank Leslie	D.O.W.	12/5/17	France
3210	Pte. BOSMA, Henry John William (M.M.)	D.O.W.	25/8/16	France
208	Pte. BOUCHER, Joseph William Alexander	D.O.W.	30/4/15	Gallipoli
7205	Pte. BOWDEN, Harold Leslie	K.I.A.	26/8/18	France
1061	Pte. BOWDEN, John Stirling	K.I.A.	25-29/4/15	Gallipoli
3693	Sgt. BOWEN, Warwick Young	D.O.C.	27/11/18	England
6481	Pte. BOX, Stanley John	K.I.A.	9/5/17	France
6946	Pte. BRADY, Ralph Norman	D.O.W.	2/10/17	Belgium
2340	Pte. BRADFORD, Ray Percival	D.O.I.	24/10/15	Gallipoli
675	L/Cpl. BRADLEY, Clarence Eugene	K.I.A.	25/7/16	France
772	Sgt. BRADLEY, Frederick Mark (M.M.)	K.I.A.	30/6/18	France
5973	Pte. BRALLA, Edgar	D.O.W.	6/5/17	France
550	Pte. BRAMMY, George Howard	K.I.A.	2/5/15	Gallipoli
6708	Pte. BRANNAN, Ellis Hyndman	K.I.A.	7/5/17	France
7364	Pte. BRAVENBOER, William	K.I.A.	28/6/18	France
6856	Pte. BRIGGS, Oswald Leonard	K.I.A.	17/12/17	Belgium
2731	Pte. BRITTON, Norman	K.I.A.	21/9/17	Belgium
4446	L/Cpl. BROADBENT, Leslie Herbert (M.M.)	K.I.A.	18/9/18	France
1313	Pte. BROCK, Leslie Salvador	D.O.C.	10/10/16	Belgium
1453	Pte. BROKENSHIRE, William James	K.I.A.	6/8/15	Gallipoli
722	Pte. BROUGHTON, Frederick John	K.I.A.	27/4/15	Gallipoli
3697	Pte. BROWN, Arthur Tennyson	D.O.W.	26/8/18	France
2807	Pte. BROWN, Frank	D.O.W.	25/8/16	France
2600	Pte. BROWN, Frederick	K.I.A.	25/7/16	France
110	Sgt. BROWN, Harry Cecil	K.I.A.	10/8/18	France
2116	Pte. BROWN, James Centennial	K.I.A.	15/7/16	France
2788	Cpl. BROWN, Lawrence Victor	K.I.A.	23/8/16	France
2599	Pte. BROWN, William Henry	K.I.A.	29/6/16	France
3700	Pte. BROWNETT, Reginald	K.I.A.	19/12/16	France
797	Pte. BRUCE, Jack McCulloch	D.O.W.	29/7/15	Gallipoli
3705	Pte. BRYAN, Thomas	K.I.A.	7/11/17	Belgium
1725	Pte. BRYANT, Harry	D.O.W.	11/4/18	France
2601	Pte. BUCKENARA, Lawrence Alfred	K.I.A.	19-23/8/16	France

THE FIGHTING 10TH

Regt. No.	Rank.	NAME. (Showing Decorations)	Nature of Casualty.	Date of Casualty.	Place of Casualty.
6719	Pte.	BUDER, Edwin Walter	K.I.A.	21/9/17	Belgium
3702	Pte.	BUDER, William Albert	K.I.A.	20/8/16	France
5646	Pte.	BULLOCK, Frank Melville	K.I.A.	6/5/17	France
1120	Pte.	BURKE, John Francis	D.O.I.	6/3/15	Egypt
6483	Pte.	BURNETT, Leonard Ward	D.O.W.	1/3/18	Belgium
3465	Pte.	BURRETT, James Robert	K.I.A.	23/8/16	France
2119	Pte.	BURROWS, Percival Charles	D.O.W.	18/9/18	France
886	Pte.	BURTON, Reginald	D.O.W.	2/10/17	Belgium
2342	Spr.	BUTTERICK, George Arthur	D.O.W.	23/7/16	France
2343	Pte.	BUTTLE, Samuel Leonard	D.O.I.	10/8/15	Egypt
1907	L/Cpl.	BUTLER, Albert	K.I.A.	8/4/17	France
	Lieut.	BYRNE, Albert John	K.I.A.	25/4/15	Gallipoli
1121	Pte.	BYRT, John Thomas	D.O.I.	20/1/15	At Sea
79	L/Cpl.	CADE, Harold Frederick	K.I.A.	21/8/16	France
3707	Pte.	CAIN, John	K.I.A.	28/9/16	Belgium
224	Pte.	CAMERON, Richard	K.I.A.	2/5/15	Gallipoli
2582	Pte.	CAMERON, Robert	K.I.A.	20/8/16	France
1317	Pte.	CAMP, John	D.O.W.	15/5/15	Gallipoli
6130	Pte.	CAMPBELL, Daniel George	K.I.A.	11/8/18	France
4449	Cpl.	CAMPBELL, Thomas (M.M.)	K.I.A.	8/4/17	France
7216	Pte.	CAMPBELL, William Young	K.I.A.	10/8/18	France
1920	Pte.	CAMPION, Gerald Gordon	D.O.W.	10/10/17	Belgium
2051	Pte.	CAMPION, Willie Edmond	K.I.A.	8/10/17	Belgium
7465	Pte.	CANNY, John Francis Joseph	D.O.W.	4/6/18	France
5063	Pte.	CARMAN, Roland Clarence	K.I.A.	8/4/17	France
1922	Pte.	CARMICHAEL, David	K.I.A.	14/8/15	Gallipoli
5832	Pte.	CARN, James Patrick	K.I.A.	24/4/18	France
6487	Pte.	CARRISON, Albert William	D.O.W.	9/1/18	Belgium
5064	Pte.	CARRUTHERS, William James	D.O.I.	9/9/19	S. Aust.
473	Pte.	CARTER, Sydney Mervin	D.O.I.	4/5/17	France
3261	Pte.	CARTER, Thomas Henry	D.O.I.	2/1/16	Egypt
7327	Pte.	CARTER, William	D.O.W.	18/9/18	France
4747	Pte.	CASKEY, John Percival	D.O.W.	2/10/16	Belgium
3712	Pte.	CASS, Thomas	D.O.W.	7/8/18	France
594	Pte.	CATLOW, Thomas Norris	K.I.A.	2/5/15	Gallipoli
7468	Pte.	CAVE, Geoffrey Austen	K.I.A.	18/9/18	France
2821	Pte.	CHAMBERS, Eric Henry	K.I.A.	25/7/16	France
5672	Pte.	CHAMPION, Percy	K.I.A.	6/10/17	Belgium
3011	Pte.	CHAPMAN, Sidney Hunt	D.O.W.	12/5/17	France
6224	Pte.	CHARLESWORTH, Martin Walter	K.I.A.	21/9/17	Belgium
5673	Pte.	CHARTERS, Walter William	K.I.A.	8/10/17	Belgium
893	Cpl.	CHILD, Alfred	K.I.A.	2/10/17	Belgium
3469	Sgt.	CHINNER, Wilfred Prior (M.M.)	K.I.A.	10/8/18	France
6982	Pte.	CHRISTIAN, Walter Leslie	K.I.A.	21/9/17	Belgium
3713	Pte.	CHRISTIE, Robert Edwin	K.I.A.	23/7/16	France
3470	Pte.	CLARE, Rutherford Barker	K.I.A.	8/4/17	France
1733	L/Cpl.	CLARK, Albert Edward	D.O.W.	24/7/16	France
6986	Pte.	CLARK, Eardley Austin	K.I.A.	30/7/18	France
1322	Pte.	CLARKS, Mathew	K.I.A.	30/7/15	Gallipoli
1924	Pte.	CLUES, Robert	K.I.A.	1/8/15	Gallipoli
4452	Pte.	COAD, Reginald Bennett	K.I.A.	25/2/17	France
1321	Pte.	COATES, Edward	D.O.W.	23/8/16	France
2123	L/Cpl.	COCHRANE, George Victor	K.I.A.	25/7/16	France
928	Pte.	COCHRANE, Herbert	K.I.A.	2/5/15	Gallipoli
1037	Pte.	COCKS, William	K.I.A.	23/5/15	Gallipoli
2125	Pte.	CODLING, Sidney James	K.I.A.	23/7/16	France
4456	Pte.	COFFEY, Thomas Joseph	K.I.A.	21/8/16	France
3471	Pte.	COLBERT, Edward John	K.I.A.	15/4/17	France
2450	L/Cpl.	COLE, John	K.I.A.	11/8/18	France

ROLL OF HONOUR 277

Regt. No.	Rank.	NAME. (Showing Decorations)	Nature of Casualty.	Date of Casualty.	Place of Casualty.
2612	Pte.	COLE, Stephen John	D.O.W.	7/6/16	France
466	Sgt.	COLE, William	K.I.A.	8/10/17	Belgium
2347	Pte.	COLES, Leith Carlyle	K.I.A.	23/7/16	France
917	Pte.	COLES, William	K.I.A.	18/9/15	Gallipoli
2248	Pte.	COLLINS, Frank Edward	D.O.I.	18/10/15	Gallipoli
6981	Pte.	COLLINS, Walter George	K.I.A.	18/9/18	France
	Lieut.	COLLISON, Herbert Youngman	K.I.A.	25/2/17	France
2613	Pte.	COLLISSON, Frederick Norman	K.I.A.	1/10/16	Belgium
5330	Pte.	COMPTON, Herbert	K.I.A.	7/5/17	France
486	Sgt.	CONNOCK, Edward	D.O.W.	1/10/17	Belgium
	2/Lt.	COOMBE, Harry Heyward	K.I.A.	23/8/18	France
	Lieut.	CORCORAN, Thomas Leo (M.C.)	D.O.W.	30/5/18	France
3720	Pte.	CORNISH, Leslie Francis	K.I.A.	6/5/17	France
5072	L/Cpl.	CORRIE, Albert Ernest (stated to be Cory, Wilfred Francis)	K.I.A.	21/9/17	Belgium
3274	Pte.	COTTON, Ernest Alfred	K.I.A.	6/5/17	France
303	Cpl.	COX, Archibald	K.I.A.	6/5/17	France
7473	Pte.	COX, George	D.O.W.	2/5/18	France
1125	Pte.	COX, Horace Raymond	D.O.W.	8/5/15	Gallipoli
2129	Pte.	COX, John	D.O.W.	7/9/15	Gallipoli
6229	Pte.	CRABB, Murray John Rossiter	K.I.A.	24/4/18	France
4283	Pte.	CRONIN, Edmund Thomas	K.I.A.	7/5/17	France
186	Pte.	CROWHURST, Frank Samuel	K.I.A.	25/4/15	Gallipoli
1126	L/Cpl.	CROWHURST, Vincent Parnell	K.I.A.	9/5/18	France
	2/Lt.	CROWLE, Herbert Walter	D.O.W.	25/8/16	France
1100	Pte.	CROWTHER, Alfred	K.I.A.	25/4/15	Gallipoli
	Lieut.	CRUICKSHANK, Errol (M.I.D.)	K.I.A.	25/12/17	Belgium
463	Pte.	CULLEN, George Frederick	K.I.A.	17/5/15	Gallipoli
	2/Lt.	CULLEN, Hedley Elbert	D.O.W.	10/8/15	Gallipoli
1080	Pte.	CURLEY, John	D.O.W.	7/8/15	Gallipoli
340	Pte.	CUSSION, Christian Walter	K.I.A.	2/5/15	Gallipoli
5349	Pte.	DACK, Herbert Royden	K.I.A.	21/9/17	Belgium
2357	Pte.	DADLEFF, Herbert James	K.I.A.	19/6/16	France
1933	L/Sgt.	DALLAS, John Dunstan	K.I.A.	21/3/18	Belgium
6993	Pte.	DALY, Claude Francis	K.I.A.	21/9/17	Belgium
241	L/Cpl.	DASHWOOD, Frank Leopold	K.I.A.	25/4/15	Gallipoli
4459	Pte.	DATSON, Victor William	K.I.A.	13/12/16	France
3726	Pte.	DAVENPORT, Arthur John	K.I.A.	26/7/16	France
894	Dvr.	DAVEY, Albert Henry	K.I.A.	19/5/15	Gallipoli
1456	Cpl.	DAVEY, Claude (M.M.)	K.I.A.	6/5/17	France
6995	Pte.	DAVIES, George	D.O.W.	1/11/17	Belgium
6495	Pte.	DAVIES, George Homer Francis	K.I.A.	20/9/17	Belgium
590	Pte.	DAVIS, Alfred	K.I.A.	25/4/15	Gallipoli
4460	Pte.	DAVIS, Aubrey Rowe	D.O.W.	30/5/18	France
3478	Pte.	DAVIS, Fergus	K.I.A.	24/4/18	France
5351	Pte.	DAVIS, Gilbert Walter (M.M.)	K.I.A.	8/10/17	Belgium
755	Pte.	DAVIS, Jack	K.I.A.	30/5/18	France
825	Pte.	DAVIS, Norman Ernest	D.O.W.	31/8/15	Gallipoli
5085	Pte.	DAWSON, Alexander Henry	K.I.A.	26/8/18	France
3727	Pte.	DEACON, Sydney James	K.I.A.	25/7/16	France
1133	Pte.	De BOER, Jack	D.O.W.	24/5/16	Gallipoli
3017	Pte.	DENING, William Charles Henry	K.I.A.	28/9/16	Belgium
6235	Pte.	DENNIS, Dalby Cecil	D.O.W.	19/8/18	France
1329	Pte.	DERRICK, John	K.I.A.	6/8/15	Gallipoli
4462	Pte.	DEW, Harry Clement Linley Gratton	K.I.A.	7/5/17	France
	2/Lt.	DEY, George Roy McGregor	K.I.A.	23/8/16	France
2765	Pte.	DIGHTON, Hillary John	K.I.A.	23-25/7/16	France
1330	Pte.	DILLON, Leslie Frank	K.I.A.	25-29/4/15	Gallipoli
6236	Pte.	DOCKING, Frantz Albert	K.I.A.	6/5/17	France

278 THE FIGHTING 10TH

Regt. No. Rank.	NAME. (Showing Decorations)	Nature of Casualty.	Date of Casualty.	Place of Casualty.
6237—Pte.	DOCKING, Lionel Theodore Claude	K.I.A.	6/5/17	France
Lieut.	DODSON, William Francis Lyon	K.I.A.	19-20/9/17	Belgium
6497—Pte.	DOLLING, Charles Hermann Edward	K.I.A.	21/9/17	Belgium
315—Pte.	DONALD, George Henry	D.O.W.	29/7/18	France
7479—Pte.	DONNELY, David Daniel	D.O.I.	10/3/18	England
Lieut.	DOUGALL, Norman (M.C.)	K.I.A.	6/5/17	France
3732—Pte.	DOWDELL, Roy Vane Thomas	K.I.A.	23-25/7/16	France
725—Pte.	DUFFY, John Patrick	K.I.A.	13/12/16	France
6242—Pte.	DULDIG, Oswald Rudolph	K.I.A.	20/9/17	Belgium
1134—Pte.	DUMBRILL, Henry Walter Seymour	K.I.A.	23/8/16	France
6496—Pte.	DUNCAN, Harold Ernest	K.I.A.	3/11/17	Belgium
6498—Pte.	DUNKLEY, Leslie Leonard	K.I.A.	24/7/18	France
312—Pte.	DUNLOP, George Alfred	D.O.W.	2/5/15	Gallipoli
5088—Cpl.	DUNNE, George Alexander	K.I.A.	30/7/18	France
3737—Pte.	DUNSTAN, Edward Thomas	K.I.A.	25/2/17	France
1336—W.O.II	DYER, Stanley Alic (M.I.D.)	K.I.A.	10/8/18	France
7481—Pte.	DYSON, Norman Douglas Arthur	D.O.W.	30/6/18	France
474—Pte.	EAST, Walter Leonard	K.I.A.	15/5/15	Gallipoli
2860—Cpl.	EASTHER, George (M.M. and Bar)	K.I.A.	18/9/18	France
617—W.O.II	EBBORN, Wilfred Henry (M.M.)	K.I.A.	25/7/16	France
5357—L/Cpl.	ECKERT, John George	K.I.A.	1/10/17	Belgium
4467—Pte.	EDSON, Arthur Leslie	K.I.A.	4/7/18	France
6503—Pte.	EDWARDS, Albert James	K.I.A.	6/5/17	France
1104—Pte.	EDWARDS, Edward (stated to be Fitzgerald Edward William)	K.I.A.	25/4/15	Gallipoli
6703—Pte.	EDWARDS, Warren	K.I.A.	14/4/17	France
777—Pte.	ELLERY, William Howard	D.O.I.	6/10/19	France
2635—Pte.	ELLEWAY, Edgar John	D.O.W.	24/8/16	France
5092—L/Cpl.	ELLIOTT, Frank Oswald	D.O.W.	13/4/17	France
4468—Pte.	ELLIS, Thomas George	K.I.A.	10/8/18	France
1743—Pte.	ELY, Charles	K.I.A.	17/12/17	Belgium
4469—Pte.	ERSKINE, Leslie Victor	K.I.A.	23/7/16	France
6743—L/Cpl.	ESTICK, Sydney William	K.I.A.	30/5/18	France
63—Pte.	EVANS, Francis Gilbert	D.O.W.	31/5/16	Gallipoli
5093—Pte.	EYRE, George	K.I.A.	8/4/17	France
755—Cpl.	EYRE, Leslie Francis Robert	D.O.W.	30/3/18	Belgium
355—Sgt.	FAINT, William (M.M. and Bar)	K.I.A.	11/8/18	France
6751—Pte.	FAIRBAIRN, Edgar Colin	D.O.W.	15/10/17	Belgium
219—Pte.	FALK, Charles John	K.I.A.	25-29/4/15	Gallipoli
901—Pte.	FARRAR, Arthur	K.I.A.	2/5/15	Gallipoli
Lieut.	FARRIER, Charles Percy	K.I.A.	9/5/15	Gallipoli
631—Pte.	FEATHERSTONE, John	D.O.W.	22/5/15	Gallipoli
2366—Pte.	FEEHAN, Richard Victor Patrick	D.O.W.	22/9/16	France
2249—Pte.	FELS, Roy Cyril Conrad	K.I.A.	17/2/17	France
3484—Pte.	FERGUSON, John Montcrieff	K.I.A.	21/8/16	France
4771—Pte.	FERGUSON, Roy Albert	K.I.A.	8/10/17	Belgium
6507—Pte.	FERRES, Ernest Leslie	K.I.A.	21/9/17	Belgium
979—Pte.	FERRETT, George Clement	K.I.A.	25-29/4/15	Gallipoli
3485—Pte.	FIEDLER, John Frederick	K.I.A.	25/7/16	France
744—Pte.	FIELD, Ralph Ewart	K.I.A.	23/7/16	France
6999—Pte.	FINCH, William George	K.I.A.	6/10/17	Belgium
7579—Pte.	FINDLAY, Valentine Joseph	K.I.A.	24/4/18	France
436—Pte.	FISHER, Frank Norman	K.I.A.	2/5/15	Gallipoli
2146—Pte.	FISK, Charles James	K.I.A.	23/8/16	France
7486—Pte.	FITZGERALD, Thomas Henry	D.O.W.	9/5/18	France
2643—Pte.	FOGGO, Robert Albert	K.I.A.	1/10/17	Belgium
7000—Pte.	FORBES, David Murray	D.O.W.	2/10/17	Belgium
4918—Pte.	FORD, Cecil Roy	D.O.W.	1/10/17	Belgium
Lieut.	FORD, Rufus Philip	K.I.A.	7/10/17	Belgium

ROLL OF HONOUR 279

Regt. No.	Rank. NAME. (Showing Decorations)	Nature of Casualty.	Date of Casualty.	Place of Casualty.
6248	Pte. FORD, Thomas Patrick	D.O.W.	20/9/17	Belgium
321	Pte. FORDHAM, Horace Utting	D.O.I.	11/2/15	Egypt
2/Lt.	FORDHAM, Roy Ogilvie	K.I.A.	8/4/17	France
3747	Pte. FORREST, John	D.O.W.	22/11/16	France
2148	Pte. FORSE, John	D.O.I.	11/9/16	France
2867	Pte. FOSTER, Charles	K.I.A.	27/3/18	Belgium
747	Cpl. FOSTER, Frederick	D.O.W.	6/5/15	Gallipoli
2150	Pte. FRANKCOM, Richard Charles	K.I.A.	20/6/16	France
6745	Pte. FRANKLIN, Charles	K.I.A.	6/5/17	France
1141	Pte. FRASER, Robert William	K.I.A.	8/8/15	Gallipoli
	Capt. FRAYNE, William Stanley	K.I.A.	6/8/15	Gallipoli
3493	L/Cpl. FREEMAN, Bert	K.I.A.	10/8/18	France
6998	Pte. FREEMAN, Clarence	K.I.A.	2/10/17	Belgium
316	Pte. FREEMAN, Fred (P.O.W.)	D.O.W.	8/4/17	France
5461	Pte. FRERICHS, Frank Frederick	D.O.W.	9/11/16	France
7234	Pte. FROST, Frank Frederick	D.O.W.	30/5/18	France
4475	Pte. FULLER, Frederick Chalmers	K.I.A.	25/2/17	France
1461	Cpl. FULLER, Ruben	K.I.A.	23/8/18	France
1937	Pte. FURNER, Samuel George	K.I.A.	6/5/17	France
2615	Sgt. GARDEN, Robert Venables	K.I.A.	23/7/16	France
3494	L/Cpl. GARDNER, Edgar	K.I.A.	10/8/18	France
3495	Pte. GARNER, Frank	K.I.A.	19-23/8/16	France
3496	Pte. GARNISH, William James	D.O.W.	3/6/18	France
1447	L/Cpl. GIBBONS, William James	K.I.A.	25-29/4/15	Gallipoli
6128	Pte. GIBBS, William Charles	K.I.A.	10/8/18	France
6462	Pte. GILCHRIST, William Carson	D.O.I.	6/2/17	England
7438	Sgt. GILES, Robert Summers	K.I.A.	30/5/18	France
5099	Pte. GILES, William Benjamin	K.I.A.	9/5/17	France
2771	Pte. GILL, Garnet Cyril	K.I.A.	21/9/17	Belgium
5366	Pte. GILL, Leslie Ira Mervyn	K.I.A.	4/6/18	France
4477	Pte. GILLISPIE, Thomas Hunter	K.I.A.	19-23/8/16	France
461	Sgt. GILPIN, Anthony Simpson	K.I.A.	25/4/15	Gallipoli
495	Cpl. GLADES, Alexander	K.I.A.	25/4/15	Gallipoli
3756	Pte. GOLLAN, Septimus	K.I.A.	1/10/17	Belgium
3501	Pte. GOODALL, Charles Ernest	K.I.A.	23-25/7/16	France
3567	L/Cpl. GOODE, Alick Ferguson	K.I.A.	20/9/17	Belgium
450	Pte. GOODE, Eric Ralf	K.I.A.	27/4/15	Gallipoli
3757	L/Cpl. GOODENOUGH, Ernest Willie	K.I.A.	6/5/17	France
7489	Pte. GOODIER, Frederick Hall	K.I.A.	18/9/18	France
96	Cpl. GOODYEAR, Harry	K.I.A.	22/8/16	France
1144	Pte. GORDON, Kenneth Douglas	K.I.A.	25/4/15	Gallipoli
332	Pte. GOWER, John Lewis	K.I.A.	25/4/15	Gallipoli
2158	Pte. GRAHAM, Alexander	D.O.I.	24/9/15	Gallipoli
1143	Pte. GRANT, Thomas Watt	K.I.A.	15/5/15	Gallipoli
6516	Pte. GRATWICK, Robert William	K.I.A.	7/5/17	France
6254	Pte. GRAY, Frederick Thomas Robertson	K.I.A.	21/9/17	Belgium
1343	Pte. GRAY, John	K.I.A.	20/9/17	Belgium
2660	Pte. GRAY, Sydney James Oswald	K.I.A.	23/7/16	France
2662	Pte. GREEN, Edward Louis	K.I.A.	8/10/17	Belgium
3333	L/Cpl. GREEN, Harold Tamperly	D.O.W.	30/7/18	France
7491	Pte. GREEN, Harold William	D.O.W.	26/4/18	France
3505	L/Cpl. GREEN, Henry Frederick	K.I.A.	20/9/17	Belgium
3506	Pte. GREEN, Herbert	D.O.W.	23/8/16	France
	Capt. GREEN, Keith Eddowes	K.I.A.	25/4/15	Gallipoli
902	Pte. GREENHILL, Percival Charles	K.I.A.	25-29/4/15	Gallipoli
2663	Pte. GRIGG, William Joseph	K.I.A.	23/8/16	France
1344	Pte. GRIVELL, Arnold Clifford	K.I.A.	20/8/16	France
2664	Pte. GROSS, Robert Carn	D.O.W.	2/3/18	Belgium
6463	Pte. GROVES, George Eaton (M.M.)	D.O.W.	31/7/18	France

280   THE FIGHTING 10TH

Regt. No.	Rank. NAME. (Showing Decorations)	Nature of Casualty.	Date of Casualty.	Place of Casualty.
3761—Pte.	GROVES, John Farthing	D.O.W.	14/8/16	France
6756—Pte.	GROVES, Philip Walter	D.O.W.	18/5/17	France
2665—Pte.	GUNTHER, Ernest Alfred	K.I.A.	9/11/16	France
5106—Pte.	GURR, James Henry	K.I.A.	13/12/16	France
1751—Pte.	GURRY, Joseph	K.I.A.	19/5/15	Gallipoli
4185—Pte.	GUTHRIE, David Glen	K.I.A.	25/2/17	France
5370—Pte.	GUY, Philip Gawler	K.I.A.	10/8/18	France
2481—Pte.	HABNER, Lloyd Francis	K.I.A.	19-23/8/16	France
2666—Pte.	HALES, Stanley Russell	D.O.W.	25/7/16	France
213—Sgt.	HALL, Anthony Basil	K.I.A.	18/5/15	Gallipoli
Capt.	HALL, Sydney Raymond	K.I.A.	25/4/15	Gallipoli
7008—Pte.	HALPIN, Joseph Cyril	K.I.A.	30/7/18	France
1491—Pte.	HAMPTON, Henry Percival	K.I.A.	4/10/15	Gallipoli
1345—Pte.	HANCOCK, John	K.I.A.	25-29/4/15	Gallipoli
3331—Pte.	HANLEY, Daniel Henry	D.O.W.	2/7/18	France
2167—L/Cpl.	HANNAFORD, John Charles	D.O.W.	27/10/16	France
665—Pte.	HANNAFORD, Lancelot Ramsay	D.O.W.	22/5/15	Gallipoli
2381—Cpl.	HANSEN, William Edmund (M.M.)	K.I.A.	10/8/18	France
6259—Pte.	HARKIN, Dennis Neabo	K.I.A.	24/4/18	France
4484—Pte.	HARRISON, Charles Henry	K.I.A.	20/9/17	Belgium
2890—Pte.	HARRISON, Clement	K.I.A.	25/7/16	France
7494—Pte.	HARRISON, Frank Francis	K.I.A.	11/8/18	France
6948—Pte.	HASS, Albert Fred	K.I.A.	20-21/9/17	Belgium
2/Lt.	HASTWELL, Hugh Norman	K.I.A.	30/6/18	France
3515—Pte.	HATCH, Harry Joshua	K.I.A.	21/8/16	France
6765—Pte.	HAWES, John Edward	D.O.I.	27/4/17	England
3068—Pte.	HAYES, Robert	K.I.A.	13/6/16	France
6262—Pte.	HAYLOCK, Frank Harold	D.O.I.	25/11/16	England
2675—Pte.	HEATH, Clinton Randolph	K.I.A.	7/6/16	France
1530—Pte.	HENDERSON, David Alexander	K.I.A.	19/5/15	Gallipoli
2383—Pte.	HENDERSON, John	D.O.W.	21/3/18	Belgium
2619—Cpl.	HENNESSY, James Henry	K.I.A.	24/4/18	France
4490—Pte.	HENRY, Charles	K.I.A.	7/10/17	Belgium
3172—Pte.	HENSON, Thomas (P.O.W.)	D.O.I.	25/10/18	Germany
Major	HENWOOD, Horace Norman (M.I.D.)	K.I.A.	1/3/18	Belgium
Lieut.	HERITAGE, Felix Hereward Gordon Norfolk (M.I.D.).	K.I.A.	20/9/17	Belgium
2678—Pte.	HEUZENROEDER, Gerhard Leopold	K.I.A.	23/7/16	France
2676—Pte.	HEUZENROEDER, Harman	K.I.A.	22/8/16	France
3224—Sgt.	HEWETT, Harry Bruce	K.I.A.	23/7/16	France
765—Pte.	HEWETT, Roy Sylvester	D.O.W.	24/8/16	France
3707—Pte.	HIGGS, Horace	D.O.W.	7/10/17	Belgium
Lieut.	HILL, Alfred Thomas (M.C., M.I.D.)	D.O.W.	30/5/18	France
3517—Pte.	HILL, Leslie Norman	K.I.A.	22/7/16	France
1085—Pte.	HILL, Raymond Davenport	D.O.W.	28/4/15	Gallipoli
5120—Pte.	HILL, William Charles	K.I.A.	19/12/16	France
Lieut.	HILLIER, Robert James Bradley	K.I.A.	25/7/16	France
1553—Pte.	HIRSCHAUSEN, Allen William	K.I.A.	15/4/17	France
5378—Pte.	HOCKEY, Leslie James	K.I.A.	3/11/17	Belgium
7331—Pte.	HOCKING, Samuel Roy	K.I.A.	28/6/18	France
978—Pte.	HOLDEN, John	K.I.A.	25-29/4/15	Gallipoli
4495—Pte.	HOLLAND, John William	K.I.A.	8/4/17	France
5331—Pte.	HOLLIDAY, William	K.I.A.	1/10/17	Belgium
2685—Pte.	HOLLYWOOD, Leo Francis	D.O.W.	24/7/16	France
6520—Pte.	HOLMES, George Frederick	D.O.I.	6/2/17	England
Capt.	HOLMES, Louis Gordon	D.O.W.	23/6/15	Gallipoli
1357—Pte.	HOLT, Sydney Brooks	K.I.A.	29/5/15	Gallipoli
Capt.	HOOPER, Charles William	K.I.A.	25/7/16	France
1565—Pte.	HOOPER, Frederick Richard	K.I.A.	19/8/16	France

ROLL OF HONOUR 281

Regt. No.	Rank. NAME. (Showing Decorations)	Nature of Casualty.	Date of Casualty.	Place of Casualty.
	Lieut. HOOPER, Robert James Mansfield	K.I.A.	27/4/15	Gallipoli
5121—L/Cpl.	HORNER, Ernest George	K.I.A.	24/4/18	France
3031—Pte.	HOWARD, Laban Cyril Joseph	K.I.A.	23/7/16	France
5123—Pte.	HOYLE, Fergus Sydney	K.I.A.	7/5/17	France
118—Pte.	HUGHES, Frank	D.O.W.	3/8/15	Gallipoli
3520—Pte.	HUGHES, Leonard Headland	K.I.A.	23-25/7/16	France
3779—Pte.	HUNN, Samuel Ernest	K.I.A.	11/6/16	France
498—Sgt.	HUNT, Charles Lawrence	K.I.A.	25/4/15	Gallipoli
1362—Pte.	HUNT, Harold Pearce	K.I.A.	23/8/16	France
5384—Pte.	HUNT, Ivan Cecil	D.O.I.	4/5/16	At Sea
836—Sgt.	HUNTER, Albert Charles	D.O.W.	22/5/17	France
505—Sgt.	HUNTER, Thomas	D.O.W.	31/7/16	France
888—Pte.	HUNTLEY, George Henry Stuart	K.I.A.	25/4/15	Gallipoli
4498—Pte.	HURLING, David Thomas	K.I.A.	20/8/16	France
1960—Pte.	HURN, George Sylvester	D.O.W.	5/7/18	France
1146—Pte.	HURRELL, George Edward	K.I.A.	22/7/18	France
1961—Pte.	HURRELL, Horace Claude	K.I.A.	23/7/16	France
1533—Sgt.	INWOOD, Robert Minney	K.I.A.	24/7/16	France
	Lieut. JACKSON, Albert Heyward (M.M.)	K.I.A.	24/4/18	France
2693—L/Cpl.	JACKSON, Arthur Harold	K.I.A.	2/10/17	Belgium
941—L/Cpl.	JACKSON, Harold Edgar	K.I.A.	7/5/17	France
7017—Pte.	JACKSON, Norman Edward	K.I.A.	30/7/18	France
66—Sgt.	JACOBS, Arthur Abraham	K.I.A.	7/10/17	Belgium
1149—Pte.	JAEHNE, Clarence Vincent	D.O.I.	14/1/15	At Sea
1150—Pte.	JAMES, Frank	D.O.W.	4/5/15	Gallipoli
5273—L/Cpl.	JAMES, Frank	D.O.W.	24/4/18	France
826—L/Cpl.	JAMES, Tudor	K.I.A.	23/8/16	France
2622—Pte.	JEFFERY, Frederick Sampson	K.I.A.	23/7/16	France
2178—Pte.	JEMISON, Robert Glendinning	K.I.A.	8/4/17	France
872—Pte.	JENKINS, Sydney Herbert	K.I.A.	3/1/18	Belgium
1368—Pte.	JENZEN, Edgar Harold	D.O.W.	3/5/15	Gallipoli
5131—Pte.	JESSOP, Hedley	K.I.A.	28/9/16	Belgium
2047—Pte.	JOHNSEN, William	K.I.A.	8/10/17	Belgium
1569—Pte.	JOHNSON, Aleck	D.O.W.	26/4/18	France
801—Pte.	JOHNSON, Arthur Sydney	D.O.I.	6/3/17	England
358—Pte.	JOHNSON, Frederick Aloysius (stated to be Rundle, Joseph Aloysius)	K.I.A.	19/5/15	Gallipoli
3528—Pte.	JOHNSON, Knut Einer (stated to be Johansson, Knut Einer)	K.I.A.	29/5/15	Gallipoli
1108—L/Cpl.	JONES, Ernest	K.I.A.	10/4/17	France
1941—Pte.	JONES, Ernest Vickery	K.I.A.	26/6/16	France
945—Pte.	JONES, Frederick Wallis	D.O.W.	2/5/15	Gallipoli
5716—Pte.	JONES, Norman Nicholas	D.O.W.	30/4/15	Gallipoli
1523—Pte.	KARNEY, William James	K.I.A.	1/8/15	Gallipoli
555—Pte.	KEEN, Alfred William	K.I.A.	20/9/17	Belgium
1967—Pte.	KEEN, Joseph Beers	K.I.A.	25/7/16	France
3182—Cpl.	KELEY, Arthur Harold	K.I.A.	21/9/17	Belgium
1021—Pte.	KELLY, Thomas	K.I.A.	25/7/16	France
132—Pte.	KELLY, William	K.I.A.	25/4/15	Gallipoli
881—Pte.	KENNEDY, Martin	D.O.W.	8/8/15	Gallipoli
2703—Pte.	KENNETH, Ernest	D.O.I.	31/3/17	France
	2/Lt. KENT, Edgar	K.I.A.	22/8/16	France
4505—Pte.	KENT, Richard Henry	K.I.A.	23/8/16	France
380—Pte.	KENT, William	K.I.A.	2/5/15	Gallipoli
2897—Pte.	KEOGH, Kevin Aloysius	K.I.A.	30/5/18	France
2704—Pte.	KINDLER, Johann Carl	K.I.A.	20/4/16	France
556—Dvr.	KING, Charles	K.I.A.	6/8/15	Gallipoli
2723—Pte.	KING, Frederick Rupert	K.I.A.	23-25/7/16	France
1370—Pte.	KING, George Austin	K.I.A.	25/4/15	Gallipoli

THE FIGHTING 10TH

Regt. No.	Rank. NAME. (Showing Decorations)	Nature of Casualty.	Date of Casualty.	Place of Casualty.
955	Pte. KING, Leo	K.I.A.	21/8/16	France
2048	L/Cpl. KINMOND, Robert Marshall	K.I.A.	23-25/7/16	France
	Lieut. KINNISH, Henry Arthur	K.I.A.	21/8/16	France
5456	Pte. KNEALE, Roy Rutherford	K.I.A.	3-9/10/17	Belgium
7508	Pte. KNIGHT, James Gemmel	K.I.A.	4/7/18	France
508	Pte. KNIGHT, Joseph James	K.I.A.	13/8/15	Gallipoli
5139	Pte. KNOWLING, Ernest Leslie	D.O.I.	27/5/16	Egypt
7509	Pte. KOEHNA, Oscar Herman	D.O.W.	30/5/18	France
7510	Pte. KRUGER, Albert Rheinold Heinrich	K.I.A.	30/7/18	France
2709	Pte. KRUSS, Jasper Clifford	D.O.W.	31/7/16	France
7512	Pte. LAMBERT, Thomas (stated to be Davidson, Thomas Scott)	K.I.A.	28/6/18	France
6535	Pte. LAMSHED, William Horace	K.I.A.	20/9/17	Belgium
2398	Cpl. LANCHESTER, John Albert	K.I.A.	6/10/17	Belgium
2715	Pte. LANGLEY, Clarence Frederick Thomas	K.I.A.	1/10/17	Belgium
3220	L/Cpl. LANGLEY, James Alexander Robert	K.I.A.	24/7/16	France
3793	Pte. LANTHOIS, Ernest George	K.I.A.	23-24/7/16	France
341	Pte. LAPTHORNE, Victor Walter Athelstone	K.I.A.	27/4/15	Gallipoli
4551	Pte. LARKIN, James Phillip	K.I.A.	7/10/17	Belgium
7023	Pte. LARKIN, John Arthur	D.O.I.	3/2/19	France
1499	Pte. LARKIN, Thomas	K.I.A.	28/5/18	France
454	Pte. LASHMAR, Allan John	K.I.A.	2/5/15	Gallipoli
1154	Pte. LAST, Henry Stewart	D.O.W.	21/5/15	Gallipoli
2063	Pte. LATHAM, Jack (stated to be Latham, Walter Martin)	K.I.A.	3/8/15	Gallipoli
	Lieut. LAURIE, Leonard Buxton	D.O.W.	27/4/18	France
7025	Pte. LAWRIE, Allan Harcourt	K.I.A.	20/12/17	Belgium
2712	Pte. LAYCOCK, Julius	K.I.A.	23/7/16	France
1975	Pte. LEACH, Herbert John	K.I.A.	23/8/16	France
2905	L/Cpl. LEAK, Hugh Phillips	K.I.A.	5/8/16	France
6779	Pte. LEAK, Reginald Arthur	D.O.W.	9/10/17	Belgium
1710	Pte. LEAN, Horace	K.I.A.	1/3/18	Belgium
	Lieut. LEAVER, Graham Holland	K.I.A.	20/9/17	Belgium
959	L/Cpl. LEE-THOMAS, Henry	K.I.A.	8/1/18	Belgium
1372	Pte. LEECH, Samuel	K.I.A.	25-29/4/15	Gallipoli
1153	Pte. LEES, David	K.I.A.	24/4/18	France
3796	Pte. LEHMANN, Herman Carl	K.I.A.	25/7/16	France
7032	Pte. LESTER, Francis Joseph	K.I.A.	1/10/17	Belgium
689	Pte. LEWIS, David	K.I.A.	25/4/15	Gallipoli
	2/Lt. LEWIS, Ernest Stanley (D.C.M.)	D.O.W.	2/10/17	Belgium
21	Pte. LEWIS, James Llewellyn	K.I.A.	25-29/4/15	Gallipoli
601	Pte. LIERSCH, Alfred	D.O.I.	5/2/15	Egypt
936	Pte. LIESCHKE, George Albert	D.O.I.	3/5/15	Gallipoli
	Lieut. LIMB, Arthur (M.I.D. 2)	D.O.I.	7/5/20	France
1977	Pte. LINDNER, Arthur	D.O.W.	7/8/15	Gallipoli
1973	Pte. LINDNER, Edmund Charles	D.O.W.	28/8/15	Gallipoli
2189	L/Cpl. LINDSAY, John Glendinning	D.O.W.	26/7/16	France
641	Pte. LITHGOW, Mark Holman George	D.O.W.	3/5/15	Gallipoli
3254	Pte. LITTLE, Alexander	K.I.A.	4/6/18	France
6282	Pte. LLEWELYN, David Lindsay	K.I.A.	21/9/17	Belgium
1149	Pte. LLOYD, Sydney George	K.I.A.	7/5/17	France
155	Sgt. LODGE, Wilfred Francis Huggett	K.I.A.	25/4/15	Gallipoli
1156	Pte. LOUGRAN, John	K.I.A.	28/4/15	Gallipoli
923	Cpl. LOVELL, Ernest Charles	D.O.W.	30/6/18	France
3393	Pte. LOWE, Thomas	D.O.I.	28/11/15	At Sea
1998	Pte. MABEN, David	K.I.A.	21/8/16	France
6109	Pte. MACDONALD, Gordon	D.O.I.	14/4/17	France
649	Cpl. MACDONALD, Roderick Francis	K.I.A.	30/7/18	France
441	Pte. MACEY, William Henry	K.I.A.	23/8/16	France

ROLL OF HONOUR 283

Regt. No.	Rank. NAME. (Showing Decorations)	Nature of Casualty.	Date of Casualty.	Place of Casualty.
407	Sgt. MacGILLIVRAY, Ivor Eric	D.O.W.	26/4/15	Gallipoli
3561	Pte. MACKENZIE, William Alexander	D.O.W.	22/8/16	France
7518	Pte. MACKERETH, Sydney Roy	K.I.A.	24/7/18	France
1774	Pte. MADDIFORD, Frederick	K.I.A.	3/8/15	Gallipoli
4515	Pte. MADDISON, Joseph Foster	K.I.A.	22/8/16	France
6287	Pte. MADLAND, William Spencer	K.I.A.	20-21/9/17	Belgium
2649	Sgt. MAHONEY, Joseph David	K.I.A.	8/4/17	France
2704	Pte. MAHONEY, Lloyd Leonard	D.O.W.	28/7/16	France
3536	Pte. MALCOLM, George James	K.I.A.	19-23/8/16	France
3124	Pte. MALONE, Anthony James Lawrence	K.I.A.	25/7/16	France
6132	Pte. MALONE, John Joseph	K.I.A.	18/9/18	France
6789	Pte. MANGELSDORF, Wilfred Harold	K.I.A.	20/9/17	Belgium
6618	Pte. MANN, William	K.I.A.	7/5/17	France
3538	Pte. MANOEL, Ernest John	K.I.A.	25/7/16	France
6783	Pte. MANSER, Walter Charles (M.M.)	K.I.A.	18/8/18	France
1161	Pte. MANSFIELD, Harold Osborne	K.I.A.	25/4/15	Gallipoli
124	Pte. MANUEL, William Owen	D.O.I.	24/12/16	France
2267	Pte. MARA, John Clarence	K.I.A.	23/8/16	France
3539	Pte. MARCUS, Robert Struan	K.I.A.	19/6/16	France
4640	Cpl. MARION, John Mott (M.M.)	K.I.A.	24/4/18	France
246	Pte. MARKS, Bernard Ernest	D.O.W.	28/4/15	Gallipoli
1991	L/Cpl. MARLOW, Kenneth Cullen Downing	K.I.A.	25/7/16	France
774	Pte. MARRIOTT, Percy George	K.I.A.	8/8/15	Gallipoli
3540	Pte. MARSH, James	D.O.W.	30/7/16	France
1050	Pte. MARSHALL, Aitken	D.O.W.	24/8/18	France
1011	L/Cpl. MARSHALL, Andrew Kirkland	K.I.A.	25/2/17	France
3648	Pte. MARTIN, Ernest	K.I.A.	6/5/17	France
	Lieut. MARTIN, Frederick William Scott (M.M.)	K.I.A.	20/9/17	Belgium
1990	Pte. MARTIN, Percy Wilfred	K.I.A.	1/8/15	Gallipoli
6544	Pte. MATHEWS, Ernest Arthur Wilfred	D.O.W.	27/6/18	France
6133	Pte. MATTINSON, Edward Victor	K.I.A.	30/6/18	France
2000	Pte. MAYFIELD, Alfred Irvine	K.I.A.	23-25/7/16	France
2858	Pte. McASKILL, Archibald Gordon	D.O.W.	25/7/16	France
3828	Pte. McBEATH, Robert Donald	K.I.A.	23/8/16	France
4533	Pte. McBEATH, William Henry	K.I.A.	25/2/17	France
866	Pte. McCAFFREY, Michael	K.I.A.	25-29/4/15	Gallipoli
5409	Pte. McCARTNEY, James	K.I.A.	10/4/17	France
3556	Pte. McCAULEY, James Joseph	D.O.W.	19/9/18	France
1049	Pte. McCONNACHY, Albert	K.I.A.	25-29/4/15	Gallipoli
511	Pte. McCUBBIN, Alexander	K.I.A.	25/4/15	Gallipoli
1391	Pte. McDONALD, Reuben Donald Stanley	K.I.A.	20/8/16	France
1157	Pte. McDONALD, Victor George Robert (D.C.M., M.I.D. 2)	K.I.A.	21/8/16	France
2740	Pte. McDONNELL, Peter	K.I.A.	19-23/8/16	France
509	Pte. McEWAN, George	K.I.A.	25-29/4/15	Gallipoli
5802	Pte. McFARLANE, Alexander Henry	K.I.A.	8/4/17	France
585	Pte. McGUIRE, Reginald Francis	D.O.W.	29/4/15	Gallipoli
	Lieut. McINERNEY, John Morris	K.I.A.	28/6/18	France
3419	Pte. McINERNEY, Nicholas Leo	K.I.A.	23-25/7/16	France
23	L/Cpl. McINTOSH, Victor Charles	D.O.I.	13/1/15	Egypt
580	Pte. McKAY, Albert John	D.O.C.	15/6/17	France
5410	Pte. McKAY, Ronald John Leslie	D.O.W.	15/8/18	France
2191	Sgt. McKECHNIE, John Adolph	K.I.A.	23-25/7/16	France
2948	Pte. McKENZIE, Daniel Humphrey (D.C.M.)	K.I.A.	25/2/17	France
263	Sgt. McLAREN, Clarence Roy	K.I.A.	23/7/16	France
5413	Pte. McLEOD, Donald	K.I.A.	10/4/17	France
5414	Pte. McLEOD, George Kenneth	K.I.A.	28/9/16	Belgium
6796	Pte. McLEOD, Norman Love	D.O.I.	14/6/17	France

284   THE FIGHTING 10TH

Regt. No.	Rank (Showing Decorations)	NAME.	Nature of Casualty.	Date of Casualty.	Place of Casualty.
751	Pte.	McLINTOCK, John Sloan	K.I.A.	25-29/4/15	Gallipoli
181	Cpl.	McMAHON, Michael John	D.O.I.	8/1/17	Lemnos
7047	Pte.	McMILLAN, William	K.I.A.	20-21/9/17	Belgium
3838	Cpl.	McNAUGHTON, Edward Frank	K.I.A.	20/21/9/17	Belgium
4538	Pte.	McNEIL, Samuel Philip	D.O.C.	8/9/16	Belgium
381	Pte.	McTAVISH, James	K.I.A.	2/5/15	Gallipoli
70	Pte.	McWILLIAM, Joseph Glaister	K.I.A.	2/5/15	Gallipoli
304	Pte.	MEADE, John Henry	K.I.A.	13/8/15	Gallipoli
1780	Pte.	MEADOWS, Albert Percy	D.O.W.	26/7/16	France
6298	Pte.	MEPSTEAD, Percy	K.I.A.	7/5/17	France
3807	Pte.	MERITON, John William	K.I.A.	21/8/16	France
1381	Pte.	MERRY, James Samuel	K.I.A.	7/10/15	Gallipoli
5798	Pte.	MEYER, William Carl	K.I.A.	21/9/17	Belgium
6117	Pte.	MEYERS, Herbert Leslie	K.I.A.	7/5/17	France
7039	Pte.	MILDREN, Frederick Onesimus Hewett	D.O.W.	9/5/18	France
5731	Pte.	MILDRUM, Bertie	D.O.C.	13/2/17	France
2546	Pte.	MILLARD, Walter Edmund	K.I.A.	20/8/16	France
3547	Cpl.	MILLER, Alexander	D.O.W.	11/8/18	France
	Lieut.	MILLER, Alexander Lorimer	D.O.W.	8/5/17	France
7526	Pte.	MILLER, Ernest	D.O.W.	29/9/18	France
4621	Pte.	MILLER, William Henry Melbourne	D.O.W.	24/8/16	France
3809	Pte.	MILLHOUSE, Rupert Victor Mayfield	K.I.A.	30/6/18	France
6541	Pte.	MILLS, Albert Edward	K.I.A.	6/5/17	France
5154	Pte.	MILLS, Harold	K.I.A.	10/4/17	France
	Lieut.	MILLS, Sydney Sylvanus (M.C.)	K.I.A.	20/9/17	Belgium
3810	Pte.	MILNES, Archie Lambert	K.I.A.	21/9/17	Belgium
6792	Pte.	MITCHELL, Frederick Walter	K.I.A.	4/7/18	France
3649	Pte.	MOBBS, Herbert George	K.I.A.	8/10/17	Belgium
791	Cpl.	MOORE, Andrew John	K.I.A.	12/5/18	France
3548	Pte.	MOORE, Charles Thomas	K.I.A.	23-25/7/16	France
1992	L/Cpl.	MOORE, Robert	K.I.A.	24/4/18	France
3819	Pte.	MOORE, Stanley Roy	K.I.A.	19-23/8/16	France
2411	Pte.	MOREY, James Laurence	D.O.I.	20/11/15	Gallipoli
4524	L/Cpl.	MORGAN, Harold Clifford	K.I.A.	4/7/18	France
2412	Pte.	MORLEY, William	K.I.A.	7/5/17	France
1030	Pte.	MORPHETT, Glenton Stuart Victor	K.I.A.	29/4/15	Gallipoli
1993	Pte.	MORRIS, Alfred Harold	D.O.W.	15/8/18	France
6793	Pte.	MORRIS, Raymond Francis	K.I.A.	24/4/18	France
5799	Pte.	MOSS, Wilfred Joseph	K.I.A.	8/4/17	France
3822	Pte.	MUGFORD, Albert John	K.I.A.	23/7/16	France
3824	Pte.	MUMFORD, Louis Rupert	K.I.A.	11/8/18	France
3550	Pte.	MUNRO, David	K.I.A.	23/7/16	France
522	Sgt.	MUNRO, William Henry	K.I.A.	25/4/15	Gallipoli
4530	Pte.	MURPHY, John Clare	K.I.A.	8/10/17	Belgium
1163	Pte.	MURPHY, John George	K.I.A.	19/5/15	Gallipoli
2943	Pte.	MURRAY, Robert Gordon	D.O.I.	31/1/16	Egypt
3563	Pte.	NAIRN, William Fred (P.O.W.)	D.O.W.	21/9/16	France
702	Pte.	NASH, Brunel John	K.I.A.	2/5/15	Gallipoli
4541	Pte.	NATION, Clifford Story	K.I.A.	6/5/17	France
2747	Pte.	NEALL, Albert Edward	K.I.A.	8/10/17	Belgium
3564	Pte.	NEARY, John	D.O.W.	26/8/16	France
685	Pte.	NEAVE, George Danford	K.I.A.	13/9/15	Gallipoli
608	Pte.	NEEDHAM, Harman Oliver	K.I.A.	19-23/8/16	France
6305	Pte.	NEIL, William	K.I.A.	9/10/17	Belgium
5164	Pte.	NELSON, Eric William	K.I.A.	10/4/17	France
2416	L/Cpl.	NELSON, Frank David	K.I.A.	30/7/18	France
3843	L/Cpl.	NELSON, Walter John Clinton	K.I.A.	24/4/18	France
6803	Pte.	NEWBERY, Ralph George	K.I.A.	26/3/18	Belgium
6805	Pte.	NEWTON, Herbert	K.I.A.	9/10/17	Belgium

ROLL OF HONOUR 285

Regt. No.	Rank. NAME. (Showing Decorations)	Nature of Casualty.	Date of Casualty.	Place of Casualty.
1575	L/Cpl. NICHOLLS, Ernest John	K.I.A.	9/5/17	France
3565	Pte. NICHOLSON, Edward James	K.I.A.	23/8/16	France
2423	Pte. NIELSEN, William Ernest	K.I.A.	25/7/16	France
3066	Pte. NIEMANN, Otto Christian	K.I.A.	23-25/7/16	France
7045	Pte. NINNES, William Edward	D.O.W.	2/1/18	Belgium
5419	Pte. NOBLE, Alan Campbell	D.O.W.	9/5/17	France
5251	Pte. NOBLE, Thomas Nicholas Rowe	K.I.A.	11/8/18	France
3842	Pte. NORMAN, Roy Spencer	K.I.A.	18/9/18	France
3220	Pte. NORRIS, Frederick James	K.I.A.	7/5/17	France
5741	Pte. NORRIS, John	D.O.I.	30/5/17	France
7530	Pte. NORTH, Cecil Joseph Rice	K.I.A.	4/6/18	France
5742	Pte. NORTON, Bert Henry	D.O.I.	11/12/16	France
5168	Pte. NOYES, Keith Hayden	D.O.W.	8/11/16	France
3846	Pte. OAKES, Hubert Lancelot	K.I.A.	23-25/7/16	France
6088	Pte. OBORN, Hartley Morrish	K.I.A.	3/10/17	Belgium
3847	Pte. O'BRIEN, Cyril	D.O.W.	20/9/18	France
4547	Pte. O'BRIEN, John	K.I.A.	25/2/17	France
	2/Lt. O'BRIEN, William	K.I.A.	9/4/17	France
1577	L/Cpl. O'CONNELL, Michael John	K.I.A.	23/7/16	France
7531	Pte. O'GRADY, Victor Thomas	D.O.I.	14/2/18	England
3568	Pte. O'KEEFE, William Percival	K.I.A.	25/7/16	France
1140	Pte. OLDEN, John Peter Henry	D.O.W.	11/11/16	France
3651	Pte. OLDFIELD, Sydney Herbert	K.I.A.	10/8/18	France
	Major OLDHAM, Edward Castle	K.I.A.	25/4/15	Gallipoli
1398	Pte. OLSEN, Charles	K.I.A.	19/5/15	Gallipoli
3569	Pte. OLSTON, Francis Arnold	K.I.A.	21/9/17	Belgium
3570	Pte. O'MALLEY, Timothy Cassimor	K.I.A.	19/5/16	France
7051	Pte. OPIE, Percy John	K.I.A.	23/7/18	France
5743	Pte. O'RIELY, Edward	K.I.A.	6/5/17	France
7110	Pte. O'SULLIVAN, Eugene Augustus	K.I.A.	6/10/17	Belgium
7533	Pte. OSWALD, John Lawson	K.I.A.	28/6/18	France
472	Pte. PACK, Simon George	K.I.A.	17/2/17	France
4549	Cpl. PADE, Charles Victor	K.I.A.	30/5/18	France
904	Pte. PAGAN, Joseph Burt	K.I.A.	25/7/16	France
949	Sgt. PAGE, Norman Livingstone	K.I.A.	8/10/17	Belgium
3571	Pte. PALMER, Alfred Edward	K.I.A.	23/8/16	France
433	Pte. PALMER, Raymond Roy	D.O.W.	2/5/15	Gallipoli
3573	Pte. PALMER, Samuel John Thomas	D.O.W.	17/8/18	France
677	Pte. PALMER, Thomas George William	K.I.A.	27/4/15	Gallipoli
1579	L/Cpl. PARKER, Charles Alexander	K.I.A.	8/10/17	Belgium
7360	Pte. PASCALL, Howard Henley	K.I.A.	9/5/18	France
6810	Pte. PATZEL, Laurence Ralph	D.O.W.	12/10/17	Belgium
823	Sgt. PAUL, John	D.O.W.	15/8/16	France
1034	Pte. PAYNE, Elford Athol	D.O.W.	20/5/15	Gallipoli
	2/Lt. PEARCE, Alfred Alexander	K.I.A.	10/8/18	France
679	Pte. PEARCE, Ambrose Stanley	K.I.A.	25-29/4/15	Gallipoli
3156	Pte. PEARCE, Arthur John	K.I.A.	19-23/8/16	France
2756	Pte. PEARCE, Edward Leslie	K.I.A.	19-23/8/16	France
3856	Pte. PEARCE, George Sydney Baxter	K.I.A.	3/6/18	France
3857	Pte. PEARSON, Ernest Victor	K.I.A.	19-23/8/16	France
4551	L/Cpl. PEARSON, Thomas William	D.O.W.	22/9/16	Belgium
1964	Pte. PEDERSEN, Nils Christian	K.I.A.	30/5/18	France
1793	Pte. PEDERSON, William	K.I.A.	19-23/8/16	France
2422	Pte. PENDLE, Alfred James	K.I.A.	19-23/8/16	France
6563	Pte. PENDLE, Hugh McIntyre	K.I.A.	1/10/17	Belgium
2758	Pte. PENGEL, Archibald	K.I.A.	2/10/17	Belgium
2423	Cpl. PENNA, Herbert	D.O.W.	5/5/18	France
3577	Pte. PENTECOST, Alan	K.I.A.	22/8/16	France
2209	Pte. PEPPER, Leonard William Percy	D.O.I.	2/2/16	Gallipoli

286   THE FIGHTING 10TH

Regt. No.	Rank. NAME. (Showing Decorations)	Nature of Casualty.	Date of Casualty.	Place of Casualty.
2006	L/Cpl. PERRY, Frank	D.O.W.	2/10/17	Belgium
2759	Pte. PETHERICK, Ormonde Leslie	K.I.A.	23/7/16	France
3861	Pte. PFUHL, William Thomas	K.I.A.	25/7/16	France
417	Sgt. PHILLIPS, Albert Edward	D.O.W.	14/12/15	Gallipoli
7059	Pte. PHILLIPS, Albert Victor	D.O.W.	21/9/17	Belgium
5178	Pte. PHILLIPS, George	K.I.A.	28/6/18	France
814	Pte. PHILLIS, Horace Vincent	D.O.W.	29/6/15	Gallipoli
5746	Pte. PICKEN, John	K.I.A.	21/9/17	Belgium
4555	Cpl. PICKER, William Patrick	K.I.A.	18/8/18	France
7538	Pte. PICKERING, Angus Cameron	K.I.A.	26/6/18	France
92	Sgt. PICKERING, Roy	K.I.A.	19-23/8/16	France
311	Pte. PINKNEY, Frederick James	K.I.A.	8/5/15	Gallipoli
6567	Pte. PITT, Roy Henry	K.I.A.	11/8/18	France
831	Cpl. PLAYER, Henry John	K.I.A.	25/7/16	France
1069	Pte. PLEW, William John	K.I.A.	23/7/16	France
469	Pte. PLUMMER, James Willis	K.I.A.	25/4/15	Gallipoli
3083	Pte. POLGLASE, William James	K.I.A.	25/7/16	France
527	Pte. POOLE, John William	D.O.I.	28/9/14	S. Aust.
3864	Cpl. POWELL, Edward Archie	D.O.I.	18/11/16	Egypt
3075	L/Cpl. POWNALL, Francis George Hyde	K.I.A.	23/8/16	France
6135	Pte. PRATT, Walter Fitzroy	K.I.A.	21/9/17	Belgium
3584	Pte. PRETTYJOHN, Hurtle Charles	K.I.A.	6/1/18	Belgium
2211	Pte. PRICE, Percy	K.I.A.	6/8/15	Gallipoli
5254	Pte. PRICE, William Henry	K.I.A.	30/5/18	France
793	Pte. PUGH, Walter Ernest	D.O.W.	18/8/15	Gallipoli
5184	Pte. PURVIS, Henry James (M.M.)	K.I.A.	20/9/17	Belgium
150	Pte. PYBUS, Frederick Hagedorn	K.I.A.	8/10/17	Belgium
5185	Pte. PYLE, John	K.I.A.	15/4/17	France
3074	Pte. PYM, Percy Laurie	D.O.W.	2/3/17	France
2428	Pte. PYNE, Octavius John	D.O.W.	17/3/17	France
973	Pte. PYNE, Patrick Thomas	K.I.A.	25-29/4/15	Gallipoli
1800	C.Q.M.S. RADBONE, Henry Gilmore (M.M.)	D.O.W.	30/6/18	France
	2/Lt. RAE, Albert Norman	K.I.A.	8/10/17	Belgium
2009	Pte. RAINEY, Harold	D.O.W.	7/8/15	Gallipoli
7289	Pte. RAMSAY, George	K.I.A.	30/7/18	France
7061	Pte. RANDELL, John Cuddeford	K.I.A.	23/7/18	France
1170	Pte. RAPKINS, Frank	K.I.A.	19/5/15	Gallipoli
1171	Pte. RAPLEY, John Albert	D.O.W.	8/5/15	Gallipoli
1407	L/Cpl. RATTIGAN, Peter	K.I.A.	22/8/16	France
1508	Pte. RATTRAY, Frederick Norman	K.I.A.	19-23/8/16	France
3079	Pte. REARDON, Joseph Bertram	K.I.A.	4/6/18	France
1974	Pte. REES, Francis Sidney Willyama	D.O.W.	3/6/18	France
7541	Pte. REGAN, James Edwin	K.I.A.	10/8/18	France
3876	Pte. REGNIER, Oscar Hugo Berghold	K.I.A.	8/11/16	France
3590	L/Cpl. REICH, Edgar	K.I.A.	2/10/17	Belgium
743	L/Cpl. REID, Frederick Charles	K.I.A.	25/4/15	Gallipoli
7284	Pte. RETCHFORD, Norman Leslie Albert	D.O.W.	28/8/18	France
3880	Pte. REVELL, Clarence Henry David	D.O.W.	8/4/17	France
6575	L/Cpl. RHUE, Thomas Edward Lindsay	K.I.A.	10/8/18	France
4506	Pte. RICE, David William	K.I.A.	30/6/18	France
533	Pte. RICHARDS, George Victor	K.I.A.	18/6/15	Gallipoli
557	Sgt. RICHARDS, Vyvyan Henry	K.I.A.	26/9/16	Belgium
7382	Pte. RICHES, Leonard William	D.O.W.	25/4/18	France
616	Pte. RICHMOND, Alexander	K.I.A.	18/5/15	Gallipoli
2771	Pte. RIEBE, Roland Hermann	D.O.W.	4/10/17	Belgium
1806	Cpl. RIEDEL, Charles W.	K.I.A.	21/8/16	France
2259	Pte. RIGNEY, Frank	D.O.W.	4/9/16	France
6872	Pte. RILEY, Bernard	D.O.W.	17/5/17	France
3883	Pte. RILEY, Frederick William	D.O.W.	22/8/16	France

ROLL OF HONOUR

Regt. No.	Rank. NAME. (Showing Decorations)	Nature of Casualty.	Date of Casualty.	Place of Casualty.
2772	Pte. RIMMER, James	D.O.W.	22/11/16	France
986	Pte. RIVETT, Alfred	D.O.W.	24/7/15	Gallipoli
3884	Pte. ROADS, Andrew	K.I.A.	25/7/16	France
2213	Pte. ROBERTS, Arthur Edward	K.I.A.	23/8/16	France
6816	Pte. ROBERTS, John	K.I.A.	3-9/10/17	Belgium
2683	Pte. ROBERTS, John James	K.I.A.	1/3/18	Belgium
4563	Pte. ROBERTS, Richard Lawrence	K.I.A.	20/8/16	France
4562	Pte. ROBERTS, Stanley Arthur	K.I.A.	20/8/16	France
4564	Pte. ROBERTS, Walter	K.I.A.	22/8/16	France
654	Pte. ROBINSON, Duncan Markham	D.O.W.	31/5/15	Gallipoli
48	Pte. ROBERTSON, Ivan Scott	D.O.W.	25/5/15	Gallipoli
5808	Pte. ROBERTSON, James	K.I.A.	17/2/17	France
638	L/Cpl. ROBIN, Philip de Quetteville	K.I.A.	25/4/15	Gallipoli
3885	Pte. ROBINSON, Arthur Wadsworth	K.I.A.	17/2/17	France
179	Pte. ROBINSON, Christopher Keith	D.O.W.	27/4/15	Gallipoli
2214	L/Sgt. ROBINSON, Francis	K.I.A.	24/4/18	France
3886	Pte. ROBINSON, William James	K.I.A.	23/8/16	France
2221	Sgt. ROE, Richard David	D.O.W.	10/4/17	France
1412	Pte. ROE, Sydney Clarence	K.I.A.	14/7/15	Gallipoli
6318	L/Cpl. ROFE, Rollo John	K.I.A.	3/6/18	France
701	Pte. ROKE, John	K.I.A.	8/4/17	France
1413	Pte. RONALD, Andrew	K.I.A.	23/8/16	France
2745	Pte. ROSSER, Hubert	D.O.I.	27/12/15	Lemnos
5428	Pte. ROSSER, Roy Leonard	D.O.W.	30/4/18	France
2778	Pte. ROWNEY, Albert Ross	K.I.A.	8/10/17	Belgium
455	Pte. RULE, Charles (M.M.)	K.I.A.	15/4/17	France
166	Pte. RYAN, Patrick Francis	K.I.A.	2/5/15	Gallipoli
3895	Pte. RYAN, Thomas Philip	D.O.W.	27/1/18	Belgium
5870	Pte. RYAN, Thomas William	D.O.I.	9/12/17	France
1067	Pte. SALE, Charles	K.I.A.	6/5/17	France
1816	Pte. SALTER, John	K.I.A.	16/6/15	Gallipoli
1362	Pte. SAMPLE, Henry Ewart	D.O.W.	14/10/17	Belgium
6581	Pte. SAMPSON, Clem Roy Clarence	D.O.W.	15/5/17	France
3594	Pte. SANDERCOCK, Wilfred James	K.I.A.	25/7/16	France
738	L/Cpl. SANDFORD, Albert William	K.I.A.	25/7/16	France
3595	Pte. SANDFORD, Walter Murray	K.I.A.	23-25/7/16	France
	Lieut. SANDLAND, Arnold Cooper	D.O.W.	4/8/16	France
4570	Pte. SAVAGE, Charles	K.I.A.	7/5/17	France
2783	Pte. SCHANTZ, Frank Allen	K.I.A.	20/9/17	Belgium
2784	Pte. SCHROEDER, Stanley Henry	D.O.W.	20/4/16	France
1414	Pte. SCHWARK, Charles (P.O.W.)	D.O.W.	22/8/16	France
	Lieut. SCOTT, Cleve James (M.C.)	K.I.A.	22/7/18	France
3899	Pte. SCOTT, Donald	K.I.A.	25/2/17	France
	Lieut. SCOTT, Frank John (M.I.D.)	K.I.A.	8/10/17	Belgium
7065	Pte. SCOTT, Stanley Kenneth	K.I.A.	9/5/18	France
101	Cpl. SEAMAN, Walter Batley	K.I.A.	19/5/15	Gallipoli
6831	Pte. SIEGERT, George William	K.I.A.	21/9/17	Belgium
1091	Cpl. SELLICK, George	K.I.A.	25/7/16	France
	2/Lt. SHARPE, Frederick	K.I.A.	23/8/18	France
5753	Pte. SHARRARD, Walter John	D.O.W.	14/2/17	France
	2/Lt. SHAW, Harold Baker	K.I.A.	19/5/16	France
354	Pte. SHAW, Hurtle Charles	K.I.A.	25-29/4/15	Gallipoli
420	Pte. SHEEDY, James John	K.I.A.	27/4/15	Gallipoli
2864	Pte. SHEEDY, William Patrick	K.I.A.	24/7/16	France
3905	Pte. SHEFFIELD, Frederick Stanley	D.O.I.	1/10/17	France
5854	Pte. SHEPHARD, Thomas Frederick	D.O.I.	2/8/16	At Sea
2058	Pte. SHEPLEY, Reginald Brushfield	K.I.A.	20/8/16	France
3907	Pte. SHIERS, William Henry	K.I.A.	23-25/7/16	France
6821	Pte. SHILLABEER, Andrew William	K.I.A.	8/10/17	Belgium

THE FIGHTING 10TH

Regt. No.	Rank.	NAME. (Showing Decorations)	Nature of Casualty.	Date of Casualty.	Place of Casualty.
2812	Pte.	SHIMMIN, Walter John	K.I.A.	19-23/8/16	France
1544	Pte.	SHIPLEY, Arthur Edward	K.I.A.	18/9/18	France
6098	Pte.	SIMMONDS, John Andrew	K.I.A.	15/4/17	France
2788	Pte.	SIMPSON, Alexander Galbraith	D.O.I.	12/11/18	England
2787	Pte.	SIMPSON, Charles Archibald	K.I.A.	19-23/8/16	France
3603	Pte.	SIMPSON, Frederick	D.O.W.	18/9/18	France
619	Sgt.	SINCLAIR, John Mitchell	K.I.A.	30/7/18	France
334	Pte.	SKINNER, Henry	K.I.A.	2/5/15	Gallipoli
6020	Pte.	SKUSE, Arthur Frederick	K.I.A.	24/7/18	France
2439	Pte.	SLADE, Charles Henry	D.O.W.	19/8/16	France
3911	Pte.	SLATER, Stanley Gordon	K.I.A.	23-25/7/16	France
2793	L/Cpl.	SMALL, George	K.I.A.	20/4/18	France
100	Pte.	SMART, Jesse	D.O.W.	15/5/15	Gallipoli
2794	Pte.	SMELT, Charles Harold	K.I.A.	19-23/8/16	France
	Lieut.	SMITH, Colin Macpherson	D.O.W.	6/10/17	Belgium
538	Pte.	SMITH, Cyril Charles	K.I.A.	25/4/15	Gallipoli
	Lieut.	SMITH, Eric Wilkes Talbot (M.I.D.)	D.O.W.	30/4/15	Gallipoli
7306	Pte.	SMITH, Francis Harmer	D.O.W.	30/5/18	France
427	Cpl.	SMITH, Francis Rodney Thomas	K.I.A.	7/5/17	France
6100	Pte.	SMITH, John	K.I.A.	2/10/17	Belgium
6580	Pte.	SMITH, Lester Bryce	K.I.A.	12/5/18	France
286	Pte.	SMITH, Malcolm Teesdale	K.I.A.	27/4/15	Gallipoli
7551	Pte.	SMITH, Percy James Arnold	K.I.A.	22/7/18	France
644	Pte.	SMITH, Peter Vincent	K.I.A.	25-29/4/15	Gallipoli
3609	Pte.	SMITH, Thomas George	D.O.W.	23/8/16	France
537	Pte.	SMYLIE, William Miller	K.I.A.	25/4/15	Gallipoli
	Lieut.	SMYTH, Trevor Owen	K.I.A.	16/5/15	Gallipoli
771	Pte.	SOMMER, Emil Nicholai Martin	D.O.W.	26/1/19	France
1810	Pte.	SPOONER, Walter George	D.O.C.	31/10/15	Egypt
	Lieut.	SPROTT, John (M.M.)	K.I.A.	24/4/18	France
3612	Sgt.	SPURRITT, Robert Henry	D.O.W.	2/10/17	Belgium
297	Pte.	STANBRIDGE, Charles Roy	K.I.A.	28/4/15	Gallipoli
1808	Pte.	STANLEY, Henry James	D.O.I.	31/7/16	At Sea
2797	L/Cpl.	STANTON, Ernest Ross Bishop	K.I.A.	21/9/17	Belgium
178	Sgt.	STEER, George Colin	K.I.A.	10/8/18	France
3925	Pte.	STEVENS, Caleb Jasper	K.I.A.	8/4/17	France
3491	Pte.	STEVENS, Robert Cydric	K.I.A.	19-23/8/16	France
1813	Pte.	STEWART, George	K.I.A.	19-23/8/16	France
40	Pte.	STOKES, Francis Herbert	K.I.A.	27/4/15	Gallipoli
2575	L/Cpl.	STORY, Archibald George	K.I.A.	22/8/16	France
790	Pte.	STRANG, William Andrew	K.I.A.	25-29/4/15	Gallipoli
2799	Pte.	STREETER, Walter	K.I.A.	23-25/7/16	France
7071	Pte.	STRINGER, Horace Edward	K.I.A.	6/10/17	Belgium
5459	Cpl.	SULLIVAN, John	D.O.I.	18/2/19	England
56173	Pte.	SURMAN, William (stated to be Surman, Bedwell William)	D.O.I.	20/10/18	England
2800	L/Cpl.	SUTCLIFFE, Alexander	K.I.A.	11/8/18	France
3931	Pte.	SUTCLIFFE, William	K.I.A.	6/11/16	France
558	Pte.	SUTHERLAND, John Donald	D.O.W.	4/10/17	Belgium
1423	Pte.	SWAIN, Frederick Job	K.I.A.	10/5/15	Gallipoli
5434	Pte.	SWAIN, Lawrence Arnold	D.O.W.	26/2/17	France
5219	Pte.	SWANSON, Arthur Wilhelm	K.I.A.	10/4/17	France
6829	Pte.	SWIFT, Lance	K.I.A.	21/3/18	Belgium
669	L/Cpl.	SWITZER, William Arthur	K.I.A.	22/7/18	France
2753	Pte.	SYMONDS, William Edwin	K.I.A.	21/6/16	France
3617	L/Cpl.	TAIT, Andrew Stevenson	D.O.W.	8/4/17	France
7076	Pte.	TAMBLYN, Charles David	D.O.W.	30/6/18	France
4585	Pte.	TAYLOR, Arthur John	D.O.I.	16/7/16	England
128	Sgt.	TAYLOR, Gordon Clyde	K.I.A.	16/4/18	France

ROLL OF HONOUR 289

Regt. No.	Rank. NAME. (Showing Decorations)	Nature of Casualty.	Date of Casualty.	Place of Casualty.
2255	Pte. TAYLOR, Guy Holbrook	D.O.I.	6/10/15	Gallipoli
5220	Pte. TAYLOR, John James	K.I.A.	24/4/18	France
1187	Pte. TAYLOR, Herbert Morton	K.I.A.	25/4/15	Gallipoli
1584	Pte. TAYLOR, James Southwick	K.I.A.	23/8/16	France
2252	Pte. TAYLOR, Wilfred Arthur	K.I.A.	30/9/15	Gallipoli
185	Pte. TAYLOR, William	D.O.W.	18/9/18	France
2807	Pte. THOMAS, Daniel Columbus	K.I.A.	20/8/16	France
1077	Pte. THOMAS, Horace James	K.I.A.	24/7/16	France
5763	Pte. THOMAS, Ronald George Albert	K.I.A.	8/10/17	Belgium
6122	Pte. THOMAS, Seymour Jacks	K.I.A.	8/10/17	Belgium
2809	Pte. THOMAS, Walter Victor	D.O.W.	18/4/17	France
4588	Pte. THOMAS, William John	D.O.I.	13/3/17	France
3936	Pte. THOMPSON, John	K.I.A.	23/8/16	France
4589	Pte. THOMPSON, Peter John	K.I.A.	7/5/17	France
915	S/Sgt. THOMSON, George William Wyville	K.I.A.	24/4/18	France
3621	Pte. THORN, Reginald Samuel	K.I.A.	24/7/16	France
761	Pte. THORNE, Garnet Whypoole	K.I.A.	27/2/17	France
1184	Pte. THORPE, Benjamin Thomas	K.I.A.	19/5/15	Gallipoli
2224	Pte. THREADGOLD, Ernest William Sharman	D.O.W.	23/8/16	France
2803	Pte. TIDSWELL, Clarence Tom Horatio	K.I.A.	2/10/17	Belgium
2435	Pte. TIESTE, Joseph Henry	K.I.A.	22/8/16	France
6150	Pte. TOWNSEND, Albert John	K.I.A.	18/9/18	France
7559	Pte. TOWNSEND, Benjamin Blackburn	K.I.A.	24/4/18	France
6592	Pte. TREGLOWN, George	D.O.W.	7/5/17	France
1822	Pte. TRENWITH, Arthur Aubrey	K.I.A.	17/2/17	France
3941	Pte. TREVILYAN, Hedley	K.I.A.	10/6/16	France
280	Pte. TRICHARD, Henry Daniel (stated to be Swaneport, Henry David)	K.I.A.	2/5/15	Gallipoli
1511	Pte. TRINNE, Benjamin Waldemar	K.I.A.	22/7/16	France
292	Pte. TUCKER, John Stewart	K.I.A.	2/5/15	Gallipoli
2027	Pte. TUCKER, Leslie Everard	D.O.W.	18/11/15	Gallipoli
203	Pte. TURNBULL, John Sanderson	K.I.A.	6/7/15	Gallipoli
1185	Pte. TURNER, Bassie	D.O.W.	26/8/15	Gallipoli
7561	Pte. TURNER, Cecil Edward	K.I.A.	24/4/18	France
1431	Pte. TUTT, Henry Dawson	D.O.W.	27/4/15	Gallipoli
5862	Pte. TWIGDEN, Cyril Roy	K.I.A.	10/4/17	France
5440	Pte. TYLER, George	K.I.A.	20-21/8/17	Belgium
5765	Cpl. VARCOE, Robert Neil (M.M.)	K.I.A.	26/7/18	France
6844	Pte. VAWSER, William Herbert	D.O.W.	8/10/17	Belgium
2819	Pte. VEITCH, William	K.I.A.	11/6/16	France
965	Pte. VENNING, Percy William	D.O.W.	28/4/15	Gallipoli
1042	Pte. VICK, William Henry	D.O.W.	27/4/15	Gallipoli
3946	Pte. VIDEON, Walter Lloyd	K.I.A.	21/8/16	France
1715	Pte. VIGAR, Norman Joseph	D.O.W.	21/9/17	Belgium
2821	Pte. VIGAR, Oscar Vincent	K.I.A.	9/10/17	Belgium
2230	Pte. VINCENT, William Goldsborough	K.I.A.	23/7/16	France
	2/Lt. VIRGOE, Randal Gordon	K.I.A.	21/12/17	Belgium
1832	Pte. VOGEL, Frederick	D.O.W.	26/2/17	France
2822	Pte. VOLERECHT, Henry Richard	K.I.A.	23/7/16	France
6594	Pte. VON DITTMER, Herbert John	K.I.A.	6/5/17	France
7116	Pte. VOUMARD, William Hippolyte	K.I.A.	24/4/18	France
1836	Pte. WADDINGTON, Frank	D.O.I.	12/10/17	England
979	Pte. WADE, Eric Arnold	K.I.A.	25/7/16	France
2463	Pte. WADE, Reuben Harold	D.O.I.	18/7/15	At Sea
582	Pte. WAGNSEN, Khristian (stated to be Vognsen, Kristian)	K.I.A.	26/6/15	Gallipoli
2039	Pte. WAIT, Edward Walter	K.I.A.	11/7/15	Gallipoli
2971	L/Cpl. WALD, Stanley Lykke	K.I.A.	23/8/16	France
	Lieut. WALKER, Alexander Ralph	D.O.W.	23/8/16	France

290 THE FIGHTING 10TH

Regt. No.	Rank. NAME. (Showing Decorations)	Nature of Casualty.	Date of Casualty.	Place of Casualty.
4629—Pte.	WALKER, Clarence Leslie	K.I.A.	13/12/16	France
1436—Pte.	WALLIS, Aver William Mitchell	K.I.A.	19/5/15	Gallipoli
Lieut.	WALSH, Douglas John (M.C.)	D.O.I.	12/8/18	France
3626—Pte.	WALSH, John Joseph	D.O.I.	6/7/16	France
1076—Pte.	WARD-PROCTOR, Dudley	D.O.I.	25/6/15	Gallipoli
1547—Pte.	WARHURST, Frederick Keith	K.I.A.	3/11/17	Belgium
4596—Cpl.	WARK, Reginald Fergusson	K.I.A.	30/6/18	France
337—Pte.	WARMING, Frederick James	D.O.W.	6/8/16	France
4595—Pte.	WARNER, Edward	K.I.A.	20/8/16	France
7565—Pte.	WARNEST, Johanis Ernest	K.I.A.	24/4/18	France
6031—Pte.	WARREN, Francis Oliver	K.I.A.	21/9/17	Belgium
592—Pte.	WASHINGTON, James Roy	K.I.A.	11/5/15	Gallipoli
7108—Pte.	WATERS, Maynard Septimus	K.I.A.	20-21/9/17	Belgium
856—Pte.	WATERSTON, Edward Alexander	K.I.A.	23-25/7/16	France
6105—Pte.	WATKINS, Edgar Bruce	D.O.W.	22/9/17	Belgium
240—Pte.	WATSON, George	K.I.A.	27/4/15	Gallipoli
7119—Pte.	WEATHERSPOON, Herbert Leonard	K.I.A.	24/4/18	France
1098—W.O.II	WATSON, Joseph Charles	D.O.W.	12/5/17	France
1191—Pte.	WEAVER, William Alfred	D.O.W.	25/5/15	Gallipoli
5237—Pte.	WEBB, George Frederick Howard	D.O.W.	15/11/16	France
988—Pte.	WEBB, William Arthur	D.O.W.	27/4/15	Gallipoli
2041—Pte.	WEEN, Albert Robert	K.I.A.	23/8/16	France
3629—Pte.	WELCH, Frederick Andrew	K.I.A.	19-23/8/16	France
1192—Pte.	WELCH, William John	K.I.A.	7/10/17	Belgium
7087—Pte.	WELHAM, George Walton	K.I.A.	30/4/18	France
2973—Pte.	WELLS, Rowland Robert	D.O.W.	27/3/18	Belgium
18—Pte.	WEMYSS, Robert	K.I.A.	24/4/18	France
2/Lt.	WENDT, Kenneth	K.I.A.	6/5/17	France
2257—Pte.	WESTERBERG, Holge William	K.I.A.	24/4/18	France
1586—Pte.	WESTON, Leonard Herbert	K.I.A.	25/6/15	Gallipoli
3209—Pte.	WHITBREAD, Edward	D.O.W.	25/7/16	France
Lieut.	WHITE, Alexander Deucher	D.O.W.	18/9/18	France
3630—Pte.	WHITE, Franklin Ebesworth	K.I.A.	19/6/16	France
543—Pte.	WHITE, George Oliver	K.I.A.	25-29/4/15	Gallipoli
4601—Pte.	WHITE, Horace (P.O.W.)	D.O.W.	19/12/17	Belgium
255—Sgt.	WHITE, Herbert Hurtle	K.I.A.	28/9/16	Belgium
2556—Pte.	WHITE, John (stated to be Struss, John)	D.O.W.	26/4/18	France
451—Pte.	WHITE, John Alexander	D.O.I.	28/9/15	Gallipoli
364—Sgt.	WHITE, Roy Neville	D.O.I.	6/12/18	England
5240—Pte.	WHITE, Wilfred Ambrose	K.I.A.	21/9/17	Belgium
Lieut.	WHITEFORD, Clarence George	K.I.A.	25/2/17	France
1946—L/Cpl.	WHITING, Thomas Frederick (Italian Bronze Medal)	K.I.A.	4/7/18	France
47—Pte.	WHYTE, Thomas Anderson	K.I.A.	25/7/16	France
2/Lt.	WICKHAM, Lindsay Claude (M.M.)	K.I.A.	25/7/16	France
3651—Pte.	WICKS, George	K.I.A.	20/8/16	France
1193—Pte.	WIGGINS, Percy Frederick	K.I.A.	23/7/16	France
855—Sgt.	WILCOCK, John	K.I.A.	25-29/4/15	Gallipoli
1055—Pte.	WILKINSON, Frederick Charles Erasmus	D.O.W.	24/9/17	Belgium
3645—Pte.	WILLIAMS, Albert	K.I.A.	11/8/18	France
2700—Sgt.	WILLIAMS, Charles Allen (M.M. and 2 Bars)	D.O.W.	28/4/18	France
3961—Dvr.	WILLIAMS, Charles Thomas	K.I.A.	27/2/17	France
5449—Pte.	WILLIAMS, David Newland	D.O.W.	5/6/18	France
1195—Pte.	WILLIAMS, Edwin George	K.I.A.	23/7/16	France
3163—Pte.	WILLIAMS, Ernest	K.I.A.	27/3/18	Belgium
2836—Pte.	WILLIAMS, Frank	K.I.A.	25/7/16	France
1443—Cpl.	WILLIAMS, Harold	D.O.W.	18/9/18	France
7313—Pte.	WILLIAMS, Henry	D.O.W.	10/9/16	Belgium

ROLL OF HONOUR

Regt. No.	Rank. NAME. (Showing Decorations)	Nature of Casualty.	Date of Casualty.	Place of Casualty.
2036	Cpl. WILLIAMS, James Henry	D.O.W.	10/9/16	Belgium
2258	Pte. WILLIAMS, John Howie	K.I.A.	30/5/18	France
2837	Pte. WILLIAMS, Llewellyn	K.I.A.	8/11/16	France
3963	Pte. WILLIAMS, Norman Leslie	K.I.A.	28/6/16	France
3120	Cpl. WILLIAMS, Reginald Wilfred	K.I.A.	1/10/17	Belgium
3964	Pte. WILLIAMS, William	K.I.A.	22/8/16	France
	2/Lt. WILSDON, Walter Harry (D.C.M.)	K.I.A.	8/10/17	Belgium
2238	Pte. WILSON, Leslie	D.O.W.	23/8/16	France
5453	Pte. WINCKEL, Alfred Otto	D.O.W.	6/11/17	Belgium
175	Pte. WINFIELD, Harry Moseley	K.I.A.	23/8/16	France
3968	Pte. WINKLER, Charles William	K.I.A.	11/8/18	France
3969	Pte. WINTER, Percy Charles	K.I.A.	13/8/16	France
1838	L/Cpl. WINTON, Louis Mayne	K.I.A.	23/8/16	France
4606	Pte. WISE, Frank Swainson	D.O.W.	14/8/18	France
2875	Pte. WITCOMB, John Francis Trafford	D.O.W.	27/8/18	France
5246	Pte. WOOD, Arthur	K.I.A.	31/12/16	France
1025	Cpl. WOOD, Robert	K.I.A.	29/12/17	Belgium
2241	Pte. WOOD, William Ferguson	K.I.A.	6/8/15	Gallipoli
2446	Pte. WOOD, William Richard	D.O.W.	17/4/18	France
5454	Pte. WOODING, William	D.O.W.	16/11/16	France
3973	Pte. WOODINGS, George William	K.I.A.	6/5/17	France
449	Pte. WOODS, Charles Julian Tenison	D.O.W.	23/7/16	France
1849	L/Cpl. WOODS, Harry Joshua	D.O.W.	28/7/16	France
1446	Pte. WOODS, Thomas	D.O.W.	30/6/15	Gallipoli
3974	Pte. WORTHINGTON, William Jeffrey	D.O.W.	25/8/18	France
604	Pte. WRIGHT, Harry Taylor	D.O.W.	3/5/15	Gallipoli
4608	Pte. WRIGHT, John Henry	D.O.W.	23/8/16	France
7092	Pte. WYE, Sydney William	K.I.A.	20-21/9/17	Belgium
1448	Pte. WYLD, Roy	K.I.A.	25-29/4/15	Gallipoli
2843	Pte. WYLIE, Percy Sidney	D.O.W.	6/10/17	Belgium
1198	Pte. YOUDS, Howard Lealand	K.I.A.	30/7/15	Gallipoli
	Capt. YOUNG, Robert Percy (A.A.M.C.)	K.I.A.	18/9/18	France
3312	L/Cpl. YUILL, James Anderson	K.I.A.	22/8/16	France
	Lieut. YOUNGER, John James Affleck	K.I.A.	10/8/18	France
804	Cpl. ZANDER, Charles Oscar	K.I.A.	22/8/16	France
4312	Pte. ZIMMERMANN, Charles Rudolph	D.O.W.	23/7/16	France

ANALYSIS OF 10TH BATTALION ROLL OF HONOUR.

In the foregoing *Roll of Honour* the "Place of Casualty" means the country in which the casualty originated, and not necessarily the place in which the death or burial subsequently occurred. Many members of the Battalion who died of wounds or injuries received whilst serving on Gallipoli subsequently died at sea, or in Egypt, Malta, etc., whilst others who evacuated France with wounds or injuries died in England or elsewhere. The Honour Roll and the appended summary do not convey this information.

Place of Casualty	Officers	Other Ranks	Total
South Australia	—	2	2
Egypt	—	11	11
Gallipoli	11	196	207
Lemnos	—	3	3
Belgium	15	158	173
France	35	556	591
Germany	—	1	1
England	—	15	15
At Sea	—	7	7

Grand Total—61 Officers, 949 Other Ranks = 1,010.

"HOW SLFFP THE BRAVE, WHO SINK TO REST,
BY ALL THEIR COUNTRY'S WISHES BLEST!"

William Collins.

XXIII

NOMINAL ROLL OF ORIGINAL BATTALION

Embarked at Outer Harbour, South Australia, per H.M.A.T. A11 *Ascanius* and H.M.A.T. A12 *Saldanha*, October 20, 1914.

Arranged numerically and according to Companies, etc.

HEADQUARTERS.

ADMINISTRATIVE.

C.O.—Lieut.-Colonel Weir, Stanley Price
2nd in C.—Major Hurcombe, Frederick William
Adjt.—Capt. Lorenzo, Francis Maxwell de Frayer
Q.M.—Capt. Minagall, Charles Francis
1—R.S.M. Whitbourn, Wesley Armstrong

2—R.Q.M.S. Magenis, George Charles
3—O.-R. Sgt. Leane, Benjamin Bennett
4—Pioneer Sgt. Heritage, Felix Hereward Gordon Norfolk
5—Sgt.-Cook Parker, John Goldsack
128—Bugler-Sgt. Taylor, Gordon Clyde
141—Arm.-Sgt. Provis, Claude Oswald

SIGNALLING SECTION.

Captain Hall, Sydney Raymond
6—Sgt. Walker, Leonard Reid
8—Pte. Gill, Charles Dunderdale
9—Pte. Spry, Gordon William
15—Pte. Leahy, Raymond Benjamin
16—Pte. Massey, Thomas

17—Pte. McAulay, Hector Percival
20—Pte. Clarke, George
37—Pte. Murphy, Reginald William
394—Pte. Truman, Wilfred
715—Pte. Robinson, George Alfred

TRANSPORT SECTION.

2nd Lieut. Smyth, Trevor Owen
445—Sgt. Gill, Edward Charles
52—L.-Cpl. Hurcombe, Roy Kintore
42—Dvr. Lloyd, William
49—Dvr. Warren, Frederick Arnold
78—Dvr. Bennett, Francis Harold
83—Dvr. Lingwood-Smith, Albert
119—Dvr. Woods, Sylvanus Samuel
165—Dvr. King, Albert James Henry

217—Dvr. Mooney, James
226—Dvr. Coley, George
423 Dvr. Cox, Robert Emmanuel
721—Dvr. Young, Phillip
745—Dvr. Stewart, William
861—Dvr. Shearer, Elliott Leaney
869—Dvr. Jones, Edward
909—Dvr. Warren, William Patrick
1103—Dvr. Ross, John Thomas

MEDICAL SECTION.

Capt. Nott, Harry Carew (A.A.M.C.)
172—Cpl. Davinett, Charles Beauchamp (A.A.M.C.)
144—L.-Cpl. Becker, Jean Pierre
89—Pte. Canaway, Leslie St. John (A.A.M.C.)

114—Pte. Smith, Donald Lang Talbot (A.A.M.C.)
118—Pte. Miller, Leonard (A.A.M.C.)
173—Pte. De Jong, Edward Meyer (A.A.M.C.)

MISCELLANEOUS DETAILS.

79—Pte. Cade, Frederick Harold
103—Pte. Simpson, Harry North
289—Pte. Crowder, William Thomas
586—Pte. Roberts, Malcolm Howard

952—Pte. Jacobs, Herbert Edward
954—Pte. Jones, Eric Clifford
955—Pte. King, Leo
1073—Pte. Alford, Gordon James

MACHINE GUN SECTION.

2nd Lieut. Robley, Vernon Hermann
7—Sgt. Sawer, Edgar Geoffrey
10—Cpl. Edgar, William
23—L.-Cpl. McIntosh, Victor Charles
25—L.-Cpl. Harden, James Stanley
28—Dvr. Forsyth, Francis Davison
1001—Dvr. Williams, Harold Lennox
12—Pte. Coughlan, Alma
22—Pte. Reid, John Thomas

24—Pte. Monks, Vivian Cyril
26—Pte. O'Callaghan, John
29—Pte. Hall, Robert William
158—Pte. Hooper, James Richard
437—Pte. Roach, Eric Mervyn
475—Pte. Andrews, Ronald Ernest
820—Pte. Tonkin, James
1000—Pte. Kethro, Joseph
1072—Pte. Mackie, Robert

NOMINAL ROLL OF ORIGINAL BATTALION

"A" COMPANY.

Major Beevor, Miles Fitzroy
Lieut. Hosking, Herbert Champion
2nd Lieut. Rumball, Clarence
45—Col.-Sgt. Oliver, Thomas Brown
159—Sgt. Gordon, John Rutherford
209—Sgt. Rigney, Sydney Earl
320—Sgt. Henwood, Horace Norman
396—Sgt. Tidy, Tom Stuart
43—Cpl. McAulay, John Albert
319—Cpl. Barclay, Charles James
626—Cpl. Dunk, Melville Basil
656—Cpl. King, Frederick John
664—Cpl. Cromwell, Victor
32—L.-Cpl. Annis, Cecil Edgar
39—L.-Cpl. Inglis, Eric Murray
239—L.-Cpl. Vallis, Arthur James
370—L.-Cpl. Clarke, Hubert
675—L.-Cpl. Bradley, Clarence Eugene
205—Bugler Witcomb, Oscar George
722—Bugler Broughton, Frederick John
740—Dvr. Raffen, Percy Edward Leonard
956—Dvr. Brokenshire, George Reginald
30—Pte. Balfour, Claude Frederick
31—Pte. Blackburn, Arthur Seaforth
33—Pte. Fisher, Guy
34—Pte. Holloway, Percy Edgecumbe
35—Pte. Holland, Frederick
36—Pte. Hutson, Aubrey Victor
38—Pte. Jose, Oswald Wilfred
40—Pte. Stokes, Francis Herbert
41—Pte. Meldrum, Eric Douglas
44—Pte. Wearne, Samuel Arthur
46—Pte. Neil, George
47—Pte. Whyte, Thomas Anderson
48—Pte. Robertson, Ivan Scott
50—Pte. Smith, Stanley Rupert
160—Pte. Harrison, Richard Temple
189—Pte. Schofield, Arthur
203—Pte. Turnbull, John Sanderson
204—Pte. Tydeman, Basil
206—Pte. Walters, Walter Hetley
207—Pte. Bennett, Garnet Wolseley
208—Pte. Boucher, William Alexander Joseph
286—Pte. Smith, Malcolm Teesdale
287—Pte. Edwards, Harold
288—Pte. Sharrad, Victor Wallace
290—Pte. Quinnell, Stanley
291—Pte. Smith, Stanley
292—Pte. Tucker, John Stuart
293—Pte. Moore, Allen Samuel
314—Pte. Hanton, Harold Hardy
318—Pte. Johnston, Frederick Roy
321—Pte. Fordham, Horace Utting
323—Pte. Johnston, Thomas Edmund
339—Pte. Elliott, Charles Herbert
381—Pte. McTavish, James
384—Pte. Ricken, Jack
385—Pte. Banks, Harold Alonzo
388—Pte. Allchin, Frank Edmund
393—Pte. Ey, Richard Ernest
397—Pte. Crouch, Leonard
398—Pte. Sharrad, Joseph Willie
399—Pte. Everall, Henry
401—Pte. Ehlers, Henry Frederick William
402—Pte. Appleby, Robert
403—Pte. Graham, Archibald
421—Pte. Westbury, William Charles
434—Pte. Dunhill, Avelyn Clarence
435—Pte. Pendle, Walter Vincent
436—Pte. Fisher, Frank Norman
444—Pte. Sharpe, Frederick
628—Pte. McNiece, Cecil Joseph George
636—Pte. Evans, Andrew David
637—Pte. Hearne, John Edwards
638—Pte. Robin, Philip de Quetteville
639—Pte. Halstead, Alick
640—Pte. Mercer, Arthur William
641—Pte. Lithgow, Mark Holman George
643—Pte. Wilson, William
644—Pte. Smith, Peter Vincent
645—Pte. Knutsen, Nils Andreas
646—Pte. Worthley, Harry
647—Pte. Francis, Rupert Stanley
648—Pte. Langridge, Charles
649—Pte. Riley, John
650—Pte. Kaerger, Frederick Ludwig Paul Albert
651—Pte. Haines, Cephas Ratchne
652—Pte. Lee, James Campbell
653—Pte. Harvey, Henry George
654—Pte. Robertson, Duncan Markham
657—Pte. Murray, William
658—Pte. Johnston, William
660—Pte. Hall, Harry James
662—Pte. Scott, Frank
663—Pte. Shepherdson, Ernest John
665—Pte. Hannaford, Lancelot Ramsay
666—Pte. Long, Charles Otto
668—Pte. Holloway, John Leonard
676—Pte. Pascall, Howard Henley
677—Pte. Palmer, Thomas George William
718—Pte. Westley, Benjamin
730—Pte. Davis, Frederick Gordon
946—Pte. Wormwell, Jesse
947—Pte. Ross, George Donald
948—Pte. Rayney, Robert Allan
949—Pte. Page, Norman Livingstone
950—Pte. Hurford, Frederick
951—Pte. Harrison, Alfred Cornelius
957—Pte. Hope, Albert
958—Pte. Nunn, Walter Hardman Bates
959—Pte. Lee-Thomas, Henry
960—Pte. Nunn, Albert James
961—Pte. Swan, Nicholas
1018—Pte. Gatfield, William
1021—Pte. Kelly, Thomas
1035—Pte. Watson, Samuel James

294   THE FIGHTING 10TH

1039—Pte. Rambert, George Robert
1040—Pte. Smith, Angus Archer

1055—Pte. Wilkinson, Frederick Charles Erasmus

"B" COMPANY.

Capt. Shaw, George Dorricutt
2nd Lieut. Stopp, Eric John Carl
2nd Lieut. Farrier, Charles Percy
51—Col.-Sgt. Hassam, Oscar Donald
54—Sgt. Howe, Sydney John
55—Sgt. Jarrett, Adolphus Wilmot
61—Sgt. Lister, Charles
566—Sgt. Hall, George
58—Cpl. Whitbread, Albert Alfred Osmond
60—Cpl. Prince, George Debney Lloyd
417—Cpl. Phillips, Albert Edward
546—Cpl. Cheney, Edward
823—Cpl. Paul, John
57—L.-Cpl. Westwood, Cecil Roy
212—L.-Cpl. Jolley, Cyril
545—L.-Cpl. Spinkston, Royce
841—L.-Cpl. Carroll, Donald McDonald
968—Bugler Gordon, Thomas Stanley
1041—Bugler Hill, Edward Richard
164—Dvr. Spencer, Henry Law
612—Dvr. Allen, John James
13—Pte. Robertson, Herbert John
56—Pte. Mackay, Harold Oswald
59—Pte. Nock, Ronald Ashton
63—Pte. Evans, Francis Gilbert
82—Pte. Loader, Percy
161—Pte. Horsefield, Cyril
162—Pte. Dommett, Wilfred
210—Pte. Wray, James Searle
211—Pte. Walker, Richard Ernest
243—Pte. Hall, Herbert William
312—Pte. Dunlop, George Alfred
395—Pte. Andrew, Archibald John
447—Pte. Wickham, Lindsay Claude
466—Pte. Cole, William
467—Pte. Kirk, Archibald George
468—Pte. Coombs, Tressilian Herbert
469—Pte. Plummer, James Willas
544—Pte. Webster, Albert Edward
567—Pte. McMahon, Nicholas
568—Pte. Johnson, Theodore
569—Pte. Wilson, Archibald
570—Pte. Carlson, Nicholas
571—Pte. Jensen, William Laurence
572—Pte. Fulton, William
611—Pte. Nutall, Percy Edward
613—Pte. Cox, Josiah
614—Pte. Fennell, Joseph William
615—Pte. Howse, Frederick Thomas
616—Pte. Richmond, Alexander
617—Pte. Ebborn, Wilfred Henry
618—Pte. Castle, William
621—Pte. Lewis, Ernest Stanley
623—Pte. McCormick, Thomas
624—Pte. Lock, Cecil Bert Lovell
667—Pte. Wilson, Edward Roy
669—Pte. Switzer, William Arthur
670—Pte. Kirk, Albert
671—Pte. Harvey, Charles William
672—Pte. Copeland, Robert
673—Pte. Winyard, Richard
674—Pte. Fisher, Thomas
678—Pte. Holthouse, Reginald Herbert
679—Pte. Pearce, Ambrose Stanley
680—Pte. Crocker, Thomas Arthur
682—Pte. Feige, Kurt Gerhart
683—Pte. Link, Albert Ernest
684—Pte. Leonard, Arthur Henry
685—Pte. Neave, George Danford
686—Pte. Anderson, John Albert Ellis
687—Pte. Simpson, Stamford Wallace
688—Pte. Weatherly, Leonard Walker
689—Pte. Lewis, David
806—Pte. Cheney, Henry Arundel
807—Pte. Wallbridge, Harry George
817—Pte. Macfarlane, Horace Edward
818—Pte. Horley, Frank Harry
819—Pte. Pendleton, George Henry
821—Pte. Ramsay, George
822—Pte. Long, Francis Edward
824—Pte. Langley, Thomas Edward
825—Pte. Davis, Norman Ernest
826—Pte. James, Tudor
827—Pte. Goard, Joseph Reginald
828—Pte. Beeson, Albert
829—Pte. Ayers, James
830—Pte. Smith, James
831—Pte. Player, Henry John
832—Pte. Foster, Albert Ernest
833—Pte. King, John Charles
835—Pte. Smallacombe, Stewart
836—Pte. Hunter, Albert Charles
837—Pte. Graves, Stanley Edward
838—Pte. Craig, Thomas
839—Pte. Nickless, Albert John
840—Pte. Bence, Vivian Clarence
842—Pte. Kay, Thomas
844—Pte. Mensforth, Arthur
845—Pte. Gifford, William
846—Pte. Robertson, Alexander
847—Pte. Henry, James
849—Pte. McVey, Robert George
944—Pte. Richardson, Frederick Herbert
945—Pte. Jones, Frederick Wallace
962—Pte. Parkinson, Clifford Roy
963—Pte. Partridge, John Leslie
964—Pte. Court, Arthur James
965—Pte. Venning, Percy William
966—Pte. Carter, George Box
967—Pte. Coffen, Harry Hughes
969—Pte. Smythe, James Hugh
1008—Pte. Scott, Leslie William Arthur
1030—Pte. Morphett, Glinton Stewart Victor
1042—Pte. Vick, William Henry

NOMINAL ROLL OF ORIGINAL BATTALION 295

1043—Pte. Casey, Patrick
1044—Pte. Stagatitch, William James
1070—Pte. Scott, Thomas Stephen

1075—Pte. Merritt, Benjamin John
1092—Pte. Trevor, Paul William

"C" COMPANY.

Lieut. Green, Keith Eddowes
Lieut. Sexton, Eric James
2nd Lieut. Hooper, Robert James Mansfield
74—Col.-Sgt. Aspinall, Charles Alfred
77—Sgt. Backman, Charles James
113—Sgt. Fry, Leslie Kenneth Temple
213—Sgt. Hall, Anthony Basil
338—Sgt. Courtenay, James
76—Cpl. Kolb, Oswald
92—Cpl. Pickering, Roy
101—Cpl. Seaman, Walter Batley
180—Cpl. Mollett, Clarence Harcroft
214—Cpl. Wilson-Todd, Robert William
97—L.-Cpl. Foggarty, Michael
108—L.-Cpl. Ruddock, Stephen
114—L.-Cpl. Youds, Clarence Gordon
425—L.-Cpl. Cussion, Charles Colin
633—L.-Cpl. Read, Walter Gordon
712—L.-Cpl. Nagle, William John
717—L.-Cpl. Coughlan, Michael
88—Bugler Manchip, Walter Stanley
632—Bugler Noble, Thomas Lindsay
75—Dvr. Bergin, Walter
359—Dvr. Lynch, Hurtle John Watson
14—Pte. Holden, Joseph
80—Pte. Blackburn, Watkins William
81—Pte. Marriott, Thomas William
84—Pte. Klenner, Arthur George
85—Pte. Kennedy, John McGain
86—Pte. O'Reilly, John James
90—Pte. Quinn, Henry
91—Pte. Pilkington, Francis William
93—Pte. Hester, Percy George
95—Pte. Hooper, William Thomas
96—Pte. Goodyer, Harry
98—Pte. Emmott, Thomas Ernest
100—Pte. Smart, Jesse
102—Pte. Slaughter, Percy Charles
104—Pte. Shelley, William George
109—Pte. Whitelaw, Arthur John Leslie
110—Pte. Vennermark, Carl William
112—Pte. Smith, William James
115—Pte. Waller, Arthur Roy
116—Pte. Wilson, Edward George
117—Pte. Williams, Alfred Parmer
118—Pte. Hughes, Frank
166—Pte. Ryan, Patrick Francis
182—Pte. Liddiard, John Percy Henry
328—Pte. Castles, George Herbert
336—Pte. Havey, Francis
337—Pte. Warming, Frederick James
340—Pte. Cussion, Christian Walter
341—Pte. Lapthorne, Victor Walter Athelstone
342—Pte. Watson, Thomas
343—Pte. Burns, Jack
344—Pte. Thorn, William

345—Pte. Shelley, Edmund
346—Pte. McLaren, Sydney
350—Pte. Welch, Leslie
351—Pte. Wood, Arthur Douglas
353—Pte. McGrath, Walter Leonard
354—Pte. Shaw, Hurtle Charles
355—Pte. Faint, William
356—Pte. Taylor, Frederick
358—Pte. Johnson, Frederick Aloysius
360—Pte. Morgan, Arthur George
362—Pte. King, Robert
363—Pte. Wells, Ronald Charles
365—Pte. Doley, Samuel Edmund
366—Pte. Ryan, Charles
367—Pte. Purdie, Edward Driver
369—Pte. O'Meara, John James
627—Pte. Chilman, Percival John
631—Pte. Featherstone, John
690—Pte. Organ, Harry
711—Pte. Lambert, Stanley
713—Pte. Brook, Donald Hamilton
714—Pte. White, Albert Henry
716—Pte. Watson, Alfred John
741—Pte. Whyte, George Rennie
808—Pte. Smith, Charles
896—Pte. McVicar, John Kenneth
897—Pte. Corcoran, Thomas Leo
898—Pte. Green, Lincoln Llewellyn
899—Pte. Bradford, John William Archie
901—Pte. Farrar, Arthur
902—Pte. Greenhill, Percival Charles
903—Pte. James, John Rodda
904—Pte. Pagan, Joseph Burt
905—Pte. Evans, Erle Charrington
907—Pte. Stanford, William Edwin Arthur
908—Pte. Morrison, Jack
911—Pte. Hepburn, John
912—Pte. Macklin, George
913—Pte. Hanrahan, Thomas Michael
914—Pte. Watts, Gordon Stanley
915—Pte. Thomson, George William Wyville
917—Pte. Coles, William
919—Pte. Sast, Alexander
972—Pte. Gray, Alfred James
973—Pte. Pyne, Patrick Thomas
975—Pte. Hoare, John Murdoch
977—Pte. Ward, Oliver
978—Pte. Holden, John
979—Pte. Ferrett, George Clement
982—Pte. Knight, Ernest Barrington
1009—Pte. Francis, Bryan Maurice
1031—Pte. Trebilcock, Frederick Norman
1032—Pte. Middleton, Mervyn Merritt Bath
1054—Pte. Waine, Joseph
1056—Pte. Wheatley, Frederick

296 THE FIGHTING 10TH

1057—Pte. Kay, James
1079—Pte. Barnes, John
1080—Pte. Curley, John
1084—Pte. Smith, Frank Palmer
1086—Pte. Fisher, Richard
1087—Pte. Edmonds, George William
1088—Pte. Waterton, Albert
1089—Pte. Winter, Walter William
1090—Pte. Morgan, Rowland Claude
1095—Pte. Smith, Clement James Drummond

"D" COMPANY.

Capt. Herbert, Mervyn James
2nd Lieut. Todd, David Leslie
2nd Lieut. Frayne, William Stanley
133—Col.-Sgt. Coward, Henry
124—Sgt. Newlands, Alan John
131—Sgt. Neave, Albert George Ferdinand
405—Sgt. McCann, William Francis James
407—Sgt. McGillivray, Ivor Eric
125—Cpl. Outerbridge, Stanley Alexander
371—Cpl. Boyle, John
883—Cpl. Blunt, Edward Keith
939—Cpl. Oliver, Edward Bruce
126—L.-Cpl. Tippett, George
169—L.-Cpl. Kent, Harold
404—L.-Cpl. Addison, Herbert
746—L.-Cpl. MacNeil, Alexander William L.
170—Bugler Battye, James
389—Bugler Edis, William Taylor
860—Dvr. Barnes, Victor Malcolm
870—Dvr. Gabriel, Harold
94—Pte. Howard, George Clemont
121—Pte. Harnden, Roy Rupert
122—Pte. Green, Cyril Patrick
123—Pte. O'Connell, John
127—Pte. Wilson, Leonard Bartlett
129—Pte. Redpath, Archibald
130—Pte. Pearson, Raymond Arthur
132—Pte. Kelly, William
167—Pte. Harper, Archibald Salvador
168—Pte. Hamilton, Robert John Joseph
173—Pte. Wickens, Harold Gordon
175—Pte. Winfield, Harry Mosely
324—Pte. Mead, Frederick James Stanley
325—Pte. Shaw, John
326—Pte. Hendry, Charles
327—Pte. Rockwell, Reginald George Anstey
386—Pte. Darrock, Gordon David
390—Pte. Benton, Robert Bruce
391—Pte. Murray, James
406—Pte. Butterfield, Alfred Hall
415—Pte. Button, Arthur Irvine
456—Pte. Weatherill, Joseph Cook
470—Pte. Guthrie, George
471—Pte. Kelly, Harry
472—Pte. Pack, Simon George
547—Pte. Anderson, Douglas
549—Pte. Cox, Robert John
550—Pte. Brammy, George Howard
551—Pte. Bates, Glen Roy
552—Pte. Beasley, Frederick
553—Pte. Baker, Arthur Robert
554—Pte. Moncrieff, James
555—Pte. Keen, Alfred William
556—Pte. King, Charles
557—Pte. Richards, Vyvyan Henry
558—Pte. Sutherland, John Donald
559—Pte. Toovey, Leslie Clarence
560—Pte. Westall, Harry Thomas
561—Pte. Wilson, Joseph Henry
573—Pte. Arnold, Frederick Michael
575—Pte. Breeding, William Clarence
576—Pte. Daniell, Frederick Charles
577—Pte. Everett, Harry Blair Everett
578—Pte. Fennell, David
580—Pte. McKay, Albert John
581—Pte. O'Donnell, John Patrick
582—Pte. Wagnersen, Kristian
742—Pte. Nelson, Edward Charles
743—Pte. Reid, Frederick Charles
744—Pte. Field, Ralph Ewart
804—Pte. Zander, Charles Oscar
813—Pte. Taylor, James
862—Pte. Richardson, Herbert James
864—Pte. Jones, Harry Richard
865—Pte. Hawkes, George William
866—Pte. McCaffrey, Michael
867—Pte. Douglas, Gordon Walter
868—Pte. Docherty, Patrick
871—Pte. Milne, Learmouth
872—Pte. Jenkins, Sydney Herbert
873—Pte. Seary, Thomas
878—Pte. Dillon, Daniel
881—Pte. Kennedy, Martin
882—Pte. Baker, George Ernest Anthony
885—Pte. Sheridan, James
886—Pte. Burton, Reginald
887—Pte. Sharp, Adam James
892—Pte. Carson, Alfred Gibbon
893—Pte. Child, Alfred
932—Pte. Sheppard, William Alfred
933—Pte. Mueller, Reginald Henry
934—Pte. Robertson, John Modley
935—Pte. Couston, Alec
936—Pte. Lieschke, George Albert
937—Pte. Howe, Ernest Edward
938—Pte. Doddridge, George Ernest
941—Pte. Jackson, Edgar Harold
953—Pte. Schmidt, Peter
983—Pte. Mossop, Percy Fairlees
984—Pte. Allen, Charles Henry
985—Pte. Carr, David
986—Pte. Rivett, Alfred
987—Pte. Maccini, Joseph
988—Pte. Webb, William Arthur
1016—Pte. Cusack, Patrick

NOMINAL ROLL OF ORIGINAL BATTALION

1017—Pte. Walker, Samuel Hurtle
1019—Pte. Cavanagh, John Percy
1023—Pte. Durrant, Harry
1025—Pte. Wood, Robert
1033—Pte. Howard, William Harry
1034—Pte. Payne, Elford Athol
1038—Pte. Van Veen, William Carl
1048—Pte. Staker, Stanley Botham
1068—Pte. Ternan, Walter Percy
1069—Pte. Plew, William John
1081—Pte. Delaney, Edward
1097—Pte. Chadwick, Benjamin
1098—Pte. Watson, Joseph Charles

"E" COMPANY.

Capt. Oldham, Edward Castle
2nd Lieut. Heming, Hector Roy
2nd Lieut. Sommerville, Alfred Cyril
135—Col.-Sgt. Jones, Charles Henry
65—Sgt. Bates, Charles Joseph
177—Sgt. Tucker, Alfred Martin James
178—Sgt. Steer, George Colin
231—Sgt. Pearce, John Ellis
142—Cpl. Beresford, William Russell de la Poer
181—Cpl. McMahon, Michael John
216—Cpl. Kinnish, Henry Arthur
424—Cpl. Rixon, Frederick
619—Cpl. Sinclair, John Mitchell
191—L.-Cpl. Sandland, Arnold Cooper
192—L.-Cpl. Timcke, Karl Frederick
228—L.-Cpl. Davidson, Walter Harold
329—L.-Cpl. Reading, John Forrest
791—L.-Cpl. Moore, Andrew John
172—Bugler Bartholomaeus, Herbert Alexander
316—Bugler Freeman, Fred
137—Dvr. Hooper, Archie Gordon
774—Dvr. Marriott, Percy George
11—Pte. Bastard, Robert Stanley
19—Pte. Durham, Patrick James
21—Pte. Lewis, James Llewellyn
64—Pte. Geddes, Joseph
66—Pte. Jacobs, Arthur Abraham
134—Pte. Knox, Alexander
136—Pte. Johnson, Arthur William
138—Pte. Bray, George
139—Pte. Tobin, William Francis
140—Pte. Rosewarne, Leonard James
171—Pte. Churton, Alex Roper
176—Pte. Scudds, Howard Wilson
179—Pte. Robinson, Christopher Keith
190—Pte. Edmonds, George Francis Charles
193—Pte. Williams, William James
194—Pte. Winnicott, Charles Henry Jackson
195—Pte. McInerney, Michael John
197—Pte. Scott, Joseph William Arthur Laurence
215—Pte. Moffitt, Frank Granville
218—Pte. Fleetwood, Harold Leslie
219—Pte. Falk, Charles John
220—Pte. Giblin, Leo
222—Pte. Harrison, Frank Hugh
223—Pte. Claridge, Ralph Elesmere
224—Pte. Cameron, Richard
225—Pte. Donald, William
229—Pte. Paget, Harry S.
232—Pte. Robertson, Stanley James
244—Pte. Glover, Archie
245—Pte. Fairburn, George
246—Pte. Marks, Bernard Ernest
247—Pte. McKiernan, Bernard
330—Pte. Mort, Joseph
332—Pte. Gower, John Lewis
347—Pte. Toster, George
373—Pte. Nation, Henry Albert
418—Pte. Bott, Herbert Allen
536—Pte. Ryan, Walter
620—Pte. Fisher, David
709—Pte. Clark, Charles Edward James
758—Pte. Hoggarth, William Paton
759—Pte. Sayer, Walter Albert
760—Pte. Kennerick, John Henry
761—Pte. Thorne, Garnet Whayfoote
762—Pte. Rae, Albert Norman
763—Pte. Blackford, Harold
764—Pte. Lace, George William
765—Pte. Hewett, Roy Sylvester
766—Pte. Rapley, Reginald
767—Pte. MacLennan, Robert Sharp Galbraith
768—Pte. Conway, John James
769—Pte. Wright, John Dixon
770—Pte. Jackson, Peter Henry
771—Pte. Straney, Patrick
772—Pte. Bradley, Frederick Mark
773—Pte. Adam, Robert Sangster
775—Pte. Mann, Thomas Rule
777—Pte. Bradley, Henry
778—Pte. Hockey, Emmanuel Victor
779—Pte. Garland, Herbert Victor
780—Pte. Spry, Stanley Percy
781—Pte. O'Neill, Thomas
782—Pte. Sealey, Harry
783—Pte. Russell, James
784—Pte. Shields, Richard Thompson
785—Pte. Smith, Ernest Archibald
786—Pte. Robins, William
787—Pte. Bradshaw, William Arthur
788—Pte. Anstey, John Trenn
789—Pte. Wickham, James William
790—Pte. Strang, William Andrew
792—Pte. Oates, Irwin Harry
793—Pte. Pugh, Walter Ernest
795—Pte. Lennard, William Charles
796—Pte. Gibbons, William James
797—Pte. Bruce, Jack McCulloch

798—Pte. Peardon, Percival King
799—Pte. Hunter, Robert
800—Pte. Reid, Allan Ivier
920—Pte. Snow, Frank
923—Pte. Lovell, Ernest Charles
924—Pte. Lovell, Benjamin Frank
942—Pte. Chapman, Charles George
991—Pte. Bowers, Thomas William
992—Pte. Tyndall, Sydney Howard
1006—Pte. Walkley, Alfred Rascoria
1007—Pte. Bateman, Valentine Thomas
1027—Pte. Topliffe, Arthur Gordon
1028—Pte. Black, Harold Frederick
1029—Pte. Huselius, Ernest Ferdinand
1037—Pte. Cocks, William
1047—Pte. Hayward, Bernard William
1063—Pte. Peters, Thomas Edward
1066—Pte. Sanders, John
1076—Pte. Ward-Proctor, Dudley
1082—Pte. Johnson, John William
1085—Pte. Hill, Raymond Davenport
1101—Pte. Hill, George

"F" COMPANY.

Capt. Redburg, George Ernest
Lieut. Holmes, Louis Gordon
Lieut. Smith, Eric Wilkes Talbot
708—Col.-Sgt. Coombe, Samuel Walter
183—Sgt. Clarke, Tennyson George
691—Sgt. English, Charles Frederick
695—Sgt. Virgo, Claude Arnold Percival
850—Sgt. Tomlinson, Charles Albert
333—Cpl. Coffey, Stanley Clarke
377—Cpl. Cowan, Geoffrey
392—Cpl. Gellert, Leon Maxwell
706—Cpl. Storey, Thomas Victor
707—Cpl. Martin, Thomas Ernest
67—L.-Cpl. Manning, Arthur
368—L.-Cpl. Mayman, Rupert Livingstone
699—L.-Cpl. Adams, Thomas Henry
853—L.-Cpl. Davidson, James
696—Bugler Stewart, Thomas
1022—Bugler Flood, John Michael
736—Dvr. Marshall, Joseph Thomas
926—Dvr. Boag, Edward Henderson
18—Pte. Wemyss, Robert
68—Pte. Moyse, Gerald Albion
69—Pte. Denman, Henry Spencer
70—Pte. McWilliam, Joseph Glaister
71—Pte. Amber, Charles William
72—Pte. Ellmer, Samuel
73—Pte. Allard, Alfred Donald
145—Pte. Woods, Douglas Griffen Tenison
146—Pte. Du Rieu, Desmond Theodore
147—Pte. Hicks, Ernest
148—Pte. Rhodes, Randall Lance
184—Pte. Fordham, Roy Ogilvie
185—Pte. Lennell, Roy
186—Pte. Crowhurst, Frank Samuel
187—Pte. Barker, Oliver Albert Mortimer
334—Pte. Skinner, Henry William
348—Pte. Jones, Denis
353—Pte. Allen, William James
375—Pte. Glover, Roy
376—Pte. Durbin, William John
378—Pte. Chase, Walter Vernon
379—Pte. Herriott, Hubert Ronald
380—Pte. Kent, William
387—Pte. Ash, Arthur Addison
420—Pte. Sheedy, James John
443—Pte. Wauchope, Ernest John Luther
449—Pte. Woods, Charles John Tenison
450—Pte. Goode, Eric Rolfe
454—Pte. Lashmar, Allen John
455—Pte. Rule, Charles
473—Pte. Carter, Sydney Mervyn
474—Pte. East, Walter Leonard
564—Pte. Mosel, Frederick Frank Ernest
692—Pte. Thomson, James
693—Pte. Marsh, Albert Arthur
694—Pte. Gaskell, Wilfred Samuel
697—Pte. Hansen, Andrew
698—Pte. Marchant, McCord
700—Pte. Ryan, Thomas Henry
701—Pte. Roke, John
702—Pte. Nash, Brunel John
703—Pte. Biggs, Stanley
705—Pte. Lowe, Alfred
710—Pte. Colbey, Frank Hammond
719—Pte. Wells, Edward James
720—Pte. Barry, Max William
723—Pte. Basnett, Leonard
725—Pte. Duffey, John Patrick
726—Pte. De Graaf, Henry Charles
727—Pte. Tume, Walter William, same as Kendrick, Edward John
728—Pte. Mackay, Percy Alexander
729—Pte. Ritchie, Thomas
731—Pte. Adams, John Albert
732—Pte. Munro, Douglas Stewart
733—Pte. Pointing, William Henry
734—Pte. Ashenden, George Henry
735—Pte. Mantell, William Henry
737—Pte. Huddy, Arthur
738—Pte. Sandford, Albert William
739—Pte. Hunter, Hugh Hamilton
801—Pte. Johnson, Arthur Sydney
802—Pte. Ross, William Gordon
809—Pte. Olifent, Douglas Roy Elson
810—Pte. Antram, Harry
811—Pte. Gale, Keith St. Clair
812—Pte. Taylor, Francis Thomas
814—Pte. Phillis, Horace Vincent
815—Pte. Altwood, William Charles
816—Pte. Lindop, George William
851—Pte. Bushell, Alfred Ernest
852—Pte. Bushell, John Spencer
854—Pte. Ward, Peter John
855—Pte. Wilcock, John

NOMINAL ROLL OF ORIGINAL BATTALION

856—Pte. Watherston, Edward Alexander
857—Pte. Cryer, George Samuel
859—Pte. Morgan, Joseph
875—Pte. Beames, George Darley
876—Pte. Braithwaite, John Bowman
888—Pte. Huntley, George Henry Stuart
889—Pte. Palmer, Claude Ernest
890—Pte. Edwards, Hartley James
925—Pte. Farrell, Sydney Frederick James
927—Pte. Hocke, Leonard Wilms
928—Pte. Cochrane, Herbert
929—Pte. Robertson, George

993—Pte. Gaffney, James Hugh
996—Pte. Rogers, James Keith
997—Pte. Brown, Robert Service
998—Pte. Isbell, William
1050—Pte. Marshall, Aitken
1060—Pte. Pinson, Clarence Victor
1061—Pte. Bowden, John Stirling
1064—Pte. Sargent, George Aron
1065—Pte. Wilson, William
1067—Pte. Sale, Charles
1093—Pte. Sheldrake, William James
1094—Pte. Edwards, James
1099—Pte. Pierce, Frank

"G" COMPANY.

Lieut. Giles, Felix Gordon
2nd Lieut. Loutit, Noel Medway
2nd Lieut. Perry, William Howard
234—Col.-Sgt. Henderson, George Francis
150—Sgt. Evans, William Horace Lionel
155—Sgt. Lodge, Wilfred Francis Huggert
157—Sgt. Duncan, Andrew Stewart
411—Sgt. Ford, Francis Charles
188—Cpl. Rule, Thomas Esson James
199—Cpl. Blake, Walter Henry
237—Cpl. Searcy, John William
255—Cpl. White, Herbert Hurtle
269—L.-Cpl. Hazelwood, George William Edward
276—L.-Cpl. Robinson, Arthur Harold
383—L.-Cpl. Batty, William Reginald
414—L.-Cpl. Franklin, Rodney Vernon
594—L.-Cpl. Catlow, Thomas Norris
1036—L.-Cpl. Kent, Edgar
605—Bugler Smith, Ernest
803—Bugler Evans, John
259—Dvr. Ogilvy, James
442—Dvr. McKinnon, Roderick
120—Pte. Creighton, Edward William
149—Pte. Cook, Elsley Arthur
151—Pte. Sudbury-Smith, Harold George
152—Pte. Winchester, John
154—Pte. Lazarus, Joseph
156—Pte. Lee, Leonard Walter
198—Pte. Bertram, Charles
200—Pte. Gallagher, Martin
201—Pte. Cato, Leonard Frederick
202—Pte. Malone, Michael
233—Pte. Opie, Henry Heyworth
235—Pte. Harris, Walter Geoffrey
236—Pte. Hamilton, Walter
238—Pte. Wells, Stephen Claude
240—Pte. Watson, George
241—Pte. Dashwood, Frank Leopold
242—Pte. Darrell, Edward
248—Pte. White, Arthur
249—Pte. Waller, Leonard John
250—Pte. Watkins, Fred
251—Pte. Tombs, Percival Charles James
253—Pte. Vincent, Herbert

254—Pte. Vanderweg, Arent
256—Pte. West, Charles
258—Pte. Osborn, Alfred Ernest
260—Pte. Moss, Alfred Hector
261—Pte. Masters, Leslie Edgar
263—Pte. McLaren, Clarence Roy
264—Pte. McLeod, Roy
266—Pte. Lanchester, Donald Thomas
267—Pte. Liddle, Albert
268—Pte. Halliday, William George
270—Pte. Hall, Harold
271—Pte. Howie, Leslie Bryant
272—Pte. Gibson, Lionel George
273—Pte. Carmichael, Gordon
274—Pte. Parsons, John Gordon
275—Pte. Phelan, Thomas P.
278—Pte. Scott, Frank John
279—Pte. Taylor, George
280—Pte. Trichard, Henry Daniel
281—Pte. Beard, Arthur Earnest
282—Pte. Affleck, James Carlyle Wells
283—Pte. Chilman, Roy
284—Pte. Daley, Robert
349—Pte. Hanley, Justin Thomas Augustine
364—Pte. White, Roy Neville
412—Pte. Ellerton, Douglas William
413—Pte. Curran, Gerald Patrick
416—Pte. Reed, Sydney Hayter
426—Pte. Lynn, Segmore Breadstropp Powell
427—Pte. Smith, Francis Rodney Thomas
428—Pte. Lines, Joseph James
430—Pte. Dawes, Raymond Oswald
431—Pte. Dawes, Ernest
432—Pte. Fuller, Basil
433—Pte. Palmer, Raymond Roy
438—Pte. Smith, Albert James
439—Pte. King, Harold Newton
440—Pte. Box, Walter
441—Pte. Macey, William Henry
451—Pte. White, John Alexander
452—Pte. Wright, Arthur Thomas
584—Pte. MacPherson, Norman Allan-Wallace
585—Pte. McGuire, Reginald Francis

587—Pte. Franks, Albert Ernest
589—Pte. Leach, William
590—Pte. Davis, Alfred
591—Pte. Alston, Harry
592—Pte. Washington, James Roy
595—Pte. Stevens, William John
596—Pte. Richards, Albert
597—Pte. McCoy, Frank
598—Pte. Watson, Frederick Robert
599—Pte. Pike, William
600—Pte. Brooks, Edward Samuel
601—Pte. Liersch, Alfred
602—Pte. Wills, Sydney
603—Pte. Franks, Wilfred Henry
604—Pte. Wright, Henry Taylor
606—Pte. Harmer, Walter James
607—Pte. Gregory, William

608—Pte. Nedham, Harman Oliver
609—Pte. Taylor, Leonard Benjamin
634—Pte. Hincks, Cecil Stephen
891—Pte. Lines, Cecil Roy
931—Pte. Tritton, Reginald Arthur
999—Pte. Dakyns, Thomas Lort Mansel
1010—Pte. Jackson, Albert Heyward
1011—Pte. Marshall, Andrew Kirkland
1045—Pte. Stidston, Lancelot Lyndhurst Tudor
1046—Pte. Harvey, Stanley Robert
1058—Pte. Wellcoat, Hugh Joseph Simpson
1059—Pte. Botten, Edwin
1062—Pte. Vivian, Nicolas Archibald
1077—Pte. Thomas, Horace James
1078—Pte. Toovey, Claude Henry St. Leonard

"H" COMPANY.

Capt. Jacob, Ross Blyth
Lieut. Byrne, Albert John
2nd Lieut. Hamilton, John
1015—Col.-Sgt. Shaw, Harold Baker
461—Sgt. Gilpin, Anthony Simpson
481—Sgt. Baynes, Roy George
498—Sgt. Hunt, Charles Laurence
522—Sgt. Munroe, William Henry
479—Cpl. Baynes, Ambrose Henry
520—Cpl. Molloy, Peter
906—Cpl. Edwards, Albert John
1014—Cpl. Mitchell, George Deane
310—L.-Cpl. McNeil, Robert Finlay
514—L.-Cpl. Montgomery, William Rockliff
538—L.-Cpl. Smith, Cyril Charles
747—L.-Cpl. Foster, Frederick
748—L.-Cpl. Chisholm, Donald
510—Bugler McNeil, John
1052—Bugler Slee, James Gilbert
460—Dvr. Kelly, Thomas Edward
482—Dvr. Bottom, Alfred George
294—Pte. Midwinter, John George
295—Pte. Tobin, William
296—Pte. Stewart, Gordon Brodie
297—Pte. Stanbridge, Charles Roy
298—Pte. Morison, Jack
299—Pte. Atwell, Thomas Arthur
300—Pte. Steuve, Henry
301—Pte. Bridley, Alfred Charles
303—Pte. Cox, Archibald
304—Pte. Meade, John Henry
305—Pte. Mills, Alfred Henry
307—Pte. Chabrel, Victor William
308—Pte. Tune, John Armstrong
309—Pte. Van Driel, W.
311—Pte. Pinkney, Frederick James
313—Pte. Russell, Sydney Herbert
315—Pte. Donald, George Henry
453—Pte. Sampson, James Henry
457—Pte. Williams, Gustav Cyril Milton
458—Pte. Rae, Peter

459—Pte. Cook, Albert
462—Pte. Clayton, John
463—Pte. Cullen, George Frederick
464—Pte. Thomas, William John
465—Pte. Peebles, Joseph
477—Pte. Batt, Frank
478—Pte. Bryant, Sydney
480—Pte. Bice, Herbert Alexander
483—Pte. Bailey, William
484—Pte. Cameron, Colin
485—Pte. Cairns, James
486—Pte. Connock, Edward
487—Pte. Connell, Frank
490—Pte. Daly, William
491—Pte. Delaney, Horace Hurtle
492—Pte. Fessey, John
493—Pte. Green, Leslie Alfred
494—Pte. Gainsburg, Thomas William
495—Pte. Glades, Alexander
496—Pte. Gluyas, Percy
497—Pte. Hunt, Eustine Charles
499—Pte. Hackett, Herbert Bruce
500—Pte. Hill, Thomas
501—Pte. Harley, George
502—Pte. Hodder, Henry
503—Pte. Holland, Ernest Alfred
504—Pte. Holmes, Richard Henry Arthur
505—Pte. Hunter, Thomas
506—Pte. Inwood, Reginald Roy
507—Pte. Kent, Joseph John
508—Pte. Knight, Joseph James
509—Pte. McEwan, George
511—Pte. McCubbin, Alexander
512—Pte. McCallum, Robert
518—Pte. Moran, Edward
519—Pte. Macarty, Humphrey Warren Baker
521—Pte. Maxwell, Edward Richard
523—Pte. Norminton, John
524—Pte. Olsen, Bernard James
525—Pte. Perry, Albert Richard
529—Pte. Reith, John

NOMINAL ROLL OF ORIGINAL BATTALION

530—Pte. Ross, Alex
531—Pte. Randell, Eric Lyle
532—Pte. Rawlins, William James
533—Pte. Richards, George Victor
534—Pte. Randall, Arthur William
535—Pte. Retallack, John James
537—Pte. Smylie, William Miller
539—Pte. Shaughnessy, Albert G.
540—Pte. Sykes, Reginald
542—Pte. Wilson, James
543—Pte. White, George Oliver
565—Pte. Melvin, Duncan
635—Pte. Dobbin, Leonard
750—Pte. Bateson, William Henry
751—Pte. McLintock, John Sloan
752—Pte. Gillett, John William
753—Pte. Thompson, Herbert
754—Pte. Weyler, William Joseph
755—Pte. Burrell, James Andrew

756—Pte. Miller, James
757—Pte. Mather, James
894—Pte. Davey, Albert Henry
895—Pte. Leahy, Thomas
930—Pte. Alexander, William James
1003—Pte. Sleader, Frank
1004—Pte. Harding, Leslie Elliott
1005—Pte. Pavey, Walter
1012—Pte. Thompson, Andrew Jamieson
1013—Pte. Rice, Frank Edwin
1049—Pte. McConnachy, Albert
1051—Pte. Anderson, William
1053—Pte. Mitchell, James Robert
1071—Pte. Christopherson, Martin
1074—Pte. Gray, Frederick
1091—Pte. Sellick, George
1096—Pte. Harrison, James
1100—Pte. Crowther, Alfred

MISCELLANEOUS FACTS CONCERNING ORIGINAL BATTALION.

The original Battalion represented an aggregate of 28,855 years, the average age being 25 years. The oldest member was Lieut.-Colonel S. P. Weir, aged 48 years, and the youngest was Bugler E. R. Hill, aged 18 years, of "B" Company; 615 members of the Battalion were born in South Australia, 176 in other Australian States, 12 in New Zealand, 202 in the British Isles. 12 in various parts of the British Empire, and 10 in foreign countries. There were 903 single men, 96 married, 8 widowers, and 1 divorcee; 581 members made allotments in favour of dependents or next or kin, whilst 446 drew their pay in full; 180 members were serving with the Australian Military Forces at date of enlistment, whilst many had served in the British Army or in the Australian Forces; 567 were Anglicans, 120 Roman Catholics, 145 Methodists, 95 Presbyterians, 31 Baptists, 14 Congregationalists, 10 Church of Christ, 2 Salvation Army, 2 Lutherans, 1 Unitarian, 37 unclassified Protestants, 1 Seventh Day Adventist, 1 Jewish, and 1 atheist. The first death occurred on September 28, 1914, when No. 527 Pte. John William Poole, of "H" Coy., died of illness. Early in 1915 23 members of the Battalion were returned to South Australia as medical cases and 17 as disciplinary cases. Two men of the original Battalion overstayed their leave at Fremantle and were left behind. The number of "originals" serving with the Battalion gradually dwindled, until in the Jeancourt operation of 18/9/18 only thirty were left. It was a fitting coincidence that before proceeding on 1914 Anzac Leave they had participated in the last engagement of the Battalion. Seventeen members of the original Battalion are buried in the A.I.F. Cemetery, at West Terrace, Adelaide. No original officers of the 10th have died since demobilization. Ex-No. 425 Lance-corporal Charles Colin Cussion, of Owen Street, Seaton Park, has named his second daughter "Mena," after the celebrated Mena where the Battalion was encamped. Ex-No. 687 Pte. Stamford Wallace Simpson is keeping up the old traditions of the 10th, his present address being "Tiger's Tooth", Penneshaw, Kangaroo Island.

XXIV

ORGANIZATION OF CONVOY, FIRST A.I.F. CONTINGENT, NOVEMBER, 1914

ESCORTING WARSHIPS.

H.M.A.S. *Melbourne*. Position—one mile ahead of convoy.
H.M.A.S. *Sydney*. Position—port beam, one mile distant.
Japanese Cruiser *Ibuki*. Position—starboard beam, one mile distant.

A.I.F. TRANSPORTS.

Each division of transports was four cables from the other, and each transport was two cables length ahead of the one following.

No.	Name.	Tonnage.	Speed.	Officer Commanding Troops.
	1st Division (Central).			
A3	Orvieto	12,130	15	Lieut.-Colonel D. S. Wanliss (Flagship of G.O.C.)
A27	Southern	4,769	10½	Lieut.-Colonel R. T. Sutherland
A4	Pera	7,635	11	Lieutenant E. W. Richards
A26	Armadale	6,153	11	Major P. W. Smith
A12	Saldanha	4.594	11	Lieutenant P. A. McE. Laurie
A13	Katuna	4,641	11	Major S. Hawley
A1	Hymettus	4,606	11½	Major A. A. Holdsworth
A23	Suffolk	7,573	12	Lieut.-Colonel C. F. Braund
A25	Anglo-Egyptian	7,379	12	Lieutenant W. Standfield
	2nd Division (Port).			
A18	Wiltshire	10,390	14	Lieut.-Colonel L. Long (Divisional leader)
A7	Medic	12,032	13	Major A. J. Bessell-Browne
A11	Ascanius	10,048	13	Lieut.-Colonel S. P. Weir
A15	Star of England	9,150	13½	Lieut.-Colonel R. M. Stoddart
A2	Geelong	7,951	12	Lieut.-Colonel L. F. Clarke
A17	Port Lincoln	7,243	12	Lieut.-Colonel F. N. Rowell
A10	Karoo	6,127	12	Captain H. L. Mackworth
A21	Marere	6,443	12½	Captain C. H. Spurge
A6	Clan MacCorquodale	5,058	12½	Major A. J. Bennett
	3rd Division (Starboard).			
A14	Euripides	14,947	15	Colonel H. N. McLaurin (Divisional leader)
A8	Argyllshire	10,392	14	Major S. E. Christian
A9	Shropshire	11,911	14	Colonel J. J. T. Hobbs
A19	Afric	11,999	13	Lieut.-Colonel L. Dobbin
A24	Benalla	11,118	14	Lieut.-Colonel W. K. Bolton
A22	Rangatira	10,118	14	Lieut.-Colonel C. Rosenthal
A16	Star of Victoria	9,152	13½	Lieut.-Colonel J. B. Meredith
A20	Hororata	9,491	14	Lieut.-Colonel J. M. Semmens
A5	Omrah	8,130	15	Lieut.-Colonel H. W. Lee
A28	Miltiades	7,814	13	Major C. T. Griffiths

NEW ZEALAND TRANSPORTS.

No.	Name.	Tonnage.	Speed.	No.	Name.	Tonnage.	Speed.
	1st Division.				2nd Division.		
3	Maunganui	7,527	16	10	Arawa	9,372	12
9	Hawkes Bay	7,207	13	11	Athenic	12,234	12
8	Star of India	6,800	11	6	Orari	6,800	12
7	Limerick	6,827	13	5	Ruapehu	7,885	13
4	Tahiti	7,585	17	12	Waimana	10,389	14

ORGANIZATION OF FIRST A.I.F. CONVOY

DISPOSITION OF UNITS OF THE 1st DIVISION IN THE CONVOY AND PLACES OF EMBARKATION.

No.	Name.	Tonnage.	Speed.	Embarking at—	Troops.	Officers.	Men.	Horses.
A1	*Hymettus*	4,606	11½	Sydney, Melbourne, and Adelaide	A.S.C. and horses	5	106	686
A2	*Geelong*	7,951	12	Melbourne and Hobart	Mixed	47	1,295	—
A3	*Orvieto*	12,130	15	Melbourne	G.O.C. Infantry and details	94	1,345	21
A4	*Pera*	7,635	11	Sydney	Horses	5	90	391
A5	*Omrah*	8,130	15	Brisbane	Artillery horses	43	1,104	15
A6	*Clan MacCorquodale*	5,058	12½	Sydney	Infantry and A.S.C.	6	113	524
A7	*Medic*	12,032	13	Adelaide and Fremantle	Two companies Infantry, Artillery, A.S.C., and A.M.C.	28	977	270
A8	*Argyllshire*	10,392	14	Sydney	Artillery	32	800	373
A9	*Shropshire*	11,911	14	Melbourne	Artillery	42	794	433
A10	*Karoo*	6,127	12	Sydney and Melbourne	Signallers and A.M.C.	13	388	398
A11	*Ascanius*	10,048	13	Adelaide and Fremantle	Infantry	65	1,728	10
A12	*Saldanha*	4,594	11	Adelaide	Horses	4	52	274
A13	*Katuna*	4,641	11	Sydney and Hobart	Horses	5	94	506
A14	*Euripides*	14,947	15	Sydney	Infantry	29	2,202	15
A15	*Star of England*	9,150	13½	Brisbane	Light Horse	25	487	457
A16	*Star of Victoria*	9,152	13½	Sydney	Light Horse	26	487	461
A17	*Port Lincoln*	7,243	12	Adelaide	Light Horse	19	351	338
A18	*Wiltshire*	10,390	14	Melbourne	Light Horse and A.M.C.	35	724	497
A19	*Afric*	11,999	13	Sydney	Infantry, A.S.C., and Engineers	48	1,372	8
A20	*Hororata*	9,491	14	Melbourne	Infantry	66	1,986	118
A21	*Marere*	6443	12½	Melbourne	Horses	4	80	443
A22	*Rangatira*	10,118	14	Brisbane	Artillery, Infantry, and A.M.C.	15	430	450
A23	*Suffolk*	7,573	12	Sydney	Infantry	32	979	8
A24	*Benalla*	11,118	14	Melbourne	Infantry and A.S.C.	49	1,185	10
A25	*Anglo-Egyptian*	7,379	12	Brisbane and Melbourne	Horses	6	105	492
A26	*Armadale*	6,153	11	Melbourne	Lines of communication	—	—	—
A27	*Southern*	4,769	10½	Sydney and Melbourne	Horses	5	136	281
A28	*Miltiades*	7,814	13	Sydney and Melbourne	Imperial Reservists	—	600	—

XXV

MISCELLANEOUS BATTALION ORDERS

BATTALION ORDER No. 79.
By
Major F. W. Hurcombe,
Commanding (Temp.) 10th Infantry, A.I.F.

Transport A11 T.S.S. *Ascanius*.
At Sea. 3/11/14.

PART I.

1. **Duties.**
   Captain of the Day—Major M. F. Beevor.
   Next for Duty—11th Infantry.
   Battalion Orderly Officer—Lieut. E. J. Sexton.
   Next for Duty—Lieut. A. J. Byrne.
   Ship's Orderly Sergeant—11th Infantry.
   Next for Duty—
   Battalion Orderly Corporal—Cpl. Mollett, C. M.
   Next for Duty—Cpl. Whitbread, A.

2. **Guards.**
   Guard for to-morrow will be supplied by 11th Infantry.

3. **Orderlies.**
   O.C. "F" Company will detail one man to report to Ship's Adjutant at 8.30 a.m.

4. **Detail.**
   "B" Company. No. 624 Pte. Lock, C. B. L., is detailed as permanent orderly for Orderly Room.

5. **Parades.**
   Companies will parade as under. Companies mentioned first will parade on Port side.

"D" and "F" Coys.	8.30- 9.30 a.m.
"G" and "H" Coys.	9.30-10.30 a.m.
"A" and "B" Coys.	2.0 - 3.0 p.m.
"E" and "C" Coys.	3.0 - 4.0 p.m.

   Work for to-morrow:—
   Half-hour, Musketry Instruction; half-hour, Physical Training. (Note) Companies that have not already drawn Hill-Siffken Targets from Q.M.'s stores will do so.

   2. The inoculation parade detailed for "C" and "D" Companies for Tuesday having been cancelled will take place at same time and place on Wednesday.

   3. Officers' Parade. Boat Deck, 7.30 a.m. Dress, Physical Training.

PART 2.

6. **Punishments.**
   1. Part 2 B.O. 76 is cancelled and the following substituted:—

Coy.	Reg. No.	Rank and Name.	Offence.	Award.	To date.
....	....	....	....	....	....

MISCELLANEOUS BATTALION ORDERS 305

2. The following punishments have been awarded by the Commanding Officer:—

Coy.	Reg. No.	Rank and Name.	Offence.	Award.	To date.
......	....	....	....	....	....

3. Reduction of Fine: "F" Company, No. — Pte. ——. Fine reduced from 2 days' pay (*i.e.*, 12/-) to 10/-.

(Signed) E. W. Talbot Smith, Lieut.,
Asst. Adjt. 10th Infantry, A.I.F.

BATTALION ORDER No. 86.
By
Major F. W. Hurcombe,
Commanding (Temp.) 10th Infantry, A.I.F.
Transport A11 T.S.S. *Ascanius*.
At Sea. 10/11/14.

PART 1.

1. Duties.
   Captain of the Day—Capt. Herbert.
   Next for Duty—11th Infantry.
   Ship's Orderly Sergeant—Col.-Sgt. Hassam.
   Next for Duty—11th Infantry.
   Battalion Orderly Officer—Lieut. Stopp.
   Next for Duty—Lieut. Heming.
   Battalion Orderly Sergeant—Sgt. Steer.
   Next for Duty—Sgt. Lodge.
   Battalion Orderly Corporal—Cpl. Pickering.
   Next for Duty—Cpl. Rule.

2. Guards (see also para. 11).
   10th Infantry supply Guard to-morrow as under:—
   Officers of Guard: Capt. Redburg, Lieuts. Rumball and Perry.
   Sergeants of Guard: Sgts. Virgo, Neave, and Tucker.

3. Orderly.
   "E" Company supply Orderly for Ship's Adjutant. Report at 8.30 a.m.

4. Parades.
   Companies parade as under; those mentioned first, B.D.P.
   "A" and "B"   8.30 to 10.0 a.m.
   "C" and "D"   10.5 to 11.35 a.m.
   "E" and "F"   1.15 to 2.45 p.m.
   "G" and "H"   2.50 to 4.20 p.m.
   Work: Half-hour each Physical Training, Musketry and Rifle Exercises.
   Sergeants' Parade, 6.30 a.m., B.D.P., Physical Training.
   Officers' Parade, 7.0 a.m., B.D.P., Physical Training.

5. Discipline.
   Company Officers must impress strongly upon their commands that nothing which will float must be thrown overboard. This order is most important and must be adhered to.

6. **Smoking.**
    No smoking whatever is to take place on hatch gratings, owing to the danger of sparks falling on troop-decks below. Troop-Deck Sergeants will see that Mess Orderlies are detailed to be on duty at all times as a watch. The Provost Staff will see that no smoking takes place on gratings.

7. **Blankets and Hammocks.**
    No blankets or hammocks, except those of sick men, and then only as the direct order of the Medical Officer, will be allowed on deck after 6 a.m.

8. **The *Emden*.**
    The O.C. Troops desires it to be notified for general information that the German Cruiser *Emden*, which was put out of action by H.M.A.S. *Sydney* yesterday morning, crossed in front of the fleet during the previous night, but owing to the excellent manner in which the ships were darkened she did not notice their proximity. Had she observed the fleet it is probable that she might have caused considerable damage before her exit.

9. **Inspection.**
    At inspection to-day the following irregularities were noticed and must be immediately rectified. The shelves under tables were filled with boots, towels, dirty clothes, etc. These shelves are to be used only for small personal necessities such as books, writing material, etc. Some black kit-bags were seen on troop-decks; any kit-bag found on troop-deck at inspection to-morrow will be treated as evidence of direct disobedience of orders, and the owner will be dealt with accordingly.

10. **Promotions.**
    Until further orders all promotions will be provisional. Subsequent confirmation will depend upon knowledge of work, general ability, attention to duty, and capability of handling troops.

11. **Guards.**
    The following will supply N.C.O.'s and men for Guard to-morrow:—
    "D" Company, 2 Cpls., 43 men; "E" Company, 2 Cpls., 44 men; "F" Company, 2 Cpls., 43 men.
    The Guard will fall in to be inspected during daily inspection by the O.C. Troops.

PART 2.

1. **Promotions.**
    No. 1014 Cpl. Mitchell, G. D., is promoted to be Sergeant (prov.), to date 9/11/14, and is attached to "C" Company for duty.
    B.O. 68, para. 7, is amended to read:—
    "No. 514 L.-Cpl. Montgomery, W., "H" Company, is promoted to be Corporal in "H" Company, and is appointed Acting-Sergeant. To date 23/10/14."

MISCELLANEOUS BATTALION ORDERS

2. Punishments.
   The following punishments have been awarded by the C.O.:—
   Coy.   Reg. No.   Rank and Name.   Offence.   Award.   To date.
   ....

(Signed) E. W. Talbot Smith., Lieut.,
Asst. Adjutant, 10th Infantry, A.I.F.

NOTICES.

No. 151 H. G. Sudbury-Smith, of "G" Company, is appointed Librarian.

Library Book No. 626, "The Dream Ship," is reported missing. Finder please return to Library or Orderly Room.

A tobacco pouch has been lost on Boat Deck. Finder will please return to Ship's Adjutant's Office.

BATTALION ORDER No. 97.
By
Major F. W. Hurcombe,
Commanding (Temp.) 10th Infantry, A.I.F.
H.M.A.T. A11 T.S.S. *Ascanius*.
At Sea. 21/11/14.

PART 1.

1. Duties.
   Captain of the Day—Captain Herbert.
   Next for Duty—Captain Croley, 11th Infantry.
   Ship's Orderly Sergeant—Col.-Sgt. Hemingway, 11th Infantry.
   Next for Duty—Col.-Sgt. Shaw.
   Battalion Orderly Officer—Lieut. Sexton.
   Next for Duty—Lieut. Byrne.
   Battalion Orderly Sergeant—Sgt. Gilpin.
   Next for Duty—Sgt. McCann.
   Battalion Orderly Corporal—Cpl. White.
   Next for Duty—Cpl. Coffey.
2. Guards.
   11th Infantry furnish guard to-morrow.
3. Orderly.
   "H" Company detail orderly for Ship's Adjutant for to-morrow.
4. Divine Service.
   Church Parades will be held to-morrow the same as last Sunday.
5. Detail.
   In view of the fact that Captain E. T. Brennan, A.A.M.C., is senior to Captain H. C. Nott, A.A.M.C., Captain Brennan is appointed Senior Medical Officer of the Transport.
6. Collision.
   The O.C. Troops desires to express his appreciation of the cool and collected manner in which all ranks behaved when the collision occurred at 4.25 o'clock this morning. The behaviour was splendid, absolute silence and perfect order being maintained. One might easily have imagined that the turn-out was a practice one. It is indeed

gratifying to know that no lives were lost on either boat. The attention which all ranks had paid to previous collision drills has certainly borne excellent fruit.

(Signed) E. W. Talbot Smith, Lieut.,
Asst. Adjutant, 10th Infantry, A.I.F.

NOTICES.

The following articles have been found. Owners can have same on application to Office:—

One small wristlet watch (gunmetal).
One small black leather purse.

Rifle No. 7341 is reported missing. Any man who has it in his possession will please return it to Office at once.

BATTALION ORDER No. 107.
By
Major F. W. Hurcombe,
Commanding (Temp.) 10th Infantry, A.I.F.
H.M.A.T. A11 *Ascanius*, Suez.
1/12/14.

1. Duties.
    Captain of the Day—Capt. Shaw.
    Next for Duty—Capt. Herbert.
    Ship's Orderly Sergeant—Col.-Sgt. Hemingway, 11th Infantry.
    Next for Duty—10th Infantry.
    Battalion Orderly Officer—Lieut. Loutit.
    Next for Duty—Lieut. Perry.
    Battalion Orderly Sergeant—Sgt. Virgo.
    Next for Duty—Sgt. Hall, A. B.
    Battalion Orderly Corporal—Corporal Boyle.
    Next for Duty—L.-Cpl. Cussion.

2. Guard.
    (1) Ship's Guard for to-morrow will be furnished by 11th Infantry.
    (2) Special Armed Guard will be mounted when passing through the Canal. 10th Infantry mount guard on Boat Deck Starboard at time to be notified later. Guard will be issued with 20 rounds ball ammunition, but must be warned that on no account must they fire unless the ship is fired on, and then only on the order of the Officer in Command of the Guard. The Guard will remain on duty until relieved. Detail as under:—
        Officer of the Guard—Lieut. Heming.
        Sergeants of the Guard—Sgts. Tomlinson and Munro.
        "H" Company will supply 2 corporals and 24 men.

3. Sleeping.
    Until further orders all ranks will sleep in cabins or on troop-decks.
    No one will be permitted to sleep on any upper deck.

4. Disembarkation.
    Instructions have been received that troops will disembark at Alexandria. The actual time is not yet published.

5. Orderly.
"B" Company will detail one man as Orderly for Ship's Adjutant to-morrow.
6. Parades.
Officers', N.C.O.'s, and other parades will be as per schedule.
7. Appointments.
The following appointments have been approved by the Commanding Officer, to date 1/12/14:—
To be Lance-Corporals—
"C" Company, No. 365, Pte. Doley, S. E.
"C" Company, No. 110, Pte. Vennermark, C. W.
(Signed) E. W. Talbot Smith, Lieut.
Asst. Adjutant, 10th Infantry, A.I.F.

SPECIAL BATTALION ORDER.
By
Lieut.-Colonel M. Wilder-Neligan, D.S.O., D.C.M.
(*Re* Minor Operation carried out by 10th Battalion on night of May 29-30 in Merris Sector with object of advancing line and capturing certain enemy posts.)

I am directed by Lieut.-General Sir B. B. Y. de Lisle, K.C.B., C.M.G., D.S.O., Corps Commander, to congratulate all Officers and other ranks for the very excellent operation carried out last night.

General de Lisle paid a personal visit to the Battalion Headquarters this morning to offer his congratulations and thanks.

Major-General Sir H. B. Walker, C.B., D.S.O., the Divisional Commander also visited Battalion Headquarters this morning to express appreciation of the conduct of all ranks during last night's operations.

The General considers the operation one of great excellence. In addition I have received the following letter from Brigadier-General H. G. Bennett, C.B., C.M.G., our Brigade Commander:—

"The work done by your Battalion last night was splendid, the operation being a great success. The organization was very good, and the manner it was carried out shows that the fighting spirit and the determination to 'get there' is stronger than ever. It is only necessary to set a task and its achievement naturally follows. Again we have proved that our men are better soldiers than the enemy. I wish to thank you and all concerned for your good work."

You, one and all, know what I think of you myself, so I need not add to the expression of goodwill offered by our General. All I can say is:—

"Don" Company, you have burnished your escutcheon again.
"Beer" Company, we thank you for your loyal and ready support.
"Connie," your parties were magnificent.
"Headquarters." Well, I withdraw my Battalion parade remarks.
I don't know what we would have done without you and your battery.
(Signed) M. WILDER-NELIGAN, Lieut.-Colonel.
Commanding Tenth Aust. Infantry Battalion.
30/5/18.

XXVI

MISCELLANEOUS SPEECHES, A.I.F. ORDERS, ETC.

FIRST INSPECTION OF 10TH BATTALION
By
Colonel E. G. Sinclair-MacLagan.
Friday, August 28, 1914, on Morphettville Race-course.

Colonel E. G. Sinclair-MacLagan arrived from Melbourne and reviewed the Battalion. After the inspection he said: "I am more than pleased with the material drafted into my command. They are a good lot of men, deep-chested, strong, and keen. Many of them still have to learn much in the way of drill, but I was particularly impressed with the physique of the South Australian quota of the 3rd Brigade and their alertness."

REVIEW OF 10TH BATTALION
By
Governor-General (Right Hon. Sir Ronald Crauford Munro Ferguson) and Major-General Sir William Throsby Bridges, September 4, 1914, on Morphettville Race-course.

The Governor-General and the Commander of the 1st Australian Division arrived in Adelaide that morning, and visited the Morphettville Training Camp. During the morning all A.I.F. units in South Australia were inspected on the Morphettville Race-course, the parade state being:—

Headquarters	36
3rd Light Horse	381
Ammunition Supply Column	85
10th Battalion	1,064
12th Battalion	71
A.S. Divisional Train	84
A.S. Supply Column	79
3rd Field Ambulance	85
	1,885

(Including 68 officers and 1,744 other ranks.)

The A.I.F. troops were later drawn up in hollow-square and addressed by the Governor-General, who said: "Colonel Weir, Colonel Irving, and officers and men of the Expeditionary Force—I congratulate you upon the appearance of the camp; on the appearance also of this parade; in the discipline shown by every unit of it; and on the rapidity with which these preparations have been carried through. I recognize in that rapidity the energy, the resource, and the adaptability of the officers, of the men, which will all make of this Contingent an invaluable element in the British Forces. I am also glad to see in the ranks so many who have a knowledge of war: that is an advantage; that is, an advantage which is possessed by no other army in the world. You will find when you reach the front a high standard of personal leadership and of efficient organization, which has been set up by men like your Colonel-in-Chief, Lord Roberts. You will find we have got the generals, we have got the troops, and we shall have the victory. Each individual must learn to endure and to fight as if the victory depended upon the effort of each one of you.

MISCELLANEOUS SPEECHES, A.I.F. ORDERS, ETC. 311

The whole future of the Empire depends upon the defeat of a strong, arrogant, and unscrupulous foe. The fate of free institutions is in the balance against military tyranny. I shall be able to report, and shall report to the King that his Australian Forces have lost no time in preparing themselves to come into line with his regiments, who are already upholding the renown of the British arms at the front, and who have stood the first shock of battle. It is for you now to win his thanks through a glorious triumph. May all good luck and good fortune attend you, and may you return victorious."

Following this inspiring address the 10th Battalion passed the saluting base, and then headed back to the Morphettville Camp, and were dismissed on the Battalion parade ground. Before leaving for Melbourne that afternoon, General Sir W. T. Bridges said: "I am more than pleased with the show put up by the South Australian Contingent to-day. The physique of the men was more than creditable, and their extreme adaptability will more than counterbalance their lack of training. I think they will uphold the reputation held by corps from the Mother Country when the serious business of warfare has to be contended with. Apart from their physique, the right spirit is showing; there is a desire generally to gain credit, even in these initial stages. I want also to say that I think the Broken Hill men were a particularly fine company."

PRESENTATION OF 10TH BATTALION COLOURS
By
His Excellency the Governor (Colonel Sir Henry Galway),
At Morphettville Race-course, Friday, September 19, 1914.

At 10 that morning his Excellency handed over the blue and gold regimental flag on behalf of Mrs. Jury and the people of Glenelg. The Governor said: "Colonel Weir and Men—I know every man will do his utmost to guard and keep it clean. It should be carried high, upholding those traditions which have made the British Empire. I trust you will all return with peace in your helmets and victory in your eyes." The flag was taken over by a subaltern and colour party specially selected from the 10th for the occasion. The flag was four feet square, and saxe blue and gold were predominant. The word "Australia" was emblazoned in the centre, and the magpie and laurel were conspicuously represented.

COLONEL S. PRICE WEIR'S FAREWELL MESSAGE TO THE SOUTH AUSTRALIAN PUBLIC.
October 20, 1914.

Before embarking on the *Ascanius* Colonel S. P. Weir left the following message for the South Australian public. In heartily thanking the Y.M.C.A. and generous citizens for the gifts and kindnesses they had shown the Battalion from its inception to embarkation, he said: "I am very proud of my command, and consider that I have every reason to be so. We have been under canvas for over two months, and during that time have worked hard under very unfavourable conditions as far as the weather was concerned, for the dust at times was abominable and the heat most trying. Notwithstanding this, the men have worked well, and with the exception of a few minor offences, such as drunkenness and breaking leave, no serious crime has come before me. This is a record to be proud of in a camp of one thousand men. I hope we shall give a good account of ourselves at the front, do our best, and comply with His Excellency the Governor's advice, 'Keep a stiff upper lip under all circumstances,' and follow the King's advice to his British troops when they were leaving England for the front, 'To stand united, firm, resolute, and trusting in God'."

SIR GEORGE REID, HIGH COMMISSIONER FOR AUSTRALIA, REVIEWS THE 1st AUSTRALIAN DIVISION, AT MENA, EGYPT.
December 31, 1914.

Sir George Reid, K.C.M.G., arrived from London, and accompanied by General Sir John Maxwell, G.O.C. British Troops in Egypt, and other British officers, visited Mena Camp, and during the afternoon inspected the 1st Australian Division, which was drawn up on the sands of the Libyan Desert. Sir George's address to the A.I.F. troops was the finest piece of oratory delivered to any Australian soldiers during the whole of the Great War. He said: "Sir John Maxwell, General Bridges, Officers and Men—I am glad to see you all. Anxious mothers have asked me to watch over you. Alas! it is impossible. We are all glad to see here the Officer Commanding all the forces in Egypt, that distinguished soldier, Sir John Maxwell. I am deeply grateful to General Bridges for the rare compliment he has offered me as the High Commissioner for Australia in London. The youngest of these august Pyramids was built 2,000 years before the birth of Christ. They have been the silent witnesses of many strange events. Can they ever have looked down upon a more unique spectacle than this splendid array of Australian soldiers massed in their defence? Who can look upon these majestic monuments without emotion, without regret? How pathetic, how tremendous, how useless have been these gigantic efforts to preserve the bodily presence of Egyptian Kings from the fate to which all mortality is doomed. Dust must return to dust. It is the soul of men's lives and the deeds that live for ever. Imperishable inspirations may spring from nameless graves on land and sea, when stately sepulchres are dumb. The homes of our Imperial race are scattered far and wide, but the breed remains the same, as staunch, stalwart, and loyal in the East and West and South as in our Northern Mother Land. What brings your army here? Why do your tents stretch across this narrow parting of the ways, between worlds old and new? Is it a quest in search of gain, such as led your fathers to the Austral shore? Do you seek to invade and outrage weaker nationalities in a lawless raid of conquest? Thank God! your mission is as pure and noble as any soldiers ever undertook—to rid the world of would-be tyrants. Do remember, in this bright and peaceful clime which tempts so strongly the awful task so near you, the fearful risks you are approaching, the desperate battles long drawn out you have to fight and win. Do not forget Lord Kitchener's warnings. Do not forget the distant homes that love you. Remember Australia's good name and unstained honour, which she has given to your keeping in a supreme sense. A few wrong ones can besmirch the fair name of a whole army. The unworthy, if such there be, must be shunned, must be thrust out. Your first and best victories are those of self-control. Hearts of solid oak, nerves of flawless steel, come that way. Lord Kitchener

MISCELLANEOUS SPEECHES, A.I.F. ORDERS, ETC.

will send you to the front when you are fit. It is you who must get fit and keep fit. Think of the generous rivalries that await you. Think of the glorious soldiers of the British Isles and the British Empire who long to greet you at the front. Think of the heroes of Belgium, France, Russia, Servia, and Japan. Think of the fleets watching on every sea. If any stains come on your bright new flags they must and will be stains of honour won by valour. Wide and vital as the Allied interests are, there are interests wider and more vital still. The whole world's destinies are at stake. Are the hands of fate to point backward to universal chaos or forward to a lasting peace? Backward, surely it cannot be; true culture crowned with chivalry will prove too strong once more for savage tricks and broken faith. Good luck! May God be with you each and all until we meet again." After this splendid address the 1st Australian Division defiled before him in a grand march past. His eloquent stirring sentiments have long been remembered by officers and men of the 10th Battalion.

SPECIAL ORDER
By
GENERAL SIR IAN HAMILTON
Commander-in-Chief of Mediterranean Expeditionary Force.
(Issued prior to landing at the Dardanelles, April, 1915.)

Soldiers of France and the King—Before us lies an adventure unprecedented in modern war. Together with our comrades of the Fleet we are about to force a landing upon an open beach, in face of positions which have been vaunted by our enemy as impregnable. The landing will be made good by the help of God and the Navy. The positions will be stormed, and the war will be brought one step nearer to a glorious close. The whole world will be watching our progress. Let us prove ourselves worthy of the great feat of arms entrusted to us.

(Signed) IAN HAMILTON, General.

AUSTRALIAN AND NEW ZEALAND ARMY CORPS ORDER
April 19, 1915.

Officers and Men—In conjunction with the Navy we are about to undertake one of the most difficult tasks any soldier can be called upon to perform, and a problem which has puzzled many soldiers for years past. That we will succeed I have no doubt, simply because I know your full determination to do so. Lord Kitchener has told us that he lays special stress on the role the Army has to play in this particular operation, the success of which will be a very severe blow to the enemy—indeed, as severe as any he could receive in France. It will go down to history to the glory of the soldiers of Australia and New Zealand. Before we start, there are one or two points which I must impress on all, and I must earnestly beg every single man to listen attentively and take these to heart.

We are going to have a real hard and rough time of it, until, at all events, we have turned the enemy out of our first objective. Hard, rough times none of us mind, but to get through them successfully we must always keep before us the following facts. Every possible endeavour will be made to bring up transport as often as possible; but the country whither we are bound is every difficult, and we may not be able to get our wagons anywhere near us for days, so men must not think their wants have been neglected if they do not get all they want. On landing it will be necessary for every individual to carry with him all his requirements of food and clothing for three days, as we may not see our transport till then. Remember then that it is essential for everyone to take the very greatest care, not only of his food, but of his ammunition, the replenishment of which will be very difficult. Men are liable to throw away their food the first day out, and to finish their water bottles as soon as they start marching. If you do this now, we can hardly hope for success, as unfed men cannot fight, and you must make an effort to try and refrain from starting on your water bottles until quite late in the day. Once you begin drinking you cannot stop, and a water bottle is very soon emptied.

Also as regards ammunition—you must not waste it by firing away indiscriminately at no target. The time will come when we shall find the enemy in well-entrenched positions, from which we shall have to turn them out, when all our ammunition will be required. And remember:

Concealment whenever possible;
Covering fire always;
Control of fire and control of your men;
Communication never to be neglected.

(Signed) W. R. BIRDWOOD,
G.O.C., A.N.Z. Army Corps.

SPECIAL ORDER
By
COLONEL E. G. SINCLAIR-MACLAGAN,
Commander Third Infantry Brigade.
April 21, 1915.

I had hoped to have been able to see the battalions of my Brigade personally and to put these few matters before you. Circumstances have prevented this, so I am asking your Commanding Officer to read you this letter.

It is necessary that you should understand that we are about to carry out a most difficult operation, *viz.*, "Landing on an enemy coast in the face of opposition." Such an operation requires complete harmony of working between the Navy and Army and unhesitating and immediate compliance with all orders and instructions.

You have been selected by the Divisional Commander as the covering force, a high honour, which we must all do our best to justify. We must be successful at any cost. Whatever footing we get on land must be held on to and improved by pushing on to our objective, the covering position which we must get to as rapidly as possible, and once obtained must be held at all costs and even to the last man.

In an operation of this kind there is no going back. We shall be reinforced as the Navy can land troops, and meantime "Forward" is the word, until on our position, when "Hang on" is what we have to do, until sufficient troops and guns are landed to enable us to push on.

We must be careful not to give the enemy a chance of any kind; no smoking or lights or noise from midnight onwards till after daylight. Take every chance of reorganizing (under cover if possible). Attacks must be as rapid as the ground will allow. You will probably have to drop your packs; but carry tools forward as far as you can, it may mean saving many lives later in the day. Until broad daylight the bayonet is your weapon, and when you charge do so in as good a line as possible; one or two good pieces of bayonet work now may stand us all in good stead later on.

Every man must keep his eyes skinned and help his Officers and N.C.O.'s to the utmost by reporting quickly things seen. Look out for your flanks. After taking a charger out shut the cartridge pocket. Once ashore don't be caught without a charger in the magazine. Look after each cartridge as if it was a ten pound note.

Good fire orders, direction, control, and discipline will make the enemy respect your powers, and give us all an easier task in the long run. Wild firing only encourages the enemy. Keep your food and water very carefully; we don't know when we shall get any more. Don't show yourselves over the skyline, and give your position away, if you can avoid it.

We must expect to be shelled when in our positions, but remember that is part of this game of war, and we must "stick it," no matter what the fire. One thing I want you to remember all through this campaigning work is this, and it is most important: You may get orders to do something which appears in your positions to be the wrong thing to do, and perhaps a mad enterprise. Do not cavil at it, but carry it out wholeheartedly and with absolute faith in your leaders, because we are after all only a very small piece on the board. Some pieces have often to be sacrificed to win the game, and after all it is to win the game that we are here. You have a very good reputation you have built up by yourselves, and now we have a chance of making history for Australia and a name for the Third Brigade that will live in history. I have absolute faith in you, and believe few, if any, finer brigades have ever been put to the test.

(Signed) E. G. SINCLAIR-MACLAGAN,
Colonel Commanding 3rd Infantry Brigade.
21/4/15.

AUSTRALIAN AND NEW ZEALAND ARMY CORPS ORDER.
April 26, 1915.

The G.O.C., Australian and New Zealand Army Corps wishes to place on record his appreciation of the gallantry and dash with which the 3rd Australian Brigade carried out the difficult operation entrusted to it of landing in face of opposition on an open beach.

In spite of the enemy being ready, and of heavy casualties inflicted at short range, the Brigade pressed on carrying successive positions in face of heavy fire, and completing a hazardous operation in a manner reflecting the highest credit on the commanders and on the troops engaged.

During their advance the Brigade captured three Kruppe guns.

The G.O.C. Army Corps is sure that all will be gratified to hear that the Australian submarine has succeeded in passing the Narrows of the Dardanelles and sinking a Turkish warship there.

(Signed) W. R. BIRDWOOD,
G.O.C., A.N.Z. Army Corps.

CONGRATULATORY MESSAGES TO THIRD BRIGADE.

From Royal Artillery,
    To Colonel MacLagan.
    The R.A. Officers and men second squadron congratulate you and your brigade. 26th April, 1915.

From *Queen*,
    To C.O. Third Brigade.
    Well done, Third Brigade, you have done magnificently. We are all proud of you. Open helio. communication as soon as possible.

EXTRACT FROM DIVISIONAL ORDERS
By
Major-General W. T. Bridges, C.M.G.,
Commander 1st Australian Division.

    Headquarters, April 28, 1915.

"The G.O.C. wishes to convey his most grateful and deep thanks to all ranks for their magnificent work during the last three days. It is almost an unprecedented feat for a landing to be effected on a hostile shore in the face of determined opposition, and the manner in which the covering force carried out their landing and at once advanced against a large hostile force through a most difficult and jungle-covered mountainous country is a fact of which any army ought to be justly proud. The hardships and the difficulties the troops have sustained since then have probably been quite on a par with what their comrades have probably been sustaining in France."

    (Signed) C. B. B. WHITE,
    Lieut.-Colonel,
    General Staff.
    1st Australian Division.

EXTRACT FROM VICE-ADMIRAL SIR J. M. DE ROBECK'S DESPATCH,
Dated July 1, 1915, and released by War Office on August 16, 1915.

Re LANDING OF COVERING FORCE BY 3RD BRIGADE.

"The service was one which called for great determination and coolness under fire, and the success achieved indicates the spirit animating all concerned. In this respect I must specially mention the extraordinary gallantry and dash shown by the 3rd Infantry Brigade (Col. E. G. Sinclair-MacLagan, D.S.O.), who formed the covering force."

EXTRACT FROM GENERAL SIR IAN HAMILTON'S FIRST DARDANELLES DESPATCH.
Dated August 5, 1915.

"The attack was carried out by the 3rd Australian Brigade under Major (temporary Colonel) Sinclair MacLagan, D.S.O.

The beach on which the landing was actually effected is a very narrow strip of sand, about 1,000 yards in length, bounded on the north and the south by two small promontories. At its southern extremity a deep ravine, with exceedingly steep, scrub-clad sides, runs inland in a north-easterly direction. Near the northern end of the beach a small but steep gully runs up into the hills at right angles to the shore. Between the ravine and the gully the whole of the beach is backed by the seaward face of the spur, which forms the north-western side of the ravine. From the top of the spur the ground falls almost sheer except near the southern limit of the beach, where gentler slopes give access to the mouth of the ravine behind. Further inland lie in a tangled knot the under-features of Sari Bair, separated by deep ravines, which take a most confusing diversity of direction. Sharp spurs, covered with dense scrub, and falling away in many places in precipitous sandy cliffs, radiate from the principal mass of the mountain, from which they run north-west, and south to the coast.

The boats approached the land in the silence and the darkness, and they were close to the shore before the enemy stirred. Then about one battalion of Turks was seen running along the beach. At this critical moment the conduct of all ranks was most praiseworthy. Not a word was spoken—everyone remained perfectly ordered and quiet, awaiting the enemy fire, which sure enough opened, causing many casualties. The moment the boats touched the land the Australians' turn had come. Like lightning they leapt ashore, and each man as he did so went straight as his bayonet at the enemy. So vigorous was the onslaught that the Turks made no attempt to withstand it, and fled from ridge to ridge, pursued by the Australian Infantry.

During this period parties of the 9th and 10th Battalions charged and put out of action three of the enemy's Krupp guns.

From 11 a.m. to 3 p.m. the enemy, now reinforced to a strength of 20,000 men, attacked the whole line, making a specially strong effort against the 3rd Brigade and the left of the 2nd Brigade. This counter-attack was, however, handsomely repulsed with the help of the guns of H.M. ships. Between 5 and 6.30 p.m. a third most determined counter-attack was made against the 3rd Brigade, who held their ground with more than equivalent stubbornness.

During the night again the Turks made constant attacks, and the 8th Battalion repelled a bayonet charge; but in spite of all the line held firm. The troops had had practically no rest on the night of the 24-25th; they had been fighting hard all day over most difficult country, and they had been subjected to heavy shrapnel fire in the open. Their casualties had been deplorably heavy. But despite their losses, and in spite of their fatigue, the morning of the 26th found them still in good heart and as full of fight as ever."

IAN HAMILTON, General,
Commanding Mediterranean Expeditionary Force.

XXVII

DISPOSITION OF WARSHIPS AND TRANSPORTS OFF ARI BURNU, APRIL 25, 1915

DISPOSITION OF REAR-ADMIRAL SIR C. F. THURSBY'S No. 2 SQUADRON OF THE EASTERN MEDITERRANEAN SQUADRON which was delegated the duty of actually landing A.I.F. Troops and covering the Landing at Anzac on Sunday, April 25, 1915, and the Transports employed in the operation.

BATTLESHIPS AND CRUISER.
Delegated the duty of covering the landing by gun-fire.
Majestic.   *Triumph.*   *Bacchante.*

BATTLESHIPS.
Delegated the duty of landing troops.

Queen, landed "A" and "B" Companies of 9th Battalion and General Birdwood and Staff.

Prince of Wales, landed "B" and "C" Companies of 10th Battalion and General Bridges and Staff.

London, landed "A" and "C" Companies of 11th Battalion.

DESTROYERS.
Delegated the duty of landing troops.

Beagle, landed "C" Company of 9th Battalion and ½ "C" Company of 12th Battalion.

Colne, landed "D" Company of 9th Battalion and ½ "C" Company of 12th Battalion.

Foxhound, landed "A" Company of 10th Battalion and ½ "B" Company of 12th Battalion.

Scourge, landed "D" Company of 10th Battalion and ½ "B" Company of 12th Battalion.

Usk, landed "B" Company of 11th Battalion and ½ "D" Company of 12th Battalion.

Chelmer, landed "D" Company of 11th Battalion and ½ "D" Company of 12th Battalion.

Ribble, landed "A" Company of 12th Battalion and 3rd Field Ambulance.

SEAPLANE CARRIER.
With seaplanes delegated the duty of observing for *Majestic*.
Ark Royal.

BALLOON SHIP.
With captive balloon delegated the duty of observing for *Triumph* and *Bacchante*.
Manica.

AUXILIARY CRAFT.
Fifteen trawlers were employed in the operation, and twelve rowing-boats were allocated to each troop-carrier, each troop-carrier's complement of rowing-boats subsequently being made up into four tows of three each.

A.I.F. TRANSPORTS (FIRST DIVISION).

(Over 150 vessels were required to convey the M.E.F. from Egypt to the Dardanelles.)

Third Brigade Transports.

Malda, with 9th Battalion, transferring "A" and "B" Companies to *Queen* and "C" and "D" Companies to *Beagle* and *Colne*.

Ionian, with 10th Battalion, transferring "B" and "C" Companies to *Prince of Wales* and "A" and "D" Companies to *Foxhound* and *Scourge*.

Suffolk, with 11th Battalion, transferring "A" and "C" Companies to *London* and "B" and "D" Companies to *Usk* and *Chelmer*.

Devanha, with 12th Battalion and 3rd Field Ambulance, transferring "A" Company and 3rd Field Ambulance to *Ribble* and "B," "C," and "D" Companies to *Beagle, Colne, Foxhound, Scourge, Usk,* and *Chelmer*.

Second Brigade Transports.

Novian, with 2nd Brigade Headquarters, and 5th Battalion.
Galeka, with 6th and 7th Battalions.
Clan MacGillivray, with 8th Battalion, etc.

First Brigade Transports.

Minnewaska, with General Birdwood and Staff, and General Bridges and Staff (subsequently transferred to *Queen* and *Prince of Wales*) and 1st Battalion.
Derfflinger, with 2nd and 3rd Battalions.
Michagan, with 4th Battalion, etc.

Other Transports.

Mashobra, with Engineers and Ambulance.
Pera, with Indian Mountain Batteries.
Hessen, with Indian Mountain Batteries.
Hindoo, with 2nd Australian General Hospital, subsequently transferred to *Gloucester Castle* and *Devanha*.
Nizam, with 10th Battalion Transport Section, etc.

Hospital Ship.
Gascon.

Transports Improvised as Hospital Carriers.

The majority of transports which had conveyed the 1st Australian Division and the New Zealand and Australian Division from Egypt were converted into temporary hospital ships. The following vessels carried wounded from the Dardanelles during the first week of the operation:—

City of Benares	*Clan MacGillivray*	*Devanha*
Derfflinger	*Dunluce Castle*	*Galeka*
Hindoo	*Gloucester Castle*	*Ionian*
Itonus	*Lutzow* (conveyed Gen. Godley and New Zealanders)	*Mashobra*
	Seang Choon	

XXVIII

ENVOI

"Men are we, and must grieve when even the shade
Of that which once was great is passed away."

The 10th Battalion, A.I.F., was a great infantry regiment composed of great-hearted volunteers who were loyal men to their King and Country, and as such participated in the Great War of 1914-18. This was the verdict of the women who bore them, the considered opinion of the authorities who raised, trained, and led them, and the judgment passed upon them by numerous contemporaries. Practically every town and place of importance within the State of South Australia was represented within its ranks, and many were the homes which, either directly or indirectly, had contributed a male member of the family towards its strength. Its men, its history, its traditions aspired to greatness. Its achievements during the whole of the Great War period were keenly followed by numerous South Australians and also applauded by countless Britishers throughout the length and breadth of the Empire. It worthily accomplished the great purpose for which it was so hastily raised, and as a unit of the A.I.F. set an example of which no South Australian need ever feel ashamed. It is generally recognised that even though the time will come when the officers and men who made it famous will pass away, the actual name of the Battalion itself and the deeds which earned it renown will never be relegated to obscurity.

THE TENTH.

(A South Australian recruiting poem by L.W.N., published 6/8/15.)

For evermore will their undying fame
   Be theme for poet, and the deathless deed
   Adorn historic pages. They who read
Will evermore revere the glorious name
Of those who justly earned a world's acclaim
   And died to serve their country in its need.
They knew the path of duty there must lead
To certain death, yet died and overcame.
Oh, not in vain their noble blood was shed!
   E'en now their brothers muster through the land
To follow where the glorious Tenth has led.
   No more can Austral's sons inactive stand,
But hasten to avenge the martyred dead
   Who call them from Turkey's blood-stained strand.

www.ingramcontent.com/pod-product-compliance
Lightning Source LLC
Chambersburg PA
CBHW031133160426
43193CB00008B/129